MRS GRUNDY

THE ORIGINAL SIN

After a painting by Hugo van der Goes, about 1460, in the Imperial Gallery, Vienna.

Mʀs GRUNDY

A HISTORY OF FOUR CENTURIES OF MORALS IN GREAT BRITAIN AND THE UNITED STATES INTENDED TO ILLUMINATE PRESENT PROBLEMS

BY

LEO MARKUN

ILLUSTRATED

Our fathers, in time past, distinguished right and wrong plainly enough, and it is our wisdom to be taught by them.

—Gyges the Lydian

D. APPLETON AND COMPANY
NEW YORK   LONDON

1930

Republished, 1968
SCHOLARLY PRESS ▪ 560 Cook Road ▪ Grosse Pointe Woods, Michigan 48236

Library of Congress Catalog Card Number 30-13518

Paper used in this edition is
an acid-free, permanent/durable paper
of the type commonly referred to as
"300-year" paper

PREFACE

THE casual observer sees fewer feminine knees than he did a few months ago; a Federal commission considers it necessary that the Prohibition laws be enforced, although taking cognizance of the fact that the American tradition of disregarding unpopular laws is well established; the question whether *damn* and *Hell* may properly be used in nonreligious discourse by a radio broadcaster is being seriously debated; the sale of cigarettes in the United States, especially to women, has risen amazingly since the World War of 1914 to 1918; the Massachusetts Watch and Ward Society is being severely criticized for the tactics of its agent, but the convictions he has recently obtained in Cambridge stand, while an effort is being made to liberalize the law directed against obscene literature; a meeting of American farmers is told that the diminishing birth rate of the country threatens the future prosperity of agriculture, especially since the immigration laws will probably be made more rather than less stringent in the near future. Such matters as these, which we can find discussed in to-day's newspaper, are not entirely comprehensible without some knowledge of their historical background.

To provide such knowledge has been my task. I have tried to perform it honestly, but I cannot hope that I have avoided all mistakes of fact and interpretation. I am indebted to several hundred secondary writers, but there is hardly a page of this book that does not depend to some extent upon primary sources. These include official records, memoirs, letters, sermons, books of etiquette, and literary works of all kinds.

I am grateful to Mr. E. Haldeman-Julius for his courteous promptitude in granting me permission to make free use here of the material contained in such of my earlier publications under his imprint as cover, though on a lesser scale, parts of the present ground. Hardly any of the phraseology of *Mrs. Grundy*, however, has been carried over from these.

LEO MARKUN

CONTENTS

[vii]

CONTENTS

ILLUSTRATIONS

ILLUSTRATIONS

[x]

ILLUSTRATIONS

[xi]

ILLUSTRATIONS

M<small>RS</small> GRUNDY

M<u>rs</u> GRUNDY

CHAPTER I

THE INCARNATIONS OF MRS. GRUNDY

WHEN Mrs. Grundy was an ancient Spartan, she insisted that the freeborn boys should be taught to steal, for she knew their courage and self-reliance would otherwise be imperiled. It seemed to her entirely fitting and proper that they should occasionally go out in bands and murder a few members of the hereditary slave caste, for the better maintenance of class distinctions. She knew the importance of exposing ugly and deformed children to die, in order that the Lacedæmonian breed might remain at a high level. In Sparta, as indeed elsewhere in Greece, trickery and deceitfulness seemed to her true manly virtues. Yet in Persia, at the same time, she taught young men to avoid lying as the greatest of all evils.

Some of Mrs. Grundy's friends and admirers are fond of telling us that she has always been essentially the same. Skirts may be abbreviated, one of them remarked a few years ago, but not morality. But if we are to believe the learned gentlemen who decipher old records and the travelers who visit far countries, Mrs. Grundy's outlook is by no means the same in all places and at all times. In fact, there is not a single definite rule for moral conduct that has always and everywhere prevailed among men.

Let us consider "Thou shalt not kill," on the face of it that one of the Ten Commandments acceptable to moral men everywhere, of any religious faith or none. The words will be accepted by probably all my readers as presenting an indestructible and essential rule regulating social behavior. Yet, if we turn to specific applications of the commandment, it will readily appear that they are not unanimous in their views.

For example, should the agents of the State kill a man because he has committed murder? Is it noble or base to shoot the soldiers of a country against which one's own has declared war? Is it moral or immoral to slaughter an animal other than man for food? If an infant is born that is destined to live, if at all, as a helpless, monstrous idiot, should any great effort be made to prevent its death? Most of my readers (at least those living in the twentieth century) will no doubt consider infanticide wrong and properly to be dealt with as a crime. But is the use of drugs and mechanical devices that prevent conception immoral? Is artificial abortion always to be considered a form of murder? Again, is a husband justified in killing the man he finds in his wife's bed? At a given time within the United States, we find Mrs. Grundy approving such jealousy and revenge in one community, sternly shaking her head against it in another.

In the inland regions of New Guinea, where women are cheap, it is considered perfectly proper for their husbands to put them to death in response to the merest whim. On the coast, the female sex is more respected because it is costlier. Wherever slaves are abundant at low prices, public opinion allows them to be barbarously mistreated. Mrs. Grundy respects pounds-shillings-pence even in interpreting "Thou shalt not kill."

In some savage tribes the woman who bears twins is killed or driven into the forest, perhaps with one or both of her infants. Such treatment is not a crime, but a highly moral expression of the general will. In ancient Rome girl children were often exposed. Infanticide has been and is approved among peoples at many different cultural levels all over the world. Children are allowed to die because begotten in illicit unions; considered physically unattractive; born with the head first or, elsewhere, with the feet first; born during a storm; unlucky enough to sneeze soon after birth or to be the first child or the fourth one; or simply because they have been born in a barren region where an increase of population would be disastrous. Parents may even be forced by law to put their infants to death.

"Can he be clean again," Zoroaster is supposed to have asked, "who has eaten of the carcass of a dog or the corpse of a man?"

Yet dogs and men have been eaten by eminently respectable people, though, to be sure, few if any of them have had the benefit of visits from Zarathustrian missionaries. There is no need for us to examine in detail the fluctuating minutiæ of the ethics of cannibalism, but we must remember that it is a proper, and even a hallowed, institution in most of the communities where it commonly occurs. It takes place openly (though women may be excluded from the scene), often with elaborate cere-monies presided over by chiefs and kings.

Herodotus tells us of various Asiatic tribes among whom the custom of killing the diseased and the infirm prevailed. There was a tradition among the Romans that in the early days of the city aged people had customarily been flung over a bridge into the Tiber. In many tribes of North American Indians old people were killed or proved morally self-conscious enough to kill themselves when the proper time came. Extremely wide-spread under varying cultural complexities has been the usage of killing the king or the high priest at the first indication of senility or feebleness on his part. An excellent reason for this is usually stated: to keep a weak ruler or medicine man would mean the departure of the gods and spirits of fertility, and the result would be a barren soil.

Suicide is regarded by some communities as always sinful and perhaps criminal, while others insist upon the duty of killing oneself under what seems elsewhere comparatively light provoca-tion. Thus, Lafcadio Hearn tells of a Japanese lady who quite properly committed suicide in the exact manner prescribed for gentlewomen after her husband had failed to keep his promise to support a certain candidate in an election. It has been a feudal duty in Japan to kill one's children if by doing so one's master's children might be saved from death. In some other lands it pleases Mrs. Grundy for the aggrieved person to kill others rather than himself. Such a case is recorded, for example, of British New Guinea, where two brothers were driven by their moral instinct to kill men after the death of their pig.

It is extremely improper in many circles to slaughter certain animals which are held to be sacred or taboo. The people who live in the Siamese protectorate of Nan suffer much from the depredations of tigers because it is sinful to kill them. Similarly, in southern India there is a taboo against harming snakes, though poisonous varieties abound. In other lands Mrs. Grundy frowns upon the killing of bears and deer. The ancient Egyptians had a long list of sacred animals, including the cow, the sheep, the ichneumon, the ibis, the vulture, the crocodile, and certain sorts of fish. To slay any of these was a dreadful crime.

All over the world there are complicated laws about the eating of certain foods or the abstinence from them. Orthodox Jews still regard pork with abhorrence, and a great many other peoples have maintained an interdict on the flesh of swine. The fact that raw or insufficiently cooked pork often causes disease probably has something to do with the prohibition. A tribe of Bushmen living where goats are abundant refuse to eat them. Some African negroes eat no vegetables; others reject the milk of cows and goats, even for infants. Various peoples in Asia and Africa have considered the eating of oxen proper, but not of cows.

Hindus refuse to eat food prepared by members of castes lower than their own. They hold that leather defiles, and consequently never wear shoes while cooking. Their women do not join the men at the dining table but eat the left-overs by themselves. Brahmans abstain from meat, eggs, garlic, onions, mushrooms, and fish. In the Andaman Islands every person is supposed to have his own list of foods which he never eats (travelers fail to connect this rule with a desire to reduce weight). In the Warramunga tribe of Australia young men are not permitted to eat wild turkey, emu, or bandicoot; these delicacies are reserved for the aristocracy of middle age and old. Class distinctions with regard to food are often fixed definitely; more usually, economic considerations determine them in an automatic way.

It is not mere convenience that determines what food should properly be conveyed to the mouth with the fingers, what is within the province of the spoon, what should be taken with the fork or the knife or chopsticks. There are European districts in which it is customary for all who sit at a table to derive their food from the same central receptacle; in others, it is a gross breach of etiquette to take anything except from the plate set directly before the eater. Unconventionality as to such matters may be a great sin; at the least it is considered a sign of eccentricity or boorishness.

The rules that regulate fasting and feasting change as we cross boundary lines or pass from one age to another. The Jews, who attach much importance to sobriety, consider it proper to get drunk on the Purim holiday. At least in some European and American circles it is a breach of civic duty to remain sober on New Year's Eve. Such customs must be honored if one is to remain in good social standing, even in the instances where they conflict with statute law. Generally, the criminal courts support the moral standards of their communities. Sometimes the laws shift automatically with Mrs. Grundy's whims, as with us in the case of those against the publishing of indecencies. What would have been treated as lewd and disgusting a generation ago is not necessarily regarded as such now. A book which would corrupt the young in Great Britain is given a clean bill of health in the United States; another one that stands without emasculation in England is purged by the American publishers.

In one place, it is right for a woman to reveal part of her pectoral charms at an evening party, though ruinous to her reputation to show more than the lowest inch of her legs. In another, it is most important for a decent woman to hide her face except from her own husband. Mrs. Grundy sometimes considers it insolent for a maiden to embellish her middle with clothes. In other incarnations she tells virgins never to reveal themselves naked, even to their own eyes.

As Bernard Shaw has recently remarked, nakedness is not a means of sexual attraction where it is customary. Richard Burton said long ago in *The Anatomy of Melancholy* that "the greatest provocations of lust are from our apparel." Still in many places the unmarried girls go naked while the married women wear more or less clothing. In those parts of the world where it is customary to wear only a little clothing, there is no unanimity as to what part of the body is to be covered. Sometimes it is the men, sometimes the women, who are more fully clothed.

In many Australian tribes a garment is thrown over the shoulder in cold weather, but the regions below the chest remain naked. In various islands of the Pacific, as well as many sections of Asia and Africa, though some clothing is worn, the genitals are not hidden. Curiously, neighboring tribes have sometimes very different ideas as to what constitutes propriety in clothing. An African people which insists men should cover their knees as well as their loins lives next to others among whom the male sex is untrammeled by clothes. Where Mrs. Grundy smiles benignantly upon nakedness, it may cause shame to don a blanket. Indeed, Westermarck cites many instances where clothing seems to be used to call attention to the sexual organs rather than to conceal them. And there are tribes whose women permanently remove their clothing after marriage or after the bearing of a child or two.

The position of women is by no means uniform under varying codes of morality. There is a story about a Filipino saved from a boat, who held up first his pig, then his child. He was stepping out himself, leaving his wife for last, when rebuked by a person under the influence of a more chivalrous system of propriety. Yet among some peoples of a less complex culture than his own, the men are dominated by the women.

More often, to be sure, the female sex is under numerous disabilities, but the extent of the control exercised over women by men varies widely. It may extend to the right of enslaving or killing a daughter, a wife, or a widowed mother without any formalities. Such a privilege, under the name of *patria potestas,* belonged for a time in ancient Rome to the head of the family with regard to all his children, slaves, and other dependents.

In some savage and barbaric tribes the women do practically all the work, but there are also parts of the world in which the men cook and wash. There was once an Asiatic people whose women (apparently the prototypes of the legendary Amazons) took care of the hunting and fighting. Among certain Arabs needlework is the task of the male sex. There is an African people among whom wives must get down on their knees, crawling on their hands, to talk to their husbands. According to some foreign travelers, the exact reverse of this custom prevails in a North American country know as *die Vereinigten Staaten* or *les Etats-Unis*.

It is especially evident in the sphere of sexual morality that Mrs. Grundy can wear very different aspects. Prostitution, always a dreadful sin in some places, is an accepted convenience in others, a sacred duty in still others. Herodotus tells us of an old Babylonian law requiring every woman to yield her body to a stranger in the temple of the goddess of love once before her marriage, and though the accuracy of his account has been assailed, there seems no good reason for doubting that the custom did for a considerable period exist. There have been regular temple prostitutes in many countries, and their venery has been as sacred to divine powers as the chastity of, let us say, the Vestal Virgins in Rome.

The incest rules forbidding marriages between fathers and their daughters, brothers and their sisters, seem always to have been very common, but they are not universal. The usage that requires the father to deflower his daughter when she reaches nubile age is not at all rare. Brother-sister marriages have often been required of royalty, as with the Ptolemies of Egypt, and in one or two cases encouraged among the people generally. The laws setting forth what persons may be married are among many simple peoples almost unbelievably complex. Some are excluded because they are too close—related by blood or marriage or in some ceremonial way, bearing the same name, belonging to the same clan or to a group having the same totem; others are too remote—belonging to a lower caste, speaking a foreign language, worshiping strange gods, living too far off, having insufficient property to pay the bridal price or the dowry.

Homosexuality, which has been regarded with extreme horror by the most important Christian churches, direct allusions to which even in scientific books seemed impossible a few short decades ago in the English-speaking countries, has enjoyed great respectability. The island of Tahiti possessed special gods of homosexual love, and it has been bound up with religion in many places. John Addington Symonds writes of the old Greeks as "a great and highly-developed race not only tolerating homosexual passions, but deeming them of spiritual value, and attempting to utilize them for the benefit of society." He points out that Platonic love was originally tender feeling between men, not between men and women.

Among the Hindus the woman is regarded as an "arable field" upon whom almost all the forms of sexual enjoyment, not merely those looking toward reproduction, may and should legitimately be exercised. Scratching, biting, and beating as acts of love are recommended and carefully considered by an ancient sage of India whose work is still venerated. In that country, as in many others, the relations between religion and sex are important and frank. The sexual orgy as a fertility rite is widespread.

Religion is sometimes taken to require sexual indulgence on the part of everybody, and a character in one of the great epics of India says that whoever denies a woman's request for intercourse is the murderer of an unborn child. The dominant religion among the Hebrews attached much importance to the duty of increasing and multiplying, though it sternly forbade sterile forms of sexual indulgence.

Out of a Judaic sect, influenced also by several other religions, rose Christianity, with strong ascetic tendencies. For the mediæval Jew, family life was noble, the begetting of children was an act of piety. For the mediæval Christian, though marriage had formally become a sacrament, it was a sign of human imperfection. And celibacy was but one form of abstinence and self-torture among the many indicated for the perfect Christian.

Religious asceticism originates to a large extent in the fear of divine powers and the desire to propitiate them. The Israelites in their Holy Land offered animal sacrifices, and several passages in their Scriptures seem to indicate that at one time, like their neighbors, they included human beings, even their own children.

An adjacent priesthood offered up its virility. Perhaps, as some sociologists have supposed, circumcision (a rite which extends far beyond Hebrew influence) is symbolically reminiscent

[8]

THE FLAGELLANTS

After a painting by Carl Marr.

of a greater sexual sacrifice. Literal eunuchism seemed to a few men who lived in Palestine at the opening of the Christian era a way of hastening the birth of the Kingdom of Heaven.

Otherworldliness is not the only reason for asceticism. The history of this word carries us back to the Greek athletes training for the games. But the abstinence of the athlete, the warrior, and the hunter depends to a considerable extent upon religio-magical notions. In many a savage community the soldiers and the fishermen refrain from intercourse with their wives before going off on an expedition, thus thwarting malignant spirits and invoking the aid of beneficent gods.

The early Christian monks were often tempted by Satan. But they fought the good fight, as well as carnal weakness permitted, against the delights of women and fine food and drink and warm, pleasant baths. Those who held out were comforted by the thought of endless joys to come as well as by the pleasures flowing directly from their very pains. Sometimes they flogged themselves voluptuously, sometimes they enjoyed the prick of sharply pointed consciences, the bittersweet of absolute submission to authority. Out of such alchemy a very few managed to distill ineffable bliss.

The great mass of Christians, in and out of the monasteries, sought more direct roads to joy than the Via Dolorosa. The monastic orders attracted many men and women who fled from carnage and insecurity and serfdom and toil, not from sensuous pleasure. Such a learned and devout Catholic historian as Montalembert is forced to lament that the regular orders did not long retain their pristine purity.

Christendom in general feasted and boozed and wenched and fought lustily, little concerned with fears of divine retribution on earth and in the life to come. In the lands bordering on the Mediterranean which have been considered the special home of inverted love, it is doubtful if Christianity ever for any long period reduced the prevalence of homosexuality. New economic and social conditions put an end to the elaborate Roman gladiatorial games and circuses, but the delight in human suffering seems to have increased together with masochism in the Christian

[9]

Middle Ages. Religion usually frowned upon the pride of secular knowledge, but that sprang up, stimulated by Moorish and Jewish rationalists. Mrs. Grundy was not everywhere the same, nor at all times, though she invariably made the sign of the cross before formulating her more important decisions.

PART I

THE OLD WORLD

CHAPTER II

THERE WAS A MAN SENT FROM GOD, WHOSE NAME WAS JOHN

§ 1

NEITHER Christianity nor Judaism was the first religion to restrain the "natural" man from unbridled pleasure-seeking. Taboos are as old as magic and undoubtedly older than the worship of any deity. Asceticism had a prominent place in heathen Greece and Rome. Many of their philosophers and religious leaders considered self-denial and self-torture necessary for the propitation of the gods or for the living of a perfect life. The very hedonists insisted upon the restriction of human conduct, and the most prominent of them, Epicurus, marked out a very narrow field of desirable behavior.

Every human society of which we possess any knowledge has had standards of action and abstention. These have varied so greatly, as we have seen, that not one universal principle of morality can be pointed out. But because of religious and other factors, the chief moral rules prevailing in England and the countries settled from it have changed little for some centuries. To consider but one instance, monogamy was regular in Elizabethan England and remains so in Hooverian America. There have been and there still are other countries in which we can find very different matrimonial arrangements, all perfectly proper according to their own criteria.

Great Britain in the period with which we shall be chiefly concerned here and English-speaking America since its foundation have been Protestant as well as Christian countries. In applying the second adjective I do not mean to say that their peoples have literally observed the commands attributed to Jesus in the New Testament, and I recognize the fact that the conception of a good Christian has varied almost as much as that of a virtuous man.

The Roman Catholic Church during the Middle Ages used to admit a limited freedom of theological speculation. It officially held that not all believers were to the same extent obliged to perform divinely pleasing works, a "counsel of perfection" having been given for comparatively few.

The ordinary man in mediæval Christendom was satisfied to derive his notions of right and wrong from a parish priest. They were supposed to be drawn from the Bible and especially from the words of Jesus, but the interpretation which the Church placed on one or another passage might change entirely from one century to the next. It was once a great sin for a Christian to be a soldier; it later became a merit to take up arms against the heathen and even to fight for a feudal lord's very mundane desires. There was a time when all Christians considered poverty essential to salvation; then the duty of remaining penniless was imposed only on those who had taken special vows. A number of religious limitations on the conduct of business still remained. Strict moralists declared that every Christian who took interest on money committed the deadly sin of usury. Still, economic necessity brought about evasions, among them the pressing of wealthy Jews into service as bankers.

Some of the Fathers of the Christian Church set forth extreme ascetic doctrines. Basil, for instance, considered laughter sinful. From the beginning there was also an opposite dogma that the followers of Jesus, alone being assured of eternal bliss, should be particularly merry. While many Christian preachers insisted upon the importance of abstinence from sexual intercourse, there were Christian groups addicted to the forms of enjoyment denounced in the Old Testament as unnatural and abominable.

The conflict between antinomians and Christian Judaizers which arose in the Apostolic Age was never fully settled. The official position of the Catholic Church represented a compromise: some of the Mosaic laws were rejected, while others were accepted, often in a somewhat changed form. The authority of the hierarchy to interpret the Scriptures was vigorously asserted.

The bishops were human, and in many instances far from saintly. They often used their power for the advantage of their orders and themselves. To commit any act threatening the position of the hierarchy was, according to the priests, to sin against God. Neither the illiterate peasants nor their seldom more literate lords often ventured to doubt the tenets held at Rome after the important early heresies had been suppressed. Yet there was always Christian opposition to the Roman Catholic Church, the eastern Orthodox branch breaking away long before the Protestant Revolution. It has been maintained that a widely organized anti-Christian or Satanical church had a continuous existence in Europe for several centuries. This seems doubtful, though certain pagan rites were long persistent almost everywhere on the Continent. Jews lived in many parts of Christendom, and Moors in a few. Aside from such exceptions, people were born into the Christian Church as now into national states.

Almost every conceivable human action was regulated either by ecclesiastical or by civil law. The system of auricular confession enabled the priests to pry into matters necessarily hidden from the secular authorities. Their greatest strength arose out of the general belief that Christianity as officially interpreted and administered offered the only road to salvation. There were skeptics in the Middle Ages, but they rarely exerted any considerable influence.

The first of all duties was that of worshiping in the accepted manner. Hence, sacrilege and heresy were the most deadly of sins. In comparison, fornication or even theft was a mere trifle, though, to be sure, the civil authorities considered the latter offense a hanging matter.

The teaching of Cyprian and Ambrose that almsgiving could bring about the forgiveness of sin became one of the pillars of ecclesiastical power. The care of the poor was taken over by the clergy, and it was considered quite as charitable to support the Church as to feed the penniless. A general belief was fostered that if people were only sufficiently generous in their contributions to the Church treasure chests, they would enter into

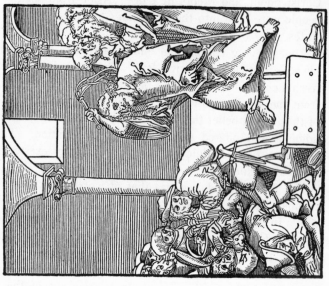

ANTICHRIST SELLS INDULGENCES

whereas Christ drove the money-changers from the Temple. From Lucas Cranach, *Passional Christi und Antichristi*, 1521.

the delights of Paradise as soon as they died, no matter what sins they had committed. Pardoners promised that all who bought their indulgences would have their souls washed clean. Officially, confession and repentance were added requirements.

Celibacy came to be prescribed for all Roman Catholic priests, as it had been from the first for members of monastic orders. The theory was that the holiness of a priest depended to a large extent upon his chastity. Not all who were supposed to be chaste were so in fact. England in the centuries preceding the Protestant Revolution was one of the countries where the sexual life of the clergy was particularly unrestrained. In many instances priests lived with women who were their wives in all but name. The illegitimate children of such unions sometimes rose to high rank in the Church. Clergymen who lived in virtual monogamy were preferred in a community to those who flitted from one woman to another.

Dissatisfaction with the priests or with the Church in general appeared on occasion during the Middle Ages. Some of the movements for the correction of abuses were frankly heretical, and these were almost always put down by force. Of another nature was that begun by simple Francesco or Francis of Assisi in the thirteenth century. He decided it was his duty to obey Jesus by going forth in utter poverty to heal the sick and cast out devils. The Roman authorities adroitly turned Francesco's somewhat dangerous enthusiasm aside. After his death little remained for the work he had done but three monastic and lay orders, whose members did not always practice what they preached.

The clergy objected to unlicensed revivalists because they did not want to share their privileges with the laity. Yet one of their most cherished rights, which was so valued that it was referred to as "the benefit of clergy," was extended to all who could read and write. This was chiefly the exemption from capital punishment in certain cases. Very few laymen, especially in the early Middle Ages, were able to read the Bible or any other book.

Many feast and fast days reminded ordinary people of their Christianity. In the sixteenth century the eating of meat was

[17]

unlawful on about two hundred days a year. The lower classes were perforce vegetarians almost always, unless they were within easy reach of fish, and meatless days affected them little. But there were many feast days, when labor was suspended and everybody sought amusement. The mediæval period was by no means one of unmitigated gloom. Though the horrors of Hell and Purgatory and the delights of Heaven were little doubted, the contemplation of future rewards and punishments seems to have had little influence on behavior.

Because morality was supposed to be derived from the divine will, represented on earth by the hierarchy, it was held that nothing that promoted the welfare of the Church could be wicked. Hence, it was a positive virtue to put unbelievers or imperfect believers to death, and it was established in the case of John Hus that faith need not be kept with heretics.

The mediæval religious reformers generally conceded the perfection of Christian ethics, but sometimes ventured to wonder if the precepts of Jesus were actually being carried out. Chaucer, the authors of *Piers Plowman,* Dante, Boccaccio, and Petrarch were among those who pointed out abuses. They said that the monks, the priests, and the nuns were not always exemplars—that many of them were gluttonous, lascivious, covetous, and indifferent to their duties. In addition to such writers as these, there were popular preachers toward the end of the Middle Ages who contrasted the words of Jesus with the actions of some Christian leaders. The Bible was translated into several of the vernacular idioms of Europe. And there were unsuccessful Luthers enough. Wycliffe, Hus, and others prepared the way for more fortunate rebels against the Catholic Church. Heresy persisted although great hosts of heretics were slain.

The reformers seldom attacked Christian asceticism. Rather, they complained that neither clerical nor lay men and women were willing to give up the transitory pleasures of the senses. The attack on otherworldliness belongs not to the Protestant Revolution but to the Renaissance. This "rebirth" was a turning to those pagan ideals which were little or not at all represented in the official Christian philosophies.

The Renaissance means more than the study of non-Christian literature. The scientific awakening, though it owed most to ancient Greece, was largely stimulated by Moorish and Jewish intermediaries. During a large part of the Middle Ages western Europe had important intercourse with the Orient. Contacts with the civilization of Spanish and Arabian Mussulmans and with that of Cathay and India really began the Renaissance.

THE CELLARER

After an initial in a manuscript of the fourteenth century.

It was already established in Italy by the fourteenth century. Thence its full influence spread westward and northward. The great physical and intellectual explorations that followed menaced the authority of the Catholic Church. Even popes found it possible to be skeptical about the whole religious and moral structure of Christianity. Men came to St. Peter's chair who considered it hardly necessary to conceal their hedonism and their contempt for otherworldly ideals. Earlier pontiffs had sinned, but the Renaissance popes scoffed at the ethical standards of the Church.

Mediæval manners, which seem to us indelicate and gross, were not entirely driven out when Oriental luxuries and antique philosophies became prominent in western Europe. Verbal taboos are, of course, dependent on time and place, and references to sexual and excretory organs and functions were common in the politest society of the Middle Ages.

In the inns of the sixteenth century, men and women who were entire strangers to each other were lodged in the same bed-room, on occasion in the same bed. Members of both sexes bathed together naked. Indeed, bathhouses sometimes served as brothels, and moral ordinances in certain districts forbade mixed bathing.

The drinking of water was rare in the sixteenth century, except among the very poor. Sir Thomas More drank water, but he also wore a hair shirt and scourged himself. Wine and beer were the common beverages. Emperor Charles V, who was not considered a drunkard or an immoral man, was accustomed to take a quart of wine at a draft. In the days before coffee, tea, and soda pop were introduced to Europeans, only extreme ascetics considered the drinking of intoxicants reprehensible. Drunkenness was a deadly sin, but so was gluttony.

The Renaissance spread luxuries among temporal and ecclesiastical lords. When bishops assembled to discuss weighty problems of dogma and Church government, the most elegant of prostitutes flocked to the meeting place. A new sort of harlot appeared. She was called *una cortigiana,* that is, a woman of a princely court. The word (our *courtesan*) is simply the feminine of *cortigiano* or *courtier.* The literature of the period reveals the courtesan as a beautiful woman, often with artistic taste and ability, attended by troops of retainers and living in great splendor. Kings and dukes visited the most attractive courtesans at their homes, and cardinals vied with artists and bankers in heaping attentions upon them.

The Italian Renaissance set up new ideals of enjoyment. It brought wealth to many who purveyed objects of luxury. Makers of beautiful things found patrons more than generous. It was not a time of anæmic æstheticism, but rather of great joy in life, of passionate desire to make the most of sublunary existence. This produced at once bejeweled courtesans and consummate artists. Out of the Renaissance arose Benvenuto Cellini, who was forgiven his murders because of his artistic skill. The *bravo* or "brave man" who assassinated with the dagger was as characteristic of the period as the courtesan and the painter or sculptor.

In Germany, under the influence of the Renaissance, rich citizens and nobles turned assiduously to sensual delight. Wealthy bishops and abbots vied with them in luxury. The country had a considerable reputation for gluttony and drunkenness. The beautiful, prosperous city of Nuremberg maintained a public wagon to carry home burghers who were unable to lift themselves out of the gutter. Dukes and counts celebrated great occasions with drinking contests.

The preachers found much to denounce. Clothing was too elaborate, and the fashions changed too frequently. Women's gowns revealed their breasts or their legs. Men wore articles of dress which distinctly suggested the phallic. There was too much eating of fine foods and drinking of costly wines. The coarse manners prevalent in Germany troubled the moralists less. Ladies and gentlemen amused themselves at parties by flinging filth at one another. The preachers themselves used language which would not bear repetition now. Moreover, the fact that they were often addicted to the very sins against which they thundered placed them at something of a disadvantage in their moral endeavors.

The most important of all Christian pietists in the period just preceding the Protestant Revolution was an Italian Dominican friar, Girolamo Savonarola. In his time, the second half of the fifteenth century, there were many complaints that the conduct of the clergy was looser than that of the laity. The common people of Italy had little interest in pagan philosophies and not much opportunity to share in the luxuries of the time.

Savonarola preached eloquently about the horrors of Purgatory and Hell. He denounced the pleasures of the aristocracy and supported the interests of the masses. Perhaps he was a superstitious fool, certainly he had in him much of the spirit that was later to be represented in Puritanism. Mediæval Christians considered the beautification of churches and religious services important, and the Italian Renaissance did not turn art away from the service of God. Savonarola insisted that the magnificent furnishings and splendid music of the churches were diverting attention from worship. He separated the sexes in his church as well as in his sacred processions through the streets of Florence.

He preached against gambling, horse racing, public dancing, and the license of the carnival season. These diversions were much older than the Renaissance. At carnival time the Dominican friar's numerous followers built a huge "bonfire of vanities" in the public square of Florence and cast into it all sorts of things which he denounced as sinful—false hair, expensive clothes, gambling devices, books and pictures which portrayed the delights of the flesh, amulets and symbols of the old religion which had survived into Christian times.

Even the aristocrats of Florence became hysterically pious. The children were formed into morals police, and they tore the veils from the faces of ladies who ventured to wear such abominable luxuries in public. Gamblers fled, leaving their dice behind, at the approach of Savonarola's boys. But the friar's triumph did not last long. His views about secular and ecclesiastical politics brought him into conflict with the Pope, and his pretended miraculous powers did not save him from public execution. The pontiff who brought about his downfall and death was a Borgia, a representative of the less savory side of the Renaissance.

The dominant intellectual spirit of Italy in the early sixteenth century appears in the writings of Niccolò Machiavelli. We are wont to think of him as brutal, but he defended the use of cruelty on the part of his ideal prince simply because he considered it necessary for the unification of Italy. While Machiavelli ignored the claims of the Catholic Church, he felt

DEATH OFFERING YOUTH THE CHOICE BETWEEN HEAVEN AND HELL

From Savonarola, *L'Arte del Ben Morire*, 1496.

that an established religion, whether true or false, was needed in an absolute monarchy.

The Church at this time possessed much temporal power, and most members of the hierarchy considered the discouragement of learning necessary for the protection of their vested interests. The Reuchlin-Pfefferkorn controversy was one of the conflicts between the defenders of ignorance and the new humanists. Pfefferkorn, himself a Jewish apostate, advised the burning of all Hebrew books except the Old Testament. Then the University of Mainz proposed that the Hebrew Scriptures should also be flung into the fire, since the authority of the Church was derived from the New Testament alone. And this, it was held, should be read in the Latin Vulgate version rather than in the Greek original.

Many priests were familiar with only scraps of Scripture. Carlstadt, Luther's colleague, said he first saw a complete Bible after he had been admitted to the doctorate in divinity. Ordinary people, even if they had access to the Bible in a language they could understand, were held incapable of interpreting its meanings, literal and allegorical. The Church was the guardian of truth, and no man might presume to explain the Scriptures in an unusual manner.

§ 2

A German monk named Martin Luther, who found at Rome abundant reasons for doubting the sanctity of the papal court, began to wonder about some of the official doctrines of the Church. He gradually reached the conclusion that the Bible has only a literal meaning, which all the people should be permitted to find for themselves. Then, in 1517, he revolted against the authority of the Pope. The time was favorable, for almost all classes in Germany were dissatisfied with the power, wealth, and moral tone of the clergy and Church.

Martin Luther, like most of the other Protestant reformers, wanted to enforce a strict morality. The fact that some of the things he said and wrote would appear gross and disgusting to our daintier ears is beside the point, and the imputation that he organized the revolt because he could not otherwise satisfy his sensual desires is absurd.

At times, Luther felt that men might lawfully enjoy almost all the pleasures available to them, providing they did not go beyond the limits of moderation: "If our Lord God may make excellent large pike and good Rhenish wine, I may very well venture to eat and to drink. Thou mayest enjoy every pleasure in the world that is not sinful: that, thy Lord forbids thee not, but rather wills it." In at least one case Luther approved of bigamy, and he went so far as to suggest that a woman with an impotent husband might quietly call another man to her assistance, attributing any offspring to her own husband. He denounced prostitution, and he saw in marriage the solution of nearly all sexual difficulties. The vow of celibacy he considered inherently void, and he himself, a former monk, married a woman who had been a nun. Later, Luther's conception of sex changed somewhat, and he began to speak of indulgence as sinful, even if necessary because of human frailty.

Although Luther was actuated by a moral purpose, his work, as he himself sadly confessed, brought about a general relaxation in behavior. For a time, confusion replaced rigid authority, and moral measuring rods were gone. The Bible remained, and acquired immense importance, but it lent itself to varying interpretations. Before long the Lutheran Church was officially teaching what it meant.

Luther's summons to freedom brought forth a response in Germany and elsewhere which did not entirely please him. Since he said that faith in Christ is the only thing that matters, some Christians felt that they might do whatever seemed good to themselves, or whatever the Bible seemed to command them. Part of them joined the Anabaptists, who all believed in adult baptism but who split up into groups according to their acceptance of other rites and doctrines. In most Anabaptist communities no individual property rights were recognized. Some held that Christians should hold women as well as goods in common. While Münster remained a center of Anabaptism, an ordinance required all persons of suitable age to marry. Because there were three times as many women as men in the city, this brought about polygyny.

The predecessors of our present Baptists almost invariably favored religious toleration. This position was forced upon them by their doctrine of individual Scriptural interpretation and more particularly by the fact that they were everywhere surrounded by hostile power. Luther believed that heretics should be silenced; the Catholic Church and most Protestant leaders thought they should all be put to death.

Luther relied rather on the princes than on the people to spread and defend his ideas. He denounced Anabaptism, which suggested disorderly democracy and seemed to be responsible for the revolt of the peasants in southern and central Germany against their lords temporal and spiritual. The princes in those regions began to turn away from the Lutheran doctrines, which they held responsible for the unrest. Luther hastened to deny his sympathy with the social aspirations of the peasants and to urge that the rebellion should be cruelly suppressed. As a result, most of the peasants of southern Germany returned to the Catholic Church, while Luther's religion acquired an aristocratic tinge.

Lutheranism made no special appeal to the middle class. The taking of interest for the use of money, which was necessary for business development, Luther denounced, saying that "the Devil invented it and the pope, by giving his sanction to it, has brought about untold evil throughout the world." Nevertheless, the Lutheran Church had finally to give a limited approval to usury.

Zwingli, the second of the great Protestant reformers and Luther's contemporary, taught that private property originated in sin, but he was a democrat rather than a communist. He introduced the Reformation into Switzerland and brought about the passage of laws in Zürich which compelled church attendance, forbade gambling, diminished the number of taverns, and created other moral restrictions. Zwingli gradually removed all music from the churches of the city. Even less tolerant than

Luther, he persuaded his followers to wage war against the Catholics of the Swiss forest cantons, and he was himself killed in a battle with them.

Luther and Zwingli paved the way for Jean Chauvin or Caulvain, whom we know better as John Calvin. He was the great French reformer, who was to seem to millions a second John sent from God to perform a divine work. His forerunner in France, Jacques Lefèbvre of Étaples, he met at the court of Margaret of Navarre, where also Farel, who was to convert the city of Geneva to the reformed doctrines, found a refuge.

Margaret of Angoulême and Valois, Queen of Navarre, is now chiefly remembered as the principal author of a book of tales called the *Heptameron,* somewhat resembling the *Decameron* of Boccaccio. She was the sister of King Francis I of France. Both Renaissance and Reformation influences were strong at Margaret's court. The two greatest men who enjoyed her hospitality and protection were François Rabelais and John Calvin. Aside from both being among the greatest prose writers in French, the two men have little in common. Rabelais presents an ideal abbey with the motto, "Do what thou wilt!" Calvin's rule is, "Do as the Holy Spirit bids thee."

Rabelais, a monk who finally "broke his cloister altogether," read the Bible and found that God is praised there for causing to grow "wine that maketh glad the heart of man." His works used to be kept on the darker shelves of bookshops, and he remains in tradition as a potbellied fellow smacking his lips over good food and drink.

Calvin, the son of an ecclesiastical lawyer in Picardy, was destined for a career in the Church. The story goes that as a schoolboy his severity and lack of warmth gave him the name of "the accusative case." Though never ordained, he held several curacies. Then, perhaps because he had come under the influence of Lutherans, he abandoned the study of theology for that of law.

At the same time he devoted himself eagerly to the Bible. His later associate, Beza, thought that overstudy in this period developed the dyspepsia which Calvin was to find very troublesome later. There is something peculiarly appropriate in the suggestion that he acquired dyspepsia and Protestantism simultaneously. These two things, together with intellectual power, go far toward explaining his career. Calvin seems to have had little capacity for tender passion, and.his coldness toward women led to the suspicion that he had homosexual tendencies.

When he was about twenty, he studied the Greek New Testament. This, and still more the Old Testament, were extremely important in his mental development. At the age of twenty-three Calvin experienced what is known as conversion. "A horror seized upon my soul," he writes, "when I became conscious of my wretchedness. Suddenly, the full knowledge of truth, like a bright star, dawned upon me. And what was left for me, O Lord, but to abjure with tears and cries of supplication the old life which I now condemned, and to flee into thy path?" Here is a mystical tendency which was often to appear among Calvin's followers. The appreciation of sin followed upon "earnest self-examination" as well as a careful reading of the Bible.

Perhaps Calvin conceived his sin to be his earlier failure to preach what now seemed to him truth and right conduct. Or he may have been thinking of the depravity bequeathed to him, according to an old theological dogma, by Father Adam. Original sin was destined to become an important part of the Calvinist system.

Calvin was determined to set up the Bible as an authority in all matters, not merely those directly pertaining to religion. Just how to bring about this reform he did not know, but he first hoped to convert a monarch. It was to King Francis I that he dedicated his chief work, *The Christian Institution,* which he wrote in Latin at the age of twenty-six and afterward translated into French. He had already given up his connection with the Roman Catholic Church, and he was in exile. The book, though otherwise highly successful, failed in its immediate purpose. The King saw in Protestantism little more than an attack upon the established order of things.

John Calvin came to the Swiss city of Geneva in 1536, in the course of a journey. There he was impressively called upon by

Guillaume Farel to remain and work for the true religion, or else to suffer the wrath of God. Calvin was impressed by Farel's earnestness, and he stayed in Geneva, except for a period of involuntary exile, until his death.

The city had about ten thousand inhabitants. It was somewhat vaguely subjected to the authority of the Duke of Savoy and the Bishop of Geneva but had become virtually self-governing. The bishop who held office when Protestant ideas were brought into the city was the son of a prostitute and a priest.

A SWISS EPICURE

A drawing by Hans Holbein in a copy of Erasmus, *The Praise of Folly,* Basle, 1514.

Opposition to Farel's preaching came from loyal Catholics and from those who considered his moral standards too strict. At one time he was driven out of Geneva, and he sent in another preacher before he dared to return himself. Then gaining control of affairs, he abolished all the Church festivals except Sunday and prohibited such worldly amusements as dancing and masquerading.

Protestant writers tell us how exceedingly immoral Geneva was before it came under the influence of the Reformation. Moral comparisons are difficult, especially where no statistical information is available, and it is impossible to say definitely whether or not Switzerland in general and Geneva in particular were more addicted than other parts of Europe to brawling, gaming, and wenching. The city possessed a large number of sumptuary and regulatory ordinances before the Protestant preachers came. One of them enacted in 1534 forbade men and women to attend the same baths. Most citizens of Geneva were undoubtedly people who were in the habit of obeying the law and treating their neighbors fairly, but who worried little about the wrath to come.

In Calvin's eyes the city was immoral. The asceticism which the Catholic Church sought, not always very urgently, to impose upon persons consecrated to religion, Calvin wished to enforce on all Christians. The one concession he made to human nature was the abolition of compulsory celibacy, even if, or perhaps just because, he considered sex a sign of the innate sinfulness of mankind. For Calvin, the Old Testament, especially in the passages which enjoined sorrow, was more essential than the New: "Unto the woman he said, I will greatly multiply thy sorrow and thy conception: in sorrow thou shalt bring forth children; and thy desire shall be to thy husband, and he shall rule over thee."

Calvin was logical, and if there are contradictions in his creed, it is chiefly because there are contradictions in the Bible upon which he built. We can find in the Scriptures the idea that all human actions reflect the divine will, the doctrine that men are saved only by faith in Jesus Christ, and definite laws for the government of the Jews, perhaps for that of Christians also. Calvin felt that faith is the one essential, but that it is necessarily reflected in the actions of the believer.

The people of Geneva, though they called themselves Christians, permitted prostitutes to roam about in search of patrons and tolerated many wineshops and gambling houses. They stopped work on saints' days and enjoyed themselves at singing and dancing. They had artistic embellishments in their churches which Calvin denounced as violating a definite command in the Old Testament. He considered the music of their religious services equally sinful.

Effective opposition to the theology of Farel and Calvin soon disappeared in Geneva. The citizens came docilely in groups of ten to subscribe to a fairly short and simple statement of Protestant views. But matters of ritual aroused a struggle. Calvin and Farel were banished in 1538 for refusing to administer the sacrament with unleavened bread. While ritual disagreements constituted the immediate cause of their exile, it was above all their moral severity that made them obnoxious to many Genevans.

The departure of the two preachers might have meant the end of Calvinism, even the end of Protestantism, in Geneva if it had not been for the refugees who poured into the city. They were fanatical Protestants who had made great sacrifices for their faith. Zealots almost invariably triumph over Laodiceans if the parties are about equal in number; and so it came to pass in Geneva that Calvin's friends became stronger while he was away. He had an opportunity to demonstrate his ability as a Protestant apologist, and he was called back to the city. He brought with him a wife, the widow of an Anabaptist preacher whom he had married at Strassburg after he had carefully consulted his friends about the desirability of the match. The matter of love played no part in the marriage.

For more than two decades Calvin dominated Geneva, despite the fact that he had almost as many enemies as friends there. The city never had a population of more than twenty thousand, including the refugees, but the period of Calvin's rule is of great historical importance. Among the foreigners who came to study at his feet were a few of energy and ability approaching his own, who returned to their homes full of his doctrines. His influence was finally to extend not only to the churches calling themselves Reformed, Congregational, or Presbyterian, but to all Protestantism and even beyond its limits.

Calvin taught that the Church has no power to punish offenders except by excluding them from communion. Among the sins that should be dealt with in such a way he included quarrelsomeness, prize fighting, drunkenness, extravagance, fornication, adultery, perjury, slander, blasphemy, and idolatry. However, in the case of some of these offenses repentance might bring readmission to the Church. Under the conditions then prevailing, excommunication was very disagreeable, but we must not suppose that it was ordinarily the sole penalty. The sinners of Geneva were turned over to the secular arm, and Calvin's authority extended to the magistrates as to the ecclesiastical officers.

The Genevan laws regulating the expenditures and the most intimate actions of the people were not new in principle, for such legislation was common all through the Middle Ages. The difference was one of severity: Calvin seemed to be determined that every butcher and apprentice carpenter in Geneva should be a saint, no matter how much the lash and the noose had to be used for the attainment of this desirable end.

A girl who struck her mother was put to death. A boy was whipped by the public executioner for calling his mother a thief and a she-devil. A gambler was made to stand in the pillory with a chain about his neck. Drunkards were sharply punished, though moderate drinking of light wine was neither a sin nor a crime. A man who swore by "the blood and body of Christ" was pilloried for an hour. Another was imprisoned for calling his son Claude (the name of a Catholic saint) instead of Abraham, as his minister desired.

The law regulated the number of guests who might be received at a wedding and the courses that might be served. It forbade unseemly displays of joy, all dancing included. Indeed, dancing or watching others dance was a crime on any occasion. There were long lists of fabrics and styles which Genevans were not permitted to use in their clothing. For example, gold and silver chains, embroidered or silk-lined doublets and hosen, embroidered sleeves, and hats of certain shapes were forbidden. It was punishable to appear on the street after nine o'clock in the evening, to neglect saying grace before and after meals, to sing "foolish" songs, and to read such courtly romances as *Amadis of Gaul* and other books which were considered immoral or frivolous.

Ministers were very carefully guarded, and they were exceedingly sensitive to real and imaginary insults. A young woman was summoned before the authorities to clear herself of the charge that she had glanced amorously at a clergyman. Three men were imprisoned for laughing while a sermon was being preached. Another was banished from the city for three months because he had said of an ass, "He brays a beautiful psalm." A woman was flogged for singing a secular air to a psalm tune.

Although it was exceedingly dangerous to criticize Calvin, Beza tells us that dogs were named after him in Geneva and that he was often referred to as Cain. In truth, he had few genuine friends, but many supporters who considered his stern rule necessary. We are told of a banker who, just before his execution for adultery, declared that he was being rightfully punished. Apparently the majority of the people did share Calvin's moral views; yet a widespread disrespect for law arose, and there is evidence to support the opinion that sexual offenses actually increased in Geneva during this period. Certainly the city was considered licentious in the succeeding century, when Milton spoke of it as one of "these places where vice meets with so little discouragement, and is practiced with so little shame."

Geneva was presently to be distinguished for religious liberalism, too, in spite of the stern doctrines that were taught and the precise forms of worship that were enforced under Calvin's rule. Willingly or unwillingly, people had to listen to two long sermons every Sunday as well as to other ministerial discourses during the week. Some of the Genevans yearned for the rites of Catholicism or found it difficult to break themselves of old habits. An old woman was severely whipped for lighting a candle and muttering a litany. Many persons of doubtful orthodoxy were banished from the city; some others, who were considered more dangerous, suffered the punishment of death.

The most famous victim is Servetus, a Spanish Unitarian or pantheist, who fled from Catholic tribunals and was caught in Geneva. He had committed no crime at all within the jurisdiction of the city, but the fact that he had written against the Holy Trinity obviously made it necessary for Calvin to have him put to death. Calvin's defenders maintain that he did not want to have the heretic burned alive, which is improbable, and they declare that most of Calvin's contemporaries were no less intolerant than he, which is true.

In addition to heretics, a number of people were executed at Geneva as witches or willful carriers of the plague. Rationalism was decidedly out of favor. Calvin considered it a sin against religion to deny that the earth is the center of the universe. The

CALVIN AT THE BURNING OF SERVETUS
After a caricature of the sixteenth century.

Reformation, and especially Calvinism, checked the tendency toward freedom of thought and expression without which scientific advancement is impossible. We are told that the Protestant Revolution ultimately favored the growth of tolerance and even of rationalism. Perhaps this is true, but its immediate result was a great stimulation of heresy-hunting all over Europe.

Buckle has suggested that Calvinism is largely responsible

for the spread of democratic ideals, a theology based upon salvation by faith alone being especially suitable for the poor and the weak, while the rich and powerful prefer one of good works. As a matter of fact, Calvinism actually increased the religious importance of all sorts of daily actions. Calvin's attack upon the saving power of good works was inspired, no doubt, by the idea prevalent in Catholic countries that salvation could be bought; but this was not aristocratic, since the widow's mite was held to be quite as efficacious as the rich man's bag of gold.

Calvinism ultimately had a certain effect in promoting social and political democracy because it encouraged the growth of the middle class. Vicarious piety was abolished, and all Christian believers were supposed to be consecrated to the service of God. The consecration was to be shown not only in their specifically holy acts, but in everything they did. It was a dreadful sin to waste money for any luxury. Hence, excess earnings were applied to capital. The Church needed comparatively little, since it rejected fine buildings and elaborate ceremonials with horror. As for charity, the prime consideration was that it should not be extended to the able-bodied and lazy. Working and saving came to be the primary virtues in Calvinistic countries.

Calvin considered usury sinful, but he did permit the charging of a low rate of interest, under elaborate restrictions. The Reformed ministers sometimes quarreled with the business men who held the principal civil offices in Geneva. Avarice, manifested in usury and fraud, was one of the offenses punishable by exclusion from communion. The merchants did not object, as long as the definition of avarice suited them. At one time the ministers asked for an order forbidding the export of wine, contending that the price in Geneva was too high. The magistrates refused to lay such an embargo, on the ground that wheat could not be imported if wine were not sent out. When, shortly after Calvin's death, the clergy complained that debtors were being subjected to double usury because the purchasing power of money was rising, the authorities stood fast for the rights of the creditor class.

Calvin did not trust the people, but he helped the growth of democracy. He considered wealth and virtue incompatible, but his work stimulated the rise of industrial capitalism. The liberal theologies he detested presently arose out of Reformed and Congregationalist churches.

§ 3

A long series of religious wars resulted from the Protestant Revolution, and the Christian virtue of turning the other cheek was much neglected. If the killing of human beings is immoral, even when inspired by pious zeal, the Reformation was morally harmful, at least in this one respect. The blame cannot be put on the Catholic party alone, though the massacre of St. Bartholomew and the slaughter of the Inquisition are wont to come to mind first. Calvinists and Lutherans showed themselves equally intolerant and unscrupulous, and the bitter quarrels between Protestant groups enabled the Roman Catholic Church to regain much lost territory. Hundreds of thousands of people perished in the religious wars and persecutions which began during the sixteenth century. The toleration which now exists is of fairly recent origin and cannot be considered a direct result of the Protestant Revolution.

In general, the Reformation depressed the status of women. The Renaissance encouraged their education, and put on a much firmer basis the chivalric idealization of the sex which had struggled all through the Middle Ages against a conception of feminine weakness and sinfulness. Some of the men of the Italian Renaissance said things about the position and the capability of women which would seem radically feministic even now. Learned women were common in the nobility as well as among courtesans. While some of the early Protestant women were good scholars, the tendency of the Reformation was to take away from them the opportunity to study and assert themselves. The reformers laid much stress upon the Scriptural passages which pronounce the female sex inferior and command wives to obey their husbands.

Catherine de Medici, who is usually held responsible for the massacre of St. Bartholomew, is also credited with the introduction of the corset in something like its present form. The primitive forerunner of this garment seems to have been intended to conceal the feminine bosom, but its effect was just the opposite. The popularity of the corset in the late Renaissance period is an evidence of women's influence: in the harem lands, where masculine convenience alone is considered, women do not flaunt their charms in public. But perhaps the majority of women, as distinguished from great and from courtly ladies, made no particular gain at this time. They remained subject to the rod of the father or husband, in the good old-fashioned way. And in all cases, in Catholic as well as in Protestant countries, the end of the Renaissance meant the waning of feminine power, which was to revive under non-Christian and partially anti-Christian influences in the eighteenth century.

One result of the Protestant Revolution was the Counter Reformation within the Catholic Church, which had important moral aspects. The Medici popes, with their Renaissance sympathies, were succeeded during Luther's lifetime by a pontiff who hated antique hedonism. Fig leaves were supplied for the nude statues in the Vatican, and Michelangelo's "Last Judgment" was made respectable by the addition of painted drawers. Pietism and prudery generally ruled at Rome thereafter, and Catholic opposition to "immodest" clothing and "immoral" books has been still greater since the attacks on the Church of the Enlightenment period.

Some of the reforms met with strong opposition. Thus, all the prostitutes of Rome were banished in 1566, but the public revenue suffered so seriously from their departure that they were soon invited to return. Prostitution was of immense economic importance toward the end of the Middle Ages, and attempts at suppression usually were fruitless.

To complicate the moral problems involved, a great wave of syphilis spread over Europe. The disease was probably introduced from America by Columbus's sailors. Other venereal disorders were as old as history in the eastern hemisphere, but they were seldom feared. Syphilis became a dreadful scourge in the last few years of the fifteenth century and the early decades of the sixteenth. The mortality was very much higher than it is now, for means of dealing with the disease were little understood, and, apparently, no racial immunity had yet developed against it in Europe. It quickly became known that the infection spread from brothels, and there were hygienic as well as conscientious reasons for closing them. Syphilis is as much responsible as the Protestant Revolution for some changes in moral standards which have taken place in modern times.

§ 4

The question of Sunday observance was brought into prominence by the Reformation. As the name of the first day of the week implies, it used to be consecrated to the sun and its god. The Roman Emperor Constantine, whose conversion from Mithraism to Christianity determined that Europe should finally accept the new religion, had his old faith at least half-consciously in mind when he commanded his subjects to rest on "the venerable day of the sun." At about this time Christians were ceasing to consider Saturday especially sacred. It was agreed that Sunday should be observed in honor of the Resurrection of Christ.

At the third council of Orleans, 583, agricultural labor was forbidden on Sunday, and the bishops were authorized to punish those who violated the order. During the late Middle Ages the Roman Catholic Church insisted on the necessity of worship every Sunday morning but did not forbid harmless sports and amusements in the afternoon.

Most Protestant reformers of the sixteenth century were content with this arrangement. Calvin joined the young men of Geneva in bowling on Sunday, and sometimes allowed military drills between sermons. Some Protestant leaders tried to revive the sanctity of Saturday, and one or two thought that it made no difference which day of the week was set apart for rest, recreation, and worship.

The Reformation eliminated most or all of the saints' days and festivals which shared holiness with Sunday in Catholic Europe.

Though it reduced the labor done on the first day of the week, it abolished a large number of holidays. Calvinism went furthest in this direction, an additional reason why it was a suitable creed for the industrial middle class.

CHAPTER III

MRS. MAC GRUNDY OF SCOTLAND

§ 1

A T the beginning of the modern era much of Scotland was still barbarous. The lack of centralized power increased during the fifteenth and sixteenth centuries. When the Scots were not fighting against England, there were always private wars between Highlanders and Lowlanders or between the feudal lords and the burghers, the peasants, or rival nobles.

But there were intervals of peace and prosperity for the cities. An important literature flourished while English poetry, following the death of Chaucer, was at a low ebb. The Scottish writers of this and earlier times knew little of prudish scruples. Their country had no serious objection to pleasure-seeking and merriment.

The existence of handfasting, a sort of trial marriage, shows that moral standards were not extremely rigid. Extravagant vices, however, were put beyond the reach of the masses of the people by the comparative infertility of the soil. The growing middle class attached great importance to sobriety and thrift. Many sumptuary laws were enacted toward the close of the Middle Ages, among them one denying persons below the rank of earl the right to use foreign drugs and confections at their weddings.

The Scottish priests, who gained popularity for a time by supporting the national hero, Robert Bruce, despite his excommunication by the Pope, fell into general disfavor before Luther's time. As Dr. Preserved Smith says: "In no country was the corruption greater. The bishops and priests took concubines and ate and drank and were drunken and buffeted their fellow men. They exacted their fees to the last farthing, an especially odious one being the claim of the priest to the best cow on the death of a parishioner. As a consequence the parsons and monks were hated by the laity."

King James V of Scotland married Mary of Lorraine, whose brothers were the chief leaders in the anti-Huguenot movement in France. Mary, Queen of Scots, married Francis II, King of France. These alliances, which were considered necessary to protect Scotland against its "natural enemy," England, brought many French influences into the country, and also a host of French nobles, soldiers, and priests. The Scottish burghers liked the French ecclesiastics even less than their own.

Meanwhile, as we shall see in the next chapter, there was a great upheaval in the Anglican Church. Henry VIII of England considered it desirable to increase religious unrest in Scotland, and he allowed the smuggling of Lutheran books and English Bibles into that country. He helped in another way to heighten Scottish interest in the Reformation. By giving monastic property to his nobles he aroused the cupidity of the Scottish lords.

The persecuting zeal displayed by the ecclesiastical and civil authorities of Scotland failed to stamp out Lutheranism. In response to a demand which could not be denied, the reading of the Scriptures in English or a Scottish dialect was made lawful in 1543. If we can believe a contemporary Protestant writer, the priests were angered by this permission because few of them had read the Bible themselves, and some believed the New Testament to have been written by an archheretic named Martin Luther. It is said that a bishop proudly boasted he was too pious to know anything of either the Old or the New Testament.

The Protestant Revolution in Scotland was largely the accomplishment of John Knox. Trained in the law after he had been admitted to the minor orders of the Church, Knox was at the age of forty a very obscure person, simply the tutor of a laird's son. He became the disciple of a Lutheran heretic who was buried alive at St. Andrews. By way of revenge a group of Protestants murdered Cardinal Beaton. Knox approved of their act. Soon he was preaching that the Pope was "ane antichrist."

A French expedition captured the castle of St. Andrews, and

Knox was among those carried off. He then spent nineteen months as a galley slave, his hatred of Catholicism steadily growing. His release was perhaps due to a request by Edward VI, King of England. He went to that country, where a bishop with Roman Catholic sympathies tried to persecute him. Himself offered an English bishopric, Knox declined to accept it on the ground that the Church still retained too much of the popish taint. Soon after Mary Tudor was crowned Queen of England, Knox found it necessary to flee.

At the age of forty-eight Knox married an English girl, apparently after having fallen in love with her mother. Tongues wagged when she left her husband for a time to stay at Geneva with Mr. and Mrs. Knox. At Geneva, it is more important to note, Knox came under the influence of John Calvin and the Calvinistic theology. Thenceforth Scottish Protestantism can no longer be described as Lutheran.

John Knox was less coldly logical and more emotional than Calvin, but he seldom swerved from the task he believed that God had assigned to him, that of destroying popery in Scotland. Carlyle's description is admiring: "But a true, loving, illuminating laugh mounts-up over the earnest visage; not a loud laugh; you would say, a laugh in the *eyes* most of all. An honest-hearted, brotherly man; brother to the high, brother also to the low; sincere in his sympathy with both. He has his pipe of Bourdeaux, too, we find, in that old Edinburgh house of his; a cheery social man, with faces that loved him."

Knox laughed most heartily at the sufferings of his enemies. However, there were many trials for him to experience before his final triumph. As the pastor of a congregation of English refugees at Frankfurt-am-Main his radical Calvinism was found too extreme for the majority, and he was driven from the city. He was able to visit Scotland, but chose flight in preference to martyrdom after nine months there. He wrote a book particularly attacking Mary of Guise, Mary of England, and Catherine de Medici; and he was indiscreet enough to make two generalizations in it which were obnoxious to Queen Elizabeth of England: first, that no woman is fit to govern; second, that birth alone without the approval of God does not make a monarch. Elizabeth showed her displeasure by refusing to let Knox pass through England when in 1559 he returned once more to take up his work in Scotland.

His fiery sermons proved very effective in strengthening the Protestant cause. At Perth his denunciation of the papacy caused a mob to sack the monasteries. However, Knox refused to assume the responsibility for their disorder, no doubt realizing that the violence of the rabble would be obnoxious to the nobles whom it was necessary to win over. The support of a foreign monarch to cope with the French armies in Scotland also seemed essential. Elizabeth's dislike for Knox almost prevented her from helping the Reformers, but she finally sent troops into Scotland. Then, by agreement, both the English and the French forces were withdrawn. The Protestant Revolution was free to proceed.

In the year 1560 the Scottish Calvinists subscribed to a confession of faith. One of the articles was as follows: "We utterly abhor the blasphemy of those that affirm that men who live according to equity and justice shall be saved, what religion soever they shall have professed." The Protestants were strong enough to secure the passage of a law forbidding the celebration of the mass, under penalty of flogging and the confiscation of goods for the first offense, banishment for the second, and death for the third. Mary and Francis reluctantly signed it.

The triumph of the Reformed party, thus concretely demonstrated, at first brought little reward to the new ministers. The assembly of 1576 formally permitted ministers and readers to add to their income by working as tapsters in taverns, provided that they conducted themselves decently.

The part Knox played in the Scottish Reformation was such as to add prestige to the Protestant clergy. Despite Calvin's advice to be more cautious, he boldly opposed his will to that of the Queen. Mary Stuart returned to Scotland, a widow, in 1561. The Reformed leaders were as much opposed to her love of pleasure as to her Catholicism. Soon Knox was preaching violently against the Queen and her court, heaping scorn and invective upon the gaiety of the palace. When Mary sent for him, he denounced her to her face. He did not absolutely condemn dancing and other amusements, he said, but she and her courtiers were carrying matters to excess in order to scandalize God's chosen people, the Scottish Calvinists. According to Knox's own account, he "merrily" told the court ladies that, despite all their luxuries, their bodies would soon be eaten by worms. The Queen feared him, and her handkerchiefs were often drenched with tears at the end of their interviews.

John Knox, as a widower of fifty-nine, married Margaret Stewart, the seventeen-year-old daughter of a lord. It is interesting to notice that such a disproportion of age between bridegroom and bride was forbidden in Geneva under the Calvinist régime. But Knox was still vigorous, and Margaret bore him three sons. He suffered a stroke of apoplexy at the age of sixty-five, but kept on preaching and working as long as he lived.

Mary Stuart was not destroyed by Knox, but rather by passion in herself and others. She married her half-cousin, Darnley, who put to death an Italian favorite of hers whom he accused of adultery with her. A new lover successfully dynamited the house in which her husband lay asleep, and it was soon reported that she intended to marry him. Perhaps more because she was suspected of intending to suppress Protestantism by force than for causing Darnley's murder, Mary was imprisoned and made to abdicate in favor of her infant son. She escaped, only to meet a tragic death in England.

§ 2

Although the government and the nobles of Scotland seized most of the spoils of the Roman Catholic Church, the Protestant clergy gradually acquired power much greater than the priests had ever possessed. The office of bishop was abolished in 1580 and the Scottish Church established on a democratic basis. Thereafter the mass of the Scottish people associated prelacy with popery. Ministers derived little influence from the rank or wealth of their parents. It was the voice of God speaking through them that mattered, and their business was the establishment of a divine kingdom on earth. Yet there was a crowned monarch at

JOHN KNOX ADMONISHING MARY QUEEN OF SCOTS

Edinburgh, with opinions of his own. James VI acquired a strong distaste for Presbyterianism, the theocracy of which menaced his rights as king. More than that, he had several narrow escapes from death at the hands of the nobles whom the ministers egged on against him.

During the seventeenth century, theology was the chief intellectual interest in Scotland. It was made to embrace most ethical and political problems, for the ministers knew how to find far-reaching authority and rules of action in the Bible. Although Scriptural interpretation occupied the best minds in the land, nothing at all resembling the higher criticism was permitted.

The ministers were seldom rich, but Scotland was a poor country, and they fared much better than the working classes from which most of them sprang. They wore plain clothing and enjoyed few luxuries, it is true, but gaiety and display and even comfort were rare things in seventeenth-century Scotland. The Protestant clergymen had, except in the mountain fastnesses where feudal loyalty and Catholicism lingered on, immense power throughout the land.

They denounced the godless tyranny of monarchs and nobles, but the ministers were the real tyrants. To pass a reverend gentleman on the street without giving him a properly respectful salute was a punishable act. To speak slighting words of a minister was a still greater offense, and to differ with him on any subject whatsoever might be construed as heresy. The Calvinist representatives of God claimed far more personal holiness than the Catholic priests had ever ventured to ascribe to themselves. They represented that divine revenge would fall upon anyone who arrested a minister or brought a civil action against him.

The ministers were very eloquent in representing the horrors certain to fall upon sinners in this world and in the next. A man who mocked at a Scottish presbyter might expect, for instance, to have his cattle carried off by Highland brigands, to perish miserably, and then to be tormented in Hell with fire and ice and lashes and all sorts of tortures too cunning for mortals to conceive.

WITCHES IN THEIR LIGHTER MOMENTS

The Witches' Sabbath as envisaged in a sixteenth-century engraving in the Bibliothèque Nationale, Paris.

Europe as a whole was very superstitious in the seventeenth century, and rationalism meant rather less in Scotland than it did in England or France. There were a few skeptics, it seems, who ventured to doubt if witches actually roamed about the world. The zealots denounced them as Sadducees. For most Scotchmen the world was full of invisible marvels. When a disease epidemic came, the ministers preached sermons on the sins that had provoked God to send such punishment.

One of the foremost duties of every Scot was listening to the divine word as it was expounded by the minister of his parish. A bit of stormy weather was no excuse at all for staying away from church. Spies went from house to house to make sure that no one who could walk or be carried missed the sermon. There was great edification in some of the discourses, which lasted for three or four hours. On fast days relays of half a dozen ministers preached about brimstone and angry devils from dawn to twilight. The majority of the people rather liked being terrified so. The objectors were grievously punished.

The Scottish ministers identified the natural with the sinful. They held up their Kirk as the standard of earthly beauty, denouncing all profane æstheticism. The Protestant Revolution checked the development of church architecture in Scotland, as it did in other countries. Catholicism stimulated music and the arts, though within somewhat circumscribed forms, whereas Calvinism made these things sinful. Sculpture and painting were particularly suspect because they served the popish adoration of the saints. Still, some Scots came under Renaissance influences during the seventeenth century, among them George Jameson of Aberdeen, the first great British painter in oils.

The ministers called on their parishioners to live in such a way as to please a jealous divinity who could not approve of frolicsome conduct, who would surely send a dreadful plague if wedding guests danced and joked and enjoyed themselves in the good old Scottish way. The Reverend Mr. Abernathy said, "Pleasures are most carefully to be avoided, because they both harm and deceive." His objection was not to some particular forms of enjoyment. "Beat down thy body," he preached, "and bring it into subjection by abstaining, not only from unlawful pleasures, but also from lawful and indifferent delights." He denounced the alternation of feast and fast days as a popish iniquity. Scots were to fast often, but never to feast, to weep often, but never to laugh. The Reverend Mr. Rutherford pointed out that Christ had never laughed, and he suggested the desirability of following such an example.

Celibacy, indeed, was no part of the Calvinistic discipline. In theory, sexual intercourse was not to produce any satisfaction except that of fulfilling the divine command to increase and multiply. It resulted in pain for the parturient woman, according to God's word in Eden.

Calvin attacked the theatre, and even the more liberal Luther spoke of it as "fools' work" which might be dangerous under some circumstances. John Knox was once present at a wedding where a play was acted, but this was in the nature of propaganda for the Reformed doctrines. The Scottish Book of Discipline made it a punishable offense to attend any theatrical performance whatsoever.

In 1603 the Presbytery of Aberdeen ordered the head of every house to keep a rod always ready for correcting his wife, his children, and his servants if they used objectionable language. The ordinance was chiefly directed at the profane use of divine names and words suggestive of holy things. Swearing was held to be very close to popery. Similarly sinful was the singing of traditional songs on New Year's Day.

Toward the end of the seventeenth century a horrified outcry arose when the courts in Edinburgh were adjourned for the last week of December. Was there to be a revival of the old pagan and popish holiday of Christmas? Calvin thought the anniversary was one that might well be kept, though he frowned upon many of the traditional usages connected with it. The Scottish Presbyterians went further, and there are still Scotchmen who regard the celebration of Christmas with suspicion.

The holiness of Sunday was carefully guarded. Swimming and other recreations which the less pious were permitted to pursue during the week, if their ministers were not very strict, might not be indulged in at all on the Lord's Day. A sad countenance was held to be part of the Sunday garb. Markets were kept closed on Saturday and Monday lest the spirit of profane business should approach too close to Sunday. For some of the Presbyterians it was an enormity to speak of Sunday and Wednesday, or of January and March, since the names were obviously derived from those of pagan gods. The proper thing was to substitute First-Day (or the Lord's Day), Third-Day, First-Month, and so on.

Religious toleration was conspicuously absent. It was a crime at law to give any hospitality to a Catholic, whether in a private house or an inn. Scots were advised not to travel abroad, at least into Catholic countries, because he who touches pitch is defiled.

The ministers enjoyed a virtual monopoly in teaching and moralizing. During the greater part of the seventeenth century most of the law courts were under their control. The prison, the pillory, the whipping post, and the halter were used to enforce their standards of conduct.

During the late mediæval period sexual relations were very loose in Scotland. The long list of incestuous degrees issued by the Church, which might keep a man from lawfully marrying any woman in his neighborhood, did something to bring such a condition about. The fact that the Catholic clergy as a class was only nominally celibate also added to the relaxation of sexual morals. The Presbyterian ministers, in their anxiety to suppress adultery and fornication, established a system of espionage and caused severe penalties to be applied to delinquents. They were subjected to public shame in the churches, excluded from the communion table, heavily fined, flogged, ducked in the pond, and otherwise punished. Such severity, which did little to reduce sexual irregularity, certainly made the spectators more brutal. Infanticide was very common in Scotland while the compulsory church penance of unmarried mothers continued.

Hard drinking was firmly established as a Scottish custom. The early Calvinist ministers, though they concerned themselves with all sorts of domestic affairs, had little to say against the use of whiskey. Very strict religionists deplored the habit of arising early for the special purpose of imbibing strong drink, but even the clergymen who denounced all pleasure did not think of urging their parishioners to give up alcoholic beverages, for these were considered essential to human life. A song of the time has to do with "four drunken maidens," who do not seem to have been altogether exceptional members of their sex. The elders who were commissioned to suppress drunkenness sometimes had unsteady legs of their own to worry about. Before going to sit for hours in damp, unheated churches almost everybody took a nip or two.

Children were kept in hand with stern measures, and Solomon's wisdom about the sparing of the rod was one of the best-known passages in the Old Testament. An act of Parliament passed in 1551 provided that boys and girls who ran about in church should be whipped. A beadle armed with a red wand watched them and also roused sleepy adults.

§ 3

The personal union of Scotland with England brought about a great deal of ecclesiastical commotion in the northern kingdom. The excitement came to a climax when Archbishop Laud tried to restore episcopal church government in Scotland, along with the celebration of Christmas and the playing of games on Sunday. He approved also of auricular confession and prayers for the dead. Laud realized how strong the sentiment against such restorations was, and he hoped to divert it by encouraging crusades against witchcraft and abstract denunciations of the Roman Catholic Church. While the Scots eagerly took up the persecution of witches, they did not forget their hatred of Laud and the bishops. Rebellion could not be averted.

As the price of Scottish support in his abortive bid for the throne after the execution of his father, the Covenanters exacted from Charles II a pledge to establish Presbyterianism in both Scotland and England. During the years when England and Scotland were kingless, the Calvinist ministers exercised great power in both countries. In 1650 the Synod of Fife established a morals police force, with an elder in charge of each of the seventeen quarters in every parish. These officials were required "to take notice of all disorderly walkers, especially neglecters of God's worship in their families, swearers, haunters of ale-houses, especially at unreasonable hours and long sitters there and drinkers of healths," reporting delinquents to the Sessions.

THE SCOTTISH GRINDSTONE

From a broadside of 1651, "Old sayings and predictions verified and fulfilled, touching the young King of Scotland and his gude subjects."

Sports of all kinds were associated in seventeenth-century Scotland with papacy or episcopacy, and the prejudice against athletic games was long-lasting. Cleanliness of the skin was by no means honored next to godliness. We have, indeed, accounts of ministers who changed their shirts after every sermon, because their vigorous preaching caused them to sweat abundantly. Muscular exertion in the pulpit seemed proper enough.

The Civil War gave prominence to the opponents of Presbyterian strictness in Scotland. This group became vocal, for example, in the physician and poet Archibald Pitcairne. He received part of his education at Paris and Leyden, becoming familiar with alien ideals. Pitcairne's writings are chiefly remembered for their ribald satirical treatment of the Presbyterian ministers.

In Scotland as well as in England the restoration of Charles II seemed to mean the complete triumph of the hedonists. The Merry Monarch's reign opened with a great banquet at Edinburgh, where three hundred glasses were gleefully broken. Thereafter the two opposing parties were clearly defined. Generally speaking, the Whigs were stern Presbyterians, while the less ascetic Jacobites were loyal to the House of Stuart and the Episcopal Church. The bulk of the people, especially in the towns, were Whigs. The Jacobites consisted mainly of a few aristocrats and the feudal groups loyal to them.

Religious toleration had little support in seventeenth-century Scotland, though new Protestant sects began to appear. Walter Scott, an ancestor of the novelist, became a convert to Quakerism, whereupon he was confined in prison and (1665) his children were taken from his control to be educated in the official faith. Under Charles II and James II there were bishops in Scotland. The zealous Presbyterian Covenanters drove them out after James fled to France.

The extreme Presbyterians, dour, mirth-hating men, seem to have been driven to outdo themselves in fanaticism by the carousals which the Jacobite cavaliers enjoyed in the time of their triumph. The old ascetic attitude was even intensified among the Cameronians. One of them, Patrick Walker, used language which seemed to imply that he considered dancing worse than murder. "Whatever be the many foul blots recorded of the saints in Scripture," he said, "none of them is charged with this regular fit of distraction."

Scotland as a whole became much more liberal and tolerant during the eighteenth century. Yet the old stern standards and the superstitions of the preceding period lingered on. In 1730 we find William Forbes, professor of law at the University of Glasgow, talking of witchcraft in the same tone he would have used if he had referred to murder. When, six years later, the laws condemning witches to death were repealed, many pious people bemoaned the sinful skepticism of the times. The belief in special providences remained with most Scots through the eighteenth century, and there are still good men and women in Scotland who think a disease epidemic can best be fought with fasting and prayer.

Theological liberalism and radicalism came into Scotland from England and France during the eighteenth century. Philosophy, economics, physical science, and poetry flourished, much to the disgust of the religious zealots.

Seventeenth-century pietism was such as to encourage hypocrisy among those who were not inherently saints. This fact was pointed out by the skeptics as soon as it was safe for them to express themselves openly. Erskine of Grange, who sat on the bench in the early part of the eighteenth century, enjoyed the inquisitorial task of routing out vice, but he was himself guilty of hanging matters. Such discrepancies helped to bring about the reaction which is shown in the writings of Pitcairne and then of Burns.

Some of the first bold protesters had to suffer for their daring. Erskine prowled about Allan Ramsay's circulating library in Edinburgh, trying to suppress it because it supplied light worldly literature instead of Calvinistic theology. Ramsay's theatre was forced to close by the passage of a special law. However, the opposition of the Kirk was not long effective against the drama. In 1756 the Reverend John Home's tragedy of *Douglas* was produced in Edinburgh. He had to give up his charge at Athelstaneford as a result, but many ministers were frequent attendants at the playhouse a few decades later. Music and dancing came slowly into respectability. Several athletic games, although denounced from many pulpits, were taken into popular favor.

The spread of skepticism affected Sunday observance hardly at all. In the eighteenth century most Scotchmen still accepted without question the idea that it is necessary to suffer for being a Christian. Many churches remained seatless and unheated, and stern elders considered the installation of a stove equivalent to the approval of a new heresy. Religious services were frequent and lengthy. In "The Holy Fair" Robert Burns describes the annual religious meeting which was such a great social event for the peasants. At the end:

> There's some are fou o' love divine;
> There's some are fou o' brandy;
> An' mony jobs that day begin,
> May end in houghmagandie
> Some ither day.

The pride that almost all Scots take in Burns and his poetry shows that the backbone of the stern Calvinistic theology has been broken. His writings are distinctly opposed to the older religion and morality. "A Poet's Welcome to his Love-Begotten Daughter" is still a defiant title. Burns had friends among the liberal clergy. It is in his "Epistle to the Reverend John M'Math" that he declares:

> An honest man may like a glass,
> An honest man may like a lass.

The crusade against fornication raged on in the first half of the eighteenth century, and it continued, somewhat abated, in the second half. Peasant lads and even proud lairds flocked to church when an attractive girl had to sit on the stool of repentance, but it does not appear that either piety or chastity was promoted by such edifying sights.

The revenue laws of this period were universally considered unjust, and smuggling was the chief occupation in many a Scotch village. Loss of life often resulted when revenue agents attempted to make arrests. As a result, contempt for law in general was somewhat encouraged.

Tea and whiskey became popular Scotch drinks in the latter half of the eighteenth century. Tea was denounced as a vile drug which would be the ruin of the country. Good Scotch whiskey has always enjoyed a certain respectability in the land of its manufacture. Clifton Johnson says of a small town at the beginning of the twentieth century that "even a church elder could stagger after a visit to Perth without losing caste." Prohibitionists have won minor skirmishes in Scotland, but they have never been able to convert the country as a whole to their view. Scotch moralists are wont to speak more harshly of fornication than of drunkenness. Still, heavy drinking seems to be much rarer now than it was toward the end of the eighteenth century.

The rate of illegitimacy in Scotland has been comparatively high. In 1855 many people who thought that the Calvinistic severity which still prevailed in a large part of the country guaranteed good morals were surprised to find that the first official statistics on the subject showed the bastardy rate to be a little above that of England and Wales, considerably above that of Ireland. Illegitimacy per thousand births was higher in some Scotch counties than anywhere in France except Paris. Bastardy has since shown a tendency to diminish, for reasons which we shall consider later.

The recent moral history of Scotland has been affected by many of the same forces that have been at work in England and the United States. Smoking became popular with both men and women in the eighteenth century. Though cards are still known in some parts of the country as "the Deil's beuks" (the Devil's books), gambling is widespread.

Heresy-hunting did not entirely die out in the eighteenth century. Within the last hundred years ministers have been disciplined for teaching that the possibility of salvation is open to all and for applying critical tests to the Bible. However, little remains of the old religious intolerance except the insistence upon Sunday quiet. The observance of the day is especially strict in some of the rural districts. From one of them comes the story of the boy who wished aloud, one Sunday afternoon, that he were a vegetable. Asked why, he replied that then he "wad be oot."

CHAPTER IV

FROM A MANY-WIVED KING THROUGH
A VIRGIN QUEEN

§ 1

PERHAPS the Protestant Revolution really began with the work of John Wycliffe, an English priest of the fourteenth century. His followers, the Lollards, became very numerous, and the Biblical translation for which he was responsible enjoyed a wide circulation. Because Wycliffe's teachings were held responsible for an agrarian revolt, they fell into bad repute with the authorities. Nevertheless, their influence remained in many parts of England during the fifteenth and sixteenth centuries. Lollardry made the path easier for later ecclesiastical reformers on the European Continent also.

The priests, and more especially the upper clergy, of England retained great power and wealth. Some ardent royalists lamented that they were richer than the king. The jurisdiction of the Church courts extended to all sorts of civil and criminal cases arising out of domestic relations. There were numerous complaints about corrupt practices in the administration of the canon law; and a struggle arose over the question of submitting appeals to Rome, where gold offered in the proper places could alone bring success.

At the beginning of Henry VIII's reign the House of Lords comprised eighty-four members, of whom forty-eight sat by virtue of their ecclesiastical offices. The clergy controlled the universities and education in general. They were in charge of almost all the charitable institutions. They acted as ministers and advisers to the King.

Priests and soldiers were the most influential people in England during the Middle Ages. When the Wars of the Roses ended, the merchants and master artisans, assured of internal peace, were in a position to acquire consequence and authority. The old feudalism died out, and though the aristocracy of land-owners was destined to remain intrenched for centuries behind vested privileges, the middle classes had visions of self-assertion. Many of its members leaned toward Lollardry, though rejecting the egalitarian doctrines associated with it. Their *bourgeois* love of law and order by no means extended to an admiration of the hordes of hungry monks and friars who seemed to them to be devouring the country. They wanted above all a unification of power which should make petty feudal wars entirely impos-sible, and they considered brawling abbots and bishops as objec-tionable as belligerent barons. The middle classes embraced royalism and nationalism.

Luther's work attracted much interest in England. A scholar named William Tyndale, discouraged by his bishop from a plan to translate the New Testament into English, went to Germany. There he prepared and published a new version of the principal books of the Bible, having six thousand copies smuggled into England. Scriptural study was strongly revived at the universi-ties and in London.

The most loyal of Catholics could not deny that ecclesiastical abuses existed. An English Parliament which showed itself thor-oughly hostile to heresy protested against several of them, includ-ing the excessive number of holidays on which no work might be carried on. Henry VIII himself appeared as a controversialist against the Lutheran doctrines. The Pope, grateful for his orthodox zeal, bestowed upon him and his successors the title of Defender of the Faith. In spite of Henry's defense, heresy remained uncrushed. It even crept into England, where it was not at first treated as a capital offense.

Shortly before Luther nailed up his defiant theses, a prom-inent Englishman, Sir Thomas More, wrote in favor of religious toleration. In *Utopia* he imagined a country of great social per-fection, where liberty of religion was freely permitted and only atheists were ineligible to public office. Such tolerance was extremely rare in More's time. Yet he was a zealous Catholic who finally lost his life for refusing to deny the papal supremacy.

In mid-Victorian days an Irish judge, John O'Hagan, wrote of him: "When Thomas More was Lord Chancellor and went each morning to take his seat in Westminster Hall, it was his invariable custom to enter the court of King's Bench where his father sat, to kneel down and ask his blessing. What in our time would excite unmeasured ridicule was then a simple act of filial and religious piety."

It was undisputed that children owed great respect and absolute obedience to their parents. More says of the Utopians: "The husbands chastise their wives, and the parents their children, unless they have committed so horrible an offense that its public punishment contributes much to the advancement of good morality." He meant, of course, to express his approval of such a usage, but it was by no means utopian. In the best families of England, grown daughters were beaten until blood ran from cheeks and back. The thrashing of wives was not uncommon in any social class.

The people of England were accustomed to see naked men and women flogged at the cart's tail for petty crimes. They had yet to acquire a reputation for prudery. In Utopia, the Land of Nowhere, it was the practice for "a sad and honest matron" to show every prospective bride, whether maid or widow, unclothed to the wooer. More, a sort of primitive eugenist, thought that blemishes and marks of disease should not be hidden from the prospective bridegroom. He was also an enemy to extramarital sexual experiences, and he caused the fornicators of Utopia to be severely punished.

Sir Thomas More's book contains a list of the moral evils prevalent in the England of his day: "for not only gentlemen's servants, but also handicraftsmen, yea, and almost the ploughmen of the country, with all other sorts of people, use much strange and proud novelty in their apparel, and an excess of riot and sumptuous fare at their tables. Now bawds, queans, whores, harlots, strumpets, brothels, stews, wine-taverns, ale-houses, with so many naughty, lewd, and unlawful games, as dice, cards, tables, tennis, bowls, quoits; do not all these send the haunters of them straight to stealing, when their money is gone?" More's

HENRY VIII, PATERFAMILIAS

Henry, Catherine Parr, and Prince Edward. A portrait attributed to Guillim Stretes at Hampton Court. Courtesy of the Metropolitan Museum of Art, and by gracious permission of His Majesty the King.

opposition to pleasure was somewhat extreme, but his indictment reminds us that puritanical morality existed in England before the Puritans arose.

Many sumptuary laws existed when Henry VIII came to the throne, and a number of important ones were added during his reign. The right to play the games which More calls illegal was indeed very much restricted. However, it was found that young men who were kept from bowling and playing tennis amused themselves in more mischievous ways, and it was usual to wink at violations of the law.

Sir Thomas More, despite his anxiety over cards and quoits, used to boast of his own skill in casting a cock-steel. It is said, too, that grave old Roger Ascham, also a renowned moralist, ruined himself by betting on cockfights. Animal combats have interested the English for many centuries.

The law of the land regulated the clothing that members of the various social classes might wear. Black genet was a fur reserved to royalty. Only nobles above the rank of viscount were permitted to wear sable, and trimming of marten or velvet distinguished persons with an annual income of over two hundred marks.

The fashionable masculine costume of Henry VIII's day included tight hose emphasizing the shape of the upper legs and a conspicuous pouch or braguette, which was often highly decorated and adorned with jewels. Women wore tightly-laced dresses which called attention to their breasts. The laws on the subject of clothes were intended to keep the poor from aping their betters, not to preserve chastity or modesty.

According to the standards of our degenerate age, the amount of good English ale consumed under Henry VIII was gargantuan. The Queen's maids of honor were each allowed four and a half gallons daily. They were obviously not expected to drink water, a liquid then in little favor.

Ale-drinking ceased to be the chief occupation of the royal court when piquant food for gossip was supplied. King Henry became deeply interested in Anne Boleyn and discovered that he had been living in sin because of Queen Catherine's previous

marriage to his elder brother. His application for an annulment
of the marriage met with serious difficulties. It would make
Princess Mary illegitimate and put the Queen to great shame.
Her nephew, the Emperor Charles V, practically made a prisoner of the Pope, who was forced to quibble and evade the issue.

Thomas Cromwell, a minister of state with Machiavellian
ideas, persuaded Henry to break away from ecclesiastical control on the part of the Pope. Parliament declared the King to
be "the Head of the Church and Clergy of England, so far as
the Law of Christ will allow." He secretly married Anne Boleyn,
and the Archbishop of Canterbury's court declared his previous
marriage with Catherine invalid.

Henry looked with disfavor upon the monasteries because
some of them had opposed the annulment, and he envied them
their wealth. Proceeding cautiously, he sent out agents to report on their condition. The "Black Book" which they presented to him charged that vice and crime were prevalent in
about one-third of the monasteries of England. The charges
were by no means unfounded. With few exceptions, the monks
were enemies to Renaissance learning. Sir Thomas More tells
us of their general indolence. Religious zeal was rare among
them; but no doubt they did beneficial work as well as evil,
and many poor people depended upon them for alms. Good
or bad, they were driven from their monasteries. The spoils
were distributed among a great many nobles and some commoners, who became staunch defenders of the independence of
the Anglican Church.

The Lutherans, considering Henry their enemy, denounced
him for cohabiting immorally with Anne Boleyn. The King
decided to suppress their doctrines, which were being heard more
openly in England, with the utmost vigor. He caused burning
alive to be made the penalty for denying the real presence in
the mass, and even refusing to confess to a priest became a felony. At the same time it was a capital offense to say that the
King was not the supreme head of the Church in England. Both
Protestants and Roman Catholics, therefore, were put to death
for expressing their opinions. There were hundreds of martyrs,

HENRY VIII WITH HIS NEW BIBLE SPURNS THE POPE

From John Foxe, *Ecclesiastical History*, 1576.

but most people accepted the new religious regulations indifferently or with satisfaction. A certain amount of agnosticism and indifference to religion appeared among the educated.

The King did not live happily ever after with Anne Boleyn, who was put to death on a charge of adultery. Her successor, Jane Seymour, died in childbirth. For political reasons Cromwell then arranged a marriage with a fat, ugly German princess. This was the true work of treason that ruined and killed the minister. After Anne of Cleves had been quietly divorced, Henry took a fourth wife, who was executed for adultery, and a fifth one, who had the good luck to outlive him. Three children survived Henry VIII: Mary, by Catherine of Aragon; Elizabeth, by Anne Boleyn; and Edward, by Jane Seymour.

§ 2

Edward VI was nine years old when he came to the throne in 1547. The chief regent, his mother's brother, is known in history as the Duke of Somerset. Inclination and policy alike made Somerset support the party which stood for further ecclesiastical change. So far the people of England had hardly felt the effects of the Reformation. A few had benefited from the suppression of the monasteries. Some resented the destruction of statues and sacred relics which had taken place in the churches. But under Edward much greater innovations appeared. The Archbishop of Canterbury openly ate meat during Lent. Clergymen were permitted to marry, and many availed themselves of the permission. Religious services were much altered.

It is generally agreed that a moral relaxation occurred during the reign of Edward VI. Perhaps his father's domestic scandals were in part responsible for the change. Under Edward the courtiers were reputed to be especially loose in their sexual behavior. Moreover, the great changes in religion and ecclesiastical government brought about widespread restlessness. Henry and Somerset both appealed to greed in carrying out their policies. The common people, especially those who had been accustomed to receive alms from the monasteries, resented the

enrichment of the comparatively few. Dissatisfaction and disorder increased. Vagabonds swarmed over the kingdom.

Somerset was much too hasty in introducing dogmas and ceremonies which were acceptable to only a small part of the people.
However objectionable some Roman Catholic abuses might be,
the forms of worship had all sorts of old and dear associations.
And Somerset showed no willingness to tolerate religious differences. Yet the heresy laws of Henry VIII were no longer
applicable, and the delay in putting new ones into effect miti-
gated somewhat the persecution of devout Catholics.

The sudden change from a Catholic priesthood to a Protestant
ministry did not bring into sudden flowering a body of educated,
altruistic, and pious clergymen. There were landowners who
made their illiterate servants bear the clerical titles while they
kept the tithes for themselves. Although not all the new ministers were of this sort, very few were distinguished for moral
zeal, and fewer still for learning. Conditions would probably
have changed in a few years if Edward had lived. The shadow
of impending death hung over his reign, and it appeared probable that Catholic Mary, despite her bastardization, would be
his successor.

When Edward died, after a reign of only six years, the radical
Protestant movement quickly collapsed. In religious affairs there
was a reversion to the conditions existing at the close of Henry
VIII's reign, and Queen Mary wished to go much further. She
insisted that the taint of heresy should be entirely wiped out.
Among those burned alive for Protestantism during the few
years she reigned were five bishops, fifty-five women, and four
young children. No person was too high in rank, none too low,
to be condemned to death by the ecclesiastical courts. The persecutions failed utterly in their purpose, since they added a
little to the numbers and much to the zeal of the Protestant
party. The half-hearted and the timid conformed to the official
Roman Catholic worship. Again there was a feeling that death
would mend matters.

The Catholics, and, at first, many Protestants as well, denied
that Anne Boleyn had ever been Henry VIII's lawful wife. It

was Mary's unpopularity in the last year of her short reign that legitimated Elizabeth in the eyes of most Englishmen. Anne Boleyn's daughter found her most determined enemies among Catholic zealots, and though she was inclined to be conservative, she had to go at least as far as her father in religious change. Events turned out so that fidelity to the independent Church of·England became a patriotic duty for her subjects.

A LAMENTABLE SPECTACLE

of iij women, with a sely infant brastyng out of the mother's wombe, beyng first taken out of the fire and cast in againe, and so all burned together in the Isle of Garnesey, 1556, July 18." From John Foxe, *Ecclesiastical History*, 1576.

The Anglican Church split into two factions. One was radically Protestant, and this, in Elizabeth's mind, was associated with disrespect for authority. She thought her subjects should be content with the religious usages which she, as their ruler, prescribed for them. At the beginning of her reign in 1558, the great majority of Englishmen were willing to worship under any form fixed by law. Loyalty to the Queen became a primary consideration, extending into all religious groups. Although the

Pope excommunicated her and denied her right to the throne, English Catholics flocked to the colors and fought against the Catholic but foreign invader.

Agnosticism and atheism became much more important in Elizabeth's reign, gathering force from the ideas of the Italian Renaissance as well as from the sight of people turning their religious coats at frequent intervals to please new rulers. The Queen herself was suspected by those close to her of indifference to religion, but she considered conformity essential to strong government.

Many matters which are now purely secular were then connected with the Church. Ecclesiastical law governed marriage, sexual relations, inheritance, and even the taking of interest on money. It was an accepted principle that clergymen and law officers should work together in enforcing desirable modes of conduct. Almost all thinkers of the time agreed that anarchy would result if the subjects of a monarch were not forced to worship in a uniform manner. Thus it came about in England that the extreme Calvinists were treated almost as harshly as the Roman Catholics, though the loyalty of the former was undoubted, while the latter were suspected of being engaged in a conspiracy to murder the Queen.

Although Elizabeth did not duplicate the bloody persecutions of her half-sister Mary, she was hardly more tolerant in principle. In the early part of her reign it became a criminal offense to practice the rites of the Roman Catholic Church. However, Elizabeth was forced by political considerations to respect the religious differences of her subjects. She dared not marry either a Roman Catholic or a Protestant prince. Because she could not bring herself to wed any of her subjects, she remained all her life "the Virgin Queen."

During the first eleven years of Elizabeth's reign no Catholic was put to death for religion. A number were executed later, but upon conviction of treason rather than heresy. Two Dutch Anabaptists were burned alive in England in 1575. English Anabaptists or Baptists were at this time quite rare.

It is difficult to pick a definite date for the beginning of Puritanism. In many ways, Lollardry was the same thing. Then came the first radical Protestants of Henry VIII's reign. Their party was favored under Edward VI, when it became Calvinistic. The Marian persecutions only served to widen the breach between it and the more conservative Protestant group.

Some of the bitterest arguments raged over the question of clerical costume. The early Puritans were horrified to see ministers attired in garments suggestive of those worn by Roman Catholic priests. As objectionable to them as white surplices were the singing of litanies in church, the sign of the cross in baptism, the use of the ring in marriage, and kneeling while receiving the Lord's Supper. These were all popish ceremonies, they felt.

In Elizabeth's reign and for some time after we find the radical Protestants complaining that all worthy and pious people were opprobriously called Puritans. The term was not yet one of honor; it implied excessive claims to personal sanctity. The Puritans later found it appropriate, because, they said, they wanted to purge the English Church of all Romish abominations and leave it purely Christian. Most of the Protestant refugees from France and Flanders who settled in English towns were Calvinists. They strengthened the position of Puritanism among the industrial middle classes.

Popular superstition was stimulated rather than destroyed by the religious changes. It was in Henry VIII's reign that Parliament made witchcraft a felony. There was a certain amount of witch-hunting under Elizabeth, though some rationalists were denying the existence of diabolic spirits. At first these bold skeptics were little heeded, even by the learned, and then they were denounced as atheists.

The Renaissance and Reformation movements in England were at most points diametrically opposed to each other. However, some scholars and writers who learned much from pagan books were nevertheless devoted to Christianity and to narrow sectarianism. Scholarship was encouraged to a certain extent by the Protestant doctrine of individual priesthood and Biblical interpretation; but this dogma was much restricted in application, since it appeared that equality and anarchism could be justified by quotations from the Scriptures. At this time most Puritans would have brusquely swept aside the idea that all men are created equal as a mere Anabaptist heresy, capable of producing the greatest evils. Authority was stressed in learning as well as in domestic and political relations.

§ 3

In the poetry of Edmund Spenser we find early Puritanism tinged with the Renaissance spirit. The feeling for sensuous pleasure which derives from the latter is bound up with moralizing, which we are wont to associate with the former. Writing to Sir Walter Raleigh a letter which served as preface to the first part of *The Faerie Queen,* the poet announced his purpose: "The general end therefore of all the book is to fashion a gentleman or noble person in virtuous and gentle discipline." Of course, "gentle" here is not a pacific adjective, as everybody who has read through the descriptions of the numerous fights in the poem knows. *The Faerie Queen* is an epic at once of Puritan and of feudal ideals.

Spenser's earlier poem, *The Shepherd's Calendar,* expresses more definitely the religious aspiration of the Puritans. It attacks the idle, lazy, and vicious ministers, some of whom had been priests under Mary, who had no principles of their own and did not mind changing the doctrines to which they subscribed. There is much evidence to the effect that the clergymen of Elizabethan days were actually looser in their morals than the lay population. Laxity in sexual matters was encouraged by the uncertain status of clerical marriage. The Queen once told an archbishop's wife that she could not call her by the title of a married woman. But the celibacy of the clergy in the Anglican Church was no longer compulsory at the end of her reign.

Spenser lived for a time in Ireland, where his high moral ideals did not keep him from approving the barbarous measures then being used in an attempt to Anglicize the country. The Irish

[67]

were treated as savage rebels because they desired to keep their own language and customs and the usages of the Roman Catholic Church. Some very moral Englishmen thought the Irish natives should all be exterminated and their property divided among loyal English Protestants.

Ethical precepts were much in favor, and not only among the Puritans. In 1565 Sir Henry Sidney, then Lord Deputy of Ireland, wrote a letter of advice to his son Philip at Shrewsbury School. Temperance, the great Greek virtue, formed the burden: "Use moderate diet, so as after your meat, you may find your wit fresher, and not duller; and your body more lively, and not more heavy. Seldom drink wines, and yet sometimes do; lest, being forced to drink upon the sudden, you should find yourself inflamed." Beer was the boy's accustomed drink.

"Give yourself to be merry," the letter went on, "but let your mouth be ever void of scurrility and biting words to any man." And there was an injunction of unbending morality: "Above all things, tell no untruth, no not in trifles." Sir Philip Sidney acquired along with military and with literary skill a sense of the obligations imposed by nobility. The story goes, and it may well be true, that, being offered a drink as he lay dying on a foreign battlefield, he asked that the water should be given to a common soldier instead: "His need is greater than mine." Chivalry could be revived for a brief period by Sir Philip Sidney and a few of his kind, but the development of firearms destroyed the supremacy of the knight. Trade flourished, and the morality of the middle classes became more and more the dominant standard in England.

In the days of Sidney and Spenser a lady sat upon the throne to inspire chivalrous deeds. Elizabeth was physically attractive in her youth, and conscious of her attractions, too. Though fond of pleasure, she read almost daily, in the original, the New Testament and the great works of Greek literature. For in her time, before the sun of the Renaissance set, it was considered proper that women of high station should be educated in the classics and even in theology.

Queen Elizabeth was especially proud of her astuteness in

THE VIRGIN QUEEN

A portrait by an unknown artist in the possession of the Duke of Devonshire.

the arts of diplomatic trickery. She did not believe, with Sir Henry Sidney, that a lie is always loathsome. We are told that she sometimes swore like a fishwife, and the fish-sellers of London really knew how to swear in those days. Elizabeth's favorite oath is said to have been "By God's son!"

She petted young squires and court favorites quite openly. She was wont to boast that she could kick high when she danced, even higher than her cousin, Mary Stuart. When she disliked the color of a courtier's coat, she expressed her displeasure by spitting at the offender. In part her freedom of manners was typical of the times, but it was to some extent her own.

Many grave men complained that the manners and morals of England had deteriorated because of the influence of the Italian Renaissance. Under Elizabeth, more especially in those upper circles which cared little for the moral creed of the Puritans, Italy set the example in a number of ways. According to hostile critics, it was teaching atheism, voluptuousness, cruelty, and extravagance to Englishmen. "An Italianate Englishman is an incarnate devil," was a common saying in Italy as well as England.

At the same time the English acquired much wisdom and feeling for beauty from the Italians. It is difficult to account for the flowerings of Elizabethan poetry unless we give credit to a fertilization from Italy. Indeed, the one great pre-Elizabethan poet of England, Geoffrey Chaucer, owed much to Italian masters. The Italianate Englishman was generally interested in coarser forms of pleasure. We often find him accused of "unnatural vice," by which we are chiefly to understand homosexual practices. He was sometimes said to have learned in Italy the art of murdering with poison.

Moral infection was supposed to be conveyed by Italian books, especially those which were translated. It is curious that a Puritan who advocated very strict moral standards, Geoffrey Fenton, made an English adaptation of Bandello's *Tragic Tales*. Fenton did, indeed, change the book greatly, inserting Biblical allusions, disrespectful references to the papacy, and an argument that husbands should use the rod to keep their wives properly subordinate. The Puritans did not object to prose fiction if it conveyed a moral lesson.

Italian voluptuousness, which we can find even in *The Faerie Queen*, stands out more clearly in Marlowe's *Hero and Leander*. Hero is portrayed with

> Her wide sleeves green, and border'd with a grove,
> Where Venus in her naked glory strove
> To please the careless and disdainful eyes
> Of proud Adonis, that before her lies.

The story of Venus and "proud Adonis" appears in one of Shakespeare's poems, and the manner of *The Rape of Lucrece* is similar. A catalogue of Elizabethan poets who wrote what later and more precise ages were to consider indecent would be a long one.

Marlowe, one of the very greatest of English dramatists, died in a tavern brawl, the result of a quarrel over a wench. Worse still, in the eyes of some of his contemporaries, he was an atheist. Many of the poets and playwrights lived wild lives and were familiar with all the criminal haunts and thievish tricks of London. Their interests were reflected in their writings.

The Prologue to John Day's *Isle of Gulls*, which was produced early in the reign of James I, asks, "What should chaste ears do at a play?" Mediæval naïveté was gone, and the shocking of Puritans had become one of the pleasures of the sophisticates. The dramatists often made direct attacks upon the Puritans, laughing at their claims to moral excellence. The latter found even more reason to complain about the licentiousness of the stage as the Renaissance period moved toward its close. Arthur Symons would apply to Middleton's plays as a whole, and perhaps some of us would apply to the whole age, the following passage from *The Phoenix*:

> What monstrous days are these!
> Not only to be vicious most men study,
> But in it to be ugly; strive to exceed
> Each other in the most deformed deed.

The Elizabethan comedy was concerned even more than the tragedy with sex, and a brothel or low tavern was often the principal setting. While the influence of Latin and Italian plays accounts to some extent for this fact, the English dramatists were familiar with such haunts; and they put on the stage the stews of Elizabethan and Jacobean London rather than the conventional classic lupanar.

Whore, cuckold, and other words of the same sort appear in the titles of the plays. We must remember that some words which our dictionaries brand as "not in decent use" came as readily to the tongues of moralizing Puritans as to those of Renaissance frolickers. They had not yet been displaced from respectable society by substitutes or silence. Moreover, euphuism and similar movements toward daintiness of language, which testified to the importance of feminine influence, were chiefly efficacious in driving out rough, rude words. While the Protestant preacher denounced the whore, the hedonist labeled her a courtly lady and decked her out as such.

Shakespeare's *Measure for Measure* deals with a strict moralist (he happens to be a Catholic) much in the manner of a recent play, *Rain.* It turns out that Angelo is actually not

> a man whose blood
> Is very snow-broth; one who never feels
> The wanton stings and motions of sense.

There is a passage in the play which seems to reflect the poet's own attitude—as it undoubtedly does the attitude of his audience —toward Puritan morality. A comic character asks the magistrate who is charged with enforcing a law that makes fornication a capital offense: "Does your worship mean to geld and splay all the youth of the city?" "No, Pompey." "Truly sir, in my poor opinion, they will to't then."

It was very dangerous to present open skepticism upon the stage in Shakespeare's day. Still, it seems to be clear that he had little faith in personal immortality or in the Judæo-Christian God. Although Shakespeare spoke disrespectfully of the Puri-

ELIZABETHAN MIMES AND MORRIS DANCERS

From Douce, A Dissertation on the Ancient Morris Dance.

tans, he showed no particular animosity to Catholics, High Church Anglicans, or pagans as such.

Early in Elizabeth's reign strong opposition to the popular amusements of the time appeared. In 1572 Parliament grappled once more with the problem of vagabondage, which had been acute since the suppression of the monasteries. The House of Commons included actors and minstrels along with bearwards and fencers under the heading of vagabonds, who were to be severely punished. The Lords objected, but the Commons had their way. However, it was provided that the monarch, the peers of the realm, and certain officials of the royal court might license and protect companies of actors.

It was not difficult for reputable troupes to be exempted from the penalties of vagabondage. Indeed, there is little evidence that the law interfered seriously with bear baiting or with exhibitions of skill in fencing and juggling. Companies of boy players were formed from the choristers of St. Paul's and the royal chapel and from the students of Westminster School. Actors frequently presented their plays before the Queen. At the accession of James I, Shakespeare was one of the actors marching in procession to welcome him.

Women and girls did not perform in public, and their parts were taken by boys. The ladies who appeared as spectators at the playhouses concealed their faces with masks. Many of the females who came to the theatre with piquant disguises had felt the smart of the beadle's whip. The intimate association of prostitution with the playhouse was one of the reasons why the Puritans spoke bitterly of the latter.

Theatres were not welcomed within the city limits of London. The municipal authorities expressed fear of danger from fire, rioting, and contagious disease. Besides, Puritanism and the stern morality which became increasingly identified with it grew rapidly in London. The theatres were erected in suburban districts where brothels and pits for the baiting of animals flourished.

Attacks upon the drama as pagan and immoral began in the earliest days of Christianity. One offshoot of the Roman comedy, the mime, was closely connected with prostitution. In the Middle Ages the Catholic Church adapted dramatic representations for religious purposes. Such a use of the stage seemed to Puritans just as objectionable as the sexual orgies that sometimes formed part of the mimes. The theatre, they argued, was historically identified with lascivious paganism and popish abominations, and it had grown no better.

The Puritans objected particularly to the performance of plays on Sunday. They accused the actors who took the part of women of violating a Biblical command. Though Elizabeth forbade religious and political discussion on the stage, it soon became evident that the dramatists all stood for the Renaissance spirit as opposed to Puritanism.

The zealots of London were not able, during the Elizabethan period, to prevent stage plays from being acted in and about the city. In some of the smaller towns the Puritans succeeded in abolishing traditional plays and pageants. The London players kept their playhouses open on Sunday and during Lent despite a prohibitory law. The Blackfriars Theatre was built in a neighborhood renowned for its piety, and crowds of bejeweled gentlemen stepped out of dazzling coaches to flaunt their extravagance before the eyes of sober business men. Worst of all, apprentices were encouraged to ape their betters, being admitted into the theatre for a low fee.

The stage was fiercely attacked in sermons and pamphlets. One of the first Elizabethan denunciations to arouse wide interest was Stephen Gosson's *The School of Abuse, containing a Pleasant Invective against Poets, Players, Jesters, and Suchlike Caterpillars of a Commonwealth.* Gosson, an Oxford man who came to London and tried to make his fortune by writing pastorals and plays and perhaps by acting also, became converted to Puritanism and wrote against his old manner of living. He impudently dedicated his work to Sir Philip Sidney, who replied in the *Apology for Poesie.* Thomas Lodge wrote a book in defense of the drama, poetry, and music, which he published surreptitiously because the Puritans were by this time strong enough to prevent the issuance of a license. The Lord Mayor of London encouraged the printing of various tracts which attacked the theatre.

A Puritan clergyman named John Stockwood assembled objections to the drama, dancing, gambling, Sunday sports, and other "evils" of the same general nature. "It is better," he thought, "to be subject to magistrate under whom nothing is lawful than under him to whom all things are lawful." Yet he might have observed that when many things are unlawful, much is unlawfully done. The fact that the legislators and the enforcement officers of the Elizabethan period often had different notions of right and wrong added to the complexity of the problem.

The Virgin Queen's subjects were, indeed, accustomed to having their actions regulated at every turn. Parliament made sumptuary and mercantile laws intended to foster English manufactures, to preserve badges of rank and wealth, and to bring about other beneficial results. Outer garments of crimson were restricted to royalty, while the wearing of velvet except in sleeves was forbidden to the lower classes. Town corporations dealt harshly with idle apprentices, workmen who were disobedient to their masters, and women who showed insufficient respect to their husbands. Where the local authorities sympathized with Puritanism, the use of profane language was sharply punished. The prosecution of this sin became vigorous after 1600.

Elizabeth's England was generally prosperous. New opportunities in commerce and industry brought wealth to many individuals. Partly under Italian influence, extravagance of all sorts flourished. The fashions changed with great rapidity, mutability and gaiety being as characteristic of men's clothes as of women's. We are told of young heirs who sold their estates and put the proceeds on their backs.

The middle-class Puritans bemoaned the wasteful shifting of fashions, with great destruction of value as one mode after another became obsolete. They felt sure that England was going to the dogs, with its plays and books and breeches so strongly tinged with Italian abominations. The Queen made use of rouge and false hair, and her example was widely followed. Cosmetics of all sorts were highly prized. Huge ruffs made necessary the employment of starch, which the Puritans named "the Devil's liquor." Fashionable men and women used large quantities of perfume, but little soap and water.

The dandies of Elizabethan England showed off their finery at balls and many different kinds of social functions. Masquerades became fashionable, allowing opportunities for licit and illicit love-making. The sumptuary laws were widely violated. However, the very poor were not able to engage in many of the pleasures forbidden by law. They had to be conservative in dress because they could not afford to throw garments away when the winds of fashion shifted.

Philip Stubbs, the Puritan author of *The Anatomy of Abuses*, found it necessary to explain that his critical remarks about the wearing of fine clothes were not intended to reflect upon "any either noble, honorable, or worshipful," and that he conceded the right of persons belonging to the upper classes to adorn themselves as they chose. At the same time he wrote about many "abuses" which were necessarily confined to the wealthy. He was certainly thinking of the courtiers, though he did not dare to mention them.

In the first edition of his book (1586) Stubbs said he objected only to the abuse of pleasure, not to its proper use. He admitted, for instance, that some plays might teach valuable lessons, and he thought that private dancing might do no particular harm. In later editions he identified himself with the Puritan extremists by omitting such exceptions. Almost everything enjoyable became a sin in his eyes. Stubbs denounces the use of cosmetics on the ground that the women who buy them "deny the Lord to be either merciful or almighty, or both, and so consequently no God at all; for if he could not have made them fair, then is he not almighty; and if he could and would not, then is he a merciful God?"

There appeared in Elizabethan days certain Puritan rumblings about the sin of drunkenness. Still, Englishmen of all shades of religious belief drank beer in quantities which made visitors from abroad gasp in astonishment. Malt beverages, usually brewed at home, were drunk freely by both sexes and all ages. When the

Earl of Leicester entertained the Queen, 365 hogsheads of beer were consumed. The importation of wine increased considerably, but its use seems to have been condemned less than that of such other luxuries as forks and glass windows, which appeared sure to make England weak and effeminate. Distilled beverages began to acquire a certain popularity under Dutch and German influences. Tobacco had its enemies when it was introduced from America, but the circle of smokers steadily increased. Feasting was one of the chief amusements of the upper and middle classes: the huge amounts of food ingested at banquets showed that forks, window glass, and tobacco had not noticeably enfeebled the English.

Merry England liked sports in which animals were tormented. Bulls and bears were tied to stakes and worried by dogs or, in another form of the diversion, they were flogged to death. Queen Elizabeth is said to have been fond of bear baiting. The rural population cherished other traditional forms of diversion. The people inherited a large number of holidays from the Middle Ages. One of the most popular was May Day, when the May-pole was set up. The Puritans called it a "stinking idol." It was a tribute to a phallic god and a symbol of fertility. May Day observances in the Elizabethan age still preserved some elements of the old orgies connected with phallic worship. For the most part, only symbolism remained, but this was clear enough to disturb the zealots. Other holidays of pagan or popish origin were equally frowned upon by the Puritans.

The Protestant radicals of England always believed God to be active on their side. When a defective scaffolding about a bear pit broke on a Sunday, causing death and injury to many spectators, the Puritans triumphantly announced that divine retribution had fallen upon the Sabbath-breakers. It was God's wrath, too, that caused accidents in theatres, whereas miraculous providences saved the godly.

Toward the end of the sixteenth century, Sunday observance became a matter of prime importance to the Puritans. The Sabbath laws of the Hebrews were taken over with minor changes as bases for the observance of the first day of the week by English Christians. Almost all classes treated Sunday as more or less different from other days. For example, Queen Elizabeth did not kick so high then. But she ordered the clergy to preach that it was no sin to work on Sundays and holidays during harvest time.

The Puritans considered Sunday labor sinful, even if waste would be caused by its omission. Some of their ministers proved from Scriptural texts that it is a deadly sin to ring church bells more than once in summoning people to attend services on the first day of the week. "Sabbath-breaking" was denounced as a crime worse than murder. It included, for the radical Calvinists, almost all Sunday activities neither specifically religious nor essential for the preservation of life.

During Elizabeth's reign Parliament often sat on Sunday, the majority of moderate Puritans not yet having been converted to extreme views about the sanctity of the day. Under James I, however, the Sunday sittings were abandoned. One of the leading Puritan pleas for Sunday observance, by Dr. Bound, makes the usual class distinctions, arguing that feasts should not be given on the Lord's Day "except by lords, knights, and persons of quality."

The life of Elizabethan Englishmen in general, though, was little affected by the sermonizing of the more precise Puritans. Ballad-singers and dancers, jugglers and idlers and wandering prostitutes continued to stroll or reel along English roads, though with a wary eye for Puritan justices of the peace, all through the reign of good Queen Bess. Even where the Puritans succeeded in having May-poles destroyed, love awakened with the spring, and the old phallic god continued to be worshiped behind English hedges.

Apparently, lawlessness and cruelty increased in England during Elizabeth's reign. The popular love of blood was satisfied not only in the baiting pits, but in the theatres as well. Some of the tragedies contained dozens of murders apiece. Many heroes of the day grew rich at piracy; the Queen knighted Francis Drake, and she was not above sharing in the spoils he had seized from a country with which England was technically at

THE MAY-POLE

After a painting by J. Nash.

peace. There was much political corruption, despite the wave of patriotism which swept through the country.

Religious persecutions were by no means unknown, but the great mass of Puritans suffered little or not at all from them. They went to church every Sunday and holiday, as required by law, and they worshiped according to the prescribed forms. They wanted to "purify" the Anglican Church, not to separate from it.

The Catholics suffered, and so did various Protestant sectaries, most of whom may be described as extreme Puritans. They were Brownists or Independents and Baptists who wished to form separate congregations of true believers. Finding themselves hopelessly in the minority, they argued for toleration and sought Scriptural texts that seemed to deny the right of the government to persecute for religion. They declared that true Christians must always be few, for which reason the Church should reject all attempts to force the entire population to join it. These separatists were, in Elizabeth's day, hardly more influential than syndicalists and anarchists are now in the United States, and they were regarded with the same sort of horrified wonder.

The main body of Puritans by no means desired religious toleration. Thomas Cartwright declared, for example, that heretics should be put to death even if they professed repentance of their errors. He was an outstanding Calvinist who lost his professorship at Cambridge because he argued in favor of presbyterian church government and numerous ritual changes. By this time religious toleration was not a mere theory. It actually prevailed in the newly independent Netherlands. Brownists and others who could not worship as they wished in England were made welcome across the North Sea.

CHAPTER V

THE ENGLISH REVOLT AGAINST CHRISTMAS

§ 1

WHEN Elizabeth died, unmarried and childless, in 1603, James VI of Scotland became also King James I of England. James was thirty-seven years old at his accession to the English throne. He had struggled long and not always successfully against the Scotch Presbyterian ministers and had acquired considerable skill in theological and political theorizing. Believing firmly in the divine right of kings, he considered the Anglican form of church government, with the monarch ruling by means of the bishops, the acme of perfection. English Puritanism reminded him unpleasantly of the Scotch Presbyterian clergymen and the theocracy they had established. James was an admirer of the middle way between Roman Catholicism and Presbyterianism. He wanted, that is, to preserve the Church of England in the condition it had officially held under Elizabeth.

The people of England had definitely turned away from the Roman Church. There were exceptions, of course; but, generally speaking, Protestantism and patriotism were closely identified at the time of Elizabeth's death. And a majority of the Protestants seemed to have gone over to the Puritan position. There was no exact definition of Puritan ideals, however, though we can find the opinions of individual Puritans set out at length.

At the very beginning of his reign King James was offered what was known as the Millenary Petition. This contained the signatures of some eight hundred ministers, or about one-tenth of the clergy of England. It asked chiefly for revisions in the church service. According to the desire of the petitioners, clergymen should not be required to wear cap and surplice, the cross should not be used in baptism, the monotony of services should be lessened, and various ceremonies which they considered popish should be eliminated. They humbly asked the King, also, "that the Lord's day be not profaned: the rest on holidays not so strictly urged."

James was not pleased with the petition. All the things that were requested reminded him of Scotch Presbyterianism and of the tyrannical way in which the ministers had treated him, their king. He feared the democratic tendencies associated with the new religion in Scotland. "No bishop, no king," he used to say. If the Church were organized on an equalitarian basis, there could be no true monarchy in the State.

As a matter of fact, very few of the English Puritans were levelers. Almost all were desirous that class distinctions should be maintained and vested interests safeguarded. But many did believe that there was a law of God, revealed in the Holy Scriptures, higher than the royal will. This was a dangerous doctrine, as James knew by experience. If the ministers were accepted as the interpreters of this divine law regulating mundane affairs, then their authority might easily become greater than the king's. If individuals decided for themselves, after reading the Bible, what was wrong and what right, anarchy might result.

Parliament, more especially the House of Commons, became the recognized leader in the Puritan movement. The Commons represented the middle classes, urban and rural, rather than the people as a whole. James was constantly denouncing "Puritans and Novelists," that is, those persons who were asking for new ecclesiastical dogmas and rites. The religious and moral questions that were involved soon became tangled with political issues.

James willingly granted one Puritan demand, that for a new translation of the Bible. Our familiar Authorized or King James Version was not altogether original, for it owed much to earlier English translations; yet a great deal of it reveals literary skill on the part of the Jacobean translators. Though it did not entirely satisfy the Puritans it was better adapted than any other English version to suit the needs of Protestants with widely varying theological views, and it became lastingly popular. It is perhaps worth noticing at this point that the King James Version is inaccurate in many passages, and that pious people desirous of believing the Bible literally, but unacquainted with the original Hebrew and Greek or with more scholarly versions, have often been misled. The chapter headings do not, of course, occur in the original languages at all. The Authorized Version has remained in common use so long that many of its words and idioms have shifted their meanings or become obsolete, with a resulting increase in ambiguity.

The King James Version is still printed with a long dedication to the high and mighty prince who was, "by the grace of God," ruler of three countries (with one of which he had very little to do) and Defender of the Faith. The Tudor kings and queens had proceeded on the assumption that God had given the paramount authority into their hands, but few of them had philosophized about the matter. They had remained generally popular. Mary had been hated by the Protestants and by many of her subjects who objected to her Spanish husband, but even she had been an Englishwoman and the daughter of an English king. Elizabeth had been idolized by most of the people, and indeed had seldom insisted upon unpopular measures.

When James came to the throne, England was more nationalistic than it had ever been before, and there was much quiet resentment of the fact that a foreigner was to be king. James was not handsome. His intellectual ability was little appreciated, except by scholars. The Bible translators spoke of his "many singular and extraordinary graces." It was, obviously, a matter of conventional flattery. The French King called James "the wisest fool in Christendom," because he was learned and could write and say clever things, but usually did foolish ones. James was proud of his logic and his rhetoric, but these very things made deeper the impression of the people that he was pedantic and unkingly.

Elizabeth had taken sides against the Puritans quite as clearly and as vigorously as James. She had not, however, gained their personal animosity to such an extent. The zealots, very soon after the Scottish King came to rule over them, began to wonder if it were not time to proclaim the fallibility of monarchs.

Rumors spread of drunkenness and dreadful sins in the royal palace. It was said that when the King of Denmark paid James a visit, both monarchs became intoxicated. And we hear much of the tears that James was accustomed to shed on the mornings after his debauches, when he thought of how sinful he had been. Probably these stories are much exaggerated: the King drank, but usually not more than he could easily handle. However, there was a great deal of drunkenness among the courtiers and the nobles of England. The common people drank deeply, mostly of home-brewed beverages.

James sometimes indulged himself in mouth-filling oaths, which were dreadful to Puritan ears. The King admitted the sinfulness of swearing, and hoped that he would be forgiven because he swore only when he was in a passion.

As we have seen, one of the "vices" which the Italianate Englishman brought home with him was homosexual love. According to the Old Testament view, accepted without question by the Puritans, pederasty was a sin which should be punished with death. King James had a number of male favorites, to one or two of whom he wrote love letters and for whose sake he gave expensive entertainments at court. Sometimes he mingled love and religion. To Buckingham, one of his minions, he addressed pious advice and meditations on the Lord's Prayer.

James also published a book containing moral precepts. This was the *Basilikon Doron,* supposed to teach his son the proper principles of social and political conduct. The King was deeply interested in witchcraft. He had no doubt at all about the existence of witches, although it is said that he became more skeptical late in life. His enemies said that he was himself something of a sorcerer, or at least that he had encouraged courtiers to practice black magic within the palace. Men who were very close to the King were implicated in a poisoning scandal. In fine, James acquired a very evil reputation. It is but fair to add that the Puritans laid on their colors pretty thickly when they painted persons whom they did not like. It might be argued, too, that the King's least lovable traits were largely due to bad education at the hands of the Scotch Presbyterian ministers. From them he acquired many of his superstitious beliefs, though, to be sure, English tutors would probably have told him also that it is the duty of a Christian to recognize the existence of witches and wizards, along with diabolical powers in general.

Among the King's literary works was *A Counterblast to Tobacco*. Smoking had become almost universal in the upper circles of society. James disliked tobacco, as he also disliked

CONSTERNATION OF THE SMOKER'S FAMILY
A print of the time of James I.

pork, and he tried to justify his repugnance with wise and witty arguments. But it is said that he was finally forced to smoke himself, in order not to feel out of fashion among his courtiers. When he spoke harsh words about tobacco, he was on the Puritan side, for smoking was held by the zealots to be an unnecessary luxury, and the seeking of new pleasurable titillations was considered displeasing to God.

With regard to Sunday observance James held views almost

directly opposed to those of most Puritans. In 1618 he issued his Declaration of Sports, in which he commended the games and festivities of old England and declared it to be his royal desire that dancing, archery, and various other sports and exercises should be practiced after the Sunday church services were finished. He forbade the baiting of bulls and bears as well as the playing of interludes and dramatic performances on Sunday. The Puritans no longer considered these prohibitions sufficient. Some of them openly asserted that to carry out the King's will with regard to Sunday sports would be to disobey the law of God.

It appears that the Catholics in some parts of England were saying that the Protestant religion kept people from enjoying life. James argued that the Papists would win back a majority of the inhabitants of the country to their creed if the Puritans, gaining full control of the Anglican Church, should insist upon too stern a moral code. He insisted, too, that if the working people, who had no free time except on Sunday afternoons, were kept from practicing archery then, England would be unprepared for war. English military greatness had been based upon the skillful use of the bow, and the musket was not yet considered dependable. James pointed out, too, that all attempts to restrict play and pleasure inevitably brought about increased drunkenness and other undesirable results. And besides, he, the King, wanted people to enjoy themselves and to keep up the good old merry games on Sunday afternoons. If Puritans and Precisians did not feel satisfied with the royal order, why, he would harry them out of the land.

A passage from the Declaration will disclose how utterly wicked (in Puritan eyes) it was: "And as for our good people's lawful recreation, our pleasure likewise is that, after the end of divine service, our good people be not disturbed, letted, or discouraged from any lawful recreation, such as dancing, either men or women, archery for men, leaping, vaulting, or any other such recreation, nor from having of May-poles, Whitson ales, and Morris dances, and the setting up of May-poles, and other sports therewith used, so as the same be had in due and convenient time, without impediment or neglect of divine service; and that women shall have leave to carry rushes for the decorating of it, according to their old custom. But withal we do here account still as prohibited all unlawful games to be used upon Sunday only, as bull and bear baitings, interludes, and at all times in the meaner sort of people, by law prohibited, bowling."

The sports that were specifically permitted on Sunday were intended for good people who attended the Anglican churches, not for Roman Catholics or for Puritan recusants. How bitter the Puritans became over attempts to keep the observance of Sunday fairly liberal may be judged from the fact that, in 1621, Parliament expelled one of its members because he had argued that the Sabbath referred to in the Old Testament was without a doubt Saturday, and that the Hebraic Sabbath observances had nothing to do with the Christian Sunday. This critic was also guilty of expressing the view that dancing might possibly be harmless, since David had danced before the Ark. Apparently, the royal will prevailed, and people who wished to enjoy the legally permissible Sunday sports were, in most parishes, permitted to practice them. Nevertheless, the position of the monarchy was much weakened by the struggle, because the Puritans considered the encouragement of recreation on the "Lord's day" one of the worst of the Stuart tyrannies.

Puritanism, which had begun as a dissatisfaction with certain Anglican rites as being unchanged, or insufficiently changed, from those of the Roman Catholic Church, shifted its emphasis somewhat toward matters of general morality. There was a time when many Puritans found nothing wrong in seeing a play, for instance; but it gradually was accepted that all those who wanted to "purify" the Church wanted also to "purify" morals by establishing and enforcing more rigid standards of behavior than had prevailed under popish control.

Calvinism as a theology did not distinguish Puritans clearly from High Church Anglicans, because many elements of Genevan doctrine were, temporarily or permanently, adopted as official by the Church of England. King James believed in foreordination, even though he approved of surplices and of Sunday sports.

But, as we have seen, military drills sometimes took place in Calvin's Geneva between Sunday services. In some respects the moral requirements of the English Puritans went beyond those of the Calvinists on the Continent of Europe. James I was willing enough that the behavior of the common people should be regulated. He did not object when, in 1614, the Lord Mayor of London took strong repressive measures against the brothels and also reduced the number of alehouses in the city and limited the amount of beer which might be sold in each. All through the kingdom, drunkards of low degree were put into the stocks or the pillory or punished in other ignominious ways. Gentlemen, of course, became intoxicated with impunity.

The growth of English commerce, by bringing many seamen into the ports of the kingdom, somewhat relaxed the prevailing morality. In those days voyages were long, and some forms of abstinence were necessarily prolonged as well. Liquors, both fermented and distilled, were indeed available to the sailors on board ship, for they were considered fully as essential as the hard bread and salt meats which were staple elements in maritime diet. Yet sailors indulged themselves in drunken sprees, just as they do now, after having been paid off in port. Commerce retained intimate connections with piracy. Almost every good and brave Englishman considered it virtuous as well as profitable to raid Spanish treasure ships, and Elizabeth had encouraged this ambition. Not so King James, who was anxious to maintain peace with Spain.

James was considered to be friendlier to the Catholic than to the Protestant powers of Europe, and frequent rumors arose of his having been converted to Catholicism. Early in his reign, by way of disproving such a report, James ordered the severe enforcement of the laws which made the observance of Roman Catholic rites illegal. A number of English Papists, consequently made reckless, determined to carry out a wild plot. They managed to introduce a quantity of gunpowder beneath Parliament House, intending to blow up the members and the King when he should come to open their session by addressing them from the throne. The plot was discovered in advance, and the extent of the conspiracy was much magnified. Protestants thought that all the Catholics of England shared in the guilt. The anniversary of the Gunpowder Plot became a regular holiday, which helped to preserve an attitude of hostility to the Roman Catholic Church. Guy Fawkes and his gunpowder thoroughly frightened the King too. He was confirmed in his Protestantism and brought somewhat closer to the Puritans.

Few Englishmen stood aloof from sectarian fanaticism. Even the enlightened Francis Bacon wrote against religious toleration, though he believed that "the temporal sword is to be drawn with great circumspection in cases of religion." He insisted upon the importance of keeping away from the common people the right to persecute for religion. "Let that," he said, "be left unto Anabaptists and other furies." Bacon knew little about the Anabaptists, evidently, for most of them believed in toleration. He thought that because they were democrats, they were obviously wicked people. Writing about superstitions, in 1625, he refers apparently to the Puritans in saying, "Therefore care would be had that, as it fareth in ill purgings, the good be not taken away with the bad; which commonly is done when the people is the reformer."

Were there any real democrats, any genuine equalitarians, in England at this time? Very few, and mostly confined to small, despised sects. And even they were hardly ready to concede that women ought to be treated as the equals of men. It was generally accepted that children should be very respectful to their parents, that wives should submit to the authority of their husbands, and that servants and apprentices should be absolutely obedient to their masters. These principles the Puritans strongly approved, and sometimes they complained that the rod was not sufficiently used for the purpose of keeping natural inferiors in their places.

Commoners had long looked upon the royal authority as something which preserved the peace and saved them from the tyrannies of feudal lordlings. They were very reluctant to undermine it. They were accustomed, also, to look with respect upon the landowning aristocrats, though sometimes with suspicion as well. It was generally believed that differences in rank were divinely ordained.

Nevertheless, the emphasis which Calvinism laid upon God's will had a certain tendency to encourage leveling doctrines. For it was taught that those whom God had elected for salvation would have eternal bliss, while those whom God had set aside for reprobation would, no matter what wealth or power they possessed on earth, be damned to the eternal torments of Hell. In the face of the infinite superiority of divine strength all men seemed to be puny. What did it matter that one was a king and one a beggar, when God was so much greater than both that the difference between them was unimportant in his eyes? Such reasoning had given John Knox the courage to denounce what he considered the wickedness of his Queen. The salvation of one soul mattered as much as the salvation of another. At the same time, the Calvinistic belief in divine decrees led to the inference that men should be content in the positions which God had assigned them.

In the reign of James I the pious members of the trading and industrial classes saw with satisfaction that the divine will had raised them up to general prosperity. After the fall of Antwerp in 1576 there had been a steady growth in the commercial importance of London and in the wealth of individual English merchants. The middle classes feared God and walked in the strait way of righteousness, looking with contempt upon the wicked courtiers of the King. As the traders and manufacturers grew rich, their political power grew. The great nobles and the courtiers turned up their noses at the citizens, utterly unable to conceive of the possibility that tanners and shopkeepers might soon be ruling England. They saw, indeed, that the Puritans controlled the House of Commons, but it seemed that King James was almost always able to do as he pleased.

And yet the middle classes sometimes were victorious in their struggles against royal tyranny. Bacon was disgraced not so much because he was more wicked than other judges as because the people happened to be highly indignant at the moment when his acceptance of presents became known, and somebody had to suffer in order that they should be satisfied. Of course, Bacon's excuse that all the King's judges were in the habit of taking gifts from litigants was not one to satisfy strict moralists. Public corruption in England did not arise under James I, by any means. It had existed, perhaps to an equal extent, under beloved Queen Bess. But the Puritans were hostile to James and his favorites. They were jealous of his usurpations of rights which Parliament supposed to have been gained by its predecessors as permanently belonging to the representatives of the commons and the privileged classes. Elizabeth had believed in the royal prerogative, but she had usually yielded when confronted by united public opinion. James was more stubborn. Dissatisfaction was manifested on all sides, usually in private conversation, for public criticisms of the King were likely to invite prosecutions for sedition.

The growth of Puritan influence showed itself by certain changes in manners and morals which took place in all classes. In the preceding century Erasmus had written of the women of England: "If you go to any place, you are received with a kiss by each one; if you depart, you are dismissed with a kiss; you are kissed on your return; kisses are exchanged on visits; a kiss is the first thing when they leave you, and a kiss all around at the last." As the Puritan sermonizing increased, it became less and less respectable to indulge in such promiscuous kissing There is no clear evidence that the kissing freedom had encouraged fornication and adultery, or that illicit sexual relations decreased when the Puritans made bussing a sin. It is, obviously, difficult to make accurate comparisons of such a sort, and the historian may easily be led to reveal his own prejudices in drawing conclusions from scanty evidence. This much is certain, that extramarital sexual relations were common under Henry VIII and also under James I.

In the days of Elizabeth and James the Puritans were not the only ones who wanted moral reforms or restrictions. The Queen's ecclesiastical commission, which had dealt harshly with nonconforming Calvinists, had also proceeded against adulterers. James approved of various measures designed to keep appren-

KING JAMES I AND HIS SON CHARLES FEASTING THE SPANISH
AMBASSADORS

November 18, 1623. After a rare print in the British Museum.

tices out of mischief, even though he considered their attendance at the theatres and their practicing archery on Sunday afternoons desirable or at least harmless diversions.

Theology became the leading intellectual interest under James, gradually overshadowing the Renaissance interest in beauty and joy. The habit of taking pleasure sadly, which foreigners have spoken of as typically English, came into fashion at this time. There was much talking and thinking about sin, a great deal of conscientious self-tormenting and repenting, much fear of strange diabolic forces. All sorts of skepticism were rare. From the death of Marlowe until the time when Hobbes rose into public notice, there was no important atheist or agnostic in England. Bacon's essay on atheism reveals that there were people in the reign of James I who scoffed at revealed Christianity. However, they exerted no influence on the thought of their own or later time.

A great many different religious influences were brought into England from the Continent of Europe. Several sects which were to be of later importance arose in half-private congregations. At Scrooby, a small place some forty-five miles south of York, about fifty men and women came together to preach and pray in the manner which they believed to be particularly pleasing to God. They were simple folk, farmers and their families for the most part. Their leader was William Brewster, who had come under strong Puritan influence at the University of Cambridge. The district around Scrooby had been little infected by Puritanism. Many of the people living in the neighborhood belonged to the Roman Catholic Church, and rumors of popish plots frequently circulated among the Protestants.

The members of the Scrooby conventicle were Puritans: that is, they opposed a large number of ecclesiastical usages which seemed to them relics of the Roman Catholic establishment. They differed, however, from most of the people to whom the same name was applied in that they were separating themselves from the Church of England and in that they favored congregational self-government. They were opposed to the episcopal system and also to a presbyterian church organization. In short, they were Independents or Separatists. They might, in contempt, also have been called Brownists, although they would have repudiated the name because Browne had returned to the Church of England after founding independent congregations. Those who shared their opinions about ecclesiastical government were later to be known as Congregationalists.

The Independents of Scrooby suffered practically no official persecution. Their neighbors laughed at them and heaped insults upon them, and they found the situation unbearable. Moreover, they feared that the bishops would deal harshly with them eventually, although their obscurity had protected them for a time. Most of the Puritans gained exemption from punishment by accepting the religious tests which were officially set up and by conducting services in the prescribed manner. The Scrooby conventicle stood somewhat apart from the aristocratic tendencies of Calvinism and from the timid conformity of the ordinary Puritans. It was influenced to some extent by equalitarian Anabaptist and Digger views. The little congregation of Scrooby is interesting because the Independents emigrated to the Netherlands, from which some of them afterwards went to Plymouth in North America. Congregationalism was soon to become of consequence in England as well.

The moral ideals of these sectaries were pretty much the same as characterized other Puritans. They were not quite so intolerant, perhaps, but certainly they did not believe that the open exercise of the Roman Catholic religion should be permitted. And if they spoke in favor of the toleration of all Protestants, it was because they were conscious of their own weakness.

§ 2

King James was succeeded in 1625 by his son, Charles I. Especially because of the contrast with his father, Charles seemed a very exemplar in his personal morals. He was reputed to be faithful to his wife and to set a good example to his courtiers. He seldom drank heavily, and he disliked deep drinkers. The people of his court, however, derived little benefit from having such a model to look up to. The Queen had a light reputation. A story is told in this connection which is said to have the authority of G. Clarke, who held responsible positions at court and was presumably in a position to know about such matters. Thomas Carew, the poet, was a gentleman of the privy chamber, and as such it was his duty to bear a candle before the King when Charles entered the Queen's bedroom. The story goes that one evening, while Carew was engaged in this duty, he saw Jermyns, Lord St. Albans, with his arm around Her Majesty's neck. He had enough presence of mind to stumble and put out the light before the King could notice what was going on. St. Albans escaped, and Carew received many favors from the Queen.

The Queen, known in English history as Henrietta Maria, was a French princess. Because she had been brought up as a Roman Catholic, the Puritans were willing to believe the worst about her. Before the marriage Charles had promised not only that she would be permitted to exercise her religion freely, but that all the Catholics of England would be tolerated. The promise was one that he could carry out only by ruling despotically. The great majority of the people and of the members of both houses of Parliament favored the complete suppression of Catholic worship. They were willing to yield so far as to let the Queen have her private chapel, but not to go much further. The Puritans had been extending their number until there was no doubt that they were more numerous than High Church Anglicans, and the latter too had little sympathy with Papists.

Charles was engaged in a struggle from the very beginning of his reign. He believed, like his father, in the divine right of kings. He could not help seeing, though, that he might have to fight for his prerogative, whatever its origin. He was confronted with opposition from Puritan theocrats who stood in the way of his greatest desires. How to contend with them he did not know. Despite all his father's fine theories, the King saw that he could not simply crush the opposition. He grew into the habit of answering disagreeable demands with subterfuges and lies and pretended concessions. If in chastity and sobriety Charles was (according to the Puritan standards of his time or the usual tests of our own) morally excellent, he was also exceptionally selfish. He was possessed of a reasoned egoism, largely based upon the exalted view of his own status which had been communicated to him in his childhood.

Despite his selfishness, Charles was found lovable by all who knew him well. His appearance was attractive, and he had a rather agreeable fondness for the good things in life. As King of England in a less troubled time he would probably have enjoyed the respectful admiration of his people. He had practically none of the pedantry and interest in theological controversy characteristic of his father. Instead, he was a patron and a genuine connoisseur of the fine arts.

Rubens came to England as a diplomatic agent from Philip IV of Spain, dividing his time there between matters of state and painting. His "Venus and Cupid" was painted on English soil. Charles knighted Rubens and treated him with great generosity. The King could not, however, persuade him to remain in England. Rubens found equally objectionable the Puritanism of the people and the corruptness and licentiousness of the courtiers.

Charles then welcomed Van Dyck to his court. He fell in readily with the free and easy ways about the palace. It is said that on one occasion King Charles asked him discreetly if he knew how it felt to be short of money, and he replied, "Yes, sire; when a man keeps an open table for his friends and an open purse for his mistresses, he soon reaches the bottom of his money-chest." The King scolded him in a good-natured way for his moral failings, and arranged a match for him with a lady of honor to the Queen. Charles did not enforce his own standard of conduct upon his courtiers, but certainly he did not encourage laxity.

The King's friends and supporters, especially those about the court, came to be known as the Cavaliers. In politics, they stood for royal power; in religion, they were opposed to innovation and to undue zeal. They thought that gentlemen should be content to go to the established churches and worship according to the manner prescribed by the ecclesiastical authorities, without any ado; and the rabble, they felt, should certainly not be consulted about such matters. In moral standards and practice the Cavaliers varied, but as a class they were much less austere than the Puritans.

While the main body of Cavaliers was devoted to the Church of England, some of the King's friends leaned toward Rome, and a few were discreetly skeptical. More were simply indifferent to religion. They looked upon the Church as a political force which should be employed to prevent the growth of democracy. The party in favor of religious toleration appeared to be all on the King's side. The influential Puritans did not favor a diversity of religious expression and worship, but desired uniformity under pretty much the same ritual system that Calvin had set up at Geneva. Most of them were willing to maintain the episcopal hierarchy, if only the bishops were such as sympathized with their views. There were, indeed, Puritans who insisted upon the importance of church government by equal presbyters, and a few radicals clamored for congregational independence.

It is difficult to generalize about either the Cavaliers or the antiroyalists in such a way as to include all the members of these parties. The people opposed to royal prerogative were mostly, but not all, Puritans. And there were Puritans not merely among the urban middle classes, but also in the nobility and among country folk of all degrees. When civil war broke out, the supporters of the King were not confined to any one social class. There were even instances in which members of the same family fought on opposite sides. All the people had been taught the duty of loyalty to the King. The most Puritan of preachers had insisted upon that, no matter how much they might regret that Charles was married to a Papist and surrounded by wicked men. To justify rebellion, appeal was made to the divine law, infinitely higher than the royal will. "God with us!" was the battle cry of the Parliamentary army.

In the early part of the Civil War most of the military commanders opposed to the royal forces considered it unwise to defeat the King decisively. For they had no thought of abolishing the monarchy: that, they thought, would bring about a

ENGLAND'S WOLFE

with eagle's clawes, or the cruell Impieties of Bloud-Thirsty Royalists, and blasphemous *Anti-Parliamentarians*, under the command of that inhumane *Prince Rupert, Digby*, and the rest." From a broadside of the Civil War.

state of anarchy. They simply wanted to frighten the King into granting concessions to Parliament. It was difficult to fight the royal armies effectively while such an attitude remained.

And the antiroyalists came little by little under the control of the Puritan radicals with more or less democratic views.

On the whole, though, the Civil War represented a matching of strength between the King and the upper nobility on one hand and the middle classes on the other. Matters were complicated by the fact that persons of all classes who held the ideals of the Renaissance above those of the Reformation generally joined the Cavalier side, because they considered the danger from a pietistic ochlocracy greater than that from a fairly benevolent and enlightened autocracy. There were still many rural tenants and laborers whose feudal loyalty led them to follow their own lord, whichever side he took.

We think of the Cavaliers as a frolicsome, irresponsible lot. Some of them spoke out openly against precise morals, and this was their great sin in Puritan eyes. To do wrong was human, as the zealous Calvinists would have been the last to deny; but the gay young courtiers insisted that it was right for them to seek all sorts of worldly pleasure. The Puritans would fain have quickened their conscience with the beadle's lash as well as with threats of terrors in the world to come. The stern zealots thought there was something diabolical about people who could sin without repenting, and who were even capable of boasting and joking about the things they had done. A Christian might play a game on Sunday; nay, he might even commit adultery, but he ought to be troubled with nightmares and with visions of Hell all the rest of his life. But Thomas Carew, who served the King (and the Queen, too, as we have seen), could write "The Rapture" and other poems devoid of shame. He could address a woman with the words,

> The giant Honor, that keeps cowards out,
> Is but a masquer.

Such a Cavalier seemed to believe in a single standard of morals, but in an opposite sense to that of the Puritans. He answered all the sermonizing of the Roundhead precisians with the verse,

> We only sin when Love's rites are not done.

[97]

It is sophistication that Carew presents, not mere innocent and careless promiscuity. He tells us that he has chosen to eat of the tree of knowledge.

Such writing as this leaves to a posterity which professes to believe in strictly controlled behavior the impression that it was written in an immoral age. On the other hand, quiet fornication and adultery or even unquiet drunkenness, not recorded in such a defiant way and without the record of a hedonistic philosophy, soon pass into comparative oblivion. For the age of Charles I we have, too, a host of moralizing chroniclers with exceedingly ascetic standards, dealing with the gay people in no spirit of tolerance.

Carew's freedom of language aroused the ire of many of his contemporaries, as we might expect. It was reproved, for instance, in *The Great Assizes Held in Parnassus by Apollo and His Assessors,* a pasquinade which was not published until several years after Carew's death, although it evidently circulated in manuscript before this time. The Cavalier poet is here stigmatized as looser than Aretino. This attack on Carew was perhaps written by George Wither, who had been imprisoned in the previous reign for seditiously criticizing the court. Wither is notable besides for having, though a Puritan, enjoyed the Christmas season in his youth and for having found no impropriety in writing a lusty poem about the Yule.

A number of poets may be ranged with Carew as illustrative of the Cavalier spirit, for example, Sir John Suckling and Richard Lovelace. Lovelace ends "A Loose Saraband" with the verse,

> Leave me but love and sherry.

He wanted woman and wine, and song he made for himself and those he loved. Carew sometimes wrote as though there were no prudish bounds to speech at all, or as though he wanted the prudes to fall into apoplexy. Lovelace implies that there are limits when he proposes to quench the fire of his beloved

> in Rhenish
> Or what we must not name.

A greater poet than these, one, too, who was more serious than these typical Cavaliers and further removed from court influences, was Robert Herrick. He said of himself, "jocund his Muse was, but his life was chaste"; and he spoke apologetically in later life of his "unbaptized rhymes." Herrick was a minister who was deprived of his living when the Puritans came into full power. "Gather ye rosebuds while ye may" conveys the note of his secular verses; but this line is the beginning of a poem advising girls to marry, not bidding them to forget the giant Honor and to care for Love's rites alone. Nor did Lovelace despise honorable ideals, which, as he said, made him leave his darling's "chaste breast" to go to war:

> I could not love thee, Dear, so much,
> Loved I not Honor more.

Among the anti-Puritan ministers of religion we find piety, religious enthusiasm, asceticism, and mysticism. By no means all were cold and worldly and indifferent, as their opponents charged. Herbert and Vaughan wrote impassioned religious verses. And there were many devout men scattered through the land who were content to preach and pray in the prescribed manner. From the tracts of the Puritans we get the impression that their opponents were all wicked and impious people. "Atheist" often means no more, in their writings, than one who is not a zealous Puritan.

§ 3

Just as royalists and High Church Anglicans differed widely in character and ideals, the Puritans were of many sorts. We should not consider Edmund Spenser a typical Puritan, and John Milton was in many ways different from our ordinary conception of the Roundhead. But Milton's career covered the Puritan growth to political power and its subsequent decline; besides, his participation in the movement as a propagandist and pamphleteer and also as a Secretary of State entitles him to a place in any outline of the history of Puritanism.

Milton was born in London, of middle-class parents. Renaissance influences were still strong, and some of the greatest of the Elizabethans were in their prime. Ben Jonson was holding his gay meetings at the Mermaid Tavern, which was perhaps located on Bread Street, where the Miltons lived. It is possible that John, as a boy, sometimes saw Shakespeare.

His parents did not teach him to look upon all poets as impious because of their craft. His father was fond of music, had some ability as a composer, and even versified a little on occasion. There was religious earnestness in the Milton home, to be sure, but this did not shut out an interest in culture and a readiness to enjoy those pleasures which were considered harmless. The Psalms interested and influenced young Milton, he owed much to the Puritan-chivalric idealism of Spenser; but he also drew upon Chaucer, Drayton, Shakespeare, Jonson, and, especially in foreign languages, upon some poets whose philosophy was far from that of Puritans and precisians. If there is a narrowness about the outlook of Milton's mature work, at least it is not due to ignorance.

Milton attended Christ's College, Cambridge, and there he did not show any very pronounced Puritan tendencies. Getting into trouble at college, for some obscure reason, he was sent away for a short time. From London he wrote a letter in Latin verse to his friend Diodati, in which he said, "When I am weary, the pomp of the clanging theatre awaits me, the garrulous stage and the clapping hands." Some commentators have supposed that Milton was merely telling about having read the plays. This is unlikely from the words he uses. He must actually have heard the hands come together, and perhaps the young man joined the audience in expressing his approval. It is improbable that he considered the theatre wicked at this time.

The same letter tells of the fair English girls he saw in the park, lovelier than the maidens of whom the classic poets wrote. At the age of nineteen he told in a Latin poem how he had fallen in love with an unknown girl in London. In his postscript to the Latin elegies he later set down an apologetic reference to "vain trophies of idleness," explaining that his youthful lightness no longer existed. Even as a boy at college he found the love of pleasure becoming more and more at variance with his stern moral standards and his great ambitions; and it was the hedonism that he ruthlessly stamped out.

He set out early in life to prepare himself to be a great poet. Occasionally he wondered if asceticism on his part were necessary to attain this end. At the age of twenty-one he wrote in a Latin epistle to Diodati, "But why do you imply that a poet must keep aloof from drinking and feasting? Song loves Bacchus, and Bacchus loves Song." Then he added that the man who aspires to be an epic poet, he who would write of "wars, and of heaven under adult Jupiter, and of pious heroes, and of half-divine leaders," must discipline himself by means of sparse living. "Herbs must furnish his innocent food; clear water in a beechen cup, sober draughts from the pure spring, must be his food. His youth must be chaste and inoffensive; his manners and morals strict; his hands stainless."

The story goes that Milton was known at college as "the Lady of Christ's" because of the austerity already manifest in him. But that he was little attached to the Puritan party at seventeen is shown by the fact that he then wrote a poem lamenting the death of Dr. Launcelot Andrewes, Bishop of Winchester, and setting forth a dream in which he saw the Bishop received by the hosts of heaven. Andrewes was one of the bitterest foes of Puritanism. Later in life, Milton wrote of him in an altogether different spirit. Some of Milton's early poetry was written under the influence of John Donne's hotly erotic verses. He thoroughly appreciated the genius of the great men of the English Renaissance. At a time when Shakespeare's reputation had not yet put him practically beyond the bounds of moral criticism, when, indeed, the strict Puritans were denouncing him no less than other poets and dramatists, Milton addressed him as "Dear son of Memory, great heir of fame."

Milton's companion poems "L'Allegro" and "Il Penseroso" show the conflict between hedonism and otherworldly asceticism in him. In the first of these he praises the beauty of the country; and he expresses his delight with "Jonson's learnèd sock" and the dramas of "sweetest Shakespeare, Fancy's child," as well as with tales of romance and chivalry and with sweet, voluptuous music. In the second, he praises tragedy, but it is as one way of developing an atmosphere of sadness. The poem is really a commendation of the pleasures that come out of pain and sorrow and self-deprivation. Later, in "Lycidas," we find a deep Puritan note.

Milton's masque of *Comus* moralizes too much to suit the taste of to-day. Nevertheless, the fact that he wrote a dramatic piece, even one intended to convey a good lesson, is significant. We have already seen something of the Puritan objections to the theatre, and we shall presently resume the history of the attack on the drama and allied forms of amusement. Prynne's *Histrio-mastix* had raised something of a furor shortly before the time when Milton wrote his masque for the Earl of Bridgewater, who was celebrating his appointment as Lord President of Wales. Milton thus proclaimed that he was not one of the fanatical extremists of the Puritan party. He was willing to write a libretto in honor of "saintly chastity." It is perhaps worthy of mention that here, as in other of his works, Milton mingles Christian and pagan imagery. This alone was sinful in the opinion of some pietists.

Comus, the son of Bacchus and Circe, is represented as a lover of beauty and of cruelty. He speaks eloquently for the Renaissance doctrine of hedonism. The Lady (played by a young daughter of the Earl's) argues against him in favor of "the holy dictate of spare Temperance." The Attendant Spirit speaks of

> Bacchus, that first from out the purple grape
> Crushed the sweet poison of misusèd wine.

Did Milton mean to imply that all wine is misused and poisonous? This is possible, though it is more likely that he meant to call wine poisonous only when misused, that is, used to excess. Not everyone to whom he spoke through the masque intended to become an epic poet, and therefore necessarily confined to the drinking of pure water. But he pointed out that wine was dangerous because "most do taste through fond intemperate thirst." Light beer had at the time much more respectability among severely moral people than wine. Yet there is no evidence of the existence of an important movement for the prohibition of wine or of distilled liquors. As for wine, it was mostly consumed by noble and worshipful people, whose taste it was still a little dangerous to criticize. But the Earl of Bridgewater was evidently satisfied to have the evils of intemperance pointed out.

Milton lived for several years a life which some Puritans would have denounced as one of ungodly idleness. In his father's country place at Horton he read and studied much, and did a little writing. Then he went off for a trip through Italy, but he was in no danger of becoming an "Italianate Englishman." However, he did fall in love discreetly with two or three Italian ladies. He was proud, too, of the praise which a cardinal of the Roman Catholic Church bestowed upon his Latin verses. Hearing of the outbreak of the Civil War in England, he shortened his European trip somewhat, but he did not hasten to plunge into the fray. Indeed, he had little of the military hero in him.

After some time Milton became a propagandist for the Puritan-republican cause. His personal experiences also brought about some pamphleteering on what was practically his own account. He married a pleasure-loving girl of seventeen, the daughter of a Cavalier squire, when he was twice her age and immersed in serious business. After she had left him, he wrote a plea for divorce in cases where husband and wife are of incompatible temperaments. The doctrine was denounced as being not only radical, but heretical as well. Milton's wife was induced to return to him, and the two lived together until she died. During the time of their separation Milton announced his firm opinion that husband and wife who could not live together were actually divorced, whatever the law might say; and he is said to have gone so far as to propose marriage to a second young woman while legally married to the first. But such a flouting of law and public opinion was avoided by the return of his wife, to whom he seems to have been sincerely and continuously attached.

Out of the divorce controversy grew the *Areopagitica,* a defense of uncensored publication and of freedom to express one's views without governmental interference. Milton's plea for liberty was far in advance of public opinion on the subject, and it exerted little influence at the time.

In other moral questions Milton's position was more orthodox. When he was assigned the task of defending Charles I's execution, he considered it necessary to list among the blots on that monarch's memory his fondness for Shakespeare. The poet had gone a long way from the admiration of his own youth.

Like most other Puritans, Milton changed his mind about the advisability of retaining the episcopal hierarchy. But he did not remain long satisfied with the presbyterian system, discovering that

New Presbyter is but old Priest writ large.

He then became a Congregationalist, but not an orthodox one; for he was not satisfied with the Calvinistic theology, and was inclined to accept the doctrine of free will. He leaned, also, toward the end of the life, close to the Unitarian position. In his latter years he believed thoroughly in religious toleration. He was then a blind old man to whose opinions little attention was paid. It is generally said that Milton lost his sight because of his close application to his duties as Latin secretary and defender of the Protectorate. Perhaps he could have saved his eyes by giving up his work, but he considered it divinely willed that he should continue.

While Cromwell was in power, Milton had the disappointment of finding the two nephews whom he had himself taught among those who expressed dissatisfaction with Puritan strictness and clamored for a restoration of the monarchy. One of the young men wrote *A Satire against Hypocrites* and *A Miscellany of Choice Drolleries,* because of which he received a sharp reprimand from the Protector's Council. And Milton lived long enough to have all his hopes for a permanent republic shattered by the

Restoration, and to hear "the barbarous dissonance of Bacchus and his revellers." His friends and his blindness enabled him to escape revenge on the part of the victors.

Necessarily removed from all public affairs, Milton set himself seriously to the work of writing poetry. He called upon the Spirit to illumine him that he might "assert Eternal Providence and justify the ways of God to men." He had long hesi-

The Orthodox true Minifter,   the Seducer and falfe Prophet.

CHURCH AND CONVENTICLE

From *A Glasse for the Times*, a tract of 1648.

tated about the choice of a subject for his epic. It might easily have been a secular theme, perhaps similar to that of Spenser's *The Faerie Queen;* but there can be little doubt that a moral purpose would have appeared in any case. Milton's early notes for *Paradise Lost* show that he considered for a time treating it dramatically instead of epically. Perhaps it was the Puritan prejudice against the stage that determined its final form. *Samson Agonistes* is a drama, however, even though it is not suitable for acting. Milton's defense of tragedy prefaced to this work shows that he understood he would offend some Puritans by writing even a religious play, and one which was not likely to be put upon the stage.

§ 4

Another Puritan, somewhat less exceptional than Milton but also of considerable interest, is revealed to us in the *Memoirs of Colonel Hutchinson*, written by his wife, Lucy. Or, rather, we should say that Mrs. Hutchinson's book shows us two interesting Puritans, for she was herself an unusual person. She was renowned in childhood as a prodigy, and at the age of seven had teachers in "languages, music, dancing, writing, and needlework." Mrs. Hutchinson demurely spoke of "man's nobler sex," but I venture to read mental reservations to this conventional modesty. Very few people in the seventeenth century dared to assert that women are naturally equal in mental capacity and in social rights to men. Milton thought that the wife should live (for God) in and through her husband. Still, there is a passage in one of his divorce pamphlets which proposes that in the exceptional cases where the woman is wiser than the man to whom she is married, she shall be the ruler of the house.

Lucy Hutchinson had the Puritan habitude of attributing even minor and ordinary occurrences to the particular desire of God. She was, therefore, constantly thanking the divinity for his favors to her or wondering what she had done to merit a divine punishment. This attitude, like a great deal in Puritanism, derives from the Old Testament. Man was the center of things for the Hebrews and for the Puritans. It has been suggested that Milton, although familiar with Galileo's new opinions about the solar system and perhaps willing to accept them, retained the geocentric astronomy in *Paradise Lost* because it admirably fitted the Puritan assumption that human behavior and destiny are the primary concerns of God. Pious men used to say that they would like to be as a right arm to God, that is, to be no more than means by which the divine will could be carried out. This was the moral meaning which predestination had for the Calvinists, who never saw the doctrine as an excuse for doing what they pleased.

Young Lucy, as we have seen, was taught dancing and music. Mrs. Hutchinson says of her childhood days: "I thought it no sin to learn or hear witty songs or amorous sonnets or poems, and twenty things of that kind, wherein I was so apt that I became the confidant in all the loves that were managed among my mother's young women; and there were none of them but had many lovers, and some particular friends beloved among the rest." Later, she learned to give up all such frivolities, and after her marriage she divided her time between praising God and managing her husband's household.

She also found time for praising her husband, and the *Memoir* is chiefly a eulogy. At the head of Colonel Hutchinson's virtues, we are told, was his Christianity. "By Christianity I intend that universal habit of grace which is wrought in the soul by the regenerating Spirit of God, whereby the whole creature is resolved up into the divine will and love, and all its actions directed to the obedience and glory of its maker." According to this, no man is a Christian who ever does anything which does not express the desire of God and contribute to divine satisfaction.

"He hated persecution for religion," says Colonel Hutchinson's widow, "and was always a champion of all religious people against all their great oppressors." We can hardly take this literally. Mrs. Hutchinson calls the Duke of Newcastle an atheist for no apparent reason except that of his having enlisted Roman Catholics in his army. "Religion" was for her very nearly synonymous with Puritanism: it included the faith of Baptists and Independents, but not Catholicism.

Much emphasis is laid upon Hutchinson's love of truth and honor. ("Honor," to be sure, had not precisely the same meaning for a middle-class Puritan that it had for a Cavalier.) Mrs. Hutchinson goes on to say that her husband never indulged in any excesses: "His whole life was the rule of temperance in meat, drink, apparel, pleasure, and all those things that may be lawfully enjoyed." As a young student he was not addicted to "wine, nor gambling, nor the converse of wicked and vain

women." If he had a fault, his widow thought, it was that of
caring too much for learning. For knowledge and wisdom were,
of course, only valuable as they led to God. Like his wife,
Hutchinson had been taught dancing and music in his youth.
Not all the Puritans objected to the moderate use of such forms
of diversion.

Mrs. Hutchinson uses strong language about James I and his
court, but has some words of praise for Charles. She says that
in his time "the nobility and courtiers, who did not quite abandon
their debaucheries, yet so reverenced the King as to retire into
corners to practice them." Charles, she says, believed "that an
honest man might be saved in any profession [that is, religious
belief] but he had a mistaken principle that kingly government
in the state could not stand without episcopal government in the
Church."

When the paintings and other works of art that had belonged
to Charles and the Cavalier nobles were offered for sale, Hutchinson is said to have been one of the few Englishmen ready to purchase them. His widow tells us that a number of important
works would have been sent out of the country had it not been
for him. The Puritans in general had little appreciation of music
and the fine arts.

§ 5

We have seen how, in the golden age of the English theatre,
when Elizabeth sat upon the throne, godly men began to raise
an outcry about the wickedness of stage plays. Early in the
reign of James I noblemen were deprived of the right to license
companies of actors. However, the professional players of London came under the protection of the crown, and they seemed
to be permanently assured of immunity from the hostility of
Parliament and also of a respectable and honorable status. Thus
sheltered, and definitely engaged on the royalist side, they began
to mock the Puritans more freely than ever, and also to defy
them by their emphasis upon bawdry. The zealots developed
more and more hatred for the theatre.

An Oxford man named William Prynne, who was a lawyer by profession and a very prolific writer by avocation, took up the work of defending the Puritans and routing their enemies. His first book was an apologia for the Calvinistic doctrine of foreordination as against the Arminian one of free will. Then began his fiery denunciations of the manners of his time. He attacked passing fads and fancies as though they had been new varieties of murder or rape. Prynne proved conclusively, for instance, that it is extremely sinful to drink to the health of friends. This custom, however, was not a new one. He showed, quoting Biblical chapter and verse, that for men to wear their hair long is "unseemly and unlawful unto Christians," while for women to wear theirs short is "mannish, unnatural, impudent, unchristian."

About 1624 Prynne set to work on a book intended to prove that no good Protestant country should tolerate stage plays. In 1629 a company of actresses brought from Paris was pelted from the stage at Blackfriars. Even the godless wretches who were accustomed to attend the theatre could not abide such a piece of immorality as putting women upon a public platform, though degenerate France permitted it. Mr. Prynne was still at work on his book about the theatre. He inserted an allusion to the fact that the females of the stage are always "notorious whores." In 1630 he obtained a license for the publication of His *Histrio-mastix;* but the book, over a thousand pages long, did not appear until November, 1632.

As may be judged by the length of Prynne's book, it assembled a great mass of evidence, and it proved beyond the shadow of a doubt (at least, for those who already agreed with the author) that stage plays had been condemned by the Holy Scriptures, by the Fathers of the Church, by all modern Christian writers whose opinion was worthy of serious consideration, and by the wisest of the pagan philosophers. He showed, too, that the theatre was a breeder of all forms of vice and irreligion.

Unfortunately for William Prynne, Queen Henrietta Maria was, at the end of 1632, rehearsing a play. She had brought over some professional actresses from France, and she and some of her court ladies were to appear with them on the stage. In calling all the women who showed themselves on the stage whores, Prynne was considered to have grossly insulted the Queen herself. Perhaps the Puritan author really had a low opinion of Her Majesty's virtue, but it is pretty clear that he did not intend to reflect upon it in print. Nevertheless, he suffered severe punishment, which included the slicing off of his ears.

There was little public excitement about the matter, since many Puritans felt that Prynne's punishment was deserved. Two years later Milton wrote *Comus*, showing that he did not share the extreme view about the sinfulness of all dramatic representations. But Puritan sentiment on the subject quickly changed, even the moderates beginning to denounce the theatre and everything connected with it. When Prynne was again severely punished, this time having the remaining fragments of his ears trimmed off, he and the other Puritans who suffered at the same time were regarded as martyrs.

Prynne was an ardent martyr-masochist, who afterward attacked the Independent congregations as fiercely as he had denounced the bishops and the players. He was a Presbyterian, but not a republican. He gained a certain amount of favor after 1660 for his royalist propaganda, and yet he managed to get into trouble again. The plays of the Restoration, he found, were by no means more godly than those of the reign of Charles I.

The triumph of Puritanism closed the theatres, or at least made them illegal. Stage plays were suppressed in 1642; and a few years later more stringent ordinances were adopted which provided that all persons caught at the acting of plays should be flogged, while the spectators should be fined. Later, modified forms of the drama were licensed for semiprivate performances, and there was considerable reaction in favor of the theatre before the restoration of the Stuart kings made it fully legal.

The Puritans objected not only to stage plays, but to a great many other forms of diversion. Macaulay's statement that the Puritans were opposed to bear baiting "not because it gave pain to the bear, but because it gave pleasure to the spectators,"

HISTRIO-MASTIX.
THE
PLAYERS SCOVRGE,
OR,
ACTORS TRAGÆDIE,
Divided into Two Parts.

Wherein it is largely evidenced, by divers *Arguments,* by the concurring Authorities and Resolutions of *sundry texts of Scripture;* of the *whole Primitive Church,* both under the *Law* and *Gospell;* of 55 *Synodes and Councels;* of 71 *Fathers and Christian Writers,* before the yeare of our Lord 1200; of above 150 *foraigne and domestique Protestant and Popish Authors,* since; of 40 *Heathen Philosophers, Historians, Poets;* of many *Heathen,* many *Christian Nations, Republiques, Emperors, Princes, Magistrates;* of sundry *Apostolicall, Canonicall, Imperiall Constitutions;* and of our owne *English Statutes, Magistrates, Vniversities, Writers, Treachers.*

That popular Stage-playes (the *very Pompes of the Divell* which we renounce in *Baptisme,* if we beleeve the Fathers) are sinfull, heathenish, lewde, ungodly *Spectacles,* and most pernicious Corruptions; condemned in all ages, as intolerable *Mischiefes* to Churches, to Republickes, to the manners, mindes, and soules of men. *And that the Profession of Play-poets,* of *Stage-players;* together with the penning, acting, and frequenting of *Stage-playes,* are unlawfull, infamous and misbeseeming Christians. All pretences to the contrary are here likewise fully answered; and the unlawfulnes of acting, of beholding Academicall Enterludes, briefly discussed; besides sundry other particulars concerning *Dancing, Dicing, Health drinking,* &c. of which the *Table* will informe you.

By WILLIAM PRYNNE, *an Vtter-Barrester of* Lincolnes Inne.

Cyprian, De Spectaculis lib. p. 244.
Fugienda sunt ista Christianis fidelibus, ut iam frequenter diximus, tàm vanâ, tàm perniciosa, tàm sacrilega Spectacula: quæ, etsi non haberent crimen, habent. in se et maximam, et parum congruentē fidelibus vanitatē.
Lactantius de Verò Cultu cap. 20.
Vitanda ergo Spectacula omnia, non solùm ne qu'd vitiorum pectoribus insideat, &c. sed ne cu'us nos voluptatis consuetudo delineat, atque à Deo et à bonis operibus avertat.
Chrysost. Hom. 38. in Matth. Tom. 2. Col. 299. B. & Hom. 8. De Pœnitentia, Tom. 5. Col. 750.
Immo vero, his Theatralibus ludis eversis, non leges, sed iniquitatem evertetis, ac omnem civitatis pestem extinguetis.: Etenim Theatrum, communis luxuriæ officina, publicum incontinentia gymnasium; cathedra pestilentiæ; pessimus locus; plurimorumque morborum plena Babylonica fornax, &c.
Augustinus De Civit. Dei, l. 4. c. 1.
Si tantummodo boni et honesti homines in civitate essent, nec in rebus humanis Ludi scenici esse debuissent.

LONDON,
Printed by *E. A.* and *W. I.* for *Michael Sparke,* and are to be sold at the Blue Bible, in Greene Arbour, in little Old Bayly. 1633.

TITLE PAGE OF WILLIAM PRYNNE'S *HISTRIO-MASTIX*, 1633

is not far from the truth. The sin of cruelty to animals was one which gave little worry to the people of the seventeenth century. The baiting of bulls and bears was a favorite English sport, and its prohibition was displeasing to many people of all degrees. Cockfighting, hunting, fishing, dancing, gambling with cards and dice, came to be vices in the eyes of most Puritans. Wrestling, shooting, bowling, and bell-ringing, along with practically everything else capable of yielding pleasure to normal people, became unlawful on Sunday, and they were more or less frowned upon on week days also. In fact, the working people had no time then to take part in them. Hours in field and workshop were long, and the Puritan régime especially emphasized the importance of diligence.

The number of sins and vices (consequently, the number of sinners and vicious people also) increased immensely as the Puritans extended their political power. A law was passed that all the May-poles in England should be cut down at once. Betting was made a penal offense. Masques, puppet shows, and horse races were all frowned upon in the days of the Commonwealth.

Dear to the English was the old holiday of Christmas, with its mince pies and its yule logs and all the ceremonies which had been characteristic of the day for centuries. Some of them were, in fact, older than Christianity. The extreme Puritans decided to abolish Christmas as a popish or pagan holiday unworthy of true believers. In 1644 Christmas fell on a Wednesday. This day was supposed to be one of fasting every week. The Long Parliament ordered that the twenty-fifth of December should be kept as a strict fast day, considering it peculiarly appropriate that men should make due amends for the fun and frolic which they and their ancestors had enjoyed in honor of the unholy day called Christmas. It was going a little too far for the mass of the people. The next year serious riots broke out on Christmas Day.

Strict precautions were taken to prevent the decorating and the opening of churches on the traditional holidays. On Christmas and the other sacred days which the Church of England had taken over from the Roman Catholic Church, shopkeepers were ordered

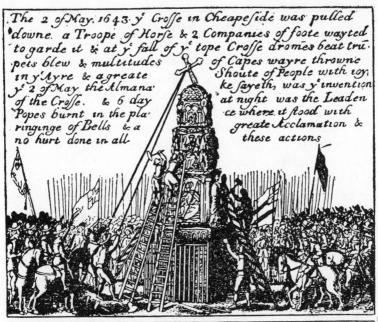

The 2 of May. 1643. ye Crosse in Cheapeside was pulled
downe. a Troope of Horse & 2 Companies of foote wayted
to garde it & at ye fall of ye tope Crosse dromes beat tru-
pets blew & multitudes of Capes wayre thrownie
in ye Ayre & a greate Shoute of People with ioy:
ye 2 of May the Almana ke sayeth, was ye invention
of the Crosse. & 6 day at night was the Leaden
Popes burnt in the pla- ce where it stood with
ringinge of Bells & a greate Acclamation &
no hurt done in all these actions

10 of May the Boocke of Spartes upon the Lords day was bu
rnt by the Hangman in the place where the Crosse stoode, & -
at Exchange

DESTRUCTION OF THE CHEAPSIDE CROSS AND BURNING OF THE
BOOK OF SPORTS

An etching by Wenceslaus Hollar, 1643.

to display their wares as usual, and apprentices were forbidden to stop work. It was finally found necessary to grant monthly holidays to school children, servants, and apprentices instead of the traditional days of rest which had been taken from them. For the Puritans by no means decreased the number of working days when they insisted upon Sunday observance. On the contrary, they added about fifty annually.

It was found impossible to suppress altogether the old way of praying and worshiping, despite laws which went so far as to forbid the reading of the Anglican Church prayer book in private houses. In remote districts a few churches used the official Episcopalian service. Even Roman Catholicism did not entirely disappear from England. The Puritans did their best, however, to tear out all traces of popery. When they gained possession of the royal collection of paintings, they burned all that contained representations of Jesus or the Virgin Mary.

The Puritans took a great deal from the Old Testament, but they were not accustomed to make any moral rules less rigid to conform to Israelitish practice. For example, they did not adopt concubinage and polygyny. In 1650 capital punishment, without benefit of clergy, was adopted for those twice convicted of fornication. This law did not last long, for Charles II considered it inconvenient. Adultery was a still more abominable crime, in Puritan opinion. Yet it is pretty sure that sexual offenses continued to be frequent while the Puritans ruled. The difficulties of dealing with them penally were great. Sober old men could make laws, but they could not enforce them upon the young people. Complaints about disrespect for authority grew, and many zealots complained that their children were possessed by devils.

Such men as Milton and Hutchinson were rather displeased with the badges of godliness which Puritan enthusiasts sometimes assumed. The pious folk had cant phrases and words of which they made frequent use. They were constantly sprinkling their speech with "surely" and "verily" and "yea verily." The Puritans were spoken of by the Cavaliers as Roundheads, since most of them cut their hair short—"with so many little peaks," says Mrs. Hutchinson, "as was something ridiculous to behold." Because Colonel Hutchinson had a fine crop of hair to which he refused to allow the shears to be applied, some of his fellow Puritans accused him of being absorbed in worldly vanity.

Broad-brimmed hats, boots with wide tops, and ruffs of plain linen were characteristic of the Puritans. The colors of the clothes worn by the men were very sober in comparison with those worn by the Cavaliers, but still a good deal more bright and variegated than men's clothing is to-day in England and America. Women's dress, too, became far less gay under Puritan influence. Perfumes and cosmetics, widely used by both sexes in the reigns of Elizabeth and James I, were under the ban. As early as 1599 Ben Jonson wrote of the Puritans as having

> Religion in their garments, and their hair
> Cut shorter than their eyebrows.

Some of the zealots even embroidered Scriptural texts upon their garments as visible signs of their conversion to true Christianity. Their speech and their correspondence bristled with phrases out of the Bible and repeated expressions of thankfulness to God.

Sunday observance, before it was rigorously enforced by law, served as a mark of distinction between the godly and the profligate. This is the one thing that has been transmitted unchanged, though now somewhat weakened, to present-day England and America from the original Puritans. The journal of Sir Simonds D'Ewes tells how, in March, 1640, a certain Mr. Stone, rector of Abchurch Clements in East London, was summoned before the Grand Committee for Religion of the House of Commons. There were various accusations against this minister, as that "he had been frequently drunk and was a common haunter of stage plays." He was accused also of having said "that God would not hear prayers in private houses, but was bound to hear prayers in churches." The most serious charge brought against him was that of having said that "Sunday compared to Christmas Day was but as chaff compared to corn."

The Committee declared Stone incapable of holding any ecclesiastical office.

During this session of 1640 Rudyard complained of rascals who had "branded all good Protestants under the name of Puritans." The term was still one of reproach. It then became honorable for a time, and was later to become an insulting name once more.

THE LAMENTABLE COMPLAINTS

of Nick Froth the tapster and Rulerost the cooke, concerning the restraint lately set forth against drinking, potting and piping on the Sabbath Day, and against selling meate." From a tract of 1641.

The Puritan soldiers in the Civil War stood, to some extent, in a class by themselves among military men. Soldiers have not in general a reputation for moral strictness. They can take literally the advice to "eat, drink, and be merry, for tomorrow ye die." And the Cavaliers spent much of the time when they were not fighting at wenching and drinking. But some divisions of the Puritan Army were altogether different. Soldiers were heavily fined for being found drunken or for drinking at all after nine o'clock in the evening, for playing games on Sunday, or for absenting themselves from religious services. When, in 1655, the Puritan major-generals became the police chiefs for the whole country, they made serious efforts to enforce the great mass of prohibitory laws which had been enacted in the two previous decades. They had actors whipped, caused jest books to be destroyed, and made gamblers pay fines of double their winnings.

A number of Puritan sects emerged into prominence during the Civil War. Parliament became dissatisfied with the episcopal system of church government, largely because Archbishop Laud had made himself hateful to the Puritans both for his leanings to what were considered popish practices and for his support of royal absolutism. Then the Scots insisted that England should go over to a presbyterian system like their own. The Church of England was, then, governed by presbyters while the Puritans were at the head of affairs. But Independent and Baptist and various other congregations not connected with the official body openly held services.

Cromwell took all sorts of pious Puritans into his Army, without troubling himself about their attitude toward ecclesiastical government or their minor theological opinions. The military triumphs which his hymn-singing sectaries won compelled the granting of a certain amount of religious toleration. Cromwell displeased many Puritans and seemed ridiculous to the Cavaliers because he allowed able men, whatever class of society they originated in, to occupy the positions they were capable of filling.

The republic was made possible, though for just a short time, only by Cromwell's Army, which consisted largely of men from the lower and middle classes of society who called themselves Independents or Anabaptists. These men's desire for religious tolerance did not extend either to Roman Catholics or to Episcopalians. They often broke into churches, destroying clerical costumes, crucifixes, sacred images, stained glass, prayer books, and other ecclesiastical paraphernalia of which they did not approve. Sometimes they attacked clergymen whom they found wearing the hated surplice. They had strong moral zeal, too.

When Cromwell connived at something which bore a suspicious resemblance to theatrical performances in London, the soldiers invaded the playhouses, stopped the shows, and broke up the furniture.

One of the new sects of this period we know as Quakerism. The Quakers, although they were Puritans, differed from other groups in that they attached more importance to a mystical communion with God than to the verbal inspiration of the Bible. Their first leader was George Fox, who became dissatisfied with the godliness of the orthodox Puritans because they considered it no great sin to linger over a jug of beer. When he was a young man, in the 1640's, most of the Puritans were still accustomed to drink healths. Indeed, they permitted that old usage to continue which required any person who could not drink as deeply as the rest of the company to pay for all. Fox became convinced that the Episcopalian and Presbyterian Puritans had too lax a moral system. And he began to denounce even those forms of pleasure which they allowed. "I was moved also," he says, "to cry against all sorts of music, and against the mountebanks playing tricks on their stages, for they burdened the pure mind and stirred up people's minds to vanity."

Some of the sectaries were at this time preaching antinomianism, contending that Christians were bound by no moral law at all, since Christ had struck off all such bonds; and a few of them attempted to practice their preaching. It was a period when extremes met. The Quakers would hardly have suffered if their only peculiarity had been a rigid moral standard. The Puritan majority made it illegal to drink healths, and Fox was considered by no means eccentric when he petitioned for restrictions on the public houses. But the Quakers wore especially drab clothes, refused to use such names as Wednesday and March because they were derived from heathen gods, and stood apart from the mass of Puritans in many other ways. Also they refused to take oath, even in court, and they considered it improper to use titles of respect. A man was a man, they said, and no one was entitled to a plural or honorific "you." The sense of distinction between "you" and "thou" or "thee" was still keen.

The Quakers or Friends rejected also such titles as "Reverend" and "Right Worshipful" and "Master" or "Mr."

Some of the Quakers were extremely zealous in prophesying. They imitated the prophets of the Old Testament in trying to gain attention for their denunciations of wickedness. We are told, for instance, of two young girls who ran naked through the streets of Oxford, denouncing the hypocrisy of the people and calling upon them to abandon their sins. The Quaker chroniclers tell us how modest and virtuous these girls were; nevertheless, they were whipped by the authorities for causing a public scandal.

There were a number of other sects, some of whose adherents held views and committed acts not less interesting than those of the Quakers. Most of them have failed to survive into our time, though some lasted into the eighteenth or even the nineteenth century. Lodowick Muggleton, one of the most curious founders of religion, declared God to be exactly six feet tall and his habitation to be four miles distant from the earth. There were, naturally, some people who gladly accepted such precise theological information, but others declared that it was blasphemous to inquire into matters of that sort. In some cases religious extravagances were sharply punished. Naylor, for instance, aroused intense indignation by acting out the life of Christ according to the Gospel of John, as though laying claim to being a second savior. Many members of Parliament favored his death, and comparatively few desired his complete pardon.

§ 6

Oliver Cromwell was, in matters of religion, one of the most tolerant men of his time in England. He allowed Jews to enter the country, though they had been shut out for centuries. Yet his treatment of the Irish Catholics can hardly be characterized as anything but atrocious. Apologists for Cromwell have racked their brains to find excuses for his conduct in Ireland; but these are all in vain unless we concede the desirability, or the excusability, of killing those whose religious and political views do not happen to coincide with our own. This, of course, was admitted by most people who lived in Cromwell's time.

The Puritan ·general put to death Catholic priests simply because they were such. He wrote scornfully of their claim to be called "clergymen." I am not writing here the history of Cromwell's campaigns, and I cannot pause to point out the instances in which he granted a certain amount of mercy to Irish noncombatants. It is enough to say that "the curse of Cromwell" remained for centuries in Ireland as a horrible imprecation.

Later, and at least partially for diplomatic reasons, Cromwell did his best to secure some measure of toleration for English Catholics; but even at the height of his power it was more than he could do. His strength arose mainly from the ability to control his army; and the soldiers, although they were willing that nearly all the Protestant sects should be on a basis of full equality and privilege, were bitterly opposed to the Roman Catholic Church and to Episcopalianism, which they considered pretty much the same as popery.

Despite his imperfections, which were many, Oliver Cromwell was one of the greatest of the Puritans. His enemies invented stories about a wild youth, and he himself seems to confirm them by saying he was "the chief of sinners" as a young man. This sort of exaggerated expression we often find in Puritan autobiographies. It may mean no more than that he sometimes allowed his thoughts to wander from divine things. There is little solid basis for the charges of laxness in sexual conduct and intemperance in drink.

One of his letters to a daughter-in-law is a little sermon about the duty of trusting in God. A brief postscript alludes to her recent miscarriage, as though by way of afterthought. This is typical of Cromwell's correspondence, which constantly harps, in true Puritan fashion, upon the will and the love of God.

The first account we have of Cromwell tells how he rose to speak in Parliament, wearing "a plain country suit, which seemed to have been made by an ill country tailor; his linen was plain and not very clean." And there was a speck of blood or two on his little neckband, presumably caused by no worse accident than a cut produced when he shaved himself. In the plainness of his clothing he was the Puritan; and he was a Puritan, too, in his belief that all his victories were direct expressions of the will of God, who wished his armies to wipe out his enemy for the fulfillment of some divine purpose.

Cromwell differed from many Puritans in finding the pleasures of the world not altogether ashen. He liked music, was fond of horses, enjoyed hunting and hawking, and sometimes played at bowls. He was not a connoisseur of the fine arts, as King Charles had been, but he preserved many of the important royal paintings. He allowed himself to be painted by several artists, including Robert Walker and Peter Lely. The story goes that he told Lely to paint him truly, warts, pimples, and all, if he expected to be paid.

There were many protests about the statues of Venus, Cleopatra, Adonis, and Apollo in the gardens at Hampton Court—"monsters which are set up in privy gardens," according to a zealous Puritan lady—but Cromwell allowed the statues to remain where they were. When the Protector's daughter Frances married, forty-eight violins played, and the dancing and merrymaking continued until five o'clock in the morning. Mrs. Hutchinson tells us that his "court was full of sin and vanity, and the more abominable because they had not yet quite cast away the name of God, but profaned it by taking it in vain upon them."

Perhaps it made some difference to Cromwell that he was the ruler of England. He departed from the simplicity with which he would have been content in a lowlier position and took over a little of the pomp associated with monarchs. And he grew more tolerant, in matters of morality as well as religion, toward the end of his life—not that he ever approved of anything even vaguely approaching libertinism, or that he gave up the habit of listening for hours to sermons which the irreverent might characterize as tedious.

Cromwell's political system crumbled and fell when he died. His sons possessed neither his earnestness nor his strength. In 1660 there were many who considered Puritanism utterly destroyed. "True religion was now quite lost, even among the religious party, and hypocrisy became an epidemical disease, to the sad grief of Colonel Hutchinson, and all true-hearted Christians and Englishmen." Many wild schemes had been tried in government and religion. The levelers and the Puritan despot supported by force of arms had had their day, and almost everybody was anxious to welcome back to England the son of that legitimate king whom his subjects had put to death.

What remained of Puritanism? We shall see in the succeeding chapters that it was not by any means entirely annihilated when a Stuart prince returned. It remained, perhaps more intimately than ever, with the middle classes, especially in London and in such industrial towns as Birmingham, Gloucester, Exeter, and the clothing centers of Lancashire. The aristocrats of the late seventeenth century and of the eighteenth could see little sin in dueling, elegant idleness, or any of the thousand other things which the Puritan ministers denounced by the hour. The honest burghers properly appreciated the enormity of these sins, though. For them, labor and service remained duties to God. And their star was still rising.

Faithful Puritan preachers remained. Richard Baxter was at the height of his powers when the Merry Prince came back to his kingdom. Baxter tells how, as a boy, he was disgusted by the worldliness of the clergy. The Church of England readers he knew then were stage players and gamesters and ignorant drunkards, and they were so immersed in sin that they seemed utterly incapable of appreciating the wickedness of a May-pole. Baxter himself had been a little of a gambler at one time, but despite his good fortune, the grace of God had turned him away from this enormity.

"A confirmed Christian," Baxter wrote, "is one that taketh self-denial for one half of his religion," the love of God being the other half. He vividly described the torments of Hell, and emphasized their intensity by calling attention to the fact that "the principal Author of them, who is God himself," takes pleasure in inflicting them. "The torments of the damned must be extreme, because they are the *effect of divine vengeance.* Wrath is terrible, but revenge is implacable."

According to Baxter, people who want to avoid God's vengeance should take care not to sin and not to be made slaves to their appetites. In addition, they should fulfill all their duties as Christians. "Not only the open profane, the swearer, the drunkard, and enemies of godliness will prove hurtful companions to us—though these indeed are chiefly to be avoided; but too frequent society with persons merely civil and moral, whose conversation is empty and unedifying, may much divert our thoughts from Heaven." Next to godliness, Baxter said, is working at the appointed task as well as you can, with due attention to possible monetary profits. If you "choose the less gainful way, you cross one of the ends of your calling, and you refuse to be God's steward."

CHAPTER VI

BACCHUS AND HIS REVELERS

§ 1

SHORTLY after Charles II landed in England, Samuel Pepys wrote in his Diary: "The King's proclamation against drinking, swearing, and debauchery was read to our ships' companies in the fleet, and indeed it gives great satisfaction to all." On the very night when Charles was happily installed in his royal palace, he chose Barbara Villiers to share his kingly couch. Pepys and others who were further removed than he from the gossip of the court soon knew that the King was gathering a little seraglio about him.

Charles was very fond of comfort and pleasure. His primary desire was to keep from having "to set out on his travels" again. If his good subjects wanted him to utter warnings against vice, well and good. But surely it was not necessary for himself and his courtiers to pay any heed to strict standards of conduct. Very few of the noblemen who habitually surrounded the King were moral precisians. The courtiers as a class had long been deprived of what they considered their right to enjoy life, and they were entirely willing to make up for lost time. Many of the young men had been brought up by grooms and lackeys and initiated into the moral code of the stables or had wandered about aimlessly on the Continent in the company of professional gamblers and charlatans. Now that they were restored to their own again, they looked forward to unrestrained merrymaking. They were to enjoy indulgences denied to apprentices and shopkeepers. Moreover, they attached great importance to the things that outwardly distinguished them from the rabble, especially to clothes and manners.

So far as good manners went, the King himself set the example.

Charles was a clever fellow, although he possessed little of the ordinary book learning of his time. Perhaps his chief delight was in witty conversation, and though a number of his courtiers excelled in this little art, Charles usually managed to hold his own in repartee. He gambled, drank, toyed with his mistresses, idled about his gardens, played with his dogs, and displayed very little of the Puritan desire to do a day's work before every sunset. Charles had been preached at in his youth by Presbyterian ministers, but they never succeeded in developing an overnice conscience or an intense fear of Hell in him. "I cannot think," he remarked, "that God will make a man miserable for taking a little pleasure out of the way."

Though he worried little about divine vengeance, the King sometimes wondered how the House of Commons would take his lazy hedonism. England was thoroughly tired of war and disorder, and most of the people, just then, were disgusted with extreme Puritan morality. Many who were opposed to despotism and to laxness of conduct nevertheless liked King Charles. And he did not seem to be a very dangerous person. His languid air was thoroughly disarming. He flaunted no elaborate theory of divine right, concerned himself little with the details of government. He was so easy-going that his mistresses were said to be chosen for him by others. But this may be a slight exaggeration.

Or we may consider it a courtly jest. For wit, recommended by the King, became very fashionable. One of the most noteworthy laws of his reign, the Habeas Corpus Act of 1679, which historians consider an important step in the movement toward personal liberty, is supposed to have passed because of a rather— well, let us be witty ourselves and say—thin joke. According to Burnet, the tellers laughingly counted a fat peer as two, and but for this the law would have been defeated in the House of Lords.

Charles and his brother, the Duke of York, were reputed to be much less addicted to hard drinking and to gambling for large stakes than some of their courtiers. The first royal mistress, Barbara Villiers, better known as Lady Castlemaine, is supposed to have lost £15,000 one evening at play, and to have won £25,000 on another occasion.

Some of the courtly pleasure-seeking was pretty reckless. On occasion certain nobles and gentlemen acted as though the common people had no rights at all which they needed to respect. For example, it was pretty reliably asserted that the Duke of Monmouth frequently engaged in drunken frolics, and that on one such spree he helped to murder a watchman, who had not provoked the attack in any way. This wild boy was the son of Lucy Walters, who became a concubine to Charles on the Continent. Monmouth was supposed to be the King's son as well, but it is certain that Lucy had dallied with more than one other man, and it is consequently somewhat doubtful who the young Duke's father actually was. He was curiously popular with the Puritans, many of whom believed that Charles had secretly married Lucy Walters and that Monmouth was their legitimate son and the heir to the throne.

The King begot other children upon his mistresses. They received fine titles and became founders of important noble families. The baton sinister, derived from a king, in the shields of many proud houses afforded an example of royal morality which necessarily influenced the behavior of English aristocrats in the succeeding generations.

Nell Gwynn is probably the most celebrated of the King's mistresses. The daughter of a London fishmonger, she became as a young girl an orange-seller in the theatre. The orange girls sold more than fruit. A bawd had Nell taught how to read and write and how to sing. Then one of the girl's lovers who was an actor coached her in the dramatic arts, and she went on the stage. Though she was not particularly talented, she sang and danced passably well, and her saucy, pretty, vivacious face gained her many admirers.

One of them was His English Majesty, the Defender of the Faith, who promptly summoned her to his palace. Nell bore him two sons, one of whom became the Duke of St. Albans. Charles liked her merry, half-insolent ways. The people, too, preferred her to his other mistresses. The most objectionable of them in

CATHOLIC AND PROTESTANT: LOUISE DE KEROUALLE AND NELL GWYNN

After portraits by Sir Peter Lely.

popular eyes was Louise de Keroualle, Duchess of Portsmouth, to whose liaison with the King the house of Richmond owes its origin. Louise was sent by the King of France to win Charles over to his interests. The mob suspected her because she was French and hated her because she was a Roman Catholic. We are told that the rabble of Oxford once heaped threats and insults at Nell Gwynn, thinking she was the Duchess of Portsmouth. Nell leaned out of her coach window and bade them be quiet, explaining, "I am the Protestant whore."

Practically the whole system of palace courtesans was borrowed from Italy by way of France. Of similar origin was a wave of homosexual love. Much of the evidence about the existence of sodomy in this period has to do with the upper classes of society. Rochester's play *Sodom* represents that it was common in military circles. A number of brothels for male homosexual prostitution were opened in England. *Sodom* was played before King Charles and his court.

Yet, by and large, it does not seem that the Restoration brought about a general relaxation of morals in England. Small lapses from chastity and sobriety were more indulgently regarded, no doubt; and there was a great increase in frankness about the pursuit of pleasure. Still, such changes were marked only in the upper circles of society. The majority of the people continued to spend long hours at work, and the lower classes were by no means encouraged to imitate the morals of the great.

Brothels were opened once more in London, and every once in a while mobs of apprentices showed their pietistic zeal by raiding and wrecking them. After such an occasion King Charles asked mildly, "Why do they go to them, then?" Perhaps the trouble was that they did not have money enough to go to them very often. Still, Charles was right: if these houses had not received the patronage of the people, they would soon have closed without any interference from police officers or from moral apprentices.

So far as I can learn, the severe penalties provided by law for bawds and harlots under the Commonwealth had not reduced illicit sexual intercourse, and the repeal of such legislation did not bring about an increase in fornication. As for the apprentice lads, they were glad to inflict damage under the cloak of high ethical purposes. This sort of moral rioting has been common enough in the English-speaking countries.

The Puritan régime encouraged hypocrisy, and this remained after 1660 in spite of the brutal frankness which became fashionable in the highest circles. England as a whole remained much as it had been. Mr. Pepys records an illuminating incident. Bab May stood for Parliament at Winchelsea, "with the Duke of York's letters, not doubting to be chosen, and there the people chose a private gentleman in spite of him, and cried out that they would not have a court pimp to be their burgess."

James of York did not possess his brother's popularity, which was capable of excusing transgressions of the Puritan moral code. But there was talk enough about the looseness of court conduct, even on the part of some who (judged by a criterion derived from the New Testament) had no right to cast the first stone. Garrulous, half-Puritan Samuel Pepys was one of these, although he became much more tolerant as he worked his way closer to royalty.

We derive the impression from Pepys' Diary that he was a hard worker and, judged by the standards of his own time, a sober man. Certainly he made fine resolutions. Yet he was, as he said, often foxed, and once in a while he found it inconvenient to read prayers in his household, fearing to disclose his tipsiness to the servants. He didn't want to set a bad example to the housemaid and the coachman. But the servants weren't deceived. They knew that Mr. Pepys was no less human than themselves. At the same time they realized that if they didn't conceal their vices, they ran the risk of being well basted with a broomstick.

While the servants were watching Mr. Pepys, Mr. Pepys was watching the Duke of York. We are told that the Duke preferred not to make a public display of his concubines. Mrs. Price used to go to and from his rooms by way of the back stairs. Lady Denham, when the Duke of York fell in love with her, insisted that her position as his mistress should be publicly known. She did not consider it a disgraceful one. James went, therefore,

THE LONDON COURTESAN

A drawing by Marcellus Laroon, from Tempest's *Cryes of the City of London*, 1688.

"at noonday with all his gentlemen to visit her at Scotland Yard," where she lived. The concubines of the King and the heir presumptive enjoyed the sensation of power. They were courted for official positions and for other favors. And they did not find it embarrassing or undesirable to be known for what they were.

Broad allusions were common in the conversation of court circles, the King setting the fashion. Charles was present at a session of the House of Lords when Shaftesbury made coarse jokes about the Queen's childlessness, and the King laughed louder than the rest. Shaftesbury had been a good moral Presbyterian in the days of the Commonwealth. Then he was for a time chancellor to Charles, and he fell in with the spirit of the court by flinging away the old morality. He admitted once to his royal master that he was "the wickedest dog in England—for a subject." Wickedness was very fashionable.

King Charles was chary of oaths: "Odds fish" was his favorite exclamation. This was exceptional. Most noblemen and gallant gentlemen of his time considered it necessary to bring divine and diabolical names into their discourse as frequent punctuation marks or ornaments, by way of proving that they were not religious fanatics. The Puritans considered swearing extremely sinful.

The King patronized horse races and cockfights and was very fond of plays. These amusements became popular with his courtiers and those who aped the customs of the palace. However, they worked their way back into popular favor rather slowly. The squires threw off the shackles of Puritan morality with a certain amount of haste at the Restoration. The urban middle classes maintained the old standards, together with the old deviations in practice.

The citizens' wives of London, if they were attractive enough to arouse the interest of the courtiers, were led into temptation. Pretty girls found the honor of being on familiar terms with a duke or a baron seductive. All who pretended to be in fashion had to flirt and ogle in the palace manner. However, the majority of the people were frankly unfashionable.

Pepys records his displeasure at seeing the maids of honor dressed in riding habits of a mannish cut. Short skirts, too, were worn in the upper social circles. They were short, to be sure, by comparison with what had gone before, and we should consider them ridiculously long. The court ladies wore dresses which revealed the beauty of their bosoms. But even among the men and women of the court the clothing worn in public showed a stricter sense of modesty than that which had prevailed under Henry VIII. Nudeness in art was perfectly acceptable to the courtiers, though. And Lely's painting of Nell Gwynn, clothed only in her loveliness, was displayed in the royal palace.

Many men who, under Puritan influence, had worn their hair cut short, were confronted after the Restoration with the task of suddenly acquiring long locks with which to display their royalist zeal. The periwig was introduced for this purpose, and it remained fashionable after its emergency usefulness had departed. Men put on great quantities of ribbons and frills. They wore muffs, suspended from the neck by ribbons.

Large-scale beer drinking came back into respectability, though the court circles preferred foreign wines. A naval chaplain who was at sea in the years 1675 to 1679, chiefly for the purpose of escaping from his creditors, tells us how he was first received on shipboard with a large quantity of punch. He speaks of "punch like dishwater," referring not to its strength but to the prodigality with which it was dispensed. When the chaplain joined his ship, he found a large number of riotous women on board. They were put ashore, thoroughly drunk, at Dover. Sailors were severely punished for drunkenness and swearing, but their officers and chaplains, no less guilty, went unscathed. The aristocrats had discovered that Puritan morality, or some phases of it, might well be retained for the lower orders.

Still, we hear of poor people who bet £5 each on a cockfight, an immense sum considering the wage scales which then prevailed. Cockfighting was, in the reign of Charles II, considered mainly a sport for the higher orders, and the price of admission put the spectacle out of the reach of most workmen. The baiting of bulls and bears, for the time being unfashionable, attracted only the rabble. Gambling at cards and with dice was popular in all circles. John Ashton, in his history of games of chance in England, considers the period of the Restoration the time when gambling was at its height.

Tobacco was taken not alone for pleasure, but as a supposed preventive and cure for various diseases. The account books of a pious Quaker family which have come down to us show that the women sometimes smoked pipes, evidently for the purpose of keeping off the plague. There has never been a time since without some female smokers in England, although the practice has not always been considered respectable.

Dueling, which had been strongly condemned under the Puritan régime, became the duty of a gentleman in the reign of Charles II. However, not all persons of high degree adhered strictly to the code of honor. Hired bravos often were used to satisfy an insult or to revenge a slight. When a nobleman became angry with a commoner, he sometimes sent his servants to administer a caning to the offender. A country member of Parliament who, in the course of a debate, spoke harshly about the royal amours, aroused the ire of Charles and his courtiers. The King could hardly engage in a duel with one of his subjects, but he might have sent a defender to fight the obnoxious Puritan. Instead, he had a gang of ruffians waylay him and slit his nose. Parliament, thoroughly indignant, convicted the bullies by a special act and refused to allow the King to pardon them. Charles II's connection with this outrage served to hasten a decline in his popularity, which became evident toward the end of his reign. As vacancies occurred in the House of Commons, they were usually filled by men known to be unfriendly to him.

The Church of England taught that the king could do no wrong: that is (for the phrase has now a different meaning), no matter what the monarch might do, his subjects had no right to offer resistance. It was officially denied that his actions might be criticized in the light of a higher or divine law. The king, as head of the Church, was also the judge of his own moral and religious obligations. Fear of the anarchy occasioned by the Civil War caused many people, including some with no strong

THE YOUNG MEN'S COFFEE HOUSE
From *The Works of Mr. Thomas Brown*, 1730.

religious convictions, to support this doctrine. It was best stated by Hobbes, who was a religious skeptic. Hobbes especially emphasized the idea that the Church must be subordinate to the monarch, and that ministers of religion are therefore not justified in putting their interpretations of the king's duty to God above his own. In his *Leviathan* he shows from Biblical texts that the Kingdom of God is not intended to be established in the mundane present, and that those who support a theocracy should be punished as traitors to the monarch and the State.

King Charles oscillated between religious agnosticism and an allegiance to the tenets of the Roman Catholic Church. It is sometimes said that he looked favorably upon Catholicism only because of its strong, compact organization, which he considered eminently compatible with absolute monarchy. Certainly he favored episcopal church government for this reason; but it is difficult to see how the Church of England, which recognized him as its supreme earthly head, was less adapted to his exercise of complete power than allegiance to a Roman bishop would have been. The Catholic priests as a whole were more favorable to royal absolutism than the Anglican ones, because they knew that the majority of the people were fiercely intolerant of popery. But the real reason why the King, when he was religious, looked to Rome seems to be that, tiring of doubt, he wanted authoritative answers, and these the papacy professed to give. Charles did not venture to proclaim himself a Roman Catholic. On his deathbed, in 1685, a priest was smuggled in to him. The dying King received absolution and felt sure that his love of pleasure would be forgiven him. Thinking of one whom he loved, he said to his brother, "Do not let poor Nellie starve."

James became a zealous Catholic convert in 1672, and he was very unpopular thenceforth in consequence. During Charles II's reign Parliament several times considered barring the Duke of York from the throne. Once a bill for this purpose was passed by the House of Commons, but it was rejected by the Lords.

At the Restoration the Parliament which welcomed Charles had been strongly Presbyterian. The Puritans afterward remained in control of some important local governments, but they lost the leadership of Parliament to ardent Cavaliers, who insisted upon conformity to the Church of England. Neither Anglicans nor Presbyterians, with rare exceptions, favored the toleration of Roman Catholics; nor did they consider with pleasure the probability that Charles II, dying without legitimate children, would be succeeded by his Catholic brother.

Charles had given the Presbyterian leaders who worked for the restoration of the monarchy to understand that there would be no insistence upon conformity of worship. But, despite his promises and, it is pretty clear, in spite of his desire, it was made a penal offense to attend any except an Anglican (Episcopalian) church. There had been an unsuccessful attempt to work out a plan of ecclesiastical government and ritual which should be satisfactory to the moderate Puritans as well as to the High Church Anglicans. Even conservative sectaries could hardly be expected to consider the Church of England satisfactory unless many of the usages were considerably changed; and there was little hope of attracting Muggletonians, Quakers, Baptists, and Independents by any sort of compromise. The Presbyterians, much against their will, were forced into the position of having to choose between disobeying the law and attending High Church services. Those Puritans who were elected to municipal offices found themselves unable to occupy them without first taking the communion according to the rites of the Established Church and swearing allegiance to the Church of England as well as the king.

The Act of Uniformity of 1662 forbade all persons except those who had been ordained by Anglican bishops to exercise the function of ministers of religion. It provided also that no book or method of prayer should be used save the official prayer book of the Church of England. Under the pressure of such legislation and a change in public opinion, most Puritans of the upper and middle classes conformed to the worship and usages of the Established Church. The fact that large numbers of them became Anglicans eventually brought about great changes within the Church of England.

The Bible, for example, became the book of books, and a

certain amount of original interpretation was allowed. The fact that people of varying theological beliefs were members of the Established Church prevented the development of a complex system of dogma with an official sanction. Piety, or the pretense of piety, and claims to high morality became typical of the urban, middle-class members of the Church of England.

The opponents of Puritanism appeared to have won a complete triumph in 1660, but they were unable to do away with rigid Sunday observance. In fact, zealous Christians of all the classes and shades of belief, or almost all, afterwards joined in demanding that Sunday should be given over to religious observance. In 1676 a law was passed forbidding all labor on the first day of the week, except work of necessity or charity. The same law provided that "no drover, horse-courser, waggoner, butcher, higgler (they or any of their servants) shall travel or come into his or their inn or lodging upon the Lord's Day, or any part thereof, upon pain that each and every such offender shall forfeit twenty shillings for every such offense." It also made boating on Sunday a misdemeanor.

All forms of recreation on Sunday were under the ban of the godly, though the revelers of the court generally felt free to amuse themselves every day in the week. Pepys expresses the surprise of the people at finding that the palace was not observing the Puritan Sabbath: "I did find the Queen, the Duchess of York, and another one or two, at cards, with a room full of great ladies and men, which I was amazed at to see on a Sunday, having not believed it; and, contrarily, having flatly denied the same a little while since to my cousin Roger Pepys."

Roger was an out-and-out Puritan, while Samuel was usually willing to drift with the times. The diarist tells how his cousin heard Lady Castlemaine's negro boy swearing at a dog and angrily exclaimed that if it had been his servant, he would have whipped him until the blood came for such cursing. By way of reaction from this attitude, the Cavaliers considered it the prettiest thing in the world to hear young girls utter blood-curdling oaths.

Out of the great moral and religious differences which prevailed in Restoration days, a new attitude toward toleration gradually evolved. In 1662 about one-fifth of the clergymen of England were driven from their parishes. These conscientious Puritans and the laymen who supported them had, during the time when their influence was at its height, mostly sought to preserve religious conformity. Now they were forced to become advocates of toleration which should extend at least to all Protestants. In Charles II's time they were violently opposed to sharing toleration with Roman Catholics, and they opposed the King when he tried to abolish all religious tests for public officers.

The Protestant Nonconformists seem to have feared that if Catholics were once admitted to Parliament and to executive positions in the State, the Marian persecutions would quickly be resumed or England would be betrayed to the popish powers. The fear that a foreign allegiance would necessarily bring about disloyal actions on the part of Roman Catholics who might be placed in offices of trust was very slow to die out in Great Britain. It is still of political importance in the United States. In the days when Charles II reigned, it was very easy to convince the people of the existence of popish plots to bring in French armies and roast the Protestants alive.

Not far to the west was Ireland, where the natives had very little reason to love English and Scottish Protestants. There was in England little inclination to redress the wrongs which had been inflicted upon the Irish Catholics by Cromwell and other conquerors. Hence, it is true that in any clearly defined conflict between English Catholics and Protestants the Irish would have taken the Catholic side. But the danger of such a civil war was minor, because the number of Roman Catholics in England, although rising under Charles II and James II, remained very small in comparison with the number of Protestants. Better founded was the fear that English and Irish Catholics would be found on the side of royal absolutism if it came again into combat by arms with Puritan and democratic forces.

There seemed to be a genuine danger that Protestant dissent from the Church of England might be forcibly extinguished.

Several laws bore down heavily upon the Nonconformist clergy. Baxter was one of the ministers who suffered severely from the persecutions. The Puritans, whether or not they conformed to the Established Church, began to turn away from the doctrine that the State should make absolute prescriptions of religious formulas and rituals.

The social position and the influence of the clergy declined sharply after 1660. Interest in theology decreased, and, in spite of periods of revived attention to religious matters, it never regained the position it had held in the early part of the seventeenth century.

For some time after 1660 the ministers still were able to mold public opinion. Few of the people read newspapers, and illiteracy was generally prevalent. Among the educated, secular intellectual interests were growing. All through Europe religious warfare was coming to an end, and the great conflicts after 1650 were usually brought about by dynastic and commercial rivalries. Even in the time when the Puritans ruled England, wars of religion were succeeded by wars of trade. A new half-Puritan spirit arose, looking toward the profits of industry and making chief use of religion to help business. In Defoe, who was born shortly after the Restoration, we find the first great apostle of the New Puritanism. Baxter's insistence that God wants Christians to do what will bring them the greatest economic profit is typical of the transition period.

Religious agnosticism became rather fashionable in high social circles in the Restoration period. Even churchmen were infected, and some of them expressed the opinion that skepticism was less to be feared than lack of conformity in worship. Nevertheless, it remained somewhat dangerous to express in public doubts about the truth of Christianity. The bishops refused to allow Hobbes' *Leviathan* to be reprinted, and the price of secondhand copies took a leap upward. Although this philosopher's religious views were pretty widely known, he used discretion in his writings. His rationalism did not keep him from bolstering up his arguments with Scriptural texts, and *Leviathan* does not exhibit any opposition to revealed religion.

Sir William Temple was supposed to hold irreligious views; nevertheless, he was elected to Parliament by the University of Oxford, which is to say, chiefly by clergymen. But the Oxford graduates did object when Temple spoke favorably of the religious toleration which was practiced in Holland. A great many English rationalists since 1660 have considered it their patriotic duty to defend the Church of England and to sneer at the members of the dissenting denominations. Like Hobbes, they have defended the Church although sometimes openly hostile to religion.

For the lower clergy the period of the Restoration was not favorable. Although a great many Puritan ministers were driven from their livings, the fortune of those who remained loyal to the official views of the Church was not improved. Clergymen who did not occupy high positions were considered inferior to gentlemen. Some of them drifted into domestic chaplaincies, where they were treated as servants. If they were permitted to dine with their patrons, they usually had to leave the table when the dessert was served. They had barely enough money to live on, and they were not considered too lofty to marry chambermaids. In fact, there was a law, which had been passed in an earlier reign, that no clergyman should marry a servant without the consent of her master or mistress. It sometimes happened that a country squire arranged a match between his cast-off concubine and his domestic chaplain. The wife of a poor minister and the mistress of a rural landlord were about on the same social level, and the latter was usually better off so far as material things went.

In the city, clergymen enjoyed a better position, economically and socially, than the rural parsons. Those whose sermons were popular or who could rise in the hierarchy by manipulating political wires stood in an altogether different category. It is noteworthy, however, that very few men in orders have held high office outside the Church since the Restoration.

Considered as a whole, the conforming clergy acted as an important conservative force, opposed to change except under extreme provocation. The chaplains were mere puppets, but they repeated the views of their masters, the country nobles and squires, who were almost always desirous of maintaining the old order of things. The middle classes, growing rapidly in importance, had more reason to demand changes in the social and political organization of England. For the first time we see a source of opposition between the industrial interests and the Protestant clergy. While many Puritan ministers were supporters of middle-class political and economic interests, it was in this period that anticlericalism began to develop among the persons interested in commerce and industry. Yet religious doubt was until late in the nineteenth century to be anathema in ordinary *bourgeois* circles.

In the intellectual history of England the rise of scientific interest under Charles II is of the utmost importance. The King encouraged experimentation in the natural sciences, which he found far more interesting than either theological or philological hairsplitting. It was the time when the Royal Society arose and Sir Isaac Newton flourished. Inductive truth-seeking brought about, for the educated, a diminished bondage to the authority of the Bible, or to any other intellectual authority. It finally resulted in a freedom of thought and discussion which made such a man as Voltaire look enviously across the English Channel. The growth of the scientific attitude was slow, its spread among the masses still slower, and prejudices against it have not disappeared to this day.

In 1664 the learned Sir Thomas Browne, author of *Religio Medici,* helped to convict two women of witchcraft. But educated men in general were even then turning away from the superstitions of their ancestors, refusing to believe in the evil eye and in possession by demons, denying that disease epidemics and great fires were to be explained merely as punishments sent by God because of the sins of the wicked. The masses clung tenaciously to such old ideas, and many Puritans felt that the disasters which came to England in the 1660's were divinely intended to rebuke the court for its levity. The notion that God requires religious offenders to receive on earth a foretaste of the eternal burning which awaits them in Hell was formally abandoned in 1677, when the death penalty for heresy was abolished in England. No heretic had actually been burned alive since 1612.

§ 2

After 1660 Nonconformity depended for the most part upon the support of the lower and the lower middle classes. John Bunyan stands out as a representative and teacher of the poor sectaries in the Restoration period. Though he was drafted into the Commonwealth Army during the Civil War, his Puritan zeal was at that time undeveloped. In his autobiography, *Grace Abounding to the Chief of Sinners,* Bunyan agonizes over his youthful depravity, but does not very clearly define it.

According to the Puritan creed, all sinfulness was deadly. "It was my delight," says Bunyan, "to be taken captive by the Devil at his will." But even in his childhood, if his later recollections are to be trusted, sin and repentance came close together. Let us see how he offended. "I had but few equals (especially considering my years, which were tender, being few) both for cursing, swearing, lying, and blaspheming the holy name of God." Since we are furnished with no examples of the language which the lad used and the memory of which horrified him later, it is impossible to know how vicious the moralists of our day would consider it.

At any rate, young Bunyan had visions of Hell and dreadful thoughts about the fate which must finally be his. Nevertheless, as he tells us, he had "lusts" until he was married, and was "the very ringleader of all the youth" with whom he associated "in all manners of vice and ungodliness." His language makes us think of fornication and drunkenness, with a little assault and battery or theft by way of variety. But the tangible acts of vice may have consisted in watching a dog fight a chained bear and dancing about a May-pole.

There were times when he worried little about "saving and damning"—a dreadful state of affairs, as he pondered over it later. Luckily, he was led to think about divine things when he several times narrowly escaped death. It seemed to him God interposed for some special reason, keeping him from being drowned in his youthful rambles and from being killed in the Civil War. At a siege his successor at a sentry post was killed immediately after Bunyan had left the place.

John Bunyan was moved to wonder why God had saved his life. For what work was he preserved? He looked inward, trying to determine if he was worthy of carrying out a divinely ordained task. And then he began to see how many of the things he had enjoyed were sinful. In his unregenerate days he had taken delight in bell-ringing, although even then troubled by the fear that God would make the bells tumble down on his unholy head.

He played tip-cat, until he heard a voice from Heaven which convinced him it was sinful to engage in that sport. A godly woman heard him swearing dreadfully and persuaded him to curse no more. But it seems that some of the fine resolutions he formed did not prevent relapses. "All this time I knew not Jesus Christ, neither did I leave my sports and plays."

Then he became interested in the Old Testament, and he wondered how he could be sanctified unless he was one of the Chosen People. His father assured him emphatically that he had no Israelitish blood. Bunyan was much perplexed. In his bewilderment he was almost seduced by some antinomian Ranters, who assured him that Christ had abolished the entire Mosaic law, and that he might do almost anything he wished without arousing the divine wrath.

Worse was still to come. He had dreadful doubts about the very existence of God. These were, of course, diabolically inspired. After the doubts were seemingly overcome, he wondered if he really possessed faith. No matter how he tried, he could not perform any miracles. Mountains did not move, waters did not become dry, at his command.

He came upon one of Luther's Biblical commentaries, and it gave him comfort. (Calvin's writings would have been unintelligible to this unlearned man.) He fell again into troubled thoughts. Had he not committed the sin of Judas, the unpardonable sin against the Holy Ghost, in denying Jesus? Sometimes he heard reassuring divine voices but he remained long in doubt.

After deciding that he had reformed sufficiently and that his conduct was satisfactory to God, he received a summons to preach: "I suddenly felt this word to sound in my heart, *I must go to Jesus.*" He joined a Baptist church at Bedford, but he never laid much stress upon the doctrinal differences between the evangelical sects. The important thing for him was the Bible, and he disliked religions which relied chiefly upon either a church tradition or mystical experience. Yet he was something of a mystic himself.

Bunyan was a tinker by trade. When he married, at the age of twenty, he had forgotten the little knowledge of reading and writing that he had once possessed. His wife became his teacher, the Bible being the principal textbook. Bunyan the writer reveals in almost every sentence how deeply the English Scriptures impressed him.

He became an unlicensed preacher and an author of religious works as well. After five years of undisturbed work he was ordered to stop usurping the functions of ordained ministers. He refused, and he was lodged in jail. There he remained for many years. He read the Bible and Foxe's *Book of Martyrs,* he made tagged laces, and he wrote a great deal. One of the books he wrote was *Pilgrim's Progress.* Because some of his friends considered the fictional form frivolous, he delayed its publication fifteen years.

The book became immediately popular with the lower-class Dissenters. Then its vogue spread into all social classes and among persons of all the creeds. For some time it was not admitted by scholarly critics among great works of literature, but it gradually won a place among the accepted classics. *Pilgrim's Progress* is distinctly a product of its own time, when the godly Nonconformists found almost insuperable obstacles in the way of their carrying out what they conceived to be their duty to God, and when religious indifference seemed to be the great fashionable vice. The allegory refers to this situation, and it is applicable only in a general way to other Christian pietists. Nevertheless,

there is a Catholic version of the book, with Bunyan's disrespectful allusions to the Pope removed. *Pilgrim's Progress* has lost
some of its old popularity. A recent critic, who objects also to
Milton and to Dante, has spoken slightingly of it. But, aside
from its genuine merit as a piece of literature, it represents the
last great expression of the old Puritanism in England. One or
two powerful Puritan voices were still to be heard in British
America.

The Quakers did a great deal of writing in the days of Charles
II and James II, though few of their works are now read. They
defended their faith, chiefly against such Evangelical Puritans as
Bunyan and Baxter, they recorded their mystical experiences,
and they denounced worldly luxury. Readers of Pepys' Diary
often come upon the name of Admiral Penn. His son became a
leader of the Friends, and one of the writers who denounced
hedonism. William Penn is known to Americans as the founder
of Pennsylvania. A Quaker named Samuel Fisher published in
1666 a book of eight hundred quarto pages called *Rusticus ad
Academicos*. This deals in an advanced way with Biblical manu-
scripts and the canon of the Holy Scriptures. The higher criticism was coming to life in England.

§ 3

A large part of the literature of the Restoration is saturated
with the Cavalier spirit. One class is chiefly interesting for its
satires against the Puritans. The best-known work in this category is a long poem, *Hudibras,* by Samuel Butler. Butler was
born only four years later than Milton, and his prime of life was
spent in the period when the Puritans ruled England. He was,
indeed, for a time a sort of upper servant to a Presbyterian country gentleman, whom he satirized as Hudibras. This Presbyterian knight performs a number of mock-heroic actions, in a
manner suggested by Cervantes, Rabelais, and Scarron. He goes
off, like a true hero, "to keep the peace twixt dog and bear," or,
in prosaic language, to stop bear baiting, and continues with
various other deeds of derringdo.

Puritanism is laughed at in all its aspects. It is represented as

> A sect, whose chief devotion lies
> In odd perverse antipathies;
> In falling out with that or this,
> And finding somewhat still amiss:
> More peevish, cross, and splenetick,
> Than dog distract, or monkey sick:
> That with more care keep holy-day
> The wrong, than others the right way:
> Compound for sins they are inclined to
> By damning those they have no mind to:
> Still so perverse and opposite,
> As though they worshipped God for spite.

Hudibras became at once a very fashionable book. Even those who were unable to appreciate its cleverness had to read it if they had any claim to being in the courtly vogue. King Charles was delighted with the poem, and he made a present to the author. The direct profits of authorship were not great, and Charles has been blamed for not being more generous to Butler.

Dramatic writing was often profitable and sermons sometimes brought large sums to the ministers who wrote them, but literature in general was a poor paymaster. Most of the leading Cavalier poets enjoyed independent incomes. One of them was John Wilmot, Earl of Rochester. Mulgrave, in his anonymously published *Essay on Satire*, spoke of Rochester as

> Mean in each action, lewd in every limb.

The Earl believed John Dryden to be the author, and he had a gang of hired bravos administer a beating to Dryden. Rochester is said to have confessed to Burnet that he "cared not" for morality. Probably he is remembered more distinctly as a drunkard and lover of pleasure than as a poet.

Whibley remarks of the Cavalier writers: "They had learned in Paris how to temper their magnificence with wit and *politesse*, and, in the glamour of beauty and courage, they forgot the long, dark days when all the decorative arts of life had been banished, when even the smile of irony was deemed a disgrace." The contrast is somewhat exaggerated. The Puritans had sometimes made good use of irony and of wit. Humor, indeed, had been almost entirely lacking, but we find little of it at the Restoration court. For humor requires sympathy, and both Puritans and Cavaliers were usually incapable of understanding the feelings of the opposite side.

We find flashes of humor in Butler, because he was not a perfect Cavalier. To him, who loved the Golden Mean, the reaction to Puritanism, with its wild excesses, was as objectionable as Puritanism itself. Butler did not approve of Sedley's running naked through the streets any more than he approved of the pulling down of May-poles by his old master, the Presbyterian colonel.

During the Restoration period there was a mass of political and religious satire notable for its disregard of prudery and of delicacy in expression, but not otherwise remarkable. The Cavaliers took particular delight in scandalizing Puritan precisians.

Music, architecture, and the fine arts in general revived at this time, finding generous patrons, royal and noble. Wide public support for the arts was still unknown, but the foundation for it was laid by the diminution of interest in religion and theology.

§ 4

Since Charles II left no legitimate children, his crown descended at his death to his brother, the Duke of York, who reigned for a short time as James II. James enjoyed attending to the business of state: all the details which Charles had gladly relinquished to others, he was willing to take upon himself. Publicly known to be a Roman Catholic, he had resigned from his admiralty when the Test Act forbade those who did not worship according to the Anglican rites to hold public office. Many English Protestants had considered James to be involved when a certain Titus Oates invented a widely believed tale about a popish plot to murder Charles and force the Roman Catholic religion upon England. Oates had, after many vicissitudes and shifts in his profession of faith, been thrust out of the Jesuit order, and he told his story to obtain revenge and also the perquisites of a national savior. He brought ruin and death down upon a number of English Catholics. Public opinion ran so high that James was forced to leave England for a time, and, as we have seen, he narrowly escaped being excluded by Parliament from the succession to the throne.

Though the Duke of York was narrow and methodical and hard-working, he had his mistresses, just like his brother. Sometimes he was inexplicably attracted to women whom other people considered very plain. One of these was Arabella Churchill, maid of honor to his first wife. Arabella's brother John benefited from the connection. He is better known in history as the Duke of Marlborough. Churchill is said to have engaged in an amour with a royal mistress, the Duchess of Cleveland. Once, when he was with her and King Charles arrived unexpectedly, John Churchill was forced to jump through the window. The story goes that the Duchess afterwards presented him with £5,000, the prudent investment of which laid the foundation for his future fortune.

The Duke of Monmouth had been put forward during his putative father's reign as a possible successor to the throne, and many Englishmen preferred to see a Protestant crowned, even though his right to the kingship might be very shaky, rather than a Catholic. There were a number of complications. First, it was pretty clear that Monmouth was a bastard, despite all the pretended evidence that his mother had been married to King Charles. Secondly, James had a daughter, Mary, who had been brought up as an Anglican and who was married to a Protestant prince, William of Orange. If it was unsafe to let any Roman Catholic wear the crown of England, Mary's claim to it was the best. William and Mary, out of policy or filial attachment, were determined not to work against James of York, and though they showed no hostility to Monmouth, they were anxious that he should not become king.

As soon as James came to the throne, in 1685, he proclaimed his determination to "preserve the government both in Church and

State as it is now by law established." This assurance that he had no hostile designs against the Church of England was favorably received. The greater part of his subjects remained loyal when Monmouth raised the banners of rebellion and Argyll rose in Scotland. Argyll's forces were quickly crushed. Monmouth's lasted little longer.

James was anxious that all the rebels, not merely the leaders, should be punished with great severity. Many of Monmouth's soldiers were put to death on the battlefield while begging for quarter. Then Chief Justice Jeffreys was sent to be the King's principal agent in the work of revenge and terror. Loyal subjects were horrified at the punishments which were inflicted upon men and women more or less remotely connected with Monmouth's aspirations. Jeffreys was reputed to be a great drunkard. It is certain that he showed little impartiality or judicial poise on the bench. He mocked at his victims, gloated over the sufferings they were to endure, stormed at the lawyers and witnesses who tried to deny or minimize their guilt.

Women were put to death for the crime of harboring rebels. Schoolgirls were convicted of treason because they had presented a banner to Monmouth. Jeffreys was a pathological sadist, a man who experienced unusual pleasure in the infliction of pain, and his royal master had similar tendencies. They enjoyed causing the death of scores of rebels. Large numbers suffered minor punishments, being horribly flogged or sold as slaves to the planters of the West Indies. The roads of England were lined with the quarters of executed rebels. Women were whipped from town to town for no greater crime than that of having expressed sympathy for the Protestant pretender to the throne. Economic interest was added to passion, and a traffic in convicted traitors reached considerable proportions. The parents and friends of indiscreet schoolgirls paid all they had to keep the children from being sold into slavery, and court ladies were among those who pocketed the proceeds.

Brutality was characteristic of the times. Gentlemen made up little pleasure parties to see the prisoners flogged in the houses of correction. Perhaps some good-looking harlots would be stripped to the waist to receive castigation in the gentlemen's presence, if they were lucky. In the next century a visitor to Bridewell described how he saw the men who supervised the corporal punishment of the prisoners lay their hands upon women's backs and breasts to judge how severely the whip might be applied.

Jeffreys, ordering a woman to be whipped at the cart's tail exclaimed gleefully, "Hangman, I charge you to pay particular attention to this lady! Scourge her till the blood runs down! Scourge her soundly, man! It is Christmas, a cold time for madam to strip in. See that you warm her shoulders thoroughly."

Baxter, charged with publishing seditious matter, was unfortunate enough to be brought before the Chief Justice. The Puritan minister, who enjoyed the veneration of a large body of Englishmen, was then in his seventieth year. He was convicted by a specially selected jury. Jeffreys abused him as though he had been a truant boy, then sentenced him to imprisonment and the payment of the heavy fine. It was rumored at the time that Jeffreys would have liked to have him flogged through the streets but was dissuaded from such a sentence by his associates on the bench.

The people of England were horrified by some of Jeffreys' actions. It was not alone a question of his cruelty: a generation which was accustomed to see men fight each other with swords for small prizes, and which flocked eagerly to see the baiting of animals, objected little to that. The Protestants did not object to Cromwell's bloodthirstiness in Ireland. But it was feared that Jeffreys intended eventually to wreak his cruelty upon all Englishmen who did not join the Catholic Church. Certainly he was a loyal servant to the King, and James would have liked to bring England back to the Roman fold, if the thing were at all possible. Jeffreys became Lord Chancellor of England. Yet the time was to come when he would be glad to be locked up out of reach of the mob.

James had experienced abundantly, before his accession to the throne, the strength of English opposition to popery. Nevertheless, his sense of royal power ran so high that he dreamed at times of reëstablishing the old Church. At the very least he wanted Roman Catholics to enjoy the same political rights as members of the Church of England. He found great difficulties in the way when he tried to put his Catholic friends and supporters into public office. He explained that he desired general religious toleration, yet he permitted the Scotch Presbyterians to be persecuted for failure to attend the Episcopalian services. It was not against his will that men and women were put to death in Scotland for nonconformity and that the Highlanders were encouraged to rob and murder the Covenanters of the Lowlands. The persecutions in Scotland were partially political, it is true, but religion and politics were so intermingled that the attack seemed to be primarily directed against freedom of conscience, or even in favor of the Roman Catholic Church.

In England King James was at first disposed to persecute the Dissenters in the same way. His ruthless zeal in dealing with the Monmouth rebels was due in part to the fact that many of them were Nonconformists. Then he saw that it was necessary to gain the support of the Protestants who did not belong to the Church of England, or at least to make much of the gap between them and the Anglicans. He became especially friendly to the Quakers, conceiving that their doctrine of nonresistance might be useful in certain contingencies. But they and members of the other Protestant sects looked with no sense of pleasure at the Catholic priests and monks who were now walking about the streets of London in their ecclesiastical garb. James became dependent, through his attempts to rule without Parliament, upon subsidies from Louis XIV of France. Louis had revoked the Edict of Nantes which protected the Huguenots and was engaged in prosecuting them bloodily. The Protestants of England had, therefore, a certain basis for their fears.

The most important state positions were gradually given over to Catholics. The disabilities resting upon Dissenters and Catholics alike were suspended by royal order. However, the Puritan leaders who benefited by the new tolerance were for the most part suspicious. Baxter, released from imprisonment, expressed no sense of gratitude; instead, he labored earnestly to unite Anglicans and Nonconformists against what seemed to be a menace to them both. Bunyan denounced the King. Those Dissenting ministers who accepted favors from James and then toned down their habitual harsh words about popery found themselves without influence. Their congregations slipped away, going to churches where the clergymen proved they had not been bribed by damning the Pope and the Church of Rome.

James made a few attempts to replace the dignitaries of the Anglican Church and the university officials (who were also practically officers of the Church of England) with actual Roman Catholics or with men who were not strongly opposed to Catholicism. It did not take him very long to realize how strong the parties he was antagonizing actually were. The Anglicans wavered in their doctrine of the illegality of resisting the king when they, not alone the Dissenters, were affected by his tyranny. If they allowed James to carry out his will, they saw they might quickly find that the Anglican Church was once more a branch of the Catholic Church headed by the Bishop of Rome.

James finally issued a proclamation in which he announced that he favored the permanent toleration of all shades of religious opinion. Neither the doctrine of unqualified tolerance itself nor the King's supposed motive in taking such a position found favor with the masses of the people. Most of the clergy refused to read the proclamation. They did not want Roman Catholics to hold public office.

The King had two Protestant daughters, Mary and Anne. Mary's husband, William of Orange, became the hope of all the Protestants in Europe when he was made Stadtholder or chief magistrate of the United Provinces. When James II's wife, Mary of Modena, gave birth to a son, it was certain that the heir apparent to the English throne would be brought up as a Catholic. There was no longer any basis for the old hope that James would, in the due course of events, be succeeded by Anglican Protestants.

Ten days after the prince was born, William of Orange received an invitation to come over and take the English throne. James was vaguely conscious of the storm that was gathering. Mis-

THE PROTESTANTS' JOY

After a ballad of 1689 in the British Museum.

trusting the Protestants in his Army, he recruited many Irish Catholics. A derogatory song about the new Irish soldiers, "Lillibullero," spread rapidly through the country. William finally landed in England and, after a brief period of doubt, gathered an English Army about his small Dutch force. James professed his willingness to make all sorts of concessions, but it was too late. He ran away, was captured, and was permitted to escape to the Continent. After much rioting and squabbling William and Mary became joint sovereigns of England.

When James had fled, London mobs attacked Catholic houses of worship and the homes of certain diplomats from popish countries. William, who was sincerely devoted to religious toleration, did all he could to save the Catholics from attack, but his authority and power were limited until the ambiguities about his own title were cleared up. He was a grandson to Charles I, but he owed his kingship chiefly to his wife. People in England were suspicious of him as a foreigner. Besides, the Dissenters were largely responsible for his accession to the English throne. The Toleration Act of 1689, which was somewhat defective even in the provisions intended to apply to Protestant Nonconformists, did not give any relief at all to Catholics or to persons denying the doctrine of the Trinity. William would have liked to make the law far more comprehensive, but he had to yield to the desire of Parliament. The Revolution of 1688 which had made him king was primarily of importance in showing that the royal will was no longer dominant. It was by virtue of an act of Parliament that William and Mary sat upon the throne.

A law passed by the English Parliament in 1691 definitely subjected Ireland to the Protestant minority there. Almost all the Irish Catholics favored the cause of the deposed King, and many of them bravely supported James in his unsuccessful efforts to regain the throne. Political and religious considerations together kept the native Irish subordinate to persons of English and Scotch origin, whom they looked upon as usurpers.

The Revolution brought about a great split in the Church of England. After James ran away, there was a tendency to forget and forgive his faults. The doctrine that it was wicked to resist the legitimate king sprang up into prominence again. To be sure, there was some question about which king deserved the allegiance of the English people. The doctrine of nonresistance, as stated by Hobbes, applies to the *de facto* ruler; but some of the clerical legitimists denied that the king over the water had forfeited his right to the throne by running away.

No less a personage than the Archbishop of Canterbury stood at the head of the Nonjurors, who refused to swear allegiance to the new King and Queen. They were ejected from their positions, but they and the men whom the bishops among them ordained had many supporters then and well into the next century.

The eviction of the Nonjurors brought many new men into the high ecclesiastical positions, as a class, liberals in religion and in politics. Indeed, the first requirement was that they should approve of the Revolution. Tillotson, who became Archbishop of Canterbury, was the author of a treatise *Against the Eternity of Hell Torments*. His sermons were immensely popular, but many good people were aghast at the idea of his being permitted to teach that sinners would not burn forever. They feared that such a doctrine could not fail to destroy public morality.

In 1696 Parliament voted against the censorship of the press. This was one of many indications of a growing freedom of thought and discussion. But the fear of popery remained. In 1701 the Act of Settlement, which provided that Anne should succeed William (Mary having already died) on the throne and that the Hanoverian princes should be next in the line of succession, specifically forbade the crowning of any Roman Catholic. The fear that a Catholic Stuart might possibly come to the Scottish throne removed most of the opposition to the uniting of England and Scotland. The two were joined into the Kingdom of Great Britain in 1707.

Except for a slow movement toward the toleration of minority opinion, there were few moral changes under William and Mary. Perhaps the most important fact for a history of moral standards and practices is the continued growth of the middle classes. The urban commercial and industrial interests developed steadily.

Moreover, the middle-class ideals of right and wrong remained different from those of the great landowning nobles and gentlemen. It was an aristocratic and feudal tradition, for instance, that questions of honor should be settled by the duel, even though, in strict law, one who killed another in the course of such a combat was a murderer. Many shopkeepers thought that a few duelists should be hanged and the practice of private justice with the sword entirely wiped out.

People of recognized position had in effect many privileges which were denied to their inferiors. Especially in the country the nobles, squires, and landowners in general had things pretty much their own way. Nobody thought of putting them in the stocks when they grew boisterous over their drink. It was seldom dangerous for a lordling to seduce a servant or a tenant's daughter.

Under James II Jamaica rum had become a fashionable drink. By way of tribute to William, or because of the growth of trade with the Netherlands, Hollands gin went into vogue, and it became thoroughly nationalized in England. William himself had the reputation of being a hard drinker, and the moral precisians found little encouragement in his way of life. At court, gambling was supposed to be proper only in the short period between Christmas and Epiphany, but it actually extended far beyond this fortnight. The lords and the common people of England continued to play cards and to bet on cockfights, as they had done in the reign of Charles II. The production of distilled liquors in England rose steadily, being in 1714 nearly four times as great as in 1684. At a reception given in honor of King William at Warwick Castle, we are told, nearly 120 gallons of punch were consumed in the process of wishing His Majesty good health. When a lord wished to celebrate an anniversary or great event in a lavish way, he usually let his servants as well as the members of his family have enough liquor to get them thoroughly drunk. While imported wines were expensive, homemade ale as well as the more potent distilled beverages were available to people of very moderate wealth.

Whatever William's private life might be, he encouraged the

London authorities in their efforts to discourage heavy drinking, swearing, and working or playing on Sunday. He told his bishops and the ministers of the Anglican Church to preach against these sins and against sexual irregularities. In 1692 the Society for the Reformation of Manners was formed by half a dozen moral gentlemen, with the encouragement of the Queen. The chief obstacle in the way of the development of this and similar organizations was the reluctance of Anglicans to work together with Dissenters, even for what they considered important causes. Yet the differences in moral outlook between the two parties were decreasing. The societies for the promotion of virtue accomplished little. In London an attempt was made to suppress Bartholomew Fair. This and other fairs brought together gamblers, jugglers, harlots, and others whose business it might be to add to the pleasure of the visitors but who certainly were interested in lightening their purses.

During the reign of William and Mary social manners were, in general, such as we should consider extremely gross. Spitting, for example, was free and generous, though the dandies kept little silver bowls in their pockets, which they took out at need and into which they spat ever so daintily. Forks had not yet completely won their way into general acceptance. Foreigners complained, too, that all the persons at a table rinsed their hands in the same basin of water after meals.

There were still moralizers who considered tea unworthy of a Christian family. Light beer was the usual beverage, even for children hardly out of their infancy. Water was still in disfavor as a beverage, and its use for cleansing purposes remained limited.

§ 5

What is known as the Restoration drama of England has not yet been considered here, because some of its most important phases arose after the time of Charles II and James II, and its history can best be examined as a whole. We have seen how the Puritans closed the theatres as diabolic haunts where sin was taught and apprentices were seduced from their labors. In the controversies and in the war between king and Parliament the actors were almost always found on the royal side. In the Commonwealth period various attempts were made to evade the laws that forbade stage plays: for instance, farces and drolls were produced under the pretense that they belonged in another category. D'Avenant was permitted to produce operas before the Restoration. After 1660 all forms of the drama were openly allowed, but there was no great revival of interest in the theatre under Charles II. For years the courtiers and those persons who aspired to be courtiers or who aped the manners of the palace made up the principal patrons of the stage. One or two theatres were enough for London in the years between 1660 and 1700, although the smaller population of James I's reign had supported as many as six.

Since the middle classes held themselves aloof, plays were written to suit the taste of aristocrats and dandies. The Restoration tragedy deals in a highflown way with chivalric aspirations, and the comedy has to do with real life in the fashionable world. It was a world in which *savoir vivre* was the prime consideration. Morality, especially Puritan morality, was either ignored or mocked at.

In 1661 Pepys expressed surprise at the production of Jonson's *Bartholomew Fair*. It then seemed an unusual piece of daring to revive this dramatic attack upon the Puritans. But the new playwrights were to go even further than the Elizabethans in heaping contempt upon the zealots and the things they most cherished.

And the appearance of women on the stage, which had been so objectionable a few decades before, became a commonplace matter. Charles II expressed the opinion that the morality of the drama would be much improved if all the lines assigned to female characters were actually spoken by women and girls. Possibly he had his tongue in his cheek when he said this. Anyway, few actresses of the time laid great stress upon chastity, in word or deed. A general knowledge of this fact added to the piquant naughtiness involved in going to the theatre. We read of clergymen taking off their canonicals to attend the play, and it seems that the more dignified members of the profession, even if they were not of the Puritan party, seldom or never went.

The plays which were popular in the years directly following the Restoration were revivals of the Elizabethan-Jacobean drama,

THE RESTORATION COMIC STAGE
From Francis Kirkman, *The Wits*, 1672.

adaptations chiefly from the French, and new works more or less modeled after these. Gentlemen of the court and professional writers both turned out comedies in which chastity and sobriety were laughed at.

It is not advisable to assemble here a collection of passages from the Restoration comedy illustrative of the tendency to flout Puritan standards of verbal propriety. Perhaps a few excerpts from critical-moral remarks about the English comedies that were produced in the five or six decades following 1660 will give some idea of their general tone. Professor Schelling, after speaking of Sedley and Etherege, says: "With examples such as these among writers who pretended to gentle manners and birth, and with Dryden descending to the dramatic stews, it is not surprising to find lesser writers and stage hacks throwing decency to the winds and substituting sheer scurrility for wit, and brutality for force of passion." Professor Allardyce Nicoll, another critic of our time, remarks: "There are, certainly, passages in the comedies of manners which overstep all bounds of decency and good taste, where the dramatists have gone beyond even the excesses of the society of their own time, and such passages can now be relished by none save a deliberate lover of pornographic literature." Nicoll adds that the "determined intellectualism" of some of the dramatists "takes away to a certain extent from the evil effects of particular scenes."

Macaulay, writing in what was probably the most prudish period of the Victorian age, says that there is nothing in the Restoration comedies quite so bad as some of the classical works which were still being read at the universities: "Plato has written things at which Sir George Etherege would have shuddered." Then he goes on to remark that the fault of the Restoration drama "is not a mere coarseness of expression." It is rather that immorality is glorified. Of the scene presented in comedy after 1660, he says: "Morality constantly enters into that world, a sound morality, and an unsound morality; the sound morality to be insulted, derided, associated with everything mean and hateful; the unsound morality to be set off to every advantage, and inculcated by all methods, direct and indirect." It is hardly necessary to say that Macaulay is here begging the question, assuming that the ethical code of the Cavaliers was unsound and that of the Puritans fundamentally sound, even though some of its implications might be highly ridiculous. Whether Macaulay was right or wrong in such an assumption it is no part of the present work to decide.

The Restoration comedy-writers almost all took it for granted that a handsome, witty London dandy was committing no serious sin when he added the art of seduction to his other accomplishments. As Macaulay truly says, "The hero intrigues just as he wears a wig; because, if he did not, he would be a queer fellow, a city prig, perhaps a Puritan." As for the Puritan characters, they are represented as having and seeking to fulfill carnal desires, too: only they are more hypocritical, and their intrigues are seldom successful.

Among the dramatists of Charles II's time there was a female adventuress named Aphra Behn. Some moral historians of literature, perhaps all the more indignant to find a woman in such company, call her the worst of the lot. But "Astræa," as Mrs. Behn was called, by no means conceived of her sex as being naturally chaste. In one of her tales, "The Fair Jilt," she presents an extreme Mrs. Potiphar type, and many of her female characters have strong sexual desires. "The stage how loosely does Astræa tread," wrote Pope a generation later. Yet Mrs. Behn often set out to teach moral lessons.

One of the first, and one of the most interesting, of the Restoration dramatists was William Wycherley. Evelyn said of him:

> As long as men are false and women vain,
> While gold continues to be virtue's bane,
> In pointed satire Wycherley shall reign.

Wycherley (who no longer reigns, perhaps because men are no longer false, and so on) learned how to compose comedies from Spanish as well as French writers. His plays deal chiefly with wenching and cuckolding. Wycherley is remarkable, though, for his implication that it would be easy enough to laugh at Cavaliers as well as Puritans. One of his characters says, "For your bigots in honor are just like those in religion; they fear the eye of the world more than the eye of heaven; and think there is no virtue, but railing at vice, and no sin, but giving scandal." Evidently "the honor of a gentleman" could, like "godliness" and "true Christianity," degenerate into a mere cant phrase.

Wycherley laughed at the new versions of the "Englishman Italianate," the people who returned home with the borrowed manners and fashions of France or of Spain. Mr. Horner is made to remark to a mixed company that he has just come from France, but "I have brought over not so much as a bawdy picture, no new postures, nor the second part of the *École des Femmes,* nor—" Wycherley's *The Plain Dealer* is ironically dedicated to Lady B——, that is, to Mother Bennett, a well-known procuress. Another of his plays is dedicated, without irony, to the Duchess of Cleveland, mistress to His Majesty and friend to promising young men.

Some of the greatest of the "Restoration" comedians flourished under Dutch William. Congreve is usually considered the most important dramatist of the whole period. The critics who use ethical balances tell us that Congreve is less gross than Wycherley but more immoral. In truth, the words and phrases which later generations have found objectionable reappear in Congreve, but his touch is usually lighter. "Ay, ay, in old days people married when they loved; but that fashion is changed, child," one of his characters explains to the girl whom he supposes to be innocent and whom he is trying to seduce. But the fashion was, in Congreve's time, swinging back. Respectability was coming into vogue again, and above the tumult of gallant conversation good Mrs. Grundy's voice could sometimes be heard.

To be sure, the moral standards of the Restoration comedy-writers had never gone entirely unchallenged. We find Dryden apologizing as early as 1671, in the preface to *An Evening's Love:* "It is charged upon me that I make debauched persons (such, as they say, my Astrologer and Gamester are) my protagonists, or the chief persons of the drama; and that I make them happy in the conclusion of my play: against the law of Comedy, which is to reward virtue, and punish vice. I answer, first, that I know no such law to have been constantly observed in comedy, either by ancient or modern poets." Dryden goes on to explain his unwillingness to be known as a glorifier of libertinism. He wanted to be considered virtuous; but he was also anxious to make money, and spicy comedies were then the wear.

In 1698 a nonjuring clergyman named Jeremy Collier issued *A Short View of the Immorality and Profaneness of the English Stage*. In politics Collier was diametrically opposed to the Puritans. The fact that he was not identified with extreme moral views no doubt caused his arguments to be heard more attentively. However, he repeats the same arguments that had been employed by the old Puritan enemies of the theatre.

Collier derived some of his ideas from Thomas Rhymer, a petty critic who considered Shakespeare unimportant. With this view, too, Collier agreed. Much of the *Short View* I think we need not hesitate to call entirely absurd. Its author objects when wicked people are represented on the stage as saying and doing wicked things. He does not think that even the villain of the piece should be permitted to ascend the stage and say that Sunday observance in England is too strict. He would not allow Christian ministers or even the priests of other religions to be brought into the theatre or light literature at all, whether presented in a favorable or in an unfavorable manner. He points out the sinfulness of introducing Biblical characters or of using on the stage a long list of words which he considers sacred. This list includes *martyr* and *inspire*, even when they are used to express secular ideas.

We are sometimes told that it was Collier's attack that overthrew the Restoration drama. It is true that King William was impressed by it, and it helped in bringing about his proclamation against debauchery. The Master of the Revels began to censor plays, but he was actuated by political rather than moral considerations. A great pamphleteering war arose, which called public attention to the standards of the London stage and perhaps hastened a change which had already begun.

Dryden, though rejecting some of Collier's arguments and conclusions, admitted that he had erred: "But I will no longer offend against good manners: I am sensible as I ought to be of the scandal I have given by my loose writings; and make what reparations I am able, by this public acknowledgment." This sentence is found in the preface to a collection of translations and adaptations of stories in verse by Homer, Ovid, Boccaccio, and Chaucer. Dryden asserted that he had chosen only such as conveyed an edifying moral.

The Restoration drama continued for some time after Collier's attack, with the production of old plays and of new ones in the same tradition. Farquhar, one of the last writers of the Restoration comedy, was capable of forgetting his own definition: "Comedy is no more at present than a well-framed tale handsomely told as an agreeable vehicle for counsel or reproof." In fact, he usually wrote without any moral purpose. The Restoration comedy really died when the sentimental comedy became popular. In 1703 Steele's *The Lying Lover* was generally disapproved as being too pious. But the Cavalier attitude in the theatre lost its dominating position during the eighteenth century. The stage began to cater to the middle classes.

Colley Cibber, who was born in 1671 and died in 1757, saw great changes take place in the public estimation of the theatre and its players. When he first became connected with theatrical management, all actresses were judged to be prostitutes because of their profession. Cibber says that they were actually not all promiscuous and some of them valued their chastity highly. But he tells about a titled lady whose family had cast her off because of her indiscretions. She asked to be accepted as an actress. The managers were then given to understand that they would make powerful enemies if they gave her employment. Her relatives felt that her appearance upon the stage would be a public advertisement of her frailty. Cibber in his youth wrote a number of plays more or less tolerant of looseness in sexual morality. Later he was more careful not to give any cause for offense.

Queen Anne was rather hostile to the stage, and she was not accustomed to attend the theatre. Yet she consented to see, within the royal palace, such a play as Dryden's *All for Love*. She several times issued proclamations against the presentation of irreligious or indecent matter on the stage. Just where she drew the line between decency and indecency, it is hard to tell. The Restoration cynical attitude still appeared in some of the new plays produced in her reign. Anne was anxious to reduce the connection which existed between the theatre and prostitution. She ordered the Master of Revels to see that no person of good quality went upon the stage or behind the scenes before or during the performances, that no masked women should be permitted to sit in the audience, and that no women should be admitted free of charge.

§ 6

The old English kissing customs, which had lost their respectability under the Puritan rule and come back with the Restoration, flourished in Queen Anne's day. There were, to be sure, some people who laughed at them or denounced them as iniquitous, but they went unheeded. In high social circles the gentleman who entered a room was supposed to kiss all the ladies he found there. Both unmarried and married men and women took part in games in which kisses were the forfeits. On St. Valentine's day, men and women were paired off, usually by lot; the man gave his valentine kisses and gifts, even though she might be married to someone else. He was permitted to call on her while she still lay in bed.

The formal levee, or bedroom reception, was introduced from France. Ladies received gentlemen while they lay or sat up in their beds, in their nightclothes or partially dressed. The custom was not scandalous, or at least it was not considered so in the circles where it prevailed, because it was the latest fashion. Moreover, the fine lady was chaperoned by a host of maids and hairdressers. Men and women did not need to be intimate with the hostess to receive invitations to a levee. Casual acquaintances swarmed about.

Weddings were occasions for much gaiety and rude jesting. It was part of the duty of the bridegroom's attendants to pull off the bride's garters. However, these were usually unfastened and slipped down in advance, the old custom being modified by a growing delicacy. A great deal of the ceremony of undressing the

THE LAUGHING AUDIENCE
An etching by William Hogarth, 1733.

couple still remained, perhaps as a relic of an older usage which required the marriage to be consummated before witnesses. The bridesmaids sometimes remained in the bridal chamber while the groom climbed into the bed where his bride already lay, and we are told that they were supposed to show a reluctance to leave even after the pair had drunk the traditional posset. Joking about what was to take place afterward was not frowned upon.

In the time of Charles II his mistresses and some of the other court ladies scandalized the people by wearing mannish riding habits. Under Queen Anne it became fashionable for women to wear bifurcate garments when they went riding. In general, the female sex had a great deal of freedom.

Society in the narrow sense, the *beau monde*, had a considerable development in Queen Anne's reign. Ladies and gentlemen became adept at the art of fashionable idling. They lay abed all morning (unless they went to visit their friends in their bedrooms) and spent half the night gossiping and playing cards.

Fashions for ladies changed so fast it was difficult to keep up with them. It took an expert to know, at a particular moment, whether hats were supposed to resemble mountains or pancakes, to be decorated with wagons or with rosebushes. Low bodices were the rule, but a tucker or modesty piece of lace partially covered the breasts. Toward the end of Anne's reign this garment grew smaller and went entirely out of fashion. Stern moralists complained that men were being too much tempted. Masks, which had been worn by fine ladies under Elizabeth and the Stuarts, now became the distinguishing marks of prostitutes.

Cosmetics were widely used, and many different varieties came upon the market. Together with perfumes they concealed to a certain extent the lack of bodily cleanliness which was then usual, even in the highest circles. In the lower ranks of society the same shirt might be worn for months, or until it fell apart. Among persons of social pretensions clean linen was more in demand. But bathing did not become common in England until the middle of Victoria's reign.

Queen Anne's reign was an age of hard drinking. The wealthy drank wine, the poor, beer and ale, in large quantities. Brandy and other distilled liquors were available in penny drams. In a letter to the lady whom he called Stella, Swift wrote about being with Harley, later Earl of Oxford, "and, among others, William Penn the Quaker: we sat two hours drinking as good wine as you do." The journal-letters to Stella are full of references to drinking bouts, mostly in the company of prominent statesmen and writers. Macaulay in his panegyric on Addison alludes to the fact that he sometimes got drunk, and adds: "The smallest speck is seen on a white ground. Of any other statesman or writer of Queen Anne's time, we should no more think of saying that he sometimes took too much wine, than that he wore a long wig and a sword." The weekly allowance of a seaman in the English Navy included seven gallons of beer, for part or all of which smaller quantities of wine or spirits might, under certain circumstances, be substituted.

Snuff-taking was general, on the part of women as well as of men. We hear, too, of women who smoked clay pipes. Even in schools a recess was sometimes called so that the children might smoke. It seems that tobacco was still believed to have important prophylactic qualities.

Playing for heavy stakes was characteristic of the upper social circles. A law was passed against excessive gambling, but the State itself held lotteries. Ashton tells of women who prostituted themselves to pay card debts. The Queen encouraged horse racing, and ran horses under her own name. She did this with the intention of improving the breed of English horses. The races, too, afforded opportunities for gambling. Another sport which had an important place in English life, before it was replaced by boxing, was fighting for prizes with sticks, daggers, swords, and other weapons.

Dueling seemed to be on the increase. A number of young bloods formed gangs for committing acts of mischief or worse. The most notorious of these were the Mohawks or Mohocks. They enjoyed Homeric jests, as for instance setting women on their heads or rolling them in barrels and carving up honest people with their swords.

This age had its moralists, too. Addison and Steele worked

together on the *Spectator,* a paper intended to combine pleasant reading with good advice. It was addressed to women at least as much as to men, and it was intended to teach both sexes that virtue was not necessarily priggish and Puritan. Usually the paper was concerned about the improvement of manners rather than with the more serious moral problems. But Mr. Spectator, we are told, visited Spring Garden, which was later to be known as Vauxhall, and he complained that he found more strumpets than nightingales there. Perhaps Steele's morals were themselves not above reproach: in addition to the drunkenness which was characteristic of the times, he had a constitutional inability to resist petticoats, and he is said sometimes to have been less than scrupulously honest and considerate of the rights of others. The moral standard of his writings was high, though.

In the days of Queen Anne the Dissenters were still, as a class, rather more scrupulous than members of the Church about Sunday observance and some other moral questions. But this difference was disappearing, especially because many of the Puritans had returned to the Establishment. And we have seen how it was a High Church and ultraconservative minister who delivered the most important attack upon the Restoration comedy. But Swift complained about having to walk in London on Sunday because neither boats nor hired coaches could be had.

The Dissenters of London were usually the leaders in clamoring for enforcement of the Sunday laws and for the suppression of the fairs. Mayfair was abolished in 1709, but there is no evidence that there were thenceforth fewer prostitutes in and around the city. Women who had been convicted of petty offenses were then often let off on condition that they should be attached to the Army as camp followers, and the soldiers themselves were, to a considerable extent, convicted criminals. The conditions of military life for privates were so disagreeable that ordinary methods of enlistment did not suffice. The state of the Church was not quite the same as that of the Army, but much laxity existed; and many of the ministers, especially private chaplains, were poorly paid and little respected. A few clergymen were influential behind the political scenes. Probably the Church of

SOUTHWARK FAIR

An engraving by William Hogarth, 1733.

England was both more popular and more pious that it was to become under George I.

The Dissenting bodies grew, and fear was expressed that they might swamp the State Church. Defoe, in *The Shortest Way with the Dissenters,* ironically proposed that all their preachers should be hanged and all their members exiled. When it was realized that Defoe's intention was to mock the High Churchmen, he was severely punished for seditious libel. But his Nonconformist sympathizers did their best to make his pillory a flower-garlanded place of honor. Just before Anne's death in 1714 an act was passed which forbade Dissenters to act as teachers, even to their own children. This was repealed in the next reign, when the Whigs, who were more sympathetic to the independent churches, came into power.

Among the Tory High Churchmen of Queen Anne's reign the one great literary genius was Jonathan Swift. Swift was a good deal of a skeptic, yet he considered religious toleration a nasty Dutch custom. Conformity seemed to him and to the Tories in general necessary if Church and State were to be maintained in their old perfection. Swift once remarked that religion may arise, like love, from the pretense of having it. That it arose within him in this way, to any considerable extent, is doubtful. His *Tale of a Tub,* which was perhaps intended to satirize religious hypocrisy and superstition, seemed to many of his contemporaries to be an attack upon all the branches of Christianity. Because this book offended the Queen, Swift never obtained the bishopric he so ardently desired.

Some of the passages in his personal life were, for a professional man of religion, not unexceptionable. *Gulliver's Travels* has now, by a freakish irony of fate, become a children's book, though with many deletions. Swift enjoyed dwelling upon the likenesses between human beings and the brutes, especially in the excretory functions. It does not appear that he thought much about the close connection which, as a minister, he might have found between men and the angels.

Swift tells something about the fashionable irreligion of his time in a letter to Stella: "I was early with the secretary to-day, but he was gone to his devotions, and to receive the sacrament; several rakes did the same; it was not for piety but employments; according to act of Parliament." Because these men cared nothing at all for religion, they were quite content to take the sacrament according to the Anglican usage to comply with the law. They confessed semipublicly their indifference to Christianity. However, they were loyal to the Church of England, in which some of them held office. Persons who sincerely objected to the rites of the Established Church, though they were earnest Christians and Protestants, were excluded from positions of trust in the government. They did not even enjoy the right of teaching their own children. It was no wonder that some moralists considered hypocrisy the great fault of the age.

CHAPTER VII

A NEW AND METHODICAL ST. JOHN

§ 1

ANNE STUART was succeeded on the English throne by her cousin, George of Hanover. The new King soon took advantage of his position to turn two German favorites into peeresses of England, under the titles of the Countess of Darlington and the Duchess of Kendal. George I had little interest in Great Britain except as a source of income for himself and his concubines.

As a German princeling he had neglected his wife for a number of rather ugly mistresses. Then it had been discovered that the Princess was having adulterous relations with a bold adventurer. Her lover had been assassinated, and she remained shut up in a castle for thirty-two years. Thus did the gander disapprove of the use of his sauce for the goose.

The aristocrats of England laughed at the King because he was a foreigner, knew practically no English and made no effort to improve himself in the language, and, worst of all, ignored the pretty girls of his kingdom in favor of unattractive German women. George saw no need of changing his old habits and casting off the mistresses to whom he was accustomed simply because he had become a king. Like many other petty princes of Germany, he had learned that the first duty of a monarch is to amuse himself; but he never acquired, or tried to acquire, the graceful and artistic hedonism characteristic of Versailles.

The first two Georges exerted little political influence in Great Britain. The principal man in affairs of state was a Whig, Sir Robert Walpole. Like his royal masters, though not quite to the same extent, Walpole was devoted to pleasure, and he resembled them also in that his manners were not particularly delicate. He talked noisily and with the utmost frankness about his affairs with women, and a large part of the time when he was not busy with politics was given up to such conversation. To be sure, he had to reserve part of his leisure for the consumption of wine, beer, and punch. And like a true English gentleman, he was fond of dogs and hunting. There were people in Walpole's own time who called him coarse, irreligious, and worldly, but they did not disturb him. He found boon companions in abundance, and his manner of life did not jeopardize his position as Prime Minister of Great Britain.

George I seldom tried to speak English at all, and his son had a pronounced German accent. Besides, neither of them was much interested in books or in ideas as such. Consequently, conversation ceased to be one of the arts encouraged in the palace. It was, to a considerable extent, replaced by card playing. Under the leadership of George II gambling for large stakes, which had become slightly less respectable in the time of Queen Anne, was restored to full favor in the upper social circles. Both of the first two Georges played in the palace, especially during the Christmas season. The office of Groom Porter, which involved the control of gaming within the royal buildings, lasted until 1772, when George III abolished it.

During the reigns of the Georges the authorities of London continued to look with disfavor upon games of chance. Many women peddlers used to carry dice with which they gambled, both with adults and children, usually for fruit and nuts. The Lord Mayor ordered, in 1716, that any who continued this practice should be arrested. Under the second George a number of laws against various forms of gambling were passed. In 1745 we find the Baroness of Mordington complaining that the police were going too far in interfering with her gambling house, since she enjoyed special privileges as a peeress of the realm. Her protests went unheeded. Many houses were raided, and a great deal of expensive apparatus was destroyed. Private lotteries were put under the ban of the law in 1721, but those of which the profits were used for public purposes continued to flourish. Despite the prohibitory laws, interest in gambling of all varieties rose among all classes during the first half of the eighteenth century. For this the attitude of the first Hanoverian kings was to some small extent responsible.

There were years under the first two Georges when all signs of the old Puritanism, in fact, of religious and moral zeal in general, seemed dead in England. The populace occasionally mobbed Dissenters, but not out of piety. Hardly anyone seemed to have any sincere interest in religion. Such was the impression which foreigners received, but perhaps it was not entirely accurate. For there were always zealots, in and out of the Church of England. And if the Nonconformists had not attached any importance to their own peculiar religious usages and dogmas, they might have avoided annoyance and worse than annoyance by leaving their conventicles and joining the Established Church.

A landmark in the history of rationalism was the repeal, in 1736, of the law making witchcraft a felony. However, some educated men still believed in the existence of diabolically possessed persons. The Church was weakened by the fact that bishoprics and other ecclesiastical dignities were occasionally sold at private auction. There remained, too, a political split. While the bishops were Whigs, supporters of the Hanoverian kings and Walpole's régime, most of the lower clergy were Tories, and some of them were working for the Stuart King over the water.

Private chaplains were still marrying servants or cast-off concubines, still leaving the table when sweets and wine were served. But they did not flee from the wine because of any scruples against the use of alcoholic beverages. "Be not righteous overmuch" was during most of the eighteenth century a favorite text with Anglican preachers. And most of the people, of all degrees, agreed that the injunction was a wise one.

George II had the advice of his wife Caroline in selecting his mistresses. Perhaps that is why they suited the public taste better than his father's imported concubines had. His Queen was a clever woman, and she had advanced ideas, at least about religion; but she did not venture to doubt that her husband might enjoy a moral freedom denied to her. As for George, he seemed to consider it a duty belonging to his position in life to maintain a seraglio. There is no doubt that he felt genuine sorrow as he stood by Caroline's bed and watched her slowly dying. She said she hoped he would remarry. *"Non, non, j'aurai des maîtresses,"* he sobbed—"No, no, I will have mistresses." Prince Frederick, who married the Princess of Saxe Gotha and who loved his wife just as his father had loved Caroline. also kept a number of concubines.

But the popular interest in the royal court and its affairs which had prevailed in the reigns of the Tudors and the Stuarts hardly existed under the Hanoverian Georges. The middle classes hurried into prominence. Manufacturing and commerce made many people rich. Colonial adventurers, planters, and officials came home loaded down with wealth and attracted public interest to easy ways of acquiring a fortune. In 1720 and 1721 there was a wild speculative orgy centering around the stock of the South Sea Company. Many public officials were involved in scandal when the bubble burst.

It was of great importance that the aristocrats of England became interested in securities and, even though thoughtlessly and superficially, showed general curiosity about commerce, invention, and industry. The distance between gentlemen of leisure and the middle-class traders and manufacturers grew appreciably less. This was not the result of the South Sea bubble alone. Rather, the speculative orgy was one of the symptoms of a great burst of expansion which improved the position of the middle classes.

The Commercial Revolution was largely responsible for the old Puritanism, the Industrial Revolution for the Evangelical awakening of the eighteenth century. John Kay's fly shuttle, James Hargreaves' spinning jenny, and James Watt's steam engine play a larger part in the history of morals in the English-speaking countries than all the sermons and tracts of the Puritans. They insured that the wealthy and influential men of England and North America should lay great stress upon the virtues of thrift, industry, and sobriety.

Yet the first great growth of factories seemed, indeed, to be contributing to the development of religious and moral indifference. The factory hands in new overgrown towns were allowed to grow up with little or no instruction in Christian dogma and ethics.

The Dissenters kept up some of their zeal. When, toward the end of Queen Anne's reign, all the hackney coaches of London were permitted to operate on Sunday, it was the Nonconformists who uttered a great cry of horror at such ungodliness. And they continued during the early Hanoverian period to work for Sunday observance despite the diminished interest of the Anglican ministers in such matters. They had the advantage that abstinence from Sunday work and play had already become habitual in England. And the Sunday laws were pretty strictly enforced. During the first half of the eighteenth century there was very little traveling on the first day of the week. Even highwaymen fell into the custom of taking their rest then. Presumably it was because they found it unprofitable to watch the roads when few people were to be found there, but some of them may have been pious folk who did not care to profane the day. So important a person as Chancellor Harcourt was stopped by a constable of Abingdon for trying to pass through the town while Sunday services were going on. In 1757, in the midst of a war and with an urgent need for soldiers existing, the Nonconformists raised an outcry because the militia was being drilled on Sunday, and they were influential enough to have the practice stopped.

The upper-class Anglicans, in general, cared little about Christian duties on any day of the week. They had no high standard of decorum when they went to church. If, as often happened, the preacher read an uninteresting sermon in a lifeless way, Lady This was likely enough to while away the time by whispering a naughty story to Lady That or, it might even be, to Lord Tother. The priests of the Anglican Church were too deeply conscious of their own inferiority to protest at inattention in church or misbehavior elsewhere on the part of persons who had benefices to give away or who were friendly with landowners possessing the avowdson, donation, presentation, and free disposition of various rectories or parsonages and the rights and appurtenances thereof. A few zealous clergymen ventured to rebuke their patrons for un-Christian behavior, but most of them were too indifferent or too anxious to assure food and lodging to their (often very large) families to protest in any case. And some could not, with any good grace, pretend to teach moral lessons at all.

Cabinet councils were held on Sunday while the four Georges reigned, since the political leaders had no great fear of defiling the day. The playing of cards and other quiet recreations went on as usual. But it was considered a daring innovation when a lady introduced Sunday concerts at her house in London. The virtuous mob might easily have been induced to break her windows. In the country, landowners had more freedom in such matters. It was usually the lord of the manor who determined how strict his tenants and dependents should be about Sunday observance and many other things which came into public notice.

The time of the first four Georges was one of deep drinking. The story goes that George III once remarked to a courtier, "They tell me, Sir John, that you love a glass of wine." "Those who have so informed Your Majesty have done me a great injustice," was the mock-indignant reply; "they should have said a bottle." And it was true that men seldom reckoned a day's drinking in glasses. We are told of two Englishmen who on an ordinary occasion consumed a gallon and a half of champagne and burgundy between them at a sitting.

Dr. Samuel Johnson, that great defender of Virtue, spoke with considerable contempt of claret, on the ground that "a man would be drowned by it before it made him drunk." He was persuaded to drink a glass so he might tell if his prejudice was a fair one. Then, as Boswell tells the story: "He shook his head, and said, 'Poor stuff! No, sir, claret is the liquor for boys; port for men; but he who aspires to be a hero (smiling), must drink brandy. In the first place, the flavor of brandy is most grateful to the palate; and then brandy will do soonest for a man what drinking *can* do for him.'"

Poor Bozzie reminded his hero how the two used to drink wine together when they were first acquainted, the Scotchman invariably having a headache after each night's session. Ap-

A MODERN MIDNIGHT CONVERSATION

An engraving by William Hogarth, 1733.

When Cromwell ... at something which bore a suspicious resemblance to theatrical performances in London, the soldiers ... the playhouse, stopped the shows, and broke up the ...

... of the new sort of ... period we know as Quakerism. The Quakers although they ... were Puritans differed from other ... in that they attached more importance to a inverted ... with God than to the verbal inspiration of the Bible ... its leader ... George Fox ... became dissatisfied with ... coldness of the orthodox Puritans because they regarded ...

... most of the Puritans were still accus ... Indeed, they professed that ...

... that the Quakers ... and Presbyterian Puritans had ...

... playing tricks on their stages, for they burdened the ...

... the Quakers were forced by ... short ...

parently Dr. Johnson was somewhat displeased to have the subject brought up, and he suggested that Boswell's headache came, not from the wine, but from the sense which he, Johnson, had put into it. "What, sir! will sense make the head ache?" "Yes, sir, when it is not used to it." Johnson expressed the opinion, in the 1770's, that drinking was on the decrease. "I remember," he said, "when all the decent people of Lichfield got drunk every night, and were not the worse thought of. Ale was cheap, so you pressed strongly." He thought that the growing popularity of wine, because of its greater expense, made for temperance.

Johnson, though he had no objection to the moderate use of intoxicants, spoke harshly of tobacco and was glad of what he considered its disappearance. "Smoking has gone out," he said. "To be sure, it is a shocking thing." The use of tobacco actually did lose much of its respectability toward the end of the eighteenth century, and it did not regain its place in English high society until the last decades of the nineteenth.

What wine was, in the days of the first three Georges, for those who could afford it, beer still remained for the laboring classes. Benjamin Franklin, when he was employed as a printer in London, had as his companion at the press a man who "drank every day a pint before breakfast, a pint at breakfast with his bread and cheese, a pint between breakfast and dinner, a pint at dinner, a pint in the afternoon about six o'clock, and another when he had done his day's work." Franklin objected especially to the cost of all this, which ran to four or five shillings weekly.

For those who were anxious to feel the effects of alcohol, there was a cheaper and much quicker method. The production of distilled liquors in England went up from two million gallons in 1714 to nearly five million in 1734. About halfway between these two years the use of geneva or gin, a potation distilled from grain and flavored with juniper berries, became almost epidemic among the lower classes of London. The total consumption of distilled spirits in England and Wales rose from thirteen and a half million gallons in 1734 to nineteen million gallons in 1742. Some taverns offered to give a man enough liquor to make him drunk for a penny, or dead drunk for twopence, and provided, without additional charge, enough straw for their patrons to lie down upon until they felt lively enough to spend another penny or two. Well might the sagacious Dr. Johnson remark, "Sir, there is nothing which has yet been contrived by man by which so much happiness is produced as by a good tavern."

TEA

"My wife had tea ready for him which it is well known he delighted to drink at all hours, particularly when sitting up late. He showed much complacency that the Mistress of the House was so attentive to his singular habit, and as no man could be more polite when he chose to be so, his address to her was most courteous and engaging, and his conversation soon charmed her into a forgetfulness of his external appearance." An etching by Thomas Rowlandson, accompanied by the above quotation from the *Journal of a Tour to the Hebrides*, for *The Picturesque Beauties of Boswell*, 1786.

Little objection was raised to wine-drinking on the part of the wealthy, but the spread of drunkenness among workingmen was felt by the authorities to constitute a menace to the prosperity and integrity of England. In 1736, therefore, a tax intended to be practically prohibitive was laid upon gin, rum, and brandy. The drinkers of gin were not, in any genuine sense, represented in Parliament. They could not threaten to elect members pledged to repeal the tax. But as true liberty-loving Englishmen they expressed their resentment by shouting, rioting, and violating the law. An important smuggling trade in geneva quickly grew up. In fact, the smuggling trade in general, and lawlessness in other directions as well, were stimulated by the high liquor tax. Artisans and apprentices did not consider it very wicked to avoid paying the excise rate; they could not afford to get drunk very often if they bought tax-paid liquors. Besides, they knew that the great were cheating the government still more effectually. In short, the law appeared to be an utter failure, and much milder restrictions were substituted for it. About the middle of the century the consumption of spirits fell off somewhat, and the moderate legislation was considered at least partially responsible for effecting this result. But perhaps the increased popularity of tea and coffee was the chief reason for the drop in the use of all forms of alcoholic beverages which appeared at this time.

The people who lived in England during the eighteenth century had many habits which would appear gross and disgusting to us now. Mud and filth were everywhere. The daily bath had not yet become the distinguishing mark of an Englishman. Table manners were crude. Aristocratic young ladies sometimes used language which would make a longshoreman of our degenerate days turn pink behind the ears. The name of the Deity, which the Puritans had reserved for the most sacred occasions, which the Quakers refused to utter in courts of law, was invoked on all occasions. The English soldiers in Flanders were regularly known as the "Goddams," and they were not far ahead of the civilian population in the ready flow of their profanity.

There were always moralists enough, and they found plenty to preach at. In 1739 we find a writer in *The Ladies' Library* complaining that women "are for throwing away the very fig-leaves; they have already uncovered their shoulders and breasts, and as they have gone so far in a few months, what may they not do in years?" Thackeray, accustomed to the many-layered feminine clothes of the Victorian age, says in a tone of surprise about the middle of the eighteenth century: "The girls used to run races clad in very light attire; and the kind gentry and good parsons thought no shame in looking on." At this time it was considered effeminate for a man to carry an umbrella in the streets of London, but the beaux were vying with the belles in the use of rouge and other cosmetics.

England was merry, and thought little of Heaven and Hell. Extreme piety was unfashionable. Public expressions of agnosticism were not common, but some of the staunchest supporters of the Church of England were known, at least to their friends, to be deists or atheists. It was an age of reason, and rationalism was the keynote to the thought which was then dominant, even in theological writings. (I do not mean, of course, to imply that superstition was dead or that accurate thinking was widespread.) According to general opinion, the greatest offense against religious propriety was "enthusiasm," or emotionalism, including mystical ecstasy. The ministers of the Church of England were, for the most part, anxious above all not to be too different from the laity. When we find the contemporary biographer of Isaac Watts praising him because his sermons contained not a single expression "that could raise the faintest blush upon the cheeks of modesty," we learn something about the ordinary preaching of the time.

There were, indeed, some Anglican clergymen who did not share the worldliness and rationalism of the time. William Law's works are still read by persons who are interested in mysticism. But few Englishmen of the eighteenth century agreed with Law that "our bodies and all bodily pleasures are at one dash struck out of the account of happiness" by the Scriptures. In *A Serious Call to a Devout and Holy Life,* a book perhaps most important because of the influence it exerted upon John Wesley, there is a sentence which sums up Law's teaching: "Whether a man die before he has writ poems, compiled histories, or raised an estate, signifies no more than whether he died an hundred or a thousand years ago."

In 1726 Law published *The Absolute Unlawfulness of Stage-Entertainment Fully Demonstrated.* Thus was continued, still on the High Church side, Collier's attack on the theatre. Perhaps there was then less reason for a moral onslaught on the theatre than there had been in William III's reign. The last important "Restoration" comedy, Farquhar's *The Beau's Stratagem*, had been produced in 1707; and since then virtue had become fashionable upon the stage. There were some exceptions, as John Gay's *The Beggar's Opera*, which made out the life of doxies and highwaymen to be quite attractive if somewhat dangerous. But, in general, the drama had become very, very moral by the time that Law wrote against it. Some of the words which were used may now appear indelicate, for fashions in verbal taboo shift about as much as those in clothing, and about as inexplicably. Still, it is clear that the actors were no longer catering to the sophisticated aristocracy alone, but were trying to please the urban middle classes by showing virtue triumphant.

Colley Cibber tells us how matters had changed: "In 1725, we were called upon, in a manner that could not be resisted, to revive *The Provoked Wife*, a comedy, which, while we found our account, in keeping the stage clear of those loose liberties it had formerly too justly been charged with, we laid aside for some years. The author, Sir John Vanbrugh, who was conscious of what it had too much of, was prevailed upon to substitute a new-written scene in the place of one, in the fourth act, where the wantonness of his wit and humor had (originally) made a rake talk like a rake, in the borrowed habit of a clergyman; to avoid which offense, he clapt the same debauchee into the undress of a woman of quality. Now the character and profession of a fine lady, not being so indelibly sacred as that of a churchman; whatever follies he exposed, in the petticoat, kept him, at least, clear of his former profaneness, and were now innocently ridiculous to the spectator."

To Mrs. Grundy in her present incarnation it may represent little or no advance that the rake talks like a rake in a fine lady's petticoat rather than in the gown of an Anglican minister. But the audience was satisfied, we are told, and that was what Colley Cibber cared most about. That there were at the time many rakes who talked like rakes and who habitually wore the clerical garb was, of course, beside the point. A lady of quality's petticoat covered a multitude of sins, we are led to infer. And the "play being thus refitted for the stage, was," as honest Cibber tells us, "called for, from court and by many of the nobility."

William Law's moral ideas did not coincide with those of the noble and royal persons who went to the theatre. "The playhouse is as certainly the house of the Devil," Law thought, "as the church is the house of God." He considered all actresses harlots and all theatres the reception rooms of brothels. Yet Cibber and his colleagues were at this time anxious to be considered quite as decent as the members of other professions, and they were doing all they could to acquire respectability. The stage was held almost exclusively by moralizing plays, farces, and comedies in which even the most modest of maiden aunts could find nothing to blush at.

In 1737 Walpole's act for the licensing and censoring of plays was passed. It seems to have been intended rather to keep the theatre from being used for attacks upon the government than to insure its moral purity. The strictures of Law and others — for example, Arthur Bedford, who discovered blasphemy in Addison's *Cato,* and who believed that pagans ought to talk like pious Christians when they appeared upon the stage—had little influence upon public opinion. To be sure, there were people who considered it wicked to attend the playhouse. Such feeling had never died out since it first became prominent in Queen Elizabeth's day.

The masquerade ball became important in the social life of the English aristocracy during the early Hanoverian period. In 1749 George II attended such an affair, which was signalized by the appearance of a maid of honor, Miss Chudleigh, representing Iphigenia and very scantily garbed. Some of those who attended were scandalized, though they were accustomed to see women in the slums who were forced by poverty to wear equally revealing clothes.

The lower orders often showed their staunch support of virtue by rioting or by flinging stones and overripe fruit at offenders.

THE RAKE'S REVELS

After a painting by William Hogarth for "The Rake's Progress," 1735.

to have lost £1,000 one evening at play and to have won £5,000 on another occasion.

Some of the courtly pleasures of the age were indulged against certain nobles and gentlemen even as though the common people had no rights at all which they needed to respect. For example, it was pretty reliably asserted that the Duke of Buckingham frequently arranged to duck, to probe, and even to confess he helped to murder, fellow men who had not done the attack in any way. He was boy who was the real culprit who became a constant guest at Whitehall until his death was reported to be one-fifth as well as the king that James had dallied with more than one lady and was, frequently, somewhat familiar with the young ladies other attendants. He was generally popular with the ladies ... it was believed that Charles and another blamed the other ... after Monmouth and their legitimate son and the so on.

The king ... was ... minister as being his favourite ... about two times and became a matter of importance ... either ... was ... King, as well as a king to the most ... the ... it was officially acknowledged ... until ... his ... and when it was too, heart double ... when it was ever ...

There follows in general the next successor ...

The Grub Street Journal for May 6, 1731, tells how a notorious bawd fared: "Yesterday the noted Mother.Needham stood in the pillory in Park Place near St. James's-Street and was severely handled by the populace. She was so very ill that she lay along the pillory, notwithstanding which she was severely pelted, and it is thought that she will die in a day or two."

We find the heroine of Hogarth's "A Harlot's Progress" beating hemp at Bridewell while an overseer threatens her with his rattan. However, repressive measures did not check the growth of prostitution. The fear of the pillory and the lash did not keep procurers and procuresses from pursuing their search for fresh country girls with whom to please jaded appetites.

A marriage act which became effective in 1754 was intended to prevent young men and women from marrying in undue haste. It provided, among other things, that no persons under the age of twenty-one might be married without the consent of parents or guardians. This law applied to England alone. Gretna Green in Scotland was to become the mecca of English elopers.

Much moral indignation was manifested about the middle of the century over the increasing number of divorces. Yet it was infinitesimally small by comparison with the numbers to which we are now accustomed. Every divorce required a special act of Parliament, and the cost put it beyond the reach of all except the wealthiest. That the good middle-class Christians were horrified was probably due in no small degree to the fact that the luxury was beyond their reach.

If we could see eighteenth-century England in all its details, we should, no doubt, be impressed most of all by the prevalent callousness to suffering, in part rather to be characterized as a positive pleasure in others' pain. But many humanitarians appeared before 1800, and they initiated movements which were to become powerful in the age of Victoria. Some of the reformers were influenced by the religious revival with which we shall presently deal, and their humanitarian zeal often went hand in hand with pietism.

When the jails of England were reformed, the improvements which were introduced included the separation of the sexes, the exclusion of the prostitutes who had formerly been permitted to visit the male inmates, and the abolition of the little gin shops within the walls. In the good old days a condemned man who had a little money might enjoy the pleasure of drunkenness during the last days of his life and attain partial oblivion before he was made to dance on air. Then the preachers began to insist that the condemned men should be kept sober during their last days on earth. They should be tortured with visions of Hell, for the greater good of their souls.

Bernard de Mandeville, in *The Causes of the Frequent Executions at Tyburn,* describes an early eighteenth-century crowd out to see a hanging: "No modern rabble can long subsist without their darling cordial, the great preservative of sloth, geneva, that infallible antidote against care and frugal reflection; which, being repeated, removes all pain of sober thought, and in a little while cures the most tormenting sense of the most pressing necessities. The traders who send it among the mob are commonly the worst of both sexes, but most of them weather-beaten fellows that have misspent their youth. . . . The intelligible sounds that are heard among them are oaths and vile expressions, with wishes of damnation at every word, pronounced promiscuously against themselves, or those they speak to, without change in meaning."

Mandeville had a good word to say for Vice at a time when all the world was praising the great god Virtue. His book called *The Fable of the Bees; or Private Vices–Public Benefits* aroused considerable scandal and even occasioned a public prosecution. Mandeville thought that "fraud, luxury, and pride" contribute to the good of the State if they are "by justice lopped and bound." His paradox was resented. People did not object so much to fraudulent and proud and sensual actions as to the suggestion that there was no clear line between vice and virtue.

§ 2

When George III ascended the throne, in 1760, a strong stimulus was given to the practice of the middle-class moral excellences in England. Yet the third of the Georges seems not to have been entirely different from his great-grandfather, his grandfather, and his father. To be sure, he did not make a flaunting display of concubines. But John Hoppner the painter (who was born 1759 in a royal palace, where his mother was a sort of upper servant) claimed to be the King's son. It is known that George paid for his instruction in art, though he did not often go out of his way to encourage budding genius.

It is not important, for our present purpose, to pry into the details of George III's domestic behavior. What does matter is the fact that his reputation was different from that of the other of the first four Georges. He is supposed to have been greatly impressed by the death of his uncle, the Duke of Cumberland, at the age of forty-four. This was attributed to Cumberland's grossly intemperate habits of eating and drinking. George laid down for himself certain rigid rules of conduct, intended to check all leanings toward excess. He never permitted himself to be complimented on his abstinence, probably fearing to be considered a prig. " 'Tis no virtue," he was accustomed to say. "I only prefer eating plain and little to growing sickly and infirm."

Whatever his motives were, and we have no good reason to consider them "higher" or different from those he assigned, the fact remains that George III lived more like the middle-class Londoners than like the great nobles. He even possessed a certain amount of pietism with a Nonconformist tinge. The attitude of the aristocracy of his time is fairly well represented in Lord Chesterfield's letters to his son, which show strongly the influence of contemporary French thought.

When Voltaire visited England, in 1766, he declared he could discover practically no evidence of the existence of religious feeling. This might well be the case, since most of his contacts were with men of letters, scientists and scholars, and with the leading statesmen and high nobles. These people were nominally Christians, Protestants, and Anglicans, but they privately expressed skeptical views. The Puritan tradition, already much distorted, remained with the mercers and brewers of London.

Though the King's personal influence was exerted to make some moral standards more rigid, though his example helped to form an unfavorable public attitude toward drunkenness, gluttony, swearing, and perhaps lechery, he did nothing to reduce political corruption. To be sure, bribery and the sale of public offices for money or promises of support existed in England long before the Hanoverian kings sat upon the throne. Walpole, however, made corruption into an elaborate system for maintaining himself in office. Monarchy was definitely replaced, except in form, by the rule of the skilled politician, and the skill of chief importance was that of using the control of the treasury and other branches of the State to perpetuate the politician's power.

George III, finding the danger from the Stuart legitimists practically over, revived the old formula of the divine right of kings. However, he was not too stupid to see that his birth and his coronation had given him only a limited amount of authority. He proceeded to become a politician and to use the system of trickery and chicanery devised by Walpole and continued by his successors. Being the king, and finding it possible to gain back a small part of the royal prerogative which his great-grandfather and his grandfather had given up, he thought he could manage matters to suit himself. He had the right to appoint public officers, and he selected those who were willing to work for his favorite schemes. Having much money at his own disposal, he laid out large sums in buying the votes of members of Parliament. Since he possessed the right to create peers, he filled the House of Lords with "the King's friends." The frank purchase of votes and offices disgusted the rising middle classes, most members of which found that they could exert no political power. If the King had been able to increase the glory of Great Britain, much might have been forgiven him; but his royal ambitions were generally disastrous, most conspicuously so in the case of the thirteen American colonies which won their independence and became the United States.

The third George did not, then, purify politics, and he was

TEMPERANCE ENJOYING A FRUGAL MEAL
A caricature of the parsimonious George III by James Gillray, 1792.

not very successful in preserving the morals of his own relatives. The Duke of Cumberland, his brother, was made, in 1770, to pay damages amounting to £10,000 to the husband of a woman of whom he was found to have had carnal knowledge. Cumberland was later known to be keeping up illicit relationships with more than one married woman. George III's sister, the Queen of Denmark, was disgraced and for a time imprisoned for adultery. Her paramour, too, was punished, and there was a great scandal with unpleasant echoes in England.

King George himself was in many ways a good Puritan. He objected to the painting of St. Paul's Cathedral, on the ground that it would be popish to use anything but whitewash in a house of worship. He discontinued the Sunday receptions in the palace and forbade the courtiers to gamble.

King or no king, games of hazard remained popular with the mass of the people. Betting on horse races became firmly established. The boxing ring developed into a great center of interest for betters and others, gradually driving out the old method of prize fighting with swords and canes as well as the baiting of animals.

George had no objection to the theatre, and he was a fairly frequent visitor, but he could not abide anything serious. He liked bluff English humor of the most primitive and obvious sort. In fact, he laughed with almost dangerous heartiness when he watched a clown struggling with a string of sausages or clumsily falling over after he had been kicked in exactly the right spot.

King George liked dancing, too; he sometimes whirled about to a single tune for three hours. But no matter how late he stayed up to indulge himself and his party of perhaps a dozen couples in this amusement, he never had supper served. The court people grumbled at the lack of refreshments, you may be sure. One can get pretty thirsty dancing so long to the same tune. Yet George remained anxious not to die in gouty middle age, even though it was necessary for him to preserve his health at the expense of his appetite.

Under the four Georges, though agnosticism was prevalent in

high society and among the learned, Virtue was generally worshiped. This does not mean that moral practice was unusually severe, for it certainly was not, but simply that ethical didacticism had a prominent place. For instance, we find it elaborately explained in Hogarth's engravings that honesty is the best policy. The same thing is true of a large part of the poetry and fiction of the period.

Both Fielding and Richardson were devoted to Virtue, though they differed widely about the nature of moral excellence. Fielding's most famous hero, Tom Jones, permits his wealthy mistress to help him with money and does many other things which Richardson's Sir Charles Grandison would consider abominable. Richardson's advocacy of masculine chastity seemed laughable cant to Fielding. And Grandisons were certainly rare in high society, though Mr. Richardson the printer might have met one or two among his middle-class friends. Even in the novels of the time we can see clearly that two ethical streams existed and that the methodical John Wesley was not a Moses who drew one of them out of solid rock.

The manner which Richardson employed to glorify chastity has seemed to some critics, of his own and later times, essentially immoral in effect. It was not merely that he dwelt upon the details of seduction in a way to suggest our modern confession magazines. In *Pamela* he seemed to be emphasizing unduly the commercial value of chastity. In his other novels his Puritan whining cant— or what such a man as Fielding considered to be the cant of a London tradesman—while it did not keep most ladies of his own time from enjoying themselves with sentimental tears, has operated to destroy Richardson's popularity with later generations. The lesson which is conveyed in *Clarissa* we find expressed in a short poem by Goldsmith, contained in *The Vicar of Wakefield:*

> When lovely Woman stoops to folly,
>   And finds too late that men betray,
> What charm can soothe her melancholy,
>   What art can wash her guilt away?

> The only art her guilt to cover,
> To hide her shame from every eye,
> To give repentance to her lover,
> And wring his bosom, is—to die.

A writer of our own time might rather show the betrayed woman suing her lover for breach of promise. One modern author has parodied Goldsmith's poem by making the lovely Woman express the emotion of her betrayal in smoothing her hair with automatic hand and putting a record on the gramophone.

Clarissa dies of grief, though she can only be reproached with indiscretion, not with deliberate wickedness. Lovelace, though a very villainous villain, is redeemed to some extent by his fear of Hell. A deist, or a Christian who denied the doctrine of future rewards and punishments, would have been too depraved a person for Richardson to make into a major character.

Smollett, whose works now appear unduly frank, was also criticized for the same reason in his own time. But he, too, loved Virtue, as he was careful to explain: "That the delicate reader may not be offended at the unmeaning oaths which proceed from the mouths of some persons in these memoirs, I beg leave to premise, that I imagined nothing could more effectually expose the absurdity of such expletives, than a natural and verbal representation of the discourse in which they occur."

He also insisted that he was depicting libertinism only in order that it might be subjected to indignation. There seems to be little doubt that, at least in theory, Smollett disapproved of French moral standards and considered the English nation the best behaved in the world. Despite the fact that his language is gross and unseemly, judged by the usual criteria of our age (which is not quite so prudish as it might conceivably be), Smollett was anxious to be considered a moralist. We must remember that the verbal taboos of his time were less rigid than our own and that some of his phrases which seldom appear in print now were then respectable. Of course, his novels are not now read for moral edification.

Smollett was a Tory, and as such a defender of the ancient rights of the Church of England. We find, in a private letter of his, that he favored the Church "not as a religious but as a political institution." He was anxious to dispel the suspicion that he had "imbibed priestly notions."

The most important work of genuine pornography that has been published in English appeared in 1750. This was John Cleland's *Fanny Hill, or the Memoirs of a Woman of Pleasure.* It had an enormous sale and made the publisher wealthy, though the author only received twenty guineas for it. Cleland was summoned before the Privy Council to answer for the licentiousness of his book, but his plea that he had been driven by poverty to write it was accepted. No action was taken against the publisher. A bookseller accused of inserting passages more objectionable than those the author had written into some copies was convicted in 1757 and had to stand in the pillory.

The comedies of Richard Brinsley Sheridan are sometimes credited with putting an end to the "Restoration" comedy and to the glorification of gallantry and seduction on the stage. As a matter of fact, Virtue had gained control of the theatre some decades before his works were first presented. However, Sheridan's plays do help us to understand the moral tone of England in the 1770's.

Lydia Languish, who is somewhat akin to the flapper of our own day, is shown in *The Rivals* to be reading novels quite as daring as any which now appear. When Lydia hears Mrs. Malaprop coming up the stairs, she cries to her maid: "Here, my dear Lucy, hide these books. Quick, quick!—Fling *Peregrine Pickle* under the toilet—throw *Roderick Random* into the closet—put *The Innocent Adultery* into *The Whole Duty of Man*—thrust *Lord Aimworth* under the sofa—cram *Ovid* behind the bolster—there—put *The Man of Feeling* into your pocket—so, so—now lay *Mrs. Chapone* in sight, and leave *Fordyce's Sermons* open on the table."

Mrs. Malaprop insists that "thought does not become a young woman." Of course, this was the exaggeration of a comic character, but many people held opinions which were not very different. During the eighteenth century we often find the view expressed that a girl should not have any preferences among her suitors but should accept the man of whom her parents approve. Love was almost universally considered rather vulgar. In Richardson's novel, Clarissa is rebuked by her mother for considering "the person" of handsome Lovelace and preferring him to repulsive Soames. Still, elopements were pretty frequent in real life, and comedy plots were often built around them. Old-fashioned people insisted on the duty of obedience to parents and considered that young men and young women who insisted on choosing their own mates were very wicked. Great respect and formality were expected of children in their relations with their parents.

Although Sheridan's plays are definitely not of the Restoration class, they are not such as might have satisfied the Reverend Jeremy Collier. The farce called *St. Patrick's Day* contains an honest "damn" spoken by a husband to his wife and various other pieces of rough language. Lieutenant O'Connor tells us something about the fashions of the time when he complains: "The London ladies were always too handsome for me; then they are defended, such a circumvallation of hoop, with a breastwork of whale-bone." The beaux wore padded stockings to show a handsome leg. Wigs were, at the moment, out of fashion.

A Trip to Scarborough shows us Sheridan as a moralist. He argues here in favor of a single strict standard of sexual morals and presents the dangers of flirtation. *The School for Scandal,* that wittiest of comedies, is in many ways suggestive of the plays of Congreve and Wycherley, but differs from them in that Virtue emerges triumphant.

Fitzpatrick's prologue to *The Critic* contrasts

> those gay days of wickedness and wit
> When Villiers criticized what Dryden writ

with "our more pious, and far chaster days." Within the play we have an explanation of literary puffing, in which one of the forms, of an indirect nature, is said to be the denunciation of the

THE COCKPIT

An engraving by William Hogarth, 1759.

work in question by friends or paid agents. Thus, it is said of a new book, in order to stimulate the sale: "The severity with which certain characters are handled is quite shocking: and as there are many descriptions in it too warmly colored for female delicacy, the shameful avidity with which this piece is bought by all people of fashion is a reproach on the taste of the times, and a disgrace to the delicacy of the age." Modern advertising methods are, it seems, not all new.

Such puffing might appropriately be applied to some of the eighteenth-century books written by men in holy orders. Swift, whose most important works were published in the reign of George I, has already been mentioned. The Reverend Laurence Sterne's writings lean even closer to the pornographic. The adjective "Rabelaisian" is sometimes applied to them, recalling the fact that Rabelais, too, was a clergyman. Both Swift and Sterne, while they held offices in the Church, published books which we can easily imagine as causing criminal prosecutions if they were published for the first time to-day. Sterne's *Tristram Shandy* came out volume by volume in the years between 1760 and 1767, while an eager public waited for the succeeding parts. To be sure, a certain amount of moral indignation about the book was manifested, but not enough to matter. Sterne became a social lion, and—this tells us something of the age in which he lived—he used his fame to dispose profitably of a volume of sermons.

I do not, of course, mean to imply that all Church of England ministers were equally lax in expression, though it is certain that a great many, of lesser fame, were. Clergymen could not safely say and do all the things that others might. Sterne himself complained that his black cassock deprived him of many pleasures.

Dr. Johnson, who was fairly representative of the pious High Church Englishmen of the eighteenth century, had rather high notions of clerical propriety. Once, talking of a dignified and respected man, he said, "I should as soon think of contradicting a bishop." His respect for the clergy was, to a considerable extent, a reflection of his Toryism. Like most other Tories of his day, he had ceased to look toward the banished Stuarts and was loyal to George III. His allegiance to the King extended also to the Established Church, and he believed that the State ought to impose uniformity of worship upon all its members.

Johnson considered it "mighty foolish" of the government not to repress infidel writings. He expressed the opinion that the skeptics were immune from prosecution because they were all Whigs, adherents of the party just then in power. The struggle for liberty of expression had by no means been won. To name merely one instance out of many, after the American colonies had won their independence, it was impossible to publish in Great Britain any history which was considered to give an account of the Revolution unduly favorable to the successful rebels.

It was the age of fox-hunting, wine-bibbing ministers. Samuel Johnson did not approve of them. He once said: "Sir, the life of a parson, of a conscientious clergyman, is not easy. I have always considered the clergyman as the father of a larger family than he is able to maintain. I would rather have Chancery suits upon my hands than the cure of souls. No, sir, I do not envy the clergyman's life as an easy life, nor do I envy the clergyman who makes it an easy life."

Boswell tells us that "Johnson's profound reverence for the hierarchy made him expect from bishops the highest degree of decorum; he was offended even at their going to taverns; 'A bishop (said he) has nothing to do at a tippling-house. It is not indeed immoral in him to go to a tavern; neither would it be immoral in him to whip a top in Grosvenor Square. But, if he did, I hope the boys would fall upon him, and apply the whip to *him*. There are gradations in conduct; there is morality— decency—propriety. None of these should be violated by a bishop. A bishop should not go to a house where he may meet a young fellow leading out a wench."

Dr. Johnson and a friend were once in the company of "several clergymen, who thought that they should appear to advantage, by assuming the lax jollity of *men of the world* . . . Johnson, who they expected would be *entertained*, sat grave and silent for some time; at last, turning to Beauclerk, he said, by no means in a whisper, 'This merriment of parsons is mighty offensive.'"

Boswell asked for Johnson's opinion on the propriety of his consulting with another lawyer on Sunday. "It is not criminal," the great man thought, "though it is not what one should do, who is anxious for the preservation and increase of piety, to which a peculiar observance of Sunday is a great help. The distinction is clear between what is of moral and what is of ritual obligation." Johnson himself took Sunday seriously, considering it necessary to rise at an especially early hour, to attend church twice, to read the Bible and other Christian books of religion, as well as "to wear off by meditation any worldly soil contracted in the week."

It made the old moralist furious to hear one who "swore and talked bawdy." He showed his objection to the phrase "damned fool" by repeating it with emphasis several times. As to Johnson's prudery or lack of it, it may be defined by saying that he had the poems of Rochester castrated for his edition, but not those of Prior. In other words, he put limitations on verbal freedom, but he was not extremely strict.

Johnson sometimes spoke slightingly about the intellectual capacity of women. Nevertheless, he often extended his hospitality and his encouragement to a number of the "bluestockings" who flourished in his time. Burke said to Fanny Burney in 1782, "This is the age for women." He was referring to the great changes which had taken place in their position during his own lifetime. Miss Burney's novels were to some extent responsible for this. She had written and published them by stealth, ever fearful of violating the proprieties by asserting herself unduly. By 1800 it was much easier for women to receive recognition for their work in literature and the arts than it had been in 1750. In addition to Fanny Burney, such women as Elizabeth Carter, Mrs. Montague, and Hannah More accustomed the public to the idea that the female sex was capable of independent thought and self-expression.

Women occupied a prominent place on the stage in the second half of the eighteenth century. Actresses of the highest type were no longer regarded as simply expensive and fashionable courtesans. There were women engaged in various light forms of entertainment as well. Pictures of the time show the female wire dancers at Sadler's Wells, wearing garments which resemble the tights of to-day, but apparently somewhat padded about the hips.

Women worked hard in their homes, also in the fields, at domestic industries, and in the new factories. They were, in general, considered constitutionally inferior to men, and they seldom were allowed to fill responsible positions. Sometimes a widow managed the business which her husband had left, but more often she relinquished the management to a new husband or some other man. Few women came, by respectable and decent means, into public notice.

The chief ambitions of the female sex were matrimonial. And now it was the women far more than the men, although by no means exclusively, who developed the art of beautification. In 1770 there was actually introduced into Parliament a bill intended to prohibit all women, whether maids, wives, or widows and of no matter what rank or condition, from trying to entrap any of His Majesty's masculine subjects by using perfumes, false hair, or rouge. It provided also that offenders should be dealt with as witches, and that all marriages brought about through the use of cosmetics should be considered void. The bill was not passed; maids, wives, and widows continued to embellish themselves with paints and pomades; and bridegrooms remained as before powerless to annul their marriage when they found their brides taking off the best part of their hair before going to bed.

However, the men had the benefit of advantages accorded by law and public opinion in their relations with their wives. The principle that women were bound to obey their husbands, just as children were subject to the will of their parents, was accepted with virtual unanimity. Yet it is true that among the upper classes and to a large extent among the middle classes as well, the ancient privilege of beating one's wife was being lost, though the law on the subject remained practically unchanged. Public opinion with regard to the brutal treatment of children and

A FEMALE WIRE DANCER AT SADLER'S WELLS

After a contemporary print.

apprentices was slowly changing, but cases of gross cruelty were still very common.

Manners during this period were such as we should consider extremely rude. Some of the practical jokes we find recorded in Fanny Burney's novels, Goldsmith's plays, and other dramatic and fictional works of the time now appear disgusting rather than funny.

In 1781 a quack who called himself Dr. Graham took a suite of rooms in Schomberg House, London. He persuaded a large part of London high society to use his mud baths for the sake of improving their beauty. Dr. Graham made use of a model named Emma Lyon. Casual visitors could see Emma up to her neck in the wonder-working mud. Those of them who paid for the privilege were allowed to look at her after she emerged, clothed in her beauty, a brilliant example of the advantages of using Dr. Graham's mud. Emma was to have a most interesting career. Among other things, she became the one great inspiration of the painter Romney, the wife of a noble English diplomatist, and, as Lady Hamilton, the paramour of Lord Nelson.

§ 3

For the second time after the spread of Christianity through Europe, there was in the eighteenth century a great wave of religious skepticism. This was more extensive and more important than the irreligion associated with the Renaissance. There had been scientific progress of considerable consequence in between, some of the discoveries attacking what were considered to be fundamentals of Christian belief. But Charles Darwin had not yet appeared, the uniformitarian geology had not been firmly established, and astronomy remained somewhat inexact and unreliable. Comparative religion was in its infancy. For most European scholars it was useful simply to show how much better Christianity was than any other religion. The masses in all the European countries accepted everything in the Bible literally, except where they were taught by their clergy to read allegorical meanings accepted by the Church into some passages.

(Familiarity with the Scriptures, however, was by no means universal, even in England.) The higher criticism was little developed and not familiar even to all theologians.

The belief in witchcraft had declined and was still declining, and many people denied the existence of miracles in modern times. Yet histories of remarkable providences were widely circulated. Ordinary people were still willing to believe that if a stroke of lightning killed a sinner but left the virtuous people at his side unhurt, it was carrying out the revenge of God.

John Wesley was, above all, a man of his century. He was born in its first decade (1703) and died in its last (1791). The pietistic movement with which we associate his name represents, to be sure, a reaction from the philosophies of some of the other leading men of the eighteenth century. From one point of view, it is possible to define Wesley, in Chestertonian fashion, as the opposite of Voltaire. He appears to have little in common with such an Englishman of his time as Gibbon. Yet we find John Wesley continually insisting upon the importance of reason. There was a time when he was greatly influenced by Boehmen, Law, and other mystics, but he turned against them and denounced "enthusiasm."

While he was a very little boy, Jackie Wesley decided that it was best to assure himself of a comfortable seat near the heavenly Throne. God took special care of him, giving him a pious minister for a father and an equally religious mother. Some of the sinners whom the Reverend Samuel Wesley denounced took revenge by burning down his parsonage. Jackie had a narrow escape, which he considered the result of a special mercy of God; and he considered himself thereafter, in more than one sense, "a brand plucked out of the burning."

Nineteen children were born to Samuel and Susannah Wesley, of whom ten died in infancy. Susannah was accustomed to speak of her husband as her "master," but she had a will of her own. Quarreling with him over politics, she refused to cohabit with her husband for a time. The death of King William III in 1702 was no doubt a divine providence, for it overcame Mrs. Wesley's legitimist scruples and made it possible for Jackie to be born the next year. Both husband and wife were descended from staunch Dissenters, but they belonged to the Church of England, of which Samuel was a minister.

Mrs. Wesley and an ancient Hebrew king held very similar tenets about the relationship which should properly exist between the rod and the child. In 1742 she wrote to her son John at his request a letter summarizing the rules she had followed in bringing up her family. "When turned a year old (and some before)," the children "were taught to fear the rod, and to cry softly; by which means they escaped abundance of correction they might otherwise have had; and that most odious noise of the crying of children was rarely heard in the house; but the family lived in as much quietness as if there had never been a child among them." The little ones were seen but not heard: "At dinner their little table and chairs were set by ours, where they could be overlooked; and they were suffered to eat and drink (small beer) as much as they would, but not to call for anything. If they wanted aught, they used to whisper to the maid which attended them, who came and spake to me; and as soon as they could handle a knife and fork, they were set to our table."

John Wesley thoroughly approved of his mother's methods. We are pretty much accustomed to Rousseauan or libertarian educational methods, and to most of us the emphasis which Mrs. Wesley and her famous son laid upon the necessity of breaking the child's will must seem monstrous. According to St. Paul, a man should submit to the will of God, a woman to her husband's will, and a child to the will of its parents. It was, then, in Susannah Wesley's opinion, her religious duty to keep her sons and daughters from developing their own inclinations.

Yet Mrs. Wesley by no means submitted to her husband, and her sons never blamed her for her independence. John, when his opinion was looked up to, used his influence to improve the position of women. His mother and a number of other women played important parts in his life and were largely responsible for molding his character. It is perhaps noteworthy that John Wesley denounced wife-beating. His Journal tells about a man who thrashed his wife by his minister's advice. There were still many husbands who refused to abandon the old usage of beating their wives with a thin stick. It may be that Wesley's attitude hastened the decline of wife-beating.

With regard to the discipline of children Wesley agreed to the views of his mother: "I insist upon conquering the will of children betimes, because this is the only strong and rational foundation of a religious education; without which both precept and example will be ineffectual. But when this is thoroughly done, then a child is capable of being governed by the reason and piety of its parents, till its own understanding comes to maturity, and the principles of religion have taken root in the mind." Heaven and Hell, she thought, depend on the denial of self-will. "So that the parent who studies to subdue it in his child, works together with God in the renewing and saving a soul; the parent who indulges it does the Devil's work, makes religion impracticable, salvation unattainable, and does all that in him lies to damn his child, soul and body, for ever."

Susannah punished any child whom she found playing in church or on Sunday. Her son John went further. He thought children should be kept steadily at work or they might turn into idle and ease-loving adults. It was expressly stated in the rules of the Methodist Kingswood School that the children should never play at all. They rose at four, spent an hour in prayer and meditation, and then went about their work, classes being in session from seven to eleven and from one to five. The principal diversion was being taken on occasion to see a corpse, and this form of light recreation was defended on the ground that the children ought to appreciate their mortality as well as their immortality. Two days a week were distinguished in the school by the fact that no meat was served. Religious excitement (which sometimes brought about insanity) was encouraged every day in the week.

When Jackie Wesley went to Oxford, it does not appear, despite the rigid moral education he had received at home, that he was altogether averse to pleasure. He danced, he drank tea with the ladies, he spent money pretty freely. His reverend father, like Johnson's good clergyman, but in a more literal sense, had, despite the possession of a pretty valuable benefice, a larger family than he was able to maintain. Samuel Wesley could be extravagant on occasion, and his son John sometimes showed the same failing. He carried on several more or less mild flirtations, and it is probable that a young woman was the "religious friend" who converted him to Christian piety and turned his mind away from worldly things in 1725.

Four years later John Wesley became the leading spirit in a little group of serious young Oxford men. He was at that time a fellow of Lincoln College, exercising certain tutorial duties. As such, and as one who was already displaying some of the qualities of a leader, he naturally headed an organization consisting chiefly of undergraduates. Piety was just then very much out of fashion at the University of Oxford, and those who practiced it conspicuously were subjected to ridicule. Wesley's band was generally known as the Holy Club. Its members were derisively called the Bible Bigots, the Bible Moths, the Sacramentarianists, or the Methodists. The last name was applied because they were deemed to be too methodical about the ordering of their lives. The greater part of the students esteemed gaming and drunkenness no great crimes. The austerities of the Bible Bigots seemed to them thoroughly ridiculous.

The members of the Holy Club were all Anglicans with High Church leanings. (Dissenters were not then admitted to Oxford.) The rites and dogmas to which the Bible Moths were most strongly attracted savored a little of Rome. William Law, their oracle, thought that small monastic groups of men and women should be established in England for the sake of pleasing God and raising the general level of piety.

The Holy Club encouraged fasting and long meditations among its members. One of them died at college, and his father heaped reproaches upon John Wesley and his brother Charles, who also belonged to the group, for leading him into an asceticism beyond his strength. In the letter of justification which John wrote, he quoted from the words of his own father, the Reverend Samuel, approving of their austerities: "I have the greatest rea-

son to bless God that he has given me two sons together at
Oxford, to whom he has given grace and courage to turn the
war against the world and the devil, which is the best way to
conquer them. They have but one more enemy to combat with,
the flesh; which if they take care to do by fasting and prayer,
there will be no more for them to do, but to proceed steadily
in the same course, and expect the crown which fadeth not
away."

METHODISM OR THE RELIGIOUS HUMBUGG
From *Political and Satirical History of the Years 1756–60*

John Wesley has often been likened to some of the Roman
Catholic saints. It is not difficult to conceive that if the Catholics of England in his time had occupied a more favorable social
and political position, Wesley might have joined them. As it
was, he spent a large part of his life defending himself and his
followers, "the people called Methodists," against the charge,
repeated in many forms, that they were Papists.

Indeed, there was in John Wesley a streak of selfishness foreign (if we are to believe the official hagiologies) to the saints.

Urged by his father to come to Epworth and help him with his work in that little town, St. John the Methodist replied that he had first to consider the salvation of his own soul. Quiet contemplation at Oxford might, he thought, best prepare him for a seat near the Throne. Later he changed his mind and undertook missionary labors. He sought to spread his holiness in Georgia, where Oglethorpe had established a colony primarily for debtors and other persons who were poorly adjusted to life in England.

Aboard ship on the way to America, Wesley made the acquaintance of a party of Moravians or Brethren. These German emigrants seemed to have trained themselves better than he to despise mundane things; at least, they were able to go on quietly praying while the ship was storm-tossed. Wesley was much influenced by the Moravians, though he afterward quarreled and broke with them.

In Georgia he found that the Indians were too depraved to listen to his preaching, and he did not consider the whites much better. For the sake of his own immortal spirit Wesley fasted and walked about barefoot a great deal. He tried in vain to introduce the confessional, penances, an elaborate sacramental system, and much more that belonged to the highest of High Church practices among the colonists. They told him they were Protestants and knew nothing of such popish rigmarole. As for Dissenters, the pious young priest refused to admit them to the communion table or even to give them Christian burial. He refused also to baptize a child whose parents insisted that it should be sprinkled rather than immersed.

This new and methodical St. John was much tempted by the Devil, especially in the form of women. Sophia Hopkey of Georgia stood out above most of the rest because of her religious and moral zeal. After Wesley gave Miss Hopkey to understand that he intended to marry her, he developed doubts and consulted his friends, the leaders of the Brethren. They dissuaded him from marriage. Torn between what, at moments, seemed no more than carnal desire and a feeling that marriage would destroy his holiness, perhaps bar the way to the Throne, Wesley decided to leave the answer to God, according to the usage of the Moravians. That is, he drew lots. The oracle told him not to marry. Sophia saw that his ardency was much reduced, finally decided that he had no matrimonial intentions, and married another man.

Wesley was furious. If he was to play the monk, why should not she play the nun? His excited resentment led him to act injudiciously. As a result, he was indicted for defaming Sophia Williamson (such was her new name) and refusing without due cause to administer the sacrament to her. There was some delay about bringing the case to trial. Wesley, seeing that he could not be very useful in Georgia and no doubt fearing the result of his former sweetheart's action, quietly slipped away from the colony and sailed back to England.

In this period of his life Wesley was troubled with occasional doubts about the truth of Christianity. After much inward struggling, and aided by the teachings of the Brethren, he reached the conclusion that if he could convince himself of his intrinsic sinfulness and then believe firmly in Jesus Christ as the redeemer of mankind, he would be assured of salvation.

For a time he had followed the advice of the Moravian Peter Boehler: "Preach faith till you have it; and then, because you have it, you will preach faith." Wesley felt better when he was sure that he actually possessed faith. The change came one day in 1738. He had previously sought God through good works, fasting much, giving up meat and wine, going shoeless. Then he reached the conclusion that good works were valueless and only faith in Christ mattered. On his great day of conversion the Bible passage he came upon in the morning when he opened the book aimlessly and the title of the anthem he heard later at St. Paul's seemed to convey divine messages intended expressly to reassure him. Then, at 8.45 P.M., May 24, A.D. 1738, as he tells us: "I feel I did trust in Christ, Christ alone, for salvation; and an assurance was given me, that he had taken away *my* sins, even *mine,* and saved *me* from the law of sin and death." (The italics are, of course, Wesley's own.) The only thing that troubled him for a while was the absence of strong feelings of joy. At last he decided that one might be truly converted without experiencing any vivid consciousness of immediate bliss.

The personal religious experiences of John Wesley are recorded here because they brought about ultimately the formation of the various sects called Methodist or Wesleyan, which have played an important part in the New Puritanism, and also because Wesley's work stimulated pietism in the Church of England and other ecclesiastical groups. The founding of new religious organizations was no part of Wesley's original plan. The Dissenters remained under various political and educational disabilities. Moreover, he was attached to the Anglican Church, of which he and some of his most important disciples were priests. What he really intended to do, when he realized the extent of his influence, was to remodel the Church of England according to his ideas. But this was not to be, except indirectly and to a limited extent. The American Methodist Episcopal Church was founded during his lifetime, but his English followers did not secede from the Established Church until after his death. The Calvinist Methodists, who were led by George Whitefield and supported by the Countess of Huntingdon, had gone their separate way before this. Wesley could see in the last years of his life that the other English Methodists would soon form a distinct group. In fact, they were applying for the licenses which were given to Dissenting chapels to legalize their meetinghouses.

Much prejudice against the Noncomformists still existed. It was considered not quite patriotic to worship anywhere but in Anglican churches. In 1788 a deputation from the various sects waited on Chancellor Thurlow to ask his support for the repeal of the laws which made taking the sacrament in an Anglican church prerequisite to the holding of various offices and to a number of other privileges. He is supposed to have said to the delegates: "Gentlemen, I'm against you, by God! I am for the Established Church, damn me! Not that I have any more regard for the Established Church than for any other church, but because it is established. And if you can get your

THE SLEEPING CONGREGATION
An engraving by William·Hogarth, 1736.

damned religion established, I'll be for that, too." Many people shared this attitude, though few spoke so frankly. Here is the chief reason why Wesley hesitated so long about leaving the Church.

George Whitefield was the son of a tapster in a Gloucester inn. He was the great preacher of the Methodist movement, as Charles Wesley was the great hymn-writer and John Wesley the great organizer. Whitefield was much more successful than John Wesley in the work he did in British America. We have abundant testimony to the power of Whitefield's eloquence. Franklin tells us how the preacher wheedled him out of all the money in his pockets for a purpose which he had made up his mind in advance to consider inexpedient.

The life which Whitefield led as a young man seemed to him, in retrospect, a very sinful one. He was never so ascetic as the Wesleys. When he came to Georgia for the first time, he found that the importation of distilled liquors into the colony was prohibited, and he expressed the opinion that this was retarding its growth. And he worked against the passage of a stronger prohibitory bill by the Provincial Council. On one occasion, when he was sailing for England, he tells us that his friends brought him "wine, ale, cake, coffee, tea," and various other articles for his use on the voyage. Thomas Coke, the first American bishop of the Methodist Church, received "a few bottles of excellent old rum" as a *bon voyage* gift, and history does not record that he poured the contents overboard.

John Wesley consistently opposed the use of distilled liquors, even advancing the (certainly fallacious) argument that it was responsible for the high cost of grain. He by no means opposed the use of light beer, to which he had become accustomed as an infant. In discussing a medical book by an eccentric writer, he asks, "But why should he condemn wine *toto genere,* which is one of the noblest cordials in nature? Yet stranger, why should he condemn bread?"

When, in 1747, the Bishop of London spoke against the asceticism of the people called Methodists, Wesley wrote to him: "I presume your lordship means the abstaining from wine and animal food; which, it is true, Christianity does not require. But, if you do, I fear your lordship is not thoroughly informed of the matter of fact. I began to do this about twelve years ago, when I had no thought of 'annoying parochial ministers' or of 'captivating' any people thereby, unless it were Chickasaw or Choctaw Indians. But I resumed the use of them both, about two years after, for the sake of some who thought I made it a matter of conscience, telling them, 'I will eat flesh while the world standeth, rather than make my brother to offend.' Dr. Cheyne advised me to leave them off again, assuring me, 'Till you do, you will never be free from fevers.' And since I have taken his advice, I have been free (blessed be God!) from all bodily disorders." Wesley later resumed the use of both meat and wine, not being aware of any religious or moral obligation to abstain from either.

Tobacco and tea seemed to him far more objectionable than wine. Many others joined him in this position. Tea was very expensive, at least in view of the ordinary wages of the time; and Arthur Young toward the end of the eighteenth century complained that rural laborers were starving themselves to obtain this beverage. He found it especially shocking that men as well as women were passionately devoted to it.

In one of Wesley's sermons there is a reference to "a cup of wholesome wine." This fairly represents his general view on the subject. Of course, there was practically no opposition to the use of wine in his day. The miracle at Cana was assigned as a topic for schoolboys' compositions, and Christians did not feel any need to apologize for it. Wesley, like most Englishmen of his time, considered wine to be of ritual importance. The substitution of unfermented grape juice for it at the Lord's Supper would have seemed to him no less than blasphemy. And he used to boast about the numbers of bottles of wine consumed at the communion table over which he presided.

Wesley abstained from tea for twelve years. He disliked all forms of luxury, and he embraced under the term many things which we are accustomed to consider comforts or necessities. He objected to the passing of old English plain living, "the ancient hardiness lost, the British temperance, and scorn of super-fluities, the rough indefatigable industry, exchanged for soft-ness, idleness, and fulness of bread."

It cannot be denied that he was accustomed to practice what he preached. Indeed, he inflicted greater austerities upon him-self than he expected of his disciples. Despite his scorn of good works as a way of acquiring grace, he busied himself all through middle and old age in what he considered the service of God. He traveled hundreds of thousands of miles, and hardly a day passed in which he did not preach several times.

When Anglican parsons unsympathetic to his aims complained that he was driving their congregations mad and refused to allow him the use of their churches, Wesley followed White-field's example, preaching in the street or in open fields. Enor-mous numbers of people who were unused to church attendance, or left unstirred by the mumbled sermons of indifferent minis-ters, came under the influence of the Wesleys, Whitefield, and other Methodist missionaries. The effect was perhaps greatest in Wales, where Griffith Jones had begun his Evangelical mis-sionary labors even before the Wesleys had been converted. The Methodist work was also important in the new industrial dis-tricts of England, which were little provided with regular churches and ministers.

The sin of sins, according to Wesley, is dissipation. The dis-sipated man, he tells us, is one who is separated from God, "dis-united from his center; whether this be occasioned by hurry or business, by seeking honor or preferment, or by fondness for diversions, for silly pleasures so called, or for any other trifle under the sun. The vulgar, it is true, commonly confine this character to those who are violently attached to women, gam-ing, drinking, to dances, balls, races, or the poor childish diver-sion of 'running foxes and hares out of breath.' But it belongs equally to the serious fool, who forgets God, by a close attention to any worldly employment, suppose it were the most elegant, or of the most important kind. A man may be as much dis-sipated from God, by the study of the mathematics or astronomy, as by fondness for cards or hounds. Whoever is habitually inattentive to the practice and will of his Creator, he is a dissipated man."

It was manifestly impossible for all who became Methodists to possess the earnestness of John Wesley. And he, too, was sometimes "dissipated" by ambition or passion. The chief question for him, all through his life, was "How shall I be saved?" He sought the answer in the Bible, which he tried to interpret and accept literally. There were, indeed, some Scriptural passages which the various Methodist leaders conceived to have different meanings. Wesley was sure that all men can be saved for Heaven, Whitefield maintained that some are foreordained to go to Hell.

The Moravians, who considered themselves good Bible Christians, attached less importance to abstinence from luxury than the founder of Methodism believed to be necessary. The Scriptures, Wesley preached, "manifestly forbid Christians, those in the lower or middle ranks of life, to be adorned with gold, or pearls, or costly apparel." He denounced "elephantine hats or bonnets, those scandals of female modesty." Addressing himself particularly to those women among his hearers who aspired to be fashionable, he told them: "You kindle a flame which, at the same time, consumes both you and your admirers. And it is well, if it does not plunge both you and them into the flames of Hell." Methodist women in general were soon known for the severe sobriety of their attire.

In John Wesley, as in many another ascetic, flesh contended with spirit. He objected to expensive and fashionable clothing and jewelry, as well as to distilled liquors, on the ground that they promote unchastity. Though he finally got married, he always maintained that the Bible advises celibacy as a means of attaining to holiness. He tells us that immediately after abandoning bachelorhood he "met the single men, and showed them on how many accounts it was good for those who had received that gift from God, to remain single for the Kingdom of Heaven's sake, unless where a particular case might be an exception to the general rule." His own case was, no doubt, sufficiently exceptional. Wesley used to insist that men and

SETTLING THE ODD TRICK

After a print published in 1778.

women should sit apart during the administration of the communion. Some of his detractors consequently remarked that he was adopting Jewish as well as popish usages.

Wesley was not the most extreme of ascetics. The following verses by Herbert appeared to him "too melancholy":

> Take thy meat: think it dust: then eat a bit,
> And say with all, earth to earth I commit.

And he was not absolutely opposed to worldly learning. "Methodists," he said, "may read useful history, pious and elegant poetry, or several branches of natural philosophy. If you have time, you may divert yourself by music, and perhaps by philosophical experiments."

What Wesley thought about Sunday observance is made sufficiently clear by an entry which he made in his Journal at Athlone, Ireland: "I was in hopes even the Papists here had at length a shepherd who cared for their souls. He was stricter than any of his predecessors, and was esteemed a man of piety as well as learning: accordingly, he had given them strict orders not to work on the Lord's Day. But I found he allowed them to play as much as they pleased; nay, and averred, 'It was their duty to do so' to 'refresh both their bodies and minds.' Alas, for the blind leader of the blind: has not he the greater sin?" Wesley assured his followers that those who sought recreation on Sunday would be punished for their sin in this world and the next. There was a zealous preacher named William Grimshaw who took care of the mundane part of the punishment himself. He used to visit the taverns of his town on Sunday and horse-whip the roisterers into church to hear his sermon.

There is a passage in Wesley's Journal which shows his conception of the right way to óbserve a day of thanksgiving. It may be noted that he was not alone in this, for he wrote of an actual celebration: "It had all the solemnity of a general fast. All the shops were shut. The people in the streets appeared, one and all, with an air of seriousness. . . . There was no noise, hurry, bonfires, fire-works in the evening; and no public diversions. This is indeed a Christian holiday, a 'rejoicing unto the Lord'!"

The Methodists were taught to consider playgoing extremely sinful. And their opposition was confirmed (not, indeed, that it required confirmation) by the appearance of several comedies which mocked the movement. Oliver Goldsmith in *She Stoops to Conquer* makes Tony Lumpkin sing:

> When Methodist preachers come down
> A-preaching that drinking is sinful,
> I'll wager the rascals a crown
> They always preach best with a skinful.

Alas, it was true in some cases. Many of the people called Methodists showed themselves human, all too human. There were even some who displayed laxity in their sexual theories and practice — for instance, Westley Hall, who married one of John Wesley's sisters and made love to another. And there were Methodists who attended boxing matches and cockfights and their parochial church feasts, though Wesley taught that they would be punished for it, probably by a divine visitation on earth, and surely by burning in Hell forever. Yes, forever: Wesley displayed no sympathy with the heretics who tried to calculate the number of thousands or millions of years of burning which would be sufficient to appease the divine wrath.

Though Wesley liked to harp upon the importance of reason in religion, he and his disciples appealed particularly to the emotions. Some were so violently stirred by Methodist preaching that they fell into convulsions or became permanently insane. The most notable of these is the poet Cowper, who considered himself

> Damned below Judas, more abhorred than he was
> Who for a few pence sold his holy Master!

An ironical passage in Cowper's *The Task* shows how the geologists of the eighteenth century stirred up the controversy between the parties now known as Modernists and Fundamentalists:

> Some drill and bore
> The solid earth, and from the strata there
> Extract a register by which we learn
> That He who made it, and revealed its date
> To Moses, was mistaken in its age.

No, "God never meant that men should scale the heavens by strides of human wisdom." Scientific investigations appeared to Cowper almost as bad as telling jokes while delivering a sermon. He disposes of that sin easily enough:

> So did not Paul. Direct me to a quip
> Or merry turn in all he ever wrote,
> And I consent to take it for your text,
> Your only one, till sides and benches fall.

CHAPTER VIII

INCLUDING A FAT PRINCE

§ 1

GEORGE III and his Queen lived simply, and their example was generally in favor of the middle-class virtues. Their sons, however, did not follow them in matters of morality, and they were responsive to the fashionable vices of the day. The Prince of Wales distinguished himself early in life as a clever fellow very much devoted to pleasure. In considering certain aspects of his life we must bear in mind that during the reigns of the first four Georges the aristocracy practiced hard drinking, heavy gambling, and sexual laxity as a matter of course. The middle classes, already favoring strict moral standards, had, in a large measure, responded to the exhortation of the Methodist preachers by the end of the eighteenth century. The lower classes had then shown at least a temporary reaction in the direction of pietism. But the upper circles of society were little touched. Drinking was considered a badge of manhood, and the young noble or gentleman who could not dispose of two or three bottles of wine at a sitting was despised as a milksop.

The young Prince speedily distinguished himself as a tippler. He was a faithful subscriber to the doctrine that every potation should be tried at least once. Some drinks invited more than one sampling. Moralists who knew the lad sometimes professed not to be entirely satisfied with his truthfulness. He was criticized also for keeping low company.

At eighteen or nineteen His Highness of Wales was a chubby youth with red cheeks. He had good manners, but he did not hold himself unduly aloof from the people, and he enjoyed considerable popularity. That he liked pleasure was not generally held against him. It was taken for granted, even by moralists of considerable strictness, that persons of high rank might do a great many things which would be objectionable in the case of their inferiors. Wesley was careful not to include the upper classes in his diatribe against expensive clothes and ornaments. The Prince seemed not altogether to have wasted his time, for he could speak French and Italian and quote poetry on occasion, while his skill in singing and in playing the violoncello were (for an heir to the throne) good enough to warrant high praise.

He was already devoted to costly and flashy clothing. Thackeray, looking down from the height of his Victorian goodness, remarks sarcastically that the Prince's most important achievement was the design of a shoe buckle five inches broad. In truth, Wales had no higher ambition than that of shining as a social leader. Hence, the conception or the popularization of a new fashion was to him no small matter.

The Prince attached himself to the fashionable Whigs, and one of his particular cronies was Charles James Fox. Fox was distinguished as a hard drinker in an age when such a distinction required many hundreds of bottles to gain. In his childhood he had been taught to gamble by his father; but he was lacking in either skill or luck, for his total losses are said to have run to £200,000.

Wales spent £10,000 annually to maintain the splendor of his wardrobe, and enough on his miscellaneous pleasures to make his allowance insufficient. When the public heard about the debts he was contracting, his popularity waned. Many were resentful, also, of the fact that his relations with the Whig politicians were extremely friendly.

At about the age of eighteen the Prince of Wales entered into the first of his well-known liaisons with women. He became enamoured of Mary Robinson, an attractive actress whom he first saw when she played the part of Perdita in *The Winter's Tale* at the Drury Lane Theatre. For two years, until he wearied of his Perdita, he maintained her in an expensive establishment. The complete list of his concubines is a rather long one. Perhaps twenty women might be included, although the comparatively ephemeral duration of some of the affairs makes it doubtful how they should be classified. Women never fully took up the Prince's time. He enjoyed boxing matches and horse races, he gave long sessions to drinking and gaming with his male friends.

In 1772 the Prince fell in love with the twice widowed Mrs. Fitzherbert. Despite all his offers and importunities the pretty widow refused to enter into an illicit connection with him. Only marriage would satisfy her. Wales was sorely smitten. Mrs. Fitzherbert was a Roman Catholic. According to the act of Parliament which provided for a Protestant succession, no person married to a Catholic could ascend the British throne. Possibly this obstacle might have been surmounted, but it was also compulsory for the Prince to have the King's consent before contracting marriage. George III was not at all likely to approve of the lady whom his son loved. The Prince of Wales finally settled the matter by having an Anglican clergyman marry him in private to Mrs. Fitzherbert. Some time later, rumors were heard about this situation, with ugly anti-Romanist rumblings. At the Prince's request Fox denied the whole story on the floor of the House of Commons. Mrs. Fitzherbert (or perhaps we should call her the Princess of Wales, for the Pope assured her that the marriage was valid) became angry with Fox because of his denial. Then the Prince and Fox quarreled.

The marriage was never publicly acknowledged, and the documentary proofs of its existence were not revealed until 1905. However, the Prince of Wales did not conceal the fact that he was living with Mrs. Fitzherbert. In fact, almost all his liaisons were quite open. His model was Charles II, but he was rather a heavy, uninspired copy of the Merry Monarch. He founded a new club because some of his habitual companions were unwelcome at the old fashionable ones, and there he lost heavily at cards.

George III became insane in 1788. Some supposed that chagrin at his eldest son's conduct was largely responsible for his affliction. The Prince tried to obtain the regency with full royal powers; a squabble developed in Parliament; and before the matter was settled, the King had recovered his mental health,

THE MORNING AFTER MARRIAGE, OR, A SCENE ON THE CONTINENT

A caricature of the Prince of Wales and Mrs. Fitzherbert by James Gillray, 1788.

though only temporarily. The Prince of Wales did not become regent until 1811. In the meantime he was seldom on good terms with his father.

Young George was constantly worried by the problem of making both ends meet after they had encircled a host of luxuries for his mistress of the moment. Sometimes he adopted rather sharp practices. For instance, he issued a loan on the security of the hereditary bishopric of Osnaburg, and though he paid the interest, he repudiated the principal when it became due. And he became involved in a number of scandals, as in the instance when his jockey was accused of cheating at the races.

Finally, in order that his father might be persuaded to pay his debts and without regard for the fact that he was already married, the Prince of Wales agreed to marry whatever princess should be chosen for him. Caroline of Brunswick became his bride. He did not receive her with much enthusiasm. He was so drunk the evening of the wedding that his friends had to support him at the altar, and it was a matter of considerable difficulty to elicit the responses required on his part. Caroline said later that he had spent the nuptial night lying in a grate, dead to the world.

Soon there were quarrels between husband and wife. He was not, indeed, accustomed to remain faithful for long even to the women he chose for himself. After the Princess bore him a daughter, he informed her that he no longer intended to treat her as his wife. So long as George III possessed his health and his authority, Caroline was not entirely deprived of her rights as Princess of Wales. When her husband became regent, he heaped indignities upon her. He even took their daughter away from her and refused to let her see the child.

The Princess was not, of course, expected to console herself by following her husband's example and openly living with men to whom she was not and could not be married. Yet reports spread that she was indiscreetly seeking elsewhere the love which the Prince did not give her.

The public became interested in the domestic difficulties of the Prince and Princess of Wales, and the interest was mingled

with disgust. For married men, including princes, to have concubines was no novelty; still, to flaunt them and to abandon
one's own wife was to arouse a great deal of English indignation.
Not only the precise middle classes but the less rigorous aristocracy as well blamed the Prince of Wales for the way he had
treated his wife. Somewhat later, when one wave of scandal had
disappeared, it became known that the young princess, Caroline's
daughter, was having secret love affairs of her own. When the
Princess of Wales went abroad, she was seen to be very friendly
to Bergami, her attendant; and she went so far as to ask foreign
governments to bestow decorations upon him.

§ 2

The moral outlook of England changed a great deal under the
influence of the French Revolution. The philosophical ideas
associated with the revolution were, indeed, largely of English
origin. Voltaire, for instance, had been stimulated by the scientists and political theorists of England as well as by the governmental system of Great Britain. When the movement toward
liberty began in France, there were many sympathizers across
the Channel. They expected a limited monarchy to be established. Literary men were nearly unanimous in welcoming the
change.

"When France in wrath her giant-limbs upreared" to win her
freedom, many even of those who, like Coleridge, regretted that
"Blasphemy's loud scream with the sweet music of deliverance
strove," were on the side of the revolutionists. Events moved
fast, and soon most Englishmen were hostile to the revolution.
The Terror and the destruction of vested interests were both
calculated to alienate conservative Englishmen. In England
it had been fashionable to hold skeptical views about religion,
but not to attack the Church. There had been much playing
with political abstractions among the English, but efforts to
undermine the constitution were rare. The skeptics and open
hedonists of Great Britain belonged mostly to the aristocracy.
They were willing to philosophize freely, to encourage scientific
thinking, to laugh at Sterne's jokes and Swift's and Voltaire's,

so long as their own special privileges were safe. But they saw the very same French nobles who had encouraged the *philosophes* being stripped of their possessions, even put to death, apparently as the result of the spread of liberal ideas. It was fear that drove the English upper classes to pietism and a stern insistence upon moral duty. They wanted to be sure they were not nurturing dragons which would fall upon them and devour them.

The Methodist revival brought about a new spirit in the Church of England. Many Anglican ministers who had denounced enthusiasm finally were converted to a sense of the importance of religious emotion. They stopped worrying about the sin of being righteous overmuch. Rationalism was attacked at the same time by the Methodist fever and by the reaction against the Reign of Terror in France. Burke, who considered duty to God the foundation of all morality, became almost insanely excited about the French Revolution. Thomas Paine, who was at once an opponent of Christianity and a defender of liberty, published an answer to Burke's reflections but soon found it necessary to flee from England. Even before the revolution broke out in France, there were indications that the upper classes were veering over to middle-class standards. The swing was much accelerated in the last decade of the century.

In 1788 Hannah More published anonymously her *Thoughts on the Importance of the Manners of the Great to General Society*. Seven large editions of this book, which was intended to induce the upper classes to adopt stricter moral practices, were sold within a few months. According to the Reverend Henry Thompson, who wrote Mrs. More's biography in the early Victorian period: "A book so universally read could not fail to be influential, and its influence was soon traceable in the abandonment of many customs which it attacked. The elaborate hairdressing which employed incalculable hands during the sabbath services of the church, soon altogether disappeared, the example being set in the highest quarter; the perquisite of card-money rapidly diminished; the Christian master no longer pleaded for the practice of employing his servant to tell conventional falsehoods; and Sunday concert-parties of sacred music, even if unobjectionable in themselves, were seen to produce a large proportion of evil by the necessary desecration of the sabbath on the part of coachmen and servants. For all these improvements, society is very mainly indebted to the pen of Hannah More."

In 1790 Mrs. More issued *An Estimate of the Religion of the Fashionable World, by One of the Laity.* This was also intended to make the upper classes pietistic. She worked with the poor as well, starting a number of schools which were mainly devoted to religious and moral instruction. She had been friendly to the French Revolution at the outset; she took up the excited cry against blasphemy and atheism, helping to spread the doctrine that it was the pious duty of the English people to abhor and combat the revolutionary movement in France. In her later years Mrs. More became a violent enemy of the theatre. Her reverend and early-Victorian biographer disapproved of this last moral attack, saying that she turned respectable people away from the drama, and therefore caused it to become almost as objectionable as it had been in the time of Charles II.

We must not err with Mr. Thompson in overestimating the importance of Mrs. More's work. People listened to her because they were just ready to hear about the excellence of old-fashioned English morality. No matter how much drinking and gambling and loose living had taken place in England, John Bull always prided himself upon his moral superiority to the frog-eating Frenchman. And now it was generally agreed that irreligious philosophy was responsible for the bloody terror in France, that the failure of the nobles of England to say their prayers might result in making the lower orders turn the social organization topsy-turvy. The *Annual Register* for 1798 commented on the streams of carriages that were visible at English church doors. The country folk, who had little acquaintance with international affairs, wondered why their lords and squires suddenly became so devout.

The principal concern of the great was setting a good example. Those who had been skeptical or indifferent to religion were not (we may suppose) suddenly converted by the Reign of Terror. Unquestionably, many of them were hypocritical in their display of piety. When religious zeal is fashionable, and, more than that, when the lack of it is regarded with abhorrence, pretence invariably arises.

In the middle orders of society also pietism was strongly favored. Sir Leslie Stephen says of the New Puritanism which Methodism fostered in the last quarter of the eighteenth century that it was "a faint reflection of the grander Puritanism of the seventeenth century. The morality founded upon it showed all the old narrowness without the old intensity. The hatred of the world was too often interpreted as a hatred of all that makes the world beautiful, combined with a hearty appreciation of everything that adds to its material comfort."

A new Society for the Reformation of Morals and an Association for the Better Observance of the Sabbath were formed. The gambling laws were enforced as strictly as possible. In 1797 several noble ladies were fined fifty pounds each for playing cards, and Lord Kenyon threatened to bring some of the society women under the lash of the law by putting them in the pillory. Such extreme enthusiasm for morality did not last long. The Prince of Wales was fond of cards, and the nobles, no matter how much they were opposed to French godlessness, found it impossible to stay away very long from the gambling tables.

Stakes were often very heavy, and bets were laid upon almost every conceivable sort of contingency. There is a story, dating from this period, about a man who was run down by a carriage in front of a fashionable club. The noble and gentle persons who ran out of the club made no effort to see if they could help him. Instead, they paused at a distance to lay bets on the question of his being dead or alive.

There was a great deal of speculation in commodities and bonds. People of the highest rank followed the example of the Prince of Wales by running into debt recklessly, sometimes without any intention of making payment. Because of the uncertainties involved in such transactions, high prices were charged to the aristocracy. Some merchants who were fortunate enough to collect most of their debts grew immensely wealthy. And the Napoleonic wars provided many opportunities for shrewd or

Discipline à la Kenyon.

DISCIPLINE A LA KENYON

A caricature of three noble and notorious gambling ladies by James Gillray, 1797.

lucky traders and manufacturers to acquire fortunes with great rapidity. Some spent their money lavishly almost as fast as they earned it. Others bought land and founded important families.

Political morality remained extremely lax in the period of the French Revolution and the Napoleonic wars. Indeed, as there was more expenditure on the part of the English government, there were correspondingly more opportunities for corruption. It was no secret that peerages, offices, decorations, and votes were sold to the highest bidders.

The French Revolution brought about a suspension of freedom of expression in England. The movement for political reform, which had been fashionable under the sponsorship of such men as the younger Pitt and Fox, was, after the outbreak of the Reign of Terror, considered seditious. Conservatism which leaned backward so far that it became reaction was treated as the bulwark of English patriotism. A number of laws were enacted for the purpose of repressing even the mildest of agitators.

The Corresponding Society, a liberal body whose membership included Horne Took, Thomas Paine, Holcroft, and the poet and artist William Blake, became offensive to the authorities. A group of English and Scottish delegates met in Edinburgh in 1793 to discuss universal suffrage and the reform of Parliament. Several of them were convicted of sedition and sentenced to fourteen years of penal exile at Botany Bay in Australia. Chief Justice Eyre then delivered a charge to a London grand jury in which he made the crime of high treason include all attempts to introduce alterations into the form of government. Twelve members of the Corresponding Society were arrested. Though the evidence against them was slight, feeling against them ran so high that they were in some danger of being hanged, but not until they were dead, having their bowels drawn out before their eyes and being quartered, as by law provided for persons convicted of high treason. Godwin in a newspaper article attacked Eyre's charge, showing that high treason had never been made to include peaceful efforts to reform the government. This argument was to some extent responsible for the acquittal of those of the defendants who were brought to trial.

But the liberals and their cause remained unpopular. As early as 1791 a Birmingham mob destroyed the home and the scientific instruments of Joseph Priestley. He added to the offense of preaching Unitarian doctrines that of making chemical experiments. He suffered, however, for an enormity of which he was not guilty: he was supposed to have attended a dinner where parliamentary reform was discussed. Priestley's *History of the Corruptions of Christianity* was burned by the common hangman.

Prominent people, including orthodox clergymen and judicial officers, encouraged the people to destroy Nonconformist chapels and the homes of prominent Dissenters. Liberals and men who did not belong to the Anglican Church often found it difficult to earn a livelihood. Paine, hated both as a republican and as a deist, had to run away from England and take refuge in France. Great odium was attached to his name for several decades, and it was extended to freethinkers and free thought in general.

Englishmen who did not attend the services of the Established Church remained under a number of disabilities. Under a strict interpretation of the law no Dissenter was entitled to hold public office. When Methodism definitely parted from the Anglican Church, the number of Nonconformists rose greatly. Other independent churches were attracting members from the Establishment. A considerable part of the people who went to church regularly in 1800 belonged to one or another dissenting sect. The pious mobs which defended Church and State were often composed of men who seldom attended religious services.

Roman Catholics were, at the end of the eighteenth century, in a very weak position under the laws of England. The penal law against them had, however, been modified in 1778, and it was seldom enforced. They shared with Dissenters a number of political, social, and educational disqualifications. All the people of England, no matter what their faith, had to contribute to the support of the Established Church. Only Anglicans were admitted to the universities, except that Cambridge sometimes allowed other Protestants to matriculate but not to take degrees.

In 1800 William Wilberforce induced Pitt to refrain from presenting to Parliament (which would, no doubt, have passed it) a bill intended to give the Tory magistrates power to persecute Methodist and other dissenting ministers. The influence which Wilberforce exerted spoke eloquently of the new strength of the English middle classes. It was chiefly he who brought about the law prohibiting the importation of slaves into British possessions.

However, Wilberforce felt differently about the virtual slaves who labored in English factories. He and his fellow Evangelicals urged upon Pitt a law which made the organization of trade unions illegal. They resisted all efforts to shorten extremely long working hours and to safeguard the health of the men, women, and children who toiled in factories and mines. The Tories, being representative of the landowning interests rather than of the manufacturers, allowed themselves to become indignant about the way in which English boys and girls were lashed into fifteen or sixteen hours of work daily. A number of factory laws were passed, though the most important ones did not come into being until Victoria sat on the throne.

Where the personal profits of the Liberals were not involved, they were willing to work for reform. Conditions in the prisons were improved. The pillory and the public whipping post were abolished. The number of capital offenses was reduced. The penal flogging of women was no longer permitted. Humanitarian influence became visible in the Army, where an order of 1807 limited the number of lashes which a soldier might receive for a single offense to one thousand. Larger numbers had actually been applied in many instances before this order was issued. The primitive beginnings of a State educational system for the working classes were perhaps an indication of advancing democracy.

The French Revolution gave an impetus almost everywhere in Continental Europe to rationalism and free morality. Even in England, where this moral and religious influence was mostly inverse, the end of the eighteenth century saw many people who theorized about free loving and free living. There was an increase in the number of popular charlatans of various kinds, such as usually appear in an age of doubt. (That is to say, many people who lose one faith manage to provide themselves quickly with another.)

In 1793, when the Duchess of York was pregnant, fashionable women and girls took to wearing pads, small cushions under the waistband. It is said that this strange fashion had an influence on the formation of the French feminine mode of the Directory period. However, the short-waisted, so-called naked costumes for women which came into favor in France were supposed to be derived, by way of compliment to the ancient republics, from the old Greek feminine garb.

Scantiness distinguished the Directory fashions. Some extremists discarded shoes and all underwear, that their clothing might be more truly classical. We are told of ladies who boasted that their clothing weighed only eight ounces for each. Englishwomen never took off quite so much of their clothes as their French contemporaries, but they were, nevertheless, strongly influenced by the Directory and Empire fashions. We find moralists complaining that they allowed too much to be seen of the bosom and various other regions which the ladies of England had previously been in the habit of concealing.

Generally speaking, the French Revolution enters into the history of English morals as the cause, or one of the causes, of a reaction to extremely strict standards of conduct. Frenchmen, Germans, and Italians of the early nineteenth century, not merely content to live with mistresses or to practice promiscuous love-making, boasted about their own experiences and theorized about sexual relations in books and on the stage. It was well known that Goethe lived for many years with a woman before marrying her, yet he moved in the highest social circles.

Henry Crabb Robinson tells how, in 1804, Goethe spoke sarcastically about *moral* Englishmen. John Bull was proud of being *moralisch;* and, if Robinson had been more of a chauvinist, he would have called Goethe a damned something-or-other Dutch

THE FASHIONABLE MAMA, OR, THE CONVENIENCE OF MODERN DRESS
A caricature by James Gillray, 1796.

something-else for presuming to place his wickedness higher than British virtue. By the time that Victoria came to the throne, it was almost a badge of patriotism in England to be pietistic and prudish.

The aristocracy offered most resistance to Mrs. Grundy. During the intervals of peace between the Napoleonic wars English tourists came to know and to be influenced by foreign manners and morals. There were some impoverished gentlemen who went to France chiefly for the purpose of living inexpensively, and these often prided themselves upon having nothing to do with foreigners. Lord Nelson, who was a splendid hater of the French, was for a time (before, indeed, he had won his fame or his title) in this class. Many Englishmen returned home to boast that they were not like the immoral foreigners. But almost all had a different moral outlook, just the same, after they had come into contact with Continental standards. A little later, Germany lost some of the gaiety and sparkle, imported from Paris, which was characteristic of the Napoleonic period, and sank back into middle-class stolidity. Probably it did not become more "virtuous," though it acquired a certain amount of prudishness. At any rate, France preserved more than any other country the reputation of being pleasure-loving and lax. In the middle of the nineteenth century Englishmen thought of Germany as the home of good people, morally very much like the English themselves.

Trevelyan contrasts the gross manners of the country squires in Fielding and Smollett with the gentility of those portrayed by Jane Austen. Certainly Miss Austen's characters, if they belong to the upper or the upper-middle classes, talk with considerable stiffness and formality. It has been suggested that this is a lapse from realism, and that the novelist was anxious to mark class distinctions, even at the cost of accuracy. There is, no doubt, a certain amount of exaggeration in the highflown and intricate language her heroes and heroines use. At the same time, we must remember that formality in speech and letter-writing was carefully cultivated among genteel people in the early decades of the nineteenth century. Refinement was the dominant note: there was even a fashionable and refined way of spitting on the carpet, which ladies and gentlemen of social aspirations had to learn.

In the days of the Regency the clothes which men of fashion wore were reckoned to be of prime importance. It was the era of Beau Brummel and of a stylishly stout Prince. Gentlemen blossomed out in garments of blue and red and yellow and various other colors, some of them improvements upon the rainbow. No meaner personage than the Duke of Wellington was turned away from Almack's because he wore long trousers instead of the knee breeches regularly prescribed for the male dancers there.

Interest in hunting, racing, betting, and gay living did not die out at the end of the century; but many aristocrats added what was at least a polite curiosity about literature, music, and the fine arts. There had always been isolated wealthy patrons. Now came the development of a public demand for books, spreading from the scholarly and wealthy classes into those circles where the pursuit of wealth had, with the sole exception of religious exercises, formed the only acknowledged end in life.

Thomas Babington Macaulay was born in 1800 of Quaker and Scotch Presbyterian stock. At the age of fifteen he wrote home from school advising his mother to read Boccaccio, at least in Dryden's version, and saying that he much preferred the Italian author to Chaucer. His father, a rigid Evangelical, probably was unfamiliar with Chaucer and Boccaccio, for he never interfered with his son's reading. But he later expressed sorrow when Thomas wrote for a "worldly" periodical, that is, one not primarily concerned with the teaching of pietism. The elder Macaulay considered it sinful to take a walk on Sunday for the sake of pleasure. He belonged with Wilberforce to the circle known as the "Clapham saints." His son probably had as much moral fervor as he, but he shook off much of the old prejudice against beauty and pleasure.

Macaulay says that in 1778, when *Evelina* appeared, there was "a disposition among most respectable people to condemn novels generally." This feeling, so far as it actually did exist, was the result of the sort of novel which was then being generally published. Objections to the reading of fiction lasted well into the nineteenth century. Indeed, they have not entirely disappeared among strict Evangelicals to this day, although "wholesome" novels came into general respectability during the reign of Victoria.

The early-nineteenth-century theatres catered but little to the middle classes. They usually contained private boxes which were fitted out with sofas to serve the amours of the aristocracy. In fact, the playhouses were dedicated to Eros and to Bacchus no less than to Thalia and Melpomene and Terpsichore.

The upper classes were, save for fitful moments of official devotion to Virtue, permitted to go their own way. This might almost be said of the lower classes and their morality as well. They were, on occasion, severely punished for gaming and drunkenness, and they were often preached at; but, by and large, they were accustomed to avail themselves of all means of attaining pleasure that they found within their reach.

The formal duel was peculiar to the aristocracy. The fashion of wearing swords had disappeared early in the reign of George III, and the upper classes became a little less quarrelsome as a result. During the Regency, gentlemen settled affairs of honor with pistols. Poor people were no less belligerent than their superiors, but they fought with their fists or cudgels, weapons which were usually less dangerous. The urban middle classes were strongly opposed to the duel, as to all forms of violence. Their opposition was usually expressed on religious grounds, and they could point to the commandment, "Thou shalt not kill."

The first third of the nineteenth century was the great age of prize fighting in England. Boxing with the bare knuckles was the favorite form, but fighting with sticks and other weapons for a bet or prize still lingered on. The country magistrates charged with suppressing these matches were, for the most part, friendly to boxing, and they might sometimes be seen among the spectators. Large crowds went to remote places to see famous boxers perform. The monetary rewards of even successful fighters were usually small, though. Cockfighting and, to a less extent, bull

BULL BAITING

BEAR BAITING

From Henry Alken, *British Sports*, 1821.

baiting had their devotees, most of whom were betters. The Act against Cruelty to Animals which was passed in 1835 made the baiting of bulls illegal. This was another indication of an increasing opposition among the people of England to the grosser forms of cruelty.

Horse racing became of interest to more and more of the population. John Ashton, writing in the more sedate period when Queen Victoria was in her old age, mentions as "a curious incident of manners in the early century" the match races which were sometimes held between women jockeys. And he cites several of the names given to horses at this time as indicative of the current frivolity. One was called Jack Come Tickle Me.

The government by holding public lotteries encouraged at least one form of gambling. Private lotteries were illegal unless specifically authorized by act of Parliament, and such a license was difficult to obtain. The last public lottery in England was held in 1826; and ten years later it was forbidden to advertise any sort of lottery, whether the drawings were held within or without the country. That the laws against gambling houses could sometimes sting was shown in 1825, when Josiah Taylor, upon conviction, was sentenced to a year's imprisonment and a fine of £5,000 and was made to put up heavy securities to guarantee against a repetition of the offense. The prohibitory laws, nevertheless, did little or nothing to check the ever growing interest in games of chance.

The New Puritanism was slow to prevail against swearing, as an account in the *Annual Register* for 1834 of an incident which occurred in the Bow Street Court shows. A French cook was arraigned for disposing of red game contrary to law. "I don't know vat de devil goes up into the dining room," he is reported to have said, without rebuke. Then, after he had been fined, he remarked to the court, "Vel, I shall pay de money, but it is dam hard." Such language was evidently allowable from an inferior, or it would no doubt have been treated as contemptuous in this case. It is true that we don't find any indications of such a condition in Jane Austen's novels; but, after all, she was a maiden lady.

Thomas Bowdler, whose name has given a word to the English language, published in 1818 *The Family Shakespeare in Ten Volumes, in which nothing has been added to the original text; but those words and phrases are omitted which cannot with propriety be read in a family.* Bowdler later edited Gibbon in the same way, omitting chiefly those passages which he considered irreligious. He stated his guiding principle as follows: "If any word or expression is of such a nature that the first impression it excites is an impression of obscenity, that word ought not to be spoken nor written or printed; and, if printed, it ought to be erased."

Bowdler's work was attacked in his own lifetime for its prudishness and for its rude treatment of works of genius. Curiously, it was Swinburne who had a good word to say for Bowdler at the end of the century, declaring that this editor made it possible for imaginative children to read Shakespeare. Bowdler was not, indeed, the first to remove morally objectionable portions from classical works in reprinting them, and he was by no means the last. But whenever we speak of bowdlerizing, we are reminded of this lover of virtue and friend to Hannah More.

Literary prudery was fairly common in the early part of the nineteenth century. An "honored friend" of Coleridge's persuaded him to delete the word *bitch* which he originally used in "Christabel." The phrase *toothless mastiff bitch* became *toothless mastiff, which,* the context making such an easy change possible.

English pietists continued to attach a great deal of importance to Sunday observance. Raumer, a German who visited England in 1835, observes: "Singing, music, dancing, the drama, and all amusements which are addressed to our intellectual nature, are forbidden and denounced as schools of the Devil." He thought that such prohibitions fostered drunkenness and sexual irregularity on Sunday. A few years earlier, the elder Bulwer-Lytton declared that "the Sabbath is generally observed by all orders except the poorest." Some working people were forced to "desecrate" the day by laboring on it. There were factories in which it was customary for the regular operators of machines to clean and oil them on Sunday. It was not usual, though, for the mills to betray Sunday activity by emitting the ordinary noises.

Workmen who received their weekly wages on Saturday and then found themselves with an idle day before them usually proceeded to exchange a large part of their money for gin. The public houses were open late on Saturday night, and the law permitted them to keep open until eleven o'clock Sunday morning. Many moralists thought that the pay day should be changed.

As for the middle and upper classes, a number of observers in the 1830's agree that there was less drinking than there had been in the previous generation. Still, a quart of wine for each man after dinner was not considered excessive. An almost prohibitive war tax on beer (as high as 150 per cent of its value) was reduced for the purpose of weaning the lower classes away from distilled beverages. The high level of taxation resulting from the Napoleonic wars, together with various embargoes, had given a new stimulus to the smuggling trade, which was largely concerned with brandy and other potations.

Perhaps the example of the rich counted for something. At any rate, drunkenness declined among the poor soon after it ceased to be fashionable among the higher social orders. Gentlemen still sometimes fell under the table after dinner, but it was no longer an obligation for them to do so, except in old-fashioned circles.

The painter Isaac Cruikshank died in 1811 of alcoholism. His son George then gave his artistic talents, in large measure, to the work of preaching against drunkenness. His "Court of Love" (1812) shows Lady Hertford, drunk. on the Regent's knee, her husband looking on.

Opium-eating became, if not extremely common, a matter of general knowledge in England. In this connection, two great literary names, those of De Quincey and Coleridge, come to mind. Narcotic drugs of this class did not cause a serious moral problem until various synthetic forms were invented.

Sexual laxity prevailed in practically all walks of life during the early years of the nineteenth century. The London newspapers record a number of instances of wife-selling. An American visitor writes of the scene outside the Drury Lane Theatre in the 1830's: "Rogues, courtesans, and beggars thronged on every side, obstructed the way, and shocked the ear with words of disgusting indecency. Not satisfied with words, they assailed those who passed with gallantry of a more practical kind. Verily, there was some truth in that Frenchman, who, in explaining the difference between Paris and London, declared that it consisted chiefly in the fact that there were enjoyments which could be procured in Paris if you desired them; but in London you must submit to them, whether you would or not."

For the highest circles the lead of George, as Prince of Wales, Regent, and then as the fourth English king of his name, was paramount. A number of courtesans and concubines became enormously wealthy. Mrs. Theresa Berkeley is said to have retired from her profession with a capital of a hundred thousand pounds. To be sure, she was ingenious enough to immortalize her name by inventing the Berkeley horse, a device intended to serve the convenience of wealthy masochists and sadists. Instruments of chastisement had a prominent place at Mrs. Collett's, where the Prince Regent used to come, and at various other brothels and houses of assignation. Masochistic prostitution remained important in London long after the end of the Regency; and, in fact, it still exists.

In the days when the old Puritanism was struggling with the Renaissance Cavalier spirit, both sides were well represented in London. It was there that the merchants and master artisans looked on in horror while the courtiers went to the theatre and enjoyed numerous pleasures which could hardly be had in the country or in smaller cities. Then the Evangelical movement with which we connect the name of John Wesley won converts in London as well as in small towns and villages. But the fact remained that certain sorts of temptation were unavailable, or available only with difficulty, in the rural districts, while they were thrust upon Londoners. We find in the late eighteenth century and in the early nineteenth a number of frightened references to what Wordsworth called "the dissolute city." The romantic revival in literature was, at first, largely a turning from urban sophistication to the innocence of green fields and snow-capped mountains. Wordsworth's hero Michael was brought up virtuously in a lonely country district, but when he sought his fortune in the city, he "gave himself to evil courses" until he was driven "to seek a hiding-place beyond the seas."

The pious poet himself had once been led astray by enthusiasm for the French Revolution, and he had begotten an illegitimate daughter upon a Frenchwoman. He turned later against all things French and all things liberal and spent most of his long life "lamenting ancient virtues overthrown."

§ 3

John Keats revolted, like Wordsworth, against the eighteenth-century pseudoclassicism, but not out of any anxiety to preserve the simplicity of the English countryside. His love was Beauty, and he clutched at antique hedonism with all the sense of fresh discovery that had characterized the early leaders of the Renaissance. English prudery sometimes disgusted him, as the following extract from a dramatic critique he wrote in 1818 shows: "The names of old plays are Dantean inscriptions over the gates of Hell, Heaven, or Purgatory. Some of such enduring pathos that in these days we may not for decency utter them, 'honor dishonorable!' In these days we may but think of passion's seventh heaven, and but mention how crystalline the third is."

It might be argued with some show of reason that the inhibitions that his middle-class upbringing gave Keats improved his work. In any case, they gave him a delicacy of touch which helped to make some of his poems actually more voluptuous than anything that free-speaking Byron wrote.

Shelley loved Beauty too, but he cared more for Liberty, Equality, and Fraternity. His master, William Godwin, was an anarchist who had revolted against a stern Calvinistic creed. Godwin's moral doctrines differed widely in many respects from those generally received when he wrote (or, for that matter, from those generally received now); but though they were circulated fairly widely, they did not exert much influence except upon a few enthusiasts like Shelley. Indirectly, through Shelley's poems, they spoke and are still speaking to many impressionable, and mostly youthful, men and women.

Godwin considered truth one of the most important virtues and thought that even polite fictions about not being at home (or, as some of us would say, being "in conference") are extremely dangerous to society. So far he was no more revolutionary than Hannah More. More striking was his plea for freedom. He wished everybody to be permitted to speak and write freely and thought there should be no trials, whether criminal or civil, for libel and slander.

His most important book, *The Inquiry concerning Political Justice,* attacked the Established Church and the established State; but it was sold at so high a price that the poor could not buy it, and the authorities thought it unnecessary to prosecute Godwin. Besides, he spoke rather doubtfully about violent revolutions, as about the use of force in general.

Godwin believed in monogamous relations between the sexes, and in this he was conventional. But he did not think that a man and a woman should be sworn to love each other or even to live together all their lives. He was, in short, opposed to what is generally known as marriage, which seemed to him a form of bondage imposed by the Church and confirmed by the State. He did not think that any pattern of behavior should be forced upon people, no matter how good for them it might be.

Shelley, following Godwin, tells us in his poems that government and society are corrupting agencies, and that we ought to follow nature. The thought was Rousseau's before it was Godwin's. Shelley came under the influence of Godwin's philosophy while he was still a schoolboy. He soon learned to call himself an atheist, though this meant perhaps no more than that he refused to accept Christianity. In his poetry he played with the idea of two contending divine forces, one good and one evil.

Young Shelley set out naïvely to reform the world, to be perfectly sincere, and to be universally benevolent, according to the doctrines of Godwin. As an Oxford student he wrote and had printed a pamphlet on *The Necessity of Atheism.* It would have been bad enough if it had merely attacked Christanity. But it also put forward some of Godwin's most objectionable moral ideas, for instance; "'A husband and wife ought to continue so long united as they love each other; any law which should bind them to combination for one moment after the decay of their affection would be a most intolerable tyranny." Because of this essay Shelley was expelled from the university.

He married Harriet Westbrook; then, in accordance with his doctrine, having discovered that he no longer loved her, he went away. Harriet's suicide made it possible for him to enter once more into legalized marriage. His second wife was Mary Godwin, the daughter of his great philosopher by Mary Wollstonecraft. The Westbrooks petitioned that his two children should be taken from him because his atheistical and immoral opinions made him an unfit guardian for them. The Lord Chancellor by granting this petition confirmed the social ban on Shelley already existing.

Mary Wollstonecraft, afterward to be Mrs. Godwin, published in 1792 *A Vindication of the Rights of Women*. The book was daring, because even though the bluestockings had already appeared, it was not considered proper for a woman to make any important claims in favor of her sex. Horace Walpole described Miss Wollstonecraft as "a hyena in petticoats." Actually, she was an attractive and affectionate woman who had been forced to support herself and who saw her married sister living in a miserable, brutalized home.

Miss Wollstonecraft ventured to propose that women should enjoy opportunities for education and that they should be enabled to earn their own living if necessary. She did not suggest that men and women should be educated alike, and she never maintained that the two sexes are equal in intellectual capacity. Let us see how bold she could be: "I may excite laughter by dropping a hint, which I mean to pursue some future time, for I really think that women ought to have representatives, instead of being arbitrarily governed without having any direct shares allowed them in the deliberations of government."

Mary Wollstonecraft lived for a time, not formally married,

with an American named Gilbert Imlay, and a child was born to them. Later she met Godwin. When their child's birth was approaching, they went to church and became husband and wife. Godwin spoke apologetically to his friends about this violation of his principles. Ten days after the birth of the baby girl who was to become Mrs. Shelley, Mrs. Godwin died.

In the history of liberty, as in that of literature, a number of interesting names are connected with those of Godwin and Shelley. Of all the strange theories that came out of this circle, the feministic views of Mary Wollstonecraft Shelley have been most fully realized in practice. Indeed, her claims now seem extremely old-fashioned in their modesty, though they were bold and almost insolent in their time.

One of Shelley's friends, Thomas Love Peacock, maintained the tradition of Sterne, tinctured with Voltaire, in verse and prose satires. Hostile critics saw in his shoe "the cloven foot of infidelity." Peacock carried over into the Victorian age the spirit of aristocratic hedonism which developed in the time of the Regency.

Among the great romantic poets of the early nineteenth century, Byron stands closest to Shelley and to Keats. But Byron became a lord when he was still a boy; and, somewhat more than Shelley, altogether different in this respect from Keats, he was brought up in the aristocratic tradition. At Cambridge he found that the undergraduates were interested in pleasure much more than in scholarship. Mr. Drinkwater remarks that, at the wine parties he gave, Byron "was generally out-drunk with some ease by robuster performers." The greatest scholar who was then teaching at the university, Richard Porson, conducted himself in such a way as to disgust those who were not easily disgustable. Byron later said of Porson: "I never can recollect him except as drunk or brutal, and generally both; I mean in an evening. I have seen him, in a private party of undergraduates, take up his poker to them, and heard him use language as blackguard as his action."

Byron leaped almost overnight into prominence as a poet, and because he was a lord, public attention was all the more focused upon him. He was not, except at moments, a social idealist or even a romantic lover like Shelley. Ethel Colburne Mayne declares: "Byron, like most men of his time, was never out of intrigue, and never in love." Certainly he formed sexual attachments with a number of women in whom he had no poetic interest. He let servants and countesses, bluestockings and ignoramuses, come to him. Women forced themselves upon him, impelled by his handsome face and his fame as a poet, sometimes chiefly by the fact that he was a lord.

One of these was the eccentric Lady Caroline Lamb, addicted to extremely frank speech and to the drinking of brandy mixed with laudanum. Neither of these habits was extremely common on the part of ladies, but both had a certain vogue among the ultrafashionable.

Byron married, and then left his wife after a short period of cohabitation. It was then whispered within a select circle that the reason for the separation was Byron's incestuous love for his half-sister. This has never been proved, and in the nature of things it is unlikely that definite proof either way will ever be given. In any case, the matter is unimportant in the present connection.

The poet quickly lost his popularity in a wave of moral indignation. Macaulay wrote, not many years later, "We know of no spectacle so ridiculous as the British public in its periodical fits of morality." And he went on to point out that the feeling against Byron soon subsided. His poetic works became more popular than ever.

In at least one instance Byron played the moralist himself. Just as Sheridan had denounced the lascivious quadrille, he uttered harsh words about the waltz. This dance was, he felt sure, going to put an end to British virtue. "Now in loose waltz the thin-clad daughters leap," he declares, and some "display the free unfettered limb." Byron's concern for virtue in this instance is, at least in part, explicable by the fact that he had a deformed foot.

When English society turned against him, Byron took up in earnest the work of exposing contemporary cant and priggery.

THE WALSE

A caricature by James Gillray, 1810.

The Regency possessed an abundance of religious and moral hypocrites, and Byron's satire struck home to them. The poet sometimes seemed to enjoy playing the part of a martyr-masochist, as in the instance when he went out of the way to assert his authorship of an attack on the fat Prince which had first been published anonymously.

Byron's masterpiece, *Don Juan,* was calculated to offend British prudery, as the author knew. Moore and other friends advised him not to publish it. For a time he seemed to agree with them that this mock epic would not do for public circulation. Then he insisted that it should be printed, and without any cuts. The first edition did not, indeed, bear the name of either the author or the publisher, but there was no attempt to keep the names secret.

A great volley of abuse appeared immediately. An article in *Blackwood's Magazine* called Byron a fiend "laughing with detestable glee over the whole of the better and worse elements of which human life is composed." Byron himself said that the outcry was unprecedented and that he hardly dared to appear in public: "I was advised not to go to the theatres lest I should be hissed nor to my duty in Parliament lest I should be insulted by the way." The mob considered him immoral alike in his life and his writings; besides, they enjoyed immensely the quasi-privilege of jeering at a lord. People kept on reading Byron's poems, the "wicked" ones with the rest, but they did not approve of the poet's character. Byron's death was romantic, perhaps also heroic. Yet his statue was excluded from Westminster Abbey.

Byron's life was in various ways interlinked with those of most of the other important writers of his time. He engaged in a number of word battles with Southey, one of the men of letters who had changed violently from his liberal position as a result of the Reign of Terror in France. Southey, attacking Byron in 1821, said: "For more than half a century English literature has been distinguished by its moral purity, the effect, and in its turn, the cause of an improvement in national manners. A father might, without apprehension of evil, have put into the hands of his children any book which issued from the press, if it did not bear, either in its title-page or frontispiece, manifest signs that it was intended for the brothel." Southey expressed the opinion that "the publication of a lascivious book is one of the worst offenses against the well-being of society." In the same year that this attack appeared, a pirated edition of Southey's youthful revolutionary poem, *Wat Tyler,* was issued. Lord Eldon disposed of Southey's suit against the publishers with the ruling that he had no property rights in the book because of its immorality. This decision gave Byron ample material for satire on Southey's moral position with regard to other people's writings.

Byron's friend Thomas Moore was an Irishman and at least a nominal Roman Catholic. The legal profession was thrown open to Papists in 1793. Moore came to London to study law not many years later. He sang well, he possessed the social graces, and he wrote amorous poetry of evident merit. Soon he found himself a welcome visitor in the best circles. His *Anacreon* was dedicated by permission to the Prince of Wales, who was then still popular. His second book of poems, *The Poetical Works of the Late Henry Little,* which was published anonymously, aroused a little storm of abuse. As in the case of *Don Juan,* there was no real attempt to conceal the author's name. The *Edinburgh Review* called Moore "the most licentious of modern versifiers, and the most poetical of those who in our time had devoted their talents to the propagation of immorality"; and attributed to him "a cold-blooded attempt to corrupt the purity of unknown and unsuspecting readers." Moore thought it necessary to challenge the editor, Francis Jeffrey, to a duel; however, the police were notified in time to prevent the firing of any shots. A rumor spread that one of the pistols that were to be used in the duel was charged blank. Byron referred in a poem to "Little's leadless pistol." Again there was a challenge, but with no serious result. Moore became the friend of Byron, as he had already become of Jeffrey.

After Byron's death Moore published his biography. The noble poet was not just then very popular, and the life had a disappointing sale. Perhaps one of the contributing reasons for this was Moore's reticence about Byron's intimate life. Greville says, in his contemporary Diary: "But as to the life, it is no life at all; it merely tells you that the details of his life are not tellable, that they would be like those of Tilly and Casanova, and so indecent, and compromise so many people, that we must be content to look at his life through an impenetrable veil." In the reproduction of Byron's correspondence, asterisks and initials are often given instead of names, and many hiatuses are indicated. On the other hand, some later critics, for example, Mrs. Harriet Beecher Stowe, complain that Moore expresses no moral indignation over Byron's wickedness. He inquires quite calmly about the possibility that Byron really had a child when he wrote, while still a schoolboy, the poem called "To My Son."

Moore expressed the opinion, in 1802, that some of his own erotic poems might well, for the sake of prudence, have been omitted or modified. Yet I think that few contemporary moralists would find his treatment of love objectionable. Moore wrote enthusiastically about wine, but his drinking poems did not seem immoral in his own day. In some of his later satires Moore wrote against his old friend the Prince Regent.

For essentially this same offense Leigh Hunt suffered severe punishment. He and his brother published a political weekly called the *Examiner,* which was looked upon with suspicion by the authorities. The Hunt brothers were several times unsuccessfully prosecuted, once for an article which denounced the brutality of the floggings in the British Army. In 1812 a newspaper writer spoke of the Prince Regent as an "Adonis in loveliness." The *Examiner* thereupon pointed out that this Adonis was "a corpulent man of fifty." To this undoubted truth it was added that the Prince was, among other things, "a violator of his word, a libertine over head and ears in disgrace, a despiser of domestic ties, the companion of gamblers and demireps." The Hunts were each sentenced to a prison term and the paying of a heavy fine. Some of the most prominent literary men of the age came to visit Leigh Hunt in prison. He was well supplied with books, and he continued to edit the *Examiner.* The brothers refused to accept a pardon on the condition that they should promise to attack the Prince Regent no more.

Among the artists of this period perhaps Thomas Rowlandson most deserves our consideration. He was exceedingly fond of gambling, and he is said to have diced continuously for thirty-six hours on one occasion. In his caricatures he liked to delineate voluptuous women. As an illustrator he was most successful with Fielding, Sterne, and Smollett. Iwan Bloch says that Rowlandson would be in jail if he had first published his work in twentieth-century England or Germany.

The writers and the artist who have just been considered show us something of the moral standards that prevailed in the first third of the nineteenth century. It does not appear that they made any important changes in the lines of moral development. When, however, the Reverend Thomas H. Malthus published, in 1798, his *Principles of Population,* which was in some sort an answer to Godwin, he precipitated a discussion and brought about an interest which was to change, in an important respect, most people's conception of right and wrong. Malthus proved, or attempted to prove, that while population, unless checked, increases in geometric progression, food supplies increase only arithmetically. He earnestly desired the poor to consider that they could do away with much misery, disease, and warfare (such being the crude means used by the Divinity to keep the population of the world from growing faster than the food to feed them) if they voluntarily ceased to procreate by abstaining from sexual intercourse.

Presently others were wondering if it were not possible to limit the size of families in an artificial manner. Of course, infanticide and the use of various abortifacients and crude contraceptives had been known to men long before the time of Malthus, but Christian moralists had usually maintained that the killing of infants, born or unborn, constituted the deadly sin of murder. The Malthusian theory and the vulcanization of rubber together made the problem of population take on a new aspect.

In 1822 Francis Place issued a book in which he argued that workingmen should marry early, that they should live with their wives in the ordinary way of married people, but that they should take preventive steps to keep from being troubled with

THE SAD DISCOVERY, OR, THE GRACELESS APPRENTICE
A colored engraving by Thomas Rowlandson, 1809.

more children than they could afford to bring up. A group of radicals then began to distribute the "diabolical handbills," probably written by Place, which gave directions for preventing conception. Richard Carlisle and Robert Dale Owen were among the writers who next took up the argument in favor of what we now know as birth control. Malthus did not expect his book to produce a flock of neo-Malthusians or he probably would not have published it. It stirred up material for many wrathful sermons in another unexpected way when it led Charles Darwin to apply the Malthusian principle to the solution of a troublesome biological problem.

§ 4

From 1820 to 1830 George IV was King of England. During this decade his confidential agent was kept busy settling the debts that he had incurred as the Prince of Wales. Despite the vast sums that had slid between his fingers, George had the reputation of being rather stingy to his mistresses and others. At his accession, nevertheless, he issued instructions that his wife should be offered an allowance of fifty thousand pounds annually on condition that she should remain away from Great Britain and abandon the title of queen.

Caroline refused to accept this offer. Many in England clamored for her return. Greville tells how King George attended the Ascot races and, amid much cheering, heard a voice out of the crowd, "Where's the Queen?" At a theatre a less respectful voice cried out to royalty, "Where's your wife, Georgie?" But the King was not particularly unpopular, except with very moral people. His rough jokes and his general looseness of conduct did not hurt his reputation much with the upper classes. The fact that his manners did not improve with age was somewhat worse. There is a story about his going, when he was Regent, where he had not been invited. By way of rebuke to him, his companion was asked, "Who's your fat friend?"

When Caroline returned to England, unbidden by her husband, the London mob expressed a great deal of sympathy for her. King George decided to ask for a divorce. If it had been expedient, he might, to be sure, have shown that Caroline was not his wife, because of his marriage to Mrs. Fitzherbert. Instead, he asked Lord Liverpool to introduce into Parliament a bill of divorce on the ground of Caroline's adultery. Sporting men, who had wagered heavily that the Queen would or would not come back to England, now laid bets on the result of the King's attempt. Much evidence of a damaging nature was produced against Caroline, but the London populace and public opinion in general favored her, for the reason that her husband had never treated her fairly. If she had entered into illicit relations with other men, the great fault was still George's. It added no dignity to the kingly office to have the royal dirty linen spread out in the sight of the nation and the world, and it was finally considered advisable to let the Divorce Act drop. Caroline did much to alienate the sympathy of the people when she attempted to force her way into Westminster Abbey at George's coronation with the avowed purpose of demanding her own crown as queen. Then, five days later, she died; and she was hailed as a martyr. George IV appeared seldom in public during the last years of his life. He was anxious not to disclose his fat flabbiness. When he took off his corsets, his paunch hung down like a sack.

George's successor was his brother William, who had long been known as "the royal sailor." We meet him in Fanny Burney's Diary, forcing large quantities of champagne upon everybody at his table, using language which was represented by "— —." Suddenly elevated to the throne, he brought to it the manners of an eighteenth-century man-of-war. He is said to have cried out to his visitor, King Leopold of Belgium, "God damn it, why don't you drink wine? I never allow anybody to drink water at my table." William IV had many children, but not one among them was of legitimate birth. Perhaps his chief interest when he was king was in supporting the turf and horse-breeding.

The sons of George III gave, to the sober-minded middle classes, the impression of being all selfish libertines and blunderers. In 1809 the Duke of York's mistress had been accused of selling military commissions for her own profit and that of others. It was assumed by many that the Prince, too, had benefited by this alleged piece of corruption. William IV's rude manners then proved shocking, for the upper classes were just then paying a great deal of attention to the social graces. It was no wonder that Greville wrote in his Diary at Victoria's accession: "The young Queen behaves with a decorum and propriety beyond her years, and with all the sedateness and dignity the want of which was so conspicuous in her uncles."

Politically and socially, events moved fast in England during the years between 1800 and 1837. In 1800 Ireland was included with Great Britain into the United Kingdom. At that time Pitt proposed the removal of political disabilities from the Irish Catholics, but King George and the great majority of Englishmen and Scotchmen were then still afraid of popery. The Protestant Dissenters in Ireland had been made eligible to hold public office two decades before; but the great majority of the Irish, remaining steadfast Roman Catholics, were without political rights. In 1812 the House of Commons voted for Catholic emancipation throughout the United Kingdom. The Lords (who in this instance seem to have represented public opinion better than the Commons) were opposed. Toward the end of the next decade the last of the laws discriminating against Protestant Nonconformists in the matter of political privileges were repealed. Then it was made possible for Roman Catholics to sit in Parliament and to occupy almost any executive position in the State. George IV opposed the law admitting Catholics to public office, but in vain. The royal veto power had become merely nominal.

By 1800 the British House of Commons had lost all claim to be regarded as a body truly representing the people of England. The great cities which had sprung up as a result of the Industrial Revolution sent few or no members. Towns which had once been of importance but which had degenerated into hamlets or less than hamlets still sent representatives. These were actually controlled by various great landlords. Seats in Parliament were offered for sale at private or public auctions.

In 1809 Sir Francis Burdett met with little support when he urged parliamentary reform. He was imprisoned in the Tower for a time by order of the House of Commons after he had

MONSTROSITIES OF 1827

A caricature by George Cruikshank.

described that body as "part of our fellow-subjects collected together by means which it is not necessary to describe." Somewhat later the masses of the people became interested in the reform of Parliament. They had other grievances as well. New machines appeared almost daily, and their immediate effect was to throw thousands out of work. The proletariat gathered in mobs to clamor for bread or to burn objectionable machinery. A number of repressive acts were passed, and for several years after 1817 there was probably less freedom of expression in England than at any time in the preceding century.

William Cobbett, whose twopenny newspaper was addressed to the lower orders, found himself obliged to give up his radical propaganda and flee to America. William Hone, because he had written satirical pieces against the party in power, was accused of having blasphemously parodied the Litany, the Athanasian Creed, and the official Church Catechism; but his case aroused a great deal of public sympathy and he was acquitted. It was pointed out that some of the writers on the government side had written parodies which were no less irreverent than Hone's. Blasphemy was treated as a grave offense, and only five years before Hone's trial Lord Ellenborough had sentenced a convicted blasphemer to stand in the pillory for eighteen periods of two hours each. Richard Carlisle, a bookseller, was often in trouble for advancing heretical views. Because his employees were constantly being dragged off by the police for the crime of selling irreligious and immoral books, Carlisle finally had automatic vending devices installed in his shop. It was he who kept Tom Paine's writings in the public eye. John Stuart Mill began his labors in favor of freedom of discussion in 1823. He then wrote five articles. The newspaper which published three of them considered the rest too outspoken.

Henry Crabb Robinson recorded in his Journal for 1818 that Hazlitt, in a lecture, "drew an ingenious but not very intelligible parallel between Swift, Rabelais, and Voltaire, and even eulogized the modern infidel. So indiscreet and reckless is the man!" Six years later Robinson heard Coleridge, at a dance, speak of "the growing hypocrisy of the age, and the determination of the higher classes, even in science, to repress all liberality of speculation. Sir Humphry Davy has joined the party, and they are now patronizing Granville Penn's absurd attack on geology as being against revealed religion. It seems that these ultrareligionists deem the confirmation of the great fact of the deluge from the phenomena within the crust of the globe as inconsistent with the Mosaic account."

Hazlitt, in *The Spirit of the Age,* says that his time was one when honesty, and even the name of honesty, were exceedingly rare. Looking back, it does not seem that laughter "at the very name of honesty" was quite so common as he declares. The virtues were, nominally, much honored. Moral pretense was everywhere, and the age was willing to worship Mrs. Grundy, though not always ready to follow her advice. Outspoken libertinism was certainly on the decline soon after 1830, the year of Hazlitt's death.

If we allow for personal idiosyncrasies, we can learn something about the tendencies of the New Puritanism in the first half of the nineteenth century from Cobbett's book, *Advice to Young Men and (incidentally) to Young Women.* Cobbett spoke primarily to the lower orders but also found an audience among the middle classes. He wrote against luxury in general. For him the word included tea and coffee as well as wine. People asked him, he said, why he laid so much stress upon these things: " 'Lord, *what* is a glass of wine?' " And he told them that it is everything, because "it demands all other unnecessary expenses." Cobbett disapproved of cards and of all forms of gambling. To dancing he did not object. He felt that the theatre might become an educational and moral force, but he objected to the censorship of his day, which was intended to accomplish little more than to keep the stage from being used for attacks upon the Conservative government.

The Reform Act of 1832 put political power into the hands of the middle classes. The great masses, who had clamored for a wider franchise, found that the vote was still denied to them. In fact, the merchants and manufacturers who now became prominent in public life were not democrats any more than the country gentlemen who had controlled the House of Commons earlier in the century and in previous ages. In considering the moral history of England during Victoria's reign we must remember that the urban middle classes were dominant, at least until about 1890.

A new interest in Sunday observance appeared in the last years of William IV's reign, as an earnest of early-Victorian pietism. Parties on Sunday were frowned upon, even in the highest society; and Cabinet meetings were no longer held on that day. When the railroads were opened, vigorous attempts were made to keep them from "defiling the Sabbath." The operation of third-class cars on Sunday seemed especially objectionable, for it was still held that people who belonged to the upper classes or to the middle ranks of life were entitled to many moral privileges which it was not safe to let the lower orders have. The pietists finally succeeded in having Sunday mail delivery reduced to a minimum. There was a great deal of controversy about the right of clergymen to be driven to church in carriages. Old Testament texts were produced to show that horses should not be worked on the Sabbath, and many zealots contended that ministers ought to support the Bible by walking to and from church every Sunday.

CHAPTER IX

MRS. GRUNDY SITS UPON THE THRONE

§ 1

VICTORIA, who became Queen in 1837, had been brought up like a German girl of the middle classes. Because her uncles furnished a horrible example, particular stress was laid upon her religious and moral education. She was taught to be a good little girl and to accept the creed of the Church of England. Until she became queen, at the age of seventeen, Victoria's bed was kept in her mother's room. All her actions were closely supervised. And when she acquired freedom with her throne, it did not go to her head. She continued to try hard to be very, very good.

When Victoria was crowned, William Lamb, Viscount Melbourne, had been Prime Minister for three years. His wife was Byron's Caroline Lamb. He himself had twice been named corespondent in divorce actions, and twice vindicated. Lord Melbourne was in the habit of frequently besprinkling his speech with a vigorous "Damn!" or two. He had great difficulty in keeping back his profanity when he conversed with young Queen Victoria about official matters. Soon he was engaged in a mild quarrel with the Queen because she would not permit the men who dined in the palace to sit alone over their wine very long. Melbourne belonged to the old school of gentlemen, who thought they should not leave the table until some members of the company were under it. Victoria had been disgusted by her uncle William's drunkenness, and she therefore objected to hard drinking. She also disliked the old custom because it left the ladies to shift for themselves. Now that she was queen, she thought that she might properly insist that her male guests should join her quickly after dinner.

At Victoria's court the flippant attitude about flirtations, amours, and concubines which had distinguished the palace life of a number of previous English sovereigns went distinctly out of fashion. "We are not amused," the Queen's reply to stories and remarks which she did not consider sufficiently genteel, was enough to squelch all unduly light forms of wit and humor. When the Queen visited Brighton in 1843, she found it too gay and the inhabitants "indiscreet," for which reason she never visited the resort again.

Victoria chose her German cousin, Prince Albert, to be her consort, thus insuring that middle-class domesticity should prevail at court. Marriage did not change the Queen's high opinion of Albert's handsomeness and cleverness. He was something of a plodder, not stupid but not particularly brilliant, interested in a great many fields of knowledge, impressed with the virtue of working hard. Contemporary diaries tell us how the Queen used to sit working at her embroidery while the Prince Consort read books of history to her. Victoria, because she was a sovereign, had more reason than other women to be interested in history. Otherwise, the scene was almost typically middle-class. Victoria had a rather unqueenlike concern for all sorts of domestic matters. Wherever she went, she wanted to see the kitchens. In having a variety of intellectual interests but receiving knowledge and wisdom from the mouth of her husband, she was, to some extent, expressing the new feminism, still modest and shy, but destined to become bolder.

Admirers of the good little girl who became queen still tell us that the excellence of her character made the United Kingdom of Great Britain and Ireland very, very good. As Edith L. Elias puts it, "a virtuous queen made a virtuous people." We shall see that there were limits to the goodness of Victorian England. Besides, a noticeable increase in pietism had taken place in the years just preceding her accession. We must not overemphasize her early influence, especially in view of the fact that Victoria was not always very popular. While she was still young and inexperienced, she seemed to be involved in a minor palace scandal which made many powerful people angry. Lady Flora Hastings, who was connected with the court, was said to be with child, though unmarried. The royal physician, who enjoyed Victoria's confidence, examined Lady Flora. After much hemming and hawing he decided that she was actually pregnant. This turned out to be a mistake. Soon after, Lady Flora Hastings died. Public opinion was with her family and sharply against the Queen.

Victoria seems not to have been particularly at fault in this affair. Perhaps she is more blameworthy in some other matters which caused her to become unpopular for a time. She was never such a heroine to her people as Elizabeth had been. She was a short little girl who grew up into a plain dumpling of a woman. Her efforts to be at once good and dignified were always a little amusing. She did not stir the imagination. If poetry was addressed to her, it was didactic rather than poetic. Of course, the people who valued "virtue" above all other things were pleased that she, and not flirtatious Queen Bess, sat upon the throne in their day.

Victoria was a queen to please the middle classes. The New Puritans found that the balance of political power was with them. The rise of commerce and industry at the expense of agriculture made the honest *bourgeois* the real rulers of England. They were almost always satisfied with the homely (in both senses), industrious, uninspired woman who sat on the throne. Of course, she had little actual authority, but the urban middle classes felt that she was setting a good example.

The aristocrats were reluctant to consider the Queen their social leader. Indeed, she was not very anxious to enjoy this position. She considered the nobles as a class depraved pleasure-seekers. There was a moment when Melbourne's wrath about Victoria's careful cultivation of the proprieties burst out in an exclamation: "This damned morality will ruin everything!"

The court was seldom gay. Victoria and Albert considered it their duty to devote a large part of their time to State papers, questions of diplomatic policy, and all sorts of governmental affairs. The Prince Consort, studying English constitutional history in a half-pedantical sort of way, thought that a great deal of power still remained with the monarch. As a matter of

THE BRIDAL MORN

Victoria and Albert, February 10, 1840. After a drawing by F. Lock.

fact, George III, by using the tricks of the cheap politician, had abandoned almost all the constitutional prerogative that still remained with the king at his accession. Victoria made occasional attempts to recover it, but her own political ineptitude, her husband's wrong advice, and the growing tendency toward democracy combined to make the Queen lose (for herself and her successors) virtually all of the modicum of authority that she had inherited. Probably the best-known of the disputes between the Queen and the ministers responsible to Parliament arose over what was known as the bedchamber question. If the queen was to have any influence at all, it seemed to Victoria that she ought to be able to control her palace personnel. Yet it was customary for the ministry in power to appoint ladies of the bedchamber whose husbands were identified with the party in power.

In other words, the Queen was not permitted to decide for herself what ladies should surround her. After she had become accustomed to one set, an election seemed to require that they should be turned out and replaced by others. Precedents for this were laid before Victoria, but she insisted that the fact of her being a queen in her own right changed matters. For a while she seemed to have gained her point: Peel resigned, and Melbourne, whom she had learned to like, returned to office, keeping the old ladies of the bedchamber. But in the end Victoria had to accept the principle of responsible government, with the implication it had acquired that the Liberals were to put their own ladies into the bedchamber after they had defeated the Conservatives, and that Conservative ladies were to take charge of the Queen's apartments when their party was in power.

Several times when it became known that the Queen was attempting to meddle with foreign affairs, republicanism acquired a certain strength in England. In short, the people of England, even the middle classes, did not always consider the Queen a perfect exemplar. She was subjected to keen criticism; and Prince Albert, chiefly because he was a foreigner, was regarded with a certain amount of suspicion. Those who knew him could testify that he was anxious to promote the welfare of England, though he might blunder about a little in his efforts; one of his earliest was a study of British agriculture. Albert's figure, like Victoria's, was a drab one. The domestic virtues, which the pair personified, may be very important. They may, as ministers and political orators so often tell us, be the very foundation upon which the greatness of nations is built, the very pillars of civilization, and so on *ad infinitum*. Let all this be granted, and the fact remains that the domestic virtues are neither heroic nor thrilling. Even the middle-class Victorians were hardly able to consider them so.

Shortly after the Queen was married to her cousin, Lord Melbourne assured her that Albert would soon be flirting with the ladies of the palace, although it was still too early for that sort of thing. But Victoria never caught her husband ogling the ladies, and there is no record that anybody else ever did. To be sure, little squabbles sometimes arose between husband and wife, usually occasioned by the fact that Albert's official inferiority to his wife hurt his masculine vanity. The story goes that Victoria was once heard knocking at Albert's locked door. He asked, "Who is there?" and she replied, "The Queen." Again and again he asked the same question and she made the same reply. But finally she answered, "Your wife, Albert," and the door was opened. Such *bourgeois* tiffs in the middle-class court gave the hedonistic aristocracy and the equally pleasure-loving proletariat abundant material for laughter.

Characteristically, Albert took up the work of creating a sentiment among the upper classes against dueling, which was repugnant to the new Evangelicals as it had been to the old Puritans. The Prince Consort was especially anxious to put an end to duels between officers of the Army and Navy, and he worked out a scheme for the establishment of courts of honor to settle matters which usually led to armed combats. Though no courts of honor were set up, dueling did actually decrease, in civil and military circles alike. Perhaps Albert's agitation did not accelerate the change much. It did no harm, at any rate. Juries stopped treating deaths resulting from duels as justifiable homicides, no matter how closely the traditional code of honor had been followed. The members of the middle classes believed

PRINCE ALBERT THE BRITISH FARMER

A caricature by John Leech in *Punch*, 1843. Reproduced by permission of the
Proprietors.

that aristocrats should give up their last claims to feudal rights by bringing their differences before the regular courts instead of settling them themselves with swords or pistols.

The upper classes, too, had duties to perform, according to middle-class opinion, and the support of law and justice was not the least of these. Were not Victoria and Albert, whatever their faults might be, devoted to virtue and public service? And was it not incumbent upon peers and squires to follow their example? In these days of transition the doctrine that nobility imposes obligations—always honored largely in the breach—was in some danger of being forgotten entirely.

The boozing, fox-hunting country gentleman was slow to pass out of the picture. The line separating the upper part of the middle classes from the lower aristocracy tended to become shadowy under Victoria. Many men who became rich through industrial or commercial careers bought titles or other honors. It was even simpler for them to buy land, and the ownership of large estates was the traditional mark of an English aristocrat. The new landowners were often anxious to be horsy and solicitous about the preservation of ancient customs, by way of proving that they were not mere upstarts.

At the public schools and the universities young men who had money derived from trade were looked upon with a certain amount of condescension. But this feeling became weaker, especially when the new aristocracy and the old began to inter-marry. The middle classes were but little inclined to favor democracy. Having won political power for their own order, they did not like to extend it to workingmen. And they believed in class distinctions, though they tended to feel that wealth should be considered at least as much as ancient lineage. The Liberals became exceedingly conservative, and it was the Conservatives, led by Disraeli, who gave the ballot to the laboring man. Coventry Patmore indignantly wrote about "the year of the great crime," that is, 1867,

> When the false English nobles and their Jew,
> By God demented, slew
> The Trust they stood twice pledged to keep from wrong.

Disraeli stood out in the sober Victorian days as a blaze of color, wearing green velvet trousers and a canary waistcoat, his hair in ringlets. Perhaps this was part of his conservatism, to appear like a Regency beau when the New Puritan browns and grays and blacks were beginning to make all men seem to wear a common sadness. The time came when this gaudy, bejeweled grandson of Israel dazzled the Queen, and she came perilously close to falling in love with him.

Her own influence, to be sure, was never exerted in favor of gay costumes. She had to be careful what she wore herself, on account of her figure. Bright colors would have emphasized her dumpiness and utterly destroyed all her claims to dignity. At best, she never had much *chic* or style. Her example was generally opposed to the employment of artificial aids to beauty, and in this she was supported by the Evangelical preachers.

The use of cosmetics seemed suddenly to become unrespectable. Red and white were still added to complexions, but furtively, and often with whatever materials lay close at hand. Women tried to make the most of their natural skins and put veils, bonnets, and parasols between their faces and the sun. Englishwomen looked to Paris for the fashions, but made them soberly Victorian before adopting them. Perfumes and ointments which genteel English ladies, and gentlemen as well, had once thought it no shame to use were abandoned to prostitutes and sporty concubines. In theory, it became disgraceful for respectable women to attract men by means of bodily beauty; in fact, it was hardly conceded that ladylike females possessed such gross things as bodies.

There were, nevertheless, in the early years of Victoria's reign, women who worked nearly naked pulling coal cars in English mines. Neither in the factories nor in domestic service, almost surely not in their own homes, did working girls enjoy much privacy. In the case of the unmarried women of the urban middle classes the prudery which arose might possibly be based upon the innocence of ignorance. This could seldom be the case in the lower orders of society. Profit came first with the industrial capitalists. It seemed to be a necessary part of good business that women should be turned into naked-breasted beasts of burden. Next came morality, asserting that women are angels, not animals, and have no such unmentionable parts as legs and thighs. There were, to be sure, some moralists who did not own any stock in mining companies and who secured the enactment of laws regulating the labor of women. A willingness to remain sightless before facts and to see only conventional representations sometimes seemed to be characteristic of the Victorian period. This was displayed in such freaks of prudery as that which turned a wine-cooler, in polite speech, into a "sarcophagus."

It must not be inferred that there was no honest and intelligent idealism during Victoria's reign, or that conscious hypocrisy was far greater than it is now or than it has been at other times in England. But it was certainly true that the persons who derived personal profit from the exploitation of others were unwilling to abandon the conditions that made this possible. One or two conspicuous exceptions do not destroy the truth of this generalization.

There were limitations to the prudery of the Victorian period, as we shall see in this and the following chapter. In the early years of Victoria's reign William Etty was continuing to paint his nudes. To be sure, he usually depicted mythological scenes, by way of justifying his boldness in presenting undraped women. Still, it was evident that he was interested in the naked body, not in the Victorian plurality of petticoats. Etty prepared a scheme of decoration for a garden house at Buckingham Palace, but the Queen and others concerned could not quite bring themselves to approve his "immodesty." There were, however, many Englishmen of the time who considered it entirely proper to paint or model nudes or to look at works of art which were not bedraped by way of proving their morality. Indeed, all sorts of moral principles were in circulation, though some of them were confined to small circles.

Communication with the important cities of Continental Europe became easier, and ideas filtered in more rapidly than ever before from France, Germany, Italy, and Belgium. Probably the German influence was the greatest. This was not due entirely to the favor of Albert and Victoria. The middle classes of Great

YOUTH ON THE PROW AND PLEASURE AT THE HELM

After a painting by William Etty in the National Gallery.

Britain found their nearest kin in the *Bürgerstand* of Germany. The aristocracy generally looked toward France, with its livelier hedonism. Sometimes there was great interest in Italy because of the conflict between anticlerical liberalism and the papacy.

Many events occurred in Victoria's reign to broaden the outlook of the English people. Still, contact with foreign cultures and with new ideas did not always increase tolerance or even understanding. The travelers often returned thanking God that they were sons and daughters of Britannia, not wicked Hindus or Frenchmen or Americans. Comparatively few came back to find that theirs was not the best of all possible countries and to smile knowingly at the polite conventions. Conformity was easiest and most profitable, and the rebels against current morality had often to pay well for their daring.

Professor Foakes Jackson, in an essay on "Mid-Victorianism," remarks: "The English race has always had a bias in favor of what is known as Puritanism, not only in religion but in life. I think it may be said of us that we dislike intensely to have a thing forbidden by law, but love to have many forbidden by custom."

Let us grant at once that tea-table gossip had much to do with the maintenance of prudishness. But it cannot be denied that the authorities did their best to support Mrs. Grundy. During Victoria's reign a number of laws directed against various petty moral offenses were enacted, but the new spirit showed itself still more in the harsh enforcement of old ones. In England, as in America, it is always possible to resurrect a great deal of half-forgotten legislation in response to an indignant moral flurry. There were standards of conduct which the Victorian police labored to enforce, as there were others which belonged to particular classes or castes and for which the greatest penalty was social ostracism.

It is said that a little girl, under the rule of the good Victoria, once remarked to her governess that she had run around a lot and was sweating. She was reproved with the words: "My dear child, only animals sweat; men perspire, but young ladies merely glow." We must not forget that, while this story, literally true or not, does tells us about the manners and taboos that were cultivated in some English circles, most girls grew up without governesses to instruct them in such fine points. A great many were in such circumstances that they could by no means pretend to be merely glowing. They had to perspire like men, at the very least.

Many great inventions and applications of new scientific principles revolutionized the lives of some of Victoria's subjects. However, the domestic labors of women were not, to any considerable extent, made lighter. Housewives who did their own work had little time for the cultivation of the subtler forms of gentility. On the farms of England the animals performed their natural functions in spite of Mrs. Grundy. It does not appear that fashionable ignorance or even the urban verbal taboos had much hold upon farmers' daughters. There are to this day English country districts where new vogues penetrate very slowly and the customs of a century or two ago prevail. In such places respectability has a meaning, and usually an important one, but the standards of respectability are not precisely those which prevail in London.

During most of the nineteenth century such isolation existed in a comparatively large part of England. The gentility of the urban middle classes was without meaning for many thousands of country folk. For somewhat different reasons it was not shared by the city proletarians. They lived in crowded tenements. Their homes were not their castles, because the walls of privacy were down. They could not easily wear masks. Indeed, the one great offense among them was for an individual to pretend to be better than his or her neighbors.

With the rise of political democracy came a more clearly evinced tendency on the part of working people to regard their superiors and the moral principles they maintained more critically. To be sure, servants and laborers had always known that the middle and upper classes were humanly imperfect. Under Victoria, new educational opportunities for the poor reduced their illiteracy and enabled them to express themselves in understandable language. The general availability of schools did a great deal to blur caste lines. They still exist, of course, and the speech of the poor cockney or the rural laborer usually marks him off from the aristocrat. To have attended a board school (or what we in America call a public school) is no high social recommendation. The board schools were founded only in 1870, and during most of Victoria's reign it was difficult for the sons of the poor to obtain more than the veriest rudiments of an education.

That people should "know their places" was axiomatic, but it was an axiom applied chiefly to domestic servants and factory operatives. The middle classes displayed an increasing unwillingness to consider the aristocrats their superiors. They argued that England stood first in morality and commerce, and that the middle classes had made the country preëminent in both regards. Hostility between the upper and middle classes, especially between the landowners and the industrialists, enabled the lower classes to obtain many political and social ameliorations.

Great Britain was at peace during most of Victoria's reign—in theory, at least, for there was usually trouble in one or another part of the far-flung Empire. The Opium War against China did not seem to be invested on the British side with any high moral principles. It arose out of a desire on the part of the Chinese authorities to suppress the traffic in opium among their people. The British merchants of Canton insisted upon their sacred right to import the drug from India, and finally a pretext (or perhaps it was a good reason) for war appeared. China was forced, finally, to give Hongkong, certain trading privileges, and a cash indemnity to the United Kingdom. After a second war, China formally recognized the opium trade.

There is not room here to tell the complete story of British imperialism, and perhaps it is unnecessary to contrast the high moral standards of modern Great Britain with certain actual occurrences in countries which have not had the advantage of Christian civilization or that of the English language and tradition. I think it is fair to say that profit has always been the dominant motive in British imperialism, as it has been in the imperialism of other countries.

Good British patriots have discovered the high moral purposes which, it seems, have always distinguished the imperialism of England. The British undertook the work of spreading civilization, we are told, without regard for possible profits, without any shrinking from danger and hardship.

The loss of the important North American colonies during the late eighteenth century eventually brought about a change in the administration of the English-speaking dominions. Most of them were allowed self-rule during Victoria's reign. Australia was for a time little more than a penal settlement, but it presently came to be dominated by voluntary immigrants. There was a time when most of the servants were convicts. Practically all female domestics were virtual prostitutes, save for the Irishwomen who had been transported for political offenses. After a time Australia became as orderly and as strict in morals as any of the other self-governing dominions in the Empire.

It seemed anomalous to some people when Christian England became the ally of Moslem Turkey against Christian Russia in the Crimean War. Again it became apparent that pounds-shillings-pence played a more important part in British foreign policy than religious considerations. The days of sectarian warfare were over, although commercial and imperialistic rivalries still could give rise to hostilities.

Pious zeal did not disappear, however. It was manifested especially in strict Sunday observance. With the exception of Scotland, England observed the day more stringently than any other European country. On the Continent a great deal of business was done at Sunday fairs and markets, and recreations were almost everywhere permitted after church services. But Victorian England usually frowned upon worldly occupations of all sorts for the first day of the week.

In 1856, when a bill providing for the opening of the National Gallery and the British Museum on Sunday was defeated, Greville wrote in his Diary: "Cant and Puritanism are in the ascendant, and it will be well if we can escape more stringent measures against Sunday occupations and amusements. It is stated that the Sabbatarians are so united and numerous that they can carry any election!" Military bands gave Sunday concerts until Palmerston agreed to the Archbishop of Canterbury's request that they should be silenced. A royal proclamation prohibited Victoria's "loving subjects, of whatever degree or quality soever, from playing on the Lord's-day, at dice, cards, or any other game whatsoever," either in public or in private. It also forbade the selling of alcoholic beverages on Sunday while church services were being conducted. Taine, who visited England frequently in the 1860's, says that although the doors of taverns were closed, drinking went on in the back rooms while the sermons were being preached.

Some early-Victorian pietists considered it irreligious to build railroads or to ride on them at any time. To be sure, the resistance to railroads gradually decreased, but similar opposition was shown to various other innovations. Old-fashioned people argued that the good old English vigor and morality would be broken down if communal isolation were destroyed. Some feared that what they called the depravity of London would be extended to farms and villages. (We must not, indeed, jump to the conclusion that the moral standards of the large cities were laxer than those of the rural districts.) In such conservatism religious reasons often went hand in hand with the desire to preserve vested interests. The landlords and the manufacturers thought they would be better off if the common people were kept ignorant, provincial, and pious. The members of the upper and middle classes sometimes had a vague feeling that if the Londoners spent their Sundays like the Parisians, they would also build barricades in the streets and set up communes.

§ 2

It was a great surprise to the ardent supporters of rural isolation to discover, when the first statistics on the subject were issued, that the rate of illegitimate births per thousand births was considerably higher in certain agricultural districts than it was in London and other large cities. To be sure, the urban centers had much more prostitution, and brothel women are comparatively infertile. As between city and country the bastardy statistics did not show very accurately the relative prevalence of illicit sexual intercourse. But they did seem to show that the women in rural districts were no chaster than those of the great cities.

Some of the brothels of London, such as the one kept by Kate Hamilton, were well known in the early Victorian period. Red lights in front indicated the nature of these places. Cremorne Gardens and a number of other resorts attracted practically no women except professional prostitutes. Taine thought there were about fifty thousand harlots in London in 1870. Reliable statistics on the subject are not to be had, however. Colquhoun, a magistrate of the city, estimated that there were fifty thousand prostitutes as early as 1796. The estimates for 1840 ran as high as eighty thousand. Sometimes the figures were much lower. For example, the London Metropolitan Police thought there were 2,071 well-dressed prostitutes in brothels in 1841, only 921 in 1857; 1,994 well-dressed prostitutes walking the streets in 1841, 2,616 in the latter year; while the number of harlots "infesting low neighborhoods" went down from 5,344 to 5,063 in this same period. According to these estimates, prostitution declined somewhat, especially that carried on in brothels.

But, admittedly, the lists from which the police statistics were compiled were incomplete. Perhaps there were in London during early Victorian days ten thousand regular prostitutes in addition to many women who worked at some trade or were employed as domestic servants but who derived part of their income from prostitution. According to the common law of England, open and notorious lewdness and the keeping of a brothel were both crimes. But most Victorian Englishmen who ventured to think about such matters were of the firm opinion that prostitution was a necessary evil. There were people who disagreed sharply with this view, but many of them belonged to the class which considered it improper to discuss sex, even in vague generalities; and their views, finding no open expression, were altogether unimportant.

There was one serious attempt at the hygienic control of

prostitution, under the Contagious Disease Act of 1864. Although the experiment, so far as it was carried, was reported to be successful, the law was soon repealed, in response to an agitation led mostly by strong individualists who objected to governmental regulation. Later there was considerable clamor for the total suppression of the venereal traffic. The number of brothels, though probably not the number of prostitutes, declined. In London and other large cities it was never difficult for a man to find a harlot. Sometimes, indeed, it was hard to keep from being seized by one. Liverpool seemed, in the middle of Victoria's reign, to have more prostitutes in proportion to its population than any other important city in England. This was chiefly because of the large number of seamen always to be found there.

The procuring of attractive young women for brothels was a business of some importance. According to contemporary accounts, bawds even went to churches and Sunday schools to make the acquaintance of girls whom they might induce to become prostitutes. It is a curious commentary on the opinion that sermons and Bible lessons offer some sort of insurance against the loss of "virtue."

A certain amount of importation and exportation of girls existed during the Victorian period. While English young women were induced to go to Hamburg or Paris, German and French girls were brought to Liverpool and London. The advantages to the brothel keepers of such an interchange were several. It was felt that a prostitute far away from her relatives and friends, in a country with whose laws, customs, and language she was unfamiliar, would necessarily be docile. She would not leave the brothel to set up for herself, she could not protest effectively against being cheated by the managers. Moreover, the patrons of brothels tired of the old faces and were constantly asking for new girls. The foreign trade in women supplied this demand. It is true that fraud entered occasionally into these emigrations and immigrations, but force was very seldom used.

The Industrial Revolution brought about increased poverty and crowding in the cities. Both these factors made the recruiting

[269]

of prostitutes somewhat easier. In the sewing trades, in mid-Victorian London, women and girls had to work hard for fourteen hours a day to earn from half a dollar to two or three dollars weekly. Although many commodities were cheaper than they are to-day, such a wage was not enough to provide sufficient food and decent shelter. Very few women who supported themselves were sure of even the bare necessities of life. This condition made it easy to provide a sufficient number of harlots and concubines so that the chastity of the urban middle-class women was seldom assailed.

Occasionally during Victoria's reign the raiding of houses devoted to homosexual prostitution brought about flurries of excitement. There were also numerous brothels for masochists. In France, England was considered the particular home of the erotic birch. Perhaps masochistic prostitution was actually no more developed in London than it was in Paris and Berlin. Or it may be that the continued devotion to corporal punishment in the English schools actually contributed to the development of masochists and sadists. Discussions of the necessity for whipping boys and girls were eagerly followed, and translated into foreign languages, because of the prurient details they contained.

The Society for the Suppression of Vice in London conducted a crusade against books and pictures that were considered objectionable. The police did little to assist the agents of the Society. There were destroyed in three years, nevertheless, 279 "blasphemous and impure books," 1,162 "obscene publications," 1,495 song sheets, and 10,493 prints. The meaning of the seizures and confiscations does not appear from the mere statement of numbers. It is impossible, though, to analyze the destroyed matter and compare it with that which was seized in the United States under Anthony Comstock's direction. This much can be said, that many themes which are now unobjectionable were taboo in mid-Victorian England. And France allowed distinctly more latitude than England in the discussion of sexual problems.

With *La Dame aux Camélias* we are now sufficiently familiar under the title of *Camille*. Mahaffy in 1874 wrote of this play by the younger Dumas that it "could not be represented in England" except in the form of an Italian opera. For the English were not content with any but the highest standard of chastity: "We nowadays rate personal purity so highly that the loss of it by misfortune is hardly less excused by society than its abandonment through passion." This was said of women, of course, not of men.

Acton in his *Functions and Disorders of the Reproductive Organs,* published in the middle of the century, declared that women "if well brought up" should know nothing at all about sexual physiology. He denounced as a "vile aspersion" the idea that respectable women have sexual appetites and enjoy venereal satisfaction: "I should say that the majority of women (happily for society) are not very much troubled with sexual feeling of any kind." This doctrine, which most experts of our own time consider simply ridiculous, enjoyed considerable vogue in the nineteenth century. It was taught by leading German and Italian as well as English physiologists. Apparently, it is a curious instance of the domination of science by moral prejudice. In classical and Oriental writers we often find the view expressed that women have a stronger libido and derive greater pleasure from sexual intercourse than men. The Victorians, anxious to believe that there was a wide gulf between "good" and "bad" women, wanted to be told that while a depraved prostitute may enjoy copulation, a genteel female does not. Women were taught that they should expect to find the sexual part of wifehood an ordeal, but one which they owed it to their husbands to accept without question. Some writers of medical works thought that a woman, after being driven into a loose life by poverty or other unfavorable conditions, might then acquire an unnatural, morbid pleasure in sex.

Very few people, in or out of the medical profession, thought that a young woman ought to know anything at all about sex before she married. The idea that instruction in this field should be given to boys and girls was lightly dismissed as worse than immoral—in fact, as thoroughly absurd. However, the emphasis laid in genteel circles upon the avoidance of the subject made the interest in it all the greater. When no women or children were about, men joked freely about sexual matters. Even the demure females, when assured of privacy, sometimes ventured into the forbidden field. In early-Victorian times there were many sly jokes about "crim. con." Until 1857 one part of the elaborate course of action required to obtain a divorce was an action for damages on account of criminal conversation brought against the man who was alleged to have committed adultery with the woman in the case.

There were many popular songs about flirtations and gallantry. The following verses deal with conditions on a Thames excursion steamer in the middle of the century:

> Oh, I met her on a steamer,
>   As I journeyed to Cremorne;
> A crinoline and a pork-pie hat
>   Her figure did adorn;
> Our glances met, she smiled at me,
>   Then, as if unawares,
> My arm it slipped around her waist,
>   While on the cabin stairs.
> I asked her if she'd go with me,
>   Said she, "Yes, if I'd let her."
> 'Twas just as good as going home,
> Yes, as good, *and a good deal better!*

The sailors' prostitutes on Ratcliff Highway were very seldom disturbed, and there were many London streets through which it was almost impossible to pass without being accosted by women. Under such circumstances it is remarkable that some city women seem really to have been kept ignorant about sex and its exploitation.

The female sex was supposed to require a great deal of shielding protection. An American physician, Dr. William W. Sanger, wrote in the 1850's about the dangers to which Englishwomen were exposed if they went about alone: "The single females who frequent dancing-rooms, theatres, and other similar places in England, without friends or family escort, have very little virtue to risk. The country fairs are far more injurious; they are indiscriminately attended by all ages and sexes, and their effects upon the female agricultural population are often very pernicious. Greenwich Fair, a three days' scene of rollicking and junketing, was held at Easter and Whitsuntide, in the outskirts of London, but is now abolished. It had its uses a century or two ago, but recently has been attended by all the idlers of London, of both sexes, and was justly dreaded by the friends of youth. It is proverbial that more women were debauched at Greenwich Fair (allowing for its duration) than at any other place in England."

THE BALLET
A caricature by W. M. Thackeray.

The theatre was for a time under the ban of the middle classes. During most of the Victorian period the literary level of the drama was pretty low. There were many broad farces, vulgar enough but seldom suggestive of sex. There were also theatrical representations "for gentlemen only," which it may be that really genteel gentlemen did not attend, since they were full of double meanings and sexy jokes. In the 1860's the theatre acquired a certain amount of respectability. Ladies who had considered it improper to pass beyond the concert room in the way of public entertainment began to show an interest in the stage. The opera offered a means of transition, and it was permitted to tell stories of passion in foreign languages.

Among men, boxing enjoyed considerable favor. Special trains were operated to the places where the matches (forbidden by law) were held. Races, too, were popular. Visitors from abroad commented on the fact that a large part of the population laid bets on the results of horse races. When Victoria came to the throne, there was already in force a large amount of legislation against gambling. There were occasional raids against houses which violated the law, and their owners were sometimes severely punished. It is probable that gambling declined somewhat during Victoria's reign, though this change, if indeed it actually occurred, seems not to be due to the additional repressive laws which were enacted.

Gaming of all sorts was found wherever sporty men came together, as at race courses and boxing rings. Betting on horse races became, and has continued to be, the great "national vice" of England. In the 1850's there were in London four or five hundred betting houses. Many of them displayed stocks of cigars or other articles used by men, but all of them depended upon betting for their existence. There were many scandals about these places, and it was gossiped about that some of their managers were accustomed to bribe jockeys and in various other devious ways to insure their own profits. A law was passed making it illegal to bet against all comers. It still remained permissible to act as a betting agent, and bookmakers showed themselves openly at the tracks. The races offered a legitimate form of gambling to all classes, as the stock and commodity markets did to the rich.

Smoking was frowned upon in high society. It was considered especially unmannerly to smoke in the presence of ladies or in rooms to which they had access. Offering a cigar to any clergyman above the rank of curate was also a grave social sin. Even when men were alone and there were no deans or bishops among them, the use of tobacco was greatly restricted. Henry Adams, who was in England at the time of the American Civil War, tells us of the special grace which permitted him and other guests to smoke in his bedroom at a country house. Stables, sometimes kitchens, were ordinarily indicated as the proper places indoors for smoking. At the fashionable clubs, smokers found themselves hedged in with restrictions. Smoking was not permitted at all at White's until 1845, and then a special room was set aside for the use of tobacco. In 1866 the Prince of Wales and others formed the Marlborough Club in order that they might smoke when and where they pleased. Even military officers were restricted as to their use of tobacco, and smoking was not allowed in barracks until after the Crimean War.

It was generally much more convenient to drink than to smoke. In fact, considering that the Victorians thought of themselves as genteel and dainty people with a leaning toward the spiritual, they were remarkably fond of food and liquor. The temperance movement in England began early in the century, and the Queen consented in 1837 to become patroness of the British and Foreign Temperance Society. (Since we misuse the word *temperance*, it is perhaps necessary to add that Queen Victoria was not a prohibitionist.) One of the first laws passed in her reign restricted the sale of spirits on Sunday mornings and to children.

In Ireland one man, a Capuchin friar, the Reverend Theobald Mathew, was largely responsible for creating widespread sentiment in favor of temperance. Perhaps his preaching did not greatly reduce the prevalence of drunkenness there, but it made hard drinking lose much of its old respectability. Neither the Anglican Church nor the independent sects did very much in England to build up a temperance organization. Deep boozing became rather rare in aristocratic circles, in comparison, that is, with Regency manners. Travelers from the Continent continued to speak in tones of horror about the drunkenness of the lower classes. In the '40's and '50's rum was the staple drink in the Navy, while little beer was consumed on board the royal ships.

A treaty with France brought Bordeaux wine into wide use, in place of the much more potent brandied ports. Some members of Parliament were horrified, declaring that the morality of Madame Bovary would enter the land with the French light

A SPLENDID SPREAD

A caricature by George Cruikshank for the *Comic Almanac*, 1850.

wines. The reasons for such a feeling of alarm are not altogether clear, but the principal objection seems to have been that the wines were considered suitable to be drunk by women. Confectioners sold Bordeaux along with cakes and candies. According to one parliamentary orator, the result was certain to be that a man could find his wife drunken and his daughter dishonored in the confectioner's back room.

Equally dangerous, according to some of the people who enjoyed pointing with alarm, was the custom which grew up in the '60's of serving coffee after luncheon, ladies and gentlemen remaining together. If young men were exposed to young women's amorous glances over the coffee cups, what might not become of good old English morality? Perhaps coffee and French wines were responsible for the crumbling of taboo which took place in Victoria's old age. Who knows? Seemingly less adequate explanations have been advanced for it.

Once upon a time (and it was under the rule of virtuous Victoria) it took twelve yards of serge to make a bathing suit for a decent Englishwoman. And this was in spite of the fact that the extremely tight lacing of early-Victorian days must have reduced the average circumference of ladies. Maids were rated according to their pulling power at the laces. Then followed the era of the crinoline, when the skirt became a veritable piece of armor. Ladies were excluded from the outside seats of omnibuses, and their movements were much restricted. Walking down the stairs in such billowing garments, it was difficult to keep from showing unmentionables to the gentlemen standing below. Of course, true Victorian gentlemen did not look. A special "waved jupon" which took up comparatively little space was introduced; it had the further advantage, according to the advertisements, of preserving ladies from the necessity of blushing.

In 1872 the *Lady's Magazine* published a letter from a London greengrocer who complained that dress and fashion were ruining him. "Only picture to yourself," he wrote, "a greengrocer's wife issuing from her cellar in Drury Lane, with a monstrous hoop, exposing a pair of legs, the ankles as thick as the calf, and the calf as thick as the modern waist; her hair bepuddened, her cheeks bedaubed with red." He went on to lament that "her daughters made as ridiculous a figure."

§ 3

Let us be philosophical for a moment and consider the new democracy and feminism revealed in this complaint by the dealer in fruits and vegetables. The poor retailer's wife and daughters considered themselves as much entitled to dress up when they left their cellar as the countess when she left her town house to pay a visit to a duchess. It is interesting, also, to notice that the authority of the greengrocer, as husband and as father, was by no means absolute. He was not using a rod to enforce respect for his wishes, but expressing his sorrow in a letter to a magazine, yea, and to a magazine for women. It is true that there had always been henpecked husbands in England, even in the days when law and public opinion most strongly supported the chastisement of shrews and disrespectful wives. But now the free woman was appearing, though she had hardly begun to clamor for her rights. The fact that she applied some sort of rouge to her cheeks, perhaps even the fact that she allowed glimpses to be caught of her calves, clearly indicated her new freedom.

It would be more dignified, no doubt, to begin a discussion of the rise of feminism in Victorian England with an account of Florence Nightingale. It was not with red cheeks, not with a display of legs, that she advanced the cause of women. Miss Nightingale, who came of a reputable and well-to-do family, insisted on becoming a professional nurse. The female nurses of early Victorian days were not considered very genteel people. As a class they were reputed to be addicted to the smoking of pipes, the drinking of much brandy, and other improper or immoral practices. And they were seldom properly educated for their work.

Florence Nightingale became experienced in nursing and learned a great deal about the organization of hospitals in the various European countries. When the Crimean War broke out, she was permitted to organize a party of more than thirty nurses for work near the front. Eventually, thousands of ill and wounded soldiers came under her care. She found hospital conditions very bad, and she suffered much from the arrogance and jealousy of some of the men who were in positions of authority. But she cut endless red tape, she worked tirelessly, and she accomplished marvels. She was finally acclaimed in England as a heroine and as one who had succeeded where many of the supposedly superior sex had failed. That she had made nursing respectable was only a small part of her triumph. Far more important, she brought about a new attitude toward women. Several female writers had already won genuine recognition, but there had been a general reluctance to concede that women might have important executive ability, that they might direct other women and also men in the performance of difficult tasks. Engineers and surgeons consulted Miss Nightingale about the proper way to design hospitals. And she was asked for her advice about a variety of matters, some of them far removed from the profession of nursing. She wrote, in addition to several books on the organization and operation of hospitals, a somewhat eccentric philosophical work in three volumes, but this had only a private circulation. Like most people who have proved their ability in one field, she gained a reputation for general wisdom and was asked to stick her finger into a variety of pies.

Early in Victoria's reign the Melbourne ministry secured the passage of the Custody of Infants Act. This measure, which was really revolutionary, provided that married women who were living apart from their husbands might, if their moral reputation was good and they secured the approval of a court of equity, have occasional access to their children. Many peers objected fiercely to the law. They did not feel that a woman had any rights except those which her husband was willing to concede to her. And a woman who voluntarily left her husband, no matter how brutal he might be, was without the pale of respectability.

As for divorce, it was exceedingly difficult for a man to obtain, impossible for a woman. From the Protestant Revolution to 1858 the average number of divorces granted in England was about one a year, though the rate was higher toward the end of this period. We are told of a poor man who was brought before Mr. Justice Maule charged with bigamy. His wife had left him, eloping with a lover, and he had then married another woman to take care of his children. "Prisoner at the bar," said the judge after he had heard this story, "you should have sued the adulterer at the assizes, and recovered a verdict against him, then taken proceedings by your proctor in the ecclesiastical courts. After successful termination, you should have applied to Parliament for a divorce act, and your counsel and your witnesses would have been heard at the bar of the house." The prisoner pointed out that he could not afford such expensive procedure. Mr. Justice Maule made the sententious and crushing reply, "It is the glory of the law of England that she knows no distinction between rich and poor." His irony seems to have been intentional.

The law certainly did know a distinction between the rights of husband and wife. Even wealthy and influential women were unable to take advantage of the existing means of obtaining a divorce. A wife had no claim to exclusive cohabitation with her husband, and it was impossible for her to bring suit for criminal conversation against the women who had sexual relations with him. The wife possessed at common law no identity apart from that of her husband, and until matters were changed by statute, she consequently could not sue on her own account.

The Divorce Act of 1857 brought about 1,279 divorces in the eleven years after it was put into effect. Although it gave men the greater privileges, it allowed women to apply for a full legal separation, with the right to remarry, in certain aggravated cases of adultery. A series of laws improving the position of married women with regard to property rights followed. Women householders gained voting privileges in local elections. The new University of London and the Royal University of Ireland admitted female students and granted them degrees. Medical study was made available to women. Oxford and Cambridge were somewhat reluctant to offer their facilities to women students but finally granted them a series of privileges. Every change brought about an outburst of horror on the part of conservative women as well as men. A movement looking to the full enfranchisement of women came into general public notice. It was strongly supported by John Stuart Mill. Florence Nightingale announced that she was in favor of woman's suffrage.

Queen Victoria's opinion about the feminist movement is sufficiently shown in a letter she wrote in 1870 to Mr. (the later Sir Theodore) Martin. "The Queen," she said, "is most anxious to enlist every one who can speak or write to join in checking this mad, wicked folly, of 'Woman's Rights,' with all its attendant horrors, on which her poor feeble sex is bent, forgetting every sense of womanly feeling and propriety. Lady —— ought to get a *good whipping*. It is a subject which makes the Queen so furious that she cannot contain herself. God created men and women different—then let them remain each in their own position."

Ironically, it is quite possible that Victoria was herself to some degree responsible for the growth of feminism. She was carrying out the duties of her high office fully as well as her immediate male predecessors. Certainly she was more conscientious about them than her uncles had been. There were times when the Queen was unpopular, even times when ribald stories were told about her, but her subjects usually believed in her virtue and her ability. England prospered while she reigned, and some of the credit for the prosperity and advancement of the country was given (justly or not) to the sovereign.

While a woman sat upon the throne, Queen of the United Kingdom of Great Britain and Ireland, later Empress of India as well, many other members of her "poor feeble sex" were given lowlier stations in public or industrial life which they filled quite as well as she did hers. The hairdressing trade, which had been monopolized by men, came to a large extent into the hands of women. Girls replaced the male clerks in many business offices, especially after the introduction of typewriting machines. Men were alarmed, not merely because the tradition of women's inferiority and their belonging in the home exclusively was being overthrown, but for definite economic reasons. Women were willing to work for low wages, especially if they depended in part upon the earnings of husbands or parents, and they tended to reduce the wage levels of the men who were in competition with them. This fear hastened the growth of trades unions, which gradually acquired importance among women as well as men workers.

A softening of manners accompanied the growth of feminine influence, and this was noticeable at the close of the nineteenth

THE POLKA

From Richard Doyle, *Manners and Customes of ye Englyshe in 1849.*

century in all social classes. Verbal niceties were in some circles carried to an extreme. And in the attempt to avert occasions for quarreling, Englishmen limited their conversation to mere trifles. Mill, who had been brought up by his father as something very much like a debating machine, complained in the '60's that "all serious discussions on matters in which opinions differ" were considered "ill-bred." As a matter of fact, this reluctance to

permit freedom of expression with regard to controversial problems was not entirely confined to the drawing-room. There was
a bitter struggle over free speech and the free press.

Lord Campbell's Libel Act of 1845 permitted the defendant
in an action for libel to introduce proofs of the truth of what he
had written or of his lack of malice and desire to serve the public
welfare in uttering the statements that were considered objectionable. It became thereafter much less dangerous to criticize
the party in power and its leaders. Yet there was much fighting
to be done in gaining the right to express heretical religious
and social views. Mill, Buckle, and Huxley were among the
foremost of the fighters.

Pietism in England had been since the days of Wycliffe almost
always associated with the party opposed to elaborate religious
ceremonials and to every taint of popery. John Wesley, though
he belonged to the High Church party as a young man, had to
move a good way toward the other side before he could exert
any considerable influence. In the nineteenth century, however,
the great religious revival was associated with the High Church
group. Like the Methodist movement, it came out of the University of Oxford. This revival exerted considerable influence
on the aristocracy. The middle classes, still a little fearful about
popery, were generally led to abandon their interested and half-
sympathetic observation of this new Oxford movement when
some of its leaders went over to the Roman Catholic Church.
The revival was a reaction against rationalism in religion, and
above all against the higher criticism, which was especially associated with German scholars. Rationalism was often supported
by people of liberal moral views. The High Church and conservative standards of conduct went together. The middle
classes began to show sharp divisions over religion and morality.
Some deserted the Evangelical party for open skepticism or for
the Broad Church, that part of the Established Church which
lay between the High Church and the Low or Evangelical Church
in doctrine and ritual but was more receptive than either to
liberal theology. The asceticism of the Oxford movement, which
could easily be considered popish, worked together with the

increased wealth of the upper middle classes to stimulate a sort of modified hedonism among the merchants and manufacturers. Besides, these people began to see that industrial progress depended upon free scientific investigation, and many of them discarded the literal authority of the Bible.

There were religious conflicts within and without the Anglican Church. Some, like Arnold, favored the retention of the Established Church but wanted to eliminate from its creed practically everything that orthodox people considered fundamental. Some of the free churches went over to Unitarianism. Others stood fast for the whole list of Christian miracles and the complete inspiration of the Scriptures. The Church of England, because of its special privileges, retained in its membership people of widely varying beliefs. They could not leave the Church without forfeiting something of their social position, though most of their legal advantages as Anglicans disappeared during Victoria's reign.

One of the important workers for religious liberalism was a woman named Mary Ann Evans, who translated from the German several books expounding critical views. We know her better by the name on the title pages of her novels, George Eliot. She fell in love with a writer, George Henry Lewes, whose wife preferred another man to him. Circumstances made a divorce impossible. Miss Evans decided to live with Lewes as his wife without the sanction of law. Perhaps it was a horrible example of the demoralizing influence of the higher criticism. Or maybe it was an instance of a transition to a more intelligent moral system. In any case, George Eliot was deliberately doing what she considered right. She was herself a moralist, perhaps too much so for the complete æsthetic perfection of her novels. In flouting the conventions, or at least defying one convention, she never thought of herself as a sinner. As an interpreter of the new theology she was equally conscientious, and equally subjected to abuse.

In a year of great intellectual excitement, 1859, appeared Mill's *Liberty* and Darwin's *The Origin of Species*. Darwin presented the first cogent and systematically arranged arguments against the theory of the individual creation of species, which was at that time usually accepted by biologists and which was supposed to be supported by the authority of the story of creation in Genesis. Mill's book, written in collaboration with his wife, argued eloquently for the greatest possible amount of freedom of expression and action. (Later, notably by Herbert Spencer, the theory of evolution in its Darwinian form was to be used to support individualistic philosophies.)

These two books aroused a great deal of thought and discussion. Darwin's attracted attention at first chiefly among scientists, but it presently became a storm center. At first, biologists of repute were generally opposed to the theory of organic evolution. Gradually, however, they came to find all the evidence favoring the general theory, although the Darwinian explanation, by means of natural selection, seemed doubtful to many. By the end of the century there were few biological authorities anywhere who still refused to accept evolution as a necessary deduction from incontrovertible facts. The hottest opposition to the Darwinians came from theological writers, such as Pusey and Bishop Wilberforce. But by 1900 most churchmen were trying to reconcile the dogma of evolution with the story of creation in the Bible, or even basing a religious philosophy of constant human improvement under divine inspiration upon Darwin's theory.

Within the Church of England there were a number of attacks upon alleged heretics. A book called *Essays and Reviews,* which was written by seven ministers and published in 1860, aroused heated controversy. The Reverend Rowland Williams was brought to trial on the charge of having, as one of its authors, denied the doctrine of eternal punishment. The ecclesiastical court which first heard the case dismissed Williams from his ministry. Then the Privy Council, sitting as a court of appeals, accepted the defendant's plea that he had merely hoped God would not punish sinners eternally and that he was not presuming to deny an accepted tenet of the Church. Another contributor to the book, Wilson, was also cleared on appeal.

In far-off Natal, Bishop Colenso examined the Hexateuch,

applying the tests of the higher criticism. The Bishop of Cape Town deposed him from his see for publishing heretical views. Once again the Privy Council favored the liberal side, declaring the deposition null and void. The orthodox bishop then displayed his zeal by issuing an order excommunicating Colenso. This too was treated as invalid. But the danger in espousing heterodox religious views was seen to be considerable. During practically the entire Victorian period public opinion was on the side of the old, familiar views.

James Anthony Froude, who was later to win fame as a historian, became a member of the enthusiastic High Church group at Oxford. While still at the university his zeal for orthodoxy weakened and he slipped over to the rationalist side. When he made his new position public, he found it necessary to resign his fellowship at Oriel College. Among those whom he angered was his father, who stopped his allowance. Froude was an old man when Oxford honored him in 1892 with the Regius professorship of modern history.

Harriet Martineau, a writer whose family was devoted to Unitarian views, came to the conclusion that Christianity is a superstition which has its uses at certain stages of development but is unnecessary in a civilized country. Dickens declined to use Miss Martineau's novel, *The Missionary*, in *Household Words* on the ground that it was too favorable to the Catholics. Another Victorian novelist, George Borrow, was constantly worrying and writing about popish plots to enslave England. He thought his country was in danger from the Jews, too.

Both Roman Catholics and Jews, despite the fears of some zealous Protestants, were relieved of their last political disabilities at law during Victoria's reign. In 1871 all religious tests at Oxford and Cambridge were removed. Social discriminations against the members of the various Protestant independent sects, though they did not altogether disappear, became much weaker. But religious prejudice, especially against non-Protestants, remained. And the Anglican Evangelicals found they were closer to the Protestant Dissenters than they were to the High Church enthusiasts or Anglo-Catholics within the Church of England.

Some of the latter refused to call themselves Protestants. In 1870 Gladstone seized upon the authoritative definition of papal infallibility by the Roman Catholic Church as the basis for an argument that Catholics could not be trusted to remain loyal to their country. Probably some members of the High Church party who would otherwise have gone off to Rome remained within the Anglican Church because they did not care to acknowledge the doctrine, then made official, that whenever the Pope, speaking as such, expressed an opinion about religion or morals, his views were those of the Roman Catholic Church, binding upon all its members.

Two decades earlier there had been much shaking of Protestant heads in Great Britain when the Pope organized the Roman Catholic clergy of England into twelve dioceses, with an Archbishop of Westminster at the head. Previously there had only been bishops *in partibus infidelium*, with foreign titles. It was said that no one was entitled to call himself a bishop in England unless he had been consecrated in the legal way by the Established Church. But in spite of Gladstone and other Protestant zealots the Roman Catholic clergy gradually came to be treated with virtually the same respect, and almost with the same legal recognition, as members of the Anglican hierarchy. In semipublic documents, Manning, as cardinal-archbishop, was allowed to sign his name directly after the Prince of Wales. There had been much shaking of heads over Newman at Oxford when he entered the Roman Catholic Church, yet in 1877 his old university granted him an honorary fellowship in Trinity College. Disraeli the Jew—no matter what his political attachment to the Church of England, he was proud of his supposedly pure Hebrew blood—became a leader of public opinion and a dear friend to Her Royal and (by his favor) Imperial Majesty.

There were many shifts in public opinion during the Victorian age, and some views which were dreadfully heretical when first expressed became not merely tolerable, but popular or platitudinous, within a decade or two. Fitzgerald made a translation or adaptation of Omar Khayyam's poem of religious and philosophic doubt, which was first printed in 1859, that great year of intellectual ferment in England. He hesitated to present copies of the *Rubáiyát* to his friends, fearing they might be shocked. A few were sold at a penny apiece. But it was not long before the poem was serving as a delicious intoxicant for the young and as a sort of Bible of skepticism.

Huxley coined the word *agnostic* in 1869. It afforded a convenient label for some who hesitated to call themselves atheists and for the few who were able to maintain an attitude of suspended judgment about the existence of a God or gods. Huxley's popular expositions of science and philosophy were listened to eagerly.

Winwood Reade's *The Martyrdom of Man,* a brilliant short history of the world, was outspokenly hostile to Christianity. The *Times* of London and such magazines as the *Spectator* and the *Academy* refused to review the book at all. The reviews which appeared were made up chiefly of denunciations. Yet the history had a good sale from the outset, and new editions have often been called for since.

Early in Victoria's reign Lord Melbourne is reported to have said, "No one has more respect for the Christian religion than I have; but really, when it comes to intruding it into private life—!" It is possible to maintain that this sort of paganism declined in England during the second half of the nineteenth century. Or perhaps it was only the frankness which declined until, when the Queen was an elderly woman, a great wave of open opposition to Christianity appeared.

Not even the middle classes retained their traditional devotion to the churches. Samuel Butler meant to picture them in *Erewhon* as worshipers of Mrs. Grundy, whom he represents anagrammatically as the goddess Ydgrun. They themselves would have said that they were simply attaching the proper importance to respectability and good form. In fact, football and good form were the chief subjects of instruction at such schools as Eton and Rugby, with Latin and Greek bringing up the rear. Thomas Arnold, as headmaster at Rugby, laid particular emphasis upon what he called Christian character. It seems that his instruction did not keep the students from brutality and drunkenness, but was largely instrumental in maintaining a tendency to scoff at individualism and originality. Good form was usually held to require certain Christian observances but to inhibit deep religious feeling. In fact, displays of emotion, no matter of what sort, were considered unworthy of English gentlemen.

John Stuart Mill tells how his visits to the Continent, beginning as an inexperienced lad in 1820, made him familiar with "the low moral tone of what, in England, is called society; the habit of, not indeed professing, but taking for granted in every mode of implication, that conduct is of course always directed toward low and petty objects; the absence of high feelings which manifests itself by sneering depreciation of them, and by general abstinence (except among a few of the stricter religionists) from professing any principles of action at all, except in those preordained cases in which such profession is put on as part of the costume and formalities of the occasion." This is really a repetition of Hazlitt's complaint, although Mill puts the case more accurately. Comparatively few Englishmen were able to see the import of the English tradition of good form so clearly. Even if they went abroad, men who had been educated in the public schools were accustomed to find in contrasts of manners and morals no more than confirmations of what they had been taught to believe, that England was in all respects the greatest of conceivable countries.

Mill was himself attacked as the defender of a low ethical creed. He was, in the philosophy of morals, a prominent leader in the school which had been established long before his time in England but then became known as Utilitarian. The Utilitarians had one criterion of conduct: a man should act in such a way as to produce the greatest good to the greatest number of people; this rule, they felt, was sufficient, though the application in a particular case might present difficulties. The criterion is democratic, and it ignores the usual moral authorities.

To the democratic implications of Utilitarianism comparatively few objections were raised by Victorian moralists. Yet many of them must have felt that the welfare of a duke or a bishop is more important than that of half a dozen chambermaids or cobblers. Mill was influenced by the French socialists, especially by St. Simon. At the same time, other Utilitarians were zealous defenders of the capitalistic system. And it would be possible to make a case for feudalism or for absolute monarchy under the principle of the greatest good for the greatest number. In fact, Hobbes came close to the latter of these in the *Leviathan*. The Utilitarians found their most vigorous opponents among those who insisted that the true standards of conduct are to be found in the Bible or an innate moral sense, the moral instinct of old-fashioned psychology. It seems to me that most thoughtful ministers of religion in Great Britain and America have accepted the Utilitarian rule, though they are careful to say that the Ten Commandments and the words of Jesus provide concrete directions for acting in such a way as to insure the greatest good to the greatest number.

About 1870 Mill thought that the cause of free discussion had made vast gains, but he was not sure that they would continue. What was really taking place was an alteration in the public attitude toward two matters in which Mill was deeply interested, religion and the position of women. Religious liberalism and feminism were being regarded with friendlier eyes. Although reactionary swings have taken place since, the general tendency in England has been toward rationalism and the equal rights of the sexes. As to freedom of utterance in general, it is difficult to tell if any real gains have been made since 1870.

Several times during Victoria's reign neo-Malthusian doctrines were brought to public notice. In 1854 Dr. George Drysdale's *Physical, Sexual, and Natural Religion* was anonymously published. This book, later reissued as *The Elements of Social Science*, boldly proclaimed that the physical functions of men and women, including those which have to do with sex and reproduction, are fully as important and as noble as the mental ones. It laid down the thesis that the artificial limitation of conception is important as preventing the three great and interrelated evils of poverty, prostitution, and celibacy.

Another work expressing essentially similar ideas, Knowlton's

Fruits of Philosophy, circulated for a time without interference. In 1876 a Bristol bookseller was prosecuted for selling "indecently illustrated" copies of the book. He considered it expedient to plead guilty rather than to defend the morality of the work. The publisher, too, hastened to repudiate it. Then Charles Bradlaugh entered the case in the interest of freedom of expression.

Bradlaugh as a lad of sixteen ventured to express his doubts about the truth of Christianity. The result was that he was forced to leave home. His reputation as a freethinker pursued him, and he found it difficult to obtain work. Finally, to keep from starving, he joined the Army as a private. Later, he began to lecture and write against the Christian religion and in favor of republicanism. After two unsuccessful attempts he was elected to the House of Commons, but because he refused to take the prescribed oath on the Bible, he was refused admission. His constituents several times reëlected him, and he was each time told that he could not take his seat without swearing on the Bible. In 1886 he was allowed to take his place in the House on a simple affirmation. Toward the end of his life Bradlaugh became very popular among his colleagues and elsewhere. Parliament went so far as to expunge from the journals the resolutions expelling him.

Charles Bradlaugh was several times forced to stand trial for blasphemy and sedition. Each appearance in court meant wide publicity for his doctrines. This is why he involved himself in the matter of the neo-Malthusian pamphlet. He was joined by Mrs. Annie Besant, who later became absorbed in Oriental mysticism and repented of her interest in such grossly mundane matters as the generation of children. The two republished and circulated Knowlton's work. They were arrested, convicted, and sentenced to prison terms and the payment of heavy fines. On appeal, they escaped through a technicality. But they had accomplished their chief purpose, which was the arousing of wide interest in the control of conception.

A Malthusian League was formed, and it soon became evident that the people of England were becoming educated in the mat-

THE SCHOLASTIC HEN AND HER CHICKENS

MISS THIMBLEBEE: *"Turn your heads the other way, my dears, for here are two horribly handsome officers coming."*

A caricature by George Cruikshank for the *Comic Almanac,* 1847.

ter. Almost immediately after the trial there was a noticeable decline in the birth rate. In the 1880's this tendency was observable all over the civilized world.

The proportion of illegitimate births in every thousand total births in England and Wales fell from sixty-seven in 1842 to forty-seven, the average rate for the years 1884-1888. Undoubtedly the widespread familiarity with contraceptives arising out of the Bradlaugh-Besant case had much to do with this decline. It is doubtful if we are justified in inferring from it a decrease in illicit sexual intercourse from the early to the late days of Victoria's reign.

§ 4

This much is certain, that the prevalence of an elaborate system of verbal taboo is no certain indicator of the rarity of adultery, fornication, and other sexual irregularities and delicts. Often it does show that certain classes of society are supposed to remain chaste or that certain seasons are dedicated to continence. In Victorian England, prudery was chiefly valued as a method of keeping nubile girls virginal, mentally as well as physically, until they married. The problem was complicated by the fact that Englishwomen had a tradition of freedom. They could not very well be shut up in a special part of the house from which all male beings were excluded. It was even found that the female descendants of Miss Lydia Languish could not be kept from reading the latest novels.

Hence, according to many Victorian moralists, whatever was unsuitable for the reading of a virgin of sixteen ought not to be published at all. Yet, there was some willingness to be tolerant in the case of books which the young girl could hardly be expected to read. Early in the reign of Victoria a Roman Catholic ecclesiastic, Cardinal Wiseman, spoke in a lecture of the occasional indecency of Chaucer and Spenser. Leigh Hunt then defended the old poets in an article which appeared posthumously in *Fraser's Magazine*.

Generally speaking, the classics circulated freely despite their frankness in dealing with sexual matters. Those which were published in the original Latin or Greek were intended for boys and young men, and the chastity of the male sex was not a matter of particular concern. Many old books in English which knew nothing of Victorian prudery appeared in new, unexpurgated editions. To give but a single instance, there was a complete paper-covered Carew in 1845, followed by other reprints in 1870 and 1893.

Palgrave omitted Spenser's "Epithalamion" from *The Golden Treasury* because, as he said, he did not consider it in harmony with his age. That is to say, he felt that the inclusion of such a poem would jeopardize the success of an anthology which might be expected to have a place on parlor tables and in schools for girls. Edward Hutton, commenting on this omission in 1906, remarked that "happily manners have changed much since mid-Victorian times, and we may all read the 'Epithalamion' without being expected to blush." Curiously, one or two poems were included in Palgrave's anthology which we might expect to have been found equally objectionable with Spenser's marriage hymn.

The Victorian poet most suggestive of Spenser was Alfred Tennyson. Tennyson enjoyed reading sensual poetry, but his own work usually conformed to the strictest standards of his age. He became a moralist because morality was in demand. "The Lotos-Eaters," first published in 1832 without any ethical lesson, appeared in a revised version ten years later with a good moral attached. For the young literary radicals of our time Tennyson is almost a scarecrow representing Victorian gentility. He is remembered for such a sentiment as

> 'Tis only noble to be good,
> Kind hearts are more than coronets,
> And simple faith than Norman blood.

The Dedication of "Idylls of the King" to the memory of Prince Albert,

> Wearing the white flower of a blameless life

comes to mind. The praising of a man

> Who loved one only and who clave to her

reminds some of us of certain newspaper poets who write atrocious verses and are consequently beloved by millions.

The "Idylls" celebrate Victorian rather than chivalric and feudal ideals, obviously, and their trappings are consequently incongruous. They make us think of Knights and Dames who put on wooden swords to drive out bootleggers or to frighten newsdealers into stopping the display of *Spicy Stories*. Not that Tennyson denounces wine in his poetry. As a matter of fact, he speaks of the fermented juice of the grape with something akin to reverence. And he records, with evident approval, the old English Christmas custom of kissing girls "beneath the sacred bush" of mistletoe. He brings naked Godiva into a poem, and several times he deals with amorous passion in an understandable if somewhat indirect manner.

Personally, Tennyson was capable of eating and drinking like a robust son of John Bull, and of talking like one, too. And, like a true patriotic Englishman, he disliked the France of "Buonaparte" and the wicked city of Paris. For him there was nothing relative or changing about morality. The good knights of old acted like good Victorians, and had the same aspirations, if we are to believe his poems. If the French did not maintain the same standards as the English, why, they were wicked people. Tennyson taught,

> And, because right is right, to follow right
> Were wisdom in the scorn of consequence.

The trouble with such a doctrine (assuming that normal human beings should consent to be bound by it) is that even Victorian Englishmen were not unanimous in their opinion of what constituted right and wrong.

Browning as a moralist was somewhat more original and more daring than Tennyson. In "The Statue and the Bust" he made the nursing of unacted desire the worst of all vices. The man and the woman are held apart by fear, and that is very much to be deplored, Browning tell us, "though the end in sight was a crime." The imputed sin of "the unlit lamp and the ungirt loin," that is to say, adultery, seemed to most Victorian moralists far worse than the drawing back from such a crime because of timidity. They would, of course, have preferred a purity resulting from self-respect and love of virtue: but fear, they felt, was much better than sin.

Browning had no intention of glorifying illicit love. He simply argued that chastity, whatever may be said for it, is a less important virtue than courage and determination. Even this was a departure from the main line of Victorian morality as we find it in Tennyson. The religious orthodoxy of Browning is less questionable, for he attacked the higher criticism as well as spiritualism. He favored woman suffrage for a time but later changed his mind on the subject. Both he and his wife enjoyed reading Balzac. Mrs. Browning approved of the morality of *La Dame aux Camélias,* and she read *Madame Bovary* without any apparent horror. When the Brownings called on George Sand, the English poetess was disappointed to find no cigarette in that lady's mouth: "Ah, but I didn't see her smoke!" Great Britain did not remain entirely aloof from French moral standards, as manifested in literature and life.

The Pre-Raphaelite movement in British art, which was especially important in painting and poetry, was not primarily moral, perhaps; but it had ethical aspects. It arose in the middle of the nineteenth century, and to a certain extent it represented a protest against the crassness of the Victorian middle classes. They were in the saddle, and money was their chief concern. With the love of money was often associated a Puritanic religion, or at least an opposition to beauty which arose from the old hatred of paganism and popery.

Ruskin, Arnold, and other defenders of culture attacked this "Philistinism." Arnold declared that England had too much of the Hebraic spirit. He asked for less "strictness of conscience" and more Hellenism, with its "spontaneity of consciousness" and ability "to see things as they really are."

William Morris developed the gospel of beauty by making beautiful things of many kinds — poems, finely printed books, wallpaper, furniture. He was one of the Victorian critics who found fault not only with the æsthetic standards of the time, but also with the current economic teachings and the distributive ethics which the governing classes found acceptable.

We may consider the Pre-Raphaelite movement one aspect of a rather wide attack on Victorian standards. The painters turned, indeed, for models to a mediæval Italian group which conventionalized women with narrow, childish bosoms. But there is no evidence that they were consciously deferring to the unwillingness to face reality which was characteristic of mid-Victorian England. Soon the poetry of the Pre-Raphaelites broke through the conventions of the time. Dante Gabriel Rossetti, the leading poet of the group, who was by descent three-fourths Italian, sometimes used imagery of a sort which seemed to represent southern sensualism. But it can hardly have been a matter of race or ancestral environment, for Spenser and Keats (and, in our time, D. H. Lawrence) also make us feel, when we read them, the same sensation of touching a smooth, warm skin.

Rossetti dared to say in verse that women have bodies and breasts, and that some of them sell themselves on London streets. A poet and miscellaneous writer named Robert Buchanan published, under the pseudonym of Thomas Maitland, a magazine article called "The Fleshly School of Poetry," directed principally against Rossetti. Rossetti brooded over the attack. He surely had no immoral intention in writing "Jenny," to which Buchanan objected on the ground that it presented a prostitute as heroine. And a number of other poems which Rossetti modified for later editions of his poems, or which he removed from them, do not now seem very vicious.

Swinburne went further than Rossetti in defying the mid-Victorian conventions. Sometimes he almost seemed to be blissfully ignorant of the prudery of his times. In 1862 the young poet attended a party at which Thackeray and his two daughters and the Archbishop of York were among the guests. The poet read to a mixed company no less shocking a poem than "Les Noyades." The Archbishop soon looked worried, Thackeray's daughters giggled aloud, the poet glanced up with an annoyed look. But he kept on reading until the butler appeared and saved the situation with his announcement, "Prayers, my lord!"

The offending poem, together with others which proved to be no less offensive, was published in 1866 in a volume called *Poems and Ballads* in England, *Laus Veneris* in America. Dallas, who was chief reviewer for the London *Times*, saw an early copy of the book and immediately called on Moxon, the publisher. He insisted that Moxon should make no attempt to circulate it, saying that he would otherwise launch an attack upon author and publisher both which would have dire consequences. Moxon was afraid of Dallas' ill will and withdrew from his connection with the book, but another publisher was found. An orgy of moral indignation followed, with good people ostentatiously refraining from reading Swinburne's poems about the sea and the laughter of a child as well as those which glorify illicit passion or attack the religion of Jesus. Swinburne was influenced in his treatment of sexual themes by the Hebrew prophets, the Elizabethan dramatists, and several French writers. After him there appeared many English authors who defied the mid-Victorian taboos, but most of them began to publish their work when the old prudishness was already beginning to crumble.

Most important novelists of Victorian days, except those who came into prominence in the '80's and '90's, were willing to accept the moral limitations on literature which Swinburne resisted. Still, neither Dickens nor Thackeray—to take the two most prominent names—dealt exclusively with "good" people. As Chesterton says: "Dickens and Thackeray claimed very properly the right to deal with shameful passions and suggest their shameful culminations. . . . Dickens did not claim the license of Gride (let us say) over his purchased bride: but Dickens does not leave the reader in the faintest doubt about what sort of feelings they were. . . . Thackeray would not have described the toilet details of the secret balls of Lord Steyne: he left that to Lady Cardigan. But no one who has read Thackeray's version would be surprised at Lady Cardigan's."

Critics have remarked, too, that Thackeray's good people are usually much less clever than his bad ones. In fact, a number of

Victorian writers reveal the fact that good people were supposed to be rather simple and easily fooled. Especially for women, unsophistication, lack of cleverness, and virtue were considered to belong together. The Reverend Charles Kingsley wrote in the "Farewell to C. E. G.":

> Be good, sweet maid, and let who will be clever.

Much was made of the old simplicity of the peasants and the working classes in general. It was generally feared in the upper and middle classes that the spread of education would lead the underprivileged to make demands upon their masters. And this was (consciously or not) the sort of consideration that led Victorian men to hope that sweet maids would refrain from learning and thinking too much.

The women novelists all stood for virtue, of course; but some of them displayed great intellectual ability. It was, it still is, common to say of George Eliot that she had the intellect of a man. As a matter of fact, she displayed an independence of mind which put to shame most of her masculine contemporaries.

Even Charlotte Brontë was considered rather daring. In *Jane Eyre* she drew the portrait of a hypocritical minister. As the head of a charity school he has the girls' hair cut off—bobbed hair was not then in vogue, of course—because "we are not to conform to nature"; but his wife and daughters have theirs elaborately dressed. He has ascetic ideas, which he applies to others, but he and his family live in luxury. Miss Brontë carefully explained that she did not mean to attack religion or worthy clergymen. Perhaps she was treading on forbidden ground, too, when she represented her Mr. Rochester as once having had a concubine in the person of a French opera dancer. As might be expected from her nationality, the dancer was found with another man, and Mr. Rochester gave her up.

Charlotte Brontë had definite ideas about the limits of propriety, though. Paying a tribute to Thackeray as a satirist and social reformer, she said: "They say he is like Fielding: they talk of his wit, humor, comic powers. He resembles Fielding as the eagle does a vulture: Fielding could stoop on carrion, but Thackeray never does."

Thackeray was influenced by Fielding in a number of ways, some of them rather curious, as in making a young man of supposedly illegitimate birth his hero in *Henry Esmond*. The fact that the scene was laid in the days of Addison and Steele encouraged Thackeray to some few small freedoms of expression in this novel: still, comparatively little was made of the opportunities for introducing scenes of gallantry.

Thackeray sometimes felt galled by the verbal taboos which bound him fast. The following extract from the preface to *The History of Pendennis* shows his attitude toward them: "Even the gentlemen of our own age—this is an attempt to describe one of them, no better nor worse than most educated men—even these we cannot show as they are, with the notorious foibles and selfishness of their lives and their education. Since the author of *Tom Jones* was buried, no writer of fiction among us has been permitted to depict to his utmost power a MAN. We must drape him, and give him a certain conventional simper. Society will not tolerate the Natural in our Art. Many ladies have remonstrated and subscribers left me, because in the course of the story I described a young man resisting and affected by temptation. My object was to say, that he had passions to feel, and manliness and generosity to overcome them. You will not hear—it is best to know it—what moves in the real world, what passes in society, in the clubs, colleges, mess-rooms—what is the life and talk of your sons. A little more frankness than is customary has been attempted in this story; with no bad desire on the writer's part, it is hoped, and with no ill consequence to any reader."

When Anthony Trollope died, in 1882, he left behind an autobiography which shows that he seldom found the Victorian taboos irksome. In writing novels, he tells us, he wanted to teach his readers "that honesty is the best policy; that truth prevails while falsehood fails; that a girl will be loved as she is pure, sweet, and unselfish; that a man will be honored as he is true, and honest, and brave of heart; that things meanly done are ugly and odious, and things nobly done beautiful and gracious." There were still people who considered the reading of novels sinful, though their number was much smaller than it had been in the early years of the century, and novelists sometimes felt called upon to apologize for their craft. "I do believe," says Trollope, "that no girl has risen from the reading of my pages less modest than she was before, and that some may have learned from them that modesty is a charm well worth preserving. I think that no youth has been taught that in falseness and flashness is to be found the road to manliness; and some may perhaps have learned from me that it is to be found in truth and a high and gentle spirit."

When Trollope joined with others in founding the *Fortnightly Review*, which was supposed to be devoted to freedom of expression, he stipulated that no articles should be admitted to the magazine which should cast doubt upon the divinity of Christ. But his piety was not sufficient for the Scotch Presbyterian clergyman who edited *Good Words*. After beginning the publication of a novel by Trollope, he refused to use the remaining instalments because they contained dancing scenes.

In 1870 Trollope was venturesome enough to introduce into *The Vicar of Bullhampton* "a girl whom I will call—for want of a truer word that shall not in its truth be offensive—a castaway." As a good moralist he made this girl suffer intensely for her sins. He tells us in his autobiography that respectable young women had been supposed up to that time to remain ignorant of the very existence of prostitutes. "Whether that ignorance was good may be questioned; but that it exists no longer is beyond question." Clearly it had not lasted long.

Trollope explains that his autobiography is not of the Rousseauan variety: "If the rustle of a woman's petticoat has ever stirred my blood; if a cup of wine has been a joy to me; if I have thought tobacco at midnight in pleasant company to be one of the elements of an earthly paradise; if now and again I have somewhat recklessly fluttered a five pound note over a card-table; of what matter is that to any reader?" But perhaps this one sentence is confession enough, not merely of what

Trollope's life was like, but of what lies behind much of the decorum of Victorian literature.

The roaring girl of the Victorian age was created by women novelists in the '70's. She was capable of falling in love, she sometimes forgot her gentility so far as to talk slang and rumple her dress. Justin McCarthy described, about 1880, the type of fiction in which the roaring girl was found. At its best, he says, "it recognizes the fact that women are not a distinct angelic order of beings, but that they have their strong passions and even their coarse desires like men." It was important that the women themselves were insisting upon this point. For one thing, it turned away the force of the self-righteous criticism which was being directed against Thomas Hardy and other novelists of real life.

CHAPTER X

IN WHICH THE WALTZ BECOMES RESPECTABLY OLD-FASHIONED

§ 1

WHEN Queen Victoria's eldest son, Bertie, was a little boy, she used to hope that he would grow up to be like his "angelic dearest father." As Edward (to mention that one of his names by which history remembers him), Prince of Wales and heir to the thrones of the United Kingdom and India as well as the defendership of the faith, he was taught to remember his duties and neglect his pleasures. Her Majesty was anxious above all that Bertie should not resemble his grand-uncles. Everything that could be done to keep him from acquiring a character like that of George IV or William IV was tried.

Perhaps the careful lessons in virtue, propriety, and religion were carried a little too far. Or maybe there was a serious slip when he was taken to Paris, at the age of thirteen, on a visit to the court of Napoleon III. Thenceforth he considered the palaces of London insufferably dull, and he was constantly looking across the English Channel. Eventually he was to be acclaimed as more Parisian than the Parisians.

At seventeen or eighteen the Prince enjoyed practically no liberty. He was sent to Oxford, but not to mingle with *hoi polloi*. A small and carefully chosen group of undergraduates joined with him in his studies. Meanwhile he was under careful supervision. At the age of twenty-one he was married to Princess Alexandra of Denmark. No longer was he under the full control of his mother. There had been a time when he could not smoke without incurring the risk of being confined to his room for a month. This sort of danger disappeared with his marriage. Nevertheless, the Prince of Wales remained afraid of his mother for many years afterward. We are told how he trembled when he arrived in the palace somewhat late for dinner.

But so far as social leadership went, the Prince soon had far more authority than his mother. She had never been friendly to high society, feeling that the aristocrats were not quite what they ought to be morally. The Prince of Wales liked to associate not only with the old nobles, but with new industrial millionaires, with sporting people, and with men and women who were connected with the theatre. His influence helped to accelerate the disappearance of the taboos on tobacco which had existed in English society since the late eighteenth century. He smoked immediately after dinner, and many others followed his example. He was fond of playing cards and betting on the races, and he was sometimes rebuked in newspapers and magazines for wasting his time and money and setting a bad example to the youth of the nation.

The Prince was neither prude nor Puritan. The odor of scandal occasionally hovered about him. Once he was accused of having had adulterous relations with Lady Mordaunt; but he appeared in court and denied the charge, and his denial was accepted. On another occasion he was a witness in a case which hinged upon cheating at cards on the part of a man with whom he had had close social relations. The precisians were excited. They asked if a second George IV was going to sit upon the British throne.

Still, Edward was different in many ways from his granduncle. He never lived openly with concubines. He did not abandon his wife. He did not become grossly drunken and unmannerly. And his popularity was helped by his friendly attitude toward France. Victoria had German sympathies, which became disagreeable to her subjects as the political and industrial strength of Germany rose. Rumors which escaped about her attempt to meddle with the foreign policies of Great Britain did not increase the loyalty of her subjects.

Victoria's attachment to her faithful old servant John Brown gave rise to strange and scandalous stories. Her prudish people seized eagerly upon lascivious gossip, even when it was palpably wild. For the most part the Queen stood aloof from the course of events. In the last two decades of her life, manners and morals changed greatly, and the new ways were almost invariably disagreeable to her. The end of the century (*fin de siècle,* as the

L'ENFANT TERRIBLE

After a cartoon by Joseph Keppler in *Puck,* 1891.

sophisticates called it) was associated with the decadent movement or movements in literature and the arts. But there is no reason to suppose that the mere fact the century was drawing to a close had any particular effect on moral and æsthetic standards. Some of the things which appeared in England in the 1880's and 1890's originated in France much earlier. America also made contributions to the new spirit. Perhaps Poe's influence was mostly indirect, through certain French writers. Walt Whitman spoke directly, although in the matter of poetical technique he was to influence English writers of the twentieth century through the *vers librists*.

A great many Britons came into contact with the moral standards prevailing in remote parts of the Empire. They learned to know the customs and the rules of right and wrong prevailing in India, Egypt, and the veldts of South Africa. They met savages and also civilized peoples whose attitude toward sex was very different from that of Victorian England. We find in the fiction of the time (for example, in *Vanity Fair*—Thackeray himself was born near Calcutta) the Englishman who has returned from years of residence in India with much money, a bad liver, and morals to whose depravity sly allusions are made.

Such contacts probably helped to bring about the movement toward frankness of expression which arose during the last decades of the nineteenth century. Of course, moral standards move in cycles. Great strictness brings about hypocrisy and disgust, then a dissatisfaction with the resulting extreme looseness brings a swing back toward asceticism. And the middle classes, who had been accustomed to consider their savings as capital or potential capital, found toward the end of Victoria's reign that they had money enough for luxuries. The new scientific advances increased their wealth and also, in many cases, undermined the bases of thier religion. They no longer found mundane pleasures, merely considered as such, sinful. It is true that the most vigorous leaders in the movement against precise moral standards were at first the aristocrats. If we are fond of attributing social changes in a monarchy to royal influence, we may say that Victoria, coming to the throne after the loose reigns of George IV and William IV, brought with her extremely precise standards of purity, until her importance diminished as she retired from the limelight in her somewhat comically tragic widowhood in favor of her son; who, beginning rather fearfully, introduced innovation after innovation. But there was unrest all over Europe and America in the '80's and

'90's. It was not merely in the United Kingdom that moral opinions changed.

During the eighteenth and nineteenth centuries France was usually the great horrible example to which conservative Englishmen pointed. Verlaine and Baudelaire were not, indeed, innovators in their flouting of *bourgeois* standards in art and life. The theory of art for art's sake we find (to go back no earlier) in the Englishman Keats, the American Poe, and the Frenchman Gautier. But Gautier brought it forward to justify *Mademoiselle de Maupin,* and that made a difference. Keats and Poe wrote practically nothing which precisians could consider indecent.

Gautier's novel and (perhaps still more important) the preface to it were published before Victoria came to the British throne, but they helped to awaken the protest which took form some decades later against Victorianism. *L'art pour l'art* is itself a moral dogma: whatever is otherwise suitable for presentation in the arts, we are told, should not be barred because it does not advance the current doctrines of right and wrong. It is proper to make beautiful things, that is, without inquiring if they are ethically acceptable. The art-for-art's-sake doctrine has at times been identified with protests against conventional morality, even with the diabolical inversion of moral values. But it properly bears no such connotation. And toward the end of the nineteenth century, when destructive moral propaganda became prominent on the English stage and in English books, some clever defenders of the old morality asserted their belief in art for art's sake. Attempts to glorify the old vices were, they said, no more justified in serious artistic efforts than attempts to preserve the old virtues.

The problem is one with which critics still struggle. It is chiefly the opponents of the present organization of society who now argue against an art which is dissociated from propaganda. They follow Tolstoi, who declared Shakespeare to be lacking in the highest order of greatness because he tacitly approved the evils of his time.

Indeed, it is difficult to write fiction, poetry, and drama in such a way as to conceal one's opinions of right and wrong. And

[307]

the literature of Victorian England was certainly much concerned with ethical values. Both Dickens and Thackeray wrote novels of purpose. Dickens wanted to protest against the mismanagement of poorhouses, the brutality of schoolmasters, and so on. Thackeray laughed at snobbery and hypocrisy, though sometimes not so loudly and openly as he would have liked. There were a few writers all through Victoria's reign who showed their disapproval of the current prudery.

The masculine population of the upper and middle classes realized that propriety was a matter of public utterance rather than of private behavior. Even the known rakes of the mid-Victorian period were not cast into limbo unless they were unduly insolent in flaunting their way of life before extremely good people. As a matter of fact, young men were expected to sow their wild oats.

Victoria prided herself on keeping the impure at a distance. Yet she trusted men who were not altogether angelic. Melbourne gained her confidence in the early days of her reign. As a widow she allowed Disraeli to flirt discreetly with her. There was nothing very discreditable to her about this, I should say; but it proved (if, indeed, it needed to be proved) that she was a human being who could be swayed by affection. The passions did not disappear in the Victorian period, no matter how improper it may have been to allude to them.

"Speech was not given to woman for her to say what she is thinking," remarks Romain Rolland. "Thank God! for there would be an end of morality on earth." Some Victorians denied the thinking as well as the saying, unconsciously struggling to defend their double standard of sexual conduct. They did not mean to be hypocritical, they would have angrily denied their selfishness. And they found it difficult to understand that other peoples had different moral standards, as legitimate (in their light) as those of England. Foreign ways seemed no more than brazen wickedness.

In speaking against the provincialism of England, Matthew Arnold was really attacking English prudery and pietism. To a certain extent he understood what he was doing. Walter Pater made still clearer the issue between Puritanism and Greek hedonism. But at times he seemed to be deliberately wrapping his thoughts in a cloud. It may be that he was unduly shy and timid. Perhaps he had genuine reason to be afraid. He acted as though he had a string of pearls which it would not be well to fling before creatures which might, by some possibility, turn out to be swine.

It is true that the swinishness has been attributed to some of Pater's disciples, and even to Pater himself. Terms of contempt and abhorrence are not of interest to the historian except as they indicate wide differences of outlook—in this case, the chasm which lay between outright Puritans and absolute Epicureans. It is not necessary to examine the clues we have to some elements in Pater's personal life or to inquire what he meant by certain controversial phrases. Pater was sufficiently under the influence of Victorian taboos to deplore the "immodesty" of *Chérie,* by the brothers Goncourt, but he read and admired it; he read Zola; he gave glowing praise to the art of Flaubert.

Pater's *The Renaissance* first appeared in 1873. Some of his most pagan utterances gave dissatisfaction and were omitted from the second and third editions of the book; but, beginning with the edition of 1888, they were restored, although with certain modifications. Young men were then permitted to read that they should "burn with a hard, gemlike flame," and that they should renounce "Christian asceticism" in favor of Greek serenity with regard to "the sensuous." Pater exerted great influence upon Oscar Wilde and some of the other writers who arose at the end of the century.

George Meredith, a Victorian who was slow to find honor among his contemporaries, seems "modern" because of his manner rather than his matter. In religion, indeed, he was not orthodox, speaking against priestcraft and seeming to vacillate between pantheism and Christianity. He clung generally to the old moral system, and he never agreed with the people who defended sexual relations carried on outside the bonds of marriage. But he could not accept the mid-Victorian view that for committing a fault which would be considered easily venial in

THE ENGLISH TAKE THEIR PLEASURES SADLY

A cartoon by George Du Maurier in *Punch*. Reproduced by permission of the Proprietors.

a man, a woman should be condemned beyond the possibility of forgiveness.

Thomas Hardy attached far less value than Meredith to the Christian creed. In fact, Hardy's God or Fate is an individual or a force to be feared, but hardly capable of inspiring love. Reacting against the facile optimism characteristic of most Victorian poets and novelists, Hardy saw human beings vainly struggling for happiness against hostile cosmic powers. Such a philosophy of life was itself sufficient to make him mistrusted by ordinary good Christian people. The manner in which he dealt with sex set him still further apart from the typically Victorian writers. It was not for him something to be hinted at in vague, sugar-coated words, but a prime mover—one that often brought on a catastrophe, to be sure, and yet productive of almost everything worth having in a world of mutability and frustration. Hardy dared to call Tess "a pure woman," meaning, of course, not one who was virginal, but one who acted as it is natural for members of her sex to act.

The full possibilities of the reproductive impulses in furnishing themes for literature were seen in France. In French books appeared the woman whose husband failed to understand her, or who could never be fully content within the limitations of monogamy. The young girl was shown, not virginal, but full of all sorts of bizarre desires. Oriental works dealing with sexual phantasies and aberrations sometimes appeared in English, but in small private editions. France was more friendly to them; in fact, we find English translations of Hindu works, which were circulated only among the select few, retranslated into French and offered for general sale at a low price. Some Englishmen first became familiar with such books as *The Aphorisms of Love* through these French versions of English translations.

One man, Sir Richard F. Burton, was sufficiently daring to bring to England the full aroma of a world which knew nothing of any Anglican grundyisms. He was a cadet in the Army of India, a student of many Oriental languages, a bold explorer. Burton is primarily remembered for *The Book of a Thousand Nights and a Night,* published in ten volumes, 1885-1886, and followed by *Supplemental Nights* (1887-1888). He was more than a translator of Arabic popular stories; for he added illuminating notes of his own on certain customs of the East which were very different from those prevailing in Great Britain, and he wrote freely about many things which not all Englishmen considered mentionable. Burton derived ten thousand pounds from this Arabic translation, and though the sets were sold by subscription, they reached a fairly wide audience.

Burton's wife, an ardent and pietistic Catholic, did not altogether approve of her husband's frank language. She prepared a bowdlerized version of *The Arabian Nights*, which, I suppose, did no particular harm to anyone. Also, somewhat strangely, she permitted the translations of the *Pentamerone* and of Catullus, which remained in manuscript after his death, to be published. She destroyed a manuscript translation of the Arabic erotic work called *The Scented Garden,* and she forbade other works of his to be printed without the express permission of the secretary of the National Vigilance Society, an organization opposed to the circulation of literature which its managers considered immoral. Despite domestic and other censors, Burton helped to make educated Englishmen conscious of the existence of a world apart from their own, one where no shame was felt in deriving the greatest and most varied pleasures possible from sex.

In France, a few decades earlier, Charles Baudelaire had spoken out with almost Oriental freedom. His *Flowers of Evil,* after being rejected with horror by a number of publishers, appeared in 1857. The author was then prosecuted for an offense "against public morality and good manners" and fined three hundred francs. At this time six of his poems were specifically condemned. They were soon published at Amsterdam in a volume of *Wreckage or Stray Pieces,* but it was some time before they were restored to their old place in a regular French edition of *Flowers of Evil.*

George Moore tells us, in *Confessions of a Young Man,* how Baudelaire affected those young Englishmen who became enthusiastic about French letters in the last quarter of the nineteenth century: "Gautier had written in *Mademoiselle de Maupin* a

[312]

lyrical exaltation of the joys of the flesh; he had eloquently and unreservedly pronounced the fleshly pleasures good. Baudelaire had gone farther: he had said that Evil was beautiful, the most beautiful thing in the world—and proved it, to those who were anxious to believe it, by writing beautiful poems about every form of evil that he could think of."

Baudelaire sometimes seemed to be defending art for art's sake, as when he wrote that he declined "to confuse ink with virtue." In general, he was identified with the diabolists, whose viewpoint is most attractively presented in English in a few of Swinburne's poems. But Swinburne was far less consistent than Baudelaire, and he is usually a defender of passion rather than of evil and vice as such. He never went quite so far as some of his French contemporaries in inverting Christianity and setting up the black mass of Satan. What he particularly attacked was Puritanism. Curiously, he showed himself something of a Puritan in the last years of his life. And, similarly, some of the Satanists on the Continent ended in the lap of Mother Church. There was more real danger to the familiar standards from such men as Pater, who did not remain content with inversions or negations but looked back longingly to the hedonism of the antique world.

It is often carelessly assumed that the revolt against the old standards in English literature broke out abruptly in the 1890's and entirely as the result of foreign influences. Perhaps the latter assumption is a result of the fact that the orthodox moralists of England have almost always condemned books and customs that have seemed obnoxious to them as un-English. Italianate works, poetry contaminated with the skepticism and the indecency of France or (in our own times) of Germany and Russia have been condemned on patriotic grounds as well as on the more obvious moral ones.

The classics of Greece and Rome, however, have long enjoyed a privileged position in English education, and they have suffered comparatively little from bowdlerizing. There was once an edition of Martial for use in English schools which had "all the obnoxious epigrams," as Byron tells us, "placed by themselves at the end." The idea was that the book should be complete but still suitable for continuous reading in the classroom. The boys all read the appendix, however, even though it was not assigned.

Byron sets out, in *Don Juan*, that

> Ovid's a rake, as half his verses show him,
> Anacreon's morals are a still worse sample,
> Catullus scarcely has a decent poem,
> I don't think Sappho's Ode a good example.

These were authors whom British schoolboys read and who knew nothing of Victorian prudery. The young writers of the '90's often mingle echoes of Catullus with those of Baudelaire or Verlaine.

English versions of the Latin and Greek classics were until recently intended almost exclusively for the use of women. As a consequence, the translations are usually honeycombed with deletions, euphemistic paraphrases, and passages which are presented in the original instead of being englished with the rest. This is often the case with the newest versions published in England and America, though some faithful translations from classical writers lacking prudery appear, especially in expensive limited editions.

In the 1880's and 1890's the precise moralists of England thought that immorality was being imported from France. Tennyson in his old age took up the cry about the degenerate times. In "Locksley Hall Sixty Years After," which was published in 1886, he exclaims:

Authors—atheist, essayist, novelist, realist, rhymester, play your
   part,
Paint the mortal shame of nature with the living hues of Art.
Rip your brothers' vices open, strip your own foul passions bare;
Down with Reticence, down with Reverence—forward—naked—
   let them stare.
Feed the budding rose of boyhood with the drainage of your sewer;
Send the drain into the fountain, lest the stream should issue pure.
Set the maiden fancies wallowing in the troughs of Zolaism,—
Forward, forward, ay and backward, downward too into the abysm.

Zola became quickly known in England. In 1887 Vizetelly began to issue an unexpurgated edition of his novels in English translation. Two years later he was prosecuted. He was convicted, imprisoned, ruined, and driven to his death. The police as well as Tennyson were anxious to save the budding rose of boyhood and the maiden fancies from the troughs of Zolaism.

It was, then, a genuinely bold plan of young Havelock Ellis' to bring out complete and unbowdlerized reprints of the Elizabethan and Restoration plays in the Mermaid Series. However, the plays were English, not importations of French immorality, which may be the reason why editor and publisher were not molested. Ellis edited also the Contemporary Science Series, and the first volume he presented was *The Evolution of Sex* by Geddes and Thomson.

Havelock Ellis planned for his own writing a work on the psychology of sex. The first part that was ready, *Sexual Inversion,* appeared in 1897. In the preceding decade England had apparently become accustomed to frank discussions of sexual problems. Yet Ellis and his publisher made no great attempt to advertise the book, and it was quietly sold to a few people. A German translation was received with great interest and occasioned no prudish protests. But in England matters remained very different. In 1898 Bedborough, who was prominent in the free-thought movement, sold a copy in his private house to a detective. He was then arrested for "publishing an obscene libel," that is, selling an indecent book. He chose to plead guilty, feeling that more important concerns of his would be compromised if he stood trial. The publication of the book, and of the remainder of the work, in England was then abandoned. The series is now published by a Philadelphia firm specializing in medical works, but its sale is supposed to be restricted to physicians and lawyers. It was intended for the laity, and certainly as a serious scientific contribution, not as a piece of pornography. In French and German translations it is sold to the intelligent men and women for whom it was intended.

About the same time that *Sexual Inversion* appeared, Edward Carpenter was offering *Love's Coming of Age* to the publishers of London. He finally issued it at his own expense. Carpenter's book, even more than Ellis', was intended for the general reader. Its tone is guarded throughout. There is, indeed, a chapter on homosexual love, but the matter is treated in such a way that moralists have to go somewhat out of their way to take offense. Perhaps his contemptuous treatment of the Victorian lady, kept pure and subservient by means of ignorance and the prostitution of many women, and his plea for feminism were not less objectionable than his generalizations about love between men and between women in the eyes of the publishers who found his book unavailable. In 1911, with its success already accomplished, Carpenter wrote in the preface to a new edition an account of his early trials, adding: "And to-day people are beginning to see that a decent and straightforward discussion of sex questions is not only permissible, but is quite necessary." More explicit books than *Love's Coming of Age* now circulate freely in England.

George Moore comments ironically on the circulating library as it flourished in Victorian days with the support of the publishers, who usually printed novels in several expensive volumes each: "Pressure was brought on the publishers, and books were published at 31s. 6d.; the dirty, outside public was got rid of, and the villa paid its yearly subscription, and had nice large handsome books that none but the *élite* could obtain, and with them a sense of equality with Lady This and Lady That, and certainty that nothing would come into the hands of dear Kate and Mary and Maggie that they might not read, and all for two guineas a year. English fiction became pure, and the garlic and assafœtida with which Byron, Fielding, and Ben Jonson so liberally seasoned their work, and in spite of which, as critics say, they were geniuses, have disappeared from our literature."

They had not, as a matter of fact, altogether disappeared when Moore wrote these words, and (partly under his own influence) they have returned to a considerable extent. Moreover, English writers have not had to turn to foreign literatures to learn how to deal with "garlic and assafœtida." There was a continuous tradition, starting at least as far back as Chaucer and running up to Swinburne and Thomas Hardy, in the mid-Victorian wilderness.

Moore complained that the novelist was not permitted to say artistically what the newspapers told but clumsily and pruriently. Under the Victorian compromise between truth and "pleasant fibs," he says, "the understanding was that brutality, lust, and selfishness were to be represented as being qualities only of 'bad' people, plainly labelled as such." And he asks a question which has troubled other critics: "I wonder why murder is considered less immoral than fornication in literature." Of course, the murder mystery is read by the most moral of people without thought of shame. Still, some of our American motion-picture censors object to having men shot dead on the screen as well as to ardent love-making.

The French influence was probably the most important of those from modern Continental sources upon art and life in England at the close of the Victorian period. Next, I should say, came the Norwegian, and that was represented almost exclusively by one man, Henrik Ibsen. Ibsen, after writing lyrics, romantic plays, and dramas of a philosophical-poetic nature, became known for his treatment of controversial social questions on the stage. His problem plays began to appear in the late '70's. The first important English production of Ibsen came in 1889, when *A Doll's House* was given to an astonished audience at the Novelty Theatre in London.

Soon the battle between the English Ibsenites and anti-Ibsenites was in full swing. Clement Scott spoke of "such unpleasing realism," and these were among the mildest words of dispraise. The newspapers printed letters from readers who thought the censors should prohibit such vile stuff. George Bernard Shaw appeared as an admirer of Ibsen, but he displeased some of the Ibsenites who thought the Norwegian's poetry should be emphasized rather than his supposed teachings. Ibsen himself used to insist that he was not a propagandist but a poet. In 1891 the London *Evening Standard* called the people who had a good word to say for Ibsen's *Ghosts*, "lovers of prurience and dabblers in impropriety, who are eager to gratify their illicit tastes under the pretense of art." The censor forbade the public showing of this play, and it was not presented in the regular way in England until 1914.

Ibsen exerted an influence upon many English dramatists, including some who were loud in the denunciation of Ibsenism. Pinero, Jones, Galsworthy, and Shaw are among the playwrights whose work shows some sort of discipleship to the Norwegian. Shaw, who has sometimes been criticized as though Ibsen were the only writer from whom he derived ideas, rightly insists that his principal teacher was the Victorian Samuel Butler.

Butler's *Erewhon*, with its attack on the great god Grundy, became at once moderately popular, although his other books published in his lifetime fell flat. *The Way of All Flesh* was not presented to the public until after his death. Then it helped to arouse a feeling that the command, "Thou shalt honor thy father and thy mother," had been somewhat too sternly enforced in Victorian days. The twentieth century has, indeed, been the era of the child.

George Bernard Shaw first appeared in print when he wrote a letter to a newspaper expressing his disapproval of the methods employed by the American revivalists, Moody and Sankey, who came to Dublin in 1875. Later, Shaw became known as a musical and dramatic critic, as a socialist, an antivivisectionist, and a vegetarian. Shaw's plays began to appear in the '90's, although his great popularity did not come until the new century. Shaw differs from most of the *fin-de-siècle* writers not merely in the fact that he has lived and worked into our own time, but more essentially in that he represents the Protestant and Puritan tradition of England rather than an exotic Gallicism.

Mrs. Warren's Profession, written in 1893, was forbidden by the censor, and it was not seen in London until 1902, when it was privately presented at the New Lyric Club. This play, like most of the others written by Shaw, was meant to convey a moral and to bring about more precise sexual standards. It was considered improper by the censor because it deals with prostitution. Shaw argues that society should take steps to keep women from selling themselves for money, whether in brothels or in respectable and sacred matrimony. He offers a solution—the financial independence of women.

Shaw has fought against many usages of his time. What his success as a propagandist has been, it is difficult to tell. Some of the things for which he clamored have been realized, in whole or in part; but it is probable that they would have come about just as soon without his work. Englishmen in general regard him as an eccentric fellow, perhaps as a clever writer and a wit, but long hesitated about taking him seriously. For this impression he is himself largely responsible, because the means he has taken to arouse attention have often been such as to suggest the buffoon. Germans and Americans seem to respect his views more than Britons do.

In England his arguments against prudery and the censorship of the stage have probably aroused most attention. His earnestness about these matters results from the fact that he has himself suffered from the taboos. In the preface to *Getting Married*, which appeared in 1908, Shaw says: "When Zola tried to repopulate France by writing a novel in praise of parentage, the only comment made here was that the book could not possibly be translated into English, as its subject was too improper." Zola, too, was an uncompromising moralist, and one who was charged with immorality because of his anxiety to make his ethical lessons impressive. The same thing may be said of Ibsen, although he professed to be a poet rather than a propagandist.

Shaw complained, for instance, in the preface to *The Showing-Up of Blanco Posnet*, one of his plays which the English censor found objectionable, that the censorship did not operate to promote good morals. He said that vicious plays were allowed providing they satisfied English prejudices by having happy endings, obvious farcical scenes, and other conventional elements, while such plays as his own, which spoke out plainly for moral reform, were barred or regarded with disfavor.

Contemporary with Shaw in the '90's, but not destined to live into the new century, was Oscar Wilde. The work of the two men bears a certain resemblance, mostly superficial. Shaw was a Puritan; Wilde could be an ascetic at times, but his asceticism was, if religious at all, that of the Roman Catholic Church.

Indeed, the Oxford movement is responsible to some extent for the literary ebullition of late-Victorian times. Abel Chevalley says: "One of those invasive recurrences of French influence in manners, feeling, and expression that are almost always sequential to a revival of English Catholicism made itself felt about the year 1890." Of course, neither the High Church Anglican pietists nor those who joined the Roman Catholic Church approved of all the importations from France.

Wilde and many more of his contemporaries of whom it may safely be said that they were influenced both by France and by the Church of Rome, were at least equally responsive to paganism. As for Wilde, he wore so many different masks that almost anything may be said, with a certain amount of justification, about his character and his philosophy of life. Sometimes he was a Diabolist and could write, "What is termed Sin is an essential element of progress." He says also, in *The Critic as Artist:* "To be good, according to the vulgar standard of goodness, is quite easy. It merely requires a certain amount of sordid terror, a certain lack of imaginative thought, and a certain low passion for middle-class respectability."

Sometimes he was the champion of a sort of kid-glove æstheticism. He defended *l'art pour l'art,* saying, "An ethical sympathy in an artist is an unpardonable mannerism of style." Yet he was constantly troubled by problems of conduct. Christian consciousness of sin (or perhaps a vague fear of the evil that was eventually to overtake him) sometimes disturbed his classical hedonism, as when he exclaimed in a poem, "And Atys with his blood-stained knife were better than the thing I am."

For the thing he was, because of his recklessness, he went to prison. England collectively held its nose. His plays and his books were withdrawn, men and women who had received letters from him burned them up, respectable people were careful not to mention his name. But pirated editions of his writings were issued, and some of them were very successful. When Oscar Wilde was convicted of indulging in forbidden homosexual acts, many heard his name for the first time or with an interest never previously aroused.

Two magazines of the '90's, the *Yellow Book* and the *Savoy*, stood in the forefront of literary and artistic change. The name of Aubrey Beardsley is associated with both of them. We think of Beardsley chiefly as an illustrator, but he had ambitions as a writer as well. He set to work on a romance, *Under the Hill*, which reads in part like a fictionized version of Krafft-Ebing's *Psychopathia Sexualis*. Beardsley's drawings lay emphasis upon the breasts and buttocks of women, which appear in size much out of proportion. The science of voluptuous cruelty offered Beardsley many themes. Sadism and masochism were specialties of the period; they were associated for this artist with the black mass of Satanism. Arthur Symons speaks of the grotesque beauty which is nearest "to brutality and the spectacular vices" and which we find in Manet, Degas, and Whistler as well as in Beardsley. The Satanism of Beardsley turned into the penitence of a good Catholic on his deathbed, when he asked that the drawings which he then felt to be obscene should be destroyed. He died young, like so many artists of the '90's.

Ernest Dowson too died young, after having spent most of his life in France. And he, like Beardsley, was a Roman Catholic who could not fully adjust himself to a hedonistic way of life. Or perhaps we should rather say that his was the same seeking of tortured, sorrowful delight, the same attempt to find beautiful pleasure in the dolorous road and the way of the Cross. Dowson found sorrow in love, too: there was a simple girl from France who might have understood him had she waited instead of running off with a waiter. Tragedy was essential to him, as it was to all the sad young men of the '90's. Dowson learned much from Swinburne and from Swinburne's French masters, but he spoke for himself and for his time when he expressed a desire "for madder music and for stronger wine." Symons comments on "that curious love of the sordid, so common an affectation of the modern decadent, and with him so genuine."

There were a number of other Catholic minor poets in the late years of Victoria's reign, with varying moral outlooks.

Coventry Patmore was simply a secondary Tennyson who became converted to Catholicism and who retained the grundyisms of the middle of the century. Francis Thompson, like Dowson in his college days, was addicted to narcotics. He was familiar enough with sordidness, whether or not he loved it. His moral heresies were, indeed, actions and not words or principles.

Arthur Symons, who has written critically about the men of the '90's, also took part in the work of "bewildering the *bourgeois*." He did this admirably, for example, in the poem called "Nini Patte-en-l'-Air," which is one of a group dedicated to Charles Baudelaire. He talks about the dancer's drawers in a manner which spinster aunts must have found painfully disconcerting. He says of Nini, in words which might have been applied to himself and to many artists of the time:

> What exquisite indecency,
> Select, supreme, severe, an art!
> The art of knowing how to be
> Part lewd, æsthetical in part,
> And *fin de siècle* utterly.

In the next stanza he speaks of "this science of concupiscence." Well might the old-fashioned *bourgeois* feel bewildered.

It was the fashion to be daring—and in view of that fact it didn't require a great deal of courage to say shocking things. To be sure, there were limits, but the writers of poetry and fiction seldom found them very troublesome. Commercially there were still, during the '90's, advantages in keeping the old taboos. Conservative publishers were slow, the persons in charge of renting and free libraries were still slower, to accept the new standards.

George Moore, whose attack on the Victorian library system has already been quoted, started to write realistic novels in the '80's, under the influence of Flaubert and Zola. He has continued to shock prudes into our own time. After becoming accustomed to hear himself denounced as indecent, he found himself assailed as blasphemous because of *The Brook Kerith* (1916), and since then he has published mostly limited editions.

THE STOMACH DANCE

An illustration by Aubrey Beardsley for Oscar Wilde's *Salome*, 1893. Reproduced
by permission of John Lane, Ltd.

Thomas Hardy's boldest novels appeared in the '90's. Apparently he was affected by the moral criticisms directed against his work, and this seems to be the reason why he stopped writing novels and turned his attention entirely to poetry. Some other novelists, of much less literary importance, created about as much stir as Hardy in the last years of the nineteenth century. A journalist of Canadian origin, Grant Allen, published in 1895 a novel called *The Woman Who Did*. His advocacy of increased freedom in the relations between the sexes caused a burst of moral indignation which increased the sale of the book. Its commercial success brought a number of imitators into the market.

Several women novelists went further than those who had created the "roaring girl" in dealing with sexual problems. "Sarah Grand" or Mrs. Frances Elizabeth McFall began in 1888 to study the case of the wife whose husband commits adultery and other similar situations.

Nietzsche's inversions of moral values, his paradoxical philosophizing, and his glorification of the strong, ruthless individual (a sort of Darwinian Machiavellianism) became familiar to a few Englishmen at the end of the nineteenth century. He was still known to the "man in the street" only by smatterings and misquotations in 1914, and it was consequently possible to divide between him and the Kaiser the blame for starting the World War. Max Stirner's anarchistic doctrines were discussed in the '90's but seem to have had no important lasting influence. British egoists had, however, from 1898 to 1902, a small magazine called the *Eagle and the Serpent*.

Rudyard Kipling burst upon the British public with a somewhat different philosophy of power, which was sometimes implicit, sometimes explicit, in his tales and poems about India and then about other parts of the Empire. Men turned to Kipling, in many cases, by way of reaction from the decadents. They spoke of a world which was coming to a close; he dealt with a new vitality. Still, his moral effect was not altogether dissimilar to theirs. Kipling was Nietzschean in pleading that there might be high righteousness about the use of force.

Nietzsche, however, actually shrank from the prospect of a European war, while Kipling clamored for the day when the British forces should march against the Russians.

Nietzsche spoke, primarily to philosophers, about going beyond good and evil. Kipling makes the British soldier ask:

Ship me somewheres east of Suez, where the best is like the worst,
Where there aren't no Ten Commandments, an' a man can raise a
    thirst.

There can be no question about Kipling's having had, especially in the English-speaking countries, a far greater moral influence than Nietzsche.

Wilfrid Scawen Blunt was one of the most prominent opponents of British imperialism. He suffered imprisonment for his work in Ireland, and unpopularity in England was his almost as a matter of course. Blunt attacked conventional morality, directly or by implication, in a number of his poems. The prime mid-Victorian virtue is disposed of in "The Wisdom of Merlyn" as follows:

Chastity? Who is unchaste? The church-wed wife, without blame
    Yielding her body nightly, a lack-love indolent prize, to the lord
        of her legal shame?
Or she, the outlawed passionate soul? Their carnal act is the same.

In other words, love justifies all things, and loveless marriage is more sinful than illicit relations brought about by passion. Blunt tells in a series of sonnets how, as a young man, he attracted the interest of a French actress and how she initiated him into the mysteries of love.

Rousseauan autobiography has, indeed, gained a strong hold on many English writers since Trollope wrote the story of his life. Often authors veil their frankness with the more or less transparent disguise of fiction. Some novelists have been blamed for kissing and telling; one or two have been accused of telling without having kissed.

Now we have Frank Harris telling about his life in the manner of Casanova, and his book reaches many Englishmen and

Americans, even though not printed in an English-speaking country. James Joyce has written a book with the frankness (and some of the genius, too, I should say) of Rabelais. Though *Ulysses* was published in Paris, many copies have come into Great Britain and the United States. A somewhat abridged version has been published in an American monthly. Joyce has been denounced as a wanton pornographer, and some critics have found symptoms of his madness in *Ulysses;* but it is indisputable, at any rate, that he has not violated the current literary decencies because of a desire for money.

This cannot be said of all the English writers of shocking books in the last two or three decades. Some of them have deliberately written sexy novels because they thought they would sell. Still, until about 1912 the lists of British commercial successes were made up mostly of "wholesome" books, supposed to be suitable for family reading, and this type has by no means been driven out since.

Elinor Glyn's *Three Weeks* appeared in 1907, and the *New International Year Book* bearing that date tells us that this "detailed description of a passional episode in sensual language became more conspicuous through the controversy it created than any literary merit." The same article tells us about Galsworthy's *The Man of Property* and *The Country House,* books "full of unpleasant people whose sordidness and prejudices are described with mordant humor." Of course, I do not mean to make comparisons of literary merit in bringing these two names into the same paragraph.

Sometimes, as in *The Fugitive* (1913), Galsworthy seems to say that a revolt against conventional morals is sure to bring disaster upon the rebel. Many of the writers who have been denounced as immoral are really defending the old standards, simply violating the rules of prudery in order to be more effective. Galsworthy, indeed, is not entirely satisfied with things as they are. It is noteworthy that very few of the bold, bad novelists of twentieth-century England have found fault with monogamy, at least as a norm, though some have attacked certain aspects of conventional marriage.

Shaw, Arnold Bennett, and W. L. George are a few of the many writers who have brought harlots and concubines into their books, but there is no longer any pretense that the English maiden remains ignorant of the existence of such beings. It is now possible for young writers to deal with illicit sexual behavior almost as a matter of course, without showing any conscious desire to shock and bewilder the grocers, stenographers, and duchesses who may be expected to read their books or to see their plays. To be sure, there are many people horrified every year by some of the new books, and there are still preachers in England who find it possible to use current novels and plays as texts to illustrate the need of reticence. And the general attitude toward literary morality has probably changed as much since 1912 as it had between 1840 and 1885, or between 1885 and 1912.

In 1912 the drama of *Hindle Wakes*, by Stanley Houghton, made many Londoners angry. It tells how a working girl is seduced by her employer's son, who later offers to marry her, but she refuses because she does not love him. According to the mid-Victorian view, such a girl has been defiled, and she cannot recover her pristine purity, though she can regain a certain vestige of respectability by marrying the man who has seduced her. According to the precisians of Richardson's and Goldsmith's age, no course is open to her but a slow pining to death. Now we find writers saying that she has not been seriously injured, or at least that the wrong of a loveless marriage cannot repair the evil of a seduction.

Max Beerbohm wrote, a few years before the outbreak of the World War, of "that conscious, separate, and quite explicit desire to be a mother with which modern playwrights credit every unmated member of her [Zuleika Dobson's] sex." Even the scientific writers of that period were somewhat inclined to explain sexual desire, in women if not in men, as a longing for progeny.

More recently writers have been willing to credit women with venereal appetite and satisfaction quite distinct from, sometimes in full opposition to, a wish for children. Psychoanalysis, which has attracted novelists and general readers since the war, has opened up new fields to frankness. And though psychoanalysis as a fad (never quite so important in Great Britain as in the United States) has virtually disappeared, the new attitude toward sex has remained.

D. H. Lawrence is probably the English writer who has made the largest and most important use of Freudian symbolism in fiction. It is true that his power and his "immorality" are not dependent upon any particular psychological system, and that his books would, without much doubt, be essentially the same even if he had never heard of psychoanalysis. Lawrence makes us feel rather than think. Few writers have gone beyond him in the ability to evoke intense sensual responses. Attempts to suppress one or two of his books have given him a great deal of advertising and added to the circle of his readers. As the philosophical author of dust-jacket panegyrics for an American series of reprints remarks: "Ironically enough, it was the vain effort of a self-appointed censor to suppress *The Rainbow* that first called to the attention of the general public the enduring qualities of the book."

Since the World War many biographies have appeared in England which lack the cheaply sentimental hero worship which used to be characteristic of the general run of these books. The credit of pioneering in the new movement is usually given to Lytton Strachey, who first aroused attention with *Eminent Victorians*. Strachey's work shows a familiarity with French literature, and his wit has been called Gallic. Unlike some of his imitators, he has been neither a scandalmonger nor a purveyor of the commodity known in America as wise cracks. There are people who deny that the clay feet of idols should be analyzed, fearing that the resulting knowledge is likely to give moral indigestion to the young; and they are resentful of what Strachey has done.

§ 2

All these literary changes correspond to alterations in manners and moral outlook which have been revealed in a variety of ways. But I have chosen to deal in some detail with books and plays because it has been mostly through these that the revolt against Victorianism in England has been revealed to the American people. There are tourists enough nowadays who cross the Atlantic, and between trips to one or another shrine in England they can observe the current length of skirts and the availability of beer; but they seldom remain long enough to obtain a full realization of ethical attitudes. They learn about these, if at all, from literary works. Generally speaking, the same moral forces have been at work in England and America, though it is easy to point out certain differences, some of them rather important. The extreme pietism which is still rather common in many rural districts of the United States is not unknown in England and Wales, but it is less influential.

Opposition to the theatre was strong in England during the 1890's, and has not altogether disappeared to this day. In 1900 Mr. S. Smith, member for Flintshire, denounced in Parliament the depravity of the stage; thereupon Mr. Gibson Bowles pointed out that Mr. Smith might easily be mistaken in the matter since he had never entered a playhouse. The Methodists were then, to a large extent, enemies of the theatre; and in Wales, where Methodist and other Dissenting bodies were strong, it was well into the twentieth century before the majority were willing to consider theatregoing other than sinful.

Queen Victoria's eldest son, as Prince of Wales and then as King Edward VII, associated freely with actors, thus helping to improve their social position. Edward was very fond of pleasure, and he had none of the Puritan prejudice against the "rogues and vagabonds" who left no tangible proof that they had labored. Easily bored, he was constantly flitting from place to place, from amusement to amusement. The country was, apparently, not injured by the fact that he did not share his parents' devotion to work, did not sit for hours trying to uncover the import of involved State papers.

As Prince of Wales, Edward was hardly doing more than his duty when he maintained a stable of racing horses. Almost everybody in England was enthusiastic when, in 1896, his entry won the Derby. Racing remains respectable in England, and royalty continues to lend its support. Betting on horse races has a strong hold on the people, and whippet racing has recently aroused the interest of many spectators and betters. The dogs have served gamblers in another way, since the stocks of whippet-racing companies have been used for speculation. In general, though, people of small means in England have usually stayed away from gambling operations in securities and future contracts for commodities.

Grace Thompson gives the credit (or perhaps the discredit) for some important social changes to royalty: "King Edward regarded the best class of Hebrews with marked favor and had a warm liking for Americans, especially when they were beautiful and rich; when the King showed approval the others were not slow to turn a friendly eye. The old aristocracy, proud, narrow, sometimes a little ridiculous, but with a deeply-rooted conviction that it was responsible for the welfare of the country, gave place to a society in which wealth alone was the 'Open Sesame' and in which a sense of responsibility, however vague and in-elastic, was not required at all."

The changes here indicated had actually been going on for some time before 1901. Edward was simply recognizing an accomplished fact. The great landowning nobles whose families had arisen or been enriched through the confiscation of the monasteries under Henry VIII, or because of later royal amours, were no longer the real rulers of England. The brewers and manufacturers of liver pills had replaced them. As to the sense of responsibility, it has become as great among the industrial leaders as it ever was among the landlords. The attitude of the urban laboring classes has changed, though. They are not content to wait for the goodness and the generosity of their employers, but insist upon higher wages or upon insurance against illness and periods of depression. The English aristocracy has always been essentially one of wealth, and the important change has been the growth of nonagricultural capital.

But the commercial and industrial classes were slow to develop social pretensions. The middle classes were reluctant to give up the Puritan tradition of thrift. Merchants considered it proper to live in the same buildings where they kept their shops; and until quite recently many prominent lawyers have had their living apartments attached to their offices. During the nineteenth century many people who became wealthy through manufacture or trade bought land, by way of asserting themselves socially. Some of the newly-rich acquired titles, the outward symbols of aristocracy. The prestige of the peerage diminished gradually, and it has gone down still more in the twentieth century, especially since the Parliament Act of 1911 has much reduced the legislative power of the House of Lords.

There is no clear evidence that English society has been coarsened by the new aristocracy. Of course, it is possible to give individual instances of war profiteers and pickle manufacturers who do not feel at ease in the presence of complicated dishes and retinues of servants; but, in general, the tendency of high society has been in the direction of refinement, perhaps sometimes of overrefinement.

There has been an alteration of table manners even within the royal palaces. The story goes that Victoria was once eating chicken in the presence of a grandchild, and that the boy gazed wonderingly while she took up a bone in her hand. He had been taught the iniquity of such a way of eating by his nurse. Finally he exclaimed, "Oh, grannie, piggy-wiggy!"

Late in Victoria's reign the upper classes adopted the convention, and, to some extent, the habit, of a daily bath. All social circles raised the standard of bodily cleanliness, although the improved plumbing facilities which have made the change easy in the United States have come very slowly into English homes.

England has witnessed a brightening of clothes and manners since mid-Victorian days. Society women began in the last years of the nineteenth century to make frank use of perfumes and cosmetics, which had been abandoned to harlots and flashy concubines. This tendency gradually increased, and it took a leap upward during the World War, when, indeed, respectable women of all social classes adopted methods of allurement which had long been left to those who sold their bodies.

Earlier, King Edward's influence had been exerted in favor of a smart, gay society. And he had stimulated travel to French and other Continental resorts. But, again, it was the presence of excess wealth and the new standards of the middle classes rather than the King's personal example that added sparkle to English social life. Matters did not change when Edward was succeeded by George V. Of course, Edward's attitude toward amusements and toward life in general had counted with certain of the industrial magnates who considered the opportunity to associate with royalty the greatest reward of success.

Some of the American heiresses who married English nobles and gentlemen worked to increase the gaiety of London society. They attached importance to fashionable dress and lively recreations. It is, indeed, doubtful if they have stimulated the growth of democracy in England, though they have probably helped to improve the position of women.

The English are accustomed to speak more frankly about social distinctions than we do in America. A servant is a servant—never "help." The difference goes further than words, of course, since domestic workers in some parts of the United States are treated as equal to the lady of the house. Recently, however, the privileges of English servants have been greatly augmented. Social democracy is increasing in Great Britain; in fact, there are indications of a movement toward guild socialism.

A history of the popular dances in the English-speaking countries would tell us much about the liberalization of manners since the 1880's. The waltz, which had troubled Byron's sense of propriety, became acceptable to the Victorian age. It enjoyed a long reign, and it did not disturb unduly the formality of ballrooms. In the '90's the barn dance and the Washington post illustrated and helped to produce a looser standard of decorum. Then came the bunny-hug, the turkey-trot, the tango, the shimmy, the Charleston, and a host of others combining gymnastics and voluptuousness. The waltz, which had once been cited as an example of modern depravity, became a symbol of antiquity, of slow-going, romantic days. It was connected with a sentimen-

FIN DE SIÈCLE DANCING MEN

"Been dancin' at all?"
"Dancin'? Not I! Catch me dancin' in a house where there ain't a smokin'-room! I'm off, directly!"

A cartoon by George Du Maurier in *Punch*. Reproduced by permission of the Proprietors.

talism which seemed somewhat ridiculous to young people who learned cynicism and sophistication from Arlen and Aldous Huxley, or from one another.

During the 1890's women became interested in bicycles, and some of them began to appear on English roads dressed in knickers. A number of eloquent appeals to women to free themselves from the shackles of corsets and heavy skirts appeared during this period, but they had little influence at the time. In fact, it was considered dreadful enough that even bicycling should bring out visibly bifurcate garments. The boys of the '90's could not be kept ignorant of the fact that women are two-legged animals. Or perhaps, to judge by some sermons and editorials of the bicycling days, it was merely "shameless females" who were two-legged. The motor car partially replaced the bicycle and gave decreased occasion to women to wear mannish garments. It did, however, make shorter skirts somewhat more convenient, especially for the women who learned to drive cars. Not until the period of the World War did the stay-makers have reason to tremble.

In 1895 English young women who went skating were advised to wear "an under-petticoat of flannel," short skirts—oh, dreadfully short skirts—"at least three inches above the ankles" and "easy short corsets." At about this time there were proposals for forming girls' teams to play association football. But the sporting woman, then and for some time later, furnished much material to caricaturists and joke-writers.

During the early years of the twentieth century, ping-pong was the fashionable game for girls and women. It did not seem unduly strenuous, it permitted a graceful position, and it did not require any abbreviation of costume. Archery was favored for similar reasons, and it was supposed to be even better suited for putting young women into striking and lovable attitudes. There were fairly rapid changes in the attitude of English girls toward sport and sporting costumes. In the winter of 1913-14 the fashion magazines of England showed pictures of women at Alpine resorts who had altogether discarded their skirts for ski-running and similar exercises. Since the War the costume most suitable for any given game has usually been worn. Women tennis players still cling to their skirts, and photographers delight in showing them in action, making available for the delectation of their contemporaries and of posterity glimpses of their undergarments and the upper parts of their legs. There are defenders of modesty who think some sort of bloomers should be worn by women when they play tennis, or at least when they are photographed as they play. Female runners, football-players, and swimmers are frankly two-legged.

All over Europe, women were expected as late as the '80's to wear a plurality of petticoats. When the outer skirt was lifted, as for the purpose of keeping it free of mud or dust in crossing a street, an underskirt became visible. The requirement that at least one petticoat should be worn remained for several decades. But the changes in feminine costume which have aroused the wrath of moralists began before the outbreak of the World War. In 1911 a few extremists appeared publicly in harem or trouser skirts. Then came the vogue of very tight skirts. In 1912 and 1913 there was an alarmed outcry that women were not dressing themselves for their public appearances, but rather undressing themselves. Skirts remained long for several years afterward. In 1919 they became decidedly shorter, at the same time that waists became larger.

Perhaps there are no available statistics on the average length of skirts worn by English and American women. Some travelers curious in such matters report that the English girls have gone to greater extremes. But in 1927 and 1928 very short skirts have been frowned upon. In several English cities the passengers in tram cars have objected to the length of the skirts worn by young women, or possibly to the manner in which these have been arranged, and asked the conductors to eject these offenders.

With short skirts for women has gone short hair. The sovereign of England is reported to have said that he dislikes the docking of horses' tails and women's hair, but royal looks of disdain have not appreciably retarded the acceptance of new fashions. King George V and his Queen have shown a devotion to gentility and an opposition to innovations in manners almost as strong as Victoria's. But their son is setting up a counteracting influence, much as Edward did when he was Prince of Wales. George and Mary frown upon jazz, their eldest son enjoys it immensely; and most of the people of England seem to be on the bachelor Prince's side in the matter.

According to Mrs. C. S. Peel, "It is, perhaps, to Miss Margot Tennant"—whom we know better as Margot Asquith and as the Countess of Oxford and Asquith—"and to the bicycle that we owe the emancipation of the modern girl." The bicycle meant exercise in the open air, a daring costume, and somewhat freer relations with the masculine world.

That Margot Tennant did not fly recklessly in the face of convention is amply shown by the fact of her friendly reception by such men as Gladstone and Tennyson. She was attractive, witty, and fond of associating with people who were supposed to be interested in intellectual things. At the same time she was a lover of sport, especially of riding. "I have broken both collarbones, all my ribs," and a long list of other bones, she tells us.

Born in 1864, Margot did not marry until 1894; but she is careful to point out in her autobiography that she did not wait so long because of any lack of earlier opportunities. In 1886 she began to do social work, interesting herself in the life of working girls. She tells how she happened, during that year, to come into a low-class public house of Whitechapel, and how she sat unnoticed in a corner, "eating my sandwich and smoking my cigarette."

Because of the example given by the Prince of Wales, men were then being permitted to smoke in the presence of women in the highest aristocratic circles. But ladies were not then, nor, indeed, until after the World War, supposed to smoke in public. Since Margot says that her cigarette was unnoticed in the pub, we may infer that the lower orders put no taboo on smoking by women. Female smokers were not extremely rare at any time during Victoria's reign. In high society there were many women who smoked before 1914, although it was not quite respectable of them to do it. The War introduced the habit to women of the middle classes.

In 1908 *Punch* published a poem about the flapper, beginning:

> Her locks are confined by a ribbon,
> Her language is open and free;
> She talks like a parrot, she's glib on
> The problems that petrify me.

The versifier could hardly be expected to know how much more open and free the language of the flapper was to become in the following decade or two.

In 1910 Londoners were given the opportunity of examining a group of post-impressionist pictures sent over from Paris. Wilfrid Scawen Blunt, who was not an extremely prudish person, recorded in his Diary that he could see in the paintings only "that gross puerility which scrawls indecencies on the wall of a privy." So far as he was concerned, the exhibition was no more than a "pornographic show." It is easy enough to imagine how others expressed themselves. Of course, æsthetic as well as moral standards were involved in this case.

The next year Blunt wrote in his Diary an account of the entertainment a society lady provided for her guests, including himself. She had brought to London a group of French men and women who presented an Apache dance, much to the pleasure of the spectators. As Blunt remarked, this sort of thing would have been impossible in the England of his youth but "now delighted us all, without a suspicion of indecorum, young men and maidens applauding unrestrainedly."

The number of illegitimate births reported in England and Wales for every thousand births dropped from forty-eight (the average for 1876 through 1880) to forty (1901-1905), and the decrease was proportionately greater in Scotland. In 1892 Dr. Albert Leffingwell wrote, "There are certain sections of England and Wales where every sixth or seventh or eighth child is a bastard!" And these were rural, not crowded urban, sections. England and Wales as a whole reported in 1889 a lower bastardy rate than Italy, France, Belgium, Scotland, and the Scandinavian and German-speaking countries, but a higher one than Ireland, Russia, and the Netherlands. As the situation now stands, Great

Britain has a lower proportion of illegitimate births to total births and to total nubile female population than most, but not all, countries of the Continent. The bastardy rate is still highest in several country districts. There is almost everywhere a greater familiarity with contraceptive devices and drugs, making itself manifest in a lower birth rate, and especially in a lower rate of illegitimacy.

Up to 1885 the age of consent in England was no higher than ten years. This one fact is sufficient to show the fallaciousness of the opinion, still sometimes advanced, that the early- and mid-Victorians had strict moral standards from which England has in all respects deteriorated. Since 1885 it has been a felony equivalent to rape to have carnal knowledge of a girl under thirteen even though with her consent or after solicitation on her part; and fornication with a girl between thirteen and sixteen, unless the accused person can show that he had reason to suppose her to be over the age of sixteen, is punishable by imprisonment for not more than two years.

In the British Army, and probably in the general population of Great Britain as well, there has been a considerable decline in the prevalence of venereal disease, the rate going down pretty steadily in almost every year while the country has been at peace. Prostitution is not a crime in England, although public solicitation and the keeping of brothels are offenses against the law. There seems to be little doubt that the commercialization of illicit sexual relations is now less common than it was in 1885. Surely prostitution is less conspicuous than it was then. There was a time when in some London streets the male pedestrian had almost to fight his way through crowds of women anxious to seize upon him. Solicitation has not disappeared, but it has lost its former boldness.

Sometimes it has assumed ingenious forms. Abraham Flexner, surveying the state of prostitution in Europe just before the outbreak of the World War, commented on the London newspaper advertisements which appeared to the uninitiated to offer the services of women for massage, manicuring, or teaching, but which were really the announcements of brothels. The police, he thought, might be more zealous in some directions: "There would, for example, appear to be no good reason why a prostitute calling herself 'Nurse Dora' should be privileged to advertise herself on billboards circulating up and down Regent Street and Bond Street."

Havelock Ellis, writing about "the decrease of prostitution" in 1925, added a qualifier, "if that is what we are really witnessing." He spoke at this time in favor of "a new form of recognized sexual union" to go with conception control. Ellis and Bertrand Russell have worked earnestly to remove certain rigidities from the sexual morality of to-day. Mr. and Mrs. Russell would go beyond the American proposals of Judge Lindsey; but their followers are at present in a small minority, and it is therefore unnecessary to examine their views in detail. If the formal acceptance of their teachings about sexual freedom for both the married and the unmarried is rare, it is nevertheless true that a great many people in England act in accordance with their principles. And if prostitution has actually decreased, illicit sexual relations in general have not. Respectable young men and women are allowed to meet each other with considerable freedom. As I write, the upper social circles are reported to be insisting on chaperonage once more, but this is far less strict than it was before the War.

The World War is held responsible for much of the increased liberality of English morals. Yet the presence of hordes of prostitutes in London streets and the commotion about unmarried mothers which it occasioned also developed in some people the desire for stricter standards of behavior, perhaps to be brought about by law. Asceticism has by no means died out in England. It still shows itself, for example, in a feeling that sufferers from the venereal diseases should not be treated like other patients. If they apply for treatment in charity hospitals, they are often made to feel that they are wicked people who should be punished as well as unfortunates who should be cured.

The War brought about an increase in the number of young women employed in industry. Some employers showed concern about the moral conditions under which they worked. A number of English Quaker manufacturers held a conference in 1918 at which this was one of the matters discussed. George Cadbury, Jr., said: "In the interests of the children, no swearing, bad language, or drunken or dirty habits ought to be allowed. . . . A separation of the sexes at work is most desirable." Other speakers dissented from this last statement, expressing the opinion that the moral tone of the young men would be improved if they worked side by side with young women. It is no reflection on the Quakers in particular to say that the manufacturers who attended the conference were thinking of their own profits first, of the welfare of their employees only as a secondary matter. The report of this meeting is interesting because it shows the zeal for religion, morality, and money combined, in a way characteristic of the old Puritanism. But there was practically no evidence of sectarian narrowness.

Probably the number of people in England who attach importance to denominational differences has much decreased since 1837. Religious enthusiasm has lost some of its former importance. Excitement about moral issues seems to be far less prevalent in Great Britain than it is in the United States. There have, it is true, been waves of indignation about the white-slave traffic and the sale of narcotic drugs, and there are good people in England who are angry about "the profanation of the Sabbath" or the prevalence of drunkenness. But, generally speaking, the great moral forces are the desire to be genteel and a more or less logical ability to measure standards of conduct by their utilitarian effects.

In the matter of verbal taboo the United States and England are not exactly agreed, the varying connotations and associations of words being the chief factor of difference. Genteel people on both sides of the Atlantic call the belly "the stomach"; but the euphemism of "lady-dog" for *bitch*, which H. W. Fowler mentions, is rare in at least some parts of the United States. To be sure, Americans often omit the word *bitch* from nontechnical conversation, especially because it forms part of a phrase, harmless on the face of it, which is considered particularly foul. *Bloody*, as the equivalent of *damned*, is disapproved by the

genteel people of England; Bernard Shaw offended seriously
against the conventions when he had one of his heroines use the
word. *Sick* is frowned upon, though it is the usual word for *ill*
in the United States; to the English it calls up a picture of vomit-
ing. Joyce, in a scene supposed to take place in 1904, makes a
Dublin girl blush when her girl friend speaks of spanking a
little boy's "beeoteetom." Perhaps such a euphemism would
now be respectable enough for the most genteel reader of society
novelettes in the Free State.

Feminism has become vastly more important in England than
it was in 1884. In that year a law was passed providing for
virtually universal manhood suffrage. The woman suffragists
were disappointed when the sex limitation for voters was not
then broken down. Their efforts relaxed somewhat for several
years, though a serious effort was made in 1886 to pass a woman-
suffrage bill. The feminists had more than the franchise in mind,
and they sometimes expressed their desires rather loudly. At a
meeting in Hyde Park a few bold women said that riding astride
should not be considered immoral on the part of their sex. There
was a wave of indignation. "And *these* are the future mothers
of England!" wrote one journalist of 1892, words almost failing
him.

Early in the twentieth century the women of British Aus-
tralasia made great political gains, and the English suffragists
were spurred on to new efforts. In 1905 a number of women
began to attract attention by their militant tactics. Mrs. Pank-
hurst was then sent to jail for obstructing traffic and otherwise
breaking the peace in an effort to force Parliament to give votes
to women. The militant suffragists alienated many by their
methods. By destroying property and laying violent hands upon
politicians they convinced many men that women are too
hysterical to be entrusted with the ballot. Still, they kept Parliament from simply ignoring the question. Between 1897 and
1908 no woman-suffrage bill had been introduced. Afterwards,
the suffragists saw to it that the enfranchisement of women was
constantly kept before the eyes of the legislators. In 1907 and
1908 women forced themselves into conspicuous places in the hall

of the House of Commons and chained themselves to the grating
or resisted arrest in other ways while they waved their banners.

Mrs. Humphry Ward and other females of undoubted gentility turned up their noses, asserting that they were opposed not
merely to the tactics of the militant suffragists but to feminism
in general. Most leaders in the woman-suffrage movement
wanted the vote as a means of fulfilling other ambitions, such as

THE MILITANT SUFFRAGIST

"And to think that yesterday I burnt two pavilions and a church!"

A cartoon by Leo Cheney in *Punch*, 1913. Reproduced by permission of the
Proprietors.

equal wages and working conditions for women in industry, equal
divorce laws, and perhaps a single standard of morals for both
sexes. Some of the suffragists were anxious for severer laws
against seduction and other sexual delicts, and many of them
believed that women voters would insist upon a stricter regulation
of the liquor trade, if not upon total prohibition.

Militant methods were abandoned by the woman-suffrage
leaders of England during the World War. However, the cause
was advanced by the direct and indirect contributions to war

work which women made. Moreover, one of the great heroes of the war was a woman. Generals and other men of prominence were seldom able to display personal heroism. Edith Cavell, who was executed by the Germans for violations of the rules of war, became an object of patriotic worship.

In 1918 the suffrage was granted to a large number of women, including those over thirty, university graduates, householders, and the wives of householders. Then came a struggle about giving the vote to the "flappers" between twenty-one and thirty who did not fall into any of these qualifications. The objection was raised that full equal suffrage would give the balance of power to the women, who outnumber the men of Great Britain. The General Strike of 1926 again emphasized the ability of women to fill the positions of men in industry. In 1928, though much against the will of some Conservative leaders, women were finally given the vote on the same basis as men.

The number of divorces granted in England rose from 1,267 in 1913 to 5,763 in 1919, largely as a result of the Poor Persons' Act, which reduced the cost of obtaining a divorce for people who had previously considered it a luxury of the rich. Then came, in 1923, a law which made adultery a sufficient cause for divorce, whether committed by the wife or by the husband. Previously a man did not make himself liable to such action unless he added desertion or gross cruelty to his adultery. The same Parliament that put the sexes on an equal basis with regard to divorce passed a law making the subsequent marriage of the parents legitimatize a child born out of wedlock.

The movement to prohibit the sale of intoxicants, which once seemed to be as strong in Great Britain as in the United States, has been unsuccessful in twentieth-century England. At the moment, total prohibition seems to be absolutely impossible there. England, like America, has had its sad songs about the evils of drink. "Please Sell No More Drink to My Father" was the title of a ditty sung in England toward the end of the nineteenth century, which was better known by its refrain of "And pity the poor drunkard's child."

Malt liquors have an important place in the habits of most

Englishmen, and they are usually considered necessities of life. The *per capita* consumption of wine and whiskey, however, has long been, and probably still is, below that of the United States. Certainly the English are drinking less than their ancestors did, of both fermented and distilled beverages. Recent statistics on convictions for drunkenness appear to show wide fluctuations from year to year in the tendency to drink deep. During 1913 in England and Wales 153,000 males and 36,000 females were found guilty of intoxication; in 1915, 103,000 males and 33,000 females. By 1918 the number was down to 22,000 males and 7,000 females, but it climbed back in 1920 to 80,000 males and 15,000 females.

During the War, increasingly stringent restrictions on the sale of intoxicants were introduced. In 1916 over two million people signed a petition asking for complete wartime prohibition. Their request was not granted, and most of the emergency regulations have disappeared since the end of the War. The hours during which liquor may be sold are, indeed, still restricted. The American-born Lady Astor has been one of the most prominent of the workers for laws designed to improve temperance. She was largely responsible for the act of 1923 which deprived children under eighteen of the right to buy liquor at a bar and those under sixteen of the privilege of getting intoxicants at a restaurant to drink with their meals.

Mr. Chesterton sums up the situation thus:

But Noah he sinned, and we have sinned; on tipsy feet we trod,
Till a great big black teetotaler was sent to us for a rod,
And you can't get wine at a P. S. A., or chapel, or Eisteddfod,
For the Curse of Water has come again because of the wrath of God,
And water is on the Bishop's board and the Higher Thinker's shrine,
But I don't care where the water goes if it doesn't get into the wine.

Many agree with him, even though wine is less important than ale as a traditional English beverage. Some prominent English publications refuse to print whiskey advertisements, and the distilled beverages are by no means so firmly entrenched as British beer and ale.

THE ECONOMICS OF PROHIBITION

CHARLADY: *"Prohibition may be all right in America, Mrs. 'Arris, but it won't catch on over 'ere. It's too expensive."*

A cartoon by George Belcher in *Vanity Fair*, 1929.

The labor unions stand firmly against all attempts to take these away from the English workman, and their importance has vastly increased. It was not many decades ago that they were considered seditious. As recently as 1901 a decision of the House of Lords came close to taking away the right of striking. But since then organized labor has become very important, even more so than in the United States. Unemployed workmen receive a governmental distribution known as the "dole," and there are other provisions for labor of a quasi-socialistic nature.

The more radical social leaders fell into disfavor as a result of the Russian Revolution. All things that bear any resemblance to Bolshevism have been anathema in Great Britain, largely for the reason that the Soviet Government is working diligently to break down British imperialism in Asia. The World War and the fear of communism threatened and reduced, but by no means completely destroyed, the standards of free speech which had evolved in Victoria's time. Pacifists suffered while the War went on, as they did in most of the combatant countries; and though they are now permitted to express themselves freely and their principles are applauded in high circles, they can do nothing to interfere with the secret diplomacy which is preparing the way for new wars.

Political corruption is said, by competent observers, to be less general in Great Britain than in the United States. Civil-service reform was largely accomplished by the end of the nineteenth century, and local government has to a considerable extent been given over to the care of trained experts. The national parties have recognizable principles, and, so far at least, they are something more than patronage machines. Because of the absence of a ballot of unwieldy length, and for various other reasons, there is a closer approach to democracy than we have in the United States. Except for diplomacy, which is conducted as it was when English monarchs were nearly absolute (though now under the direction of a bureaucracy, not a king), the defects of the English system are mostly those inherent in representative government.

It is generally agreed that standards of business honesty have become more precise in England since mid-Victorian days. Fornication is less of a sin than it was in 1850, but commercial fraud is a far greater one. Comparisons have been made between the business morality of Great Britain and that of the United States; still, it does not seem that any important generalization can be offered with confidence. There is more talk about the ethics of business in America, but exactly what this means is not easy to determine. Novel methods, which may or may not savor of trickery, are usually frowned upon in Great Britain. This is especially true of sensational advertising. But the British have been quick to take over from America a wide application of instalment-plan selling. They make use of credit in some cases where it is practically unknown in the United States: thus, while speculators in securities on the American exchanges deposit a margin or cash deposit with their brokers, it is customarily sufficient in England to show that one is able to make good all possible losses without actually paying down a fraction of the amount involved in a purchase or sale. This may be an evidence of greater honesty in English commercial transactions. At least, honesty is ultimately encouraged by such methods, and by the wide use of credit in general.

Professional ethics vary somewhat in England and the United States. Thus, American lawyers are accustomed to the contingent fee, to an agreement by which they are to be paid nothing if they lose a suit but are to receive an agreed proportion of the sum gained if they win. The contingent fee is under the ban in England. No doubt there are some aspects of commercial and professional morality in which American standards are stricter than English. The whole matter is a complex one, and the mere comparison of published ethical codes leads nowheres.

The old aristocratic prejudice against trade and most of the professions has virtually disappeared in England, though there are still a few aged gentlemen who declare that British greatness died when the landlords lost control of the country to the shopkeepers and manufacturers. The opposition to modernisms of all sorts which is brilliantly expounded by Chesterton has actually not many more supporters in England than in America. Most Englishmen, like most Americans, agree that what is generally known as modern progress really means improvement, or at least brings more advantages than disadvantages.

The new industrial aristocrats maintain an old tradition by patronizing sports. Literature no longer depends upon patronage; but the millionaires are often ready to support the other arts, though perhaps they are not quite so generous in this regard as the American magnates of industry.

Pietism has declined in England, and though the English Sunday remains far different from that of France, the celebration of the day is distinctly less rigid than it has been. In the 1880's the Prince of Wales argued in vain that the British Museum and similar institutions should be opened on Sundays. The Lords voted in favor of such a proposal in 1886, but the Commons remained opposed for a decade more. Some opposition to Sunday sports still remains. In 1927 a number of pious inhabitants of Torwyn, Wales, took it upon themselves to parade through a golf course on Sunday to prevent play. The Court of Chancery granted an injunction against them, declaring that they were at liberty to spend the day as they thought fit but had no right to interfere with others.

The Church of England remains established. It consists of at least three distinct parties which are kept together by the fact of the establishment. The High Church party is, in its present form, a product of the Oxford movement. Many of its leaders deny that they are Protestants and come very close to the position of open Roman Catholics. Between 1877 and 1887 a number of High Church clergymen were imprisoned for supposedly popish and illegal practices. Since then the zealous Protestant Anglicans have used less drastic methods in fighting Anglo-Catholicism. Attempts to unite the High Church party with the Roman Catholic Church have so far failed.

It is still something of an offense against gentility in England to attend a chapel instead of an Anglican place of worship. However, the Episcopal Church was disestablished in Wales shortly after the end of the World War, and it is likely that disestablishment will follow in England within a few decades.

While rationalism and anticlericalism have played a little larger part in the intellectual life of England during the twentieth century than in that of the United States, a certain opposition to modernism yet remains. It is said that teachers in the city of Bootle, for instance, have been forbidden to teach the doctrine of organic evolution as it applies to man. But, generally speaking, nominal allegiance to the Anglican Church has been sufficient for most social and political purposes; and even this requirement is much less stringent than it was fifty years ago.

PART II
THE NEW WORLD

CHAPTER XI

THE CHOSEN PEOPLE

§ 1

WRITERS on American history often differentiate between the Puritans and the Pilgrims. However, our definition of Puritans as the English-speaking Protestants who wished to remove all traces of Roman Catholicism from their doctrines and their worship, or, as they said, to remove entirely the tai:.t of popery, is broad enough to include, along with other Separatists, those who emigrated from England to the Netherlands.

The Scrooby people who fled from the ridicule of their neighbors and the fear of persecution by their bishop were cordially received in Amsterdam. All sorts of other heretics were also welcomed there. The English exiles found Jews; they also found, among those who called themselves Christians, many who refused to admit the divinity of Jesus or, almost as bad, denied the doctrine of foreordination. The Englishmen had fled to seek toleration in the exercise of their own (true) religion, but they did not like to see falsehood propagated without hindrance from the authorities. Besides, they felt uncomfortable in a foreign country. Though England had jeered at them, they were used to the English tongue and English ways. And the problem of earning a living in Holland was not an easy one. Only those few among them who were skilled in handicrafts were sure of their daily bread.

The congregation was established at Leyden. As years went by, some of the Englishmen became absorbed into the Dutch population. The others feared that their children would forget their own language and desert their own faith. The founding of a colony which should be comparatively free from outside interference seemed to offer a solution to all their problems, and the English Separatists in Holland looked toward America.

How a number of them, together with some who came directly from England, crossed the sea in 1620 in the little *Mayflower,* is a story familiar enough. It should be noted that most but not all of the passengers in this ship were zealous Puritans. A few of them possessed little piety, but longed for adventure and for the opportunities to acquire sudden wealth which they conceived to exist in the New World. The economic motive, though sometimes subordinate, was present in most cases; and the mere desire for religious tolerance could have been satisfied amply at Amsterdam or Leyden. The leaders of the Pilgrim Fathers were Calvinists. They taught that every man has the right to read and interpret the Scriptures for himself, but they firmly believed that only wicked people could possibly discover any basis for free will and other objectionable dogmas in the Bible; and they did not intend to compromise with wickedness.

Those of the Plymouth settlers who expected to find a land flowing with milk and honey were sadly disappointed. Many who were unprepared to contend against the hardships which awaited them in New England were glad to return to their old homes at the first opportunity. To justify themselves they spoke disparagingly about the climate, the water supply, and much more in the new colony.

Governor Bradford said, in reply to those who called the water unhealthful: "If they mean, not so wholesome as the good beer and wine in London (which they so dearly love) we will not dispute with them; but else, for water, it is as good as any in the world (for ought we know), and it is wholesome enough to us that can be content therewith." In spite of the touch of sarcasm, Bradford evidently considered water less wholesome than fermented beverages. Small beer was the staple potation of the Pilgrims in England and the Netherlands, and they still preferred beer to water after they settled in America.

Tea and coffee were not in use. Wine was a luxury; and so, to a certain extent, were such distilled liquors as brandy and gin, which were also valued for medicinal purposes. Bradford's

THE EMBARKATION OF THE PILGRIMS

After a painting by E. Corbould.

opinion was, not that these things were bad, but that immigrants into the wilderness, whose primary purpose was supposed to be that of worshiping God in the most acceptable manner, ought not to be overmuch concerned about short rations of either food or drink. But newcomers were, nevertheless, advised to bring supplies enough to last for a year. Josselyn's list included a gallon of brandy and a hogshead each of English and Irish beer for every immigrant. The colonists learned the use of tobacco from the Indians.

The pious colony of Plymouth was disturbed by a near-by settlement called Mare Mount or Merry Mount. A certain Thomas Morton founded this town, and the inhabitants were mostly runaway servants and other Englishmen whose moral standards were less than austere. Since white women were scarce in Merry Mount, cordial invitations were extended to Indian girls. Morton and his men were anxious to develop a valuable fur trade. Hence they gave guns and ammunition to the Indians and taught them how to use firearms in hunting. Also, they let the Indians have distilled liquors in exchange for furs.

The Puritan settlers in New England were accustomed to give the aborigines cheap trinkets for valuable skins. The better furs went, naturally, to Merry Mount, where the Indians got intoxicants and guns for them. And a matter of safety as well as one of profit was involved. The red men were very dangerous when they could meet the whites with their own weapons, and it did not take much provocation to make them fight when they were drunk. Morton was hated by the Plymouth people with some reason, then. Perhaps the chief offense of the Merry Mounters in their eyes was that of setting up a May-pole and drunkenly singing and dancing about it. The Plymouth settlers, aided by those of Salem and other communities, finally hewed down the iniquitous symbol of paganism and sent Morton back to England. He returned, but he was not received with any exclamations of delight. Instead, he was exposed in the stocks and then put aboard ship once more. His personal goods were confiscated and his house was burned.

Plymouth Colony remained independent until 1691, when it

REVELS AT MERRY MOUNT

A drawing by W. L. Sheppard for W. A. Crafts, *Pioneers in the Settlement of America.*

was politically merged with the Puritan colonies which had spread out from Salem, under the name of the province of Massachusetts Bay. The Salem Puritans were not all Separatists when they came to America. Some of them believed in an established church governed like that of England but "purified" from all things popish. Others disliked the episcopal system. A few who came with them were not Puritans at all and were willing that the Church of England should be established in the colony without change. A sort of modified congregationalism finally became "the Massachusetts way."

The majority of the colonists did not want to subject themselves to the English bishops, who were opposed to Puritanism. They did not venture to set up a hierarchy of their own, because it would have seemed like a declaration of independence. The church government they set up, although not formally presbyterian, resembled the Scottish form more than pure Separatism. The New England ministers became extremely influential. The leading colonists considered the proper worship of God the most important of all concerns, and the clergymen were supposed to be qualified to pronounce authoritatively on theological questions. Moreover, the doing of God's will was considered to be the proper motive whatever the colonists were engaged in. Religious duty was omnipresent, and the task of suppressing the natural man in favor of the spiritual one was never completed.

§ 2

In the early days of New England it was impossible to prevent a certain amount of freedom in the relations between the sexes. There were many tasks to be done quickly, and women engaged in hard labor side by side with men. And, of course, the immigrants had brought no harem tradition with them. There were instances in the colonies in which a young man and a young woman met, courted, and were married all in a single day. Not all the lovers' meetings, however, ended in marriage. There were a great many cases of fornication and other sexual delicts. As a matter of fact, the early colonists were not so carefully selected for religious and moral zeal as some writers would have us believe. To New England, as to the other sections of British North America, came people of all sorts who had botched their lives in the land of their birth. There were big and little criminals, half-wits and paranoiacs among them. There were religious zealots, some poor, some rich. There were adventurers of all degrees, anxious to become rich quickly and not always scrupulous about the means. There were indentured servants, who were virtual slaves for a time, until they had worked out the cost of their passage.

The great change in environment enabled some men and women who had fared badly in England to do well in the colonies. At the same time, some who had led model lives in the mother country succumbed to temptation in an unfamiliar setting. They were, perhaps, far away from their relatives and friends. Besides, the pleasures to which they had become accustomed were lacking in America, and they were tempted to pursue all those which were available, whether lawful or not.

Gaiety was restricted by the necessity for hard work and incessant vigilance. But the dangers from disease, famine, and Indian attacks encouraged a certain feeling of recklessness, which was capable of leading to a laxity of conduct. Counteracting this was a moral earnestness which many of the New England colonists possessed. In the Puritan colonies most of the settlers lived in towns, and close moral supervision was usually possible.

Young men and women were encouraged to marry at an early age, and economic conditions were such as to keep this from being a hardship. Practically all men were married by twenty-one, and girls quite frequently before they had reached the age of sixteen. After a time it became usual to restrict the movements of bachelors, who were considered to be putting a strain upon the sexual morals of the community. They had, at Hartford, to pay heavy taxes. In many New England towns it was provided by law that every man who married should receive a building lot free of charge, or some other communal assistance.

In spite of this anxiety to marry off the young people, the New England authorities did not reduce the authority exercised by parents. Their consent was required not only before a wedding, but even before the courting began. In Massachusetts and, more especially, in Connecticut, the courts ordered amorous swains who began their courtship without the consent of the girls' parents to be severely punished.

There was much prying into domestic affairs in early New England. The communities were anxious that men and women should subdue the lusts of the flesh and walk in the way of God. The tithingmen used to go into houses where relatives had come for a visit to inquire into their status and motives. If a married daughter was found to be staying overnight in her parents' house, she was asked why she had not remained at home with her husband. In Massachusetts Bay Colony it was a criminal offense for man and wife to live apart.

However, a great many men came to New England after having deserted their wives. In 1647 the general court of Massachusetts ordered all such persons to return to England. Married men who were without their wives were permitted to remain only if they were making preparations to bring them over. But there was no easy way of investigating the histories of men who came over alone and announced themselves as bachelors. These men often remarried in the colonies.

Massachusetts required wives to obey their husbands, under pain of imprisonment. Men were not supposed to strike their wives except in self-defense. Still, domestic chastisements of this sort were usually permitted if they were considered to be justified and not excessive. Several times when husbands complained about their wives before the magistrates, they were told to do their own disciplining at home.

In 1631 Massachusetts made adultery a capital offense. New Haven and Connecticut Colony later followed this example. When New England husbands were called away from home on business, constables and tithingmen were authorized to enter their homes and see if their wives were entertaining other men. If men were found, even though there was no evidence of adultery, the wives might be publicly whipped.

Fornication was dealt with harshly in the New England colonies when it was discovered, and the fact that the guilty man and woman afterward married was not always considered a mitigation of their offense. The records of Plymouth Colony tell how a certain Dorothy Temple, who was unmarried, gave birth to a child, and how she was publicly whipped until she fainted. There were several cases in which a too early childbirth caused husband and wife to be dragged before the judges and punished for fornication before the marriage. Sometimes the man was given one or two public floggings and the woman was set in the stocks; in other instances it was only the woman who received corporal punishment. The New Haven records report that two men, servants to Elias Parkmore, "were whipped for their sinful dalliance and folly with Lydia Browne." Three years later, "Margaret Bedforde, being convicted of divers miscarriages, was severely whipped, and ordered to be married to Nicholas Jennings with whom she has been nought."

It was no very uncommon thing, in old New England, to see women bound to the whipping post, the blood running down their bare backs. Women as well as men were set into the bilboes, with their feet higher than their heads. To outrage the modesty of a female offender was, in the opinion of the authorities, simply to add to her punishment; and little consideration was given to the possible effects upon the spectators. Hawthorne has commented upon the coarseness of the first settlers as manifested in their punishments. He has, of course, made us familiar with the scarlet letter A which adulterous women were sometimes forced to wear.

The colonial penal codes were, to some extent, based upon the criminal laws of England. In many respects the penology of New England was less severe than that of the mother country, but it was sterner with regard to some offenses which non-Puritans considered minor. Almost all crimes against property were in England punishable by hanging; in New England a whipping was often the punishment for theft, as it was also for fornication or for whispering sweet nothings into a young lady's ear without her father's express permission. To hurt one's neighbor was, in Puritan eyes, no worse than to act in such a way as to displease

God. Perhaps the constant shortage of man power was the principal reason why hanging for larcenies did not become established early in colonial days. It may be, too, that there was less reason than in England to fear men who stole out of either hunger or a love of adventure. It was possible to incur danger without being an outlaw, and able-bodied men had little need to go hungry while land was to be had at little or no cost.

THE BRAND OF THE ADULTERESS

A drawing by F. O. C. Darley, from *Compositions in Outline from Hawthorne's "The Scarlet Letter"*

There were, nevertheless, a number of capital crimes in the New England colonies. In early New Haven the list was taken from the Old Testament. It included the worshiping of gods other than Jehovah, witchcraft, blasphemy, cursing God, bestiality, homosexual practices, adultery, and rape. It was also punishable by death for any child to strike or rebel against a parent except under extreme provocation.

In Massachusetts one or two adulterous women were actually put to death. One woman, after she had been married several years to her second husband, was accused of having committed

[359]

adultery during the lifetime of her first; and she narrowly escaped execution.

Cases of bestiality and homosexuality were not extremely rare, and probably they were at least as common as they were in England. In judging the morals of the New England colonists in the light of the official records, we must make allowances for the inquisitorial system which prevailed during the seventeenth century and for the consequent difficulty of keeping private affairs hidden. Unless we remember this, we are led to conclude that the colonists were exceptionally loose in their conduct. Offenses against chastity were constantly before the courts. In England they were usually ignored.

It is difficult in any case, after examining the records, to retain the notion that the Pilgrims and the other American Puritans always sternly rejected animal desires. We cannot assume that their delicts were always detected. When we read of the woman who was found fornicating with an Indian in 1639, we must feel that there were others who acted in the same way, but who were not discovered and consequently did not have, like her, to suffer the penalty of a flogging through the streets and the compulsory wearing of a badge of infamy upon her sleeve. And the same thing is undoubtedly true of other fleshly offenses.

In Connecticut, whenever an illegitimate infant was found dead, the law presumed that it had been killed by its mother, who was executed unless she could clearly prove herself innocent of murder. As we have seen in old Scotland, when it was ruled by its Presbyterian ministers, the penalties inflicted upon unmarried mothers were severe enough to drive them to infanticide.

There was a great horror of incest, which was made to include the marrying of a deceased brother's wife, an uncle's widow, or a wife's sister or niece. In Connecticut the law provided that persons who entered into such incestuous marriages should receive forty lashes on the bare back and be required to wear the letter I on back and arm.

The judicial records of New England in colonial days show that simple flirtations and what we should now call petting parties often aroused great wrath. In New Haven, in 1660, a maiden and a young man were fined for kissing each other and for sitting close together, "his arm being about her waist, and her arm upon his shoulder and about his neck." The girl in this case had also committed the enormity of joking about two lame people who were to be married that evening.

The morals police of New England could not be everywhere at once, but voluntary upholders of the law who reported their neighbors' misdeeds caught many a sinner. And the definition of sin was so wide that hardly any healthy person could consider himself absolutely free from it.

A sin was usually a crime also, and punishable by the authorities as well as in the wrath of the hereafter. The use of tobacco was regulated in a series of criminal laws. In 1629 the officials of the New England Company sent instructions to Massachusetts Bay Colony that the weed was not to be planted, except in small quantities for medicinal purposes. Then followed a mass of colonial legislation on the subject. But smoking became and remained popular. A Massachusetts law forbade the use of tobacco in barns, fields, or forests as well as in public houses. The fear of fire was partly responsible for this prohibition, and masters were enjoined to force their servants to obey it. Later the general court of Massachusetts made smoking unlawful except when the smoker was on a journey and five miles away from any town. Plymouth Colony forbade the use of tobacco on streets and highways and fined a number of people who violated this law. Another piece of legislation deprived apprentices of the right to smoke. For a time it was against the law to import tobacco; but since the only result was an increase in smuggling, the embargo was removed.

Connecticut made the regular exception in favor of tobacco that was used for the avowed purpose of preventing or curing disease. The law provided also that adults who had already contracted the smoking habit should be allowed to use tobacco in private, but it was forbidden to those who had not yet become accustomed to smoking and to all persons under the age of twenty. The public use of tobacco was absolutely prohibited: it was even illegal for two smokers to enjoy the weed together. The anti-

tobacco laws of New England were repeated by successive legislatures, often with increased penalties, but they were almost
wholly ineffective. Finally they were entirely dropped.

Light beer continued to be the staple drink of New Englanders
during the seventeenth century. Milk came more and more into
use, especially for infants and children, and to a certain extent it
displaced beer in the nursery. Water was held in suspicion,
whether for drinking or bathing. Drunkenness, though consistently discouraged and punished by the authorities, was pretty
common. Governor Winthrop of Massachusetts declared in 1630
that he would no longer drink healths, and he expressed the hope
that others would follow his example. It was about at this time
that the English Puritans were beginning to discover the wickedness of the old custom.

In 1676 the Reverend Increase Mather said in a sermon that
there was far more drunkenness in New England than in old
England. The governor of Massachusetts denied the fact, and it
is now impossible to tell which man was in the right. But the
fact that such a comparison was possible assures us that the
colonies were not extremely sober.

The severest legislation against excessive tippling seems to have
been passed in Plymouth. (Generally speaking, the notion that
the Pilgrims and their descendants were less addicted than the
other Puritans to the making of "blue laws" is far from the
truth.) New Haven directed innkeepers not to serve any person
with enough liquor to make him drunk. Half a pint of wine was
fixed as the maximum for any person to consume at a single
sitting, and no man was permitted to stay tippling in a tavern
for more than half an hour. The serving of liquor "at unreasonable times, or after nine o'clock at night," was also prohibited
in New Haven.

Drunkards were sometimes punished with considerable severity
in colonial New England. A Massachusetts man named Robert
Cole, several times convicted of intoxication, had to wear a red D
about his neck for a year. In a few instances the letter was
branded into the drunkard's skin.

Devices which might be used for gambling were generally

looked upon with disfavor. The first general court in Boston ordered all persons who possessed cards, dice, and backgammon tables to destroy them. In 1625 the Reverend John Cotton was asked by a member of his congregation about the religious propriety of playing cards. He answered that all forms of gambling and everything in the nature of a lottery are illegal. For example, he considered it sinful to choose a valentine by lot. His objection was that it was calling upon God to determine a trivial matter. The New England Puritans, like their brethren across the sea and also most non-Puritans of the seventeenth century, considered every event to be particularly ordained by the Divinity. Most of them believed that on solemn occasions and in matters of great importance it was proper to determine the divine will by the use of lots and similar devices. But to ask Heaven which of two idle fellows should have the other one's money, or to which of a company of women a valentine gift should be given, seemed somewhat akin to blasphemy.

A Massachusetts law of 1672 forbade the importation of playing cards and dice into the colony. The fine of five pounds imposed upon persons convicted of violating this law was divided equally between the treasury and the informer. Gambling was not altogether stopped. Yet it has been said, and with considerable truth, that funerals, trials, and executions constituted the principal diversions of colonial New England.

There was a difference of opinion about the religious lawfulness of dancing. Mr. Cotton found references to this amusement in the Old Testament, and therefore he said, "Dancing (yea though mixed) I would not simply condemn." He was careful to qualify his statement: "Only lascivious dancing to wanton ditties, and in amorous gestures and wanton dalliances, especially after great feasts, I would bear witness against, as a great *flabella libidinis*."

Most of the old dances involved little or no bodily contact between male and female. Still, public opinion went further than the Reverend Mr. Cotton and opposed all dances. Those in which both sexes participated were forbidden by law.

Amusements of all sorts were regarded with suspicion. Men and women, and boys and girls as well, were supposed to give all their time to useful things. Working and worshiping were supposed to be pleasing in the sight of God; and if people stopped to amuse themselves, it was considered certain that the Devil would gain possession of their souls. Connecticut Colony accordingly forbade the use of dice, bowls, shuffleboard and billiard tables, and quoits, no matter by whom and whether or not gambling or betting was involved.

All sorts of matters were regulated by law in the colonies, which went even further than the mother country in this respect. Shopkeepers were told what to sell and what not to sell and what prices they might lawfully ask for their wares. Husbands were told how to treat their wives and parents how to deal with their children. Indeed, the head of the house was expected to maintain his authority over his servants and his children, and few restrictions were placed upon his right to chastise them. If for any reason domestic castigations were considered insufficient, or if these dependents offered resistance to domestic punishment, they might be flogged by a communal officer at a public whipping post or in a house of correction. Until they set up homes of their own, they were virtual slaves. In Hartford a female servant who was found guilty of disobedience and disrespect to her mistress was committed to the house of correction, from which she was taken once a week to receive a public flogging.

The indentured servants were men and women who were brought from England after having signed articles which deprived them of their freedom for a term of years. Most of them came, naturally, from the lower classes; and it was usually the inability to earn a living in their native country which led them to seek a new start in America. Some were ensnared by agents working for shipmasters; a considerable number were criminals who were pardoned on condition that they should leave the country. In general, the indentured servants did not have strict Puritan moral ideals. The authorities felt that the fear of a lashing would do more to keep them on the strait and narrow path than all the sermons exhorting them to live righteously—not, indeed, that they were excused from listening to the sermons. There is a great deal of testimony to the effect that the presence of these white servants contributed largely to the sexual looseness of the New England colonies. The importation of negro slaves had a similar effect, but they were less numerous and less important than in the South.

Some of the laws regulating personal conduct applied exclusively to slaves and servants, others extended over the whole population. The community as well as the individual masters was supposed to have an interest in the behavior of the servile classes. For example, when they were forbidden to use tobacco, the enforcement of this prohibition was not left to the masters alone. The constables and tithingmen arrested offenders and whipped them unless their owners or masters paid the required fine. For a variety of minor offenses men and women of the lower classes were flogged or pilloried, while others had at most to pay a mulct. Aristocratic distinctions played an important part in colonial penology.

The presence of Indian savages in the neighborhood of the white settlements caused moral disturbances of various sorts. In Connecticut Colony it appears that some men who grew tired of obeying the laws against idleness, fowling, coasting, and smoking in public ran off into the wilderness and took up the Indian way of life. A law was passed providing that those who fell into the hands of the authorities after having deserted the colony to live "profanely" with the Indians should suffer severe punishment, including at least three years in the house of correction.

Though few of the early settlers in the colonies of New Plymouth and Massachusetts Bay were persons of wealth, fine clothes soon appeared. But they came under the public ban almost as soon as they were displayed. Under the Massachusetts law of 1634 objectionable articles of dress were subject to confiscation. Lace, silk, and thread of gold or silver were specifically forbidden. So also was clothing with the then fashionable slashes, although a single slash in the sleeve and another in the back were allowed. The law called upon all persons seeing others clothed in illegal attire to order them to remove the objectionable garments at once. In case the order was ignored, the magistrates were to be notified.

The authorities of Massachusetts continued to say in detail what might and what might not be worn. There was, for instance, an order against laces, though public decency was considered compatible with certain sorts of narrow edging. Then "the nakedness of the arm" resulting from the fashion of short sleeves aroused moral indignation and was proscribed.

Laws about clothing appeared at almost every session of the general court. Sometimes they were simply repetitions of previous legislation, with preambles lamenting the fact that the older laws were not being obeyed. The fact that these ordinances were often violated is illuminating about the public attitude of the time to the "blue laws" in general. Sexual delicts were, of course, committed in private; and violations of the laws against drunkenness, smoking, and gambling were necessarily often kept secret. But the young women who wore laces or slashed dresses did not remain in dark closets of their own homes. They appeared in the street and in other people's houses boldly displaying the evidence of their crimes. It was, then, very early in American history that the habit of openly violating objectionable laws was formed.

Nascent democracy objected most of all to the sumptuary laws which discriminated between rich and poor. Massachusetts ordered, for instance, that only persons possessing property worth two hundred pounds and the members of their families should wear lace or buttons of gold or silver. That sum was then a large one. As in England, it was considered proper that ladies and gentlemen should wear distinguishing badges of their condition.

Long hair, whether it was natural or artificial, was considered a mark of irreligion in all the men, of no matter what degree, who wore it. In 1675 the lawmakers of Massachusetts declared that the Indian attacks and other calamities which had befallen the colony were certain signs of divine anger over the fact that some of its masculine inhabitants did not wear their hair sufficiently short. We find also in the records denunciations of "naked breasts" side by side with orders against elaborate coiffures and ribbon decorations.

The New Haven code of 1660 did not detail improprieties of dress, but it gave the magistrates power to decide what might and what might not be worn. In view of the constantly shifting London fashions, which were reflected in the colonies a few months later, this provision obviated a complex series of laws. It was never easy to foresee what adornments might next appear, what bodily revelations might be made. The Connecticut authorities seem not to have been quite so severe in their censorship over clothing as those of Massachusetts. All over New England the sumptuary laws were relaxed in the last years of the seventeenth century. Men and women who had money enough to afford fine clothes insisted on buying them, and the latest fashions from the mother country were found irresistible. Slaves and servants who were employed in the fields wore the cheapest garments possible in view of the climate. But those who acted as waiters and butlers in wealthy peoples' homes wore elaborate costumes for the vicarious display of their masters' position in life.

Luxury was rare in the early days of New England not because of repressive laws but because poverty was the rule. It crept in as soon as men and women were assured of more than the bare necessities of life, and it developed with the influx of rich Puritans from England and the growth of American fortunes. The average farmer in colonial New England wore clothes which his wife had made from cloth of her own manufacture. This condition was the result of economic necessity, and it had nothing to do with moral considerations aside from the virtue of thrift and hard work. Home industry was encouraged by the authorities, and luxuries were frowned upon, it is true. But people of wealth, that is, the only ones who could afford expensive imported articles, were usually allowed to buy and make use of them. Thrift and work had different aspects for them.

There was for a time a law in Massachusetts Bay Colony which forbade bakers, under the penalty of a fine, to sell cakes and buns except for weddings, funerals, or other exceptional occasions. Most housewives prided themselves upon being able to bake these things for themselves; and when crops were good, the New England Puritans did not stint themselves of food.

There was a prejudice against mince pies because they suggested the Christmas festivities which had come down from Roman Catholic England. In general, however, feasting was one of the few forms of pleasure that the law and public opinion sanctioned.

When ministers assembled for some great celebration, they were always provided with an abundance of good food and drink. The latter was usually reckoned in barrels rather than in glasses or bottles. Indeed, to judge from the quantities of liquor recorded to have been consumed by New England colonial clergymen on single occasions, either they got thoroughly drunk or they had built up an immunity in advance.

Music was regarded with disfavor. There were laws against "singing, fiddling, piping," and other ways of producing harmonious sounds, especially in public houses. The violin was considered to be the Devil's own instrument. In this regard, as in the matter of dancing, the New England Puritans went beyond the prohibitions of the Old Testament. Music was objectionable, except in so far as it was used in religious services, because it was taken to be unproductive effort. Moreover, certain forms were associated with revelry and disorder. Other sorts of music called to mind the popish religion, and that made it very dreadful indeed for the Puritans.

They took from the Bible the doctrine that women are inferior in position and intellect to men. The women of colonial New England never seem to have rebelled against this idea. Yet there were among them a few who wielded great influence and gained extraordinary respect for their abilities.

Anne Bradstreet, for example, was one of the leading poets in a not very poetical period. Mrs. Bradstreet was very enthusiastically praised by her masculine contemporaries. In one of the prefatory poems to the first edition of her works, a certain "C. B." concedes that her sex "can surpass or parallel the best of man." N. Ward, in another song of praise, exclaims: "Let man look to't lest woman wear the spurs." The poetess herself was, or pretended to be, modest about her merits and those of her sex. "Men can do best," she said, "and women know it well."

She asked only "some small acknowledgment" of feminine ability. "The Tenth Muse," as Mrs. Bradstreet was called, aroused interest among men of letters in England as well as the colonies.

More widely influential was Anne Hutchinson, to whom we shall have to return in considering the standards of religious

THE MUSIC OF THE PURITANS

An engraving by Paul Revere in *The New England Psalm-Singer*, 1770. Courtesy of the William L. Clements Library of the University of Michigan.

propriety in New England. Many women were engaged in conducting small businesses, such as inns and retail shops. In the early colonial days, though, since nubile women were strongly urged to marry if they were maids or to remarry if they were widows, they seldom remained for long at the head of such establishments. True enough, they might be the genuine managers, but they were not formally recognized as such.

Most women, whether they also took care of business matters or not, were primarily home-makers. Families were large, and even those housewives who were able to have the assistance of servants were kept busy by a variety of homely tasks. The ideal woman of colonial days was a strong, sturdy mother. On the frontier, women had sometimes to fight against hostile Indians. Baking, spinning, sewing, and many other tasks which the middle-class housewives of our time do not perform at all, or which they carry out with the aid of labor-saving devices, kept the women of the New England colonies busy.

Some found time, just the same, to spread malicious gossip about their neighbors or to carry on flirtations of their own. And though the authority of husbands was undisputed in theory, the early records tell almost as often about men who were maltreated by their wives as about women who were beaten by their husbands.

Sexual morality was supposed to be equally strict for men and for women. Now the one sex, now the other, was punished more severely for its delicts. But women were more easily convicted of fornication than men; and the punishments inflicted upon them seem, generally speaking, to have been more severe. It was never assumed that they were mere passive agents, succumbing to masculine seduction.

It is not clear whether in early Plymouth and Massachusetts Bay colonies a woman could obtain a divorce because of her husband's adultery. In Connecticut and Rhode Island the law said plainly that either husband or wife might sue the other for divorce on the ground of infidelity. When Connecticut and then other colonies extended the grounds for which divorce might be granted, men and women continued to receive equal privileges in the matter. As we have seen, it was not until our own time that old England placed women on the same basis with men in actions for divorce.

Frontier conditions encouraged the equality of the sexes, though the colonial Puritans were far from being ready to make a theoretical acknowledgment of this fact. But they accepted it tacitly, as their divorce laws show. They tended to consider marriage a civil contract, and they were anxious to show they did not conceive of it (in the Roman Catholic way) as a holy sacrament.   While a divorce was extremely difficult to obtain in the mother country, it could be had rather easily in New England.   Both legislative and judicial bodies were authorized to sever the bonds of matrimony.   Petitions for annulment because one of the parties had left an earlier husband or wife alive in England were fairly common, and divorces were asked for a variety of reasons.

§ 3

In America, as in England, religion occupied a place of the utmost importance in the lives of the Puritans.   There was no great trust in spontaneous piety and goodness; or, at least, it was assumed that natural depravity arose in all human beings and had to be subdued.   The ministers of religion were largely intrusted with the task of developing spirituality out of sin and wicked instincts.   They were for the most part men of some learning, and few others shared this superiority with them.   The influence exerted by the clergy and the respect they commanded, making their position enviable, caused most of the promising young men of the New England colonies during the seventeenth century and the first decades of the eighteenth to be educated for the Church.

It was an essential dogma in Puritan theology that God deals with men and women according to his caprice, and that they are not to rebel against his will by seeking to enter a station in life to which they have not been assigned.   This doctrine was strongly opposed to democracy.   On the other hand, as we have seen, Calvinism tends to arouse equalitarian views, especially by developing or being suitable for the middle classes.   The leveling influences of the frontier were also at work in colonial New England.

But wealth and orthodoxy often went together during the seventeenth century in the Puritan settlements.   Rich men who could not accept the teachings and practices of the Church of

[371]

A — In *Adam's* Fall
We Sinned all.

B — Thy Life to Mend
This *Book* Attend.

C — The *Cat* doth play
And after flay.

D — A *Dog* will bite
A Thief at night.

E — An *Eagle's* flight
Is out of sight.

F — The Idle *Fool*
Is whipt at School.

MR. *John Rogers*, Minister of the Gospel in *London*, was the first Martyr in Q. *Mary's* Reign, and was burnt at *Smithfield, February* the fourteenth, 1554. His Wife, with nine small Children, and one at her Breast, following him to the Stake, with which sorrowful fight he was not in the least daunted, but with wonderful Patience died couragiously for the Gospel of Jesus Christ.

Some few Days before his Death, he writ the following Exhortation to his Children.

G Ive ear my Children to my words,
whom God hath dearly bought,
Lay up his Laws within your heart,
and print them in your thought,
I leave you here a little Book,
for you to look upon ;
That you may see your Fathers face,
when he is dead and gone,
Who for the hope of heavenly things,
while he did here remain,
Gave over all his golden Years.
to Prison and to Pain.
Where I among my Iron Bands,
inclosed in the dark,

C

PAGES FROM *THE NEW ENGLAND PRIMER*, 1727

England emigrated to such colonies as Massachusetts and Connecticut, where they were received as natural leaders. Later, when the Puritans gained control of the mother country, those aristocrats who went to America were mostly attracted to Virginia, and the New England immigration became for a time more plebeian.

Servants and others who cared nothing about Massachusetts Congregationalism presented a problem in New England from the beginning. It was especially difficult to solve when the authorities at home were hostile to Puritanism. The colonists who wished to be undisturbed in their Calvinistic tenets and practices did not have any broad ambition to accord religious freedom to persons of all beliefs. Most of them felt that it would have been wicked to do so. They were familiar enough with the ideal of tolerance, for many of them had lived in the Netherlands, but they did not approve of the Dutch way. Were they not perfectly sure that their own method of worshiping God was the one correct and acceptable manner?

But in forcing their own certitude upon others, the Puritans were perhaps not so blameworthy as they may now appear to lovers of religious toleration. For they were primarily concerned with maintaining their own beliefs intact for themselves and their children. Right or wrong, noble or wicked or ridiculous, their ideals were of the utmost importance to them. They had left their native country, given up many things which they held dear, built up new homes in the wilderness, for the sake of what they considered the truth. And they did not want the enemies of their principles to gain control of their promised land.

Some people who called themselves Christians considered it right to play the violin, to gamble, to eat mince pies, to dance around the May-pole, to use a ring in the marriage service. But if they were permitted to come to New England and do these things, perhaps they would bring in their friends holding similar views and prevent the Puritans from enjoying religious freedom. At any rate, they would seduce some of the children of the Puritans away from the faith of their parents. Had not this very thing happened to the sons of the Pilgrims in Leyden?

[373]

Citizenship in Massachusetts, the right to participate in the government, was extended only to those persons who were considered sufficiently orthodox, pious, and well-behaved to be admitted to church membership. At first the freemen or full citizens constituted a majority of the people of the colony, but later most male citizens found themselves deprived of any voice in the government. The original settlers saw the advantages of maintaining themselves as an aristocracy in ecclesiastical and civil government.

Those persons who were refused membership in the Church had nevertheless to attend the Congregationalist services. In England some of the theorists of Separatism contended that Church and State should never be united. The Puritans who found themselves in control of affairs in New England did not absolutely deny such a doctrine, but they nullified its seeming implications. (So also did the Calvinists of Geneva, France, and Scotland, but the friends of toleration gained the upper hand among the Dutch Calvinists.) The New England Puritans established a virtual theocracy. In their eyes the State existed to protect and cherish the Church, and the Church existed to enable the chosen people of God to serve him in the only proper way.

The original settlers of Massachusetts Bay signed articles which bound them "to follow the rule of God's word in all causes, ecclesiastical as political." And the Reverend John Cotton thought that the laws should smell of God, not of man. But the code which he wrote, based upon the Mosaic law, was rejected in favor of one which drew more upon the common law of England than upon the Hebraic Scriptures. The New Haven colonists were more consistent. They agreed that "the Scriptures do hold forth a perfect rule for the direction and government of all men, as well in families and commonwealth as in matters of church." For the first year, accordingly, they had no written law except the Bible. Later they changed their mind somewhat, and introduced man-made variations into the perfect and God-given rule.

One of the earliest acts of the Massachusetts Bay authorities was the expulsion of the Brownes, who insisted on using the official prayer book of the Church of England. Then came a series of other heretics. Richard Brown, an elder of the Watertown church, was reported to have committed the dreadful sin of maintaining that the Roman Catholic Church was a Christian body. According to the orthodox Puritan view, it was anti-Christian or diabolic. Perhaps in view of the fact that Mr. Brown was a respectable freeman who had not otherwise been found offending, the governor of Massachusetts and his court of assistants contented themselves with directing him to refrain from similar expressions of opinion in the future.

Roger Williams, as pastor of the Salem congregation, denounced women who went unveiled. But the authorities of Massachusetts did not agree with him. It was officially declared that the inferiority of the female sex was clear enough without any such special badge. The Salem preacher's zeal in this instance did not matter much. More alarming was his refusal to join the Boston congregation, on the ground that its members declined to make public acknowledgment of their sin in having communed with the Church of England. The colony existed, so far as its independence from the Anglican Church was concerned, merely on sufferance. Public attacks on the establishment were inadvisable. Williams incited Endicott to cut the cross out of a colonial flag as a popish symbol. Most dangerous of all, he preached that the king of England's charter was valueless, the Indians alone having the right to give or sell their lands to the colonists. The authorities wished neither to lay themselves open to the charge of treason nor to deny the only claim they had to Massachusetts.

Williams is principally remembered not for his political views about the validity of the charter, but because he asserted the true Separatist doctrine that the civil magistrates have no right to punish men for violations of the first table of the decalogue, that is to say, for strictly religious matters. He was finally ordered to return to England. Instead, he found a refuge with the Indians, whose friendship he had cultivated. Then he laid the foundation for the colony of Rhode Island, the first American province where absolute religious toleration became not merely the usual practice but an avowed principle as well.

The most interesting among the proponents of the antinomian heresy in colonial New England was Anne Marbury Hutchinson, who came to Massachusetts with her husband in 1634. Mrs. Hutchinson started a series of religious meetings, first intended for women only. Men also began to flock to hear her sermons or lectures. That a female should set herself up as a religious teacher offended the moral feelings and the sense of fitness of many people. Moreover, Mrs. Hutchinson and the group to which she belonged seemed to lay too much stress upon the personal and mystical experience of religion, too little upon the observance of the law. They were accused of saying that Christ had abolished all legalisms and left Christians free to do as their inner moral feelings directed them. For a time the governor of Massachusetts and the most influential people of Boston supported the antinomians. The rest of the colony, especially the ministers in the other towns, argued that Mrs. Hutchinson was a heretic and a presumptuous woman. They finally gained the victory, and her views were officially condemned. Most of the Bostonians agreed to renounce her heretical opinions.

The Reverend John Wainwright, an antinomian leader who was driven out of Massachusetts, founded the town of Exeter, New Hampshire. Mrs. Hutchinson, too, was forced to leave, though she was pregnant at the time. A rumor afterward spread among the orthodox and godly that she had given birth to a monster. It was a superstitious age, and people found no difficulty in believing that heretics gave such palpable indications of their connection with Satan. Mr. and Mrs. Hutchinson and their adherents founded the city of Newport in Rhode Island. After her husband's death Mrs. Hutchinson established a home for herself and her children near what is now New Rochelle, New York. It was in the wilderness. A band of Indians fell upon the house and massacred all who were in it. A Massachusetts minister, the Reverend Thomas Welde, then preached upon God's goodness in causing the violent death of this abominable female heresiarch.

Except in Rhode Island the teaching of Roger Williams that it is unlawful (according to the Scriptures) for magistrates to punish religious offenders found little favor. Elsewhere in New England, people were required to attend the services of the church established in the colony for two long sermons every Sunday and perhaps a special lecture in the middle of the week as well.

In early Massachusetts, men and women sat on opposite sides of the rude structure used for the services. We should not call it a church, because the colonial Puritans particularly objected to the word. The building was a meetinghouse, and the day when it was most used was not Sunday, but the Lord's Day. The tithingman watched carefully to see that nobody was disorderly or sleepy during the preaching of a very long sermon. The benches were adamantine in their hardness, and for many years the meetinghouses were entirely unheated. A good rousing hell-fire sermon might, under such circumstances, prove very welcome on a frigid winter day; and it is probable that some of the half-frozen children thought of eternal burning as a welcome relief from the discomforts of a cold meetinghouse.

Many of the older people looked forward eagerly to the Lord's Day, with its long sermons and thorny doctrines. Theological hairsplitting enjoyed great favor. Books dealing with abstruse matters of doctrine were given to young ladies as courtship presents; and many private libraries in colonial New England consisted exclusively, or almost exclusively, of theological works.

Sinful men and women who stayed away from the religious services were dealt with severely. Officers were authorized to enter homes while the services were going on and to arrest all persons whom they found there, except those who were too ill to be able to walk to the meetinghouse. Fines, floggings, and other penalties were imposed upon persons who failed to attend church.

Within the meetinghouse the tithingman kept order. He laid his rod upon restless boys and girls. He rudely awakened dozing adults. A certain Roger Scott was annoyed at being disturbed in his slumber, and he once struck the officer who awakened him in church. For this offense and for that of sleeping while the sermon was being preached, he was sentenced to a severe whipping. The task of flogging sinners was deemed eminently pleasing to the Lord of Hosts, and it was occasionally carried out on the Lord's Day. A Plymouth maidservant who was seen to smile in the meetinghouse was threatened with expulsion from the colony as a vagabond.

Heresy and blasphemy were considered seditious crimes in early New England. They were offensive to God, and also they were attacks upon the authority of those who laid down the official tenets and rules of conduct. The various sorts and degrees of improper, disrespectful, and blasphemous language merged into one another. They were all severely punished.

In 1656 a woman who was convicted of blasphemy was whipped at Taunton and again at Plymouth, and ordered to wear a red B for the rest of her life. A man was set in the bilboes for impatiently exclaiming, "Damn ye, come!" The use of objectionable language was often punished by exposing the offender with his or her tongue in a cleft stick. We find blasphemy listed as a capital offense in several of the New England colonial codes. And speaking disrespectfully of the civil or ecclesiastical authorities was considered almost as bad. One man for such a crime was publicly flogged, deprived of his ears, heavily fined, and banished from the colony. A woman was whipped and then made to stand for half an hour with her tongue held in a cleft stick. A New Haven man who ventured to remark that he was receiving no profit from his minister's sermons was fined and flogged. In the same city another man was severely punished for lying. He had carelessly remarked that his gun was loaded, when it wasn't.

We can read in the early records of Massachusetts that "Captain Stone, for abusing Mr. Ludlow, and calling him justass, is fined an hundred pounds, and prohibited coming within the patent without the governor's leave upon pain of death." In 1655 it was made a criminal offense in Plymouth to deny that the Scriptures afford an unfailing guide to human conduct. It was, then, all very well to express an opinion in New England, providing only that it agreed with those which were officially received. And it was safe enough to praise ministers, governors, and justices, except when they fell out among themselves and the praise of one might seem a disparagement of others. A whip-scarred back was one of the usual rewards for those persons who attempted freedom of expression.

In the early days of New England the greatest moral difference between the colonies and the mother country was probably caused by the varying conception of Sunday and holiday observance. Winthrop wrote, while still aboard ship in 1630: "After reaching New England came a sudden dropping of all reference to church holidays." Thanksgiving Day and an annual fast day became features of Puritan life in America, and Sunday took on a new importance. It was a holy day, not a holiday. In fact, vacations and periods of diversion were frowned upon. It was like forgetting to thank God for his mercies to cease even momentarily in the task of serving him. Work was a form of divine service, play was the service of the Devil.

The speech of the Puritans was full of pious asides. In their letters and journals the particular matter with which they are dealing seems, in fact, always to be an aside from a theological discussion. And their week was important because it contained the Lord's Day.

There was a great deal of discussion about the beginning and the end of the First Day. For the Hebrews the Sabbath began at sundown on Friday and ended when darkness came on Saturday evening. Some New England Puritans argued, therefore, that Christians ought to cease work each Saturday at about six o'clock in the evening and keep up the strictest holiness until the same hour on Sunday. Others thought that days properly begin and end at midnight. Still others, in order to be sure of carrying out God's will, wanted the sanctity of the Lord's Day to include both Saturday and Sunday evenings. And for a time work and play were actually interdicted for thirty hours each week.

Sport and frolic were, of course, not characteristic of the Puritans on week days. They were absolutely under the ban on the Lord's Day. It was a great sin for a child to make a remark about the squirrel it saw running across the road on Sunday morning. For anyone to walk, except to and from church, was a punishable offense. A certain Captain Kemble returned to Boston on a Sunday after three years' absence, and he was seen to kiss his wife without any regard for the holiness of the time. He was therefore sentenced to sit for two hours in the stocks.

Of course, it was not easy to stop all love-making on Sunday, especially that which was carried on behind locked doors and between husband and wife. Still, some ministers refused to baptize infants born on Sunday, for there was a theory that these had been conceived on the Lord's Day also. But when one of the foremost zealots was confronted by the fact that his own wife had given birth to twins on the Sabbath, he was forced to admit that his calculations had probably been faulty; and thereafter Sunday's children were no longer given over to the Devil.

Breaking the sanctity of the day was considered so serious that it added to the guilt of robbery or burglary; and such crimes, if committed on the Lord's Day, were more severely punished. In Plymouth a man who was found working on Sunday and who was accused of "disorderly living in idleness and nastiness" had his property taken from him and was temporarily enslaved to the governor of the province in 1638. In New Haven the law provided that ordinary cases of "profaning the Sabbath" should be punished with fines, whippings, and imprisonment. Then it went on to say: "But if the courts upon examination, by clear and satisfying evidence, find that the sin was proudly, presumptuously, and with a high hand committed against the known command and authority of the blessed God, such a person therein despising and reproaching the Lord, shall be put to death that all others may fear and shun such provoking rebellious courses."

Even in Rhode Island, the most tolerant of the New England colonies, and the views of whose founder seemed to shut out the civil compulsion of keeping any day holy, there were early laws forbidding all persons to sell liquor and to take part in any

A STOLEN FROLIC IN A PURITAN FARMHOUSE

A drawing by F. O. C. Darley for W. A. Crafts, *Pioneers in the Settlement of America.*

game or sport on the first day of the week. Throughout New England it was considered objectionable to do any cooking on Sunday, to go into a tavern for a drink, to do any traveling for business or pleasure, to engage in any sort of recreation, and even to wear a smile. In fact, there was a special law against telling jokes in the neighborhood of a meetinghouse.

Connecticut passed in 1715 "An Act to Prevent Unseasonable Meetings of Young People in the Evenings after the Sabbath Day and at Other Times." Lovers were sometimes fined for sitting together under a tree on Sunday. Fines for hunting, fishing, playing, or even working in order to keep things from spoiling on the first day of the week were very frequently imposed; and imprisonment in jails or open cages and corporal punishment were not particularly rare. Sunday laws, like those which regulated apparel, were frequently repeated with slight amendments. For a number of years the ministers of Massachusetts were required to read the Lord's Day regulations to their congregations each week.

The Boston authorities went so far as to station guards to keep people from entering or leaving the city between Saturday afternoon and Monday morning. But, especially in the larger cities, reverence for Sunday gradually fell off; and in the last years of the seventeenth century some pious people were beginning to feel that a lugubrious expression on the Lord's Day did not help to preserve holiness.

Religious opinion in New England was much influenced by the coming of missionaries who represented various sects. At first, these were Puritan Evangelicals whose creed differed usually in minor matters from that of the orthodox Congregationalists. The antinomians and other liberals were silenced or driven out, but Massachusetts and Connecticut moved over a little in their official religious doctrines toward the position of Mrs. Hutchinson. Rhode Island stood apart in allowing almost all sorts of religious doctrine to be preached.

Then came the Baptists. They were connected historically and identified by public opinion with the polygamous or promiscuous Anabaptists of Germany. The Anabaptists had practiced communism, too. Consequently, the Baptists were sternly forbidden to preach in the orthodox colonies of New England. Rhode Island alone was friendly, and Roger Williams for a short time called himself a Baptist. Then he announced that he was a Seeker, still looking into the Bible to discover the truth and the proper manner of worshiping God. Massachusetts was especially zealous in protecting its only true religion against the assaults of Baptists, and also of Quakers.

But the Friends came in, undeterred by persecution. As we have already seen, the early Quakers were willing to do almost anything to arouse interest in their preaching. Quaker men and women ran naked through the streets of Boston, and forced their way, sometimes in the same clothes of Mother Nature, into the Congregational meetinghouses. This was bad enough, but perhaps their equalitarian doctrines were still more offensive to the authorities. It was a time when common people were put into the stocks for theeing and thouing their neighbors, and the second personal singular of the pronoun was used by the Quakers as a religious duty. The Society of Friends frowned upon titles and the usual expressions of respect.

The Quaker missionaries in Massachusetts were flogged in large numbers. Many were jailed or exposed to public shame in cages, stocks, and pillories. Women were ordered whipped in the public squares of one town after another, and the trickle of blood down their backs and breasts showed that the executioner did not lay on the lash any less lightly because of their sex. The Massachusetts authorities decided that some of the women should be examined as possible witches. This meant that a committee of men stuck pins into their naked bodies in order to discover if they had "the Devil's mark," a spot from which no blood flowed when it was pricked and an infallible sign of diabolic possession. Several Quakers were kept in jail for as long as five days without being fed by the authorities, and they would have starved if sympathizers had not slipped food in through the window. The Friends who were driven out of Massachusetts after severe punishment often returned. They continued to come back even after a law was passed which provided that they should be hanged if found in the colony after their banishment. A woman, Mary Dyer, was one of the Quakers actually put to death under the terms of this law. At one time Massachusetts proposed to sell the children of Quaker missionaries into slavery in the Barbados, but no shipmaster was found willing to take such a cargo.

President Oakes of Harvard College said in a sermon in 1673: "I look upon toleration as the first-born of all abominations." And he was not exceptional in uttering such an opinion. But it was noticed that in Rhode Island, where the Quaker missionaries were met with quiet arguments instead of the lash and the noose, they made fewer converts than in Massachusetts and Connecticut. Peter Folger, Benjamin Franklin's rather eccentric maternal grandfather, was one of the Massachusetts people who spoke out in favor of the toleration of Baptists and Quakers. The Indian wars and other calamities he interpreted, as usual, as signs of divine wrath; but he attributed the displeasure of God to the penalties imposed for matters of conscience.

It was for a time criminal in parts of New England to give food and shelter to a Baptist, a Quaker, or a Roman Catholic. The Congregationalist authorities did all they could to make theirs the exclusive faith wherever it was established. The first important move for toleration came from without, when King James II issued his Declaration of Indulgence in 1687. This was held to apply to the colonies as much as to England, and it at once improved the position of Anglicans and other non-Congregationalists in Massachusetts and Connecticut.

One of the capital crimes listed in the early laws of Plymouth was "diabolical conversation," or having to do with the Devil. In 1648 Margaret Jones of Charlestown was executed after being convicted of such a crime. In 1691 and 1692 there was a witchcraft craze at Salem. Apologists for the Puritans are fond of reminding us that no one was burned alive: one man was pressed to death, and other persons, male and female, were hanged. They tell us also, what is true, that there were then and later people in Europe who believed in witchcraft. There had been an epidemic of witch-hunting in England at the beginning of the century, and rationalistic views prevailed among most educated Englishmen at the end. Yet, as we have seen, John Wesley, in the second half of the eighteenth century, still considered skepticism about the existence of diabolic possession little better than atheism. Perhaps the most interesting thing about the witchcraft hysteria in Salem was the rapidity with which it passed away. Samuel Sewall, who was among the foremost of the prosecutors, later made a public confession that he had been misled.

An attitude of doubt about the accepted dogmas of religion and ethics had been growing. Some conservative Puritans were inclined to lay the blame for the new skeptical attitude upon the rule of Andros and the suspension of the Massachusetts charter in the 1680's. The home government forced the colony to allow not only Anglican services but even the celebration of Christmas. This tolerance caused, if we are to believe the preachers of the day, an increase in drunkenness, street fighting, dancing around the May-pole, and other abominations.

The typical seventeenth-century Puritan of Massachusetts was an intensely religious man. He was interested in theological arguments, but still more in the emotional excitement which arose out of religion. Conscience and the fear of divine wrath played a leading part in his life. We find in a boy's diary an account of the terrible remorse he felt after having whittled on Sunday and of the vivid fear of eternal hellish tortures which he then experienced.

Michael Wigglesworth's doggerel verses, in *The Day of Doom*, tell how the sinners appear before the bar of Heaven and plead that they are not at fault, since they have been reprobated in advance. Christ is represented as answering them:

> Whom God will save, such he will have
> the means of life to use;
> Whom he'll pass by shall choose to die,
> and ways of life refuse.
> He that foresees and foredecrees
> in wisdom ordered has
> That man's free will, electing ill,
> shall bring his will to pass.

As for infants who died before they had a chance to do either good or bad, Wigglesworth represents Christ as promising them "the easiest room in Hell."

§ 4

Public confessions of sin were frequent in the meetinghouses. Sometimes women were compelled to arise and tell the congregations about the sexual delicts they had committed. Sometimes a respected elder arose voluntarily and announced that he had to unbosom himself of the sins which weighed upon his heart. There were many expressions of uneasy consciences, there was much violent straining after goodness.

Nevertheless, the people of New England acquired a reputation for business shrewdness sometimes amounting to sharp dealing. If it is (as some believe) a Christian duty to be poor, there was at least one duty which the colonial Puritans did not try very hard to fulfill. They did respect both wealth and power, perhaps all the more because they conceived of them as direct expressions of the divine will.

In the early class rolls of Harvard College the students were arranged neither alphabetically nor according to scholastic standing. Instead, the order of their names corresponded to the social position of their parents. And this is but one indication of the aristocratic organization of society in colonial New England. There were large numbers of indentured servants or white temporary slaves, and in some parts of New England the African slaves were also of considerable importance. But climate, soil, and other geographical factors were such in the greater part of the Northern colonies as to make the large estate unprofitable. New England became the land of small farmers. Indentured servants whose terms expired were enabled to take up farms on their own account. There were many democratic tendencies, which remained important in the New England states until the Industrial Revolution; then a great influx of foreigners changed matters.

We have seen enough of the penology of colonial New England

to convince us that the early settlers were not extraordinarily humane. In their wars against the Indians they seem to have been capable of showing quite as much treachery and vindictiveness as their savage foes. In fact, they compared themselves to the Israelites in Palestine, who were divinely commanded to exterminate the original inhabitants of the land. The New England Puritans attributed their own sadism to God. When a ship was wrecked on Sunday and a number of sailors drowned, the pious jubilantly proclaimed that this was a divine visitation upon profaners of the Lord's Day.

In the last two decades of the seventeenth century the ministers were kept busy lamenting and denouncing the decay of the old moral and ecclesiastical system. Certainly Church and State were drifting apart, though some of the effects of the original theocracy lasted into the eighteenth century and even into the nineteenth. Few sumptuary laws were added in eighteenth-century New England, but many old ones remained on the statute books. Toward the end of the seventeenth century the Puritan colonies had a reputation for extreme moral severity which they no longer merited.

Jasper Danckaerts, a Dutchman who visited Boston in 1680, wrote of the city: "Nevertheless, you discover little difference between this and other places. Drinking and fighting occur there no less than elsewhere, and as to truth and true godliness, you must not expect more of them than of others. While we were there, four sons of ministers were learning the silversmith's trade." The last sentence is illuminating as to the growth of luxury, and it hints also at a decline in clerical power and prestige.

In 1681 a dancing master began the exercise of his profession in Boston. Available amusements were at that time very few, and there was a rush to learn how to dance. Three years later, Increase Mather preached a fiery sermon against "gynecandrical dancing, or that which is commonly called mixed or promiscuous dancing of men and women, be they elder or younger persons, together." Clerical denunciations did not in the least check the rapid growth of interest in dancing. After a time it was even possible to give ordination balls in honor of new ministers. There was considerable excitement in the discussions of mixed dancing, such as usually prevails in times of moral change.

During this same period the wickedness of playing musical instruments ceased to be self-evident to some New England people. They were at first used mostly for hymn tunes, but secular airs became more and more familiar, especially after dancing had gained a firm foothold. But in the country districts such innovations were more firmly resisted. Massachusetts and Connecticut saw the lines drawn between the wicked city and the pure rural district.

In 1686 a fencing master came to Boston. The Puritans were strongly opposed to dueling; and though they permitted fencing to be openly taught, their attitude toward affairs of honor remained much the same. Duels occurred, but those persons who killed or wounded their adversaries had to flee out of the province. In 1687 swordplay was exhibited on a stage or platform in Boston. The same year a May-pole was set up in Charlestown. Romances, some of them translated from the French, came creeping into New England bookshelves together with jest books and stage plays. Books of theology were pushed to one side or even carried up into the attic to make room for Shakespeare and long French novels. In the eighteenth century the library of over a thousand volumes which Bishop Berkeley presented to Yale included a number containing plays, among them Wycherley's.

In 1706 precise Puritans were scandalized to see the British soldiers wear crosses in their hats on St. George's Day. In 1715 there was a horse race at Cambridge. Three years later Judge Sewall made a horrified entry in his Diary: "The governor has a ball in his own house that lasts until three o'clock in the morning." Taverns and coffee houses were increasing in number. There was less talk about salvation and damnation, more about politics and the honor of a gentleman and means of recreation. In 1732 the *New England Weekly Journal* of Boston printed in its columns the complete text of a play, Lillo's *The London Merchant*, to the horror of some good people, but for the satisfaction of others.

[387]

The old spirit remained in such a man as the Reverend Cotton Mather (1663-1728). His asceticism manifested itself especially in frequent fasts. On at least one occasion every month, he considered it necessary for the welfare of his soul to do without food for a day, or even for two or three days. Fasting helped him to achieve a state of religious ecstasy, in which, as he said, he heard the voices of angels. But what they told him was evidently not very reassuring, for Mather was constantly meditating suicide. He knew that the Lord still wanted him to live and that it would have been the greatest of sins to take his own life. Yet he longed to kill himself and put an end to the terrible fear of damnation. Mather saw miraculous providences all about him. He was active in the witchcraft persecutions.

Yet even he, in the last years of his life, was infected to some extent by the new rationalism. He made a happy note of the fact that all the Congregationalist ministers in Massachusetts were orthodox. Still, the bases of their faith were being undermined. A revolt against Calvinistic theology was developing in the first decades of the eighteenth century. The Puritans built up an educational system, primarily for the purpose of training orthodox clergymen; but the increase in knowledge put to flight the devils, witches, and miscellaneous spirits which had troubled the colonists in the seventeenth century.

In the generation of Cotton Mather the conception of marriage as a civil contract lost ground. The English authorities insisted that a minister should preside at every wedding. Much stronger opposition to divorce appeared. For example, Judge Samuel Sewall was unwilling that his daughter's marriage should be dissolved, even though she bore a child three years after her husband had ceased to cohabit with her.

Parents were still supposed to exercise almost unlimited authority over their children. Boys and girls, and grown people as well, were accustomed to address their parents with considerable formality in conversation and letters. Actually, the relationship was becoming much less rigid. Youth was gaining a position in America far more advantageous than it held in England.

Young people were choosing their own mates, and courtship

The Wonders of the Invisible World.

OBSERVATIONS

As well *Historical* as *Theological*, upon the NATURE, the NUMBER, and the OPERATIONS of the

DEVILS·

Accompany'd with

I. Some Accounts of the Grievous Moleſtations, by DÆMONS and WITCHCRAFTS, which have lately annoy'd the Countrey; and the Trials of ſome eminent *Malefactors* Executed upon occaſion thereof : with ſeveral Remarkable *Curioſities* therein occurring.

II. Some Counſils, Directing a due Improvement of the terrible things, lately done, by the Unuſual & Amazing Range of EVIL SPIRITS, in Our Neighbourhood : & the methods to prevent the *Wrongs* which thoſe *Evil Angels* may intend againſt all ſorts of people among us; eſpecially in Accuſations of the Innocent.

III. Some Conjectures upon the great EVENTS, likely to befall, the WORLD in General, and NEW-ENGLAND in Particular; as alſo upon the Advances of the TIME, when we ſhall ſee BETTER DAYES.

IV. A ſhort Narrative of a late Outrage committed by a knot of WITCHES in *Swedeland*, very much Reſembling, and ſo far Explaining, *That* under which our parts of *America* have laboured !

V. THE DEVIL DISCOVERED: In a Brief Diſcourſe upon thoſe TEMPTATIONS, which are the more Ordinary *Devices* of the Wicked One.

By Cotton Mather.

Boſton Printed, and Sold by *Benjamin Harris*, 1693.

TITLE PAGE OF COTTON MATHER'S *WONDERS OF THE INVISIBLE WORLD*, 1693 became a matter of importance. Sara Knight, journeying from Boston to New York and back in 1704, commented on the Puritanism of the people along the way, which would not permit kissing between unmarried young men and women. In England, as we have seen, kissing was frequent in greetings and in games. There is no good evidence that it was rare in New England, though public and promiscuous kissing was discouraged.

The custom of bundling encouraged kissing and other forms of love-making on the part of unmarried but marriageable couples. New England dwellings, especially in the early days, were small, cold houses; and this was long true of those occupied by the lower classes. Sometimes there was but a single bed in the house, which was shared by the family with all persons who asked for hospitality. In the seventeenth century, women hardly ventured to receive men when their husbands were not at home. To do so might bring a censure from the magistrates, perhaps a public flogging. Later the suspicious attitude of the authorities and of public opinion changed. A French visitor in Connecticut shortly after the American Revolution wrote: "The Americans of these parts are very hospitable; they have usually but one bed in the house, and the chaste wife, even if she were alone, would divide it with her guest, without hesitation or fear."

Chaste (or supposedly chaste) lovers, too, lay together in bed, and this with the consent and approval of their parents. Thus they kept warm without using up valuable fuel, and they had no need to burn candles. They were supposed to wear all or part of their clothing in bed, and bundling was not considered an opportunity for fornication. It was simply a convenience. For instance, a young man might walk for miles through deep snow to call on his sweetheart; he was not sent home late at night, but permitted to bundle with her.

However respectable bundling may have been, and however well-meaning the parents who encouraged it, the fact remains that a great many illegitimate children resulted from the practice. In such cases pressure was brought to bear to make the father and the mother marry promptly. Often this was impossible, perhaps because other and previous entanglements stood in the way. The country lawyers of New England derived a large part of their income from bastardy cases all through the eighteenth century. But the custom of bundling was firmly established as a folkway; and when, in the middle of the eighteenth century, the sofa was introduced for courting purposes, old-fashioned parents insisted that it was improper and that all self-respecting young people should do their wooing under the covers.

Prostitutes appeared in a few of the larger cities. Still, girls who enjoyed a certain respectability and who did not expect any direct payment were concerned in most cases of premarital sexual relations in colonial New England. Rhode Island was reputed, all through its history as a province, to be laxer in matters of sexual morality than the rest of New England. Cromwell issued a special order for the suppression of fornication and adultery there. Perhaps Rhode Island was more closely watched because of its policy of religious toleration; possibly it attracted people of loose ways of life because there was no theocracy to condemn almost all forms of pleasure. But bundling and illegitimacy appear to have been most common in Connecticut, the most intolerant toward hedonism and religious liberalism of all the colonies. There was a time in the eighteenth century when Connecticut ministers found from one-third to one-half of the unmarried young people they questioned on the subject willing to confess fornication. The bearing of illegitimate children became a quite ordinary occurrence, and unmarried mothers found it about as easy as other young women to obtain husbands.

It was in part because of the frequency of sexual irregularity that the Reverend Jonathan Edwards was led to begin a religious revival. In 1734 he was thirty-one years old and a minister at Northampton, Massachusetts. Edwards was an exceedingly earnest young man. One of his principles of action was "never to lose one moment of time, but to improve it in the most profitable way I possibly can." Another was: "Resolved to act, in all respects, both speaking and doing, as if nobody had been so vile as I, and as if I had committed the same sins, and had the same infirmities and failings, as others." One aspect of his asceticism was expressed in his principle: "Resolved, if I take delight in it as a gratification of pride, or vanity, or on any such account, immediately to throw it by."

Edwards considered it his duty to admonish the young people of Northampton against walking about at night, frequenting taverns, and seeking all manner of fleshly delight. With great eloquence he elaborated upon Hell and its torments, told of God's pleasure in the agony of sinners. Jonathan Edwards was a man of unusual intellectual power, not only a powerful preacher but the foremost American theologian of Calvinism.

In the system which he organized, the divine will is the central fact. Man is infinitely little, according to Edwards, and the virtually insignificant amount of merit which it is possible for him to acquire comes only through his acting as an agent of the divine will. Whatever man does, he must depend upon the mercy of God.

Edwards' philosophy is rather difficult. His preaching, however, was not too cold and intellectual to stir the emotions—quite the contrary. He deliberately planned to make people hysterical over religion. And to see a child of four or five in convulsions because of pious excitement was for him a source of pleasure. It showed that his work had been well done.

Edwards' work was successful enough to serve as a model for the Wesleys in Great Britain. It also stirred up a number of American revivalists. All through New England, and then in the other colonies, men and women, young and old, grew hot with religious zeal. There is evidence that some of the heat was diverted. Fornication and adultery as well as pious zeal took an upward swing. It has beeen said that Edwards made it so difficult to reach Heaven that he discouraged many thousands of people from making the attempt.

Whitefield, who was a Calvinist like Edwards, came to New England in 1740, and his preaching stirred even the stony-hearted to tears. When Whitefield preached at Northampton, Edwards' eyes were seen to be moist all through his sermon. The English Methodist worked in the other American colonies as well. The Great Revival was, perhaps, more permanently influential outside New England than within it. In Massachusetts and Connecticut it was chiefly important in helping to break down the old sectarian barriers. Baptists and Methodists became much more numerous. The Anglicans generally opposed religious enthusiasm, and the Congregationalist ministers were divided on the subject. In 1743 the general convention of Congregationalist ministers of Massachusetts Bay protested in strong language against revival methods. Edwards and his followers rather indiscreetly attacked the clergy in general, declaring that many of them were Sabbath-breaking, drunken, worldly men, who were leading their flocks straight to damnation.

Finally Edwards aroused the enmity of his own parishioners. He declared that the young men and women of Northampton were reading vicious books which caused them to indulge in lewd thoughts and conversation. Tradition has it that Richardson's very moral *Pamela* was one of the objectionable novels. Edwards proposed to discipline all the youthful offenders in public. The deacons and the leading citizens of the town supported his plan until they discovered that their own children were involved and that the shame would reflect upon themselves. Then there was a quarrel, and Edwards was dismissed from his pastorate. In the last years of his life he was president of the new college at Princeton in New Jersey.

A wave of reaction against revivalism and hysteria in religion appeared in New England. When Whitefield came into the Northern colonies again, his reception was far less enthusiastic than it had been on his previous visit. At the outbreak of the American Revolution religion and theology were still matters of importance in Massachusetts and the neighboring provinces, but they were no longer foremost in men's minds.

In morality New England was then no longer homogeneous. The cities showed a decided tendency toward liberalism, although some taboos lingered on. The districts that had been recently settled were more democratic than the older parts, and the prevailing manners were ruder. Perhaps the Puritans who moved westward were even more tenacious of their old prejudices than those who remained at home, at least in the cities. It was possible for Sir Harry Frankland, collector of the port of Boston in the middle of the eighteenth century, to take a mistress openly into his home. To be sure, an ample supply of moral indignation arose; Sir Harry was not really popular in Boston until, having been saved miraculously (as he thought) from the Lisbon earthquake with his concubine, he brought her back to Massachusetts as his lawful wife.

James Franklin of Boston, brother of the better-known Benjamin, launched an attack in his newspaper upon the Mathers and other theocrats. He was several times in trouble with the authorities, and Benjamin was released from his articles of apprenticeship to appear as the nominal editor of the paper. A group of young men who sympathized with the anticlerical views of James Franklin organized the Hellfire Club.

Card playing and theatrical performances were, in those days, objectionable to a great many people who professed to be liberal in religion and morality. Massachusetts enacted a number of laws which were intended to keep out playhouses. In Boston the theatre was not firmly established until after the Revolution. Rhode Island allowed no dramas to be publicly performed until 1762. In 1773 Bostonians were stirred to vocal disapproval when English officers played cards on the Lord's Day. The act was, of course, one to annoy precisians in the mother country as well as in the colonies. Sunday observance was not quite so strict in New England as it had been in the preceding century, but public opinion still confined most work and play to more worldly days.

Though drunkenness remained in disfavor, drinking enough to become gay and lively was common in all classes. We are told of a Lynn minister who, at a merry party, kissed all the maidens present. At ordinations and other ceremonial occasions, ministers, though perhaps never actually intoxicated, sometimes found it difficult to maintain their poise and dignity. The force of gravitation, perhaps diabolically strengthened, tended to bring them into a more or less balanced position under the table. When clergymen preached against the abuse of rum, it seems that they sometimes spoke from experience.

Rum was distilled at Boston, Newport, and other New England towns. Large quantities were drunk in the home, and it was served as a regular ration to workingmen. Cider was supplanting beer, especially in rural districts, as the staple drink of the eighteenth century. The cider was alcoholic, to be sure; and practically no opposition was manifested to the moderate use of intoxicants.

Rum was assured of a certain amount of respectability because of the important place it held in the international commerce of New England. There was a triangular trade in rum, molasses, and slaves. Rum was taken on board ship, perhaps at Newport or Providence, and carried to Africa. There it was exchanged for slaves; and in the West Indies or the Carolinas, molasses was accepted in part payment for the negroes. There has been preserved a letter sent by a New England shipowner to his captain directing him to "put plenty of water in the rum, and use short measure as much as possible." Pious merchants and ministers approved of the triangular traffic, for the excellent reason that it was profitable. Smuggling enjoyed considerable respectability for the same reason— in fact, some of our best national heroes engaged in it; and something which bore a suspicious resemblance to piracy brought pieces of eight to good people in Rhode Island and Massachusetts.

THE ABORIGINES WITHOUT BENEFIT OF CLERGY

A drawing by Jacques Le Moyne, 1564, engraved by Theodore de Bry for his edition of Thomas Harriot's *Briefe and True Report of the new found Land of Virginia*, 1591.

CHAPTER XII

SOUTH OF THE PROMISED LAND

§ 1

IN the colonization of Virginia the desire for gain was the
leading motive, with the love of adventure second. Historians agree that the majority of the early settlers were not
men of the noblest and most heroic mold. John Smith spoke
of the people at Jamestown as being "poor gentlemen, trades-
men, serving-men, and libertines." The authorities, then and for
some time later, felt that stern discipline was essential.

Under Governor Dale extremely severe "Divine and Martial
Laws" were put into effect. Especially with regard to religious
observance Dale's code was quite as harsh as any ever enacted
in New England. The population of Virginia was for many
years such as to present difficult problems. It consisted mostly
of men without families, who had come in the hope of finding
great heaps of gold at once and without difficulty. They were
extremely disappointed to find themselves confronted by the
necessity of choosing between hard work and starvation. Sir
Thomas Dale relied upon religious instruction and the fear of
dire punishment to keep the colonists in hand.

Persistent refusal to go to church was made a capital offense.
In each plantation the foreman or captain was required to have
the gates shut and guarded by sentinels half an hour before
services began every Sunday. After all the men were supposed
to be gathered in the church, the captains searched the houses
for absentees. Then they came to church with the sentinels,
laying the keys to the outer gates before the governor to show
that no one had been allowed to escape into the fields for godless meditation. In addition to two sermons on Sunday, there
was one on Wednesday. Besides, prayers were read in the chapel

twice a day, and all the people of Jamestown were required to attend. Despite the elaborate precautions which were taken to insure church attendance, there seems to have been a fear that some would contrive to evade it. Heavy penalties were provided for men found to be staying away from the religious services without adequate reason. For the first offense they were deprived of a day's food; for the second, severely whipped; for the third, condemned to the galleys for six months. Blasphemy and profanity were treated as crimes of a still more serious nature. Second offenders were punished by having a heavy needle stuck through the tongue, and third offenders were supposed to be put to death.

Governor Dale insisted that great respect should be paid to the ministers. His decree provided that any colonist who spoke disrespectfully to a clergyman should be three times flogged and thrice required to apologize in church. The same penalty was applied to those who failed to appear before the minister to receive religious instruction, and they might even be flogged every day in case of obstinacy. The laws were not merely empty threats. They were actually enforced, as in the instance when a man was put to death by exposure after being convicted of blasphemy.

In later administrations, though the authorities of Virginia remained fixed in their determination to enforce church attendance and Sunday observance, the penalties were less severe. Governor Argoll, however, dealt with the matter almost in the same way as Governor Dale, ordering that offenders should be imprisoned and kept in an uncomfortable position for terms increasing with each repetition of the delict.

In 1619 Virginia had a representative assembly, the first in British America. This body expressly announced that it recognized the authority of the Church of England within the colony, and it required the colonists to attend church services twice every Sunday.

To restrain extravagance in dress it was ingeniously provided that parish taxes should be apportioned according to the value of each man's apparel. The assessor found everybody in rags as he made his rounds, no doubt. The same legislature enacted a law fixing the price of tobacco, which was the agricultural staple of the colony. Tobacco became in effect the money of Virginia. Fines were paid in it: for instance, a hogshead of tobacco had, according to the law of 1623, to be paid for failure to attend church.

During the seventeenth century the Virginia authorities were little behind those of New England in their attempts to prevent all except specifically religious activity on Sunday. It was against the law to work, travel, hunt, or fish on the first day of the week. There were many violations of the Sunday laws. In the middle of the century the grand jury of Lower Norfolk County charged that the whole county was disregarding them.

Virginia did not long remain the home of a few settlers living in towns. As the colony expanded and the plantation system developed, the old strictness of moral policing became impossible. People were scattered over wide tracts of land, and Governor Dale's simple system of bringing everybody to church became impracticable. Besides, the landowners became almost feudal lords, with white indentured servants and black African slaves under their control; and it depended upon them rather than upon law officers how rigidly Sunday was observed.

Few of the earliest immigrants to Virginia were Puritans, but there soon came a time when it seemed that the Puritan influence would be dominant in the province. Then the triumph of the Roundheads in England brought a host of Cavaliers to Virginia. It was they who gave the tone to religion, morality, and government after the middle of the seventeenth century. The Cavaliers were inclined to be much less precise about pious observances and standards of conduct than the Puritans. They agreed that it was the duty of a gentleman to attend religious services and to support the Church, and they believed that it was the duty of his dependents to follow him; but they condemned religious enthusiasm and extreme manifestations of pietism on the ground that they were in bad taste.

Nevertheless, the Virginia courts often imposed punishment upon minor violators of the Sunday laws. The belief that the sermons helped to keep servants and other subordinates in their places and served to check crime evidently prevailed. The favorite substitute for churchgoing, which was tippling in the taverns, was not approved either by the landlords or the officers of government.

Contemporary chroniclers give almost invariably unfavorable accounts of the Anglican ministers of Virginia colony. The early reports which circulated in England about Virginia were not such as to induce successful clergymen to migrate. Ministers came to the colony because they were unable to earn a livelihood in their native land, or even because they were anxious to live where they would not themselves be under any strict moral control. The Puritan poets spoke, not without justification, of certain priests of the Church of England who interpreted the position of pastor as an opportunity to eat, not to protect, sheep. Some of the worst of these went to the American colonies. It was far different in New England, where the Congregationalist ministers were long the best educated, the most respected, and (with some exceptions) the most precise morally of all the people.

To speak disrespectfully of a Virginia minister was almost as dangerous as to commit a similar offense in Massachusetts; yet in the Southern colony the reverend gentlemen seem to have given much more occasion for scandalous gossip. It is significant that a special law which was passed in Virginia in 1629 provided that "ministers shall not give themselves to excess in drinking or riot, spending their time idly by day or night, playing at dice, or other unlawful game."

The Church of England ministers fell into general contempt. Almost all of them were worldly, self-seeking people. Taken as a class, they had more knowledge and skill in the field of fox-hunting than in that of theology. In addition, they were offenders against the various criminal laws of the colony quite as often as the farmers and merchants of Virginia.

The Congregationalist missionaries who flocked in from New England were not welcomed by the Virginia authorities, but those people who cared seriously for religion turned more and more to them and the preachers of other Nonconformist sects. For a time, Quakers, extreme Puritans, and others who refused to attend the established Anglican houses of worship were severely punished. Pious mobs participated in the persecutions, Virginians proving their zeal for Church and State by ducking Baptists in a pond or by driving Quakers out of town. Religious intolerance, so far as it applied to Protestant Dissenters, was suspended in the time of the Commonwealth; it broke out again in 1661, but was relaxed in the last two decades of the century.

Then the laws which required church attendance on Sunday were considered to be satisfied if people went to any Protestant chapel. Nonconformists were never treated so harshly in Virginia, after representative government was established, as members of the dissenting sects were in Massachusetts. No Quaker women were hanged, no children were in danger of being sold into slavery merely because of their parents' theological views. At times the Virginians displayed great zeal for religion; Governor Wingfield was accused of atheism because he had brought no Bible with him from England.

In Virginia, as in the Puritan colonies, there were frequent expressions of the view that religious instruction, especially when provided by clergymen of the Church established by law, provided the best preventive for all forms of immorality. The chief trouble with this was the fact that the ministers themselves often laid themselves open to charges of fornication, adultery, drunkenness, profane language, and so on.

As in New England, Indian massacres and other calamities were often attributed to the wickedness of the people, and prayer and fasting were said to be the best remedies. A modern critical view leaves the impression that wickedness actually was responsible for some of the misfortunes of Virginia. For instance, the Indians were cruel and constantly dangerous, not merely because of congenital depravity but largely because they were provoked by harsh treatment on the part of the colonists. Prayer and the building of forts went on together, precisely as in New England. Soldiers were drilled to fight against the

Indians; and in order that they might not provoke the divine wrath, they were ordered· not to use blasphemous or profane language. The private who took God's name in vain, whether he was drunk or sober at the moment, was forced to run the gauntlet through a hundred men. If he was found guilty a second time of this offense, his tongue was bored through with a hot iron.

From the earliest days of the colony the Virginians had the reputation of being a pleasure-loving people. In general, the provincial authorities encouraged sports and diversions, except when they were considered riotous, excessive, or untimely. Hunting was for some time useful in contributing to the food supply. Moreover, it became established as a recreation suitable for gentlemen. Racing was considered a sport for the upper classes alone, and a judicial decision of 1674 definitely established the rule that a tailor and his equals might not lawfully race horses.

Cards and dice seem to have been brought in by the earliest settlers. Certainly they were common in colonial Virginia. Heavy wagers were laid on the outcome of cockfights and races, and gambling of all sorts was much in vogue. The laws against dicing were very frequently violated, and even those which applied to the clergy were honored largely in the breach.

Means of diversion were naturally limited in the early days of the colony, and the fact that no large cities grew up made difficult the establishment of elaborate pleasure resorts. Country taverns and private houses had usually to serve as the scenes of revelry. The hospitality of Virginia became famous. Food and drink were supplied in abundance, and feasting was perhaps the most important diversion of the province. In 1686 one gentleman had stored in his cellar, for his private table, ninety gallons of rum, twenty-five gallons of lime juice, and twenty dozen bottles of wine. Others were equally well prepared to offer hospitality.

Virginia had an abundant supply of laws and proclamations which denounced drunkenness and set up penalties for drunkards. Intoxicated servants were put into the stocks, although their masters were privileged to save them from such ignominy

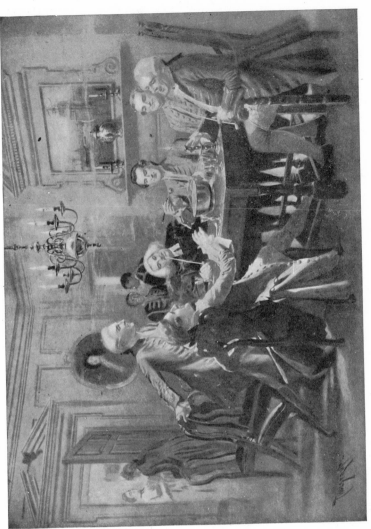

AFTER THE LADIES LEFT THE TABLE

After a painting by T. de Thulstrup.

and discomfort by paying fines for them. No one class monopolized the heavy drinking. A law of 1658 provided that all persons three times convicted of drunkenness should thenceforth be ineligible to hold any public office. And there was enacted, a few years later, a statute which forbade judges to get drunk on court days and ministers to drink excessively before ascending their pulpits. There was a complex mass of legislation regulating inns and tippling houses, much of which was intended to curb public intoxication. However, drunkenness was a very common sight in colonial Virginia.

Deep drinking was often associated with the use of profane language, which was also forbidden in a number of ordinances. In 1694 Mrs. Ann Stop was accused of having employed improper language on at least sixty-five different occasions. Although the Cavaliers of Virginia did not feel profanity to be entirely so dreadful an offense as the Massachusetts Puritans conceived it, they sometimes punished it harshly.

Also connected with drunkenness was the offense of brawling. The duel had, indeed, a natural place in the semifeudal society of Virginia, even though it was not formally authorized by law. Among the lower orders there were frequent private or free-for-all fights, in which biting and gouging were common features. So far as we can infer from the available records, Virginia had more brawls and disorder than Massachusetts and Connecticut. But it was more especially the frontier that suffered from lawlessness.

In Virginia much trouble was caused by the servants. The white men and women who were brought from England under indentures for a limited period and the Africans who were brought in to be permanent slaves both gave difficulty. The negroes were unaccustomed to civilization. Some of the tribes from which they came were at the level of savagery. Few of the colored people were accustomed to intensive agricultural labors. Their taming was done with a heavy hand, and a constant fear that they might organize a general revolt caused a series of repressive laws to be put into effect against them.

The problem of miscegenation soon arose. The authorities

exerted themselves to stop sexual relations between blacks and whites, as by making the penalty for fornication heavier in such cases. We read how, in Lower Norfolk County, a white man and a black woman had to do penance in church, standing up together dressed in white sheets and bearing white wands in their hands.

There were a great many white female servants in the colony, some of them free, others indentured. In either case they usually came to Virginia alone; and the fact that their families were far away—in the days of slow sailing ships the distance across the Atlantic was in effect much greater than it is to-day—tended to make them morally reckless. As for those who were indentured, they had little freedom of choice. Like the negro slaves, they had to do what they were told, and the laws that were intended to protect them were seldom enforced against the will of their masters. The result was a great deal of bastardy.

Free women who bore illegitimate children were, in many cases, punished by public whippings, even if they later married their lovers. In such cases Virginia usually dealt more harshly with the women than with the men. For example, there was one case in which the unmarried mother received thirty lashes on the bare back, whereas the father of her child was released after he had confessed his guilt in church. The men were often of higher rank than the women; sometimes their guilt was difficult to prove; besides, fornication and adultery were held to be worse crimes when committed by women. It was the general practice in the Southern colonies to compel maidservants to serve beyond the terms of their indenture if they bore children while still bond. The laws which provided for this were based upon the idea that the master should be repaid for the time and expense consumed in lying-in and the care of the infants. However, they operated in just the same way if the father was the master himself. The motive of profit was added to that of lust in such cases.

The people of Virginia sometimes had sexual relations with Indians as well as with negroes and white servants. In the eighteenth century Braddock's officers caused a great deal of trouble by their affairs with the wives and daughters of the red allies. The squaws had finally to be sent away from the camp.

On the whole, the laws of Virginia meddled comparatively little with personal affairs. The sumptuary legislation was much scantier than that of the New England colonies. Still, when there was an outcry about extravagance in dress, an attempt was made to keep women from wearing pearl necklaces. When a play was acted, in 1665, the actors were summoned to court; but it was held that they had violated no law, and they were discharged. Amateurs did a great deal of dramatizing; and if there was no permanent professional theatre in the seventeenth century, this was rather because economic conditions did not favor it than because of any moral objections.

The Virginia gentlemen came more and more to resemble landowners of the same social class in England. Their standards of right and wrong were little different, except as they were modified by the presence of large classes of absolute dependents. Even with regard to fashions and passing fads, the Virginians looked always to the newest importations from London. Sports were enjoyed wholeheartedly, as in rural England when it was not under the yoke of the Puritans.

Education advanced more slowly than in New England. Governor Berkeley boasted in 1671, in a report to the home government: "But, I thank God, there are no free schools nor printers, and I hope we shall not have these hundred years." A decade later a Virginian was imprisoned for venturing to print the provincial laws without special authorization. Obscurantism flourished, and a woman was ducked for witchcraft in 1705. Still, the Virginians were either too enlightened or too easy-going to conduct a campaign against witches in the Salem way, and to prove their complete literal belief in the Old Testament by hanging old women.

There was little religious enthusiasm until Whitefield came, and then it appeared to be temporary. The great religion of the aristocratic South, in colonial days and later, was chivalry. The New World conditions in Virginia made possible the revival of some aspects of feudalism which were obsolete or obsolescent in England. The great estates, which were at first of little value, became in time sources of wealth and power.

The importation of negro slaves provided a class which seemed better suited than the mediæval peasantry to labor for the benefit of feudal lords. It was soon seen that the system of indenture which brought in white servants, chiefly from England, could not be more than a temporary stop-gap. The negroes, most masters felt, constituted a permanent working class. Virginia tried to discourage the working of white women in the fields by making them free of tax in case they were only employed at domestic labor. The authorities did not object, though, when negresses were driven with the overseer's whip to hard agricultural labor.

The chivalric ideal embodied respect for the lady and gave her certain privileges which the gentlemen did not have, but it did not admit her equality with him. During the early days of Virginia, when women were scarce in the colony, they obtained many advantages which they did not enjoy in England. We are told of one young lady of the seventeenth century who capriciously broke her engagement, then refused to marry the second man upon whom her fancy fell until he consented that the promise to obey should be eliminated from the ceremony. Most Virginia people married while they were still quite young, and widows found suitors as soon as they were free. The list of distinguished Virginians who married widows includes George Washington, Thomas Jefferson, and James Madison. The widows often had, in addition to their traditional charms, valuable property left to them by their first husbands.

§ 2

The province of Maryland was settled by agents of Lord Baltimore. His principal purposes were personal gain and the provision of a refuge for Roman Catholics, who were meeting with much intolerance in England. The first settlers were gentlemen belonging to the Roman Catholic Church, who became lords of the manor in America, and their servants, most of whom were communicants of the Anglican Church. Lord Baltimore was careful to instruct his agents on board the ship that brought the first settlers that the rites of the Catholic Church were not to be celebrated openly. The governor and the commissioners were explicitly ordered to "suffer no scandal nor offense to be given to any of the Protestants."

The question has often been asked whether or not Lord Baltimore believed in the principle of toleration. In other words, would he have welcomed Protestants to Maryland if the Catholics had been at the head of the affairs in England? But it is unnecessary for our present purpose to try to answer this. Under the conditions which actually existed, it was impossible for Baltimore to make Maryland exclusively Catholic. Whether or not he believed in toleration, he found it necessary, in order that his coreligionists might have the freedom to worship as they desired in his American province, to extend the same privilege to others. And this was sufficient to account for the direction he gave to his commissioners, that they were "to treat the Protestants with as much mildness and favor as justice will permit."

We have seen how intensely popery was hated by most Englishmen in the seventeenth century. It was far worse, even to the average High Church conservative, than Presbyterianism or Independency, for the Roman Catholic Church was associated with harsh oppressions and foreign attacks. Comparatively few of the aristocratic English families remained true to the old religion in favorable and unfavorable times alike.

Full religious tolerance was not officially granted in the early laws of Maryland. Blasphemy, idolatry, sacrilege, and witchcraft were made capital crimes. It was provided, in 1649, that all persons who declared their belief in the Trinity should enjoy full political privilege in the province. But Maryland did not extend religious toleration to those who denied the divinity and divine sonship of Jesus Christ or who uttered "reproachful speeches" about the Holy Trinity. Such persons were to be severely punished. On a third conviction they were supposed to be executed and their estates confiscated Yet the earliest records of the province contain Jewish names, and it appears that persons who did not accept the divinity of Christ were unmolested and gradually permitted to extend their civic rights. It was provided by law that fines should be imposed upon persons who spoke slightingly of religions other than their own and used such terms as "Schismatic Puritan," "Roundhead Separatist," or "Popish Priest."

The persecutions which the Puritans suffered in Virginia brought many of them into the safer territory of Maryland. They settled in large numbers at a place which they piously named Providence, and which later became known as Annapolis. These Puritans, who had suffered for their faith, eventually gained control of the government of Maryland, and they proceeded to show how intolerant and how zealous for conformity they could be in their turn. The Roman Catholics had permitted them to come and enjoy the privilege of citizenship, but they conceded no such right to the Catholics. In fact, their attitude toward moral and religious standards was much the same as that of their brethren in New England. They passed a number of sumptuary laws. They had Quakers whipped from constable to constable until they were out of the province. Yet the Friends gathered many proselytes, just as they did under similar conditions in Massachusetts. When Catholic King James was frightened out of his throne, the Church of England was established in Maryland.

Here, even more than in Virginia, the reputation of the Anglican clergy as to morals was bad. At best, the ministers raced horses, hunted foxes, went to cockfights, and devoted their thoughts and time to pleasures more or less harmless. At worst, they were drunken criminals, who robbed their parishioners in order to be able to gamble and to gain the favor of women, perhaps the wives of others. Because British America was without bishops, there was no easy way to discipline ministers guilty of minor offenses or of breaches of their duty.

The majority of the people of Maryland either lost interest in religion or joined Nonconformist bodies. In 1711 a law was passed which provided that no drinking should be permitted at the Quaker conventions—proof that these meetings were attended by large and sometimes riotous crowds.

If the Friends occasionally became drunk at assemblies devoted to problems of religious work, who in Maryland was sober on ordinary secular occasions? We must, of course, make allowances for the fact that Fox's followers could not all preserve in practice the ascetic principles which he promulgated. The flesh was, in many a case, weaker than the spirit. Nevertheless, the Quakers kept to a higher level of sobriety than the members of other churches.

Sunday observance was required in Maryland, as it was in the other colonies, especially those under Puritan influence. Fines were imposed for working or playing on the first day of the week, and those who could not pay them were flogged.

Fornication, drunkenness, and profanity were crimes with which the legislatures of Maryland were much concerned. The judicial officers were kept busy with such cases. A law of 1704 forbade men and women to associate without the consent of the ecclesiastical authorities under pain of a heavy fine and whipping. Other legislation attempted to deal with the usual moral difficulties brought about in the colonies by the presence of white servants and colored slaves. The existence close by of Indians, who were averse to disciplined habits of industry, also contributed to the restlessness of the province. Young men sometimes doffed the elaborate European costume in favor of the simple Indian garb, and we hear of some who scandalized congregations by appearing in church wearing no more than a breechclout.

Maryland, except when the Puritans were in full control, was no less merry than Virginia. It had its wines and its races and its card playing. Noble gentlemen vied with each other as to the quantity as well as the quality of the potations in their cellars. They imported great hogsheads of wine from Europe.

After the middle of the eighteenth century the population of Maryland was increased by a large number of criminals sent from England. Naturally, they contributed something to the moral looseness of the province. At the other end of the social scale, the government officials were often corrupt and rapacious. In their case, as in that of the Anglican ministers, the American colonies were habitually treated as harbors for the incompetent and the reckless. Lords and favorites who were burdened by good-for-nothing younger sons felt that they might properly be provided, for at the expense of His Majesty's provinces across the sea. Such black-sheep officials joined the Maryland land-owners in pleasure parties of all sorts, and vied with them in the attempt to adopt London fashions before they had entirely lost their pristine freshness. The grosser forms of amusement were most favored.

Little attention was paid to newspapers, still less to books. Few showed any interest in philosophy, the arts, and culture in general. Some Marylanders, especially those belonging to Catholic families, sent their sons to France for their education and kept in touch with French ideas. In the eighteenth century there was a certain rise of interest in intellectual matters through-out the Southern colonies, including Maryland.

The history of women in colonial Maryland was similar to that in Virginia. In the early days of the province a woman named Margaret Brent occupied a place of particular impor-tance. When Governor Leonard Calvert died, his will named her as his executrix. In 1648 Miss Brent formally laid claim to a seat in the assembly. Although this was denied, her political influence was very great. It seems that she was an unusually attractive woman, for one of her rejected suitors left her his estate.

§ 3

Pennsylvania, like Maryland, was settled under the direction of a proprietor who was concerned with mitigating the sufferings of a religious sect. But in Penn's case there is no doubt that he believed in the principle of toleration. Englishmen and peo-ple from many other European countries, Quakers and non-Quakers, were welcomed to Penn's grant. A number of quarrels arose in Pennsylvania and Delaware between the members of various sects and national groups, but these were seldom serious. Although the proprietors, William Penn and his heirs, were consistently opposed to religious discrimination, they sometimes had to submit to public opinion and the will of the authorities in England. It was necessary, therefore, to require the Roman Catholics in Pennsylvania to keep their church services private and to deprive them of the political rights which were freely accorded to all Protestants.

There were Sunday laws in Pennsylvania province, but they were not so strict as those of Virginia, and far less stringent than those which prevailed throughout most of New England. The law of 1700 dealing with Sunday observance required worship and the reading of the Scriptures, but permitted these activities to be carried on at home by those persons who did not care to attend any of the churches in their neighborhood. Six years later, the selling of meat, milk, and fish was permitted on Sunday at stated hours and under definite restrictions. In short, Pennsylvania retained the notion that the Lord's Day should be devoted to religious exercises and that the State should keep it from being profaned; but an attempt was made to retain a spirit of tolerance in the enforcement. and a certain amount of common sense.

A great many non-Quaker pietists came to Pennsylvania, notably a number of Germans who belonged to various strict sects. In general, more religious feeling was displayed in Penn's province than in Virginia and Maryland. The Anglicans were the least pious and enthusiastic of the American colonists — though, as usual, we must make allowances for exceptional persons.

Some of the zealots of Pennsylvania went even further than the New England Puritans in adopting Old Testament laws and customs. The German Protestant pietists were sometimes described by careless observers as Jews, and this was especially true of those who kept the last day of the week as their Sabbath. There seem to have been a few genuine Jews in the region that is now Delaware even before this district passed under the control of the English and became part of Penn's tract. Under the jurisdiction of Pennsylvania they could not enjoy the full rights of citizenship, but they were free to worship as they pleased and to engage in trade on an equal basis with Christians.

Almost everybody, in the early days of Pennsylvania, was connected with some religious body, even though this was not compulsory. The various church organizations attempted to control the morals of their members and to regulate their behavior in a wide variety of ways. In the Scotch-Irish communities persons who were found to have committed sexual delicts were required to make public confession in church.

But the State did not entirely abandon matters of morality to the religious bodies. It punished fornication, like assault and larceny, with public whipping or exposure in the pillory. The laws of Pennsylvania forbade playing at cards, dice, billiards, ninepins, and many other games; and a number of statutes were enacted for the purpose of keeping theatrical representations out of the province. The very first representative assembly of Pennsylvania legislated against these things, as well as against other similar vices, such as the drinking of healths, the use of profane language, dueling, cockfighting, bull baiting, and drunken or riotous revelry. We find in the records that grand juries indicted long lists of card players and other offenders against the moral sense of the community.

But the people of Pennsylvania, including the Quakers and members of various other pietistic sects, generally became more tolerant in their attitude toward amusements and luxuries. Dueling became quite common in Philadelphia during the eighteenth century. The Quakers weakened in their opposition to expensive and fashionable clothes; and some of their women took to wearing their hair in an elaborate fashion, requiring hours of a hairdresser's time to prepare. Just before the Revolution, Philadelphia had the reputation of displaying much more luxury than Boston or any other city in the British American colonies. Its rich merchants were fond of display, and their wives appeared in public wearing evidence of wealth in the form of silks and jewels.

The manufacture of beer in Pennsylvania was one of the very

first industries to be established in the colony. William Penn himself directed that a brewery should be set up. Besides, a great deal of beer and other alcoholic beverages was made at home. On the frontier, whiskey was the favorite drink, and there were few adults who refrained from using it. The wealthy had their fine imported wines, the poor devoted a large part of their income to the purchase of beer and distilled potations. In 1744 a Philadelphia grand jury of which Benjamin Franklin was the foreman declared that tippling houses were largely responsible for poverty, a decrease in piety, and an increase in the use of profane language. It recommended, therefore, that the number of licenses issued for the sale of liquor should be cut down. Dancing lessons had first been given in the city a few years before, but they were, apparently, not held responsible for poverty and irreligion.

Benjamin Franklin himself cared nothing about the old creeds, and in his mature years he was certainly not a Christian. But he felt, like Voltaire, that if no God existed, it would be necessary to create one for the preservation of good morals. During the Indian wars he used his ingenuity to help a chaplain who complained that the soldiers were staying away from prayers. Since the chaplains were charged with the duty of passing out the daily allowance of a gill of rum to each man, Franklin suggested that this should be distributed after prayers, and only to those who had performed their religious duties. It is not clear, to be sure, that piety was increased by church attendance motivated by the desire for a gill of rum; but it was held that participation in prayer and listening to a sermon, even though involuntary, had some sort of efficacy.

Franklin possessed and valued the Puritan virtues of industry, thrift, and sobriety. He felt that the churches were justified, no matter what the truth or lack of truth of their theologies, if they inculcated these things. *Poor Richard's Almanac,* the most popular of all his writings, proves with a variety of saws, anecdotes, and wise sayings that honesty is the best policy and that the early bird catches the worm. Franklin prepared for himself a list of moral principles, and he carefuly checked

X Mon. December hath xxxi days.

She that will eat her breakfaſt in her bed,
And ſpend the morn in dreſſing of her head,
And ſit at dinner like a maiden bride,
And talk of nothing all day but of pride,
God in his mercy may do much to ſave her,
But what a caſe is he in that ſhall have her.

1	7	*Unſettled weather*	7	♓	7	21	5	☽ ſets 11 after.
2	G	Advent Sunday	8	14	7	21	5	Firſt Quarter,
3	2	*now.*	9	28	7	22	5	*God works won-*
4	3	△☉♄ *Either rain*	10	♈	7	22	5	*ders now & then;*
5	4	*or ſnow, and then a*	10	26	7	22	5	*Behold! a Law-*
6	5	7 * ſet 5 10	11	♉	7	23	5	☽ ſets 3 15 m.
7	6	*froſt comes on*	12	26	7	23	5	*yer, an honeſt*
8	7	*I know*	1	♊	7	23	5	*Man!*
9	G	1 Sund in Adv	2	26	7	23	5	Full ● 9 at nig.
10	2	☉ enters ♑ then	2h	♋	7	23	5	*He that lives*
11	3	Wint. Qu. begins	3	24	7	23	5	*carnally, wor*
12	4	& makes ſhorteſt	4	♌	7	23	5	☽ riſe 8 8 aft.
13	5	day 9 h. 14 m.	5	3	7	23	5	*live eternally.*
14	6	*Windy and clouds,*	6	♍	7	22	5	
15	7	✱ ♄ ☿	6h	20	7	22	5	*Innocence is its*
16	G	2 Sund. in Adv.	7	♎	7	22	5	*own Defence.*
17	2	7 * ſouth 8 58	8	14	7	22	5	Laſt Quarter.
18	3	*like for ſnow.*	9	27	7	22	5	☽ riſe 1 15 m.
19	4	✱ ♄ ♀	10	♏	7	21	5	*Time* eateth *all*
20	5	Days incr. 4 mi	10	20	7	21	5	*things, could old*
21	6	St. Thomas	11	♐	7	21	5	*Poets ſay; The*
22	7	*High winds and*	12	14	7	21	5	*Times are*
23	G	3 Sund. in Adv.	1	26	7	20	5	☽ riſe 5 43 mo.
24	2	✱ ☿ ♀ □ ♃ ♀	2	♑	7	20	5	*chang'd, our*
25	3	CHRIST Nativ.	2h	20	7	19	5	New ☽ at 2 mo
26	4	S. Stephen ✱ ☉ ♂	3	♒	7	19	5	*times* drink *all*
27	5	St. John *cloudy*	4	14	7	18	5	*away.*
28	6	Innocents *weather*	5	28	7	18	5	☽ ſets 8 29 aft.
29	7	*Snow or Rain will*	6	♓	7	17	5	*Never mind it,*
30	G	*now appear, and a*	6	24	7	17	5	*She'l be ſober afte*
31	2	*Froſt end the Year.*	7	♈	7	16	5	*the Holidays.*

A PAGE FROM THE FIRST ISSUE OF *POOR RICHARD'S ALMANAC*

December, 1733.

himself on the extent to which he observed the rules. His virtues were temperance, silence, order, resolution, frugality, industry, sincerity, justice, moderation, cleanliness, tranquillity, chastity, and humility.

The precept of chastity to which he tried to adhere was: "Rarely use venery but for health or offspring, never to dulness, weakness, or the injury of your own or another's peace or reputation." He tells us frankly in his Autobiography that he was not a perfectly chaste bachelor: "That hard-to-be-governed passion of youth hurried me frequently into intrigues with low women that fell my way." He refused to marry a woman because her parents haggled over the dowry to be given with her. Then he married another who had not been divorced from her first husband, but who suspected that he possessed another wife in England and that the marriage had never been valid.

Divorce was uncommon in colonial Pennsylvania, but it happened not seldom that husbands and wives were exchanged without legal authorization. The authorities tried to emphasize the sanctity of the marriage bond, as by making it illegal for widows to marry until their husbands had been dead for a year. Adultery was made a cause for divorce in 1682, and it was supposed to bring severe criminal penalties as well. The penalty for a first offense was a severe flogging and imprisonment for at least a year in the house of correction; for a second, lifelong imprisonment.

There were the usual attempts to prevent miscegenation. A white woman received twenty-one lashes on the bare back for bearing a child whose father was a negro. Benjamin Franklin's enemies accused him of having black mistresses, and certainly there were many Philadelphia men who did have them. A Pennsylvania law of 1700 provided the death penalty for negro slaves convicted of sodomy or of rape on white women. In cases of attempted rape upon women of the dominant race, they were supposed to be castrated.

The presence of transported criminals, indentured servants of both sexes, and colored men and women who had been torn away from their African homes considerably complicated matters. Perhaps the increase of wealth in the eighteenth century had a still more disturbing effect on morality. For instance, public prostitutes appeared as soon as there were enough young men willing to contribute to their support; and the opposition of the authorities did not suppress their trade. Franklin complained that such women were at once expensive and dangerous to health. As a prudent and foresighted person, he saw the advantages of getting married instead of continuing to patronize them.

Benjamin Franklin may be considered an example of the early development of the New Puritanism in America. His many-sided genius keeps us from considering him typical, however. That he was able to do important scientific work is in itself sufficient proof that much of the old bigotry was gone. He was born and brought up in Massachusetts, a colony where, a century earlier, the attempt to draw electricity out of the clouds would have brought down the wrath of the ministers upon him. Clerical influence was unimportant in eighteenth-century Philadelphia. Utilitarian principles generally prevailed in the handling of moral problems.

Although the province as a whole became less rigid in standards of conduct, this was not the case in some of the communities. A visitor to Philadelphia in 1722 commented on the fact that the kissing of young women by men seemed to be unrestricted. In pietistic German households daughters and maidservants who ventured to adopt this custom ran the risk of having the rod applied with a heavy hand. This is not to say that no women in the conservative German communities ever bore illegitimate children. Bastardy was extremely common all over the American colonies in the eighteenth century; and in many sections it exerted no serious influence upon the social standing of mother or child. Franklin's natural child became governor of New Jersey.

Among the Quakers, women were allowed from the first days of the Society to testify freely about their religious experiences. Female preachers of the word showed themselves no less zealous than the men, no less willing to incur hardships and dangers.

Where the male missionaries were whipped and hanged, the women suffered equally with them. Consequently, though there was little among the Friends corresponding to the chivalry of Virginia, the women actually enjoyed a far higher standard. It was, then, in Pennsylvania that the idea which now seems typi-

THE QUAKER SHEEP

who remains inactive but expects to derive advantage from the French and Indian War no matter who may win. A contemporary caricature, from the *Proceedings* of the Pennsylvania-German Society.

cally American, that men and women should work together for high moral purposes, first arose into prominence.

In Pennsylvania, where the Friends were in control of the legislative branch of the government, their opposition to war sometimes caused difficulties. As a matter of fact, they were not opposed to defensive actions against the French and the Indians. Still, they did not like to vote money expressly for gunpowder and other military supplies. But their conscience did not trouble them when they apportioned funds "for the King's use" or under similar indefinite headings, even though they knew that the money would be used to buy instruments of slaughter. To point out this moral quirk is not to deny that the American Quakers were more anxious than most of the other colonists to avert war. They usually did their best to remain on good terms with the Indians.

The Scotch-Irish settlers in Paxton County were of a different mind. Absorbed in the religion of the Old Testament, they actually seem to have identified themselves with the Israelites and the Indians with the Philistines, whom it was necessary to exterminate. Their Indian neighbors were harmless men and women, many of whom called themselves Christians. Yet the Paxton Boys formed themselves into a pious military band and massacred all the Indians they could reach. At Lancaster they broke into a building where the authorities had gathered a number of Indian men and women for safe-keeping, and murdered them all. Franklin succeeded in diverting them from Philadelphia, where there were some Indians whom the Moravians had converted. Many ministers in Pennsylvania praised the Scotch-Irish assassins for their courage and devotion in putting the Indians to death.

We have already seen something of the narrowness and the fanatical asceticism of the Scottish Presbyterians in the period that followed the Reformation. In Ireland the Scotch settlers cultivated also an intolerant fierceness. Their Christian religion was not one of mildness and gentleness. They never thought of turning the other cheek, but were much concerned with destroying the enemies of God. These might be Irish papists or red-skinned pagans. The savage and barbarian aborigines of America were far less bloodthirsty than the civilized Scottish Calvinists who immigrated from Ireland.

To understand the New Puritanism as it exists in our own times, we must consider the Presbyterians who came to America after a comparatively short residence in Ireland as well as the New England Congregationalists who came from England. These "Ulstermen" went, in most cases, first to Pennsylvania.

Thence they spread into the frontier districts of various Middle and Southern colonies. A few went to New Hampshire.

They were much more democratic than the Puritans of English descent: that is to say, they believed that members of their own group, or even all white Protestants, were essentially equal; and if any inferiority existed, it was displayed in lack of courage or the inefficient use of weapons. Settling as they did on the frontier, and usually moving westward with it, they were enabled to maintain such a democratic creed. No one had great wealth, no one who could shoot starved to death. Some of them went up into the Appalachian mountain chains, where they were to remain aloof from the industrial progress of the nineteenth century. Others remained in the Southern lowlands, becoming owners or drivers of slaves. These looked earnestly into their Bibles, and found that negro slavery was a divinely ordained institution. Not all of them remained Presbyterians, but most retained their faith in the complete literal truth of the Scriptures.

When the Revolution broke out, about one-sixth of the population of the colonies was of Scotch-Irish descent. The Ulstermen ceased to be aliens in America, lost something of their homogeneity, drew closer to their neighbors and intermarried with them. Still, they did not abandon their ideals and their prejudices. While the New England Puritans cultivated schools and colleges and acquired a certain amount of rationalism, the Scotch-Irish and their descendants who lived on the frontier or in remote mountain districts retained their ignorance and their suspicion of "book learning." The superstitions of their fathers were good enough for them. It should be added that the heritage of the Ulstermen did not always pass lineally. Some descendants of the Scotch-Irish escaped from the fear of books, but not from that of rationalism. Others became entirely separated from their people in cultural matters. At the same time, other people, of English or German or French Huguenot stock, became associated with the Ulstermen, taking up their way and philosophy of life.

The Scotch-Irish inclined toward asceticism, but they did not, as a class, have any objection to the use of distilled alcoholic beverages. Economic considerations made the domestic still very important to the Ulstermen in colonial times. Living for the most part far from waterways and other means of transportation, they had to make whiskey of all the grain they grew except that which served to make food for their own use.

The College of New Jersey at Princeton—of which, as we have seen, Jonathan Edwards became the head after he had incurred the wrath of his parishioners—was founded by Scottish Presbyterians. Those who remained in the settled districts were more friendly to education than the Scotchmen and Scotch-Irishmen who lived on the frontier.

The little province of New Jersey was influenced by a number of pietistic bodies, including the Quakers and the New England Congregationalists as well as the Scottish Presbyterians. It was soon provided with its full share of "blue laws." The Quakers of East Jersey were especially anxious to prevent dueling, and they prohibited the carrying of pistols, daggers, or dirks. It was due less to their desire than to that of the Presbyterians and Congregationalists that severe laws were enacted against working, traveling, or playing on Sunday. Legislation was passed against card playing, even in the home, bull baiting, cockfighting, tippling, and other forms of diversion. This was mostly modeled after that of Massachusetts. The Quakers were in general sympathy with such laws; but in the neighboring province of Pennsylvania, where they were in full control, they were usually somewhat milder in the punishments they inflicted upon those who engaged in sports that were considered improper.

New Jersey had the usual trouble with sexual offenses, and dealt with them in the ordinary colonial way. An East Jersey law of 1668 provided that adulterers should be whipped and banished, and allowed the injured parties to receive divorces in such cases. In one instance, the man received thirty strokes on the bare body, and the woman got thirty-five. A New Jersey law passed in 1719 forbade the marriage of persons under the age of twenty-one without the written consent of their parents. In East Jersey there had been more stringent legislation to uphold the authority of the father and the mother over their

children. Its laws made it a capital offense for a child to strike
his or her parents.

Perhaps mostly through carelessness, or it may have been because of Quaker influence, colonial New Jersey adopted a constitution which permitted "all inhabitants of the colony of full
age" to vote. This included women as well as aliens. A more
limited form of woman suffrage existed also before the Revolution
in parts of New England, where all freeholders had a voice in
local matters. But there was very little discussion of feminism
and the political privileges of women in the colonies. Their
rights disappeared as quickly and as quietly as they had come.

In the last days of New Jersey colony the Church of England
was supposed to be established there. Actually, it enjoyed few
special privileges; and most of the pious inhabitants belonged to
independent sects.

§ 4

The Carolinas were, in the earliest days, places of refuge for
criminals and bankrupts, who came from England or from Virginia and other American colonies. For a long time governmental
authority was only vaguely established; and consequently these
Southern provinces harbored runaway servants, men who had
left behind their wives or their creditors, and many others whose
actions or whose past lives could not bear close scrutiny.

During the first thirty years of the existence of North Carolina, the Quakers are said to have held the only religious services. Although the Church of England went slowly to work in
the Carolinas, attempts were made to establish it and force all
the inhabitants to contribute toward its support. Up to 1766
North Carolina recognized the validity of no marriages except
those performed by Anglican ministers. Though the province was
extremely illiterate, only members of the Church of England were
permitted to teach there. Dissenters were always in the majority,
and they protested vehemently against the special privileges
which the Episcopalian clergy enjoyed. In fact, the friction
brought about in most of the colonies by the compulsory payment

of tithes to the Anglican ministers, or the fear that such a compulsion might be introduced, was one of the causes of the American Revolution.

The original constitution of the Carolinas excluded from all the benefits of the law those persons, being above the age of seventeen, who did not belong to some church or religious sect. Nevertheless, many of the early Carolina settlers were without any great interest in religion. One of their primary concerns was to avoid paying any taxes or dues, whether for the benefit of Church or State.

There were laws to promote Sunday observance and the usual statutes against drunkenness and gambling, but few paid much attention to them. The immigrants to the Carolinas were of various nationalities, including, in addition to Englishmen, Scotchmen who came directly from their country or from Ireland, Irishmen, Germans, Swiss and French Protestants. Order and unified government were very slowly introduced among them.

Slavery soon became an important factor in the economic life, and Carolina planters had the reputation of treating the negroes very harshly. In a few towns of North and South Carolina an aristocracy grew up which cultivated the niceties of life even more carefully than the gentlemen of Virginia. In these colonies Puritanism and asceticism were of importance among some of the sectaries. But the people who gave the tone to high society were all hedonists. Their Epicureanism was, indeed, of various sorts. For some, alcoholic and amorous indulgences were of primary importance. Others found delight in graceful dancing and perhaps in clever conversation. There were a few who cared for the fine arts.

An aversion to labor developed early among the white people of the Carolinas, and for this the climate was largely responsible. The impecunious had less need than the poor people of the Northern colonies to worry about clothing, shelter, and food. The rich depended for all their luxuries, for their fine town houses and their imported wines, upon the labor of African slaves.

The mingling of white blood with that of Indians and negroes, though it was a sin in the eyes of the clergy and a crime before the law, was a striking feature of life in the Carolina provinces. There was also much sexual irregularity between whites.

Georgia was established as a philanthropic enterprise, under the supervision of General James Edward Oglethorpe. It was intended to offer a refuge for debtors and others who had come to grief in England but who might be expected to do better in a new country, away from slums and grogshops and other evil influences.

Oglethorpe and the trustees of Georgia forbade the importation into the colony and the sale within it of rum, brandy, and other distilled beverages. This order was confirmed by the English Parliament in 1735. Attempts were made to convince the settlers that they should be satisfied with malt beverages instead of geneva and strong waters in general. However, they resented the propaganda almost as much as the law. It was better, they felt, to be shut up in a debtor's prison with the solace of potent drink than to be free in Georgia without the cheering and inebriating bottle. Moreover, they were subject to enervating fevers, which they believed to be uncontrollable except through the use of distilled beverages. The settlers in Georgia had another grievance in that they were forbidden to import negro slaves. They considered the climate such as to make hard labor on the part of white people undesirable. It was virtually impossible to violate the antislavery law, but a great deal of hard liquor was consumed in Georgia. It was smuggled into the province and also manufactured within it. Georgia juries consistently refused to convict dealers in strong waters, and the attitude of the colonists was such that the authorities finally gave up all attempts to enforce the prohibition. For a time, many of the officials shared in the profits of the illicit trade.

When Whitefield came to Georgia, he quickly reached the conclusion that the colony was lacking in prosperity because of the prohibitions imposed upon slavery and the consumption of distilled beverages. He argued that both should be removed. They were, but it is not clear that Whitefield's agitation had much to do with the change. When he appeared before the Savannah grand jury and delivered a harangue on the "barefaced wickedness" prevalent in the province, he was entirely ignored. Neither he nor the Wesleys seemed to exert any important influence in colonial Georgia, although Methodism became an outstanding moral force in the state during the next century.

The Georgians had the reputation, like the people of North and South Carolina, of being addicted to gambling, sexual laxity, and the coarser forms of pleasure in general. At the time when the Revolution broke out, there was little aristocratic society in the province, and the refinements of such a town as Charleston were virtually unknown in Georgia.

A law of 1762 required everybody to attend some church on Sunday. Religious tolerance was the rule for all Protestants, and, in practice, for others as well. There were Catholics in the colony, and the second ship from London brought a group of Jews. It is significant that the five members of the Union Society, which was organized in 1750 to provide for orphans, were all of different religious faiths, among them a Catholic and a Jew.

The laws of Georgia forbade working, playing, and, except to and from church or for the sake of relieving illness, traveling, on Sunday. However, there is a great deal of testimony to the effect that the legislation intended to enforce religious observance was generally disregarded.

§ 5

When Henry Hudson sailed into what is now New York Bay and made the acquaintance of the Indians of the neighborhood, he proved his own friendly intentions and the superiority of the European civilization which he represented by allowing the red men to taste his strong drink. One of the chiefs became dead drunk; his friends, fearing that he had been poisoned, became threatening; but he soon recovered, and assured them that his experience had been thoroughly enjoyable.

The Dutchmen who settled the New Netherlands were fond

"THEY INTRODUCED AMONG THEM RUM, GIN, AND BRANDY, AND
THE OTHER COMFORTS OF LIFE"

A drawing by Maxfield Parrish for an edition of Washington Irving's *Knickerbocker History of New York.*

of drink; in fact, they considered alcoholic beverages, both fermented and distilled, to be among the necessities of life. When government buildings were put up, barrels of beer and cases of brandy were furnished for the workmen, and the amount paid for these was listed along with the cost of nails and timbers. In the early days of the province the Reverend Mr. Bogardus, of the Dutch Reformed Church, won the reputation of a sturdy drinker; so also did his habitual adversary, Governor Van Twiller. The contemporaries of Everardus Bogardus tell us that he frequently appeared in the pulpit under the visible influence of intoxicants. He was a cunning fellow. Finding it difficult to obtain subscriptions for a church building, he watched at a wedding for that favorable moment when good schnapps had made the guests mellow and generous. Then he obtained a long list of promises to contribute. Some of the Dutchmen repudiated their liberality when, thoroughly sober, they were called upon to make good their pledges.

The colonists in New Netherlands brought from the home country the custom of consuming a great deal of wine and beer at funerals, and this lasted well into the eighteenth century. The Dutch settlers were fond of food and drink, certainly, but there is no good evidence that they were less temperate in their use than the Puritans of New England. It is true that the New Netherlanders were little addicted to asceticism, though most of them professed the Calvinistic creed. Less worried than the Puritans about sin and damnation, they attached a certain importance to mundane pleasures.

They had the old Dutch attachment to cleanliness, and in this regard they were much stricter than the New England Puritans or the Scotch-Irish Presbyterians. Although they were fond of smoking, they took care almost always to smoke their pipes out of doors and avoid messing up their homes.

The people of New Netherlands were fond of all kinds of sports, some of them forbidden in New England. But on Sunday, until church services were over, they were not permitted to go on pleasure parties in boats or carriages, to hunt, to fish, to go nutting or strawberrying, to play at tennis, cards, bowls, shovelboard, or dice. Governor Stuyvesant tried in vain to make these prohibitions apply to the whole twenty-four hours: the city magistrates of New Amsterdam refused to publish his ordinance.

Consequently the enumerated list of diversions remained lawful on Sunday afternoons. And taverns were permitted to sell drink on Sunday from the time the services ended until the dusk, when guard was mounted. In the little city of New Amsterdam, houses where liquor could be purchased were very numerous—as many as a quarter of all the buildings, it has been said. It is evident that there was powerful opposition to all attempts to bar the selling of alcoholic beverages entirely on Sunday.

While the Puritans of New England objected to the celebration of all holidays which might possibly be considered popish, the Lord's Day or Sunday alone excepted, and observed an annual fast and an annual day of thanksgiving of their own fixing, the Dutch Calvinists on the Hudson kept many of the old feasts. They celebrated New Year's Day, May Day, Easter, Whitsuntide, Shrovetide, St. Valentine's Day, St. Nicholas' Day, and Christmas. There were ordinances, under Stuyvesant, against celebrating May Day and New Year's Day by selling liquor. It was also illegal to make noises with guns and drums on holidays, to erect May-poles, and to play the rough game of pulling the goose on the feast of Bacchus in Shrovetide. It does not appear that the stern old governor's orders did much to slacken the gaiety of holiday celebrations.

When the English took possession of New Netherlands and changed the name of the province and that of its chief city to New York, manners were slow to change. New York, especially the city, remained convivial. Gregarious drinking was the rule on almost every occasion of general interest. In the case of a woman convicted of infanticide the records show that about half the cost of trying and executing her represented the purchase of wine, beer, and brandy. The jurymen, the executioners, the carpenters who erected the gallows, and many more persons concerned in the case wet their throttles at public expense. In 1704, when the corporation of the city of New York gave a banquet to a new governor, the complete expense amounted to between ten and eleven pounds. Three pounds and two shillings of this were spent for thirty-one bottles of wine, and twelve shillings for beer and cider. When the Reverend Dr. Cooper died, he left behind a library worth five pounds and a wine cellar worth one hundred and fifty.

In 1738 James Alexander and Eventhus Van Horne spent more than seventy-two pounds to make an election run smoothly. They got for their money sixty-two gallons of Jamaica rum, eighteen gallons of lime juice, and considerable quantities of wine and brandy. Benjamin Franklin tells amusingly how he called upon Governor Clinton of New York for the purpose of obtaining cannon to aid in the defense of Pennsylvania. Clinton at first refused; then, at his dinner table, after a little Madeira had passed down his gullet, he offered to lend a few cannon. As he drank more and more wine, he offered more and more guns, until Franklin received all that he needed. In the year 1701 the customs taxes paid on wine and rum at the port of New York amounted to twice the amount of the duties paid on dry goods. The commercial importance of alcoholic beverages was very great.

Under English rule the Sunday laws were made somewhat more stringent in the province of New York. Still, Sara Knight remarked in 1704 that New Yorkers were far less strict than Bostonians about observing the first day of the week. In 1764 a cage was built in the city of New York, chiefly for the public exposure of negro slaves and white boys whose conduct on Sunday was disorderly.

The old holidays remained popular, often being marked by kissing parties and other gay observances. The week following Whitsunday, known by the Dutch name of Pinkster, was a period devoted to gambling, drinking, and fun. It became especially the holiday of the colored slaves. At other times, the negroes were closely watched, by the officers of the law as well as their masters. A law of 1692 provided that if they were noisy on the street or if they frequented public houses on Sunday, they should be tied to the public whipping post and receive twenty lashes each unless their owners redeemed them by paying a fine of six shillings. In his anxiety to prevent the sale of liquor to Indians, Governor Andros ordered that if one were seen drunken on a street and the magistrates were unable to determine who had sold him the drink, they might require all the persons living in that street to pay a fine.

While the Dutch were for the most part opposed to asceticism, some of the inhabitants of New York province frowned upon amusements. On Long Island there were a number of communities settled by Congregationalists and other English-speaking sectaries. Many of them had immigrated from New England, and were anxious to set up the moral standards of Massachusetts and Connecticut. On Sunday the constables were sent to visit the taverns and other likely haunts in the village to round up persons who had failed to respond to the drum which summoned them to church; and the offenders were fined or whipped. In the upper part of the province, around Albany, the Dutch Calvinists and Lutherans were mostly stricter about religious duties than those who lived on Manhattan Island, and some of them were opposed to the gaiety of urban life. Thus early grew up in New York the split between the wicked city and the sleepy country. It was possible, long before the Revolution, for the farmers to say that the inhabitants of the city of New York were egregious rogues gathered together from the far ends of the earth.

The Albany region was very conservative. The semifeudal conditions introduced by the Dutch when they gave aristocrats called patroons great tracts of land, together with the right to rule over them almost as palatines, were slow to die out. The language and the customs of the Netherlands lingered on past the American Revolution, too. Puritans from New England came into the upper part of the province as well as Long Island, and Scotch Presbyterians settled in some of the mountain districts. To the city of New York flocked people from all countries, and of all creeds. Most of them were less precise in their moral standards than the farmers who lived north of Harlem and east of Brooklyn.

To be sure, the rural population cherished some customs for which present-day precisians might blame them. Bundling, for example, was introduced from New England, and brought about similar consequences in northern New York. Washington Irving, in his humorous but not altogether fictitious history of the province, tells us that the Dutch maidens were willing enough to take up bundling, while their mothers "strenuously discountenanced all such outlandish innovations." As a matter of fact, the custom assumed considerable importance and respectability in the Albany district; and it is evident that the parents cannot have opposed its introduction very strongly. In the latter part of the eighteenth century it went out of fashion there as in New England. The Dutch in this part of the province (and, later, of the state) generally frowned upon balls and theatrical representations, but were willing to permit the playing of cards and billiards in the taverns.

Religious intolerance was decidedly less marked in the New Netherlands and New York than in New England. We are told how many "freethinkers" came from Massachusetts into Dutch territory, as for example the bold minister who declared in a sermon that "Abraham's children ought to have been baptized." For such a sin as this he could expect to find no forgiveness even among the liberal-minded. He was dragged down from the pulpit and pushed out of the church.

With the exception of Stuyvesant, the Dutch governors almost invariably supported religious freedom. And though Stuyvesant was unfriendly to tolerance, what he did was against the will of the home authorities. The Reverend Mr. Megapolensis of the Reformed Church and the governor worked together to prevent clergymen of other denominations from entering the colony. In 1657 the Reverend Ernestus Goetwater arrived from the Netherlands with a commission to act as pastor to the Lutherans of New Amsterdam, and he was immediately sent back.

Baptists and Quakers were persecuted under Stuyvesant, until he received orders from home that he should permit them to worship as they pleased. The town officials of Flushing were punished for refusing to deal harshly with the Friends. One Quaker was fined and, when he would not pay, was chained to a wheel-barrow to work with negroes; then he was brutally flogged with a rope when he refused to perform the required labor. Quakers were subjected to many indignities. Their form of marriage was not recognized, and they were punished as fornicators because they lived together as husband and wife without having been married by the clergymen of the established Church. Later, some of the British officials were equally harsh with them.

When England took over the government, the members of the Reformed and Lutheran churches in the colony were promised full toleration. In 1686 Governor Dongan reported that the province of New York contained a few Anglicans, a few Papists, many Quakers, some Jews, Sabbatarians and Anti-Sabbatarians; "in short, of all sorts of opinions there are some, and the most part, of none at all."

Attempts to establish the Church of England in the colony were not particularly successful, and rumors that there were plans to set up a bishop in New York invariably met with disquiet and threats of violence. But the canon law of England was of some importance in the legal system of the province, and its influence has remained to a certain extent in the judicial organization of the state. The benefit of clergy was extended in numerous cases to convicted felons who could read and write, until it was abolished in 1788.

The English fear of popery was reflected in New York province. A law was passed making it a capital offense for Roman Catholic priests to enter the colony voluntarily. In the middle of the eighteenth century, New Yorkers were thrown into a panic by rumors that negro slaves and Catholics had combined in a plot to gain control of the government. As a result of vague fears and hearsay evidence, a number of slaves were burned at the stake, and several white men were hanged.

There were other minor flurries of religious intolerance, with the mass of the people usually on the side of freedom. A Scottish Presbyterian named Francis Makemie, who earned his living as a West India merchant, gave a great deal of his time to missionary work. He preached in a number of colonies, traveling about on horseback; and his work is said to have been generally successful. In New York he was arrested for acting as a minister of religion without having the license required by law. He was acquitted, because the popular clamor and good lawyers were on his side. Freedom was vindicated also in the case of Zenger, who was prosecuted for criticizing the government unfavorably in his newspaper. New Yorkers were opposed to political as to religious tyranny.

In 1766 Mrs. Barbara Heck, a woman of German descent who had been converted by Wesley in Ireland but who was then living in New York, became indignant about the general irreligion she saw about her. One day she found her brother playing cards; she seized them and flung them into the fire. Then she persuaded her cousin, Philip Embury, to preach against gamblers and other sinners. Out of Mrs. Heck's indignation arose the Methodist organizations in America.

Another woman prominent in religious history, Ann Lee, came to America in 1774 with a small band of followers. She was the high priestess of the Shakers, a sect which attached importance to dancing as a part of worship and required celibacy of its members.

Women occupied a somewhat higher position in New York than they did in England. The Dutch colony afforded them excellent educational facilities. The Netherlanders allowed to women and children many privileges which were denied to them by the English either at home or in the colonies. The tradition which they established in the New Netherlands lasted long after the fall of Dutch authority. In the eighteenth century there were many complaints about the presumption displayed by members of both these naturally inferior classes. There was a great deal of lamentation about mannish women who took too great an interest in politics.

The American colonists, like the English people of the same period, required children to display a great deal of respect and formality to their parents. For example, George Washington's habitual salutation to his mother in letters was "Honored Madam." And about the same condition existed in the province of New York as in Virginia, despite many allusions to children's disrespect.

The story of sexual morals in New Netherlands and New York is not very different from the history in the other colonists. However, offenses against chastity were treated far less severely than was the case in the Puritan provinces. We hear of a great many couples who lived together without being married, and it was quite common for betrothed pairs to assume the status of husband and wife without any further ceremony. Part of the difficulty arose out of the fact that the authorities at times barred the rites of the Quakers and other sectaries, while many conscientious people considered it wicked to go to the established clergy to be married.

Divorce was rare. It is said that the province and state of New York had only one instance before 1786. The fact that it was impossible to obtain legally the full dissolution of the marriage bonds stimulated concubinage. It appears that New Yorkers seldom cohabited with negro slaves. Otherwise there would be no point in the statement made shortly after the Revolutionary War, that the path of the English Army across New York State could be traced by the presence of mulattoes.

In Dutch New Amsterdam one woman sued another for having said that the first one raised her petticoats more than was necessary to keep them out of the mud when she crossed the street. In 1756 the inhabitants of New York were still worried about the extent to which women's legs might become visible in public. A newspaper moralist of that year wrote of the fashionable lady:

> Cut her hair the shortest dock. . . .
> Let her hoop extending wide
> Show her garters and her pride.
> Her stockings must be pure and white
> For they are seldom out of sight.

The year before, eleven prostitutes had been publicly whipped at one time in New York. Perhaps it is pretty generally the case that respectable women allow glimpses to be caught of their garters at times when the police try to drive out harlots.

But just what bobbed hair has to do with the matter, I have been unable to determine.

§ 6

The American colonies were confronted with some moral problems peculiar to themselves. Bigamy, for instance, was not unknown in England in the seventeenth and eighteenth centuries, but it became extremely common in the colonies. The American settlements were remote, because of the poor facilities which were available for transportation, from one another as well as from the mother country. Consequently, and as a result also of the difficulties involved in obtaining a divorce, wives and husbands frequently ran away. In the Southern newspapers, advertisements for runaway wives were almost as frequent as those which promised rewards for the return of slaves and servants.

In the eighteenth century, luxury appeared almost everywhere in the colonies, and complaints of moral relaxation were general. About 1740, under Whitefield's influence, religion and the opposition to worldly recreations seemed to be much stimulated. Franklin tells how Philadelphia was aroused: "It was wonderful to see the change soon made in our inhabitants. From being thoughtless or indifferent about religion, it seemed as if all the world were growing religious, so that one could not walk through the town in an evening without hearing psalms sung in different families of every street." But this attitude did not remain very long, either in Philadelphia or elsewhere.

The British officers and men who came to fight the French were a generally gay and pleasure-loving lot, whose presence in America stimulated the growth of hedonism. The wars promoted laxity of conduct, even though they stimulated thoughts about religion and caused many preachers to ask for prayers and fasting to improve the chances of victory. The province of Maryland, in imposing taxes to meet the expenses of war, sought at the same time to reduce what were considered outstanding moral evils of the time. It was necessary to pay for the privileges of consuming light imported wines, of owning billiard tables, and (on the part of men of marriageable age) of remaining single. The colonial authorities were always anxious to prevent the growth of a large bachelor class, at once the sign of a luxury which made it expensive to support a wife and a danger to moral strictness in sexual matters. Extravagance increased in spite of war taxes and alarmed moralists.

Ladies and gentlemen of fashion in the American colonies wore fine clothes, and followed the English mode closely. Ladies devoted much time and money to cosmetics, and gentlemen did not consider it wrong to beautify themselves. Hairdressing for men was usually even more elaborate than that for women, though there were occasional fads which compelled women to spend hours under the care of a hairdresser before going to a ball.

In the 1770's the professional and amateur moralists of British America viewed with alarm the increase in tea-drinking and the feminine fondness for snuff. There were complaints, too, about the amount of alcoholic beverages being consumed and the rising popularity of various forms of gambling.

New York province outlawed private lotteries in 1747. Shortly before, it had forbidden innkeepers to admit servants, apprentices, or youths under the age of twenty-one to the use of billiard tables, shovelboards, and other devices lending themselves to gaming. There were, in the decades just preceding the Revolution, a considerable number of race tracks in New York and other colonies. Racing bets were often very heavy. There were several instances in colonial America of men who sold themselves into servitude for terms of years to pay gambling debts.

After 1750 there was a noticeable increase in the use of spirituous liquors; and whiskey, which was mostly manufactured on the frontier, came into favor. The growing of fruit trees was almost entirely for the purpose of providing materials for making cider, perry, brandy, and other more or less alcoholic beverages. The use of tobacco was everywhere common; and women, more especially those of the frontier and the lower classes, often smoked pipes.

In Philadelphia, New York, and several other cities many elaborate forms of recreation were available in the eighteenth century. There were balls, puppet shows, concerts, waxworks, and dramatic representations. In some of the colonies there was considerable opposition to the opening of professional theatres. This was, in most cases, overcome before the outbreak of the Revolution.

Williamsburg, Virginia; Charleston, South Carolina; and Annapolis, Maryland, acquired playhouses between 1716 and 1752. In the middle of the century there was a struggle in Philadelphia about the granting of a license for a theatre. In 1759 the authorities gave permission for the opening of a house in Southwark, just beyond the city limits. A theatre existed in New York as early as 1733, but the first professional troupe did not appear until 1750. It was an English company, the members of which had been treated as vagabonds in Philadelphia.

Nowhere in colonial America were actors and actresses highly respected. Many people considered them highly immoral. Others were willing enough to be entertained by them, but not to receive them in good society. The professional companies could not hope to please precisians, and therefore acted in many daring plays. And, to complete the vicious circle, the entertainments which they presented, since they could be considered immoral, intensified the opposition to the theatre manifested by pious and precise people.

By the time of the Revolution the playhouse had gained a certain amount of respectability but still met with a great deal of opposition. The Continental Congress of 1774, actuated by moral as well as by patriotic considerations, called upon all the inhabitants of the British colonies in America to "discountenance and discourage all horse racing and all kinds of gaming, cockfighting, exhibitions of shows, plays, and other expensive diversions and entertainments." The colonists were asked at this time to give up all their habits of luxury, to do without many articles which they had become accustomed to import from England, and to depend upon homemade goods. Patriots deprived themselves of many comforts in heeding this request, and sometimes showed their zeal also by compelling their lukewarm neighbors to abandon the use of imported commodities.

The schoolchildren of the United States are more or less familiar with the statement that the American Revolution broke out because "taxation without representation is tyranny." But perhaps a great many of the colonists really objected to paying any taxes at all, no matter by whom imposed. And this was one reason why some of the bold pioneer heroes moved westward with the frontier, trying to keep out of reach of the tax collector.

If the old mercantile theories were correct (and the general turning away from belief in free trade, especially in the United States, makes it almost impossible to consider them entirely absurd or iniquitous), there had to be a unified system of commercial regulation embracing the colonial dependencies as well as the mother country. It was impracticable for any body except the Parliament at London to direct the organization of such a system for the British Empire.

Justified or not, there were customs taxes to be paid at the American ports. Most of the colonists objected to paying them, and smuggling was the way out. The great merchants of America grew rich by means of illicit trade. Allied to smuggling were the closely connected industries of piracy and privateering. The latter of these was legal, providing there was an actual adherence to the terms of the letters of marque and reprisal, which were licenses to prey upon the shipping of countries with which the issuers of the letters were at war.

But privateers who carefully observed the terms of their licenses were in the minority. In 1652, when a struggle was going on between the Dutch and the English in America, it was said that Rhode Island vessels were preying without partiality upon the commerce of both countries. This sort of internationalism or (perhaps we should say) aversion to the narrow lines of nationalism was common enough among the privateers. Obviously, then, it would have taken a corps of philosophers to define the difference between privateering and piracy.

In the seventeenth century a great many American ports were friendly to pirates, permitting them to enter, take on supplies, make repairs, even to sell their prizes. The Carolinas, New York, New Jersey, and Rhode Island were especially inclined to be hospitable. Philadelphia was usually willing to offer its facilities to pirates, because they were ready to spend a considerable amount wherever they were made welcome; but some of the stricter Quakers objected.

In Elizabeth's day America was of interest to Englishmen chiefly as the place where the Spaniards got treasure and from which sailed galleons which provided rich plunder. Piracy as a quasi-respectable occupation began early in the history of the New World. The mercantile system was largely responsible for this. Spain forbade foreigners to deal directly with her American colonies. Yet it was profitable for Englishmen and English colonials to disregard the mercantilist orders. Once engaged in an unlawful trade, the British sailors decided that they might as well be hanged for a sheep as for a lamb. They ran little more risk as pirates than as smugglers.

Under Charles II the greatest of the buccaneer leaders, Sir Henry Morgan, was lieutenant governor of the British island of Jamaica. In the latter half of the seventeenth century, pirates were powerful enough to take possession for a time of Carthagena, Porto Bello, and the city of Panama. Both the French and the British possessions in the West Indies offered places of refuge to the pirates, and the colonials were usually in sympathy with them.

In the eighteenth century the British authorities decided to do all they could to break up piracy. Still, the buccaneers were not treated like ordinary thieves and murderers. They were several times offered pardon, especially if they should be willing to join the Navy. In the last years of the seventeenth century, Governor Fletcher of New York and Governor Markham of Pennsylvania were known to be friendly to pirates. Markham argued openly that the money they brought into his province helped to promote its prosperity.

There has been a great deal of controversy about Captain Kidd, a New York sailor who was given a royal commission to wage war against pirates. Certain great men were supposed to

THE BOSTONIAN'S PAYING THE EXCISE-MAN, OR TARRING AND
FEATHERING

A print published in London in 1774. Courtesy of the Metropolitan Museum of Art.

share in all the spoils he might seize from them. Kidd was eventually hanged as a pirate and manslayer; but his conviction and execution seem rather to have been due to the powerful and selfish enemies he made than for any actual crimes he committed. This much at least can be said, that pirates who were careful to share their winnings with people in authority were in little danger of being hanged. But during the eighteenth century more and more of the colonial ports which had formerly been hospitable to buccaneers were closed to them, and piracy eventually became a very risky business.

Smuggling made a great many American fortunes. Another illegal form of traffic was the selling of liquor and firearms to the Indians. This, indeed, brought about great danger to the settlers living on the frontier. When the French and the English fought each other in North America, neither side hesitated to employ Indian allies. Neither the French nor the English made any attempt to keep the Indians from murdering women and children and other noncombatants. War was thus made much more horrible for all concerned. The British colonials did not all treat the Indians in the same way, but the Paxton Boys of Pennsylvania were not the only ones who thought it proper to massacre the aborigines. It was because of such treatment that the Indians were usually willing to support the French against the Englishmen, and that in the Revolutionary War the majority supported King George against the English-speaking Americans. When it came to matters of profit-making, many of the American colonists ceased to find their consciences troublesome. This conveniently occurred in a large part of their dealings with the Indians. It is, of course, a delicate ethical problem to decide whether or not the immigrants from Europe had any right to occupy America and displace the aboriginal inhabitants. And although many elaborate apologies and rationalizations have been made for such forms of imperialism, perhaps it is not altogether unfair to say that the whole matter was one of inferior force succumbing to superior.

During the late colonial period, convictions for crime were proportionately much rarer than in England. It was easier to earn a living honestly in America, and it was also easier for criminals to escape. A great many convicts came to the colonies involuntarily. Some returned to England, others remained. It is not clear that they and their descendants became the nucleus for a permanent criminal class in America. But perhaps their presence did add to the demand for repressive laws, as for the control of drunkenness. Besides criminals of all sorts, there were in the American colonies debtors who had been brought over by philanthropists, and other persons who were deemed to be lacking in self-control. We have seen how the Georgians were deprived for a time of the right to purchase distilled liquors legally. But when they secured self-rule, the people were not willing to pass laws removing sources of temptation.

§ 7

A large number of felons and prostitutes were sent into the French possessions along the Gulf of Mexico. Some women who had been harlots in Paris became respectable wives in Louisiana. The male population there was far greater than the female, and many men were willing to overlook the past of attractive women.

New Orleans acquired, early in the eighteenth century, the reputation of being much laxer in moral matters than such a French settlement as St. Louis. It contained many concubines of negro or Indian blood. Prostitution was not particularly favored: in fact, white prostitutes were sometimes harshly punished. We read of their being mounted on wooden horses and flogged by the soldiers of the garrison. And nuns were brought into the colony from France, who established houses of detention and reform for harlots. Still, the traffic was not destroyed, and soon there were brothels in New Orleans. Most young women in French and Spanish America married while they were quite young, perhaps at thirteen or fourteen. Respectable women, whether single or married, enjoyed far less liberty than did those living in the British colonies.

In general, the French and Spanish settlers within what is

now the United States had more liberal moral standards than the English colonists. Bullfighting, horse racing, moderate gambling, and attendance at the theatre never seemed deadly sins to them. And many of them considered it no great harm if a man had a concubine or two instead of, or in addition to, a lawful wife. Gaiety was for them no sin at all, and perhaps sin was not quite the dreadful thing it seemed in the eyes of a New Englander.

Dueling was more common in Louisiana than it was anywhere in the British colonies, and the populace often engaged in rough drunken fights. Still, respect for law was soon established, and perhaps New Orleans was not quite so dreadful as it might have seemed to a Congregationalist minister of the period.

CHAPTER XIII

THE NEW REPUBLIC

§ 1

GEORGE WASHINGTON, after he had been made the commander of the Continental Army, found the problem of discipline often a very complicated one. Most of his men were unused to service in a regular army, unaccustomed to the military virtue of unquestioning obedience, and inclined to chafe at restraints. Washington tried to bring religious and moral pressure to bear on his men. He wrote to his brigadier generals: "Let vice and immorality of every kind be discouraged as much as possible in your brigade, and, as a chaplain is allowed to each regiment, see that the men regularly attend divine service. Gaming of every kind is expressly forbidden, as being the foundation of evil, and the cause of many a brave and gallant officer's ruin."

Washington was not much of a precisian. Neither was he orthodox in religious matters. But he shared the belief, generally accepted in his time, that compelling people to hear homilies on the delights of virtue would raise the level of their behavior.

The moral standards of the Continental Army varied somewhat from unit to unit, according to the origin of the men. Paul Revere of Massachusetts, acting as a colonial officer, ordered the punishment of two soldiers found playing cards on a Sunday in September, 1776. The Puritan spirit was still strong among the New England men. While the soldiers from the Middle and Southern colonies were promoting balls and other entertainments, most of the Yankees seemed to be more interested in sermons and fasts.

The Connecticut men were sometimes described as the most

democratic of all, while the New Yorkers and the Virginians had the reputation of being aristocrats. Of course, such generalizations were not perfect. There were aristocrats in Connecticut, some of whom owned large numbers of slaves; and there were democrats enough in New York and Virginia, especially along the frontier. Fisher Ames entered Harvard College in puritanical Massachusetts with the class of 1774, and his contemporaries marveled that he came through "unstained with any vice." There were moral currents and cross-currents; and, before the Revolution broke out, young people in all the colonies were rebelling against authority.

The war broke down sectional barriers to a considerable extent. Also it introduced much foreign, especially French, influence. The French officers who joined the army of the American rebels were surprised that their landladies should object to their playing ombre on Sunday. The landladies were equally surprised that brave men from a presumably civilized and Christian country should consider it proper to play cards on that day. But, especially because they were allies, it would not do to dismiss their strange moral standards with a sneer or a frown.

The practice of dueling was greatly stimulated by the presence of these French officers. It became, after the Revolution, the accepted method by which those persons who considered themselves gentlemen settled questions which they held to involve personal honor. Half-feudal Virginia had been generally favorable to the duel, and its popularity had been increased also by the presence of British officers during the wars against the French and the Indians. However, it was the French influence which made dueling fashionable in the early years of the United States. (Buckle maintains that the duel is essentially French, and that it is always esoteric among English-speaking peoples; but he does not give any clear reason for this.)

The presence of many bright uniforms—and most of the uniforms of the Revolutionary War were very gaudy indeed—caused feminine hearts to flutter. Some women abandoned their peace-time demureness, in whole or in part, and even felt that it would be unpatriotic to act too precisely toward heroes who might be dead on the morrow.

There were many stories about British and Hessian soldiers who did not wait to conquer maidens with their charms, but ravished them by force. There was some basis in fact for all the usual propaganda about atrocities, but perhaps not an undue amount. Theft, indeed, was fairly common on the part of the soldiers of both sides. When they were hungry or tired of monotonous rations, they had little scruple about seizing chickens and other food. And the buying of goods with rapidly depreciating paper money seemed little better than larceny. People were forced to accept in return for horses and foodstuffs promises to pay which they believed to be of extremely dubious value.

The Loyalists in America were very harshly treated. They could not by any gentle means be made to realize how very wicked they were. In fact, they were very proud of the fact that they remained true to His Britannic Majesty while their neighbors were taking up arms against him. Despite the fact that many families were split between Loyalists and Patriots, the bitterness displayed by the two parties was extremely great. The stories which circulated about the cruelty and viciousness of the Hessian and British soldiers increased the hatred felt for the Loyalists. The suffering which occurred in America on account of the bloodthirstiness and cupidity of the Indians and foreign mercenaries fell about equally upon those who favored independence and those who opposed it. The desire to rob and kill was not connected with any anxiety to advance one of the contending causes.

There were on both sides sincerely devoted men. Perhaps there were more who, at least occasionally, thought of their own personal advantages first of all. A few were willing to change their coats and betray the cause to which they had sworn allegiance. Many who considered themselves loyal sometimes endangered the army of which they were members in their anxiety to justify themselves, or to make sure of receiving their pay.

Washington was sometimes moved to exclaim that he could find no honest men about him. He was surrounded by plots and cabals. Some of the officers in whom he reposed the most trust tried to incite Congress against him. Curiously, many a soldier who was capable of risking his life fearlessly showed himself touchy and even sneaky about small sums of money or minor matters of social precedence. I am not painting a complete picture here: the heroes of the American Revolution and the nature of their heroism are sufficiently familiar to all who have gone through an elementary school in the United States.

Some of the heroines of the war are well known, too. A very few women actually took part in the fighting. Many had to do traditionally masculine work at home because their men were away with the armies. But feminism was not appreciably stimulated either by the women's war work or by the democratic doctrines associated with the American Revolution. Political wisdom was just then coming from France; and though Frenchwomen were exerting much influence, it was by means of wit and beauty rather than through any special privileges recognized by law. The natural equality of which the philosophers were talking was seldom taken to apply to the two sexes.

We can learn something of the way in which feminine America was looking out at the world from the journal kept in 1777 by a Quaker maid of Philadelphia, then sixteen years old. Sally Wister was of German and Welsh descent. She was temporarily living in a suburb when a number of officers of the Continental Army came to be quartered in her house.

"When we were alone," she wrote, "our dress and lips were put in order for conquest, and the hope of adventures gave brightness to each before passive countenance." Sally was constantly thinking of decorum and propriety; nevertheless, she and her friends allowed themselves a certain little freedom of manners. It is evident from her diary, and we know from other sources as well, that the Pennsylvania Quakers were no longer insisting upon extreme sobriety of costume and behavior. Most of them retained their principle of pacificism and refused to engage directly in war work. Some did not consider it wicked to make money out of the war.

According to Sally Wister, one of the American officers upon whom his friends had played a practical joke exclaimed, "You may all go to the D——l." Her comment was, "I had never heard him utter an indecent expression before." For it was almost as bad, at least in Quaker ears, to utter aloud the name of his Satanic majesty without good reason as to take the name of his divine adversary in vain. But some ideas of propriety had changed; thus, Sally spoke of a "charming collection of books" which included Fielding's *Joseph Andrews*.

Among the flirtations which Sally recorded was one with a Virginia captain who, after very short acquaintance, proposed marriage: "Had we been acquainted seven years, we could not have been more sociable. The moon gave a sadly pleasing light. We sat at the door till nine. Dandridge is sensible (and divested of some freedoms, which might be called gallant in the fashionable world), he is polite and agreeable. His greatest fault is a propensity to swearing, which throws a shade over his accomplishments. I asked him why he did so. 'It is a favorite vice, Miss Sally.' "

We are told how Captain Dandridge caught up Sally's hand while they were sitting together alone in the parlor, and how he pretended to be disappointed when she would not let him kiss her. However, she took mercy on him and allowed him to press her hand to his lips in bidding her farewell.

We can easily see from this Quaker maiden's diary that, at least while the war was going on, American girls enjoyed almost the same freedom that is theirs to-day. Foreign visitors of the period usually commented on the liberty that young women enjoyed. Sometimes they also criticized the prevalence of children spoiled by a deficiency of parental control.

Marriage changed matters for women. Thenceforth they seldom attended balls and other public entertainments and spent most of their time at home. According to foreign visitors, the married women of America were mostly chaste.

A German officer wrote home from Cambridge, Massachusetts, that the New England girls had "a very healthy complexion, without having to paint." If cosmetics were used—how did Sally Wister put her lips in order for conquest?—it was with restraint, and not in such a way as to suggest their presence. The German officer said also of the young women that they had "natural good manners, a very unrestrained way of acting, a frank, gay face, and natural boldness." He commented on the "domination of women over their husbands. This petticoat rule is spread throughout America, but here it is quite different than in Canada, where it aims at the welfare of the man, while here it seems his ruin. The wives and daughters make a display beyond the income of most of the men."

Luxury did not die out because there was a bloody civil war in the land. Sometimes, in fact, the realization that death and destruction might be impending caused a great increase in prodigality and recklessness. Congress asked the states to forbid dancing and dramatic performances. On the very day when this resolution was published, the fashionable people of Philadelphia, where Congress then sat, flocked to amateur theatricals. On the next day the governor of Pennsylvania gave a ball, which was attended by a large company. In spite of such striking violations of the desire of Congress, it was observed by the great mass of patriots.

Chastellux found that the playing of cards for money was considered improper in Boston while the war continued, and he tells us that this sentiment was salutary, because reckless gambling for high stakes had previously been the rule in the upper social circles. Though there was much moral enthusiasm associated with the war, its general effect seems to have been to relax the proprieties. Those patriotic citizens who gave up card playing during the war turned to it again as soon as the independence of the United States was assured, and eagerly proceeded to make up for lost time. Indeed, it was difficult to see how abstention from gambling helped the American armies much, and comparatively few people who had previously been habitual gamesters held out to the end in self-denial. A demoralized currency, more eloquent than the orators of Congress, encouraged gambling and speculation of all sorts. As for balls, tableaux, and amateur theatricals, the British officers promoted them wherever they went. There were, almost everywhere, women enough who were loyal to His Majesty, King George III, to keep his officers amply provided with partners. And some of the women were devoted to uniforms of all colors, flirting as willingly with Washington's soldiers as with Cornwallis'.

§ 2

The indifference to religion which became widespread in the United States after the war for independence is sometimes attributed to the Revolution. Deism had, indeed, spread widely among educated Americans before 1776. Franklin was no Christian; and Washington, though he often attended the Anglican (and Episcopalian) services, was far from orthodox. Both these men considered religious instruction a necessity for the masses.

Thomas Paine's views about the truth of revealed Christianity were no more radical than Franklin's, and they differed little from Washington's. However, he attacked the Christian religion and declared that there could be no utility in teaching error. Paine was one of the perhaps half a dozen men who did most to make the American Revolution successful. He was the most democratic of the lot, and his democracy forbade him to believe that the ordinary people should be taught what their educated masters refused to believe.

Paine took part in the French Revolution as well as the American. In France, democracy and anticlericalism were closely connected. And, just as the revolution in America influenced the French revolutionary leaders, the upheaval in France caused reverberations in the young republic of the United States. The cry of "liberty, equality, fraternity" echoed in America. True, the Declaration of Independence issued in 1776, signed by the most influential of the American rebels, tells us that "all men are created equal." It was not necessary to start with such a proposition to reach the conclusion that the American colonies were entitled to declare themselves independent of Great Britain. And some of the greatest revolutionary leaders were far from believing it. Did George Washington actually consider that his slaves, or white men who were descended from convicts or from

LADY WASHINGTON'S RECEPTION, "THE REPUBLICAN COURT"

After a painting by Daniel Huntington. Courtesy of the Hamilton Club of Brooklyn.

indentured servants, were, in any possible sense of the word, his equals?

There were serious attempts to introduce a hereditary monarchy in America; and the Constitution of many compromises which was finally adopted provided that the president of the United States should be chosen by a body of wise men, not directly by the people. The Electoral College is, to be sure, now hardly more than nominal; but this fact is the result of a great unwritten change in the Constitution.

A great and prolonged struggle soon arose between the conservative, aristocratic Federalists and the radical, individualistic or states-rights party called Anti-Federalist, Democratic-Republican, or (later) Democratic. Independence did not automatically bring democracy into the United States, even though the expulsion of the Tories seemed likely to deliver authority entirely into radical hands. Most of the original state constitutions limited the franchise to persons possessing certain qualifications in the ownership of property and in religious faith. In New York, for example, no man was privileged to vote for governor or state senator who did not have an equity of at least one hundred pounds in real estate. In South Carolina free white Protestants were privileged if, being twenty-one years old or more, they owned or paid taxes on fifty acres of land or a town lot or its equivalent.

For holding office the qualifications were usually stricter. Thus, South Carolina in 1778 forbade persons not possessed of land worth ten thousand pounds to hold the office of governor, lieutenant governor, or member of the privy council. The highest offices were closed to non-Protestants in New Hampshire, New Jersey, and the Carolinas, and to non-Christians in Massachusetts and Maryland.

A little later there was a movement toward democracy, stimulated by the growth of the urban middle classes and by the natural equality of the frontier. Numerous state laws abolishing primogeniture and entails at once indicated the importance of democratic opinion and contributed to its further development. But men of African descent, though they gradually attained their freedom in the Northern states, were seldom permitted to participate in political affairs. The liberation of the slaves north of Delaware and Maryland was not due to the greater benevolence of the people in the free states or to their more complete acceptance of Rousseau's political philosophy, but almost entirely to economic considerations. And though the negroes were set free in the North in the decades following the Revolution, they were not accepted as the social or political equals of white men.

The Americans who fought for independence were of all shades of opinion. Taken as a whole, they were less conservative in most respects than the Loyalists. The supporters of the King were driven from their homes, often penniless; and those few who were permitted to remain could not hope to exercise any political authority. But it soon appeared that many of the patriotic leaders were opposed to all changes beyond such as were necessarily connected with the establishment of a new country.

Other innovations were often of a disagreeable nature. It became evident that many people who disliked the British rule were also displeased with independent government, especially if a few aristocrats were the real rulers. There was much aversion to the paying of taxes, and Massachusetts mobs howled, "Down with government!" Shays' rebellion in that state was not the only occasion for the use of force to suppress anarchists and extreme democrats.

The rise of the Jacobins in France encouraged American ochlocrats to put fear in the hearts of the conservative Federalists. At Dedham, Massachusetts, a wandering democrat erected a liberty pole. Squire Ames then had him lodged in jail. Ames was an ardent defender of the old ways. It was as a conservative in politics rather than as a Puritan in religion that he feared the tavern and objected to popular amusements: "A gingerbread lottery, a vendue, a dance, a singing meeting, a sleigh ride, everything fills [the taverns] with young fellows, and our apprentice boys already claim the rights of men against their masters. In thriving villages the thirst for pleasure will be strong while the authority of manners remains feeble."

*Strain every nerve, our sinking cause to save —
Then shall no God alarm, no laws enslave —
O'er these dread foes, nor flag shall fly, unfurl'd,
And we, my sons, victorious, rule the world.*

FACTION

From J. S. J. Gardiner, *Remarks on the Jacobiniad*, 1795, a satire on the opponents of the Federal Constitution first published in the *Federal Orrery* under the editorship of Thomas Paine.

It made little difference whether sleigh rides were denounced as irreligious or as subverters of the established economic order. In any case, Squire Ames was unable to prevent them. He and the majority of his neighbors did not always hold the same opinions. He joined an Episcopalian church, most of the members of which are said to have belonged in order to escape having to pay the rates required of Congregationalists. In the early years of the nineteenth century, Squire Ames scandalized most of ·the Dedham people by decorating his home with greens for Christmas. As his son wrote somewhat later, most of his neighbors then considered Christmas adornments to be in the nature of a "rag of the whore of Babylon's underpetticoat." The whore herself was the Roman Catholic Church. The most interesting thing about the whole matter is that Ames, who was anxious to maintain social conservatism, did not feel that religious orthodoxy was its necessary bulwark. Or perhaps he did, and thought that all his neighbors ought to move in step with him.

Such men as Squire Ames insisted on the importance of revealed Christianity and denounced the democrats as unbelievers. A greater man than he, John Adams, did not know "what to make of a republic of thirty million atheists." Of course, this was an exaggeration. Not all Americans were atheists. There were more deists than atheists, and more Christians than either.

Harvard College authorities feared that the students were too familiar with Paine's *The Age of Reason,* and presented each graduate with a copy of Watson's *Apology for the Bible* by way of antidote. Long before the most famous set of teeth in the world unclenched sufficiently to allow the epithet "dirty little atheist" to be applied to Paine, John Adams called him filthy. There is no good evidence that Paine was either dirty or little, and he was not an atheist but a deist. Certainly he could not be blamed for the bloodshed and other excesses of the Reign of Terror in France. He was treated as an enemy by the extremists there.

Thomas Paine's pamphleteering had been extremely instrumental in causing the American colonists to work for independence. If there had been no religious complications, his right to be considered a hero of the republic would hardly have been challenged. Yet when Paine visited the United States in 1802, he was fiercely denounced by clerical and conservative organs. At the same time, there were many Americans who thought all the better of him for his attacks on Christianity.

Condorcet, Volney, Voltaire, Rousseau, and other bold philosophers had numerous disciples in America. Patriots were warned not to read the King James Bible, which might instill in them a respect for royalty. In the clerical circles of New York State it was said that the freethinkers, in their meetings at Newburgh, conducted Satanic masses in which the sacraments and other holy symbols of Christianity were mocked and defiled.

President Jefferson offered Tom Paine the use of an American sloop-of-war to bring him from France; and the New England Calvinists, as well as other conservatives all through the country, were deeply offended. Jefferson was a freethinker who aroused indignation, too, by refusing to issue proclamations for days of fasting and thanksgiving, asserting that he possessed no constitutional authority to call upon the citizens for religious observances of any sort.

In 1784, after the Virginia legislature had refused by a close vote to reward Paine for his services in the Revolution, he fared better in New York. When Paine later returned to America, it was evident that orthodox and propertied people everywhere had turned against him.

Henry Bradshaw Fearon wrote of Boston in 1817: *"Clerical* gentlemen have here an astonishing hold upon the minds of men. . . . A man who values his good name in Boston hardly dares to be seen out of church at the appointed hour." But Calvinistic Congregationalism by no means retained its old importance in New England. Twenty years earlier, President Dwight of Yale, in his "Triumph of Infidelity," denounced the

> smooth divine, unused to wound
> The Sinner's heart with Hell's alarming sound.

Unitarian doctrines first came into general notice among New Englanders at the time of the Revolution. Then they spread

[453]

fast, and were often preached from Congregationalist pulpits. It was not until 1820 that the Unitarians fully separated themselves from the Congregationalists. A year earlier, William Ellery Channing introduced Unitarianism to New York. The College of Physicians and Surgeons of that city allowed him the use of a lecture room, and was consequently denounced by the orthodox ministers for encouraging heresy.

In the early years of the republic such religious groups as the Methodists, Baptists, and Universalists expanded rapidly, winning converts by means of emotional, sometimes hysterical, evangelism. Unitarianism was most attractive to people of some education and intelligence, and its preachers seldom appealed to the feelings. Few of the early Unitarians approached the agnostic attitude which is now characteristic of many ministers and laymen who call themselves by that name. Still, to deny the Holy Trinity was an offense which in some parts of the country prevented the heretic from holding public office or even from voting.

The question is often raised whether the United States is, or has ever been, a Christian country. The very first addition to the Federal Constitution—one of the ten articles adopted in 1791 —provides that "Congress shall make no law respecting an establishment of religion, or prohibiting the free exercise thereof." And George Washington, with the consent of the Senate, signed a treaty with Tripoli containing the assurance that the United States was not a Christian country. Indeed, it cannot ever be so at law while the first constitutional amendment remains unmodified.

On the other hand, it is possible for individual states to establish Christianity, or a particular Christian sect, or any other religion. Most of the state constitutions, however, forbid the legislatures to do anything of this sort. Some of the states, early in the nineteenth century, judicially declared that Christianity was part of their common law. It has been decided by the highest English court, in our own time, that Christianity has never truly been part of the common law of England, and that no reason therefore exists why a legacy to an anti-Christian organization should be treated as invalid. But earlier judicial decisions in

England and in the United States were often directly opposed to such a conclusion. Even where courts have decided that the Christian religion is part of the common law, they have given a limited application to the principle. Thus, they have not sought to enforce the Old Testament prohibition of the eating of pork (which may or may not be Christian) or the New Testament injunction to turn the other cheek after being struck on one (a Christian duty according to almost all theologians). And adultery has not been punished as a violation of the Ten Commandments, but only if made a crime by statute law.

What the judges chiefly meant when they said Christianity belonged in their common law was that it was illegal to attack the religion or to speak slightingly of the Holy Trinity. A Pennsylvania man who was prosecuted for saying that the Scriptures contain many lies was convicted of blasphemy, and the Supreme Court of that state decided that "maliciously to vilify the Christian religion is an indictable offense." The New York courts reached a similar decision in the case of Ruggles. A Massachusetts law of 1782 provided that blasphemers should be punished with a year's imprisonment, exposure in the pillory, public flogging, and standing on the gallows with a rope about the neck. As we have seen, skepticism and democracy were intimately connected in the early days of the republic, and the Federalists tried to stamp out blasphemy for political and economic reasons.

In Virginia it was the great Democratic-Republican leader, Thomas Jefferson, who fought a long and finally successful battle to have a guarantee of religious freedom made part of the state constitution. He gained a victory also over the party, led by Washington and Patrick Henry, which wished all people to be taxed for the support of some church. There were even some who insisted that everybody should continue to pay rates to the Episcopal organization, which fell off sharply in importance when it ceased to be established. In 1817 the Virginia legislature decided that it would be a violation of the state constitution to appoint a chaplain, since he would necessarily belong to some sect, which would enjoy a quasi-establishment because of his officiating before the lawmaking body. But there was one old-fashioned Virginia representative, with powdered hair, a long queue, and a three-cornered hat, who arose and remarked, "Sure I am of one thing, that no gentleman would choose any road to heaven but the Episcopal."

Since those Americans who continued to believe in Christianity were coming more and more to the conclusion that a man might be saved in any sect, though good form might demand his going to the same church as his neighbors, the old arguments for the continuance of an established religious organization weakened. Still, the Congregationalist Church long continued to enjoy special advantages in the New England states. It remained established in New Hampshire until 1817, in Connecticut until 1818, and in Massachusetts until 1833. During this period, religion, or at least the old orthodoxy, was becoming very much weaker in New England; but the rest of the country, especially the South and the West, was turning to piety in the first decades of the nineteenth century.

John Bristed wrote in 1818: "The rapid spread of Sunday Schools, and of Missionary and Bible Societies, affords a most consolatory proof of the increase of religion in the United States. Two years have not elapsed since their first institution in this country, and they have already considerably diminished the ignorance, poverty, and vice of our larger cities." Precisely how the Sunday schools operated against poverty, it is difficult to say; perhaps Bristed meant that they discouraged drunkenness. Looking back over a century later, the great moral and economic improvements which are supposed to have taken place immediately after 1816 do not stand out very clearly. Possibly Bristed was a little too sanguine about the benefits derived from the religious organizations.

There seems to be little doubt, though, that, save in New England, pious enthusiasm really did increase at this time. In generalizing about conditions in the early republic, allowance must be made for the fact that the states were still much isolated: it took twenty days for the post to reach Louisville, Georgia, from Portland, Maine, and many communities were far from post roads and navigable streams. As a result, customs, morals, and religious conditions varied greatly. For that matter, there is even now no unity about such things in the United States. The standards of rural Indiana are far removed from those of Greenwich Village, and are by no means identical with those of rural Arkansas.

In, let us say, 1820, New England showed much less diversity than it does now; but still there were differences of interest and tradition between Boston and the farming country of Massachusetts, or even between Hartford and Providence. Harvard College, the old citadel of Congregationalism, turned away from the strict Calvinism of the Puritan fathers; and so did most of the educated, urban inhabitants of New England. Still, it is not very accurate to say that New England as a whole became less pious, or more concerned about human nobility and less about the attributes of God. What were the farmers thinking about? After all, they made up the bulk of the population in New England and elsewhere in the United States. They were reading less dogmatic and controversial theology than their ancestors, and they cared little about the logical structure erected by John Calvin (though some were reluctant to give up the doctrine of preordination); but, in general, they were attached to Christianity, and they attended some church. Religion was for them largely a matter of sentiment and habit, and they did not consider their creeds in the analytical manner of theological professors. We find, even decades later than the period now being considered, a certain intolerance in New England villages; but this was on the decrease, partly because of the growth of Methodism and Universalism.

The strict attitude toward Sunday observance which had been characteristic of colonial New England was very slowly abandoned by the rural Yankees. In 1790 Philip Freneau published in a New York paper a poem called "The New England Sabbath-Day Chase." He found it necessary to explain: "In several parts of New England it is customary not to allow travellers to proceed on a journey on the Sabbath day." The poem which followed describes "an event of this sort, which really befel Mr. P., noted performer in feats of horsemanship." The rider set out southward from Hartford on a Sunday, and came to a village:

Then, approaching the church, as we passed by the door,
The sexton peeped out, with a saint or two more.
A deacon came forward and waved us his hat,
A signal to drop him some money—mind that!

Mr. P. fled, but he was finally caught when his horse sank in the mud, and he was forced to pay a fine.

In 1802 the selectmen of Boston forbade bathing at the foot of the Common on Sunday. At this time it was illegal for hired carriages to enter or leave Boston on Sunday before six o'clock in the evening. While the church services were going on, the city authorities exerted themselves to keep all vehicles from moving faster than a walk.

Pennsylvania passed a series of laws, in 1779 and later, against Sunday recreations. In 1794 this commonwealth made it a punishable offense to buy as well as to sell goods on the first day of the week, except in certain specified cases. And religious fanatics of Philadelphia went so far as to fasten chains across the streets on Sunday in order to prevent the passage of mail coaches. It was customary in the early days of the republic both to carry and to deliver the mails on Sunday, and not until 1811 did any widespread objections to this practice arise.

Three years earlier a stagecoach driver carrying the United States mail was arrested in Massachusetts; but the Supreme Court of that state decided that the transportation of postal matter was permissible, although driving about a town to receive or discharge passengers would be a violation of the law. In fact, it was held several decades later in Massachusetts that Sunday travel between towns, save in the performance of necessary or charitable duties, was criminal. Congress, about 1830, was strongly opposed to any prohibition of the carrying and delivery of mail on Sunday, and the legislatures of Alabama and Indiana expressed their approval of this attitude.

The "Sabbath day" was then, in the period between 1776 and 1830, most sacred in New England. In 1779 the Vermont legislature passed a law providing that persons who shouted, jumped, rode, or danced on the first day of the week should be fined or whipped. In 1812 a man was fined in North Haven, Connecticut, for "travelling from house to house from one part of the town to the other and disturbing the good people of this town" on a Sunday.

Outside of New England it was common to scoff at the long and lugubrious Yankee Sabbath. In the first three decades of the century the clergymen of other states presented many petitions asking for stricter Sunday observance, but these were usually rejected. Even within New England, as the authority of the Congregationalist ministers waned, Sunday travel and play became more frequent. Innkeepers found it profitable to ignore the law and to serve drinks and supply horses to those who asked for them. Public opinion about the proper way to observe the first day of the week changed faster than the legislation on the subject.

§ 3

The records of North Haven, Connecticut, for 1812 show that on one occasion seven men were made each to pay a fine of $3.34 and costs of $1.27 for playing cards. Yet there were at this time public lotteries in a number of the states. Taxes long remained unpopular in the republic, even more unpopular than they are to-day. Moreover, it was difficult to defer the payment of public expenses through the issuance of bonds. There was comparatively little accumulated wealth for the purchase of securities in the country, and neither the states nor the nation had established a high degree of credit.

Some of the governmental buildings at Washington were paid for with the proceeds of lotteries. Harvard College added to its library in the same way. Lotteries enlarged the city hall of New York and enabled the commonwealth of Massachusetts to encourage the nascent industry of cotton-spinning.

Horse racing was, at the beginning of the nineteenth century, forbidden in Massachusetts. However, betters and gamblers were amply provided with other facilities for risking their money. The playing of cards for large stakes was common in Boston and other cities, and lottery tickets were everywhere offered for sale. The lottery has, indeed, retained a certain amount of respectability down to our own times, churches and charitable organizations still using modified forms of it.

The element of chance is never absent from agricultural and industrial operations, and the capitalistic organization of society necessitates a large amount of what is virtually gambling. Stock-jobbing, indeed, was still in a very rudimentary form during the period with which we are here concerned; but there was a great deal of speculation in land and in agricultural and other commodities. In the Southern and Middle states there was a large amount of gambling of various sorts. Horse racing was popular because of the opportunities it afforded for betting, and Virginians were fond of cockfights for the same reason.

Music, which had generally been condemned as diabolic in colonial New England, became quite respectable even in the orthodox circles of Boston. Hymns and religious music naturally became acceptable before the frivolous varieties.

But the opposition to the theatre was long earnest and fanatical. During the Revolutionary War, under the patronage of General Howe, there were amateur theatricals in no less a place than Faneuil Hall for the benefit of the disabled British soldiers and the wives and children of those who were killed. The most popular of the plays was a farce called *The Blockade of Boston,* written by General Burgoyne.

As we have seen, the Continental authorities, especially Congress, opposed such recreations while hostilities were going on. In 1778 the Continental Congress forbade all persons holding offices under the United States to attend stage plays, under penalty of dismissal. As soon as the war was ended, some of the states signified their willingness to receive professional companies of actors again. In 1785 an English company in New York, the same that had performed there before the Revolution, produced the first play of American authorship ever to appear on the boards. Somewhat surprisingly, conservative Dutch Albany admitted professional actors even before they were allowed to open their theatre in New York.

For some decades a considerable part of the population of Manhattan considered the drama inherently vicious. Regular playgoers were comparatively few, and it was necessary to present something sensational to draw large audiences.

Pennsylvania, in 1779 and 1786, passed laws against the drama. These were in some cases evaded, the managers announcing their plays as concerts or lectures. In 1789 such devices ceased to be necessary, for the state then removed the theatrical prohibition. Many of the respectable people of Philadelphia made it a matter of conscience to stay away from the playhouses. These found it profitable, therefore, to enter into an informal alliance with prostitution. In various parts of the country, pamphlet wars arose between those who defended the morality of the drama and those who opposed it. This was probably the greatest conflict of the period between the hedonists and the asceticists, for the alcohol agitation was still somewhat undeveloped.

Luxury of all sorts was denounced by the same people who attacked the theatre. They were, for the most part, strict religionists who feared that young people would not attend the churches if they went to the theatre. Of course, the fact that the playhouses became places of rendezvous for harlots added to the intensity of the indignation displayed. In Philadelphia the opposition came largely from the Quakers. Still, it was clear that many of them were not averse to enjoying the good things in life.

In 1793, when a second theatre was opened in Philadelphia, this was said to be not only the finest in America but equal to any in London. It contained about two thousand seats. While the seat of government was at Philadelphia, President Washington was a frequent visitor at the theatre. There was very little of the Puritan spirit in the man, but he possessed considerable aristocratic feeling; and he opposed, for the masses, some things which he considered proper enough for the entertainment of their betters. Aristocratic skeptics such as Washington have often insisted upon the utility of religion and pietism for holding the masses in check. Their position, which may be described as the fear of idle apprentices and lazy servants, is not always easy to distinguish from genuine ascetic otherworldliness. Sometimes, as with the Puritans, the two things were merged.

In Massachusetts the opposition to the theatre was formidable.

In 1791 a meeting was called to decide about instructing the Boston representatives to vote for the repeal of the state law which prohibited dramatic representations. Samuel Adams there argued that stage plays were immoral and undesirable. However, he was in the minority at the meeting, for most of the citizens of Boston were in favor of a legalized theatre. In the rural districts of Massachusetts, where there was no prospect of the establishment of theatres in any case, there was a decided opinion that Boston should be saved from its own evil desires.

The actors, realizing that Boston sentiment was in their favor, tried to evade the law in the manner that had already been used in Philadelphia. They advertised the plays as "moral lectures." *Othello* was offered as a sort of lay sermon on the evil effects of jealousy, and the moral teachings of other plays were set forth in the same way. But the performances themselves looked suspiciously like stage plays. There were even farces, or "entertaining lectures." Governor Hancock was opposed to these virtuous and educational lectures, and he ordered the sheriff to arrest the lecturers. Though the actors and actresses were released on technical grounds, they decided not to resume their attempts to cure Boston of its vices until they were more definitely authorized to do so. When, in 1793, Massachusetts repealed its law against the theatre, there were no longer any states which forbade the presentation of stage plays.

Individual cities and towns still had the right to refuse the issuance of licenses for the building and operation of playhouses. The abhorrence of the theatre felt in some circles remained long after the close of the eighteenth century, and it became more widespread with the growth of Methodism. Actors and actresses were still considered vagabonds or worse. Preachers still felt that it was part of their evident duty to inveigh against the stage. The attitude of the various cities toward the actors differed greatly. Baltimore was one of those which gave them a rich welcome.

In the early years of the republic only about a tenth of the people lived in cities. Since the country was so predominatingly rural and because the means of transportation were primitive, the

THE SERIOUS, MORAL AND INSTRUCTIVE TALE OF *JANE SHORE*

A theatre advertisement in the *Pennsylvania Packet*, 1788. From *The Pageant of America*, courtesy of the Yale University Press.

theatre could be of direct interest to comparatively few. There were circuses, musical entertainers, and all sorts of shows, but they were for city people. Even the wandering magicians and jugglers and exhibitors of single trained animals failed to reach the mass of the people.

Perhaps the chief popular diversion was politics, for Washington's hope that there would be no party divisions signally failed of accomplishment. In New England and the Middle states there were sleigh rides, often ending in a dance at some tavern. Dancing was still fiercely condemned by many pietists, although the amount of personal contact involved was very little. It had a large place in the formal entertainments of the South.

The days when the waltz was a novelty in New York are vividly depicted in *Salmagundi*, a paper modeled after the *Spectator*. Washington Irving and James Kirke Paulding were two of the leading spirits in *Salmagundi*, which appeared in 1807 and 1808. The city of New York was, by comparison with what it is now, insignificantly tiny and very simple. Everyone knew everyone else.

But there were complaints that the city had already become too stiff and formal. One of the characters introduced in the paper under the name of Anthony Evergreen "recollects precisely the time when young ladies used to go sleigh riding at night, without their mammas or grandmammas; in short, without being patronized at all; and can recollect a thousand pleasant stories about Kissing-bridge."

And, as for kissing, there were murmurs that some of the young ladies were beginning to rebel against the old New Year's Day usage which allowed all masculine callers to salute them on the lips. Apparently this was a Dutch custom. However, we have seen that kissing was part of many social occasions in merry old England. And it had, in the early nineteenth century, an important place in the festivities of rural New England. The good farmer at whose place a corn-husking party was held did not object when a young man found a red ear and exercised his privilege of kissing the farmer's daughter.

In New York, high society permitted kissing games for a considerable period after Irving's time. Still, moral people considered the waltz indecent; and the editors of *Salmagundi* joined in the outcry against the "loving, hugging dance." The town was dance-mad, as it has been divers times since.

French fashions had come in, and indeed the mode was changing very frequently. We find in the brief files of *Salmagundi* a campaign against tightly-laced corsets and also criticisms of the corsetless "classical" loose dress for women, without cushions or hoops or stiff bodices. While this latter vogue lasted, scantiness was the fashionable note. Old-fashioned people complained that ankles were no longer a treat, and that girls gave "every foppling" who acted as escort "a peep at the land." We are told that bare arms and necks appeared not only in ballrooms but on the streets, and that ladies found it necessary, in lifting their feet out of the mud, to permit a glimpse of the decorations they wore on their stockings. "Picnic silk stockings, with lace clocks, flesh-colored, are most fashionable, as they have the appearance of bare legs—*nudity* being all the rage." This was in the first decade of the nineteenth century, at a time when pigtails and powder for beaux had just gone out of style in New York.

Some of the other complaints in this chronicle of old Manhattan have a familiar sound—for example, that against tea-table gossip on the part of the fair sex. And if *Salmagundi* sometimes sighed for the good old unchaperoned days, it also complained that there was too much kissing and improper love-making going on despite the chaperons. There was a terrible younger set, addicted to gambling and to visiting ladies while under the influence of liquor. And young ladies, alas and alack! were reading the lascivious verses of Tom Moore. Sometimes they went to the theatre and did not stuff up their ears when jokes of doubtful propriety were cracked. Or they saw such a play as Rowe's *The Fair Penitent*. The editors of *Salmagundi* thought young ladies should discourage the production of such improper dramas by refusing to see them.

They suggested *Pilgrim's Progress* and *Pamela* as suitable reading for the fair sex. Not long before, the Reverend Jonathan

Edwards had denounced the iniquity of those young people of Northampton who read Richardson's novel; and fiction in general was still under suspicion in New England. But the enthusiastic young writers who edited *Salmagundi* were anxious to do all they could to preserve female chastity, though, as they said, it was already guarded by spirits and angels. And they believed that *Pamela* taught a needed lesson. Perhaps they felt that Richardson's insistence upon the authority of the husband should become familiar to the ladies of New York. They complained that women were donning mannish hats and gaiters, and might be expected to wear the breeches after marriage.

Such books as *Tom Jones, Roderick Random,* and Chesterfield's *Letters,* in addition to works by Voltaire and the other authors whom the American ministers were denouncing as blasphemous as well as immoral, were being sold all over the country. Perhaps it was such books, perhaps it was the Revolutionary War, which brought about a laxity of manners. Whatever the cause might be, horrified New Englanders exclaimed that young people were using language with which, in the preceding century, only sailors had been familiar. The more precise people of New England forbade their children, and especially their daughters, to read novels or plays. Such books, possessing the additional charm of being forbidden, gained in circulation.

McMaster lists among the things which New England farmers of 1784 considered abominable "to make a jest, to sing a comic song, to eat a dinner cooked on Sunday, or to give a present on Christmas Day." This is slightly exaggerated, even for 1784—dry Yankee humor had developed long before then, and many forms of amusement which then seemed diabolical soon became permissible. There were all sorts of simple country festivities in New England, with the merriment usually heightened by alcohol.

Crèvecœur says of the people of Nantucket in 1780 that music, singing, and dancing were held to be equally detestable, and that the pleasures of the table were almost alone generally acceptable at social gatherings. But, according to his account, overeating was more common than drinking to excess. This was not the case with New England as a whole.

Early marriage was the rule in the new republic, especially in the rural districts. Of the city of New York about 1790, Brissot de Warville remarks: "Luxury is already creating in this town a class of men very dangerous to society—I mean bachelors. The expense of women causes matrimony to be dreaded by men." Similar observations were made in this period about Philadelphia and other cities. But it does not appear that the number of bachelors above the age of twenty-five was large enough to cause any great danger.

In Philadelphia, between 1776 and 1830, a majority of the Quakers abandoned the traditional garb. Some took to wearing very gay and expensive costumes and discarded the old rigid standards for personal behavior. It became difficult to tell Quakers apart from members of other sects and from agnostics.

Some almanac verses of 1830 contrast the good old times of Philadelphia in 1800 with later degeneracy. The girls used to be willing and able to cook, says the versifier, but now they think only of beautifying themselves. They have adopted bizarre elephantine bonnets and other garments which are voluminous enough to contain a beau and a belle at the same time. They wear a great deal of hair which is not their own. When it comes to choosing a wife, " 'Tis wealth adds lustre to the cheek."

Fearon, writing in 1818, says that rouging was prevalent among the young ladies of Philadelphia, even those belonging to the Society of Friends. The almanac poet was not, then, dealing with a new abuse. And did Sally Wister use some primitive variety of lipstick to captivate her officers, or did she simply pinch her lips?

America as a whole did not devote a great deal of attention to good manners, but there were some social circles where fine points of etiquette mattered as much as they did anywhere in Europe. A French visitor tells us about the formality of Philadelphia high society immediately after the Revolution. A young lady who gossiped as she performed her part in a country dance

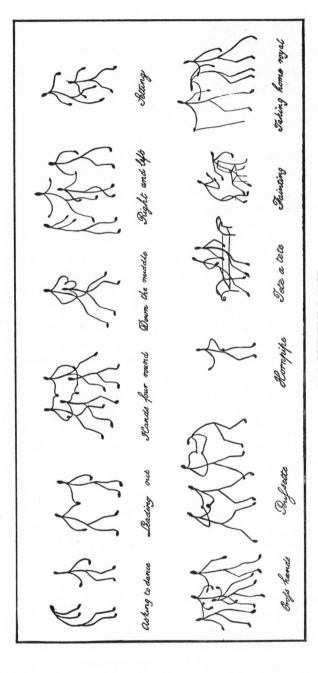

Asking to dance   Leading out   Hands four round   Down the middle   Right and left   Setting

Crop hands   Pouffette   Hornpipe   Tete a tete   Fainting   Seeing home royal

THE COUNTRY DANCE

An etching in *The Port Folio*, 1817. From *The Pageant of America*, courtesy of the Yale University Press.

found herself reproved by the master of ceremonies: "Come, miss, have a care what you are doing. Do you think you are here for your own pleasure?" It was decided not by inclination but by lot how young men and women should be paired for the whole evening of dancing. Social functions were treated as being almost in the nature of a ritual; and people attended them because it was a duty which went with their social position, not for enjoyment.

But there was much hedonism displayed in Philadelphia, nevertheless. The women wore expensive clothes, and foreign visitors tell us that many men remained single because they could not afford to support them in their accustomed luxuries. Travelers from abroad often remarked that American men had no interest in life aside from money-making. This fact (so far, indeed, as it was one) was connected with the difficulty of satisfying feminine desires for fine clothes and other extravagances. Already, too, the notion that culture was something of which the women could take care was beginning to develop.

The male sex seemed to be as much concerned with beautification as the female. An anonymous broadside against corsets which appeared in the early part of the nineteenth century indicates that "these machines of good white oak" or whalebone were used by "master and mistress," by "servant and maid."

By and large, manners in the early republic were characterized by simplicity and lack of ostentation. Still, there were conspicuous exceptions to this general fact. The battle over titles of honor and the etiquette of the presidential court waxed hot for several administrations. When Jefferson became President, he did his best to introduce the simple manners which he considered suitable for a democracy. He was anxious that the presidential mansion should not resemble a royal palace. Accordingly, he put on comfortable but very unusual and informal clothes when he received foreign diplomatists. They considered that they had been insulted. American aristocrats thought the dignity of their country was being compromised.

One of the social crimes for which Jefferson was denounced was that of accepting a cheese sent to him by a country admirer and dividing it among his friends. This particular sort of Jeffersonian crime has, indeed, been committed by most of his successors; and it would now take an exceedingly bold President to refuse cheeses, pet tigers, and other such gifts. But when Jefferson occupied the office, there was still an avowedly aristo-cratic party, which could not forgive the chief executive for recognizing the existence of bumpkins and urban plebeians.

Early conditions in the capital city of Washington were un-favorable to the development of fine manners. In the first few decades of its existence it possessed few attractive homes. Many of the congressmen and high government officials lived in boarding houses. There was a great deal of gambling among the statesmen and politicians there. Henry Clay was among those who lost heavily at play. Betting on the horse races held in Maryland was a favorite form of excitement for the Wash-ington people.

Lawmakers and high government officials often settled their differences with blows, or fought duels. But the most famous duel in American history took place away from the neighborhood of Washington. This was the combat between Aaron Burr and Alexander Hamilton, in which Hamilton was killed. His son had met death in a duel only three years before. Especially in the North, the tragic end of the meeting between Burr and Hamilton caused powerful sentiment to be aroused against the custom of settling affairs of honor by violence. Burr was indicted for murder and had to flee.

In 1820 Commodores Barron and Decatur fought at Wash-ington, Decatur being killed. Ordinarily, Congress would have voted an expression of respect and sympathy at the death of such a national hero. It indicated its disapproval of dueling by refusing to do so in this instance. However, it took no positive action in the way of censuring the practice. The New England and Middle states were confirmed in their opposition to the ordeal by battle, but the South and, to some extent, the Northwest, still accepted it as something which could not honor-ably be dispensed with.

The frontier was quarrelsome and lacking in the niceties of

an older civilization. Cleanliness was little valued. Of western Pennsylvania at the beginning of the nineteenth century, a traveler writes: "The people of the country are as astonished that one should object to sleeping two or three in the same bed and in dirty sheets, or to drink from the same dirty glass after half a score of others, as to see one neglect to wash one's hands and face of a morning."

Foreigners complained that the very common habit of smoking and chewing tobacco contributed to the filthiness of inns and public conveyances. Gouverneur Morris, while he was abroad, became accustomed to the European view that persons of social pretensions should use tobacco, if at all, only in the form of snuff. When an American asked him if gentlemen smoked in Europe, he replied, "Gentlemen smoke in no country." But such an attitude was rare in the United States. Men of all circles smoked, and spat tobacco juice as well.

In *The American Chesterfield,* a book of etiquette published at Philadelphia in 1827 and intended for the instruction of men, they are told that it is improper to elevate the feet above the head in public places. We read here about judges and lawyers who were in the habit of resting their feet on their desks in court, and of men who assumed a similar posture in church.

Henry Adams denies the charge made by a number of foreign visitors that America was altogether materialistic in the early decades of the nineteenth century. He declares that the public and private morality of those days was higher than that of Europe, and that idealism of all sorts flourished. Thomas Jefferson, indeed, seems to have held a somewhat different opinion. He wrote, in 1815, in a private letter: "I fear from the experience of the last twenty-five years that morals do not of necessity advance hand in hand with the sciences."

The country was beginning to gain a reputation for educational advantages, and even for the general intelligence of its inhabitants; but the British Tories were very reluctant to concede that any good might come out of a democracy. And there were some Americans who felt similarly. The differences between social classes were far more carefully preserved in the early decades of the nineteenth century than they have been in the corresponding part of the twentieth. Thus, before a boy could be entered in a Pennsylvania public school between 1809 and 1835, it was necessary for his parents to take a pauper's oath.

After the War of 1812 there was an increase in the rate of immigration, especially from Ireland. Germans were trickling in, not yet coming in large numbers. The immigrants of this period seem, for the most part, to have merged quickly with the earlier settlers. They became almost invariably supporters of the democratic ideal. Religion was of great interest to the people of the United States, and such opposition to the new-comers as appeared was based on the fear of staunch Protestants that the power of the Catholics in the country might be unduly increased.

Where the Irish Catholic immigrants remained under the influence of their priests, they usually supported rather precise moral standards. Their attitude toward Sunday observance, to be sure, marked them off from the strict Protestant Evangelicals. And compared with the Scotch-Irish Presbyterians, they were very liberal.

In the Southern mountains, isolated from the rest of the country, these people maintained the customs of a century before. They were especially conservative in maintaining the prejudices of their fathers. For them, there were no new ideas. They zealously preserved their ancestral opinions and superstitions. Some of the Presbyterians of Scottish origin supported an educated ministry, but the mountaineers depended for religious and moral instruction mostly upon wandering evangelists. They came largely under Baptist and Methodist influence. Theological minutiæ meant little to them, but they did like to have vigorously portrayed the flames of Hell awaiting those persons who joined in mixed dances, played the fiddle on Sunday, or otherwise transgressed the law of God.

The Scotch-Irish mountaineers had little to do with slavery, which became so important to the people of the plains. And, though they did not always live up to their own standards, they considered the aristocrats of Virginia and South Carolina wicked

ANCIENT AND MODERN REPUBLICS

The frontispiece, drawn by A. Hervieu, to Mrs. Trollope's *Domestic Manners of the Americans*, 1832.

people. Shortly after the American Revolution a French visitor, the Duke of Liancourt, referred to the Virginia "love of dissipation." With the disestablishment of the Episcopal Church, religion was in a very low state there for a time. Such freethinkers as Jefferson by no means preached laxity of morals. In fact, he regretted the beginnings of the Industrial Revolution in America because he feared that the development of factories and great cities would destroy the primitive virtues and the old simplicity of life. Unthinking hedonists, not philosophers, undermined the moral bases of Virginia.

§ 4

The Southern planters were exposed to special temptations. They had slaves, male and female, under their nearly absolute control. Perhaps in such states as Virginia, Maryland, and Delaware, although the masters were permitted to indulge their caprices with regard to the negroes, extreme cruelty was not the rule. Farther south, the lot of the slaves was generally worse.

From the first introduction of the Africans, cohabitation between white men and black women (much less frequently, between white women and black men) had occurred. By the time of the Revolution there were mulattoes and other hybrids among the slaves. Some of the women were very attractive. Moreover, they were not permitted to maintain the aloofness expected of the white ladies. They went about habitually in scanty garb, and they were not taught to cherish the virtue of modesty.

It does not appear that concubinage with slaves was altogether approved by society, for Jefferson and his friends greatly resented the charge that he had one or more colored mistresses. Nevertheless, it became very common, and came more and more to be taken as a matter of course. We hear of a few zealous moralists who gave up good businesses and moved away from slave territory because they did not want their children to be exposed to the temptations which were increasing there.

Richmond and Charleston were chief centers of the aristocratic luxury which the slave system made possible. Their gay social whirl was undisturbed by the New England inhibitions, and the pursuit of pleasure appeared to be their principal occupation. In New England the Industrial Revolution produced a class of factory girls whose low wages encouraged the growth of sexual laxity. Women already outnumbered men in these states, because of the attractions of the sea and the frontier. There were, indeed, fewer indications than there had been in colonial times of violations of the sexual code. The records of Groton, Connecticut, show that, until 1803, sexual offenders were made to confess their sins openly in church. Later, the veil of silence was cast over illicit relations, especially if, as often happened, those concerned were prominent in the affairs of the church and the community.

In the mill towns many of the pious proprietors were, at first, very careful to remove temptation from the female operatives. Still, their first consideration was low wages, and they never thought of paying the women enough to provide them with comforts and ardently desired minor luxuries. It does not appear that conditions in New England were ever quite as bad as they were in English factories in the early days of the century, but some of the causes for complaint were similar. Poor children were sometimes bound over to an apprenticeship amounting almost to slavery; and we hear of the whip being used not only upon them but upon adult women as well.

As for the millowners, they began to form something that was comparatively new in America, an industrial aristocracy. The simplicity of New England vanished, so far as they were concerned. Wealthy women advertised for poor ones to nurse their children. And the movement that carried thousands from the farms to the cities brought forth jeremiads prophesying the impending ruin of the republic.

The authority of parents, like that of ministers and communal officers, remained very great in New England; but it was diminishing steadily, and had been on the wane since early in the eighteenth century. Elsewhere the movement had gone further. A debating club in the city of New York decided in 1818 that parents had no right to interfere with the matrimonial selections of their children. There were many complaints at this time, in New York and elsewhere, that young people were abusing their freedom. Sermons and editorial remarks were much concerned with the dreadful younger generation.

In sexual morality there appears to be little doubt that the United States as a whole was stricter than Great Britain. It is true that the severe colonial penalties against fornication and adultery generally disappeared; but, so far as it is possible to judge from the available evidence on the subject, men and women by no means hurried to engage in promiscuous intercourse as soon as they were assured that they were in no danger of being hanged or publicly flogged for it. The freedom of casual intercourse between the sexes was greater than it was in the same years in England and other European countries, although it was considerably more restricted in some ways than it is now.

Early marriage was the rule almost everywhere. It was easy to get married, even without parental permission. Except in the upper circles of the largest cities, a man's economic position was usually improved when he took a wife.

Lieutenant F. Fitzgerald de Roos comments on conditions as he observed them in 1826: "In American society, there is far less formality and restraint than is found in that of Europe; but I must observe that notwithstanding the freedom of intercourse which is allowed, the strictest propriety prevails both in conversation and demeanor. It is not only permitted to young women, both married and single, to walk out in the morning without a servant, but to be accompanied by a gentleman. Walking arm-in-arm is not generally customary."

In upper-class circles chaperons were much in evidence at balls, the theatre, and social functions of all sorts. Cooper, writing of the same period as de Roos, says that the girl of high society "never rides nor walks—unless in the most public places, and then commonly with great reserve—attended by a single man, unless indeed under circumstances of a peculiar note." But when a woman traveled, she was supposed to be in need of masculine protection; and it was usual for her husband or brother, if he could not accompany her himself, to suggest some friend as an escort. Such a thing would have been scandalous in England.

Married women seldom took a prominent place in society. It was, then, girls in their teens who gave the tone to dancing parties. They were supposed to be very innocent and modest. According to Cooper, they were averse to the use of cosmetics: "Several gentlemen have gone so far as to assure me that when a woman rouges, it is considered in this country *prima facie* evidence that her character is frail."

We have evidence contradictory to this statement, and certainly it is not a generalization that covers the whole republic in the years between 1776 and 1830. Perhaps the use of artificial red was less necessary than it is now, except for city women of the leisure class. Others worked hard, and largely in the open air.

In 1827 the *American Farmer* advocated exercise for women, suggesting that dancing was especially suitable and recommending other forms as well, "with the exception of wrestling, cricket, quoits, and other sports properly termed athletic." The writer was concerned both with health and good morals: "The ladies must understand that calisthenic exercises are not good for them, unless it be that which obliges the person to run around an upright pole which has a pivot on the top, to which cords are affixed, and in holding which, while she runs, the velocity of the lady is increased by centrifugal force, until she is raised from the ground and flies, as it were, round the pole. For girls above the age of twelve such exercise may not be allowable except under particular circumstances of privacy, when no males are present."

The leg displays of which *Salmagundi* complains had disappeared, it is evident: more likely, they had never been seen in the rural districts. The only strange thing about the article from which quotations have just been made is that farmers' wives and daughters should have been assumed to need more exercise than their regular employments gave them.

The verbal proprieties tended to become more rigid during the early years of the republic. A French traveler tells of hearing the Secretary of War, Mr. Peter, sing a very "free" song of his own composition during the time of the Revolutionary War. In 1808 Chief Justice Parsons sent a lady a copy of *Tom Jones,* together with a letter commenting on the unchastity of Molly Seagrim and praising the author for plainly describing vice and thus guarding his readers against it. Parsons was a pious New Englander, and it is clear that he did not consider his gift or his letter in any way shameful.

In 1803, according to a contemporary writer, the ladies of Philadelphia, especially the matrons, were wont to use indelicate expressions and to make immoral innuendoes. "A loud laugh or a coarse exclamation followed each of these, and the young ladies generally went through the form of raising their fans to their faces." Philadelphia, which was at this time the most important city in the United States, had a reputation for luxury and debauch.

Two decades earlier, Pine created a great stir in the city when he brought from Paris a plaster cast of the "Venus de Medici." After the attempt to exhibit it publicly brought moral wrath down upon him, he showed it thenceforth only to the chosen few. In 1806 the Philadelphia Academy of Fine Arts exhibited a number of casts of nude statues in the Louvre. It was found necessary, in order to satisfy the precisians, to admit women only once a week and to prepare the "indecent" statues for their visits by carefully draping them.

In 1828, when Longfellow was at Florence, he admired the Venus of Canova for the good New England reason that it concealed what the Medici Venus revealed. "What beauty, what elegance, what modesty!" he exclaimed, certainly intending no anticlimax.

A few Americans escaped from the prevailing prudery, usually by coming under strong foreign influences. For instance, John Vanderlyn, who was born at Kingston, New York, in 1776, painted a fine nude called "Ariadne" in Paris early in the nineteenth century. He exhibited it in New York, where it was looked upon with disfavor. Vanderlyn was asked by a wealthy New Yorker to choose some famous old painting and copy it for him. He reproduced Coreggio's "Antiope." The patron of the arts looked at the finished work and cried out, "What can I do with it? It is altogether indecent. I cannot hang it in my house, and my family reprobate it."

Benjamin Franklin's grandson, William Temple Franklin, published his grandfather's Autobiography in 1817. Without indicating in any way that he was revising the original, the younger Franklin made a number of prudish changes. For example, "having got a naughty girl with child" became "having had an intrigue with a young woman of bad character." Gentility was substituted for virility. And this was in response to a movement which was visible in all the older settlements of the United States. It became necessary, in mixed company, to use the utmost care in bedraping ideas which savored in the least of nudity. The era of minced words came in.

Ladies were required to be ladies, and with a vengeance. Much indignation was displayed in 1829 when a young woman allowed herself to be publicly examined in geometry. This was in the liberal-minded city of New York. The female editor of a magazine for ladies felt that it was necessary to apologize for her boldness in filling a position which really belonged to the superior sex. She was a widow with five children, she explained, and she thought it better to subdue her modesty than to allow them to starve. In the interest of public morals, there were good people who preferred that a few children should die or that women should be forced into prostitution rather than that they should presume to display intellectual ability.

Divorces were rare in the early decades of the United States, and women were expected to submit to a great deal of maltreatment before so much as dreaming of a separation. Legally, men enjoyed a host of property rights and other privileges denied to women.

Little consideration was displayed for females of the lower classes. In 1787 a Philadelphia grand jury reported that debtors and criminals of both sexes were so crowded together in jail that debauchery and other evils resulted. Later, imprisonment for debt was abolished or made rare in all the states. And there

ARIADNE

By John Vanderlyn. Courtesy of the Pennsylvania Academy of the Fine Arts.

was some advancement in the amount of privacy afforded to women prisoners. (Complaints about deficiencies in this regard do, indeed, arise to this very day.) With the development of an urban proletariat, crowding in the slum districts, which made ladylike modesty all but impossible for the wives and daughters of workingmen, became the rule; but in the period here being considered it was still a problem affecting comparatively few.

§ 5

Poverty has never been entirely absent from the United States, even though the presence of abundant natural resources and of much free or cheap land has, until recently, assured its being less general and less acute than in Europe and Asia. Beginning in the earliest days of the American colonies, men who neglected their masters' work or dissipated their own money because of an ungovernable fondness for alcoholic beverages presented a problem.

In Puritan New England, as we have seen, while drunkenness was denounced and sometimes punished with great severity, the drinking of reasonable amounts of intoxicants—and large amounts were often held proper for ministers and magistrates—excited no serious opposition. In fact, it would have been held blasphemous to clamor against Paul's recommendation of a little wine for the stomach's sake; and theological ingenuity had apparently not yet discovered that what Jesus made out of water at Cana was unfermented grape juice.

Hard drinking increased during the Revolutionary War. In its last year the state of Massachusetts had sixty active distilleries. Both Massachusetts and Rhode Island forbade the use of grain for distilling until the end of the war, but this prohibition seems not to have worked any hardship upon the manufacturers of alcoholic beverages. The various states gave rum or beer, or both, as daily rations to their troops. The great majority of the people, including almost all medical men, felt that such beverages were essential to soldiers enduring the hardships of war. However, Dr. Benjamin Rush prepared a pamphlet which set forth the evils of excessive drinking, and this was circulated among the troops by order of the Continental Congress.

In the earliest days of the republic we find French visitors complaining that it was impossible to have water served with meals in America and that it was necessary to drink wine or whiskey. Now that this situation has been neatly inverted, we can join in a chorus of: Other times, other manners, indeed!

After dinner the ladies usually left the table while the gentlemen drank toasts for an hour or two. Tea and coffee already enjoyed a certain popularity in America, but they took away little from the established position of beer, cider, and other beverages containing more or less alcohol.

If we are to believe Crèvecœur, the women and some of the men of the island of Nantucket, where alcoholic inebriation was "unknown" in 1780, were in the habit of taking opium every morning. The sheriff, who was also a physician, took three grains of it every day after breakfast, and was unable, whenever he omitted this dose, to transact any business. I have, however, been unable to find further references to such widespread use of narcotic drugs in the United States at this early period.

There seems to have been proportionately more hard liquor consumed in America in the early days of the republic than in France or even in Great Britain, where drunkenness was at its height in all social circles at the time. The Quakers in the United States were opposed to the use of rum and other distilled liquors but had no objection to beer, porter, cider, and wine. The Methodists took pretty much the same stand, but they hesitated at times about the advisability of expelling manufacturers and retailers of liquor from the Church.

In New England most of the Congregationalist ministers were willing to consider strong drink one of the divine gifts to man. In 1784, when a clergyman was ordained at Hartford, Connecticut, fifteen bowls of punch, eleven bottles of wine, five bowls of flip, and six bowls of toddy were consumed. The next year, at another New England ordination, eighty people drank thirty bowls of punch in the morning before the meeting; and sixty-eight people at dinner made away with forty-four bowls of punch, eighteen bottles of wine, eight bowls of brandy, and some cherry rum.

The first temperance movement of any importance appeared in Litchfield County, Connecticut, in the late 1780's. A number of farmers there decided that they would no longer give their harvest hands distilled liquors, although they were willing to continue the rations of beer and cider. They were not, indeed, trying to convert the country to their views. Nevertheless, what they did was important because it pointed the way the wind was blowing, and because it made others think of battling against excess in drinking. It is significant that the opposition to distilled liquors first appeared in the form of a desire to keep workmen sober. Of course, the thrifty Yankee farmers also appreciated the saving they made when they ceased to dole out rum to their laborers.

Dr. Rush of Philadelphia, speaking after the Revolution both as a physician and a representative in Congress, continued to attack the use of distilled liquors. He insisted that the use of beer ought to be encouraged, for he considered it harmless and felt that men and women who drank it would have less craving for whiskey.

Toward the end of the eighteenth century, Congress imposed customs and excise taxes on strong drink. Then, in 1793, the Whiskey Rebellion broke out, and there were a number of less serious sporadic protests of the same kind against infractions of the sacred right to maintain unlicensed stills. Consequently, Federalists began to demand that places where liquor was manufactured and sold should be closely watched.

President Dwight of Yale, after observing conditions in the state of New York, decided that the Massachusetts practice of issuing inn licenses only to "respectable persons" was fully justified. He complained of the drunkenness and obscene swearing he found in the taverns of New York. Dwight thought, too, that the state, and more especially the city, contained an excessive number of dramshops. It appears impossible to determine if, as some then said, New England was less addicted to intemperance in drink than the remainder of the country. Perhaps it

The DRUNKARD'S PROGRESS,

OR THE DIRECT ROAD TO POVERTY, WRETCHEDNESS & RUIN.

The MORNING DRAM.

The CONFIRMED DRUNKARD.

CONCLUDING SCENE.

THE DRUNKARD'S PROGRESS

After a temperance broadside of 1826 in the possession of the New York Historical Society. From *The Pageant of America*, courtesy of the Yale University Press.

was simply that the Yankees could down greater quantities without flinching. No doubt there was less public drunkenness in New England, but much rum and applejack were consumed in the fields and at the table after dinner. This was the situation about 1800, before the beginning of any general temperance movement.

In the Carolinas and other parts of the South, physicians were saying that water should not be drunk without the addition of rum, brandy, or whiskey. They were firmly of the opinion that the water was dangerous without alcohol, and they thought the climate necessitated the use of intoxicants. A total abstinence pledge appeared in Virginia in 1800. Most Virginians kept right on drinking wine, whiskey, and other alcoholic beverages, both with their meals and at various odd times.

In New England the occasional heavy drinking of the clergy seems, more than any other factor, to have contributed to the growth of temperance sentiment. A society to work against the excessive use of intoxicants was founded at Saratoga, New York, in 1808. This led, four years later, to the establishment of a number of temperance organizations in Maine. The pledge which such societies circulated at this time did not include beer and other fermented beverages.

Cobbett, commenting on the prevalence of drunkenness in the United States and the habit of pressing whiskey on visitors at all hours of the day, remarked: "However, there is no remedy but the introduction of beer, and I am very happy to know that beer is, every day, becoming more and more fashionable." He found another consolation: "God be thanked, the women of any figure in life do not by any means give in to the practice; but abhor it as much as the well-bred women of England." We are left to our own conclusions as to women not "of any figure."

In 1818, Hector, New York, became immortal, for the temperance workers there began to offer two different kinds of pledges: one of them, later to be known as "teetotal," included not only ardent spirits, but beer and all other intoxicants as well. At about the same time the Massachusetts Society for the Suppression of Intemperance, formed through the efforts of Lyman

Beecher, was beginning to lay plans to secure legal action designed to check hard drinking.

During the 1820's the people of the United States consumed annually about seven gallons of distilled liquor *per capita*. We are told that in 1825 the 1,400 people of Shrewsbury, Massachusetts, drank 120 hogsheads of rum. That same year, Lafayette was entertained in Philadelphia by the Fishing Club. There were thirteen toasts on the program, and others were volunteered after these had been duly drunk.

When the city of New York had a population of about a hundred thousand, it is said to have contained nearly three thousand licensed drinking houses. In 1817 the Society for the Prevention of Pauperism was formed there. The managers of this organization declared that drunkenness and the lottery were the principal causes of poverty in New York.

Periods of industrial depression offered special opportunities to the individuals and organizations working to increase piety and to reduce intemperance, Sabbath-breaking, and profane swearing. In fact, it has been a general rule in American history that panics and religious revivals go together.

There were complaints in New York and some other cities that young children were permitted to buy intoxicants. It seems that some boys of five or six used to ask for gin in the saloons, as they would now ask for candy or ice-cream cones at the drug store, for their own consumption.

A large number of oyster houses were established in Philadelphia about 1820, and moralists asserted that they were dangerous places, serving as unlicensed saloons and also as brothels or houses of assignation. Many people who did not oppose the dramshops as a matter of principle thought that their number should be reduced and that illicit saloons should be closed.

By 1830 there were over a thousand temperance societies in the United States, with their greatest strength in New England and the state of New York, but extending also into Missouri, Kentucky, Tennessee, and other Southern and Western states. There was a small decrease in the consumption of distilled liquors. Perhaps the educational campaign of the temperance societies brought this about. Or it may have been due to the increasing popularity of tea and coffee and the fermented beverages.

Where the temperance orators had been most eloquent in New England, the stumps of apple orchards could sometimes be seen. These showed that some people had been sufficiently touched to destroy the sources of hard cider and applejack.

A number of church organizations had taken official stands against the use of distilled beverages, and the influence of the Evangelical churches was being rapidly extended. Between 1800 and 1850 the Methodists increased in numbers from sixty-five thousand to more than a million and a quarter, the Baptists from a hundred thousand to eight hundred thousand, the Presbyterians from forty thousand to half a million. Baptist and Methodist ministers were especially zealous and successful along the frontier.

§ 6

The men who went westward into the wilderness from New England and the other states along the Atlantic coast were mostly individualists. Many of them fled from the severe moral code which was enforced by the authorities of Church and State in closely settled little townships. Yet some of the New Englanders who occupied virgin lands were anxious to make their new homes resemble, as much as possible, those they had left behind. The stamp of Puritanism appeared in rural New York and New Jersey, then in many parts of what we now call the Middle West. And the transplanted New Englanders were sometimes more conservative about moral matters than those who remained in Massachusetts and Connecticut.

An English traveler, Thomas Ashe, was surprised to find at Marietta, Ohio, in 1806 that the payment of church rates was compulsory, there was "no fighting, no racing," and heavy fines were imposed upon persons who swore or who worked or played on Sunday. On the road between Marietta and Pittsburgh the nearest church to their own was 181 miles away. Yet the New

England settlers had built a town which was, as nearly as might be, a replica of what they had left behind.

At Wheeling, which was less godly, Ashe was told by an old Quaker "that the old settlers would be bought out in time, and the place become new and regenerated. He founded his hopes on the belief that his friends, when backed by others of the same profession, to settle in the town, will gain an ascendancy in the municipal affairs; abolish cockfighting, horse-racing, drinking, et cetera, and, above all, enforce the observance of the Sabbath, and other solemn days."

Such pious people usually followed the true frontiersman, who was often a half-barbarian, living the life of an Indian hunter. According to all accounts, the typical pioneer consumed large quantities of whiskey. Fighting was part of the ordinary life of the men who lived on the frontier. Andrew Jackson of Tennessee, when he was already a prominent leader, took part in many a rough-and-tumble battle.

Noses, lips, ears, eyes, and other human appendages often suffered severely in the frontier combats. Unless a fight was specially agreed upon in advance as a "fair" one, no holds were barred, no form of offense outlawed. Kicking, biting, and gouging were regular means of attack, and mayhem often resulted.

Gambling and drinking parties lasted for days or for weeks. Most of the frontiersmen were, until they began to respond to the emotional appeals of the missionaries, entirely indifferent to religion. Though they were seldom industrious enough to work seven days a week, they did not celebrate Sunday in a manner to satisfy the pious. They would usually visit their neighbors, who might be many miles away, and join them in feasting and drinking.

Ashe found in Lexington, Kentucky, that the churches which had been planned there had never been completed, although much work had evidently been done. The interiors had been "torn up by rogues and prostitutes who frequented them at night." He reported the principal diversions of the place to be drinking and gaming at cards and billiards.

Dr. Daniel Drake of Cincinnati, who was very familiar with

the pioneers and their way of life, described the conditions as they were about 1800, when he was a youth of fourteen. He said of the people who came into the wilderness at that time that "profanity, vulgarity, and drinking were their most eminent characteristics. All drank, though not to excess, but all of course did not participate in the other vices; yet I am bound to say that coarse jocularities were not frowned upon by any."

Almost all social gatherings came to an end in intoxication and a series of free-for-all fights. This was true of weddings and funerals as well as of casual parties. Dr. Drake could not admit that the forest and the new clearings constituted a Rousseauan Elysium: "On a calm survey in retrospect of the whole community, I am compelled to say that in purity and refinement it did not rank very high. I doubt the correctness of what is sometimes said in favor of country life among the laboring classes, and lean to the opinion that city people of a, corresponding grade as to intelligence, property, and pursuits, have, on the whole, more virtue and chaster manners."

Drake, who was probably the most celebrated physician in the West, took a prominent part in the temperance movement there. We are told of one rather long lecture on the evils of drink which he delivered at Cincinnati in 1828. An adjournment was called in the midst of it, whereupon most of the audience went out and had a little whiskey. But this does not mean that Drake's agitation was entirely fruitless.

The frontier was democratic. Women were often scarce, and this fact improved their social position. But they were not placed upon a pedestal as in the aristocratic South. They had to work hard, and often at the same tasks as the men. A wife or a half-grown child was of economic value in the new clearings. At weddings it was usual to exclaim, "Health to the groom, and here's to the bride, thumping luck, and big children!" Tennessee passed a law awarding six hundred acres of land to every father of triplets.

Girls married early, sometimes in their early teens; and marriages for money, of which there were complaints in the older settlements, were all but unknown on the frontier. Weddings were not always conducted with the full legal formalities. Sometimes there were no ministers or civil officers authorized to perform the ceremony within a hundred miles. Many couples lived together as husband and wife though they had never been formally married. And there was much trouble about women who deserted their husbands to run off with men whom they decided that they liked better. The divorces were often as informal as the marriages. In at least one case, a Presbyterian church admitted to the communion a man whose wife had deserted him, together with the second wife whom he had taken without being divorced from the first.

There were instances, too, in which women who believed or professed to believe their first husbands dead were confronted by them after having remarried. In such cases there was seldom any thought of punishing the women as bigamists. Instead, they were offered the opportunity to decide whether the first or the second husband pleased them better.

Such difficulties arose because business trips were protracted on account of the slow methods of transportation then available. One Tennessee man, it is said, was away for two years on a trip to New Orleans. On his return, he found his wife nursing an infant. He then went out and got drunk; returning, he cut off the baby's ears. This was, he explained, so he might tell it apart from his own children.

Illegitimate children were pretty common in the West. It became a matter of general remark that many of them were born about nine months after every enthusiastic camp meeting. Religious revivals on the frontier were sometimes attended by thousands who came great distances from every direction.

The years 1800 and 1828 were particularly marked by religious excitement in the new settlements. What permanent effect all the preaching and praying had, it is difficult to say. Certainly, as such states as Kentucky and Ohio became more settled and less venturesome spirits poured into them, the old freedom of manners disappeared. It is not clear that the Methodist circuit riders and the other preachers did much to bring such a result about, but probably their labors were not all in vain.

THE JERKS

From S. G. Goodrich, *Recollections of a Lifetime*, 1856.

There was a pronounced anticlerical feeling among many people of the West in the first five decades or so of the republic. The Reverend Lorenzo Dow was often attacked by hostile mobs; but, according to his own account, he was usually able to make good Christians out of those who heckled and threatened to flog him.

The revivals brought about a great deal of falling, barking, and jerking, hysterical conditions which were considered clear signs of divine favor. The intellectual elements in religion were much neglected. Still, sectarian differences loomed large. And many new sects arose on the frontier. Probably the most important of these was founded by Campbell, who professed to restore the primitive religion of Christ. The Disciples of Christ, as the Campbellites formally called themselves, were, in their moral aspirations, hardly to be distinguished from the members of other evangelical sects.

There was held at Cincinnati in 1829 a debate on the truth of Christianity between Campbell and Robert Owen. The audience at the Methodist church where it was held decided that the Reverend Alexander Campbell had proved his case, and that the Christian religion was true. It is not likely that he convinced any who were skeptical before. Still, it was about at this time that the Christian churches in the West began to make great increases in their influence.

A great many of the sects which appeared in the early decades of the nineteenth century were destined to have little or no permanent influence. Some were extremely ascetic, others favored polygamy or promiscuity. About 1815 there appeared among the westward-moving settlers a group of men and women calling themselves the Followers of the True Christ. Their prophet was said to have forbidden marriage but not sexual intercourse. They were taught that it would be sinful to cleanse or change their clothing. There were also sects of rolling Christians and jumping Christians, and some who worshiped God with dancing feet. Among them were the Shakers, whose religion bade them to be celibate. However, men and women lived in the same communities.

Numerous German pietists came to the United States. Their background was usually similar to that of the Scotch-Irish Presbyterians. Such men as Spener and Francke preached against worldly diversions, including card playing, dancing, and the theatre; and others considered even the taking of a walk for pleasure sinful, and laughter a sign of diabolic possession.

One group of Germans, who had been persecuted for their faith in Württemberg, emigrated to Philadelphia, and proceeded from there to Ohio, where they founded the town of Zoar. At

SHAKERS DANCING
From J. W. Barber, *Connecticut Historical Collections*, 1836.

Zoar they established a communistic order. The regulation of personal affairs went so far that when the number of children in the community was considered excessive, husbands were for a time forbidden to cohabit with their wives. Entertainments of all sorts, music, luxuries, and the eating of pork were frowned upon in Zoar. Tobacco, too, was under the ban. Zoar lasted as a communistic society until near the end of the nineteenth century. In the last years of its existence some of the prohibitions were disregarded, and the town had a reputation for deep beer-drinking.

St. Louis had, in the early days, a motley population including Frenchmen, Spaniards, and a variety of half-breeds. Among them were French-Canadian *voyageurs* with more or less Indian blood, who, when they returned from a successful fur expedition, were accustomed to buy fine colorful clothes and then to carouse and gamble until their money was gone. Drunken sprees and fights were common also at Mackinaw, Michigan, and other fur centers.

It was said that the moral condition of St. Louis was made much worse when the English-speaking Americans came in. Perhaps the sudden change from communities with many inhibitions to one where freedom prevailed was too much for them.

When Louisiana came under the rule of the United States, some of the inhabitants were afraid that Puritanism would be forced upon them. In the winter of 1814-15 the legislature considered a bill "For the better observance of the Sabbath; for punishing the crime of sodomy; for preventing the defacing of churchyards; for shutting the theatres and stores on Sunday; and for other purposes." One representative who spoke against it said: "Such persecuting intolerance may well suit the New England Puritans, who are descended from the bigoted fanatics of old England, who are great readers of the Bible, and consequently ignorant, prejudiced, cold-blooded, false, and cruel; but can never be fastened on the more enlightened, liberal, and philosophical inhabitants of Louisiana, the descendants of Frenchmen." The bill was rejected by a large majority.

On Sunday in New Orleans, business and pleasure were both at their liveliest. The theatre, dancing, and gambling were even more popular then than during the other days of the week. The city contained many pretty quadroon mistresses, most of them free. Although white men did not marry half-breeds, they lived with them virtually as husband and wife. There were prostitutes also, of various shades of color.

New Orleans under Spanish rule was subjected to strict standards of religious and moral propriety which were sometimes very sternly enforced. Blasphemy was punished with the loss of the tongue and the confiscation of property. If a husband

[492]

caught his wife in adultery, he was permitted to kill both her and her lover; but if he allowed the woman to live, he was not allowed to put the man to death.

Much religious zeal remained in New Orleans when it passed into the hands of the United States; but it was chiefly Roman Catholic, and therefore, in the eyes of some good American Protestants, worse than none at all. The missionaries who traveled into Louisiana reported that New Orleans was the wickedest city they had ever seen. The worst thing they found there was the availability of markets and amusements on Sunday after mass. Many Bibles were sent into the territory in an attempt to make the people recognize the errors of their ways.

CHAPTER XIV

INCLUDING A VARIETY OF REFORMERS

§ 1

IN the decades preceding the Civil War, the pious and self-righteous people of the United States kept up their opposition to the theatre. There were, during the 1830's, about a dozen genuine playhouses in the country, of which those in New York and New Orleans are said to have been the only ones enjoying consistent prosperity. Methodist, Baptist, Presbyterian, and Congregationalist ministers continued to denounce the drama.

Museums and wandering exhibitions which were represented as being educational were approved, unless a stage was annexed. The taint of the theatre was upon them in such a case. At Albany a female singer was refused the use of the only available hall, the chapel of the Female Academy, because she sometimes appeared as an actress. The influential old Dutch families around Albany were generally opposed to the theatre.

Mrs. Trollope remarked of the playhouse in Cincinnati, about 1830, that ladies and religious people made it a point to stay away. This was the situation almost everywhere in the United States. England was just then somewhat more liberal in the matter. In New Orleans the English- and the French-speaking population had separate theatres, both well patronized; but that city stood, in matters of morals, somewhat apart from the rest of the country.

Many American cities refused to issue permits for the building of theatres. In 1843 a traveling troupe of actors came to Worcester, Massachusetts. They thought that, although the local ordinances forbade the presentation of plays, a drama showing the evils of intemperance would prove acceptable. But they were mistaken, for their performance was stopped by order of the selectmen. And the officers of the American Temperance Union loudly approved this action. It was unnecessary, in their opinion, to fight against one evil with the aid of another which was equally dangerous. They did not profess to believe that the actors were impelled by any very lofty motives.

The Reverend Henry Ward Beecher told his congregation in Indianapolis that those who defended the theatres as places where good conduct was taught were not very convincing: "How does it happen that in a school of morals the teachers never learn their own lessons?" Of course, during a period when people who considered themselves respectable turned dark scowls. upon the stage, there was a natural reluctance on the part of young men and women who wanted to be looked upon as genteel to enter upon an acting career. And those who did become actors and actresses were often persons to whom public disapproval on the part of the precisians meant little.

"Those who defend theatres," Beecher said, "would scorn to admit actors into their company." But he found it necessary to admit that there were "honorable exceptions." At the same time, he refused to concede that it would be advisable to attend dramatic performances, even in case all the actors and actresses should be able to present certificates of good conduct from their pastors.

"Half the victims of the gallows and of the penitentiary will tell you that these schools for morals were to them the gate of debauchery, the porch of pollution, the vestibule of the very house of death." Closely associated with the theatre, this eloquent preacher told his congregation, were the brothel and the bar. Theatregoers wasted both their time and their money. If they were young men without a superabundance of wealth, they would nevertheless be ashamed to go to the theatre without the gold watch and the silver toothpick which others displayed there. And thus, if they once allowed themselves to be seduced into entering the devilish haunts of the drama, they would soon be thinking of dishonest ways of acquiring the luxuries they saw flaunted there.

"Let no man be led to commit adultery with a theatre, against the rights of his own trade." This sentence of Beecher's did not sound ridiculous when it was uttered, because hard workers had little leisure time. It was the familiar theme of the idle apprentice, attracted from his work and therefore going straight to Hell.

Beecher's *Idle Amusements* was circulated in a little book for many years after it was delivered by word of mouth to the people of Indianapolis. And the sentiments that it expresses are still repeated in many churches.

"I hope it is not fanaticism," said the reverend orator, "for us to judge that throwing one's heels higher than their head a-dancing, is not.exactly the way to teach virtue to our daughters; and that women whose genial warmth of temperament has led them into a generosity somewhat too great, are not the persons to teach virtue, at any rate." And then there was a reference to a popular dancer of the day: "We cannot pay for honest *loans,* but we can pay Elssler hundreds of thousands for being an *airy sylph!* . . . divine Fanny, with evolutions extremely efficacious upon the feelings."

Fanny Elssler, after having won a European triumph as a dancer, came to New York, in 1840, fearing that the American prudes would object to her abbreviated skirts. And there was reason for her fear. Only a few years earlier a Parisian ballet had caused great excitement in America. Women had screamed at the sight of skirts which did not touch the floor, and some of them had left the theatre, while it had been perfectly clear that the men were profoundly moved. But the divine Elssler, as we can see from Beecher's sarcasm, danced before large and appreciative audiences. The newspaper critics, in their ecstasy, pronounced her chaste as well as graceful and altogether agreeable. Not only in New York, but in such possibly more modest cities as Boston and Philadelphia, she scored a splendid success. If ministers spoke against her, they only did her a service by advertising her performances.

Such fiery sermons as this one of Beecher's served as the principal diversions of the pious. And the occasional spicy references to forbidden things were much bolder than the great majority of stage entertainments contained. But there were some exceptions

FANNY ELLSLER

After a contemporary lithograph.

to the generalization that the commercial showmen of this period presented generally virtuous and dull performances. In the 1840's *tableaux vivants* appeared in New York. The women who took part in them were lightly bedraped, and imaginative young men were confronted with the illusion of nudity. In one place a charge of a dollar each was made for the privilege of looking through a gauze at what were advertised to be naked ladies. A moral Bowery mob invaded such a place of amusement on Canal Street, chasing the models, who were indubitably separated from nakedness by tights, out into the street. The New York *Sunday Mercury*, in an issue of 1848, asked what had become of

> Those nice *tableaux vivants*
> Of beautiful young ladies, *sans*
> Both petticoats and pants,
> Who, scorning fashion's shifts and whims,
> Did nightly crowds delight,
> By showing up their handsome limbs
> At fifty cents a sight.

Some of the showmen had been criminally prosecuted, and others considered it advisable to tone down their exhibits.

The serious drama did not fare very well in America in the period before the Civil War. However, farces, burlesques, and melodramas in which very villainous villains came to egregiously horrible ends enjoyed a certain amount of popularity. The theatres of New York catered to the immigrants who were then pouring in rapidly, though they turned aside occasionally to offer plays which might be supposed attractive to educated people.

High society turned, in the late 1840's, to Italian opera. This was permitted to deal with illicit sexual relations for the reason that the audience was not supposed to understand exactly what was going on. Or perhaps it was respectable enough to be out of moral danger.

As for the vulgar, though the plays they saw made out chastity and virtue in general to be eminently desirable, they were confronted, in the places where they saw them, by hosts of harlots. We read of a theatre in which the gallery was empty because the manager had refused to issue passes to the prostitutes who ordinarily filled it. All the favorite minstrel songs of the period were sermons in praise of good morals. The actors and actresses were determined to prove themselves moral by what they said and sang, even though they could see painted faces and sly leers in the gallery. Obviously, the ministers had more to denounce than have those of their successors who still inveigh against the theatre. For now, though theatres present plays which mock at the Puritan virtues, they do not usually allow prostitutes to take the center of interest.

The theatregoers of the 1840's were sometimes unruly. The English actor Macready aroused the jealousy and the hatred of Forrest, who was an American favorite. Forrest's friends showed their loyalty to him by mobbing Macready. The New York crowds were always hostile to foreigners and aristocrats. And they were steadfast in the defense of virtue. Stage villains were in danger of being decorated with overripe fruit.

The New England prejudice against amusements was weakening. Merrill Ober of Monckton, Vermont, who was sixteen years old in 1848, then recorded in his Diary that he had been playing the flute for two years. And he was addicted to novels as well as to music, for he set down the fact that he had read *Jane Eyre*. On October seventh he wrote: "There was shows here last night, the Smith Boys and a Negroe. I did not go." The theatre was invading the rural fastnesses of Yankeedom.

But the country as a whole knew little of the practice of going out to have a good time. Most people were content with simple parties at home, if indeed they considered any pleasure except that resulting from the regular performance of religious duties proper. The population was shifting somewhat from country to city, and more people were coming within reach of commercialized amusements. Yet the United States was still overwhelmingly rural when the Civil War broke out.

New York had an international reputation for luxury in the period just preceding the War. Its women were reported to be very fashionably and expensively dressed. Philadelphia, which had been the gayest city in the country, was acquiring the reputation for sleepiness which still clings to it. Boston maintained its anxiety to keep youth from corruption. An orang-utan which was shown there had to have its loins decorously covered. Neither Philadelphia nor New York looked favorably upon masquerade balls when they first appeared in America, about 1830. A New York mob attacked such a ball in the interests of good morals, and a law was passed against the wearing of masks at public entertainments.

The prejudice against the theatre and against fiction that might possibly be considered frivolous ran strong in the middle of the century. In 1848 the New York *Herald* denounced the "vile and immoral literature" which was being circulated. Bulwer, Sue, and Dickens were among the objectionable authors named. The newspaper which was so anxious to preserve virtue was advertising at this time pills "which must not be used during pregnancy as they are certain to produce miscarriage during that period," as well as other abortifacients and contraceptives.

The *Herald* under the elder Bennett was what we should now call an example of yellow journalism carried to an extreme. It was said to derive its profits from blackmail and bribery. Yet Dickens was immoral in the eyes of its editors.

Scott and Cooper, too, were frowned upon by pietistic people. Some American young ladies retreated to the hayloft or other secret places to read *The Last of the Mohicans, Paul and Virginia,* and *The Vicar of Wakefield.* Nevertheless, the novelists found many readers, and many a book which now seems unbearably dull was then avidly absorbed. Clara Barton, who was born in 1821, was originally named Clarissa Harlowe Barton. The name was a tribute to a very long and homiletic piece of fiction. Later, Richardson's books lost some of their popularity in favor of the Victorian novels, which reached the American public in cheap reprints on which no royalty was paid to the authors. Byron continued to enjoy a wide circulation, although it was agreed on every hand that he was a very wicked person indeed. And, though irreligion ceased to be fashionable, there were readers of Tom Paine, mostly by way of a secret vice.

Many prominent laymen went quite as far as Beecher in condemning the theatre. The *Independent* spoke of it in 1854, as "an unmitigated evil." And there were still, at that time, American men and women who looked upon novels in the same way.

It is doubtful if the most humane of spinster aunts would now say—I don't know, though: perhaps they still do say—what Beecher exclaimed about eighty years ago: "Of cock-fighting, bear-baiting, and pugilistic contests, I need to speak but little. These are the desperate excitements of debauched men; but no man becomes desperately criminal, until he has become genteelly criminal." Bear baiting must be extremely rare nowadays; cock-fights occur secretly, though perhaps not seldom; and boxing matches are discussed on the financial page as well as in four or five pages elsewhere in a newspaper.

The rules under which prize fights were conducted before the Marquess of Queensberry devoted his genius to the task of reforming the sport may have admitted more brutality than is possible in present-day pugilistic exhibitions. Certainly the crowds that attended the matches were less genteel than those which patronize the sport to-day. In the peaceful days before the Civil War, no reformer, no prophet, no madman ventured to conceive of days when decent women would attend professional boxing matches.

Hordes of pickpockets attended the old prize fights, for the sporting gentlemen often had fat wallets. At one of the early American matches, it is said, hundreds of emptied purses were flung into the ring just before the boxers appeared. It was a not altogether pleasing exhibition of dexterity. Since it was illegal to present a boxing match, police protection for the spectators could hardly be expected.

Beecher commended the ladies of Brooklyn and Cincinnati who refused to attend horse races. It was true, he said, the English-women did watch such races, but he was glad that his female auditors were in many ways stricter than foreign women. Neither men nor women, he believed, should have anything to do with "violent amusements which congregate indolent and dissipated men, by ministering intense excitement. The reasonings applied to the theatre, with some modifications, apply to the circus, to promiscuous balls, to night-revelling, bacchanalian feasts, and to other similar indulgences."

Beecher gave special warnings to country boys who might have occasion to visit large cities. They were enjoined to guard against "lynx-eyed procurers" of all sorts of evil pleasures. They "know the city, they know its haunts, they know its secret doors, its blind passages, its spicy pleasures, its racy vices, clear down to the mudslime of the very bottom."

Such language was not, of course, meant to apply only to men who might lead the innocent country lads into brothels. Such bad company as might be found at theatres, balls, circuses, and race courses would eventually lead an honest youth into all evils. As a matter of political economy, Beecher suggested, it was unwise "to support a growing class of improvident idlers," people who produced nothing more tangible than amusement and relief from care.

At the end of his impassioned sermon Beecher addressed (only rhetorically, I should say) actors and actresses, jockeys and boxers and gamblers: "In the bosom of that everlasting storm which rains perpetual misery in Hell shalt thou, CORRUPTER OF YOUTH! be forever hidden from our view: and may God wipe out the very thought of thee from our memory."

In Augusta, Maine, between 1835 and 1840, a hot controversy raged about a woman who was prominent in matters auxiliary to the work of the Congregationalist church. She permitted a sewing society of "misses between the ages of ten and fifteen" to dance in her house with boys, while her own daughter furnished the music. The deacons became exceedingly angry over this practice, and they were not mollified even by her offer to resign from the church. They insisted that she had no right to leave it of her own accord, for they were anxious to discipline her for encouraging immoral amusements.

In some parts of the United States, lotteries were strongly condemned. Elsewhere, they were used for procuring funds to pay for public works of various kinds. In New Orleans the license fees required of gambling houses were used to support an orphan asylum.

Pennsylvania prohibited lotteries in 1833. When private enterprises of this sort were found to be about as common as before, the Pennsylvania Society for the Suppression of Lotteries was formed and undertook the task of gathering evidence against them. A number of other states passed antilottery laws in the '30's and '40's. Stock-exchange speculation was unfamiliar to most Americans in 1830, but it came increasingly into public notice during the following decades. Perhaps the fact that lotteries of the North became illicit and therefore undependable had something to do with this. But it was more intimately connected with a great industrial expansion.

When the Civil War broke out, Missouri had a state lottery, and private lotteries were permitted in Kentucky and Delaware. This form of gambling was prohibited north of the border states. The Southern states were, in general, less convinced of the need for laws against gaming.

The steamers on the Mississippi were scenes of much card playing. The stakes were reputed to be larger on those boats which passed between the slave states. The cotton planters of the lower South were very little inclined to be precise about minor moral matters. This region in 1850, as William E. Dodd says, "had been and still was an outwardly irreligious, dram-drinking, and dueling section." Neither its Catholic nor its Episcopalian clergymen were in the habit of preaching against card playing and betting on horse races. Among the poor whites of the Southern foothills and mountains religious fervor continued to be strong. These people were Presbyterians, Baptists, or Methodists. They enjoyed the spiritual drunkenness of religious revivals, and the material intoxication which often was present at the camp meetings also.

Fighting, whether in formal duels or in more or less unpremeditated affrays, was an important part of the life of Southerners of all classes. It occurred often at the revivals among the mountaineers. Many of them considered fiddling on Sunday a dreadful crime, but thought nothing of mayhem or murder. Indeed, these things were, under certain conditions, considered highly virtuous. Hard drinking remained characteristic of the

Southern mountaineers even after it ceased to be respectable in most parts of the country.

By 1830 New England Puritanism had declined to a considerable extent in the Yankee states themselves, but it remained dominant in many rural districts. The New England conscience might be seen in action not only in the villages of Maine and Massachusetts, but also in upper New York, in New Jersey, and in Ohio. Mrs. Trollope, who lived for a time in Cincinnati, reported that it was illegal there to play cards or billiards, and that any person who sold a pack of playing cards was liable to a heavy fine. This somewhat critical English observer thought, indeed, that the ministers who preached against worldly diversions had more influence with the women than with the men. Still, Cincinnati remained moral very much after the fashion of colonial New England until it was invaded by immigrants, most of them German-speaking, who brought with them a philosophy of life which transformed matters.

Some American cities, including Washington, had antigambling laws which applied only, or with particular force, to the free negroes. The tendency to lay special restrictions upon the conduct of liberated slaves, which appeared in the United States long before the outbreak of the Civil War, was destined to have great importance in the history of American legislation and moral standards.

There were many discussions, all over the country, about the proper manner of observing Sunday. In 1830, so far as surface indications went, Protestant sentiment prevailed in the greater part of the United States. Agnosticism and deism seemed to be far less common than they had been thirty years before. Most people agreed that the first day of the week should be kept sacred; by this they meant that ordinary worldly pursuits and amusements should not then be pursued, except in case of necessity. But they were inclined to be less fanatical about the matter than their ancestors had been in colonial times. At Cincinnati in 1849 the Jewish clothing dealers were permitted to keep their shops open on Sunday. This date brings us, indeed, into the period of German influence. Immigration changed many things; and it became impossible, for instance, for chains to be stretched across the streets of New York to prevent the passage of vehicles while church services were going on.

New Orleans refused to look upon Sunday through puritanical eyes. Its people went to the theatre and listened to music, which was played on the streets as well as in halls, on that day. Although many English-speaking persons came into the state of

A BROADWAY SUNDAY SACRED CONCERT IN NEW YORK

A drawing by Alfred Fredericks to illustrate one of a series of "Sketches of the People Who Oppose Our Sunday Laws" in *Harper's Weekly*, 1859.

Louisiana, they did not greatly change its moral standards. In fact, the whole region along the Gulf of Mexico was liberal.

Elsewhere, pious owners of stagecoach lines refused to operate them on Sunday. Those who were less scrupulous often found their way barred by literal or figurative chains. Some of the Sunday restrictions broke down in the 1830's. More stagecoaches and ferryboats became available for those who insisted on profaning the day, and the barriers in front of churches disappeared. Though ministers almost howled in their disapproval and disappointment, post offices were kept open for an hour each Sunday in order that mail might be received.

In 1846 New Jersey adopted a stringent Sunday law. Among the things forbidden on the first day of the week were fishing, driving, sledding, and "fiddling or other music for the sake of merriment." A decade later the *Independent* protested when the Brooklyn City Railroad Company received permission to operate its horse cars on Sunday. There was much rejoicing among the godly when the directors of the Company decided not to avail themselves of this privilege. And a number of attempts were made to keep railroads engaged in interstate commerce from being permitted to operate their trains on the first day of the week.

During the Civil War the courts of Massachusetts decided that the laws of the state required the Sabbath to be kept, even if serious waste was involved in doing this. The conviction of two brothers who had gathered up seaweed flung upon the shore in a storm was upheld, though they showed that the weed would probably have been washed away if they had waited until Monday.

§ 2

For most of the foreigners who came to the United States in the decades preceding the Civil War, the puritanical manners of America were of prime interest. Almost all the books they wrote had something to say about the morality of the country. According to the consensus of opinion of the travelers from abroad, sexual depravity was comparatively rare in the United States, or at least there were fewer outward manifestations of it in American than in English cities.

We are, of course, dealing with a country which already covered a wide area and in which manners and morals were far from uniform, and with a period of thirty-five years, from 1830 to 1865, in which many changes occurred. Making allowances for variations of all sorts, we may say that the reputation of being a libertine was a great social disadvantage in the United States. Though fornication and adultery were no longer punished by law

[505]

with the old colonial severity, they commonly led to social ostracism. Women who were known to have offended in such a regard were regarded by self-righteous people as utterly without the pale.

Frances E. Willard, in her autobiography called *Glimpses of Fifty Years*, reveals the attitude of a girl brought up in a devout Christian home: "When I was first a boarding-school pupil at Evanston, in 1858, a young woman who was not chaste came to the college through some misrepresentation, but was speedily dismissed; not knowing her degraded status I was speaking to her, when a school-mate whispered a few words of explanation that crimsoned my face suddenly; and grasping my dress lest its hem should touch the garments of one so morally polluted, I fled from the room." Mrs. Willard thought she had become more tolerant later in life, and that she would have been somewhat more kindly to the poor girl; but she assumed self-righteously that it was a sound instinct which drove her from vice and from the person who personified it for her.

America in the middle third of the nineteenth century was very proud of its own virtues. It was "God's country," marked out for moral superiority. And a feeling of material superiority was arising, as the unique resources of the United States were revealed. Other countries might starve, but the American people felt that they were under particular divine protection. When a panic came, people wondered how they had offended God; and they proceeded to devote more of their time to religion, and even to give larger contributions to the churches and the societies for the improvement of morals. The depression of 1857 was followed by a revival the next year which led Bostonians to give up hard liquor and cards and frivolous books, and which was even more effective in New York.

It was the ordinary American belief that good morals and good profits went together. Thus, in the 1830's New England employers opposed the reduction of working hours to ten hours daily because, as they said, too much free time would be an encouragement to vice. In Lowell great care was taken to preserve the chastity of the mill operatives. Girls were discharged, as one eulogist of the system proudly announced, "on suspicion of criminal conduct, association with suspected persons, and general light behavior and conversation." Girls were suspected of criminal conduct or light conversation if they were believed to be expressing dissatisfaction with the existing wages and working conditions. If one of the operatives considered the hours too long, it was evident that she was thinking of the villainies she could commit in part of the time.

Most of the mill girls came from rural homes into cities where the temptations were somewhat different, and perhaps stronger. It is hard to tell how far the elaborate precautions thrown about them by some of the pious millowners were effective. James Truslow Adams, probably the leading authority on the social history of New England, thinks that morality among the factory hands began to deteriorate after about 1840, when the stocks of the textile companies were more widely distributed. But there were other factors than the ownership of the mills at work. In the early days the superintendents and foremen enjoyed almost autocratic powers, and they could threaten refractory girls with the whip; later, they were left only with the figurative whip of dismissal.

Even this is said to have been enough to put the attractive girls at their disposal. Indeed, such a condition has not yet entirely disappeared from some New England mills. And it exists in many other industrial centers in America and elsewhere.

Southern apologists for negro slavery were accustomed to make much of the immorality which they alleged to exist in the Northern factory centers. Certainly there was much over-crowding in the tenements of Boston, Lowell, and other industrial cities. A physician reported in 1849, "I have found from six to forty or more in one house of two stories, eleven or more in one room constantly, and eight in one bed (women and men)." A Virginian who was reproached with the moral evils of slavery could retort with an account of the slums of Lowell, and ask about the chastity of eight women and men in one bed. And we, looking back eight decades or so, are forced to admit the justice of each *tu quoque*, and reflect that perhaps America was not quite so moral as she thought she was.

Thomas Colley Grattan, an Englishman who wrote of *Civilized America* in 1859, said that American girls with their "flaunting air" and "rapid, dashing step" were sometimes mistaken for prostitutes by foreigners unfamiliar with the country. But, generally speaking, the modest virgin of the United States did everything possible to distinguish herself from the woman who had "fallen" and become dishonored. It seems that such freedom of manners as actually existed was due to the fact that most of the country was close to the frontier in time and place.

Even the fashion characteristic of the frontier in colonial New England, bundling, lingered on until Civil War days, the Germans or "Dutch" of Pennsylvania perhaps remaining faithful to it longest. But side by side with pioneer conceptions of womanhood appeared a glorification of the delicate female who fainted away on the slightest provocation and would have considered it the height of immodesty to acknowledge tacitly, by taking exercise, that she possessed a body. Complaints occasionally arose that women were in danger of losing their modesty because of the foreign novels they were reading.

James Silk Buckingham thought that the United States, in 1840, knew little of romantic love. But if this was the case, at least there were compensations: "At the same time it must be admitted that there are fewer infidelities, elopements, and separations in married life in America than in most countries of the Old World." I do not think this English visitor was entirely accurate in his generalizations. We can find abundant evidence that Americans fell in love early and often. The pecuniary interest in marriage seems to have been considerably less in the United States, especially in the newer portions, than in Great Britain.

There is evidence enough to support the contention that American husbands and wives were becoming restive in the 1840's and 1850's. And it is a fact which can be verified from the public records that divorces were more common in the United States than in England in the middle of the century. Many states adopted long lists of grounds for divorce, and for a period of years Indiana judges were permitted to grant divorces for any

THE COQUETTE, STYLE OF 1851

From *Godey's Lady's Book.*

reason which they considered proper. Indiana had then such a reputation for the granting of divorces as Nevada now enjoys.

In 1860 Hundley wrote: "The socialists and free lovers argue against marriage because married people are always running off to Indiana to be divorced." Robert Dale Owen defended the state of Indiana, arguing that its laws supported good morals, while New York and New England, with less liberal divorce laws, supported hosts of prostitutes. There were no divorces at all in South Carolina, but husbands were permitted to console themselves with concubines if they tired of their wives. In a few extreme cases, married women were treated, in their own homes, as inferior to the colored slave women whom their husbands preferred.

Even in those parts of the country where divorces were easy to obtain, genteel society was usually closed to divorced people. It is true that there were many unconventional circles, and that there were agitators everywhere who questioned the ordinary standards of respectability.

Allowing for such exceptions, we may say that external morality ruled during the period we are here considering. As we have seen, a young man might go to the theatre and wink at a harlot in the gallery, but he would meanwhile hear chastity glorified by the actors. "The deep concealment of vice in the community lessened infinitely the temptation to it," Schouler writes of this period. But it is hardly true that "vice" was concealed, except in some of the rural districts. Then, as later, farm boys who did not visit the city were unlikely to see much of prostitution, but this does not mean that they were never tempted to illicit sexual relations.

On the plantations of the South it was a matter of course that a young master should choose an attractive colored woman to be his concubine. There is an account of a slave girl thus honored who went to her white minister for advice. She had learned from his sermons that chastity was a priceless jewel. The clergyman told her that her first duty was to obey her master. He could not very well have told her anything else and continued to preach in the South. Indeed, religious instruction for the

[509]

negroes was considered valuable according to the extent of the emphasis laid on the duty of obedience and submission.

The coupling of black and white was often motivated by thoughts of profit as well as by lust. Douglass tells how his owner in Maryland locked up his white foreman and a young negress in the same bedroom at night. A mulatto, above all an attractive slave woman of light color, was especially valuable. Sometimes white men were offered stud fees for the children they begot upon negresses. But in the Southern ports there were brothels with slave prostitutes, and the sailors who patronized them were required to pay, not offered the opportunity of being paid. The fertility of harlots is not great.

In the fields where the negroes worked and in the huts where they slept, little heed was paid to the maintenance of the decencies valued by white people. According to various learned jurists of the South, chastity was not a virtue for slaves, and an enslaved negress had no reputation to lose. It mattered little, then, if her rags revealed her sexual attractions instead of concealing them, or if she was never able to enjoy any privacy.

Slaves often married, but the fact that a minister united a man and a woman did not mean that their owner or owners might not separate them. In numerous instances masters paired off the blacks without bothering to inquire about their own preferences. Under such conditions it is not surprising that the slaves usually acquired an utter indifference to what white people spoke of loftily as the sanctity of marriage. Adultery on the part of a negro was practically never punished, and it was often enjoined. Prudery was practically unknown among the slaves, except the few domestic servants who were permitted to ape the manners of their mistresses and their masters.

The children of Southern planters came, very soon after birth, under the influence of mammies and of the various slaves on the place. They heard the negroes' stories of talking bunnies and haunted houses and also of love and desire. For the slaves had not acquired any taboos about such things.

One of the principal benefits which used to be attributed to the system of slavery in the South was the supposed assurance it provided for the chastity of the white women. That is to say, white men had access to negresses, and it was supposed that they would not therefore seduce or rape women of their own color.

Sexual relations between white women and negroes seem always to have been rare, although stories occasionally circulated about aristocratic ladies who gave birth to mulattoes. Some Southern women derived pleasure from flogging and torturing their slaves, male and female.

Many of the most cruel slaveowners were of Northern origin, and it may be that the opportunity to inflict pain upon human beings was one of the things that attracted them to the South. It is sometimes contended that slavery brutalized the Southern character and was responsible for the bloody duels and the indifference about human life. Not all the masters were cruel, it is true, but those who were found themselves practically unrestrained. On some plantations, women were expected to do fully as much work as the men who toiled beside them, and received the same lashing if they lagged behind. Pregnancy made little difference in the requirement. It was, however, a matter of good business not to overwork or underfeed valuable slaves, and most owners appreciated the fact.

The white women of the South were not supposed to do any gainful work at all. As a matter of fact, the wives of planters usually had a great many duties to perform. Their slaves were almost always undependable when it came to doing anything the least bit complicated. The more domestic servants there were, the greater were the difficulties confronting the housewife. On the plantations the women often found themselves very much isolated. They had to attend to minor injuries, to care for the sick, and to handle many emergencies unaided.

Perhaps the long distance between manor houses in the rural districts of the South and the difficulties of transportation were more responsible than slavery for the infrequence of adulterous relations. But relatives and friends were hospitably received, and some houses were almost always full of visitors. Married women of the South, even those who lived in the largest cities, were supposed to stay away from balls and similar functions, though their husbands might attend them. In short, their position resembled somewhat that of the wives in Oriental countries. A few ventured to complain that they were but slaves themselves, occupying a position not entirely different from that of the colored women whose charms attracted their husbands.

Especially in New Orleans, some of the mulatto and quadroon women who were concubines of white men were treated virtually as their wives. Their color barred them from going to certain places and from enjoying various privileges. However, if they had been the white wives of white men, their movements would have been still more closely regulated. To New Orleans came, from all over the country, men who were anxious to enjoy life and able to purchase luxuries. Mistresses ranging in color from black to white, with sometimes a dash of red, were easily available. So also, indeed, were women for more transitory sexual relations.

The quadroon mistresses had balls of their own, paid a great deal of attention to the latest fashions, and usually lived, if not in luxury (though this was by no means uncommon), at least in substantial comfort. Those who were slaves stood, however, always in a very precarious position. A New Hampshire man came to Louisiana and lived there for twenty years with a quadroon woman whom he treated as though she had been his wife. At his death his heirs sold his three daughters, who appeared to be of pure white blood, into slavery to be used as prostitutes.

In some parts of the South the poor white women enjoyed as a class a very poor reputation for chastity. This was especially true of those who went to work in the mills which began to appear shortly before the Civil War, or who accepted other gainful employment. If a white woman sank so low as to work in a factory, it was felt in the South of those days, she cared nothing more for her reputation. Labor belonged to the negro, and even the male "crackers" and poor whites in general felt it was below their dignity to work, except at hunting and fishing and perhaps the distilling of a little whiskey. There could, of course, be no serious belief in the dignity of labor when this was assigned to slaves.

Prostitution existed in America before the Revolution, but it aroused comparatively little attention until about 1830. In 1838 the New York *Transcript* announced: "The business of supplying brothel-keepers with unsuspecting victims has been adopted by the intelligence-office keepers in Boston."

Buckingham says that there were at this time fewer street-walkers proportionately in such cities as New York, Philadelphia, and Baltimore than in London, Liverpool, Edinburgh, and other large British cities. New York was generally reputed to be the least moral of American cities with the exception of New Orleans, which was so different that it hardly seemed to be in the same country.

Buckingham thought there were fewer opportunities for love-making in the United States than in Europe, because, among other reasons, American men seemed to be absorbed in business all day long. But he observed that revival meetings were often tinged with amorous colors. He was told that the preachers sometimes made love to excited females, and it did not excite any wonder in him that laymen used the same tactics.

President Lincoln was fond of telling a story which had a wide circulation in the West. It was about the Civil War recruit who was asked to name his father. His answer was, "Captain, sir, I guess I'm just a camp-meetin' baby."

The West of Lincoln's youth was not extremely delicate about matters of speech and behavior. The prevailing conditions did not allow the elaboration of gentility. Many a cabin consisted of but one room, and had in it only one bed. And it was not rare for the father to remove his clothing in the presence of his daughters, or even before guests, male and female. Lincoln himself, who leaned in some respects toward puritanical moral standards, was by no means a prude.

The best contemporary account of prostitution in the period here being considered is by Dr. W. W. Sanger. A large part of his *History of Prostitution* deals with a survey of conditions in the city of New York in the 1850's. Sanger had, as resident physician on Blackwell's Island, some special advantages in finding out the facts. The women were, to a large extent, recent immigrants, especially from Ireland. Others had come to New York from factory towns in New England and the Middle States. Sanger thought that poverty was the largest single factor in producing harlots. There was striking luxury in New York, but there were ragged barefoot girls on the streets who watched the splendid carriages go by. Domestic servants received, in the state of New York in the year 1850, an average weekly salary of $1.05 in addition to board. The monthly wage of women employed in the cotton mills of that state averaged $9.68; in Massachusetts it was a little higher, $13.60. To translate these figures into present buying power, perhaps we can consider them equivalent to weekly wages of the same amount as paid to-day. By way of comparison: in the 1850's as much as $9,100 annually was paid in the city of New York for the rental of a furnished house used in prostitution. The dollar of those days did not, then, go extremely far. The woman who had to pay for food and lodging out of ten dollars a month had little money for luxuries.

For the ordinary prostitute of foreign origin in New York, it was impossible to obtain as much by means of hard labor as through harlotry. Some of them were far from their friends and relatives. A considerable part had been made to emigrate from Europe by the police, or at least encouraged to go by the payment of their passage. The ships which brought immigrants to the United States took from one to three months to cross the Atlantic. During this period the women had little privacy. It is said that some of the officers and men were accustomed to seduce or even force attractive female passengers. And there were often agents on board for the special purpose of gathering recruits for the American brothels.

New York possessed all sorts of houses of prostitution, catering to various social classes and to purses of all degrees of thickness. The Germans operated and frequented quiet beer saloons where the waitresses were first of all harlots. There were dance halls which were little more than the showrooms or front parlors of brothels. There were cheap, dirty, noisy, riotous places along the waterfront frequented by sailors and poor workmen. At the other end of the scale, there were elaborate, floridly-decorated places where much champagne was consumed. And there were unobtrusive houses of assignation, where married women and extremely genteel courtesans met their lovers. There were "panel houses" where concealed doors admitted stealthy thieves at night to pick the pockets of unwary gentlemen from the country who had been attracted by pretty streetwalkers. And there were cottages in which the concubines of wealthy married men lived more luxuriously than their wives.

Venereal disease was causing concern to the public health officials, and some were proposing the establishment of a sanitary police to be charged with the hygienic regulation of brothels and other places where prostitution was carried on. Many good people felt that it would be worse for the traffic to have an implied license than it was for the harlots to spread disease unchecked because of the lack of official control. The police made occasional half-hearted attempts to extirpate prostitution, but they did not expect to have much success, and they never did. Dr. Sanger thought that prostitution was on the increase in New York in the 1850's. Times of depression seemed to add to the number of prostitutes in the city, though they cannot have increased their patronage much or made their profession more lucrative. There were many wild guesses about the number of harlots in the city, running as high as one in every thirty of the population, including men, women, and children. It is needless to say that this was much exaggerated.

§ 3

Sanger considered poverty the primary cause of prostitution, with immoral literature next. One English novelist, whom he declined to name for fear of increasing the circulation of his works, was, he said, available in many paper-covered books with lurid illustrations. These came within the letter of the law but skillfully appealed to the passions. There were, too, translations of dreadful French novels. And there were, in New York, venders of photographs which were sufficient to corrupt innocent youth. Fortunately, some of the men who suggested by means of winks and leers that they were offering obscene publications really handed over sealed packages containing religious tracts, at the same time bidding the country boys who bought them keep them concealed until reaching a private place.

Dr. Sanger was anxious that young men should be kept away from all literature dealing with vice: "And here a word in regard to the bad effects of, so called, classical studies. Are they not sometimes acquired at the risk of outraged delicacy or undermined moral principles? Mythology, in particular, introduces our youth to courtesans who are described as goddesses, and goddesses who are but courtesans in disguise. Poetry and history as frequently have for their themes the ecstasies of illicit love as the innocent joys of pure affection. Shall these branches of instruction be totally ignored? By no means; but let their harmless flowers and wholesome fruit alone be culled for youthful minds, to the utter exclusion of all poisonous ones, however beautiful."

This was no mere personal idiosyncrasy. The good people of the United States were afraid of words that were not decently bedraped, just as they were of nude statues. When Horatio Greenough made a group of "Chanting Cherubs" for J. Fenimore Cooper, the naked babies aroused great moral indignation. Then came a half-draped statue of Washington, which also brought about much sermonizing on the part of clerical and lay pulpiteers. Greenough exclaimed: "Those infantile forms roused an outcry of censure which seemed to have exhausted the source from which it sprang, since all the harlot dancers who have found an El Dorado in these Atlantic cities have failed to reawaken it. I say seem to have exhausted it, for the same purblind squeamishness which gazed without alarm at the lascivious Fandango awoke with a roar at the colossal nakedness of Washington's breast."

There seems to be something typically American about this speech, this method of defending one's own morality by showing that others who are really more vicious have not been attacked. But perhaps it is human rather than American. Yet there was a heavy note of Puritanism in Greenough's justification of nude statuary. He was not called upon to denounce female dancers. After all, the citizens of New York and Philadelphia who thought the divine Elssler more attractive than Washington's naked breast were displaying good taste, whatever may be said about the excellence of their morality.

When Captain Marryat visited Governor Everett of Massachusetts, he saw in his house a cast of the Apollo Belvedere which was ordinarily covered "in compliance with general opinion." In the 1840's "The Greek Slave" by Hiram Powers was displayed at Cincinnati. A committee of clergymen examined it to see if it was dangerous to public morality, and decided that it might safely be shown. Probably this tolerance was due to the fact that the statue aroused public indignation against the Turk whom it shows offering for sale a naked and manacled Greek Christian woman. The nudity was excused by the moral purpose. Later, other nudes by Powers found their way into American museums. And Palmer was also responsible for making the people of the United States familiar with nude statues. By 1860 there were few articulate protests against this particular form of "immorality."

Almost all the foreigners who visited America in the three or four decades before the outbreak of the Civil War commented on the prevailing prudery, which was especially characteristic of women. Mrs. Trollope tells of a resort at Cincinnati, "a garden where the people go to eat ices, and to look at roses," which had a sign representing a Swiss peasant girl. The petticoat this Swiss girl wore was indecently short, for (realistically) it revealed her ankles. The owner of the garden would have been ruined had he not hastened, as soon as the cries of outraged virtue came to his ears, to have a sign painter add a flounce to the petticoat.

Among the tabooed words in the United States, according to Mrs. Trollope, was "shirt." Delicacy was shown in a variety of ways, as by the reluctance of young men and women to picnic together on the grass. At a ball which she attended, refreshments

[517]

were served separately to the two sexes, the men being much better accommodated than the women. And this, Mrs. Trollope thought, was typical of the country. But other visitors from abroad received a very different impression about the status of women. Most of them (being themselves of the male sex) complained that the women were too much indulged. Mrs. Trollope tells us that the men of Cincinnati used to do the marketing, saving their wives a great deal of trouble. She thought American ladies were unduly fond of false hair, and she disapproved of their custom of applying large quantities of pulverized starch to their faces.

In 1837 a group of churchmen of New England especially deplored "the intimate acquaintance and promiscuous conversation of females with regard to things which ought not to be named." This is interesting, because we should otherwise find scant evidence that the women of New England at that time were informed or talkative about sexual matters. A decade later, Harriet Hosmer, who was to become renowned as a sculptor, had to go from her home in Boston to St. Louis in order to be able to study anatomy. Very few females had any accurate knowledge of the reproductive function, and most New England ladies seem to have been properly grateful that they were not defiled with such information.

American newspapers hesitated about publishing the news that a child had been born, fearing that their readers' sense of propriety would be outraged. It was with fear and trembling that a married woman went about the delicate task of informing her mother that she was with child. The husband simply had to discover the fact for himself.

"Leg" was everywhere a forbidden word, and Marryat says that it might not even be uttered with regard to the supporting members of a piano. He tells us of a visit he paid to a ladies' seminary where the pianoforte had each of its four limbs clothed in "modest little trousers, with frills at the bottom of them." J. S. Buckingham found that it was indelicate to mention the tail, the hip, or the thigh of any animal. He records that a preacher at Athens, Georgia, bowdlerized the Bible, reading "stomach" for

THE GREEK SLAVE

By Hiram Powers. Courtesy of the Corcoran Gallery.

"belly" and "a certain fowl" for "cock." "Corset" was even more objectionable than "shirt." In fact, the foreigner, unless he was familiar with a long list of words and phrases that were considered indelicate and the euphemisms, if any, that might be used for them, was in constant danger of embarrassing himself and any young ladies who might be in his company.

The Lady's Guide to Perfect Gentility, written by Emily Thornwell and published in 1856 at New York and Cincinnati, tells us a great deal about the manners considered appropriate to women in the years just preceding the Civil War. "A lady ought to adopt a decent and measured gait"; for, according to this oracle, "too great hurry injures the grace which ought to characterize her. She should not turn her head on one side or on the other, especially in large towns or cities, where this bad habit seems to be an invitation to the impertinent. A lady should not present herself alone in a library, or museum, unless she goes there to study, or work as an artist."

After twilight no young lady should walk alone, if she wanted to be considered perfectly genteel. Women who went visiting in the evening were advised to ask their husbands or other relatives to call for them—"you will, in this way, avoid all inconveniences and be entirely free from the harsh criticism which is sometimes indulged in, especially in small towns, concerning even the most innocent acts."

Young women, whether married or not, were expected to take considerable pains to keep themselves out of the reach of suspicion: "A married or young lady should never leave a party, even to go into an adjoining room, without either her mother or a married lady to accompany her." We must, of course, realize that such pieces of advice given in books of etiquette are often counsels of perfection; by no means in all social circles were the women quite so careful of their repute for discretion.

Chaperonage was strict in some parts of the North, and especially so in the aristocratic assemblies of the South. In Richmond, as De Leon says in his reminiscences of the days before the war, boy and girl were never supposed to go buggy riding alone, or to make love in a parlor from which all but they had fled. In the less pretentious families of the North the daughters of the house were usually permitted to entertain their beaux without any sort of interference or supervision on the part of their parents.

A very strict view of the careful manners required of females is presented in an anonymous book called *Etiquette for Ladies*

THE FORTE OF A FASHIONABLE FEMALE

A caricature in *Yankee Notions* of the '50's.

published at Philadelphia in 1838: "Young married ladies are at liberty to visit by themselves their acquaintances, but they cannot present themselves in public without their husband or an aged lady. They are at liberty, however, to walk with young married ladies or unmarried ones, while the latter should never walk alone with their companions. Neither should they show themselves, except with a gentleman of their family; and then he should be a near relation of respectable age."

It is indisputable, nevertheless, that genteel young ladies sometimes walked out with young men of less than respectable age, even in such conservative and decent places as Boston and Cambridge. Dr. Oliver Wendell Holmes remarks, in *The Autocrat of the Breakfast Table,* "When a young female wears a flat circular side-curl, gummed on each temple,—when she walks with a male, not arm in arm, but his arm against the back of hers,—and when she says 'Yes?' with a note of interrogation, you are generally safe in asking her what wages she gets, and who the 'feller' was you saw her with."

Observe that Holmes apparently found nothing wrong in the young man and young woman who walked out together arm in arm. They might belong to the best circles, and there would be no need to assume that the female belonged to the working classes. There was at this time, in Massachusetts almost as much as in the South, a deep chasm between women who worked and those who remained at home.

The details of ladylike behavior were many and complex, and in some instances very different from those now in effect. It was generally agreed that a lady might properly make efforts to keep the hem of her dress from being soiled by deep mud, even by lifting it slightly above the ankles, but to use more than one hand in doing this was considered extremely vulgar.

Everywhere in Europe, in the middle of the nineteenth century, women of social position were supposed to be very circumspect. Hence, when foreign visitors tell us about the free, swinging gait of the American girls, we must make due allowance for their standards of comparison. For anything that might be construed as boldness was distinctly under the ban on both sides of the Atlantic.

In the higher and middle classes of the United States, extreme formality was the rule in conversation and correspondence. Yet the books of etiquette were already advising ladies to be natural, and perhaps there was a tendency away from stiffness in the decades just preceding the Civil War. Southern ladies and gentlemen were taught to be very polite. Perhaps they carried the matter to excess in some cases. The courtesy of New Orleans owed much to French and Spanish influences.

The manners of antebellum days were in certain respects not such as to gain the approval of fastidious people to-day. Emily Thornwell found it necessary to ask: "Now what must we think of those genteel people who never use the bath, or only once or twice a year wash themselves all over, though they change their linen daily?" And we may easily imagine the truth of her remark that "they have a something about them which lavender water does not entirely conceal."

She told ladies that it was stretching delicacy too far to dine with their gloves on, "unless their hands are not fit to be seen." And genteel females whose feet perspired badly were urged to change their stockings twice a week in winter and thrice in summer, and never to wear woolen stockings in hot weather. *The Lady's Guide to Perfect Gentility* tells how to make rouge from flowers, "white salve which may be used for paint," lip salve which imparts a red color, washes to improve the breath, and many other cosmetics.

We used, not long ago, to talk about "the great unwashed." In the 1840's and 1850's the proletarians might rather have been called "the great unperfumed." If their betters bathed once or twice a year, how often did they expose themselves to the dangers of colds and chills by washing their bodies with soap and water? And they were not accustomed to apply sweet scents to palliate their bodily odors. Nor did they change their linen daily—far from it.

Etiquette books of the '40's advised "the rising generation of elegants in America" to refrain from blowing their noses with their fingers. Smoking in public, they were told, was equally lacking in gentility. In the matter of general cleanliness the people of the United States seem not to have fallen behind the British except in so far as the greater use of tobacco, especially for chewing, made things worse.

J. S. Buckingham tells how he found the church pews in America full of tobacco juice. Dickens made himself very unpopular among Americans when he wrote, in the 1840's, about the disgust which he had felt at tobacco-chewing and promiscuous spitting while he visited the United States. Somewhat earlier, Mrs. Trollope had said, "I hardly know any annoyance so deeply repugnant to English feelings as the incessant, remorseless spitting of Americans." About the time of the Civil War a Harvard professor is reported to have been in the habit of saying to his students, "Those who expectorate in my presence need not expect to rate highly in my estimation." Two or three of the older Harvard professors now wax indignant over the coughing that sometimes interrupts their lecture; but since the departure of the cuspidor, the very thought of spitting upon a classroom floor has fled from Harvard Yard.

Mrs. Trollope wrote professedly of the *Domestic Manners of the Americans*. Her principal complaints were about the lack of refinement in the United States, manifested, for example, in the current habit of conveying food to the mouth on a knife, and in that of using a pocket knife in public to remove particles of food from between the teeth. The America with which she was most familiar was close to the frontier, as Cincinnati was in the years when she lived there. Mrs. Trollope objected, even more than to the use of the knife for purposes to which she was unaccustomed to see it put, to the social democracy of the West. She found it inconvenient and incongruous not to be able to get servants, and to have to put up with "help" who did not like to eat in the kitchen, and some of whom felt themselves, as good Americans, to be superior to all snobbish Englishwomen.

§ 4

Americans were not altogether unsophisticated in the 1830's. In 1833 Dr. Charles Knowlton of Massachusetts published a pamphlet called *Fruits of Knowledge*, in one chapter of which he discussed means of preventing conception. This work was later to arouse a controversy in England and to bring about a world-wide interest in neo-Malthusianism. Before the Civil War there was a considerable decline in American fecundity.

As we have seen, agents for preventing conception or inducing abortion were advertised in the newspapers of the '40's and the '50's.

De Bow, defending the morality of the South in 1857, thought the Northern states were going the way of decadent Rome. Women there were unchaste, he declared, and they were refusing "to no inconsiderable extent to undergo the pains of child-bearing."

In the cities there was a considerable exodus from private homes to hotels and boarding houses. Newly-married couples especially were moving into such places. Attractive apartment houses did not yet exist; and bride and groom, if they did not choose to live with parents or to go to the trouble and expense of keeping up a single house of their own, had no choice but to live in a hotel. The servant problem was not much different from what it is now, though the wages commonly paid to domestic workers in the middle of the nineteenth century seem infinitesimal in comparison with present rates. White women did not like to be subservient and preferred to work in factories rather than in kitchens. Though there were many laments about the decline of home life, it is not apparent that the masses of the American people were much affected by it.

Deploring the deterioration of the young is a habit which has been firmly established in America for a number of generations. A labor paper of 1834 groaned over "the lad of fourteen who struts and swaggers and smokes his cigar and drinks rum." And in the middle of the century there were many sermons and magazine articles which expressed horror at the lack of respect shown by children to their parents.

Undoubtedly, American boys and girls were allowed more freedom and more opportunities for individual development than the children of Great Britain and the European Continent. Yet the principle that children should be seen and not heard was greatly honored in the United States, and the hickory stick was considered the principal instrument of education in school and home. But children passed early into adulthood, for comparatively few spent long periods at the universities in preparation for professional careers, and marriages were still generally entered into in the teens.

The inferiority of women was taken for granted by most members of both sexes in the days before the Civil War. Catherine E. Beecher said: "Heaven has appointed to one sex the superior, and to the other the subordinate station, and this without reference to the character or conduct of either." The Scriptures clearly ordained that wives should be subject to their husbands and children should be kept under the rule of their parents. Common sense told people (at that time) just as clearly that men were superior in strength, both physical and mental, and in authority. A Methodist preacher was, in the 1840's, accustomed to give his wife a horsewhipping every few weeks in order to keep her in subjection and to cure her of the habit of scolding. This case was not typical, and we know there were many happy marriages in which even harsh words were rare; but the inferiority of wives and their dependence upon their husbands was recognized by law and public opinion. Apologists for slavery used to say that there was nothing unique about the position of the negroes in the South. They were, like wives and children in general, divinely ordained to be under the rule of their masters.

However, frontier conditions did much to improve the position of women. They worked together with their husbands, and often they were especially cherished for their rarity. In the older sections of the country most American business men found themselves so deeply engrossed in the study of how to make money that they had no time or interest left for culture. If they did not dismiss it entirely with a sneer, they left it to their wives. The result was that the higher education of women became inevitable. But before the Civil War the conservative people of America considered feminism a crazy fad, in the same class with the temperance movement, abolitionism, vegetarianism, communism, and free love. To be sure, there were some people who believed in all these things, or in several of them. And some of the mad theories were worked out in practice. It appeared, between 1845 and 1870, that anything might happen in the United States; and many things did. Even free love was tried out, here and there, on a small scale.

Many reformers considered it their Christian duty to work for the abolition of slavery and of the traffic in intoxicants. But a large part of them considered the subjection of women also part of their religion, and refused to let females have any active part in their organizations. Yet a book written by a woman contributed to the growth of abolitionist sentiment. And Harriet Beecher Stowe was not the only member of her sex who attained prominence in reform work. For instance, Dorothea Dix did a great deal to obtain more rational and more humane treatment of the mentally diseased.

Oberlin College, a coeducational institution of learning, gave degrees in the arts to a few women in the 1840's. Other colleges were established for women and girls, or were opened to both sexes on about the same terms. The first medical college for women was established in Boston in 1848. Although comparatively few girls attended institutions of university grade before the Civil War, many graduated from high schools, academies, and seminaries.

The year 1848 was important in the American feminist movement chiefly because of the Woman's Rights Convention then held at Seneca Falls, New York. Protests were voiced there about the legal inferiority of women and the right which husbands possessed to beat their wives and to dispose of their property at will. The demands of the convention, although most of them have been granted since, then excited considerable ridicule. When Mrs. Stanton went so far as to express the opinion that women should have the right to vote, most of the convention delegates were shocked. But legislation increasing the property rights of women became popular just before the Civil War, especially in the West.

At a convention of the teachers of New York State in 1853, although the female delegates outnumbered the male, they sat quietly and allowed themselves to be instructed by men speakers. Susan B. Anthony, after struggling to obtain a hearing, ironically answered the question that was before the meeting, why the profession of teaching was little honored. Naturally it stood in low estimation, she said, since even women were admitted to it.

Miss Anthony had a genius for arousing indignation. She told a public audience that women should not allow their husbands when drunk to add to the number of their children. That a maiden lady should talk about such matters! But the men who were

BLOOMERISM, AN AMERICAN CUSTOM

A cartoon by John Leech in *Punch*, 1851. Reproduced by permission of the Proprietors.

opposed to the new feminism did not always take care to express themselves delicately. They openly considered the possibility that emancipated ladies, married or unmarried, might give birth to children in court room or pulpit, and they went so far as to name the women to whom, as they supposed, this might happen.

The peace of America was disturbed by a dress-reform movement. Women were advised to discard their corsets and their long, heavy skirts. A few bold spirits appeared in public, and even went to church, in billowing trousers partially concealed by short skirts. A Mrs. Bloomer was one of the pioneers in wearing this costume, and she was daring enough to keep on appearing in public in trousers for some years after most of the women had taken theirs off. The trousers and skirt became known as the Bloomer costume, and the trousers worn by women in gymnasiums have since been known as bloomers. The dress agitation had virtually run its course by 1860, although there were some women who ventured to wear comparatively short skirts in the next decade.

Both women and men writers of the period preceding the Civil War were much concerned with moral problems. Some sang the praises of conventionality; others wished to be leaders of revolt, and yet revealed their Puritan education. There was one man who stood apart. Edgar Allan Poe considered morality altogether out of place in artistic representations. In 1842 he criticized Longfellow's poetry for its didacticism. The *Southern Literary Messenger* in 1851 remarked: "One of the first, if not the very first, characteristic of Longfellow's poetry is his earnest and sincere devotion to moral beauty, to truth. In this respect, his whole history, as embodied by his poetical records, is directly in opposition to the absurd theory of Poe, in his 'Lecture on Poetic Principles.'"

Some of the other New England poets dealt with controversial subjects and were less popular than Longfellow. Emerson was the most important writer among those who called themselves Transcendentalists but who shared little more than the general attitude of idealism with any school of German philosophy. There were many interesting minor figures among the Transcendentalists, who advanced all sorts of novel ethical views. Emerson himself was, on most occasions, opposed to extreme asceticism and to overrefinements of the Puritan conscience. He could defend art for its own sake:

Tell them, dear, that if eyes were made for seeing,
Then Beauty is its own excuse for being.

[528]

He could praise Eros, but, after all, it was a decorous and genteel Eros that found favor in his eyes. He could sing to Bacchus and wine, but he was very fond of praising Virtue. In short, he was a descendant of the Puritans; and no matter how much he revolted against their standards, he always retained their stamp.

Herman Melville fled from the physical and spiritual presence of puritanic America to cannibals and missionaries and whales. The world seemed to him internally rotten. Melville's pessimism was less attractive to his own contemporaries than it has been in the twentieth century.

The most startling literary figure that arose in America before the Civil War was Walt Whitman. In the '40's he was a journalist in New York, a sentimentalist and a reformer. He expressed his opposition to slavery, to capital punishment, and to the use of tea, coffee, and intoxicants. Whitman held for a time a newspaper position in New Orleans, and there he is supposed to have fallen in love with a quadroon woman. He returned to the North, and in 1855 his book of poems called *Leaves of Grass* was published.

Whitman presented a copy to Emerson, who sent him a private letter full of compliments. "I find it the most extraordinary piece of wit and wisdom that America has yet contributed," he wrote. "I find the courage of treatment that so delights us, and which large perception only can inspire. I greet you at the beginning of a great career."

Leaves of Grass then contained only part of the matter which was later to be found morally objectionable. Nevertheless, Emerson had not the slightest intention that his praise of the book should be made public. He was very much annoyed when Whitman allowed his letter to be published in the *New York Tribune*. For many people felt about the book as Whittier, the Quaker poet, did when he flung the copy that had been sent to him into the fire.

Edward Everett Hale wrote in the *North American Review* for January, 1856: "For the sake of showing that he is above every conventionalism, Mr. Whitman puts into the book one or two lines which he would not address to a woman nor to a company of men. There is not anything, perhaps, which modern usage would stamp as more indelicate than are some passages in Homer. . . . For all that, it is a pity that a book where everything else is natural should go out of the way to avoid the suspicion of being prudish."

Three editions of *Leaves of Grass* were issued before the Civil War, each more daring than its predecessor. But the general reading public was still hardly aware of its existence.

§ 5

Foreign visitors were complaining in those days, even as they do now, about the crass materialism dominant in America. Referring especially to business honesty, Mrs. Trollope said: "My honest conviction is that the standard of moral character is very much lower than in Europe." She observed that Americans boasted of their high morality and of the tricky business deals they had carried out in the same breath. And they never cared about anything except dollars and cents.

This was the America which produced Emerson and Whitman. Of course, it is possible for idealism and poetic feeling to exist in a country together with sharp commercial practice; for that matter, these things can coexist in the same individual. Perhaps the chief trouble with Mrs. Trollope's observations, though, was that she had more occasion to observe the seamy side of business in America than she had in England.

There were many testimonies to public and private dishonesty in the United States. Hawthorne, after having been surveyor of customs at Salem, remarked: "Neither the front nor the back entrance of the Custom-House opens on the road to Paradise." But from his account of the conditions he found existing there, it is evident that inefficiency was more usual in the government service, and more wasteful, than deliberate dishonesty. It was a generally accepted view that those persons who did much to help elect a high official were entitled to receive public office, whether or not they were qualified to carry out the work attached to it. Hawthorne himself was given his position as a reward for political services, and he lost it when his party was defeated.

Bribery and political corruption, although they had existed in the country since early colonial days, were not yet developed into the elaborate system characteristic of the period after the close of the Civil War. But in the late 1850's New York and other cities were thoroughly familiar with political graft. Rhodes thinks that the country was less honest in commercial matters before the War than after it, whereas political dishonesty was more prevalent after the Civil War. This much can safely be said, that large-scale frauds were almost impossible in the earlier days, because both business and government were then dealing with comparatively small sums of money.

Alexis de Tocqueville wrote of the United States in the 1830's: "I know of no country in which there is so little independence of mind and real freedom of discussion as in America." Here is another one of the accusations that have been made by a long succession of foreign observers. It probably has been more justified than some of the others.

New England orthodoxy became very much weakened in the decades before the Civil War. So also did New England aristocracy. Both remained, though, perhaps not much changed save in the important respect that they were left with comparatively little influence except in some of the remote rural regions. The public schools developed, and it was settled that education should generally expand under secular authority. Moral earnestness remained marked all through New England, even in those parts from which the sons of the Puritans were largely displaced by immigrants.

The Irish Catholics who came to Boston and other cities did not rebel against the prevailing asceticism; in some respects they even showed themselves willing to intensify it. The Catholics in the United States numbered less than one in a hundred of the population when the Constitution was adopted, but were six per cent of the people in the middle of the nineteenth century. Many fears were expressed about the dire results that might be expected to result from the influx of foreigners and Papists. And some politicians therefore found it expedient to talk of the necessity of saving the country for native Americans.

In 1831 the Reverend Lyman Beecher delivered four lectures in Boston on the evils of popish doctrine and the dangers of papal interference with the affairs of the United States. Soon afterward a mob destroyed the convent of Ursuline nuns at Charlestown, with the highly commendable intention of liberating some women who, as they had been led to suppose, were being imprisoned there against their will and for no good purpose. It is not of record that these romantic persons were actually discovered. Still, other anti-Catholic riots broke out, in New York, Boston, and elsewhere.

But foreigners continued to pour into the country. Some of them, especially the Germans, were inclined to oppose certain puritanical bans. In the years that followed 1848 most of the German immigrants were people to whom liberty was very dear. In the '50's the American or Know-Nothing Party flourished. It was opposed to "French infidelity, German skepticism and socialism, and papacy." It desired the exclusion of Catholics and foreigners from public office.

The South, under the régime of the cotton kings, knew little of freedom. A man who owned slaves was everywhere permitted to flog and starve them; but in some of the states it was against the law to set negroes free. The possibility of a slave revolt occasioned much worry to the white people of the South. They had nightmares of Northern abolitionists coming to arm and lead the negroes, who would presently murder their masters and rape their mistresses in their beds.

In Louisiana a person might be imprisoned at hard labor for from three to twenty-one years, or even put to death, for using language, either in public or in private, "having a tendency to produce discontent among the free colored population of this state, or to excite insubordination among the slaves." The scope of this clause was so wide that a conversation in which sentiment falling far short of abolitionism was expressed might be construed as felonious.

Some of the Southern states forbade their citizens to teach

any negro, slave or free, how to read and write. A great deal of sensitiveness was displayed about literature which could possibly be considered unfavorable to the system of slavery. Because the books used in schools, which were published in the North, often dwelt upon the rights of man, the necessity of specifically Southern textbooks was urged. And for similar reasons many Northern periodicals were frowned upon. The Federal laws were often violated by officials of the United States in the South in their anxiety to keep abolitionist propaganda from being delivered through the mails.

The sentiment in favor of slavery was not confined to the South. Abolitionists were persecuted in various ways, and even put to death by patriotic mobs, in the North as well. But eventually the cause of abolition became bound up with that of free speech, and the use of violence to oppose it proved a boomerang. The cowardly physical attack by a Southerner upon Senator Sumner of Massachusetts was, it has been said, the real beginning of the Civil War.

The slavery question had a great deal of influence upon religion in the South. When abolitionists attacked the involuntary servitude of the negroes as opposed to Christianity, the slaveowners were moved to assert their own piety and orthodoxy. Agnosticism, deism, and religious liberalism in general went out of fashion. In 1834 President Cooper of the University of South Carolina, then eighty years old, was driven from his post for his "shameful atheism." He had been appointed fifteen years before, when the religious views of Jefferson were not sinful in the South. Cooper was a Christian, but he ventured to read the Bible and interpret it to his students critically. And though he did not grow more liberal in his old age, his neighbors became more concerned for the maintenance of the orthodox faith of their grandfathers.

There was a strong Presbyterian movement in the South, after which Methodists and Baptists forged ahead. Southerners turned to the Bible for justification of the sacredness of their "peculiar institution." After the Methodist and the Baptist organizations had each been split apart by slavery and the Southern bodies

[533]

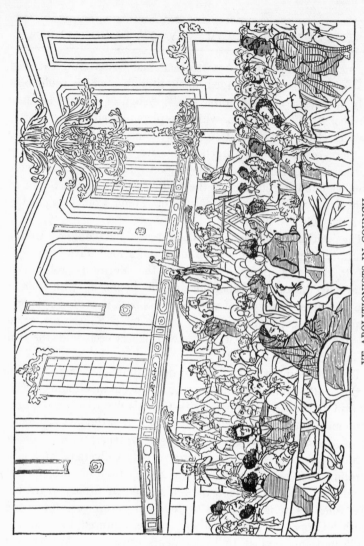

YE ABOLITIONISTS IN COUNCIL

"Ye orator of ye day denouncing ye Union, May, 1859." A cartoon in *Harper's Weekly*.

came out with definite expressions in its favor, their membership quickly increased.

Religious activity of all sorts was at a high level in the United States in the 1850's. In 1851 the Young Men's Christian Association was introduced from England. In 1857 and 1858 a great religious revival appeared. There was a great deal of old-fashioned preaching, with eloquent words and gestures expended upon death and decomposition, brimstone and molten lead and red-hot pincers.

Especially in the settlements close to the frontier, religious excitement became the principal diversion. If it was forbidden (or impossible, in any case) to see acting on a stage, it was perfectly commendable to watch a minister practice the actor's art. Foreigners spoke of the revival meeting, with its shouting and convulsions and foaming at the mouth, as typically American. It became intrenched in the South as in the West, and it was even encouraged by the authorities at Yale in the period just preceding the Civil War.

Manners were especially rude on the Western frontier. But dueling and fighting were less in vogue in such states as Illinois and Indiana than in the South. In the early '40's Abraham Lincoln accepted a challenge to a duel which arose out of a matter in which his sweetheart, Mary Todd, was involved. The Illinois community in which he lived expressed strong disapproval of Lincoln's action, for public opinion was strongly opposed to dueling.

In the South, however, it was customary to walk about armed, and it was disgraceful to decline or evade a duel. Pistols and, among the socially inferior, bowie knives settled disputes of all sorts. In 1837 the speaker of the Arkansas legislature killed a member on the floor of the house with his bowie knife. He was expelled from the legislature but was acquitted of murder. The bowie knives of Arkansas had, at this time and for a considerable period later, a pecuniary value far greater than that of the books contained in the state.

In Congress a member of the House from Maine got into a quarrel with a member from Kentucky, and the Maine man was killed in a duel. Fisticuffs in the chambers of the two houses were not uncommon. The Southern members were usually more pugnacious than those from the North and Northwest.

A blow with the hand was especially insulting ,in the South. And in a Kentucky court it was pleaded that a man who had been horsewhipped was justified in killing his attacker. The attorney said that it was so disgraceful for a white man to be flogged in a slave state that only homicide could wipe out the dishonor.

Next to the lawlessness of the South and the genuine frontier districts of the West, foreign visitors seem to have been impressed most by the use of tobacco. Women smoked, snuffed, and chewed. Southern ladies were accustomed to use a great deal of snuff, and many women of the lower classes smoked pipes.

A number of strange sects were associated with the frontier. The most important of these was Mormonism, or the Church of Jesus Christ of Latter-day Saints. Its founder was Joseph Smith, junior. Smith was born in Vermont. He received a very limited education, and as a young man he was not considered to possess any unusual talents. His neighbors said that they often saw him under the influence of drink. At Palmyra, New York, where his adolescence was spent, he came under the influence of a number of revivalists, and he changed from one sectarian allegiance to another, along with many of his neighbors. Then he was fortunate enough to see messengers sent by God, and to find in a golden box plates upon which a new divine dispensation was described.

Brigham Young, who was also born in Vermont, was a later leader of the Mormons. His strict upbringing caused a reaction in him, and when he became the head of a church, he encouraged music and dancing as harmless diversions. Brigham's near relatives all read Smith's holy book, were convinced, and became baptized.

The Mormons were from the start confronted with mob violence. This was sometimes connected with delicate moral matters. When Joseph Smith's unmarried sister became pregnant, it was declared that a miraculous conception had occurred and that a new messiah was coming. But diabolic influences were at work, and the messiah was a stillborn girl.

While Smith was living in Ohio, he received a divine revelation that it was inexpedient for the Mormons to use tobacco, coffee, tea, or any hot or intoxicating beverages. It was whispered in the 1830's that the Latter-day Saints were making up for any precise standards of conduct they might have by practicing polygamy. This was denied by the Mormon leaders. Still, the rumor could not be silenced. It was the chief reason why the Mormons were driven from place to place.

In 1843 Joseph Smith secretly took a dozen wives to himself, in response to a divine decree. Brigham Young also acquired several wives at this time. Smith is said eventually to have had at least twenty-eight, mostly young girls.

In Illinois the fact that the Mormons were polygynous was an open secret. It added to the dislike which their non-Mormon or "Gentile" neighbors felt for political and other reasons. Finally, Smith's high-handedness in suppressing criticism caused his arrest, and then brought about his death at the hands of a lynching mob. Brigham Young directed an exodus to Utah. There, in 1852, polygamy was openly pronounced to be a tenet of the Church, whereupon a violent opposition to Mormonism appeared all over the United States. Moreover, it leaked out that the Latter-day Saints were employing violence to maintain their undisturbed possession of Utah, and that their leaders went so far as to justify murder for this purpose.

Salt Lake City knew little of illicit sexual relations while the Mormons were in control and polygyny was the rule. So, at any rate, unbiased visitors reported. Brigham Young insisted that the women should wear very plain clothes. He was distinguished for the frank language he was accustomed to use in the pulpit about objectionable clothing and manners. When he denounced the tight clothes that were in fashion among Gentile men, he spoke of "fornication trousers." And as for other words which occurred in his preaching, it is best to leave them to the reader's imagination.

The Church of Jesus Christ of Latter-day Saints attracted a

THE HURDY GURDY HOUSE, VIRGINIA, MONTANA

From A. D. Richardson, *Beyond the Mississippi*, 1867.

great many members in America and abroad. It aroused the moral interest (and, usually, indignation) of almost everybody in the United States who did not belong to it. There were other sects with peculiar standards of behavior, but these were smaller and less permanent.

The history of Utah was affected by that of the country beyond. It could not remain isolated while there was a great interest in California. Gold was discovered there, near Sutter's sawmill, in 1848. Presently there came a great rush of gold-seekers. San Francisco acquired glittering bars and an array of gambling houses. It soon showed the need of a police force. The remedy appeared in the shape of a self-constituted and very drunken body of men—a remedy unquestionably worse than the disease. However, the volunteer policemen were soon driven out.

John W. Audubon was in "this pandemonium of a city" on Christmas Day, 1849. He wrote in his *Western Journal*: "Not a lady to be seen, and the women, poor things, sad and silent, except when drunk or excited. The place full of gamblers, hundreds of them, and men of the lowest types, more blasphemous and with less regard for God and his commands than all I have ever seen on the Mississippi, in New Orleans, or Texas, which gives us the same class to some extent, it is true, but instead of a few dozen or a few hundred gaming at a time, here there are thousands, and one house alone pays $150,000 per annum for the rent of the 'Monte' tables. Sunday makes no difference, certainly not Christmas, except for a little more drunkenness and a little extra effort on the part of hotel keepers to take in more money."

Here were men freed for a time from the moral bonds of their old homes. They rushed, almost all of them, to the gambling tables and the saloons. In the older settlements of the United States deep drinking was already under more or less of a taboo.

§ 6

The Prohibition movement had its real beginnings in America about 1825 or 1826; but for two or three decades it was comparatively unimportant except in New England and the settlements elsewhere which were under New England influence. In the 1830's some Primitive Baptist churches in Tennessee threatened to excommunicate those of their members who should join temperance societies.

Still, the propaganda about the evils of drink which was circulated everywhere apparently had some results. In 1837 it was commented on in the city of New York that some people were not offering the traditional distilled liquors to their New Year's Day callers. And the Fourth of July was celebrated with less hilarity than usual. In 1836 a resolution that American Methodists should not buy, use, or sell distilled alcoholic beverages failed to gain the two-thirds vote necessary for its passage; but later general conferences took a decided stand in the matter.

Friends of Prohibition have called the years between 1831 and 1837 "the Golden Age of Temperance Literature." There was an enormous circulation of tracts which purported to show the evils of drink. There were arguments intended for juvenile minds, and others meant to convince adults. It was seriously explained that drunkards are constantly in great danger because their breath may catch fire, in which case they are sure to explode. Such was the "scientific temperance propaganda" which made Americans sign temperance pledges and which induced them to vote that no licenses should be granted for the sale of liquor in their township or county.

It became general to circulate only the "teetotal pledges," which put beer and wine under the ban along with rum and whiskey. Women proclaimed that lips that touched liquor should never touch theirs. Employers began to think of the possibility of excluding hands that hoisted whiskey glasses from the control of their machines.

In the 1830's temperance workers were still divided about two matters. Many considered it unwise to attack the use of fermented beverages, because they felt them to be harmless and thought that persons who drank cider, beer, and wine could more easily be persuaded to do without distilled drinks. However, the "teetotalers" were gaining. And some felt that education alone, not legislation, should be used in putting an end to drunkenness. But the Prohibitionists were becoming more numerous, or at least more vocal.

There was a great deal of excited discussion about the need, or needlessness, of spirits in the Army and the Navy. Various experiments were made. Thus, soldiers were given the privilege of drawing coffee and sugar instead of the regular whiskey ration if they wished. Then a naval vessel was sent out without any distilled liquor on board. The regulations about the use of intoxicants in the armed forces of the United States swung back and forth as the views of Congress and the heads of the departments concerned varied. At the outbreak of the Civil War, soldiers and sailors were entitled to an allowance of strong drink, and they were allowed to buy additional liquor to what was considered a reasonable extent.

J. S. Buckingham, who was prominent in English temperance work, traveled through the South in the interest of Prohibition. He found, about 1840, much interest in the liquor problem and some legal restrictions on the sale of intoxicants. But at an election held in Mobile, Alabama, he found the drunkenness as bad as that prevailing in Liverpool on like occasions. Worse than that, he says, it could not easily have been. At Columbus, Georgia, almost all the retail establishments, including the "confectioneries," sold peach brandy, whiskey, and rum. Another strong demand seemed to exist for dirks, bowie knives, and "Arkansas toothpicks" or stilettos. These articles were prominently displayed by druggists and others.

In the West as well as in the South, rum and whiskey were associated with brawling and with political corruption. Wine and beer were little used. Consequently, it was difficult for the moral people of such states as Ohio, Indiana, and Illinois to think of beverages containing alcohol except as violent intoxicants. They could not share with the aristocrats of New York and Boston the conception of wine as an integral part of a delicate meal, valued as stirring up wit. and liveliness but no more than this. Of course, the German immigrants brought with them the habit of drinking beer and wine temperately. According to foreign observers, dinner at a hotel or boarding house, or, to a lesser extent, in a private home, was hastily gobbled by the Americans of this period. Drinking was often solitary, or it was the principal part of social functions.

On Mississippi steamers in the '50's and '60's, according to the recollections of George Byron Merrick, "whiskey was not classed as one of the luxuries. It was regarded as one of the necessities, if not the prime necessity, of life." German immigrants added to the number of drinking saloons in the West. Edward Dicey said of St. Louis, during the Civil War: "I know, in the main street, I counted out of a line of fifty houses I took at hazard, twenty were bar-rooms, or wine stores, or lager saloons." But the Germans seldom consumed enough beer or wine to become drunk. Many of them went into the business of brewing or of selling alcoholic beverages, and it became a matter of business as well as of custom to oppose the prohibition of at least the fermented drinks.

The Prohibitionists made gains in many parts of the United States, working through local-option laws. In Iowa, in 1847, all but one of the counties outlawed the saloon, a clear indication that settlers from New England were in control. Maryland the next year went so far as to order the closing of dramshops on Sunday.

The Irish temperance worker, Father Mathew, came to the United States in 1849. He asked for individual pledges, not for prohibitory laws. Mathew was banqueted by President Taylor and granted the freedom of the House of Representatives. The Senate, led by Jefferson Davis, voted against honoring him in this way, chiefly because he was opposed to slavery, but also because he was a foreigner and a Roman Catholic priest. In spite of such opposition Mathew's temperance lectures were influential, even in the South.

In 1850 duties were paid on a *per capita* consumption of two and a half gallons of distilled liquor in the United States. This represented a large reduction from the annual consumption of two or three decades before. Propaganda on the part of temperance and Prohibition workers, together with a continued increase in the popularity of tea and coffee and of fermented beverages, accounted for most of the decline.

A number of statewide Prohibition laws appeared. Maine enacted an ineffective law in 1846; then, in 1851, largely because of the efforts of Neal Dow, the state passed a strong act which forbade the manufacture or sale of intoxicants except for medicinal purposes. Some of the people of Maine who disliked the law contented themselves with becoming very ill and receiving liquor prescriptions. Others rioted. In 1855 it became necessary to call out the militia to keep a mob from seizing a quantity of confiscated liquor. Then the law was repealed, but it was soon reënacted.

There followed a wave of legislation after the model of the Maine law. In some cases the state courts held the laws to be unconstitutional, in that they disregarded property rights. Even where the laws were upheld by the courts, they did not stop the sale of liquor, though perhaps they reduced it somewhat. It is difficult to be sure about this, because hard drinking had previously been on the decline in the very states that adopted Prohibition laws.

A law passed by Kansas in 1859 is of interest as showing how feminine power was growing in the West. This forbade the sale of liquor to drunkards or, in case their wives objected, to married men. But the strength of the movement against the use of alcohol did not arise out of prohibitory and regulatory laws, many of which were very quickly repealed. It lay in the support of the principal evangelical churches—the Presbyterian and the chief Baptist bodies were sympathetic to temperance by the time of the Civil War—and in the slow growth of a respectable variety of feminism.

§ 7

The War initiated many young men who had previously known little of alcohol into the drinking habit. Distilled liquors were used in the armies and navies as medicines and as stimulants. They served to create oblivion of hardship and danger. The principal welfare organization working with the Federal armies, the Christian Commission, distributed tons of religious tracts, but no tobacco. The soldiers did not emerge from the War with any increased respect for religion, certainly not for the churches.

In the midst of the War, Andrew Johnson appeared drunk at his inauguration as Vice-President of the United States. The moralists never forgave him for it, and the enemies he then made proved troublesome later.

When the Civil War broke out, there was a tendency on both sides to give up luxuries and diversions. But in 1863 and 1864 matters changed. People flung themselves into riotous living, as though to forget their anxiety and their troubles. Much of the South was exposed to danger and famine, while the North was generally well-fed and secure. Some people grew wealthy supplying military needs or through various forms of speculation. There was a great deal of corruption among politicians and profiteering contractors.

North and South alike voiced complaints about the moral degeneration occasioned by the War. Virginia passed a law against gambling in 1863, and one against the sale of whiskey in 1864. Both were virtually disregarded. More prostitutes than ever appeared in the streets of Richmond. At Washington, toward the end of the War, it was said that congressmen supported their concubines without cost to themselves by putting them on the pay rolls of government departments, and that some of the official bureaus were little better than houses of assignation. Southerners accused the Northern soldiers of habitually raping the negresses. There were, it appears, some few men on both sides who ravished women, white as well as black. The lure of the uniform was great, and women did not always wait to be forced.

The Civil War raised the esteem in which women were held by showing that they could do men's work. In the South, where they had been sheltered, as well as in the North, women flocked to fields and factories. Many went to medical schools, and there were over 250 qualified female physicians in the North by 1864. Other professions were opened to women as direct or indirect results of the War. Clara Barton became prominent as a leader in the work of caring for the ill and wounded soldiers in the Federal armies. The result was a gain for the movement looking to the equality of the sexes before the law.

CHAPTER XV

THE AGE OF INNOCENCE

§ 1

THE Civil War stimulated the growth of industry, and eventually even more in the South than in the North. It brought about an acceleration of the movement from farm to city. Many girls who had been brought up on farms went to work in factories, and naturally these were easier to recruit for prostitution than if they had remained at home.

In 1875, Ames' *Sex in Industry* was published at Boston. The author thought that the association of young men and young women at work was the cause of much sexual vice, and he advised manufacturers to take steps to prevent this. They should, for example, keep their female employees from arranging their clothing in such a way as to provoke desire on the part of their male associates, and they should prevent them from taking up any attitude in their work which would have a similar effect.

Dr. Harry Thurston Peck says of the period following the Civil War: "The circumstance that women now worked with men, and, as in shops and factories, in complete subordination to men, was a cause of incessant temptation and a menace to chastity." But Emily Faithfull, zealous for the cause of women in industry, tells us in *Three Visits to America* (Edinburgh, 1884) that the morality of the male workers was much improved by reason of their respect for the women who now labored beside them. Perhaps the mere association between men and women in the same factory did little to promote illicit sexual relations. After all, male and female had not been kept isolated previously. But it is true that employers have had an influence over employees, and managers over subordinates, often leading to adultery or fornication in many cases where there is no question of mutual affection.

The development of industrialism vastly increased overcrowding in the cities. Tenements and slums existed before the Civil War and caused much concern then, but the problem became vastly more acute after about 1870. And immigrants poured in from a great many different non-English-speaking countries. Some of the Italians took up the occupation of bringing boys and girls into the United States and receiving the pennies that were flung to them as they fiddled and begged on the streets. The *padroni* also set up brothels, in which "fresh girls" aged ten or twelve were usually the principal attractions. Sometimes boys were substituted.

Apparently the immigration from Italy and the other countries of southern Europe increased pederasty in the United States. But it is virtually impossible to write a history of American homosexuality because of the secrecy made necessary by severe criminal laws against it as well as by the force of public opinion. It may be that the proportion of homosexual men and women to the total population has always been about the same.

Jews from the Russian and Austrian empires and the adjoining countries came to the United States in large numbers in the last two decades of the nineteenth century, and they continued to pour in during the twentieth century until their influx was made slower by immigration restrictions. The men have generally been proud of the purity of their women. Nevertheless, some Jewesses became prostitutes; and in New York and a few other cities Jews engaged in the business of maintaining brothels.

The poor immigrants who remained in urban districts usually had to live in crowded slums. Often they found themselves, against their will, surrounded by houses of prostitution. In the streets they jostled against harlots flaunting their charms. The same thing has often been true of the negroes, with their choice of residence usually limited by lack of money as well as the disinclination of genteel white people to welcome them as neighbors.

It is often taken for granted that the inflow of foreigners, with the possible exception of those loosely classified as Nordics, has greatly debased the moral tone of American life. Whether or not this is true depends to no small extent upon the criteria of moral excellence and debasement that are adopted. The newcomers have certainly not abandoned their customs and their ideas of right and wrong in passing through Castle Garden or Ellis Island. The immigrants from the Continent of Europe, even though devoutly Christian, attach less importance to Sunday observance than most Americans of Puritan or Scotch-Irish traditions do. The majority of them are in the habit of drinking alcoholic beverages—in some cases, moderately, and usually with meals; in others, often to the point of intoxication. This in itself does not, perhaps, distinguish them from the older settlers. But the very idea of Prohibition is absurd to many of these people, while some native Americans see nothing incongruous in going to the polls in a drunken condition to "vote dry." Of course, some of the immigrants have expected to find America hypocritical. This is the general opinion in central Europe about the morality of the English-speaking countries.

In some European cities and rural districts the common people consider it a waste of time and money to get married in the manner prescribed by law. Even though they live together permanently as husband and wife, their children are listed as illegitimate. And various sexual taboos which are important in the United States are unimportant or nonexistent in Continental Europe. On the other hand, the supervision of young girls is carried by some people of foreign stock to what Americans consider absurd lengths.

But among the immigrants parental authority declined as soon as the children began to learn English and to feel themselves at home in the new country. Boys and girls went to school; even if they were forced to find work at once, they were better able than their elders to acquire a working knowledge of the language and the ways of the United States. They found that their associates often gauged the merit of people by the extent to which they had cast off foreign customs. Thus measured, their parents were found wanting. If, then, immigration has really affected American morality for the worse, here is the chief cause. For patterns of behavior are not acquired in church, or from the reading of books moral or immoral, but almost entirely from the imitation of one's father and mother.

When the homes of the immigrants were overcrowded and cheerless, as they usually were in the city slums, their children had all the more reason to spend most of their free time in the streets. Often the parents, bewildered to find their authority suddenly gone, struggled to regain it by using the whip on daughters who embellished themselves with rouge and came home late at night and on sons who seemed lacking in respect. Even in foreign quarters the neighbors sometimes expressed their disapproval of such discipline as un-American, and the parents were occasionally brought before police magistrates.

The right to flog a child was more sacred in the nineteenth century than it is now, but limitations on this privilege were being stressed after the Civil War. The children of immigrants, when they felt themselves abused at home, did not often appeal to the courts. Rather, they simply went away. There was always a demand for young girls of any degree of attractiveness; and vigorous young men found it possible to earn a living for themselves, honestly or dishonestly, as they chose.

With the decline in parental authority often went, for the children of immigrants, a diminished interest in religion. They found that in the United States only the Protestant churches were considered truly American. If their parents were Protestants but worshiped in a foreign language, the churches they attended also proved unattractive.

It has been amply proved in more than one country that morality need not depend upon a religious sanction. Yet where religion and morals are closely associated in childhood, a rebellion against religion often carries with it a revolt against at least some aspects of the interrelated morality. Henry Holt, in his reminiscences, tells us that "because of the sailors on the yachts at Larchmont, who, like sailors in general, sought to have temporary wives in every port, the Protestants there had had to build a Catholic church to keep their serving maids in working condition." It is not recorded whether or not the reverend father's sermons actually decreased fornication among the cooks and second maids of Larchmont.

At any rate, it is proper to consider the possibility that a tendency to turn away from religion brought with it a changed morality on the part of the sons and daughters of immigrants. It should be added that the pietistic principles of Catholics and Jews have been and still are powerful forces in the United States. Both bodies have been striving to show themselves truly American. Some of the important Catholic periodicals have such titles as *Columbia, America,* and the *Commonweal.* And it does not appear that patriotism has a smaller place in the parochial than in the public schools.

Rabbis• and priests have worked, in and out of their pulpits, for temperance (less seldom, indeed, for Prohibition), against books and plays alleged to be immoral, against prostitution, and for many moral reforms. The tradition lingers on in New York of a rabbi who, in the manner of the Old Testament prophets, stood in the midst of an East Side street and denounced the houses of prostitution there. The Roman Catholic Church has been especially concerned with what its bishops consider indecency in women's dress. It has, of course, been among the foremost in denunciations of divorce and the control of conception.

The truth is that American communities which prided themselves upon the fact that they had remained uncontaminated by the foreigner did not maintain a morality conspicuously more precise than that prevailing in the cities where many newcomers had settled. In the 1880's and 1890's it was discovered that some New England towns which were isolated from main lines of travel had discarded almost everything that had been morally essential to their ancestors. Birth control, to be sure, was something with which they were entirely unfamiliar, and they had large families. But those who lived together as husband and wife had seldom been made such by a minister or a civil official. Sometimes they were still, at law, bound to others from whom they had obtained no divorces. There was a great deal of illegitimacy in the villages of New England. The bastardy rate in Massachusetts had a sharp rise between 1850 and 1890.

Among the mountaineers of the South a similar indifference to the legislation regulating marriage and divorce was prevalent. These people too were proud of being of old American stock. They were the descendants of the Scotch-Irish Presbyterians and others who had been poured into the same spiritual mold. Like the rural sons of the Puritans, they had large families. Most of them were indolent and illiterate. If there was any work to be done, either the women did it or it wasn't done at all. Lassitude was characteristic of the greater part of the white Southern population, due in some degree to the prevalence of endemic diseases. And the negroes as well, intoxicated for a time after the Civil War with the joy of being free and no longer subject to the lash, indulged themselves in laziness. They too came to the conclusion that work was meant largely for women folk.

In the more literate (and perhaps more intelligent) parts of the country it was observed that fecundity was declining among persons of native stock. By the end of the nineteenth century the fear was often expressed that people of non-English descent would soon constitute the mass of the population of the United States, with the negroes far outnumbering the whites in the South. But the colored people lived almost always under very bad hygienic conditions, and they kept down their numbers by dying young. The immigrants and their children showed themselves, even if they belonged to the Roman Catholic Church, willing to learn about contraceptives. In the decade or two following the Civil War there were many complaints about the frequency of artificial abortion. Abortionists advertised themselves openly, or behind very transparent disguises, in the newspapers.

Compared with the conditions now prevailing in most American cities, the prevalence of sexual irregularity was then made strikingly manifest in the streets. During the 1890's the New York police made an attempt, more determined than usual, to close the brothels; but nobody who was familiar with the conditions believed that prostitution was thereby destroyed or at all diminished. A medical observer, in the middle of the decade, wondered if even "open vice" had been reduced in the slightest degree.

Shortly after the end of the Civil War the legislature of Missouri authorized the city of St. Louis to suppress or regulate prostitution. Medical and police control over the brothels was then introduced. But the clergymen of the state objected to having the houses of prostitution officially recognized and licensed in this way. They assembled troops of "innocent virgins," dressed all in white, who trundled great petitions in wheelbarrows before the legislature. The members from rural districts succumbed to this pressure and deprived the city of St. Louis of the right to take effective precautions against the spread of venereal disease. For there was no question of driving out the brothels, however much the ministers might desire this.

Generally speaking, the legislators of the late nineteenth century took the attitude that it would defile the statute books to give any sort of license, explicit or implicit, to brothels and harlots. But the idea that it was possible to do away with such evils (evils they were usually considered), though it was slowly spreading, was characteristic of few experienced men. For whenever a brothel district was closed, streetwalkers swarmed and a large number of houses spread through the town. Women were calling for a single standard of sexual morality. It was remarked, however, that those who clamored most loudly nevertheless admired men who did not seem unduly tame.

Toward the end of the century there was a strong movement in favor of reducing the age of consent. To take an extreme instance, this was fixed in the state of Delaware at seven years until 1889; it was then made fifteen; and this was again raised, in 1895, to eighteen. Other states also raised the age, but began, in most cases, with a higher base. To have, under any circumstances, sexual relations with a girl under the age of consent was everywhere a very serious offense. Other legislation was passed against what were considered particularly objectionable forms of sexual satisfaction.

The liberation of the slaves did not altogether change the moral status of colored men and women in the South. For a time, negroes and Northern politicians controlled the legislatures of the states that were being reconstructed. In several places they repealed the laws which forbade intermarriage between the white and the colored races. When the Southern white men regained control of affairs, they made haste to bring the laws back.

Ever since the removal of Northern troops it has been a cardinal principle with Southerners belonging to the white race that the emancipated slaves must be kept not only from social equality with their former masters, but from any part in government. And the fact that the supremacy of the Democratic party is considered very important arises out of the fear that the Republicans might extend political power to the negroes.

The habit of treating colored women as persons whose feelings did not need to be considered was too deeply ingrained to disappear with the emancipation of the slaves. Such a generalization need not be taken to mean that all Southern white men, either before or after the Civil War, were accustomed to have sexual relations with negresses. But the offense involved, if indeed it was an offense at all in the eyes of public opinion in the South, was a very venial one. The idea of punishing a white man for raping a colored woman seemed very close to ridiculous. This attitude has since been somewhat modified, and the crime has at times been penalized, but almost always very lightly.

On the other hand, sexual relations between white women and men of color were, and still are, considered particularly obnoxious. It was said during the Civil War that the negro soldiers who fought on the Federal side were raping many white women. Probably there were very few such cases. Nevertheless, a great fear arose among Southerners during the Reconstruction period: the purity of white womanhood was held to be endangered. The greatest of all crimes, far worse than murder in communities where violence was usual, seemed to be a sexual assault by a negro on a white woman. Next, perhaps, was seduction in such a case; but it was hardly conceded that a woman of the dominant race would give her consent to sexual relations with a colored man.

In the border states and in the North, white women and

negroes sometimes cohabited as wife and husband or in concubinage. In one instance a white woman and a colored man lived together, undisturbed, for a number of years and had several children. Then, ignorant of the state law or defying it, they were married. And, as a result, each was sentenced to imprisonment for eighteen months.

The Chinese came into the country in large numbers after the Civil War, especially to do the common labor in connection with the building of a transcontinental railroad. Soon the dangers that American women ran from them were also worrying professional and amateur alarmists. The Chinese brought few women with them to America, and some of the wealthier ones did turn to white harlots, concubines, or wives. No one in the United States of any importance seems to have suggested that unions between white people and Asiatics might possibly be harmless. For one thing, the superiority of the white race was usually taken for granted, even before learned professors had undertaken to prove it. A few of the old abolitionists argued that color was merely superficial and that the inner man was essentially the same in Caucasian, Negro, and Chinese. But this view was not dominant in any part of the United States.

During the Civil War, a New York mob, angered by conscription, sacked the Colored Orphan Asylum in that city. The sentiment which brought about such an action did not suddenly die out when peace was declared. Economic considerations later increased Northern prejudice against the negro. But the mingling of negro and white germ cells continued after the War, in all sections of the country. This was chiefly outside of legalized marriage.

While they were enslaved, the negroes were taught that the virtue of chastity applied to them, if at all, with important reservations. In many respects their training was such as to give them a moral outlook different from that of white people. The stealing of food for their own use did not seem to them criminal. They were unaccustomed to full individual responsibility, and they had painfully to acquire the art of living as nominally free men and women in a world dominated by the whites.

The emancipation did not, of course, bring about a sudden change in their sexual habits. Adultery was still treated as a very minor sin. And the attitude of the white men was such as to help maintain the old usages. "An observant Northern doctor of divinity, fifteen years resident in one of the largest Southern cities, knowing the colored people of his city thoroughly," according to E. Benjamin Andrews, "gave it as his candid opinion that not more than one of the numerous colored clergymen of the city lived chastely."

Whether or not this statement was literally true need not detain us here. It is certain that many pious negroes and negresses lived in what was not far from a state of promiscuity. Colored women found themselves objects of interest to men of their own race and to white men as well. In fact, they were hardly permitted to resent familiarities on the part of pure Caucasian Americans. The colored woman who was honored by selection as the mistress of a white man felt herself socially superior to her old friend who was merely the wife of a negro. In certain colored circles this attitude was beginning to pass away in the late nineteenth century. It became rarer as the children and grandchildren of slaves acquired wealth and education and developed racial pride.

Old-fashioned Southerners were proud of the fact that white prostitutes were not very numerous in their cities, and they objected to the passage of laws intended to protect negresses against attentions they did not desire. It took some time before the colored people began to work against sexual laxity, and it was still longer before representative Southern men showed a willingness to coöperate with them. In some districts the negroes frowned upon adultery, although they were entirely willing to admit premarital sexual experiences. Jealousy brought about many quarrels and deadly fights. This was one of the chief reasons why the colored people were willing to consider the advantages of chastity. Whatever was accomplished in changing the sexual standards of slavery days was due almost entirely to the negroes themselves.

Northern moralists had worries of their own after the Civil

"LAST INTO BED PUT OUT THE LIGHT"

An English print satirizing Mormon polygamy. Courtesy of the New York Historical Society.

War. For instance, there was a community at Oneida, New York, which had been founded by John Humphrey Noyes. Although Oneida was of native American origin, monogamy was unknown there. "Complex marriages" were the rule, and the system which prevailed was known as "stirpiculture," the cultivation of offspring. To use a more intelligible though almost equally euphemistic expression, the Oneida community practiced free love. Under the pressure of public opinion, group marriage or promiscuity was abolished in 1879, giving way to monogamous families.

And the "Mormon Menace" occupied ethical philosophers in pulpits, editorial rooms, and village general stores. M. R. Werner, who has examined a great deal of literature pertaining to the Mormons and the attitude which Gentiles have manifested toward the Church of Jesus Christ of Latter-day Saints, tells us that "paper-covered fictions with frontispieces of semi-naked women being bathed in the Salt Lake City Endowment House by men with leering eyes came in a constant stream from the presses of the cheap publishing houses of the moral states." Gentile women and clergymen felt very much outraged by the polygyny of Utah.

The Mormon women themselves, although so much pitied, did not seem to be displeased with the system of marriage to which they were subjected. It was, they said, a religious duty for men to have more than one wife each; and the question whether it might not be more convenient and more agreeable for a woman to have a husband all to herself did not enter into the matter at all.

President Grant once remarked that it was ridiculous for polygamy to exist in a Christian country. He did not say why. At any rate, Grant was far from being an orthodox Christian himself, and he certainly did not qualify as an expert in theology. But most Americans agreed with him. Their sense of decency was outraged by the domestic arrangements of the Latter-day Saints.

Congress had passed, before the Civil War, a law outlawing polygamy in the territories. The Mormons then declared that they had only one wife apiece, the other companions of the couch being no more than concubines. The Edmunds Act of 1882 attacked this subterfuge by making it a criminal offense, within the territories of the United States, for any man to marry or to cohabit with more than one woman. Five years later woman suffrage in Utah was abolished by Congress. It had been supposed that the Mormon women, if permitted to vote, would do their best to suppress polygyny. Instead, they had used their power to strengthen it against Gentile attacks.

Between 1885 and 1890 hundreds of Mormons were sent to prison as polygamists. In 1890 a divine revelation came to the Latter-day Saints that polygyny was no longer essential or expedient. Soon after, Utah was admitted to statehood. Some Mormons kept several wives apiece long after 1890. And it was really difficult for them to solve their dilemma. The women had been married to them, in many instances, for long periods of years. It was not easy to remove them and their children to separate households, or to provide them with new husbands. Rumors persist that virtual polygyny still exists in Utah. This is also true of the Gentile parts of the United States, and it is therefore credible enough. But monogamy is the rule in Utah, as it is elsewhere, and seems to be established there as firmly as in Connecticut or Kansas.

In the period between the Civil War and the end of the century there were scattered agitators for all sorts of changes in sexual morality; but while these people served as the butts of wise and sophisticated jesters and as horrible examples for the preachers to declaim against, they never had many followers. After the war-begotten unrest had died down, the country sank into conservatism. A wave of radicalism appeared in the '90's; it did not, however, affect the fundamentals of sexual morality. At the most the question was raised if the knowledge of good and evil were not preferable to an exaggerated affectation of innocence, and if, within the limits of monogamy, some improvements were not possible.

The 1890's remained carefully virtuous. Some general hospitals still refused to receive patients suffering from syphilis or other venereal disease. There was a great deal of ostrichlike hiding from reality, and there were valiant attempts to make the American people face the truth. Efforts to bring about a certain measure of toleration in moral matters were not entirely confined to high literary circles. In 1894 there appeared a popular song called "She May Have Seen Better Days," which had a good word to say for "fallen" women.

Five years earlier a French governess in Cleveland wrote in a private letter: "The ladies talk of nothing but adultery to each other, although they never tell amusing stories of love affairs." To be sure, we have no right to assume that these particular women of wealth in Cleveland were typical of the womanhood of the country. Perhaps there was such a thing as the female innocence of which so many Americans were proud.

The old houses of assignation virtually disappeared. Their work was performed by hotels, some of which made a specialty of accommodating those women who found it inconvenient to receive their friends and lovers in their own homes.

In the state of New York the Raines Law gave hotels the privilege of selling liquor on Sunday to persons who ate in their restaurants. One result was the Raines Law sandwich, bound about with a rubber band and purchased by hundreds in a day, yet remaining whole at the close of business and ready to be served again on the following Sunday. Another was the development of small brothels or houses of accommodation about the furnished rooms which turned a saloon into a hotel.

Scandals occasionally arose about the treatment of girls and women in penal and reformatory institutions. For instance, a number of female prisoners, especially negresses, in the Georgia penitentiary gave birth to illegitimate children. Several state legislatures passed laws making it a crime to have sexual knowledge of women held in jails, prisons, and reform schools.

§ 2

After the Civil War a general reaction appeared against the extreme prudery which had previously prevailed in the United

States. We find Alex M. Gow, in *Good Morals and Gentle Manners for Schools and Families,* which was published at Cincinnati and New York in 1873, admonishing the young thus: "Indelicacy is often manifested by affectations of purity. The woman who talks about the 'limbs' of the table and the 'bosom' of the chicken is unrefined, and exposes herself to merited ridicule and contempt." He goes on to tell a story about a young woman who was injured in a railroad accident, and was asked by a surgeon what was wrong with her. "One of my limbs is broken," she replied. Then he tried in vain to learn if it was her arm or her leg. "Which is it," he finally asked, "the limb you thread a needle with?" She answered with a sigh, "No, sir, it's the limb I wear a garter on." And the disgusted surgeon expressed the opinion that "when a woman gets so fastidious as that, the quicker she dies, the better." However, the point brought out is that it is wrong to refuse to name the leg to a doctor, or in discussing poultry. This moralist would no doubt have been thoroughly shocked had he been able to hear how high-school girls now talk about legs, and to see how they display them.

The anonymous author of a more sophisticated book on etiquette, published in 1880, says: "Avoid an affectation of excessive modesty. Do not use the word 'limb' for 'leg.' If legs are really improper, then let us on no account mention them. But having found it necessary to mention them, let us by all means give them their appropriate name."

American artists who were educated at Paris in the '70's and '80's came home and found a great deal of shying from nudity. It was rather a daring person, even in New York high society, who ventured to hang a nude in his drawing room, or in any room of his house where it might be seen by casual visitors. Toward the very close of the century many Bostonians were disturbed by the Saint Gaudens decorations over the entrance to the Public Library. Still, nudes appeared in the murals of many public buildings, and gradually the people became accustomed to them. Books and works of art in general were less harshly judged if they were imported than if they were of American origin.

THE AGE OF INNOCENCE

A French traveler, de Varigny, wrote in 1895, "American journalism does not carry prudery so far as English journalism did a few years ago." In the United States there was in the period between 1850 and 1890 a great reduction in what most of us would now consider false modesty. But a considerable amount still remained in the last decade of the century. Thomas Beer has gone to the trouble of gathering together a group of words which, when used in such magazines as *Harper's* and the *Century*, brought vocal expressions of wrath and consternation from certain female subscribers. Among them are *damn, vomit, breasts, belly,* and *rape.* One woman from the country wrote that the society women of New York might like to read swear words, but the editor was very much mistaken if he supposed that others were pleased to see them. I dare say such complaints are still made.

During the '90's there were dreadful men who wrote about a w——, their intention evidently being to represent an unspeakable synonym for a woman of pleasure, that is, a fallen hussy. But matters had been changing fast. In 1880 James Schouler, the historian, wrote of "the lower extremities" of mulatto girls, which had been exposed to the view of their masters in the days of slavery. In 1895 he might have been venturesome enough to substitute "legs."

Maurice Francis Egan tells "of an evangelical lady in Philadelphia who disliked the nightly saying of 'Ave Maria' by a little Papist relative," that is to say, himself. "The fruit of thy womb, Jesus," was the objectionable phrase. But this was acceptable when rendered into Latin.

In 1873 boys and girls at school read in Alex M. Gow's book: "No girl should permit a boy to be so familiar with her as to toy with her hands, or play with her rings; to handle her curls, or encircle her waist with his arm. Such impudent intimacy should never be tolerated for a moment. No gentleman will attempt it; no lady will permit it." And many popular games of the day were condemned: "If the game requires the boys to catch, and struggle, and wrestle with the girls, or even to put their hands upon their persons, or to kiss them, it is of very doubtful propriety. Such freedom is not consistent with that respect which the sexes should cultivate for each other."

Petting and necking were firmly established in American life long before they became prominent in literature or became known under their present names. In most social circles boys and girls were permitted to associate without chaperonage and with few restrictions. As for "doorkeeper" and other kissing games, boys and girls began to play them while they were very young and continued to enjoy them at least until they were married. Teachers and ministers might mumble about the fall of Rome as they thought of these things, but they were little heeded.

When youth went out buggy riding behind a horse that was familiar with the way and did not need to be guided, it was not necessary to stop by the side of the road in order to make love. To be sure, this old-fashioned means of transportation could not carry lovers very far from home, and perhaps it did not lend itself so readily as the automobile to gross violations of the proprieties. Most people went to bed early; and young gentlemen who called on young ladies, even if they were engaged to them, were supposed to leave by ten o'clock.

De Varigny in 1895 commented on the frequent occurrence of breach of promise suits in the United States, and remarked: "The privilege of flirting is as sacred and as irrevocable in the United States as the immortal principles of 1789 are to us French." He found that American married life was very much secluded, and commented on the fact that novels dealt almost always with the unmarried. A great deal of moral idealism seemed to him to exist in the country, though actual practice was not always impeccable. Despite the fact that the streets of New York and Chicago swarmed with harlots, Americans felt sure that their country was, or would soon be made, far more virtuous than the degenerate countries of Europe. De Varigny reports the existence of a party which favored free love. Though small, it enjoyed a certain amount of public attention, for the yellow press was interested in sensations, even during the age of innocence.

The term "yellow press" is variously explained as being due to the appearance of a New York paper with a front page of that color and as being reminiscent of the *Yellow Book* which shocked the staid people of Victorian England. Before the Spanish-American War made the fortune of the New York *Journal* and before decadent poets came into general notice in the English-speaking countries, some of the newspapers in the United States were exploiting sexual scandals of all sorts.

After all, the fact that euphemisms seemed to be necessary made no difference. They conceal nothing from people who are more accustomed to them than to literal expressions. Technical terms and even old popular expressions may easily become more mysterious than the words and phrases which shocked modesty considers fit to employ to describe moral transgressions. Of course, sex is not the only stock in trade of the sensational journalist. He describes a breach of promise suit ever so absorbingly in one column, and waves the American flag patriotically in the next.

The serious writers who were held down or annoyed by the moral conventions were made particularly angry by the fact that the newspapers were not particularly reticent. Walt Whitman was familiar with journalistic ways, and he knew the importance of sexual scandals. He remained convinced of the importance of *Leaves of Grass*. Believing thoroughly in himself and his message, he seldom wavered from the position that it would be a betrayal of his own ego and of the American people if he should be led to make prudish alterations in his poems. There was in him, certainly, something of the martyr-masochist. For, glorifying his country as he did, he might have become popular in his own lifetime, despite his formal innovations, if only he had refrained from violating the taboos. As a matter of fact, some men and women whom we might have expected to keep icily aloof recognized the Puritan in him and were inclined to be friendly.

Perhaps Walt Whitman's worst offense was an attack on the vestrymen of Grace Church in New York, which he published in a Brooklyn paper. This caused pious and respectable people to look for evil rather than for good in his work. Of the character and personal habits of Whitman there is little need to speak. A number of biographers have studied them, and they are comparatively unimportant here. Indeed, the nature of his relations with certain of his close associates remains uncertain.

Leaves of Grass is widely read. Library copies show large numbers of finger marks on the pages where the more daring poems are printed. By 1881 six editions of the book had been issued. But these were all small, and Whitman was still comparatively unknown. Then James Osgood of Boston arranged to publish it. He had two thousand copies printed, and the book had a slow but steady sale. In May, 1882, the Boston district attorney informed Osgood that he considered parts of *Leaves of Grass* obscene. Whitman was notified, and he signified his willingness to make half a dozen changes or so. These were not considered sufficient, and Whitman refused to go further. Osgood turned over the remaining sheets and plates to Whitman, and a Philadelphia house took over the right to publish the book. The attendant publicity greatly helped sales, and Whitman for the first time received a substantial payment.

Indirectly responsible for the widening circulation of the book was a Boston minister, acting in the capacity of an officer in a local society for the suppression of vice. Moral indignation against the poet who dared to write of harlots and of nakedness and the delights of the flesh showed itself in a variety of ways. Whitman once lost a position in a governmental bureau at Washington after his chief had examined a copy of *Leaves of Grass* which he had left on his desk. But Whitman's friends remained steadfast. They saw that he was provided with another place. They remained loyal to him through all his adversities and rejoiced with him when some celebrity from overseas expressed approval of his work.

One of the things they admired in the man was his tolerance. During the Civil War he worked with wounded soldiers, and he gave them the tobacco for which they longed although he was not himself a smoker and had written about the evils of tobacco. The poet was one of the very few genuine democrats of his time.

He really believed in the sanctity of human beings, quite aside from their ability to accumulate wealth and honors or to obey the law. He never conceived of men and women as disembodied spirits, and he never denounced them for their imperfections.

While Walt Whitman was an old man concerned with corrupting the morals of youth, Anthony Comstock was protecting virtue and innocence. He became secretary and special agent of the New York Society for the Suppression of Vice in 1873. He was a man of little culture; it is, indeed, conceivable that culture might have interfered with his zeal. Toward the end of his life (in our own century) he proudly recited the things he had accomplished. He had, he said, caused 2,500 criminals to be convicted and brought about the destruction of eighty tons of indecent pictures and reading matter.

Comstock was chiefly responsible for the passage by Congress, in 1873, of a law which prohibited the sending of obscene matter through the mails. This law declares that information about preventing conception or inducing abortion and advertisements of objects intended for such purposes are obscene, and it makes their mailing criminal.

Some years after its passage, D. M. Bennett, founder and publisher of an anticlerical magazine, the *Truthseeker*, in New York, was sent to prison for posting a pamphlet about birth control. The commotion that appeared in England about Knowlton's little book reverberated in the United States; and the use of contraceptives spread, despite the existence of Federal and state laws designed to discourage it.

The decades just preceding 1900 were not very different from those since. Perhaps the period immediately after the Civil War was less precise than that of the '70's and '80's, and there was another relaxation in the '90's. There have been, to be sure, great changes in fashion. The safety razor has brought about the practical disappearance of the beard, and it has made the moustache cup an antique; but neither this nor any other modern invention has removed the important prejudices and taboos of the nineteenth century.

An etiquette writer of 1880 thought "there is nothing that

adds so much to native manliness as the full beard if carefully and neatly kept." The ladies who went bathing at popular resorts in that year wore loose sacques, or yoke waists, "falling about midway between knee and ankle; full trousers gathered into a band at the ankle;" as well as merino socks and water-proof caps.

There were *décolleté* dresses, though the Reverend Mr. Beecher disapproved of them. Edward Bok heard him define his attitude on the subject: "A proper dress for any girl or woman is one that reveals the lady, but not her person."

The problem which confronted Beecher remains with clerical and other censors, although it certainly has taken on a somewhat different form. Reverend gentlemen suggest that the wise an-cients allowed their women to wear loose drapery about the upper parts of their bodies but did not permit them to reveal their legs. Ladies of the Woman's Christian Temperance Union com-plain that some of the important females who sit on the platform at conventions allow their skirts to slide up too far and show too much, thus imperiling the sanctity of their cause.

In the '70's and '80's it was considered very shocking when young ladies forgot themselves so far as to mention nightgowns in mixed society. Now, in nearly all circles, American girls allude to their pajamas without finding it necessary to blush.

Many of the belles of the '80's are flourishing in the second quarter of the twentieth century; and even if they have had their hair bobbed, they have not cast away all their girlhood notions of propriety. England, especially the England of high society, has relaxed some of its social stringencies during the last forty or fifty years to a far greater extent than the United States. In the 1880's manners were conspicuously freer in America than in Great Britain. Chaperonage was usually con-sidered a pretentious importation from abroad; and if a bachelor was fit company for a maiden, his ability to take care of her and respect her purity was usually taken for granted.

And young misses were trusted with the same literature that all the family read. The result was a careful censorship of all books and magazines of wide circulation. During the 1880's

"YOUR HONOR, THIS WOMAN GAVE BIRTH TO A NAKED CHILD!"

A caricature of Anthony Comstock by Robert Minor in *The Masses*, 1915.

the novel written especially for women all but disappeared. New periodicals which were intended primarily for the feminine members of the family were published, but they recognized that the experiences and interests of women were not entirely different from those of men, and the fiction as well as some of the articles they printed were evidently intended to be read by persons of both sexes. In our own day such magazines have even featured cowboy stories by well-known authors.

In 1869 and 1870 an American female writer whose intentions were indubitably of the best caused to be printed an unsavory story about Byron. She was convinced that it was her duty to proclaim to the world that the poet had had incestuous relations with his half-sister. The moral female was Harriet Beecher Stowe, and the title of her book was *Lady Byron Vindicated.* Her avowed purpose was to defend the memory of Byron's widow, who had, she said, given her most of the material for the book. Mrs. Stowe agreed with Lady Byron that the Calvinistic doctrines taught to the poet in his youth were largely responsible for his sins. According to their theory, he felt that he was sure to go to Hell in any case, and was therefore morally reckless. Harriet Beecher Stowe was a Puritan despite her objections to preordination. She would have utterly condemned any American writer of fiction in her time who might have dared to deal with incest. But she was sure of her own righteousness and of the value of her book. Perhaps this was merely a strange quirk. Or maybe it was indicative of a general interest in the libidinous which lay not very far beneath the mask of innocence.

At about the same time, Mark Twain wrote *Innocents Abroad.* He told the story of Abélard and Héloïse, and it was to him simply an opportunity for good American moral indignation. Abélard followed his "degraded instinct," and the ruffians who castrated him should therefore have flowers put on their graves to commemorate their "just deed." Clemens was a man from the West, but his attitude was very much like that of the New England lady. He could turn, though always timidly, against priestcraft and verbal taboos of all sorts. Still, he could hardly summon up courage (especially against the opposition of his wife) to make public his disapproval of the standards of the day. In essentials he was never a rebel against the current morality. Sometimes, when he considered himself perfectly safe, he offended precisians nevertheless. Louisa May Alcott said of *Huckleberry Finn*: "Why, if Mr. Clemens cannot think of something better to tell our pure-minded lads and lasses, he had best stop writing for them."

Van Wyck Brooks holds the Civil War responsible for making the standards of spinster ladies paramount in literature and life. Many of the best young men died in battle, and the result was that a large part of the females contended with cosmic problems instead of the task of pleasing a husband and keeping a couple of babies clean. The chief weakness of this theory is that preciseness relaxed considerably in the years immediately following the War. Fitz Hugh Ludlow wrote then of a fictional couple: "They read Dickens and Thackeray with avidity; went now and then to the opera; . . . had statues in their parlor without any thought of shame at their lack of petticoats; and did multitudes of things which, in their early married life they would have considered shocking." Ludlow attributed this change in part to "the great increase of travel, the wonderful progress in art and refinement which has enlarged this generation's thought and corrected its ignorant opinions."

But it is true that, especially in New England, vitality and virility were at a low point. Men were still going westward to take up free or cheap land on the frontier. And New England was only slowly displaced from its position of authority in literary matters.

Something of a reaction did appear against the tendency toward easy divorce which had been developing before the Civil War. Maiden aunts found it difficult to understand that their married nieces might, owing to circumstances not altogether under their control, be placed in such a position that only divorce could free them from lifelong unhappiness. Divorced men were frowned upon, divorced women were beyond the pale of respectability. Most of the important churches were opposed to all dissolutions of the marriage tie, or considered divorce justifiable only in case of adultery. In addition to the Catholic clergy, the Episcopalian, Methodist, and Lutheran ministers led the movement to "preserve the sanctity of marriage." It was undoubtedly an indication of declining clerical influence that almost all the state legislatures increased the number of reasons for which a divorce might be asked, and that the number of marriage dissolutions legally granted steadily rose.

In South Carolina alone, divorce was entirely impossible, except that the legislature granted relief in a few instances in Reconstruction days. For this condition the Roman Catholic Church was certainly not responsible. South Carolina found it necessary to decide how much of his property a man might legally settle on his concubine. But in 1880 it joined some of the other states in making adultery criminal.

The moral influence of France began to percolate into the United States, as into Great Britain, in the last two decades of the nineteenth century. It was carried chiefly in literature. First, a few advanced people became familiar with Huysmans, the Goncourt brothers, and other French writers with radical moral ideas.

Then came Ibsen from Scandinavia, and the lines were drawn between the Ibsenites and their opponents almost as in England. William Winter, who was considered one of the foremost dramatic critics of New York, said of Ibsen's social dramas that they are, "with little exception, morbid, tainted, unhealthy, and distressingly diffuse of dullness, doubt, and gloom."

Winter was also distressed when Olga Nethersole, playing the part of Carmen, permitted male actors to kiss her on the lips. In a modified version of *Sapho* Miss Nethersole was carried up to what Thomas Beer calls a "theoretic bedroom." High morality (in the edition of 1900) was manifested by the arrest of the actress, but it was not strong enough to convict the charming lady.

Thomas Beer tells us how one of the actors who had a minor part in *Sapho* was notified by the headmistress of the exclusive girls' school which his child attended that she could not be kept there any longer, "as several mothers of several students have

OLGA NETHERSOLE IN *SAPHO*
Act I, Scene II. Courtesy of the Harvard Theatre Collection.

seen the play in which you are appearing and they cannot consider Margaret a fit companion for their daughters in consequence." The girl was eleven years old, and no misdemeanors of her own were charged against her. For it is not probable that she was consulted about theatrical matters. The sins of the fathers. . . .

Sapho and *Carmen* were of foreign origin; had they been originally American, perhaps they would never have been produced, even in euphemistic versions. *Harper's Magazine,* long considered thoroughly safe for family reading, published Thomas Hardy's *Jude the Obscure.* Kipling was the rage in the '90's, though he used words with which American ladies took care to show that they were unfamiliar, and though he mentioned lawless, drunken places without utterly condemning them. Harry Thurston Peck, who was influential because of his dual position as professor at Columbia and editor of the *Bookman,* stimulated the interest in Kipling. As a leader of the sophisticates of the '90's, he sang the praises of George Moore, Balzac, and other foreign writers who were considered daring.

In 1893 appeared a short novel by a young American writer which dealt with a Bowery girl who was driven from home, then fled to a gangster, lost him to another woman, and drowned herself. This was Stephen Crane's *Maggie.* The book contained no explicit preaching, but its conclusion was such as to permit the inference that he agreed with the moralists: "The wages of sin is death." *Maggie* was little noticed.

In the '90's Gertrude Atherton was one of the American writers who complained that it was necessary to eliminate almost all references to sex from fiction in order to preserve the innocence of young girls. Most popular authors were quite content to bring sweet young lovers to the altar and to leave them there with the suggestion that they lived happily ever after.

An important indication of moral change appeared in New York in 1896, when a paper first used the phrase "naughty but nice." Young people were slowly deciding that it might be time to examine critically the taboos of their parents. At the same time, ladies were walking past churches to enter theatres where they might be properly shocked by female dancers. Most of these wicked creatures still felt it necessary to conceal their legs. Still, their motions seemed lascivious to the very pure female spectators.

The first American appearance of girls wearing visible tights in a musical comedy laying some sort of claim to respectability took place in 1866, and this sort of stage costume was not at all common until the '80's. In the following decade it was still considered daring for girls to wear bloomers in the gymnasiums of schools and colleges, no matter how well they might be guarded against masculine eyes. We are told how, when this was first made compulsory, the students came in blushingly, afraid to reveal to their female companions that they were provided with two legs each. Ministers preached against the girls who played tennis. However, the popularity of vigorous sports for young women steadily increased. They went riding merrily on bicycles built for two. Because legs were not habitually revealed in public, as well as for economic reasons, the sale of silk stockings in 1900 was only one pair for each two thousand inhabitants of the United States. A materialistic interpreter of history might contend that the public display of hosiery on millions of living models became inevitable as soon as the masses could afford to buy silk stockings.

§ 3

The Civil War made a number of heroines, among them Clara Barton, its "Florence Nightingale." Miss Barton had done pioneer work as a public school-teacher and as a government clerk before becoming a nurse. She was prominent, after the war in America, as a relief worker in the Franco-Prussian War, and then as president of the American Red Cross from 1882 to 1904.

In the '70's and '80's women worked their way slowly into the world of industry. Much prejudice against employed girls and women still remained. At a meeting in New York, Mrs. Field carefully explained that the place of the female sex was not in the home alone. "Why," she asked, "is it that the thought of a

THE CYMBAL DANCE IN *LALLA ROOKH*

as presented at the Grand Opera House, New York, 1872. From *Harper's Weekly*.

lady working for money in any other sphere—even that of a teacher, so important to the family and society—is still so reluctantly accepted? To work, and to work for pay, is no disgrace."

In 1882 there were only nineteen Englishwomen registered as physicians, but there were over four hundred women practicing medicine in the United States. One of the most prominent American physicians was Dr. Mary Putnam-Jacobi. Foreign visitors were surprised to find a female minister or two among the Unitarians. The Friends had, to be sure, permitted women to testify and preach long before.

The United States had numerous women who were successful as writers and editors. Female teachers were common, and the chief point in their favor was their willingness to work for half the pay that men received. There were women clerks in the government offices in Washington, many of them having first been employed during the Civil War.

The Reverend Dr. Dix of New York lamented the indecorous efforts of women to plunge into "coarse rivalry with men." Emily Faithfull reported in 1884 that the United States had a female railroad switchman, a steamboat captain of the same sex, and even a lady colonel engaged in the work of shooting and stuffing animals. The increasing popularity of the typewriter brought large numbers of women into business offices. Female workers in factories also became more numerous in the '80's and '90's. Many of them were recent immigrants.

Some branches of the manufacture of clothing fell into the hands of people, mostly of foreign origin and provided with little capital, who operated small sweatshops. These were usually crowded and unsanitary; and success in business was held to depend entirely upon the ability to discover men, women, and children who, because of ignorance or immediate need, could be induced to work for very low wages.

Female workers received, in dollars and probably in purchasing power as well, considerably more in the 1890's than in the 1850's. Some were still in danger of starving if they depended entirely upon honest earnings in the workshop, and many more found that they could get pretty dresses and other much-desired luxuries only by engaging in occasional prostitution.

In 1889 Jane Addams and Ellen Starr opened Hull House in Chicago, chiefly for the purpose of ameliorating the condition of working girls there. A number of other settlement houses were founded in the last years of the century, and much individual work was done among the girls of slum districts. Sometimes, it is true, this was ineffective or harmful though well-meant. One or two penal institutions for the care of female delinquents came under the control of women officials.

Clubs for women developed in number and importance in the years following the Civil War. They were vigorously attacked by conservative ministers and by men who feared that they would not be able to get any supper if their wives gave up their time to attendance at meetings and the preparation of papers. In the South, where feminism developed slowly, it was asserted that the clubs were corrupting the morals of Boston women. Reconstruction conditions in the states of the old Confederacy forced many women to work for pay or to perform tasks which they would have rejected with horror in the days before the War. But Southern chivalry, recognizing or appearing to recognize a superiority in womanhood, refused to grant equality to the sex. In legal privileges the women of the North were far better off. It is not altogether unfair to say that while the Southerners were singing a song in honor of the moral and spiritual excellence of the female sex, the Northerners were actually improving the status of women.

Feminism advanced most rapidly and most surely in the West, especially in the Rocky Mountain states. These harbored a chivalry which had arisen largely because of the scarcity of women, but which did not involve putting ladies upon a pedestal or expecting them to faint to prove their delicacy and gentility. Pioneering meant hard work for both sexes. And whatever was done in the early days to advance education, morality, and culture depended largely upon feminine influence. It was in the plateau and mountain regions of the West that the woman-suffrage movement won its first important victories.

While the agitation for the rights of women was still considered queer and even anti-Christian, it attracted people of doubtful moral orthodoxy. A very few of the agitators stood for free love, a considerable number believed in easy divorce, and there were some who advocated loose forms of marriage. The churches were opposed to these things, and usually to feminism as well. It had been discovered that male ministers have a greater influence over their women parishioners than over men, but this fact was not yet bound up with the moral aspirations of the clerical leaders, except in isolated instances.

The age of American hurry-scurry definitely arrived after the Civil War, and comparatively few fathers found time to rule their families in the old patriarchal way. Leisure that could be used for cultural purposes seemed to be very rare, and success was measured very largely in terms of dollars and cents. Men who had attained wealth and social position were often content to have their interest in artistic matters exercised vicariously by their wives. It was considered a matter of common sense that men should be educated in practical matters rather than in the humanities. President Eliot contributed to this tendency by inaugurating the elective system at Harvard. Of course, he did not intend to minimize the importance of culture: has he not put it within the reach of everybody with fifteen minutes a day?

In the West, coeducation became the rule in schools of all grades and in colleges. Usually there was no alternative if girls were to be educated at all, for except in the cities it was impossible to maintain more than one school in a district. A pamphlet published in the 1880's bore the warning title, *To Educate Young Women like Young Men a Thing Inexpedient Immodest Immoral.* Perhaps the author was right; certainly it was already too late to argue about the matter.

Many women were already gathering up sufficient courage to address mixed assemblies. A large number of colleges welcomed female students on the same terms as men, and still more were considering the advisability of doing this. Many different ideas have been expressed about the moral effects of coeducation. But the fact that it has flourished in a very self-righteous country may

"GET THEE BEHIND ME, (MRS.) SATAN"

WIFE (with heavy burden). *"I'd rather travel the hardest path of matrimony than follow your footsteps."*

A caricature of Victoria Woodhull by Thomas Nast in *Harper's Weekly*, 1872.

perhaps be taken as an indication that it has not particularly encouraged striking violations of the usual taboos.

The accepted mental inferiority of women took on a somewhat legendary air when the female students often passed their examinations with average grades higher than those of the men. To be sure, the girls who went to college in the early days were particularly earnest in their desire for education. And since then, athletic and other extracurricular activities have been more important for male students than for female. But it is at least possible to contend, on the basis of college records, that women are intellectually superior to men.

Observers from abroad often remarked, in the period between the Civil and the Spanish-American wars, that the male sex in the United States seemed to be subservient to the female. The accusation had been made before, and it is still sometimes heard. It usually takes the form of a statement that the men work to provide money which their wives and daughters selfishly squander away.

Americans themselves complained, after the Civil War, that women were too extravagant, and were causing young men to hesitate about the wisdom of getting married. We must not assume that the husbands who strained themselves to deck out their wives in jewels and fine raiment were always doing so against their will. They were trying, by deputy, to show how prosperous they were.

Foreigners were amazed to find women suing for divorce on the same terms as men, and otherwise enjoying equality before the law. We find De Varigny saying in the '90's that women made insolent claims, and even neglected to thank the men who gave up seats to them in the street cars.

This statement doubtless applied to individuals. It could hardly have been true of the whole sex, any more than the accusation, made often in the decade following the Civil War, that women were making use of cantharides and other drugs in their eagerness to capture husbands. After a great war, women do cast aside some of the proprieties, no doubt; but the extent to which they do this is often exaggerated. And the feverish '90's, in

England and America, had nothing to do with an unrest brought about by war.

In the year 1869 two important associations were formed to work for woman suffrage. These were merged in 1892 under the name of the American Woman's Suffrage Association. In 1872 Susan B. Anthony expressed her belief that the fourteenth and fifteenth amendments to the Federal Constitution put an end to discrimination between the sexes in political matters. She began a test case by leading a group of women to the polls in Rochester, New York. Six years later a proposed constitutional amendment forbidding the states to deny the franchise to any person on account of sex was, for the first time, laid before Congress.

Women lawyers were beginning to appear. Some of them helped the suffrage workers in preparing bills to reduce the political and economic disabilities of women. Many of these were enacted by state legislatures. The question of full enfranchisement had been settled in the affirmative by a few states at the end of the century. It was everywhere alive. And many reformers who were chiefly interested in Prohibition or the enforcement of a single strict standard of sexual morality upon both sexes saw in woman suffrage a step toward the victory of their favorite cause.

The great freedom of the child in the United States, often previously noted, continued to interest foreign visitors during the period now being considered. The desire to protect children against cruelty and economic exploitation was developing and being manifested in a great deal of legislation, including that which raised the age of consent.

Henry James introduced in his fiction the pert American child, looked upon with wonder by Europeans. Perhaps his disrespectful self-reliance owed something to the movement away from home life which was then being much discussed. At the other end of the social scale were the street gamins in whom Horatio Alger, junior, was interested. But most American boys and girls belonged neither in the James nor in the Alger class. They were reading McGuffey's textbooks, and presumably acquiring good moral principles from them.

THE AGE OF BRASS

A Currier & Ives print satirizing the agitation for woman's rights, 1869.

§ 4

Social refinements were beginning to become important in the United States, though some circles were slow to accept them. Sir George Campbell, M. P., reported in 1879 that he had been agreeably surprised to find much less spitting in the United States than the accounts of earlier visitors had led him to expect. Perhaps, though, Campbell was more friendly than accurate, for we find him calling the American people particularly law-abiding. Emily Faithfull noticed that each congressman was provided with a cuspidor of his own, and that some congressmen·showed great skill in the chewing of tobacco and the well-aimed ejection of the contents of their mouths. It was an age when people showed their gentility by calling a spittoon a cuspidor. Probably there was less careless spitting, especially in the older parts of the country, than there had been before the War; and we can understand that readers of Dickens and Mrs. Trollope who came to America did not find manners quite so barbarous as they had been led to expect.

The etiquette books that appeared in the United States in the '70's and '80's told gentlemen that they should never enter the presence of ladies smelling of tobacco. Parsley was recommended to remove the objectionable odor. As for smoking in a room where there were ladies, even if they had given their permission, it was held to be an unforgivable breach of the conventions. In fact, gentlemen were instructed never to smoke in any enclosed place which ladies were accustomed to frequent. But I cannot learn that these rules were anywhere carried out to their full extent. They represented the British mid-Victorian attitude, not the American.

In the United States many men refrained from smoking, and some considered it wicked to smoke, especially cigarettes. But those who did smoke did not take all these exaggerated precautions to keep women from catching even the faintest whiff of tobacco fumes. Toward the end of the century a number of restrictions were placed on the sale and public use of tobacco. These were mostly made by state legislatures. And on the first day of the year 1900 three important railroads put into effect rules forbidding the passengers to smoke.

Gentlemen were constantly being reminded of the necessity of acting differently when they were in the presence of ladies. But sometimes, it seems, they went too far in this direction. According to *Our Deportment,* published in 1880, "A gentleman should never lower the intellectual standard of his conversation in addressing ladies."

This same anonymous book makes it clear that women of social position were still expected to be very careful in their choice of words: "No lady should make use of any female substitute for profanity. The woman who exclaims 'The dickens!' or 'Mercy!' or 'Goodness!' when she is annoyed or astonished, is as vulgar in spirit, though perhaps not quite so regarded by society, as though she had used expressions which it would require but little stretch of the imagination to be regarded as profane." Just what a perfect lady was permitted to say under the stress of emotion, it is difficult to imagine. But I take it that she was expected to be perennially serene.

By way of compensation, some things were permitted then which are now under the social ban. For instance, Maurice Francis Egan tells about "the best judge of Madeira in Philadelphia," who drank tea from his saucer and whose "table was always provided with little dishes, like butter-plates, for his discarded cups."

Cleanliness had become thoroughly fashionable; and the convention, if not always the fact, of a daily bath was characteristic of all persons possessing social pretensions. Sanitary plumbing was being improved, and many installations were made.

In the decades which followed the Civil War, the Americans were great eaters and drinkers, though they did not, perhaps, possess the prowess of their fathers. Henry Holt says: "Dinners in the '60's and '70's were a matter of sixteen courses and half a dozen glasses. Yet there was virtually no drunkenness among the men with whom I associated."

The attitude toward popular amusements was changing. It is true that Dwight L. Moody and other evangelists were preaching against cards, billiards, the theatre, and balls as well as against alcohol and tobacco. They agreed with Beecher about the harmfulness of such diversions. At the same time, other ministers were becoming rather more liberal-minded about them. To quote once more from the anonymous etiquette book of 1880: "The sooner we recover from the effects of the Puritanical idea that clergymen should never be seen at balls, the better for all who attend them." The inference is clear that some good Christians considered it proper to dance in public. Many people were concerned about the standards of behavior suitable for ministers of religion. Edward Bok syndicated to a group of newspapers a symposium on the question, "Should clergymen smoke?"

In many villages and rural districts of New England all music was still frowned upon except psalms and patriotic airs. And the old prejudice against the fiddle as an instrument of the Devil lingered on in many parts of the country.

Louisiana continued to bear the reputation of being a wicked state. The Louisiana Lottery was incorporated in 1868 and given a monopoly for a period of twenty-five years. By 1890 it was receiving a third of all the mail delivered in New Orleans and cashing checks and money orders to the amount of $30,000 daily. In that year Congress denied the use of the mails to lotteries. The Louisiana company was forced to resort to express service. When the monopoly period expired, there was a hard fight to secure a renewal of the franchise from the legislature. The forces of righteousness won, and the company moved to Honduras in 1894.

But ample opportunities for gambling remained all through the country. Lottery tickets were everywhere obtainable, despite the prevalence of prohibitory laws. Americans eagerly watched the results of drawings in Germany and other foreign countries, as well as of those which were clandestinely held in the United States. The churches were largely supported by raffles. Carnivals fleeced the country folk, and city people left their money in elaborate gambling houses. Gambling on the part of respectable women seems to have been somewhat unusual before 1900. Card playing was considered a peculiarly masculine vice, and it was associated with heavy clouds of smoke and the foaming suds of beer.

§ 5

The Civil War, together with the dissatisfaction felt in almost all quarters with the Prohibition laws of the '50's, brought about a pronounced reaction in favor of alcoholic beverages. And most of the immigrants who flocked into the country in the following decades were opposed to all legal restrictions on the use of intoxicants. The Germans, the French, the Italians, and the Jews boasted that they were able to drink beer and wine moderately and that their people were very seldom seen drunk.

The great strength of the Prohibition movement in the United States seems always to have arisen from the inability of many Americans to content themselves with moderate amounts of liquor. A large number of foreign visitors testify to this condition. It is significant that "temperance" has come, in the United States, to mean the same thing as total prohibition. The Prohibition leaders refuse to admit that moderate drinking is possible, even of fermented beverages with low alcohol content. Beer is as much intoxicating as absinthe, they tell us, because people drink much larger quantities of it.

Sir George Campbell in 1879 thought he saw less evidence of drinking in the United States than in Great Britain. But he added that Americans seldom drank with their meals. Alcoholic beverages were for them rather associated with the saloon, or, in some districts, the drug store, than with the home.

After the reaction of the '60's and '70's had run its course, a strong swing back to Prohibition sentiment appeared in the United States. Some enthusiasts worked right on in the years that looked least promising. In 1869 the first active Prohibitionist Party organization was formed in Ohio. A national party arose three years later, and it developed its greatest strength in the election of 1892.

What is known as the Women's Temperance Crusade took place in 1873 and 1874. Dr. Dio Lewis lectured to women in a number of towns, and he urged them to pray for Prohibition, to annoy saloonkeepers, and to take other steps to drive out Demon Rum. A group of women at Hillsboro, Ohio, decided to take his advice. Their procedure was to go to a saloon, argue with the owner, kneel down before the entrance and pray, sing hymns, and take down the names of the men who came to have a drink or two. In many other places the same thing was done, and sometimes the women actually succeeded in bullying saloonkeepers into closing their doors. The women went so far in one town as to erect a shack in front of a retail liquor shop, so that they could be sheltered from the elements while they leisurely sang hymns and noted what men ventured to defy their will by entering the saloon.

The success of such tactics depended almost entirely upon public opinion and the attitude of the police. Disorderly conduct and trespass were everywhere offenses against the law, whereas the selling of liquor, in most of the cities and towns where the "crusade" was carried out, was legal. In Columbus a number of women were arrested. There was a riot in the Loop district of Chicago when two hundred women marched from a prayer service to a meeting of the city council. The Woman's Christian Temperance Union was formed in 1874, and since then women have played an important part, perhaps the most important part, in the movement for Prohibition.

Miss Faithfull tells of the American Quaker lady who reproached a Presbyterian minister for using wine in the communion service and, she said, "making the Lord's house smell like a grog shop." Many clergymen were still finding it difficult to see what connection Prohibition had with the religious tenets presented in the Old and New Testaments. And great Biblical scholars had not yet discovered that "wine" in the Holy Scriptures always means unfermented grape juice, or possibly dried raisins, save where its excessive use is denounced. Many theologians were certain that the use of wine at the communion table was a Christian duty.

Rutherford B. Hayes became President of the United States in 1877, though there is some reason to believe that he was not honestly elected. But President he was, and he was opposed to the use of intoxicants. His influence was a strong help to the "temperance" agitators. A book of etiquette published in 1880 puts the case thus: "The mistress of the White House, Mrs. Hayes, has banished wines and liquors from her table, and an example set by the 'first lady of the land' can be safely followed in every American household, whatever may have been the former prevailing customs."

When Edward Bok, having climbed a very short way up the ladder of success, acted as reporter at a public dinner where President Hayes was the guest of honor, he refrained from tasting the wine which was set before him. Hayes noticed this, and it was the principal reason why he befriended the young man. Later, as editor of the *Ladies' Home Journal,* Bok promised Frances E. Willard and other workers for Prohibition that he would, as far as possible, keep stories containing drinking scenes out of the magazine. Once, when he found intoxicants in a story sent by Kipling, he asked him if these could not be removed. It seems that Kipling agreed, making no difficulties about the matter. But a rumor circulated among the literary wits that the author had cabled: "Substitute Mellin's Food." The story probably originated with Brander Matthews. Few of the New York *literati* had arid sympathies.

In the '80's there was a new movement for statewide Prohibition, not quite so successful as that of the '50's. Several of the New England states, after adopting prohibitory laws, repealed them in 1889. In 1881 the negro vote defeated Prohibition in North Carolina. White men in the South wanted to keep the colored population from drinking and gambling, but the new amendments to the Federal Constitution kept them from passing laws which specifically applied to the negroes alone. The best way out of the difficulty semed to lie in the enactment of legislation which should not, on the face of it, be discriminatory, but which should not be enforced upon white men—at least, upon white men of quality. But the poor whites of the South certainly did not want the wealthy owners of plantations and mills to have any special advantages with regard to the ability to get liquor.

PROHIBITION IS COMING

A cartoon by Joseph Keppler in *Puck*, 1886. From *The Pageant of America*, courtesy of the Yale University Press.

And they were largely under the control of churches which campaigned vigorously against the traffic in intoxicants.

As for the mountaineers, they stood in a class apart. They meddled little in politics, and perhaps their opinions were therefore of little importance. But they certainly had no objection to the closing of saloons. Their principal product was whiskey, and they were not accustomed to pay the taxes imposed upon distillers. Their traffic was therefore illegal in any case, and it promised to be more profitable if competition from licensed manufacturers and dealers was eliminated. The principal Southern opposition to Prohibition came from the negroes, and their disfranchisement by means of trickery and violence assured the success of the "temperance" movement, first in the states of the old Confederacy and then with regard to the country as a whole.

During the second half of the nineteenth century the Prohibitionists almost all worked against the legal sale of fermented as well as of distilled beverages. The Maine law of 1877 forbade the manufacture and sale of all intoxicants except cider. Cider was usually made and consumed by farmers, whereas beer was dispensed in wicked saloons. The people living in rural districts were thus permitted to rejoice at their own virtue without altogether having to give up the delights of intoxication.

Ernest H. Cherrington's triumphant account of *The Evolution of Prohibition in the United States* contains an interesting note about an event of the year 1890: "Leland, Iowa, passes an ordinance providing that any person who sells intoxicating liquors shall be tarred and feathered and cowhided out of the village." Perhaps such punishment was not unusual in Leland, and it may have been considered less than cruel when applied to bootleggers. No matter how wild the conjecture, it is better than the assumption that the extremely moral people of Leland chose to disregard a provision of the Constitution of the United States.

The next year a group of Prohibitionists proved their zeal for law and order: "Men and women together in a temperance crusade at Bloomville, Ohio, wreck a saloon and destroy the liquors, cigars, and billiard tables." It was such a moral mob as England and America have often been able to display.

In 1892 a negro was fined almost a million dollars for selling liquor in a "dry" part of Kentucky. Although bootleggers were already growing rich, it is not recorded that he was able to pay his fine.

Toward the end of the century South Carolina introduced a system of dispensing intoxicants from publicly owned retail stores. This plan aroused much interest throughout the country. Opposition on the part of Prohibitionists, the peculiar aspects of the liquor problem in the South, and the general mistrust of business operated by the government combined to make the dispensary system less than entirely satisfactory.

In 1893 Prohibition nominally existed in six states, as well as in various parts of other states which had local option laws. In much of this "dry" area it was usually difficult for strangers to buy intoxicants, except perhaps through the bellboys and clerks of hotels. The inhabitants had to pay fairly high prices for liquor and, if they bought it locally, often to content themselves with inferior grades. But liquor could be brought in through the mails. Where the officers charged with law enforcement thought fit, they often permitted saloons to operate quite openly. It was profitable for them to be nearsighted. Such was the state of affairs in the Prohibition districts of the country when the Ohio Anti-Saloon League was formed. In that state the opponents of the liquor traffic were largely descendants of the New England Puritans, while people with German names were among the leading anti-Prohibitionists. Good beer came out of Cincinnati, and excellent whiskey from the distilleries across the river.

The American Anti-Saloon League was organized in 1895, and it soon became an important factor in the Prohibition movement. It was able to obtain large contributions of money, which it declared necessary to combat the war chests of the brewers and distillers. Naturally, there were complaints that part of the funds clung to the fingers of League officials.

Sensationalism was sometimes employed in Prohibition propaganda. For example, at a New York meeting a paid actor represented the three stages of delirium tremens. His performance was enthusiastically received. The theatre had become somewhat more respectable, and its aid in the struggle against Demon Rum was no longer scorned. There were many songs about the evils of drunkenness. Soon after the Civil War appeared "Come Home, Father," of which the opening line still lingers on in many memories: "Father, dear father, come home with me now." But John Philip Sousa maliciously wrote the words and music of "The Free-Lunch Cadets," in praise of the viands obtainable without charge in saloons by those who bought a glass of beer for five cents.

During the last two decades of the century the Woman's Christian Temperance Union worked hard and with almost complete success to make the teaching of what was said to be "scientific temperance" compulsory in the American public schools. Pupils who did not pass beyond the elementary grades learned very little of science except that alcohol and tobacco are deadly poisons. Scientists, indeed, sometimes ventured to point out that the generalization is not true, except with such qualifications as utterly to destroy its force; but they were little heeded. It seemed to be a good democratic doctrine that truth could be made by the fiat of the elected representatives of the people. In 1899 the Indiana legislature came close to fixing the value of π at 4.

§ 6

Mark Sullivan considers the McGuffey readers largely responsible for the ethical standards prevailing in America in the twentieth century. These books, which were popular during a large part of the nineteenth, dealt much with the evils that result from drinking intoxicants. They warned the children against "the mockeries and fooleries of life."

Occasionally a child rebelled against the obvious falsehoods contained in the McGuffey readers. Thus, Gene Stratton Porter refused to be impressed by the lesson that little children should get along together harmoniously because birds in their nest agree. She had seen them fight.

Schoolbooks told young Americans how far superior their country was to all others, and how much better Christianity was than all other religions. But a number of states adopted constitutional amendments forbidding sectarian doctrines to be taught in the public schools. Like other constitutional provisions, these have been, in many districts, habitually violated. The Catholics continued to build parochial schools to keep their children from growing up godless or Protestant. Other denominations were content to give religious instruction only on Sunday, or (as among the orthodox Jews) in classes held daily after the dismissal of the public schools.

Foreigners and non-Protestants still aroused suspicion. There was a Chinese-Japanese scare in the Pacific states, and demands that immigration should be restricted arose in many quarters. Since the proportion of foreign-born residents remained very nearly constant in the United States between 1850 and 1890, the fear that the natives might be swamped does not appear to have been well founded.

Many good citizens still supposed that the Catholics were anxious to overthrow liberty in the United States. A serious attempt was made to gain President Cleveland's approval of a measure designed to bar them from the national Military and Naval academies. During the Spanish-American War a committee of Methodists and Baptists asked that only Protestant chaplains should be sent aboard American ships of war. There was much friction between the Irish and zealous Protestants of native origin. Then the Irish came into conflict with some of the other immigrants. On the East Side of New York, Jewish boys were afraid to walk in the streets where the Irish lived unless they went in large numbers. The gang wars were often between boys of different origins and faiths.

After the Civil War the religious skepticism which was prominent after the Revolution appeared again. The great orator of free thought was Robert Ingersoll, a man who was thoroughly convinced of the noxiousness of Christianity and who sacrificed a political career to the open expression of his views. Perhaps he turned comparatively few away from religion, but he made almost all educated men realize that Moses had made mistakes, which is to say that the Bible would not admit of literal interpretation.

Orthodoxy was broken. Evolution, about the truth of which the biologists had been divided, became generally accepted by men of science; but a struggle arose over the philosophical and religious inferences which were to be drawn from the fact of organic evolution. John Fiske delivered at Harvard, between 1869 and 1871, the lectures that were later presented in book form as *Outlines of Cosmic Philosophy*. He was then attacked in newspapers and sermons as a destroyer of religion. In 1872 the trustees of Lowell Institute in Boston indicated their disapproval of Fiske's views when they refused to invite him to lecture there. Nearly twenty years later Fiske was heard at Lowell Institute by overflowing audiences. He seems to have believed in God and immortality, although he was far from being an orthodox Christian, and the definitions of his faith were sufficiently vague to make the accusation of atheism possible. Fiske's later utterances were more favorable to the conception of a personal God, and therefore more acceptable to some people who had previously been shocked.

In 1876 the parsons raised an outcry because Huxley spoke at the opening of Johns Hopkins University. Later, many ministers came to accept the theory of evolution. Among them was President McCosh of Princeton, who had a perfect reputation for orthodoxy. It seemed at the close of the century that the theologians would soon all be adjusting themselves to the necessity of accepting organic evolution, as their predecessors had accepted the sphericity of the world and the new astronomy. But numerous good Christians in America knew little or absolutely nothing of Darwin. Their tranquillity indicated not assent but ignorance.

Rumblings over the higher criticism had been heard even before the Civil War. The subject was brought into general notice in 1893, when Charles Augustus Briggs was expelled from the Presbyterian ministry for professing his disbelief in certain tenets which that Church considered fundamental. He was then received by the Episcopalians and became a clergyman in the

[591]

Episcopal Church. Many ministers were wondering if they could accept literally some of the theological articles to which they had subscribed, but only a few bold ones ventured to express their doubts aloud.

While the intellectual problems of religion and theology interested comparatively few, evangelism and appeals to the emotions stirred the many. The Salvation Army was introduced into America in 1879, and it grew with great speed. The soldiers and officers of this body were sworn to renounce worldly living, to abstain from alcohol and tobacco, and to devote themselves to religious service. Moody and other popular preachers were heard by hundreds of thousands. Mrs. Eddy founded a new sect, and soon many Americans were convinced that it would be sinful to receive medical attention or to admit the existence of material evil. Spiritualism was another heresy which aroused much interest in the late nineteenth century, although the height of the spiritualist craze was not to come until after the World War.

Sunday observance became weaker almost everywhere, and especially in those cities where recent immigrants were numerous. Even New England ministers were accepting a more liberal interpretation of the duties belonging to the day. When young Edward Bok called upon the Reverend Phillips Brooks, he told him he was writing for a Sunday paper and asked whether he thought it was immoral of him to do this. Brooks answered that it depended upon the paper: he did not consider the mere fact of its appearance on Sunday sufficient to condemn it. Mark Twain felt free, in 1869, to criticize the extreme Sabbatarian views of some of his fellow pilgrims in Palestine, who tortured their mules in order to avoid the necessity of traveling on Sunday. In the '90's there was a struggle over the question whether or not the Chicago World's Fair was to be opened to visitors on the first day of the week. After two closed Sundays the managers decided that it should be open every day. Religious zealots were indignant, but they could do nothing to alter this decision.

The agitation for a stricter observance of Sunday was led by the National Reform Association and the American Sabbath Union, which later became the Lord's Day Alliance. Both these bodies have supported attempts to put an amendment into the Federal Constitution declaring the religion of the United States to be Christianity. The organ of the National Reform Association, called the *Christian Statesman,* went so far in 1888 as to argue that Congress ought to be permitted to restrain the exercise of "false" religions. These associations have been very active in the lobbies of Congress, working with particular zeal to secure very strict Sunday laws for the District of Columbia.

The irreligious frontier of one generation often became a center of piety and strict morals in the next. Samuel Bowles, editor of the Springfield, Massachusetts, *Republican,* wrote of San Francisco in 1865: "The New England elements are clearly dominant here and through the whole Pacific Coast region; softened from their old Puritanic habits . . . but still preserving their best qualities of decency, of order, of justice, of constant progress upward in morality and virtue." Much of the open laxity had disappeared: "The gamblers give way graciously to decency and respectability, and join in outward observance of the Sabbath, help to build churches, and make orderly the street life of the town. . . . Sunday is certainly as well observed as in New York."

There were still genuine frontiers in the United States. The rush into Oklahoma in 1889 brought out violence, open gambling on a large scale, and other conditions resembling those of four decades earlier in California. The sale of liquor within the territory was prohibited, but not stopped.

Some parts of the South kept up the old tradition of the blood feud. Formal dueling became rare, but the custom of shooting one's enemy in the back persisted. As late as 1900 Governor Goebel of Kentucky was shot from ambush, and some of those who conspired to kill him later received political advancement.

After the Civil War, negroes who were unaccustomed to the exercise of authority, and most of whom were illiterate, divided political power in the Southern states with voracious white politicians from the North. There were, indeed, some Northern men who came unselfishly to help the negroes, and some Southern "scalawags" who joined the Northern "carpetbaggers" in dividing the spoils. The freedmen, as was to be expected, often abused

[593]

their power. In some districts it was for a time almost impossible to convict negroes of crime; and those who were convicted quickly obtained pardons. Such conditions encouraged the white men to form lynching parties. And lynching remained long after the rule of the negroes collapsed.

The illegal killing of negroes accused of crime was at its height in the early '90's. There has been a decline since. White people in the South still sometimes say that their wives and daughters would not be safe if a colored man were not burned to death occasionally. As a matter of fact, by no means all the lynchings of negroes in the South arise out of allegations of rape or attempted rape. They have even been occasioned by slight disrespect in addressing white men, and by the refusal to be cheated by white landlords and shopkeepers.

Political corruption was certainly widespread in the South after the War, and conditions were not much better elsewhere in the United States. The Tweed Ring frauds in New York received much notice. Other cities in the North were robbed by politicians and contractors. In Columbia, South Carolina, a brothel kept by a negress was actually furnished at the cost of the State. In the North as well, public officials maintained profitable connections with gamblers, prostitutes, and liquor-sellers. During President Grant's administration many persons of prominence in Washington were involved in scandal. Grant himself was shown to be indiscreet, although no evidence incriminating him appeared.

In the South, the existence of really intolerable conditions brought about the formation of the Ku Klux Klan. Because it was secret and irresponsible, this organization became an instrument of injustice. There could be no fair trials. Negroes were whipped or murdered for very slight offenses, sometimes for none at all. Even the morals of white men sometimes interested the Klan. One or two were flogged on the charge of maltreating and failing to support their wives. The Ku Klux Klan was primarily intended to deprive the Southern negro of political power. This was made possible when Federal troops were withdrawn. There is evidence that the Southern politicians agreed to let the election

"LET US PREY"

A cartoon by Thomas Nast on the Tweed Ring, "a group of vultures waiting for the
storm to blow over," in *Harper's Weekly*, 1871.

of Hayes stand on condition that they should thenceforth be allowed to rule without outside interference.

Political dishonesty after the War represented one phase of the general response to the prevailing respect for money and for those who were "smart" enough to accumulate it. The art of getting rich and that of being genteel were the two things considered worthy of cultivation. Daniel Drew, who became rich by means of stock manipulations of a very dubious character, made himself respectable by giving a large part of his gains to various Methodist institutions. Although he eventually lost his money, his fame was perpetuated in the Drew Theological Seminary. Rhodes and others tell us, though, that the general level of commercial honesty was higher after the War than before it. And De Varigny, in 1895, commented on the unpopularity of what were considered ill-gotten gains, as manifested in the social ostracism of Jay Gould.

The expansion of commerce and industry, together with the formation of large units of business, presented great opportunities for profit. But the persons who organized trusts saw in them more than the opportunity to gain economies through large-scale operation. They often deliberately planned, and entered into agreements with one another, to destroy competition and establish monopolies. Railroads gave special rebates to favored companies. In a few instances they supplied them with information about the business their rivals were doing, in order to help put them out of business.

To the general public all trusts and large companies seemed iniquitous. Some politicians made bids for support by working to suppress the trusts. Others found it more profitable to work with and for big business. Radical movements of all sorts flourished in the '90's, and strong paternalistic tendencies were then developed in the United States. Socialism attracted many, and the single-tax theories found many supporters. But anarchism, never very popular in America, became a popular bugaboo, and some anarchists were treated with great brutality and injustice. Though conservatism was victorious in the presidential elections of 1896 and 1900, much unrest remained. Free land was virtually at an end, and this was the principal cause of discontent. Though many people in the United States were excited by the glory of a new imperialism, almost all believed earnestly in the virtues of democracy. For that was American, and whatever was American was good.

CHAPTER XVI

IN WHICH SKIRTS GROW SHORTER, AND THE INTERVALS BETWEEN DRINKS LONGER

§ 1

IT is impossible to obtain reliable statistics about the prevalence of prostitution in the United States. We can learn how many women have been arrested in one or another city for solicitation and various other offenses apparently arising out of professional harlotry, but such figures tell us more about the zeal of the police than about the extent of prostitution. However, most authorities agree that "commercialized vice" has declined since 1900. If this is true, there is more than one reason why.

Probably the primary factor is the increased economic independence of women. There is no satisfactory evidence that extramarital sexual intercourse outside of prostitution has become rarer during the twentieth century. More likely, it has become commoner. This much lies beyond dispute, that frankness about sex has vastly increased during the last three decades.

A Middle Western newspaper printed in 1928 an anecdote about a youth who called on a girl for the first time to take her for a ride. No sooner was she seated in his car than he leaned over a little and calmly asked her, "Are you a virgin?" The story, which is (or, to speak with journalistic caution, is alleged to be) true, continues with the young lady slapping his face and jumping out to take refuge in the purer moral atmosphere of her own home. The villainous seducer of old novels was never so direct. Yet now it is sometimes the respectable female who goes straight to the point. Clement Wood tells how, after he had delivered a lecture, a damsel from the audience came to him and asked, "Are you really married?" "Yes." "Well, then, let's

"NO, NO! NOT THAT!"

A cartoon by Peter Arno in *The New Yorker*, 1928.

commit bigamy or whatever they call it." To be sure, not all illicit courtship is of just this nature.

Estimates are sometimes made of the proportion of American boys and girls who have committed fornication by the time they have reached the age of eighteen or graduated from high school. These vary greatly, but they are sometimes quite high. An English reviewer of one of Ben B. Lindsey's books congratulates his countrymen on the superior chastity of their adolescents. This is very likely imaginary.

During the nineteenth century the ills supposed to arise from masturbation were much emphasized. Fathers sometimes led their young sons into brothels with the laudable desire of warding them off. It was generally held that women needed no sexual experience or information until they married, whereas the desires of men could not safely be denied. The recent tendency among medical experts has been to deny the responsibility of "self-abuse" for feeble-mindedness and the numerous maladies catalogued by Tissot. Freud has indeed made excessive masturbation or frequent pollutions responsible for neurasthenia, but comparatively few American physicians have adopted his theory. They usually accept the possibility of continence on the part of men. A certain approach has been made to a single standard of sexual morality, with women gaining privileges and men losing them in the process.

With regard to illicit relations, especially since the passage of the Mann Act, it is often the man that pays and pays and pays. By way of exception, the state of Washington adopted the law in 1919 extending the definition of statutory rape to include women, that is, making it possible to punish them severely for having sexual intercourse with boys. According to the generally prevalent theory, the man is presumed to be the seducer. In fact, the unsupported evidence of a woman of good reputation is usually enough to convict a man of rape.

"No such wholesale rebellion against the ancient conventions of sex has ever been known in the history of civilization," says Judge Lindsey. "Rubber has revolutionized morals." He includes that which is used in automobile tires. It has become possible for young people to go far from home with great rapidity, and also to evade what used to be considered the practically inevitable consequence of sexual union.

Not all the states provide illegitimacy statistics. Where they are available, they show a rather low rate for white women. In 1920, Kansas reported only seven illegitimate births for every thousand births; Massachusetts, ten; Missouri, with a considerable colored population, thirty. Of the states that made separate returns for white and colored births, Virginia showed 2 per cent illegitimate among the whites, nearly 13 per cent among the negroes; Maryland had seventeen bastards per thousand births among the whites, 195 per thousand born to colored mothers; and there were striking differences between the two races in other reports. This variation in illegitimacy is partly to be explained by a greater familiarity with contraceptive methods among the whites.

Of course, this does not entirely account for the higher bastardy rate in the colored population. Professor Jerome Dowd quotes a Southern physician about the sexual morals of the negroes: "Many girls under twelve years of age are seen by me to cohabit with men and are frequently found with venereal troubles." Some scientists contend that the sexual impulses are stronger in Africans than in persons of the Caucasian race. At any rate, the differences in environment which have existed and still exist between white and colored people are sufficient to account for the variations in moral outlook. It should be noted, too, that illegitimate children are attributed to the race of the mother, and white men still beget many children upon negresses, as well as upon mulatto and quadroon women who are set down in the records as colored.

"Still, immorality with colored women is far less prevalent than before the War," says Dr. A. W. Calhoun, referring to the war that brought slavery to an end. But he mentions the difficulty which was experienced in a Southern city about 1908 in keeping white high-school boys from having sexual experiences with negro girls. White prostitutes appeared to be becoming much more numerous in the South at this time. Dubois expressed the opinion in 1914 that they had doubled in number during the three preceding decades.

There has been an increase in the number of colored prostitutes in the North, both to provide for the great many negroes who have migrated in search of better conditions and to answer the demands of a white patronage. The negresses seldom ask high prices, and they are somewhat more willing than white women to take part in perversions. White men often find mulattoes attractive, and not seldom take them as concubines. Women with small amounts of negro blood often pass for lily-white, and marry as such. The discovery of the true situation sometimes, as in a recent case, leads to scandal.

Unmarried negroes of nubile age are rare. Colored people who lose their spouses through death, divorce, or desertion remarry more frequently than white people in similar situations. However, the bonds of matrimony are often quite loose with them. In many negro families the wife is the principal breadwinner. The husband sometimes feels that his work is done when he delivers the washing for her. This situation is due not entirely to laziness, but depends rather upon the fact that domestic labor for negresses is often easier to find than positions to which colored men are admitted. The resulting economic independence of colored women makes them unwilling to put up with marriage under unfavorable conditions. And the increased self-sufficiency of white women has also made divorce commoner than it would otherwise be in the United States.

It seems to be generally agreed by observers familiar with the facts that marital fidelity is valued less among colored people than among whites. But this condition is changing, and it is evident that the negroes are taking over the moral standards (and inconsistencies as well) of the dominant race.

At present there is more crowding among the negroes than among the whites. Poverty is common with them, and they are admitted reluctantly or not at all into districts where white people already have homes. Hence, they are usually cramped and without privacy in the cities. Even in the country a large family must sometimes get along with a one-room cabin. In

some urban districts—Harlem, for instance—rents are so high
that only the wealthier negroes can afford to have an apartment
for a single family. Lodgers usually help to pay the rent, and
to disturb the domestic tranquillity.

The immigrants living in the foreign quarters of large cities
have been confronted by a similar situation. There is a Yiddish
song of American origin about the relations existing between the
lady of the house and the boarder.

Except where they are thickly settled, negroes have few recre-
ational facilities. They are excluded from the white men's
theatres or offered undesirable seats. They are not welcomed in
parks and playgrounds except those they have been able to secure
for their own particular use. And the result often is that they
consider the various forms and degrees of love-making the only
diversions open to them.

A relic of slavery is the habit of making and breaking quasi-
matrimonial connections with the utmost informality. This
exists also in many white circles, without the same excuse. Perhaps it has been encouraged somewhat by the decision of the
Supreme Court of the United States that a man and woman living
together as husband and wife, even though they have not gone
through the regular legal formalities, are married according to
the common law, except in states that have provided otherwise
by statute. It is often difficult to tell whether a man and a
woman are guilty of habitual fornication or are to be regarded as
respectable married people. Of course, when there is no record
of a marriage, an inability to agree usually results in a full break
without a divorce suit.

Industrial booms in the South have often caused workmen and
prostitutes to join in the race for prosperity. In several instances
the wives of workmen have taken it upon themselves to wreck
the brothels to which they found their husbands attracted. The
textile mills have brought a great many girls into the Southern
cities, to work at low wages. The gains of the South have sometimes been made at the expense of New England towns and
caused distress there. But, whether in the North or in the South,
there is no clear evidence that the moral practice of the country

districts is stricter than that of the cities. The purity of the countryside is much exaggerated, and rural mothers have been heard to complain that their sons can engage in dissipation at least as easily as though they lived in the city. An automobile, which it is cheaper and more convenient to keep in a village or on a farm than in a large city, brings all sorts of pleasures within their reach.

Women of foreign birth have been far less conspicuous as prostitutes in twentieth-century America than they were when Sanger made his survey in the 1850's. Nevertheless, there have been great waves of moral indignation, fostered by sensational writers, over "white slavery." Stories were told about elaborate organizations which kidnapped girls in Europe and kept them, against their will, in American brothels. It is true that the international exchange of prostitutes existed in the nineteenth century and continues to exist in the twentieth. But intelligently conducted surveys, both in Great Britain and in the United States, have shown the number of girls brought in from foreign countries by force or the use of trickery to be very small indeed. Most of the imported prostitutes in America pursued the same profession abroad and have come here to improve their economic position.

While large brothels were numerous in such cities as Chicago and New York, it was necessary to use special recruiting agents to provide new girls for easily jaded patrons. The "cadets" and panders were not always very scrupulous in their methods. Still, they did not, except in a few exceptional instances, force young women into what may with any show of reason be called slavery. The keepers of brothels have used their old tricks to hold attractive but unintelligent women within their power, keeping them constantly in their debt and never allowing them to have a clear understanding of their accounts. But the brothel, and especially the large brothel, is now much less common in the United States than it was half a century ago.

The agitation against "white slavery" began in the early years of the twentieth century. Between 1910 and 1915 a number of laws were passed against panders and persons engaged in traffic with women. The Mann Act, passed by Congress in 1910, makes criminal, according to a Supreme Court decision of 1917, the conducting of a woman across a state line to have illicit intercourse with her, even though no economic motive is involved. It has proved a means of enriching blackmailers. Other results (said to be better ones) have perhaps flowed from this law, but there is no clear evidence of it.

The various "vigilance committees" and "social-purity" organizations which arose about 1912 volunteered a large quantity of good advice on the proper way to suppress prostitution or to reduce its evils. The fear that youth was being corrupted in motion-picture theatres led to censorship laws. The states began to pass them in 1914. Cabarets and dance halls were denounced as evil places. In 1914 the city of Detroit tried to exclude female singers from the cabarets.

Direct raids upon the brothels and attempts to do away with segregated districts appeared in response to surges of public sentiment. About 1900 a number of police judges began to discontinue the practice of imposing fines, which seemed to be license fees, upon the keepers of raided brothels, and substituted prison sentences. Another wave of purity came in 1909, and the Rockefeller report in New York brought about many wars on open prostitution in 1912 and the following years. The laws that the various state legislatures passed, the ordinances that city councils and boards of aldermen enacted at the request of earnest spinster ladies and reverend doctors, would, if placed end to end, connect all the bawdy houses in the country with broad paper roads.

Kansas made the keeping of a brothel felonious; California dealt similarly with *fellatio* and *cunnilingus*. State courts decided that various laws meant more than they seemed to say, because the legislators were too modest to mention the perversions and explain exactly what they sought to prohibit. Cleveland was agog over the proposal to abolish the red-light districts; ladies pleaded that they would be raped or seduced if no prostitutes were available; and other ladies, who felt all too secure against such dangers, wanted every bona roba driven out of town. A law was passed, and the red lights ceased to shine; but the sporting men of Cleveland boasted that they could still find Gerties and Babes enough. In many cities that had officially been cleansed, policemen wore the smile that a cat wears immediately after having eaten a canary, and aldermanic paunches grew.

Then came the War to Make the World Secure for Democracy, also known to serious historians as the War to End Wars. There was an idealist on the throne, a man proud of his descent from Scotch-Irish Presbyterians, and idealists everywhere thought that the paradisal days had come. The soldier boys went marching off on their glorious adventure. It would not do to let them wench and booze, like ordinary naughty men of war. Oh, no: if they were to die in vermin-infested trenches, they were to pass to Heaven nevertheless clothed in purity and assured of the blessing of the Woman's Christian Temperance Union. Tobacco, indeed, was not denied them, though it was complained that some of the holiest of the welfare workers demanded an exorbitant price for it.

Lecturers provided by the Young Men's Christian Association proved to the soldiers, with the aid of slides and motion pictures, that persons who abstain from sexual intercourse seldom suffer from the venereal diseases, and that syphilis may sometimes occasion very disagreeable effects. The police helped to win the War by raiding brothels, especially those in the neighborhood of the cantonments.

There were genteel and well-brought-up girls who couldn't resist the lure of the uniform, even though olive drab is far less romantic than bright blue. There were women who made a business of marrying soldiers by the dozen, collecting slices of their pay and dreaming about the German shells which would make wealthy and manifold widows of them. There were other women who displayed great generosity of one sort or another to soldiers and sailors. "War baby" came into the American vocabulary. It was a phrase of dual meaning, applied figuratively to the stocks that rose in price because of war orders and literally to children that owed their birth to war excitement.

Juvenile delinquency, including the prostitution of minor girls, increased to a considerable extent during the War, if we may judge by the frequency of arrests. Repressive measures against houses of prostitution, taken on a large scale in the time of war, continued after it was over. *The American Year Book* for 1925 tells us: "Repression of commercialized prostitution has become the course pursued in the United States, and the 'red-light' districts together with municipal toleration of open vice have virtually disappeared." Yet the next year's book has an account of the closing of five hundred brothels in Detroit, and leaves us with the wonder if there were not still a number of cities with many houses of prostitution in each. This was actually the case.

Street solicitation is still permitted in some American cities. It exists to some extent in almost every town of any size, whatever the attitude of the police toward it may be. Charles E. Miner said in 1928: "At present the segregated district is a relatively rare phenomenon in the United States." I cannot find that it exists anywhere legally, for there are a great many laws against open prostitution; but the meaning of some of the statutes and the construction to be placed upon common-law provisions may be variously construed, for which reason it would take an experienced lawyer, with access to the laws and the decisions, to interpret the status of the brothel and the streetwalker in some jurisdictions. In most communities it depends on the mayor, the chief of police, and the prosecuting attorney to what extent prostitution is openly allowed.

Occasionally, a candidate assures the voters of his unwillingness to be very severe in enforcing the laws. The phrase "an open town" is euphemistically employed in this connection. Mr. Miner tells us how the "parlor houses" in Chicago have mostly disappeared, and been replaced by small, cheap, dirty places. A single organization, not many years ago, found 120 open brothels in that city. But even in towns where large houses of prostitution are rare, there are often large numbers of unattached harlots. The decline of prostitution since 1900 is often exaggerated by people who think that an institution or condition necessarily ceases to exist when it has been put outside the pale of the law.

About 1914 George J. Kneeland began to call attention to the existence of young women of respectable and often wealthy families who habitually engaged in illicit sexual intercourse. He told the members of women's clubs (when he could get them to listen) that he had the names of three hundred such girls. They were, he said, mentally and physically normal, and they were so far from being considered vicious persons that many of them were prominent in church and Sunday-school affairs. However, they rebelled against the routine drabness of their lives by having physical love affairs. Mr. Kneeland thought that modern dancing, by bringing about intimate contacts between members of the two sexes, stimulated fornication.

Judge Lindsey, who was unquestionably in a position to know the facts, presented a picture of conditions among high-school students in Denver which shocked their parents and all the good Americans who were congratulating themselves on the moral gains brought about by repressive legislation. Attempts have been made to lighten the picture, on the ground that Lindsey's position brought him into touch almost entirely with delinquents and his viewpoint is therefore warped. And there are, of course, men and women who declare that things may be like that in Denver, but as to their own cities, why—!!

F. Scott Fitzgerald's *This Side of Paradise* brought out a number of novels on fast life in the colleges. A great deal of excitement appeared about the petting parties and the hip flasks of the younger generation, but it seemed that all possible laws had already been passed and there was nothing much to be done. Occasionally, moral indignation fell like a ton of bricks upon a young man who had been careless enough to carry his light-o'-love in his automobile over a state line.

In the feverish days after the War it was generally apparent that young women were not so passive as their mothers had considered it necessary to be. Social workers and others tried to evolve schemes for making courtship end happily with marriage. A few churches opened their social parlors for this purpose. But wooing more often took place in automobiles, and it seems that girls sometimes thought it advisable to walk home.

With the increased use of aircraft, newspaper wits began to wonder if nice girls wouldn't need to safeguard themselves by taking along parachutes.

"It has been stated," remarked Mr. Miner in 1928, "that the progress made against syphilis and gonorrhea during the past fifteen years is the greatest public-health accomplishment in history." It seems to be certain that information about the control of conception will soon be available to practically everybody in the United States who cares to have it. If, in addition, the fear of venereal disease should altogether disappear, moral standards and practices with regard to sex might easily be revolutionized.

It is probably fruitless to speculate about the future, but some observers already see signs that the United States is moving toward companionate marriage. To be sure, the childless union cannot be the sole matrimonial form if the race is to continue to exist, but the companionate and the family can flourish side by side, with the former usually preparatory to the latter.

General interest in the companionate marriage, and familiarity with the term, derive from Judge Lindsey's book on the subject (1927). Mr. and Mrs. E. Haldeman-Julius have argued in its favor, and many magazine editors have exploited the theme. The editor of *Collier's*, in a radio talk, has declared that the companionate marriage must fail because it appeals to "the baser instincts," whereas there is a pure instinct for monogamy which is certain to triumph. But there is no good reason to believe that such instincts or innate action patterns, whether good or bad, actually exist. Our opinions about marriage are the results of education, not heredity. Besides, the companionate marriage, at least as it is advocated by Judge Lindsey, is not opposed to monogamy.

He says simply that young people who wish to get married ought, especially if they cannot yet afford to bring up children, to be provided with the best available information about preventing conception; and if, being childless, husband and wife discover that they are unsuited to each other, divorce by mutual consent and with a minimum of formality and expense should be arranged. Lindsey also advocates eugenic selection in marriage, but this is a minor factor in his program. Perhaps it is the weakest element, because human beings refuse to be guided in their choice of mates by considerations of the excellence or lack of excellence of the resulting offspring. And the movement to sterilize the mentally defective has been checked by the realization that it is not always easy to separate the normal from the abnormal, as well as by a tendency to emphasize environment as much as heredity.

Divorce has become more familiar since 1900, and, at least in some circles, far more respectable. Some of the churches oppose it as much as ever, but they seem entirely incapable of checking the rising tide. William Jennings Bryan used to speak strongly against divorce, mostly on religious grounds; but, ironically, both a son and a daughter of his had their marriages dissolved in court.

Much interest has been displayed by Americans in the annulments of marriage by the Roman Catholic Rota, although not very many such decrees have been granted. The fact remains that Catholics of wealth and influence can obtain what amounts to a divorce from their Church. These are not legal in the United States without juridical action in the civil courts.

Americans have violated the laws of France in their anxiety to obtain Parisian divorces. They have used the opportunities afforded by the ample facilities for divorce in some Mexican cities. They have envied the people of the Soviet Republics, able to break matrimonial bonds by mutual consent. They have gone to Nevada for easy divorces. Some of the states make it easy enough for their inhabitants, if they are unhappily married and possess fifty or a hundred dollars for court and lawyers' fees, to become single again. The populous state of New York, although it now makes a special provision for cases where one spouse has gone away and disappeared, still formally limits divorces to those occasioned by adultery. Of course, collusion is often arranged.

A great deal of confusion arises out of the differences existing in marriage and divorce laws of the various states and the fact that the claim of residence in a particular state or country is often fraudulently made in order to take advantage of its laws. At present, though, people are reluctant to subtract anything from state rights in order to add to the powers of the Federal Government.

All the numerous attempts that have been made to induce Congress to repeal the law making it illegal to send contraceptives and information about their use through the mails have so far been in vain. In 1914 and 1915 the agitation about the right to control and limit conception came once more into general notice. The term "birth control" was then widely adopted. It has the advantage of being short and simple, as well as the disadvantage of seeming to apply to aborticide rather than to contraception. Margaret Sanger, Emma Goldman, and Dr. Ben Reitman were among those whose zeal for the cause of birth control brought them into conflict with the law.

The Catholic and Mormon churches have been most bitterly opposed to the artificial limitation of offspring. Yet their members, too, have smaller families than their grandparents had. In a few American cities there are public clinics working to develop improved contraceptive methods and to spread information. They ordinarily deal only with married women of whom it is possible to maintain that their health, physical or mental, would be injured if they could not prevent conception. There are still many physicians who know little or nothing about this work, and therefore cannot give competent advice even in cases where gestation and birth present unusual dangers.

Our moralists are in constant fear that the unmarried may learn how to prevent conception and that fornication may become even more popular than it is to-day. But, as Lindsey points out, high-school boys and girls are not quite so ignorant as they are supposed to be. In any case, extramarital relations become (by utilitarian principles) much less undesirable if it is certain that no unwanted infants will be born. Of course, they still remain vicious from the point of view of Judæo-Christian ethics.

Several religious charlatans of the twentieth century have been accused of founding free-love colonies. In no instance, though, have many people been involved. Where promiscuity has prevailed, it has always been in comparatively small circles, and it seems that wide publicity has always been fatal to such organizations. At least one female evangelist has been involved in a sexual scandal; but she has not been officially prosecuted, and most of her followers have remained loyal. In recent years southern California has proved a fruitful field for queer religious sects of all kinds, some ascetic, some voluptuous. And the headquarters of one body which advocates celibacy are in Florida.

Some parts of the country allow a certain amount of respectability to be attached to premarital sexual connections, which need not lead to marriage unless a child is born. Dr. Howard B. Woolston says that this is true of parts of Pennsylvania, settled long ago from Germany, and of certain sections of Delaware in which the old Swedish influence still remains. But he thinks the custom has become much more dangerous than it was a few generations ago: "Although such relations may be entered into today, there is not the same likelihood of marriage to legitimatize the children of such unions, and the custom probably has its effect in swelling the volume of American prostitutes." There is no evidence that it has: if the usage were general, there would be little occasion for brothels. And the danger with regard to illegitimate children has actually grown less.

Married women have gained most in the relaxation of standards since 1900. H. Perry Robinson, an Englishman who was familiar with the American proprieties, wrote in 1908 that while girls had more liberty in the United States than in England, English married women enjoyed more freedom than American ones. He quoted approvingly from *Life*: "If you marry an American girl, you may be sure that you will not be the first man she has kissed. If you marry an English one, you may be certain you will not be the last."

Matters have changed since in both countries; and young women, whether married or single, know little of chaperonage in either. There are certainly American families in which both husband and wife consider themselves free to have sexual relations with a variety of people. Whether the condition has grown since 1900, or merely the willingness to discuss it, is doubtful. In all probability, the number of adulterous husbands still greatly exceeds the number of adulterous wives, although the difference in this regard is growing steadily less. There is no unified view about the wickedness or lack of wickedness involved in adultery. Now and then a preacher speaks of it as worse than murder. And, at the same time, there are circles in which it is taken as a matter of course, or perhaps as a peculiarly modern custom, analogous to the smoking of cigarettes by women. All the tragedy of the triangle is removed when a married woman has sexual relations with several men, no one of whom she loves romantically or desires to substitute for her husband. The husband usually can, if he wishes, secure a divorce. In many parts of the country it is still allowable for him to kill his wife's lover.

Judge Robert Grant of the Probate Court in Boston wrote, a dozen years ago: "Today I hear it urged by feminists of a certain type that a wife should not be deprived of her child for mere infidelity." Judge Grant considered a sneer sufficient reply to such an idea, and some judges still agree with him. It is sometimes seen that a woman may be a good mother in spite of liking other men as well as her husband, and that, if punishment is necessary, taking away the child may mean the punishment of the wrong person. Judge Grant thought it was the female sinner that paid and paid: "Somehow the woman continues to be haled into court, while the man slips through the net in which they both were taken." But there are many who doubt the need of fining or imprisoning either. Judge Grant saw one great change: "The freemasonry of women which once was so relentless that it applied the thumbscrew of torture to offenders has happily been won to mercy." Perhaps the sex has not become less cruel, but simply more tolerant of what formerly seemed unfair competition.

§ 2

It cannot be denied that there have been moral changes since 1917, when the "Rules of the Reservation" in El Paso told the prostitutes in the segregated district that they must "not sit with legs crossed in a vulgar manner and must keep skirts down." This warning is being given to-day to the vice-presidents and executive chairmen who sit on the platforms of ladies' Prohibition conventions. They don't always heed it.

In the early years of the twentieth century, women were arrested and fined for appearing on the streets in skirts slit in such a way as to expose a few inches of the lower leg. Shortly before the European War broke out, an actress appeared in a Broadway play wearing a bathing suit partially covered by a bathrobe. Her press agent exploited her daring, and there was much commotion among genteel women. Jaded husbands in Iowa and Ohio discovered that they had business to attend to in New York.

But, since the War, some bold ministers have had lightly draped maidens present symbolic dances in their churches. Very moral clergymen have preached sensationally sexy sermons, sometimes to separate audiences of men and women. The preachers have bowed to the necessity of competing with musical comedies which present pretty chorus girls dressed in fixed smiles and shimmering beads, and with Sunday rotogravure sections which show lovely models in combination garments and winners of beauty contests dressed in one-piece bathing suits.

These papers give intimate glimpses of Mrs. Knickerbocker's knees, caught as she sits on the sand at Palm Beach or on the rail of an ocean liner. "Married women and older women generally hold a far more important place in American Society than they did a generation ago," remarked J. St. Loe Strachey in 1926. But they do not pride themselves upon their age, and they seek to conceal it as much as possible. Once upon a time, girls were proud of being old enough to conceal their legs with long skirts. That was in the almost fabulous age when women of forty-five felt it unnecessary to compete with young girls in dress and the use of cosmetics. Rouge was then chiefly employed by actresses and sporty women.

About 1913 there was great excitement in the United States over peek-a-boo waists and other translucent garments, as well as over short skirts and low-cut bosoms. Perhaps feminine intuition realized that there would be a war soon, and a struggle to win the male. And then again, maybe not; but this philosophical explanation will serve as well as another.

RELAXATIONS OF THE TIRED BUSINESS MAN

A group from Earl Carroll's *Vanities* of 1928.

In 1914 and 1915 a biology teacher in the Bronx Borough of New York was advising her freshman high-school girls to lift their skirts as they walked up the stairs, in order to keep from picking up bacilli-infested dust. The freshman boys were excited because a young teacher of English, fresh from Wellesley and making no allowance for their precocity, sat upon a table and allowed a few inches of her leg to be seen as she conducted a literary club.

Ten years earlier, a sculptor named Charles R. Lamb, addressing a group of women who made up the Rainy Day Club, urged them to wear skirts which should not reach above the shoetops. He thought this was good advice even for sunny days. But in 1914 factory girls still wore stockings of cotton. If they were very coquettish, they wore silk on rainy days, when they lifted their skirts ever so daintily to keep from getting mud on the hems.

In the spring of 1919 legs were still a treat. A young instructor at Columbia was observed to follow a girl student of the Extension Division, keeping perhaps a dozen feet behind her and gazing earnestly into the slit of her skirt. It was surely not a Barnard girl, because Barnard was very genteel.

Then came the general shortening of skirts and hair I suppose every man was shocked the first time he sat down in a street car and saw the garters of a young girl—or perhaps a grandmother—across the aisle. It became rather a point of fashion for women to display their garters. These were sometimes moved down a little, and often elaborately decorated. Sometimes there were two pairs of garters, one for show and one to hold up the stockings. Or else the stockings were rolled to somewhere in the neighborhood of the knees, and the skin was visible for some distance above. Legs which seemed to be or actually were stockingless were seen.

And even conservative magazines found no impropriety in accepting advertisements containing pictures of women who frankly possessed legs as well as arms. It was natural enough for manufacturers of stockings and underwear to use such pictures when the slogan "You just know she wears them" became obsolete. But silk-covered legs were also employed to call attention to cigarettes, washing machines, and artificial jewelry. A few

"WHERE THE HECK IS THAT TOOTH PASTE?"

Courtesy of Bost, Inc. Copyright, 1929.

periodicals of general circulation refuse to show females in combination garments, and insist that a foot or two of hosiery is
quite enough for any respectable model to reveal in an advertisement. Of course, men are less moved by the sight of knees than
they used to be.

The twentieth century has fewer verbal taboos than the nineteenth. Psychoanalysis must bear some of the responsibility for
the change. This subject had its beginnings in the 1880's and
'90's. Sigmund Freud lectured, in German, at Clark University
in 1910. American psychologists and some physicians then became familiar with his views. The general interest, culminating
in a craze, appeared in the United States after the World War.
Such words as *homosexual* and *sadism* and *exhibitionism* did not
originate with the psychoanalysts; but comparatively few people
were familiar with Krafft-Ebing and Iwan Bloch, while all the
sweet young things hurried to get popular accounts of Freud.

Newspapers in general have departed little from the taboos
which they maintained in 1910. Even the sensational tabloids
depend much upon euphemisms, though they are careful to
present their ideas clearly enough to be understood by high-
school girls. Various papers have their own lists of forbidden
words. "Rape" is very rarely seen in newspapers, except perhaps
in columns of court news intended for lawyers. "Criminal
assault" sometimes appears in its place, but cautious editors
prefer "a serious offense." However, this phrase is certainly
ambiguous, and it is sometimes used to cover sodomy and other
crimes which may not be mentioned in the presence of ears polite.
"A statutory offense" is sometimes used for these. "Prostitute"
is an embarrassing word, and for it "painted lady" or "lady of
easy virtue" is sometimes substituted. For "concubine" the
ordinary euphemism of "mistress" does not seem quite decent,
and "housekeeper" often replaces it. Such a usage may well
outrage the feelings of women who take care of the homes of
single gentlemen though not cohabiting with them. At least
equally unsatisfactory is "common-law wife" for "concubine."
There are essential differences between the two. In fact, a
common-law wife is as much married as though she had stood

before a minister, heard the strains of "At Dawning," and blushingly said, "I do."

Horace Kephart tells of euphemisms often heard in the South. A bull is there referred to as a "male-brute," and a boar as a "male-hog." Nevertheless, the mountaineers who observe these conventions use language "as coarse as the mixed-company speeches in Shakespeare's comedies and the offhand pleasantries of Good Queen Bess."

There are pruderies in commerce, too. "Hose" for "stockings" is an old euphemism which still remains. "Sanitary napkins" acquire new trade names, and special forms are printed in the newspapers to be cut out and handed to the salesman so that the embarrassment involved in asking for them may be avoided. And "toilet paper" is still further euphemized in various ways.

In 1904 Lyman Abbott suggested to Edward Bok, then editor of the *Ladies' Home Journal,* that he should deal in the magazine with venereal disease as he had already dealt with patent medicines. Bok asked the advice of a number of people about this, and he was generally advised not to meddle with the subject. No matter how he handled it, he was told, women would feel that the innocence of their daughters was threatened.

Nevertheless, Bok began, in 1906, a rather gingerly discussion of sex and the venereal diseases in the columns of his magazine. Protests quickly came, and thousands of subscribers sent in cancellations. Bok tells how he "saw his own friends tear the offending pages out of the periodical before it was allowed to find a place on their home tables." Then the editor was encouraged by the sympathetic attitude of many prominent men and women. Among those who wrote articles expressing approval of what he was doing were Jane Addams, Margaret Deland, Henry van Dyke, President Eliot of Harvard, Cardinal Gibbons, and the Bishop of London.

But most large magazines still deny their columns to serious articles about sex. Many important books on the subject have been treated by the authorities as utterly immoral, or restricted to the use of lawyers and physicians, with ministers and teachers sometimes included. Yet during the World War the Government of the United States undertook to supply information about sex. And information which "every boy should know" and "every married woman should know" is now available in five-cent as well as in five-dollar editions.

America has a reputation for prudery abroad, even in Great Britain; and this fact is due in part to the way some foreign visitors have been treated. When Maxim Gorky came with a lady who was not his wife, the hotels of New York would have nothing to do with him. Mark Twain was one of the group of American writers who cancelled the dinner they were to have given in Gorky's honor. They would not approve of immorality, not they.

Two decades later, Lady Cathcart came to the United States, told the immigration inspectors she was divorced, explained that she had eloped with one man while married to another, and was politely informed that her "moral turpitude" prevented her entrance into the country. However, since adultery was clearly not criminal in England, she was finally permitted to enter the country.

In 1904 Professor Hugo Münsterberg, in a book addressed to Germans, declared that "the moral atmosphere of the United States is much freer from unhealthful miasmas" than that of the European Continent. He considered this fact largely due to coeducation. He was referring especially to the social freedom of women and to their ability to travel alone for great distances without running much risk of being insulted.

H. Perry Robinson, commenting on the same conditions a few years later, remarked that not all American cities were alike. And he thought that the freedom from insult which, in some places, unescorted women certainly did enjoy had only recently been gained.

Foreign observers have had much to say about coeducation in the United States and about the many opportunities offered for free social intercourse between the sexes. Their objections have been of many sorts, but seldom have they said that sexual immorality is increased by the lack of separation between young men and young women.

§ 3

Doubleday, Page and Company accepted Dreiser's *Sister Carrie* in 1900. Walter H. Page wrote the author a letter congratulating him on the excellence of the book. Then it is said that the wife of another partner read it and became very indignant. The publishers could not, under their contract, avoid printing a few copies, but they took care not to sell any. In England, however, the book was successful. Some of Dreiser's later works have involved him in difficulties with the Society for the Suppression of Vice. *Sister Carrie* was objectionable because the heroine's transgressions did not bring her to a tragic end. The later novels were accused of disregarding American ideals and lacking reticence. In recent years, however, there has been a great Dreiser vogue. Many writers and readers feel thankful to Dreiser for having helped them to gain the liberty they now enjoy. He enjoys, then, a position in American literature much like Whitman's; and his artistic weaknesses, like Whitman's, are forgiven.

Ernest Boyd noted in 1922 the eagerness of many American critics to accept as great literature all that expressed a revolt against the old Puritan traditions. This now seems to be true even of many newspaper reviewers who used to speak, only a few years ago, of "gutter books" and "literary sewage." In spite of the great changes which have taken place, prudish objections remain capable of suppressing a book or a play.

In 1903 the librarians of Omaha, and in 1906 those of Brooklyn, decided that *Huckleberry Finn* was an immoral book and removed it from their open shelves. Walt Whitman's poems naturally fared still worse. *Leaves of Grass* has occasioned a number of raids on bookstores, followed by confiscations. The recent tendency, though, has been to treat it as a classic. Classics, it has been judicially decided, "are ordinarily immune from interference, because they have the sanction of age and fame and usually appeal to a comparatively limited number of readers."

There have been differences of opinion about the exemption of classics. It is sometimes contended that Rabelais is clearly "obscene, lewd, or lascivious," and, under other statutes, "filthy," and therefore unfit to become an article of commerce.

About 1921 a Georgia girl wrote to Maurice Francis Egan: "At college I looked on literature as something apart. Since I have come home to Georgia, I find that it is better to submit myself to the direction of our good Baptist clergyman, and have no books on our library shelves that I cannot read aloud to the young."

There are still many conflicting points of view, many diverging standards, in America. In fact, the test of readability to the young is a very vague one, though the conjunction with a Georgia Baptist clergyman suggests that Maxwell Bodenheim and James Joyce are excluded.

In 1907 Charles H. Caffin wrote, in *The Story of American Painting*: "Publishers are fond of preaching moderation. Both in illustration and in writing they discourage much that is original, vital, and born of convictions, fearing that they may shock the sensibilities of their public. Since the latter is overwhelmingly composed of young girls, they may exhibit an appropriate canniness, but the result upon a great deal of our literature is to confuse purity with prudishness and sincerity with dilettanteism. . . . The actual plague spot of this disease centers around the relation of the sexes in literature and the use of the nude in art, and its morbid effects spread through the whole body of fiction and painting, inducing a flaccid condition of self-consciousness and insincerity."

Caffin complained that false moral standards were bringing about a false art based on sentimentality and facile prettiness. The complaint has lost some, but by no means all, of its force since. The young girl has not ceased to rule literature, but it is precisely she who asks for a "kick." If she values the opinions of professional men of religion, she can buy a magazine in which all the stories have been approved by a board of ministers, but they are said to be capable of working upon the imagination nevertheless.

There are all sorts of quirks and mental twists in the moral attitude of the critics. H. L. Mencken denounces the Puritans and the neo-Puritans, but calls Oscar Wilde "a bounder and a swine." A great many of the books which bring down moral indignation upon' themselves are simply guilty of pointing out in forceful language the supposed fact that virtue triumphs and vice is always defeated. In fact, this point is often brought out at the expense of logical fictional development.

The New York city authorities indicated in 1928 that they would tolerate no plays dealing with prostitutes or set in brothels. However, they do not seem to be observing this as an absolute rule. One or two plays dealing with sexual perversions have made Broadway gasp.

The motion-picture censors of various cities and states have widely different standards and ways of applying them. The chief of the board in the Canadian province of Quebec says he orders the elimination of scenes showing infidelity, free love, double life, the seduction of girls, the auction of girls, adultery, white slavery, women in suggestive poses or unclothed or wearing one-piece bathing suits, as well as scenes of prolonged kissing and passionate love. He adds that he is even more severe with scenes that he considers irreligious, including mock marriages, religious burlesques, the ridicule of creed or clergy, and the representation of the clergy as immoral people. The list is pretty long, but some of the censorship boards in the United States object to the items listed above and to various others. For example, scenes implying that children are born or even that they are brought by the stork are cut out in some states. Scenes of violence are often banned. And in some states and cities everything that can be considered unpatriotic or derogatory to national heroes is eliminated.

Books have generally been allowed more freedom than stage or screen plays. The motion-picture producers, much of whose revenue comes from small towns with old-fashioned prejudices, have promised not to permit the use of "damned" and similar words. We still sometimes see, even in books, such forms as "d—" and "h—"; and such coy words as "demmit" and "helluva" are used to absorb shocks. *What Price Glory,* on the stage, used a great deal of realistic soldiers' language, which diminished during its run in New York; on the screen, this play showed "son of a gun" in a song, where it was clear that a rhyme with "itch" was indicated.

In the first decade of the twentieth century, George Sylvester Viereck was writing rather daring poetry which showed the influence of Krafft-Ebing, Swinburne, Wilde, Douglas, Rossetti, and some of the young Germans. Viereck was treated as a diabolic person during the time of the American participation in the World War, and the campaign to blot out his name met with a fair measure of success.

The New International Year Book tells us that in 1909 "novels dealing with sex problems in an unconventional manner" were being produced in large numbers, but that the lists of best-sellers were made up of "wholesome" books. That year *The Easiest Way* was produced in New York, with Frances Starr in the part of the girl who chooses it. In 1910 *Madame X* was played. In 1911 appeared Dreiser's *Jennie Gerhardt. The House of Bondage* was one of a number of novels and plays dealing in a sensational manner with "white slavery." Dostoievsky and other Russian realists began to interest considerable numbers of American readers. *Jean Christophe,* too, was attracting general notice. In 1913 *Damaged Goods* was a center of controversy. In 1915 appeared *The Spoon River Anthology,* with its air of disillusionment. At about this time the Little Theatre movement began, affording an opportunity for the production of plays which the commercial managers, sometimes because of moral considerations, did not care to produce. Eugene O'Neill was one of those who profited by it.

The War certainly quickened the movement toward literary frankness, even if it did not begin it. In 1919 came a flood of bedroom farces. In 1920 appeared Sinclair Lewis's *Main Street.* There was a great tumult over James Branch Cabell's *Jurgen,* which had been published the year before and was now denounced as obscene. The book received a juridical certificate of purity.

In 1922 a New York publisher tried to convert a very sexy magazine, which had been judged obscene in court, into a re-

pository for stories of mystery and horror. His attempt failed.
But this did not matter, because he had found a gold mine. This
was the discovery that supposedly true stories about girls who
were tempted, but who usually remained chaste, would attract
large numbers of readers. It became possible, in 1925, for a
woman writer to discuss the impotence of a Russian monarch
and to record that he once, at the dinner table, called a guest "a
son of a bitch."

Boston seems to have a stronger yearning for purity than any
other American city. (It has a greater number of prostitutes
per capita than most, but perhaps that is beside the point.) In
January, 1928, a correspondent of the *New York Times* discovered that some seventy books were barred from sale in the stores
of Boston by a mysterious censor. The Massachusetts state law
provides that a book is immoral and unsaleable if it contains any
indecent passages, no matter what its general purpose and
tendency may be. Booksellers are naturally reluctant to run
the risk of involving themselves criminally, and they very seldom display any publication of which the Watch and Ward Society does not approve. However, it is possible for Bostonians
to obtain books through the mails if they are not to be had in
local shops.

A most curious incident in the Boston "clean-book campaign"
was the arrest of Upton Sinclair for selling a copy of his novel
Oil. Sinclair is a radical in political and economic, but not
in moral, matters. It seems that the book was proscribed because of the social views it preaches, not for its love scenes.
Little remains in Boston of the old Calvinistic Puritanism.
There is a strong Catholic pietism and a political conservatism,
which is largely concerned with maintaining the present economic system.

§ 4

During the first quarter of the twentieth century the women
of the United States gained the right to vote on equal terms with
men. The first campaigns were statewide; then the possibility

of an amendment to the Federal Constitution was seen. The rural districts of the West were strongly in favor of woman suffrage. Some of the other parts of the country were much less enthusiastic about it. The amendment was carried through the various stages of its adoption on the wave of wartime idealism, even though some of the leading idealists were rather uncertain about its wisdom.

There has been a great mass of legislation to improve the rights of women with regard to property and many other matters. In most jurisdictions the wife has virtually the same privileges before the courts as the husband. The old right to his wife's obedience, which a man was permitted, if need be, to enforce with a stick, has all but disappeared. And many restrictions have appeared on the punishment of children by their parents. It is said that these old patriarchal privileges have lingered on among the negroes. Some immigrants, too, are reluctant to give up the whip with which they are accustomed to chastise their wives and children.

Capacity for business used to be denied to women. And we always have with us the joke about the lady who was indignant about the notice of an overdraft she had received when she still possessed half a dozen blank checks. Judge Grant said, not many years ago: "Women seem to be constitutionally gun-shy when confronted with mortgages, stocks, and bonds." Yet some important corporations now have more women's than men's names on their lists of shareholders. Women fill important positions in banks and industries and public departments. They have had all but the highest political honors. There are still prejudices against them, to be sure, and sometimes they are denied the titles that would go to men doing the same work.

The women's clubs have remained subject to a certain amount of criticism. Grover Cleveland wrote disparagingly of them in the *Ladies' Home Journal* in 1905, but excepted those organized for charitable or religious endeavor or for intellectual improvement from his criticisms. When we think of a men's club, we picture lounge chairs, cigars, perhaps whiskey, a gymnasium or a golf course. Clubs for women, on the other hand, are connected with some sort of aspiration to culture. It may be vague, it frequently is shoddy, of course, but perhaps the mere aspiration is worth something.

Münsterberg, at the beginning of the century, thought that the interest of American women in culture was far greater than that displayed by the men, whereas the case was by no means similar in Germany. Other foreigners have said pretty much the same thing. Only recently André Maurois remarked that "it is the women especially who read, who occupy themselves with art, with music. The men are completely absorbed in their business." Despite the virtual unanimity of such observations, there is reason to doubt their truth. Women have time during the day to attend lectures and club meetings, most American men have not. Yet men buy more books than women, in cheap as well as in expensive editions, in the field of pure literature as well as on subjects in which their interest may be pecuniary. And it is doubtful if women as a class display more intelligent interest in music and art than men do.

Middle-class housewives in the United States cannot all afford to have full-time servants. But they do possess all sorts of labor-saving devices, and most of them do only part of the work of preparing food for their families within their homes. The baker, the canner, the restaurant-keeper, and the laundryman enable them to devote a large part of their time to cards, golf, and culture. Indeed, the poems they write and the papers they prepare are seldom valuable, and the fact that they flock to see visiting celebrities while their husbands are at work proves little.

It was supposed, before the suffrage was granted to women, that they would take advantage of their privilege to destroy political corruption. Most of the time women have voted the same way as their husbands. In the exceptional instances it is not certain that the women have voted more intelligently than the men. In the public offices they have held they have proved themselves neither more honest nor more capable than men. Their principal disadvantage in this field has been lack of experience.

Morally, women display the same inconsistencies as men.

Members of the Woman's Christian Temperance Union are sometimes convicted of selling liquor illegally, just as members of the Anti-Saloon League are. The fact that a woman talks of the beauty of purity and petitions the district attorney to suppress magazines which she considers salacious does not prove that she has no paramour.

We have been learning, more and more, to think of men and women as being essentially similar in innate intellectual tendencies. The old idea that women are, by nature, morally superior to men lingers on with the gems of thought which congressmen provide for their eager constituents on the Fourth of July, but it is hardly to be reconciled with the recent observations of experimental psychologists.

§ 5

Some of the formality which in European social circles is supposed to be due when the two sexes meet is absent or rare in America. Miss D. Baker, of Harrod's staff, who visited the United States in 1927, complained: "We went to a dance at a country club, and to our horror the men took off their coats and danced in their shirt-sleeves. We were so startled that we nearly walked out." Much of the United States has a summer climate which makes the wearing of coats on the street and in offices almost unbearable. Democracy and reminiscences of the pioneer spirit also contribute to the general informality in the United States.

Perhaps there are fewer class distinctions in manners in this country than there are in Europe. The average workingman knows how to conduct himself in a restaurant, for example, and has facilities for keeping himself clean far above those enjoyed by the lower classes in Italy or even England.

Recreation has become one of the greatest American industries. Many forms of amusement are approved by the strictest of the evangelical churches. The Methodists and some other groups continue to oppose professional boxing, but this has become much more respectable during the past three decades.

Women often attend matches, and well-known politicians take prominent places, evidently without any fear that they will lose votes for this reason. The promotion of boxing matches has become an elaborate business, with securities traded in on the stock exchange. Large amounts are often wagered on the results of fights. Boxing is reputed to be more honestly conducted than professional wrestling. The fact that manipulation by gamblers is more difficult in the case of amateur sports makes them especially attractive to betters. Thus, undergraduates and others wager considerable sums on the issue of intercollegiate football games. The pools which are conducted during the professional baseball system operate usually on the lottery principle. Tickets are sold in cigar stores, billiard parlors, and saloons, as well as by agents who have regular routes or who work among their fellow employees. Other sports, such as horse racing and whippet racing, are of interest to the general public almost exclusively because of the opportunities they present for betting.

The church raffle is still one of the most familiar forms of the lottery. Even where there is absolutely no doubt that it violates the law, the authorities are reluctant to forbid it. Punchboards and gambling machines are openly displayed in many cities. In fact, the antigaming laws are no more respected in the United States than those which forbid the sale of liquor. The American people, perhaps out of sheer cynicism, often feel that gambling houses are permitted to operate because the police share in the profits, and that occasional raids on them are intended solely for political effect or to punish operators who are not sufficiently generous.

There are still some circles in the United States where the theatre and the circus are held to be wicked. The Reverend B. B. Crimm is said to have exclaimed, in the course of revival services held in 1927 at Brinkley, Texas: "I'd rather see a saloon on each street corner than a picture show there." It may be presumptuous to assume that he was talking from the point of view of a Prohibitionist.

In the province of Quebec, the Roman Catholic priests have been hostile to motion-picture theatres, though with some exceptions. They are largely responsible for an edict that children under sixteen shall not, even with the approval and in the presence of their parents, attend them. In the United States, Roman Catholic clergymen have been more liberal in the matter. Some American cities refuse to issue licenses for the building and operation of theatres. Milton, Massachusetts, which was founded in 1695 and now has a population of about 15,000, has never had any sort of playhouse. A theatre for the showing of pictures was completed in 1928, but all the churches except the Catholic opposed the granting of a license. By a close vote the town board decided to stand with the Protestant ministers. Horace Kephart says of the Southern highlands: "Most of the mountain preachers nowadays denounce dances and play-parties as sinful diversions, though their real objection seems to be that such attractions are counter-attractions that thin out the religious ones." In some of the mountain settlements practically the only amusement is going to church or camp meeting and listening to a fiery sermon. The men are often separated from the women at religious services.

Mixed dancing has been opposed chiefly because it is symbolical and provocative of venery. But the old dances which are still kept up among the Southern mountaineers present this element in a somewhat disguised form. Fashionable America has, during the twentieth century, preferred more frankly voluptuous dancing. In 1914 there was a craze for various erotic steps. Mr. Bok tells how hundreds of readers of the *Ladies' Home Journal* urged him to campaign against the shuffle, the bunny-hug, the turkey trot, "and other ungraceful and unworthy dances." He thought he could be most effective by providing substitutes, and he engaged Mr. and Mrs. Vernon Castle to work with him to bring the gavotte, the polka, and the waltz back into popularity. Mr. Bok was then accused of having fallen victim to the dancing craze himself.

The dances to which he objected went on as before. Flappers could not be convinced that the waltz was romantic; and certainly they did not imagine that, as contended by excellent authorities in such matters, it had led their great-great-grandmothers straight to perdition. Later came dances which made the 1914 varieties seem rather tame.

In the rural districts motion pictures are usually acceptable, especially if they are melodramatic or comic and free from the serious treatment of sex. Teachers are permitted to attend their showing in most communities, though their contracts may require them to go to bed at a stated hour. In many small towns they are required to stay away from dances, to wear clothes that the trustees consider modest, and to refrain from love-making, especially with their pupils. They are often required to be properly pious, and sometimes expected to teach in a Sunday school without compensation. In some districts men teachers must agree not to smoke at any time. And they must refrain from playing cards or betting if public opinion frowns upon these things.

According to the catalogue of Asbury College, a Methodist institution at Wilmore, Kentucky: "All wholesome amusements are encouraged, but questionable indulgences such as card playing, dancing, the use of tobacco, and unseemly language are prohibited." Students must be on their best behavior even while away from college: "Neither do we desire those who use tobacco during the vacation and only stop its use on entering the institution." And—since Methodist young ladies never smoke—the other sex is also provided for. "Extreme modes of dress" are discountenanced. "The reading of light and trashy literature is prohibited."

Such taboos are still accepted by a large part of the American people, though honored not seldom in the breach. It is said that they usually promote sexual indulgence, since they bar most other healthful forms of recreation to the young people where they prevail. And certainly there are many scandals about the clergy in these districts.

Some American moralists consider alcohol and tobacco equally objectionable. During the twentieth century a number of the states have placed restrictions on the sale and use of tobacco. Most of the anticigarette laws have been repealed, but the sale of tobacco to boys is generally prohibited. The nature of the campaign against it is sufficiently indicated by the following

UNDERDRESSING FOR THE DANCE, 1908 AND 1930
Courtesy of the Van Raalte Company.

sentence taken from a propaganda pamphlet: "The tobacco sot will buy tobacco to feed his degraded appetite while the bread bin is depleted, the sugar bowl empty, the milk supply inadequate, the cookie jar desolate, and the children suffer for sweets."

The United States is both the greatest producer and the greatest consumer of tobacco in the world. The *per capita* consumption is much higher than that of Great Britain, though it is surpassed elsewhere in Europe. Millions of dollars annually are spent in the United States to advertise single brands of cigarettes. But one weekly magazine, which has an enormous circulation, largely in the rural districts, finds it profitable to refuse all cigarette advertisements and all advertisements of tobacco in which its use for homemade cigarettes is indicated.

In the early years of the century, smoking on the part of women was frowned upon in nearly all genteel circles. In 1904 a woman was seen smoking as she rode down Fifth Avenue, New York, in an automobile; she was promptly arrested. Two decades later, zealous officers in small cities were still arresting female smokers, or at least warning them to throw away their cigarettes. And an Englishwoman, well known as a preacher, had many American lecture engagements canceled when it became known that she was accustomed to smoking. But so far as restaurants and night clubs in the principal cities were concerned, it was usual to see women puffing away at cigarettes. And one woman, well known for her family connections, her eccentricities, and her poetry, was accustomed to smoke big black cigars. In some rural districts of the South women were keeping up the habit of their mothers and grandmothers by smoking pipes.

Hardly anyone in the United States now justifies the use for pleasure of such narcotics as opium and cocaine, or argues that the laws forbidding their use should be repealed. Yet the addicts include men and women of prominence in literature, on the stage, in high society, and in many other fields.

Morphine was first made from opium in 1803; in the middle of the century, cocaine was first produced; and in 1898 a German chemist discovered how to make heroin, with great concentrated strength, from morphine. It is exceedingly difficult to prevent the importation and sale of these drugs for the reason that their bulk is small. That they are used now more than in the nineteenth century seems to be certain, despite the laws and the international agreements designed to prohibit their use except for medicinal purposes.

§ 6

In 1900 there were varying opinions in the United States about the right to buy and sell alcoholic beverages. Probably a majority of the people considered the moderate drinking of beer, wine, and cider entirely harmless. There was more opposition to the distilled alcoholic beverages. In the Middle West, whiskey was identified with drunkenness and drunkenness was held to be closely connected with political corruption and other evils. The cry arose that good government was impossible while the saloons remained open.

Some liberal clergymen aroused strong criticism by expressing their opinion that the use of intoxicants was quite compatible with Christianity. In 1904 Bishop Potter of the Episcopal Church dedicated a New York tavern which was to sell "only the purest" alcoholic beverages. He was assured by a large part of the religious press that a man could become drunk in this tavern as easily as in any other.

There were years in the early part of the century when the cause of Prohibition seemed to be doomed to failure in the United States. The "driest" of the states had very spotty enforcement of their antisaloon laws. In Kansas a fanatical female Prohibitionist, Carrie Nation by name, conducted raids and smashed up saloons on her own account. Most Kansans were then quite willing that the sale of liquor should be forbidden by law, so long as their own needs were supplied. In 1903 Vermont and New Hampshire repealed their Prohibition laws.

Then, in 1907, a great wave of Prohibition sentiment swept through the South. White people were in control of affairs, and they were determined to keep whiskey away from the negro laborers. In the Southwest, many people thought it necessary to deprive the Indians of intoxicants. Elsewhere, employers thought of the benefits they would enjoy if their workmen were always as sober on Monday as on Friday. They were willing enough to try Prohibition, if only they were assured of their own ability to obtain cocktails and wines.

To this sort of Prohibition both democracy and Puritanism were opposed. Mr. Mencken argues that these two are the same, or at least that they are both founded upon the desire to humble the man "who is having a better time in the world." In short, poor men felt that if they were not to have intoxicants, the rich and powerful should not have them either. And it was this idea that caused Congress, in 1913, to forbid the sending of alcoholic beverages into states where their sale was prohibited.

At this time the Anti-Saloon League was working hard to amend the Federal Constitution in such a way as to make the manufacture and use of intoxicants illegal throughout the country. In 1914 the proposed amendment secured a majority, but not the necessary two-thirds, vote in its favor. Lovers of personal liberty and, still more, persons who were economically interested in brewing, distilling, and the sale of intoxicants were alarmed. Organization was on the side of the Prohibitionists. The brewers and the distillers could not work together, for the brewers considered their cause much more easily defensible than that of the distillers. Moreover, the anti-Prohibitionists who were without pecuniary interest in the matter gasped for a moment and returned to their personal affairs. The conflict seemed to be one between selfish individuals and moral idealists.

When the United States entered the War to Make the World Safe for Democracy, Prohibition sentiment reached its height. There arose a dreadful spectre of an American sharpshooter aiming in the general direction of Kaiser Bill but, because of the glass of rum which had just destroyed all his nerve cells, utterly failing to hit him.

In 1917 Congress made the sale of liquor illegal in the District of Columbia and some of the territories. A war-emergency law provided that the whole country should do without intoxicants after July, 1919. By the end of 1917 both houses had passed the Prohibition amendment. Early in 1919 this had received the assent of three-fourths of the states and was proclaimed part of the Constitution. The Volstead Act, which forbade the sale of beverages containing more than one-half of one per cent of alcohol, was passed over President Wilson's veto and became effective in January, 1920.

There was at once a large increase in the domestic manufacture of beer, wine, and whiskey. The illicit traffic in intoxicants has, indeed, an American history which dates from before 1776; and there are parts of the country where it has always enjoyed a certain respectability. In the Southern Appalachians the revenue agent has long been considered a foe to be shot down at sight. All over the country, in "wet" as well as in "dry" territory, there were unlicensed distilleries and places where untaxed liquor was sold before 1920.

But since the Volstead Act became the law of the land, the illicit manufacture and sale of intoxicants has become hundreds of times more important. Estimates of the amount of liquor consumed in 1921 or in 1928 vary according to the bias of those who make them, but it is at least possible to argue that Americans are now drinking more beer, wine, and whiskey than they were accustomed to consume before 1920. The amount of wine grapes, malt, hops, and other raw materials and supplies now being sold supports such a contention. Both the friends and the foes of Prohibition agree that the quality of the intoxicants now available is often far below that of the tax-paid beverages formerly available. Much of the liquor sold in Prohibition days contains wood alcohol and other poisons inserted into grain alcohol under official formulas to prevent it from being used as a beverage.

So far as I am able to learn, Great Britain has had a greater proportionate decrease in drunkenness since 1900 than the United States. Canada tried the experiment of Prohibition during the War and for a short time afterward, but most of its provinces seem now to be satisfied with the sale of intoxicants under close governmental control.

Much anti-Prohibition feeling has developed in the United

". . . AND TO UPHOLD THE CONSTITUTION OF THE UNITED STATES,
SO HELP ME . . ."

A cartoon by Alfred Frueh in *The New Yorker,* 1929.

States since the Volstead Act went into effect. Many young men who were in the Army at the time that the policy of national Prohibition was adopted feel that they have had no opportunity to express their views in the matter. Those who served in France saw that habitual wine-drinkers may be temperate. Our country has been prosperous since 1920, at least as compared with those that entered the War in 1914 and wasted away much of their resources in it. It can be argued that this situation is due in part to Prohibition. But the anticipated moral benefits have not come. Crime flourishes, though the jails and prisons overflow.

In some parts of our country, bootleggers conduct their business openly, and go so far as to ask to be listed as such in the city directories. There is no area of any consequence where beer and whiskey are not to be had. And putting the sellers on a bread-and-water diet in jail, or sentencing them to lifelong imprisonment as habitual criminals, does not seem to have the slightest effect on the available supply of intoxicants.

Many Prohibitionists are much perturbed about criticism of the Volstead Act and the state laws forbidding the sale of alcoholic beverages. Some of them openly demand that all references to intoxicants shall be forbidden. They would like children to be brought up in utter ignorance that such things as gin and porter exist, and that their barbarian ancestors were accustomed to push in swinging doors. Some vaudeville circuits instruct their actors never to joke about Prohibition and drinking. The principal motion-picture producers have agreed not to show unnecessary drinking scenes. But one Southern radio broadcasting station, much to the disgust of divers moral listeners, frequently sends out a song in which a "bottle of corn" has a prominent place. The announcer often exclaims "Doggone!" and adds to the anger of the pietists.

§ 7

Much of the fiat science of our times deals with the evils of drunkenness and tobacco addiction. Legislators are almost all willing to have the children who attend the public schools warned against strong drink and cigarettes, and some of the laws they have passed require the teaching of falsehoods and of principles which, so far as anyone is yet able to tell, may or may not be true.

There is a fixed belief in the validity of the truth established by popular prejudice or the vote of elected representatives. And the result is that the various parts of the country learn very different things about the same facts. The school children of Maine and those of South Carolina are given widely divergent accounts of the Civil War. Where persons of German and Irish descent are in the majority, they want their children to learn all about the English cruelties that brought about the Revolutionary War. When the English were our brave allies, it became usual to insert fairer accounts of the American Revolution in the textbooks. Now that the War is over, these are objectionable in some parts of the country.

In 1923 Wisconsin enacted what has been called the Pure History Law. This forbids the use in the public schools of the state of any textbook "which falsifies the facts regarding the war of independence, or the war of 1812, or which defames our nation's founders or misrepresents the ideals and causes for which they struggled and sacrificed, or which contains propaganda favorable to any foreign government." And Mayor William Hale Thompson of Chicago, also in the interests of truth and patriotism, has waged war against George III and George V, to the benefit of his political career.

There are people who insist that children should be taught the cherry-tree story about Washington, whether it is true or not, because it conveys a good moral. And Prohibitionists become very angry when biographers and historians record the fact that some of the fathers of our country took at least occasional drinks, and had strong views about personal liberty. But if it was virtuous of young Washington to tell the truth without fear, may it not also be a virtue on the part of historical and scientific writers? Some scholars see that it may be a dangerous as well as a deceitful thing to tell the children in school

A MYTHICAL KICK COMING

PRESIDENT ADAM. *"Fellow myths! We are gathered here to-day to protest against the heretical utterances of one Dr. Crapsey, who repeatedly asserts that we never existed."*

A cartoon by L. M. Glackens on a contemporary heresy prosecution, in *Puck*, 1907.

that the United States has always been right, and is in every way perfect.

In this century there have been two periods in which the abuses and follies prevalent in the United States have been widely considered. The first was the era of "muck-raking," the second is that of "debunking." During the first period there were attacks on the trusts, on industries that were seeking profits by fraudulent and dangerous means, and on dishonest politicians. The "muck-rakers" almost invariably insisted that the evils of democracy could be corrected by more democracy.

Since the World War the "debunkers" have become prominent. The leading one among people who consider themselves educated is probably H. L. Mencken. As a Baltimore editor, as a writer on Shaw and Nietzsche, and as editor, with George Jean Nathan, of the *Smart Set*, he enjoyed a certain amount of fame before the present period began. But the *American Mercury* and syndicated articles have now brought his views before many thousands, and distorted accounts of them have gone to millions.

E. Haldeman-Julius has displayed less pedantry, and has shown more willingness to make himself understood by people of little formal education. He has more respect for democracy than some of the other "debunkers." Like Mr. Mencken, he believes in free speech and personal liberty. In religion, while Mencken calls himself an agnostic, Haldeman-Julius prefers to be known as an atheist. Both are anti-Christian, both agree that this is not the best of all possible worlds, and the United States not the best of all possible countries.

Rupert Hughes, turning aside occasionally from the writing of popular fiction, exposes the weaknesses of conventional religious and nationalistic creeds. Sinclair Lewis attacks many forms of American standardized stupidity in best-selling novels. Ezra Pound may be taken as a representative of other "debunkers" who, because of voluntary exile and occasional ambiguity of expression, exert little influence.

A few of the "debunkers" call themselves Christians. They are all against Fundamentalism. The Fundamentalists, as opposed to the Modernists, cling to what seem to them the essential elements in the Christian creed. They feel that the theologians who deny the inspiration and literal truth of anything contained in the Bible are breaking down the bases of Christian morality. And they insist that the stories about the creation of the world contained in Genesis contradict, and therefore prove to be false, the theory of organic evolution.

Commenting on the dominant Fundamentalism of the South, André Siegfried remarks: "If the monkey can become a man, may not the negro hope to become white? The Southerners prefer to believe that the various species have been fixed once for all, by divine wisdom, at the level that Providence has decreed."

The explanation is ingenious, but perhaps unnecessary. For the ignorant, not only in the South, and not alone in the United States, are reluctant to accept scientific facts. Those who have been brought up as Christians exclaim that the scholars have forgotten God.

For most of the Fundamentalists, evolution and atheism are identical. Man has neither descended nor ascended from any other animal form, and that's that. The world has heard about one or two state laws, but the teaching of evolution has quietly been suppressed in a number of large areas and a great many small ones in various parts of the United States. And there are American school children who are taught that the world is flat, or that human beings live on the inside of a sphere.

Nevertheless, most Americans have acquired a more critical or at least a less respectful attitude toward religion and the churches than they or their fathers had in 1900. Maurice Francis Egan, speaking in 1922 from the Catholic point of view, complained: "Unfortunately, among many of the young people, the Bible seems to be a book to be avoided or to be treated in a rather 'jocose' manner. To raise a laugh on the vaudeville stage, a Biblical quotation has only to be produced, and the weary comedian, when he is at a loss to get a witty speech across the footlights, is almost sure to speak of Jonah and the whale." College students are becoming more and more doubtful about God and immortality; and except in the sectarian institutions which grind out Fundamentalist preachers, they are either skeptical about the denominational differences or utterly indifferent to them.

There is a tendency nowadays to hook up religion with the desire to be healthy, wealthy, and respected, connected, no doubt, with the widespread publicity given to the sectarian affiliations of some of our richest men. George Santayana once heard a president of Yale cry out to the students: "Be Christians and you will be successful." And in 1925 Bruce Barton admitted Jesus Christ to the Nazareth Rotary Club.

There remains a feeling that the Protestant, and especially the evangelical, churches are particularly American and genteel. President Roosevelt, speaking to Methodists, once said: "I would rather address a Methodist audience than any other audience in America." He went on to explain that the Methodists were representative of the great middle classes. And he added: "The Catholic Church is in no way suited to this country and can never have any great permanent growth except immigration, for its thought is Latin and entirely at variance with our country and institutions."

Roosevelt was comparatively tolerant. In most parts of our country—the most conspicuous exceptions are in a few great urban centers—the Protestant churches are established in effect though not formally. To be sure, the dominant Protestantism has much less dependence upon complex theologies than it had in 1850, or even in the generation just past. Santayana, speaking with special reference to educated people in New England, says the Calvinistic creed slid gradually into a theistic optimism. What remained in 1900 was a belief that "the universe exists and is governed for the sake of man or of the human spirit."

There are, in our days, ministers and rabbis who openly profess agnosticism. Bishop William Montgomery Brown was convicted of heresy in the Episcopal Church because of his figurative interpretations of the Creed, but perhaps his Marxism was his greatest offense. Brown found a welcome in another church, though a small one.

Orthodoxy is still a force to be reckoned with. Many of Bur-

ARRIVAL OF THE REV. MR. AKED, THE NEW ROCKEFELLER PASTOR

Praise Oil from which all blessings flow!   *Praise it, all ye Standard codgers!*
Praise Oil, ye grafters here below!   *Praise Father, Son and H. H. Rogers!*

A cartoon by L. M. Glackens, in *Puck*, 1907.

bank's rural admirers turned away or heaped contumely upon him when he called himself an infidel. On the other hand, Rupert Hughes says that he received more requests for stories than ever after he had told in print his reasons for not going to church. But he has written mostly for periodicals which appeal to urban tastes. Stage plays on Broadway occasionally depict a minister who is less than perfect, but this can hardly be done on the screen. In the picture *Sadie Thompson* the missionary of *Rain* has become a lay reformer.

A number of states, most of them in the South, admit no persons to public office who are unwilling to declare their belief in God, or both in God and in future rewards and punishments. And in a few jurisdictions atheists are considered unworthy of belief as witnesses. There are many parts of the country in which non-Protestants find it impossible to be elected or appointed to public positions of any grade.

Denominational peculiarities of dress and behavior, although they still exist, are being minimized. Quakers are not to be told apart from Methodists or agnostics on the street. In October, 1927, some ten thousand Mormons met in Salt Lake City to confirm a rule permitting the wearing of short underwear, fastened with buttons instead of with strings.

There is no anticlerical political party in the United States except the numerically unimportant Communist organization. Though the people who have given up or never had connections with ecclesiastical organizations are very many, those who openly oppose the churches seem to be few. At least, they present no united front. Conflicts between anti-Christian societies and religious bodies have occasionally occurred in recent years, with the ecclesiastical forces usually winning in the rural districts and honors about even in the cities. Constitutional and legal prohibitions of sectarian teaching and the reading of the Bible in public schools are often violated.

In matters of Sunday observance many Christian laymen and ministers stand for liberality. The pietists were able to keep closed the expositions at Buffalo in 1901, at St. Louis in 1904, and at Jamestown in 1907, on Sundays. The Philadelphia Sesquicentennial Exposition of 1926 remained open on Sundays in spite of a legal attack, but the principle involved was finally decided against the management. Not until 1928 was it settled that musical concerts might be presented in Pittsburgh on Sunday. The question of permitting professional baseball games to be played and motion pictures to be publicly exhibited on the first day of the week is constantly being discussed and voted on in American states and cities. Sometimes "clubs" are formed to evade the laws forbidding commercialized recreation on Sunday. In many states and cities unpopular laws of this character are simply ignored. Where the recent immigrants and their children are influential, there is strong opposition to the Sunday of the Puritans. Elsewhere, however, there is about as much automobile riding and golf-playing on the "day of rest." The laws of New Jersey forbid singing and the playing of musical instruments on Sunday, also the use of vehicles except in going to and from church; but the ecclesiastical summer resort of Ocean Grove seems to be the only town that still puts chains across the streets.

In Tennessee many Seventh-day Adventists have been punished for refusing, as a matter of conscience, to refrain from their ordinary work on Sunday. Usually, those who keep some other day holy are permitted to labor on the first day of the week, providing that they conduct themselves quietly. Orthodox Jewish organizations are trying to make a five-day working week general, and in this they are supported by some labor organizations.

The Methodist Episcopal Church South has asked Congress to pass a law forbidding on Sunday all work by Federal employees, the operation of interstate trains, and the conduct of business by companies engaged in interstate commerce, as well as the carrying of Sunday papers through the mails. There are constant struggles in Congress over the Sunday laws of the District of Columbia. The Catholic Church in the United States has been generally opposed to strict Sunday laws. In the province of Quebec, however, it has been more pietistic and has demanded the closing of all theatres on Sunday.

Many Americans still fear that the Catholics want to turn the political control of the United States over to the Pope. The second Ku Klux Klan .(resembling not so much the first one as the old Know-Nothing Party) has capitalized the opposition to foreigners, Catholics, Jews, and negroes. Although the Klan has all but faded away, the sentiment that inspired it remains sufficiently strong to insure the continuance of the immigration restrictions of 1917, 1921, and 1924.

The second Ku Klux Klan has laid claim to high moral purposes. William Joseph Simmons rhapsodizes about the annual meetings held on Stone Mountain, near Atlanta: "It is a time in which all that is coarse and unchaste and unrefined in human life is consumed by a holy passion, and all that is noble and courteous and divine is made regnant."

The Klan has felt the purity of American womanhood to be in need of protection. In Texas one group warned men to spend more time with their own wives. A number of bands, which may or may not have been connected with the Klan, have stripped and whipped women. In Georgia a high-school principal, prominent in church work, was convicted of helping to flog a thirty-seven-year-old woman on the bare back for the alleged offense of "immorality and not going to church." In another Southern state a man was whipped by an armed band for allowing his daughter of sixteen to ride her bicycle dressed in knickers—garments that were elsewhere popular with female hikers.

Mob violence in the South certainly did not originate with either the first or the second Ku Klux Klan. It has long been an integral part of Southern life. In 1907 a struggle among the tobacco-growers of Kentucky caused a raid at Hopkinsville in which property worth $200,000 was destroyed. Industrial disputes have given rise to the shedding of blood and the destruction of property in other parts of the country as well. Recently Chicago has been the scene of many sanguinary battles between rival bootleggers and gangsters. And, speaking of the South, Kephart says: "I have known two old mountain preachers to draw knives on each other at the close of a sermon." The family feuds now cause fewer murders than they used to, but they are not entirely extinct. The lynching of whites and negroes, most common in the South, also seems to be becoming rarer.

Two decades ago Reno, Nevada, was a wild frontier town, said to have had a saloon for every twenty male adults as well as a professional gambler for every ten. The Wild West has all but disappeared now. Yet Europeans find it difficult to realize this, especially since the homicide rate in the United States is, in proportion to population, more than three dozen times as high as that of Great Britain. And the defenders of American morality cannot lay the blame entirely upon negroes and foreigners. Many of the districts where murders are most common are inhabited almost exclusively by white people of old native stock.

§ 8

By no means all of the political corruption is found in the foreign quarters of large cities. In 1911 it was discovered that the selling of votes was a matter of course in Adams County, Ohio. People of all classes, including clergymen, were found to be involved. Over a quarter of the electorate confessed having sold their votes or were convicted of this charge. This same condition prevailed in many other parts of the country. The bribing of voters is probably rarer now than it was in 1911, but it has not disappeared.

Most political machines are still built up through favors and special advantages. The spread of civil-service reform has by no means put all the spoils of office out of reach of the victors. The complexity of traffic regulations which the increased use of the automobile has brought about gives politicians many opportunities to relieve their friends of the necessity of paying fines. Sometimes more serious offenses are disposed of in the same way.

Votes are not always counted honestly. Legislators and public officials are often bribed. It is quite usual for states and cities to buy materials and services at half a dozen times what it would cost private individuals. Indeed, a complete account of the known political corruption in the United States since 1900 would fill several books the size of this. No doubt, though, there has been some improvement in the last three decades. Many units of government now lean more upon the merit system in the selection and promotion of employees. The city-manager plan has probably lessened inefficiency and dishonesty to some small extent. Still, political scandals arise frequently enough to show that perfection has by no means been reached.

Government in the United States is something between a democracy and a demagogy, with perhaps a touch of plutocracy added. Such violations of liberty as the World War and the fear of radicalism have occasioned are sometimes said to show a breakdown in the democratic system. But so far as that means the rule of the majority, it perhaps implies the right to oppress minorities. At least, the *laissez-faire* system has become merely academic in America, and the United States is no longer a nation of individualists. The important units are the corporation and the association or *bloc*.

Demagogues respond to organized public opinion, which is supposed to be capable of making or breaking them politically, and also to corporations which can give them the pecuniary benefits attached to the service of the people. There are now many natural monopolies, of which the most important must either be operated or regulated by the State. Politicians fix the rates of public utilities, and they can also relieve companies and individuals of large tax burdens, give bounties and quasi-bounties in the tariff laws, crush or insure the success of strikes, and afford many other important advantages to those whom they befriend.

Because many manufacturers gained additional profits by misbranding their products or by selling foodstuffs and medicines which were injurious to health, it took twenty-five years of agitation to enact the Pure Food and Drugs Act of 1906. Upton Sinclair, through the picture he gave in *The Jungle* of the Chicago packing houses, caused a public feeling which brought about reforms in their sanitary conditions.

During the early years of the century a fierce war was waged against the trusts. However much dismembered by the courts, they continued to flourish. Americans gradually came to accept large-scale business as an essential feature of modern life. They rode in automobiles, cultivated their farms with implements, heard music from phonographs or radio loud speakers, which they were able to buy at a reasonable price because of the methods of production which only giant corporations could introduce. At the same time, the securities of these companies became more widely distributed.

The people of the middle classes no longer listened to denunciations of the trusts. As the great American companies have extended their interests into foreign countries, the imperialism of the United States has become confirmed. For now thousands of investors, not a few, are concerned about the protection of American property in Nicaragua or Mexico or the Philippines. And it is now possible to lose as well as to gain votes by baiting the public utilities.

Both in large and in small business, Service has become a fetish. It is derived from a Calvinistic principle, but it has lost most of its theological implications. Sometimes it is a mere excuse for a service charge. Real-estate brokers and agents, by calling themselves realtors, and funeral undertakers, by calling themselves morticians, feel that they acquire the privilege of praising their usefulness to society at luncheons, and also that of raising their rates.

Service is connected with the advertising excesses of our time. A large part, sometimes the principal part, of the cost of branded articles represents advertising charges. When we pay fifteen cents for a package of Golden Mule cigarettes, perhaps three cents is for the slogan and four cents for Service on the part of the manufacturer and the dealer.

Yet, on the whole, there is more honesty (and, just as important, more efficiency) in American business than there was in 1900, far more than there was among the Puritan shopkeepers of Boston in 1700. The professional standards of behavior are much higher than they have ever been before. That they are imperfect and often violated, it is hardly necessary to say. There are dishonest and unscrupulous lawyers, physicians, and journalists. There are business men who defraud their customers, the firms from whom they purchase goods, and the insurance companies. But in spite of the fact that the opportunities for fraud and larceny are more varied than they used to be, there are probably fewer thieves.

INDEX

Acton, Dr., 271
Adams, Henry, 471
Adams, James Truslow, 507
Adams, John, 452
Adams County, Ohio, 646
Addison, 167*f.*
Adultery. *See* Fornication and adultery.
Age of consent, England, 338; America, 552
Agnostic, the term, 288. For agnosticism *see* Rationalism and skepticism.
Albert, Prince, 255, 257*f.*, 262, 294
Alcohol. *See* Drinking and the liquor traffic.
Alcott, Louisa May, 569
Alger, Horatio, Jr., 579
American Revolution, 436*f.*, 442*ff.*, 460, 479
American Woman's Suffrage Association, 579
Ames, Fisher, 443, 450-452
Anabaptists, 25*f.*, 65, 88
Anarchists, persecution of American, 596
Andrewes, Sir Launcelot, 101
Anglican Church, beginnings, 61*ff.*; under James I, 80*ff.*; its rites suppressed, 114; in the Restoration, 132*ff.*, 139; after Revolution of 1688, 153*f.*; under first four Georges, 173, 175*f.*, 191, 193*f.*; 220*f.*; under Victoria, 283*ff.*; its recent history, 347*f.*; in American colonies, 375, 384, 393, 400, 408, 421*f.*, 431
Animal combats, under Henry VIII, 59; under Elizabeth, 73, 77; and English Puritans, 110*ff.*; at the Restoration, 131*f.*; in nineteenth-century England, 232*f.*; in United States, 460; Beecher on, 500

Anne, Queen, 151, 163*f.*, 166*f.*, 169, 171
Anne of Cleves, 62
Anthony, Susan B., 526*f.*, 579
Antinomianism, 14, 118; in New England, 376
Anti-Saloon League, 588
Argoll, Gov., 398
Aristocracy, in German Renaissance, 21; Lutheranism and, 26; English, at close of Middle Ages, 57; its privileges conceded by Puritans, 76; under James I, 89; at the Restoration, 139*f.*; under first four Georges, 215*f.*, 221*ff.*; in England in early nineteenth century, 230*ff.*, 235; under Victoria, 258*ff.*, 263, 265, 267, 283; recent English tendencies, 330*f.*, 346; in colonial New England, 365, 374, 385; in Virginia colony, 405*f.*; during American Revolution, 443; in United States, 471*ff.*, 531
Arkansas, 535
Arnold, Matthew, 284, 308
Arnold, Thomas, 288, 296
Art, in Italian Renaissance, 21*f.*; and the Counter Reformation, 37; in Scotland, 47; at Charles I's court, 94; under Puritan rule, 108, 114, 121; at Charles II's court, 131; stimulated by the Restoration, 146; under Victoria, 262; in twentieth-century England, 337, 347; in United States, 477*f.*, 516, 560, 621
Art for art's sake, 307, 528
Asbury College, 630
Asceticism, religious, 8*f.*; in Greece and Rome, 13; mediæval, 18; Calvin's, 30; in Scotland, 47*ff.*; Wesley's, 212; attacked by Pater, 309; Cotton Mather's, 388; Jonathan Edwards', 391*f.*; of the Scotch-

INDEX

Lefèbvre of Étaples, 27
Leland, Iowa, 587
Levee, 164
Lewes, G. H., 284
Lewis, Dr. Dio, 584*f.*
Lewis, Sinclair, 623, 639
Lexington, Ky., 486
Literature, mediæval, 18; Margaret of Navarre, 27; Scottish, 40, 52*ff.;* Elizabethan, 67*ff.;* Puritans and Cavaliers, 97*ff.,* 143*ff.;* Restoration, 165*ff.;* under Queen Anne, 167*ff.;* under first four Georges and William IV, 189*ff.,* 195, 230*f.,* 234, 237*ff.,* 240*ff.;* under Victoria, 293*ff.;* end of Victorianism in, 306*ff.;* in colonial America, 368*f.,* 387, 410; in early republic, 465*f.;* in nineteenth-century America, 499*f.,* 515*f.,* 528*ff.,* 563*ff.,* 571; in twentieth-century America, 608, 619*ff.*
Lincoln, Abraham, 513, 535
Lindsey, Ben, 600, 608*ff.*
Little Theatres, 623
Lodge, Thomas, 74
Lollardry, 56*f.*
Longfellow, 477, 528
Lord's Day Alliance, 592*f.*
Lotteries, 172, 233; in America, 435, 459*f.,* 501*f.,* 583, 628
Louisiana, 440*f.,* 492*f.,* 532, 583
Lovelace, Richard, 98*f.*
Lowell, Mass., 506*f.*
Loyalists in the American Revolution, 444
Ludlow, Fitz Hugh, 569
Luther and Lutheranism, 24*ff.,* 41, 48, 56*f.,* 61
Luxury, in the Renaissance, 20*ff.;* frowned upon by Calvinism, 35; Thomas More complains of, 58; Wesley dislikes, 208*f.;* Cobbett disapproves of, 252; in American colonies, 367, 386, 434*f.;* during American Revolution, 447; in early republic, 461, 473*f.;* in nineteenth-century America, 498
Lynching, 594, 646

Macaulay, 159*f.,* 232
McCosh, Pres., 591
McGuffey, 579, 589

Machiavelli, 22*ff.*
Macready, 498
Magic, 9, 13
Maine, 543, 587
Makemie, Francis, 431*f.*
Malthus, 246
Mandeville, 184
Mann Act, 600, 605
Manners. *See* Etiquette and manners.
Manning, Cardinal, 287
Margaret of Navarre, 27
Marietta, Ohio, 485*f.*
Markham, Gov., 438
Marlborough, 147
Marlowe, 70
Marriage, monogamy as a norm, 13, 326; Godwin on, 283*f.;* in New England colonies, 356*f.,* 364, 386; in the other colonies, 431, 433*ff.;* in French and Spanish Louisiana, 440; in eighteenth-century America, 446; in nineteenth-century America, 475, 487*f.,.* 508*f.,* 511*f.;* common law, 603; companionate, 609*f. See also* Divorce, Wife-selling, Wedding customs, Bigamy, Polygamy.
Marriage Act of 1754, 183
Marryat, Capt., 517*f.*
Martineau, Harriet, 286
Mary, Queen of Scots, 41*ff.*
Mary I (Tudor), 42*f.,* 60, 62*ff.,* 82
Mary II (Stuart), 147, 151, 153*f.*
Maryland colony, 406*ff.,* 434*f.*
Masochism. *See* Self-cruelty.
Massachusetts, 461*f.,* 505, 551, 624. *See also* New England.
Masturbation, 600
Mather, Cotton, 388
Mather, Increase, 386
Mathew, Theobald, 275, 542
Matthews, Brander, 586
Maule, Justice, 280
Maurois, André, 626
May-poles, 77*f.,* 85, 112; in New England, 353, 387
Medici, Catherine de, 36*f.,* 42
Melbourne, Lord, 254, 256, 258, 288
Melville, Herman, 529
Mencken, H. L., 621*f.,* 633, 639
Mercantile system, 437
Meredith, 309*f.*
Merry Mount, 353